JOHN CONSTANTINE, HELLBLAZER: CRITICAL MASS

JOHN CONSTANTINE, HELLBLAZER: CRITICAL MASS

PAUL JENKINS EDDIE CAMPBELL JAMIE DELANO WRITERS

SEAN PHILLIPS PAT McEOWN ARTISTS

MATT HOLLINGSWORTH COLORIST

CLEM ROBINS LETTERER

TOMMY LEE EDWARDS COVER ART

SEAN PHILLIPS JOHN EDER ORIGINAL SERIES COVERS

LOU STATHIS Editor – Original Series
AXEL ALONSO Assistant Editor – Original Series
SCOTT NYBAKKEN Editor
ROBBIN BROSTERMAN Design Director – Books
LOUIS PRANDI Publication Design

SHELLY BOND Executive Editor – Vertigo

HANK KANALZ Senior VP – Vertigo and Integrated Publishing

DIANE NELSON President
DAN DiDIO AND JIM LEE Co-Publishers
GEOFF JOHNS Chief Creative Officer
AMIT DESAI Senior VP – Marketing and Franchise Management
AMY GENKINS Senior VP – Business and Legal Affairs
NAIRI GARDINER Senior VP – Finance
JEFF BOISON VP – Publishing Planning
MARK CHIARELLO VP – Art Direction and Design
JOHN CUNNINGHAM VP – Marketing
TERRI CUNNINGHAM VP – Editorial Administration
LARRY GANEM VP – Talent Relations and Services
ALISON GILL Senior VP – Manufacturing and Operations

JAY KOGAN VP – Business and Legal Affairs, Publishing
JACK MAHAN VP – Business Affairs, Talent
NICK NAPOLITANO VP – Manufacturing Administration
SUE POHJA VP – Book Sales
FRED RUIZ VP – Manufacturing Operations
COURTNEY SIMMONS Senior VP – Publicity
BOB WAYNE Senior VP – Sales

JOHN CONSTANTINE, HELLBLAZER: CRITICAL MASS

DC Comics, 1700 Broadway, New York, NY 10019
A Warner Bros. Entertainment Company
Printed in the USA. First Printing.
ISBN: 978-1-4012-5072-0

LIBRARY OF CONGRESS CATALOGING-IN-PUBLICATION DATA

Jenkins, Paul, 1965-
  John Constantine, Hellblazer. Volume 9, Critical Mass / Paul Jenkins, Eddie Campbell, Sean Phillips.
    pages cm
  ISBN 978-1-4012-5072-0 (paperback)
  1. Graphic novels. I. Campbell, Eddie, 1955- illustrator. II. Phillips, Sean, illustrator. III. Title. IV. Title: Critical Mass.
PN6728.H383J46 2014
741.5'973--dc23
                        2014015086

SUSTAINABLE
FORESTRY
INITIATIVE

Certified Sourcing
www.sfiprogram.org
SFI-01042
APPLIES TO TEXT STOCK ONLY

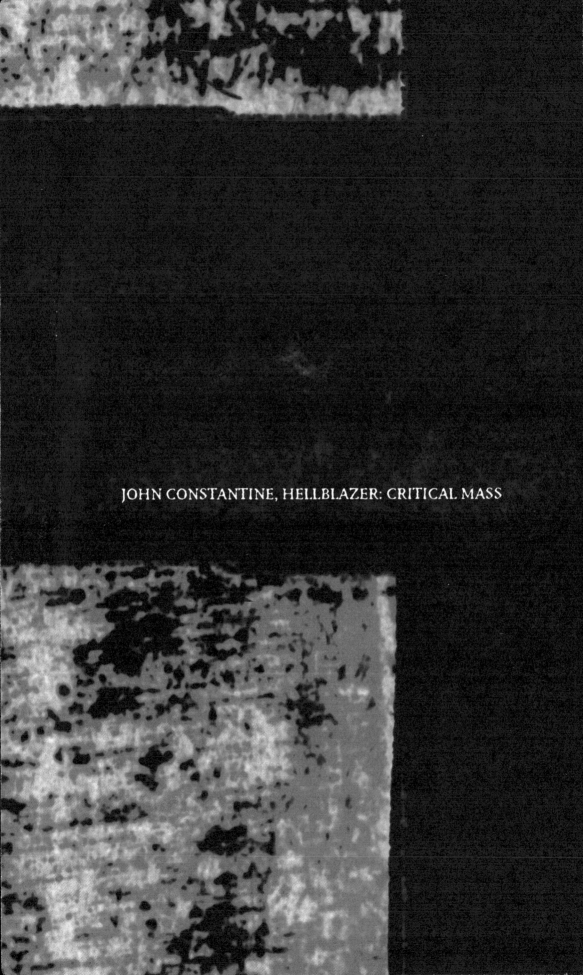

JOHN CONSTANTINE, HELLBLAZER: CRITICAL MASS

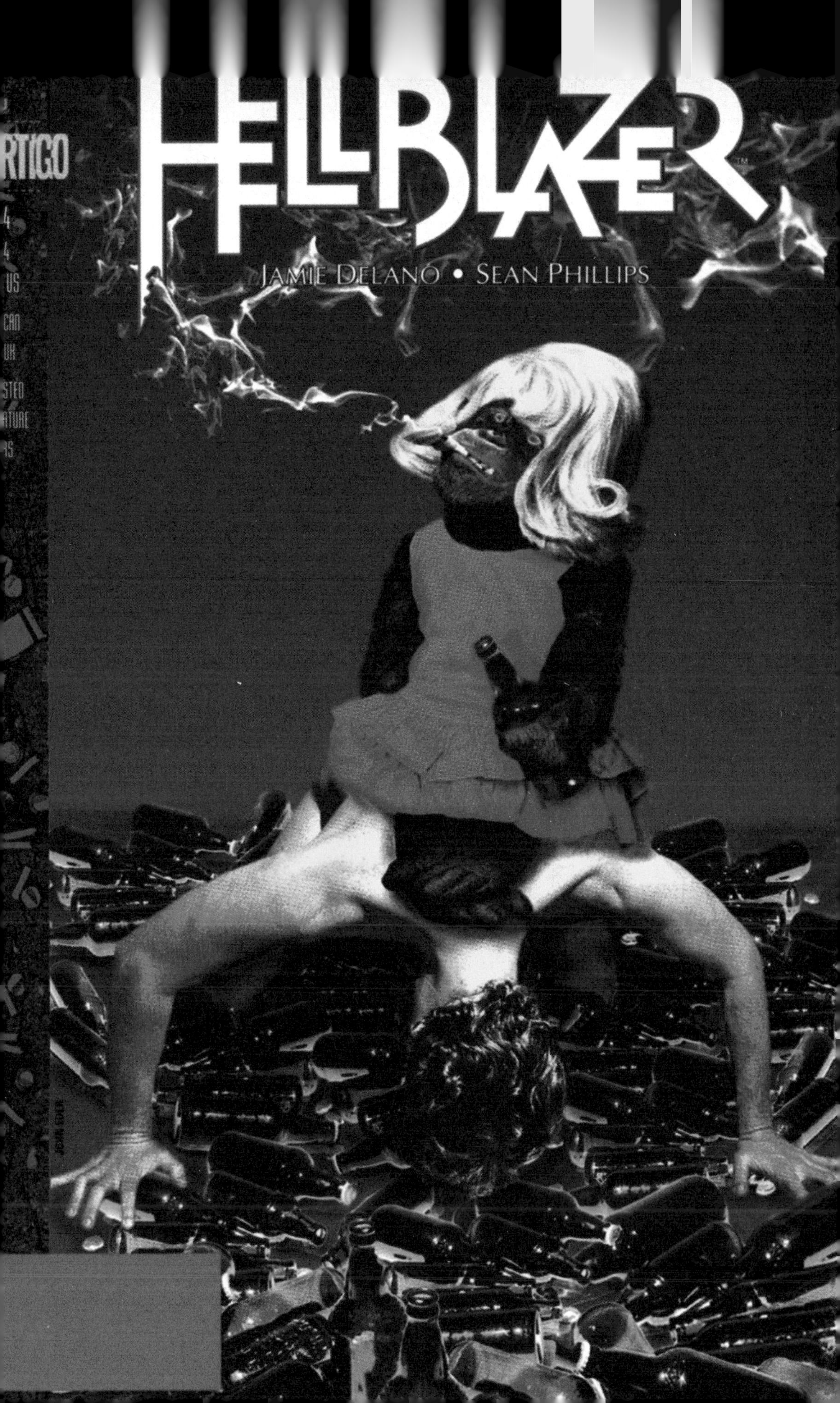
HELLBLAZER
JAMIE DELANO • SEAN PHILLIPS

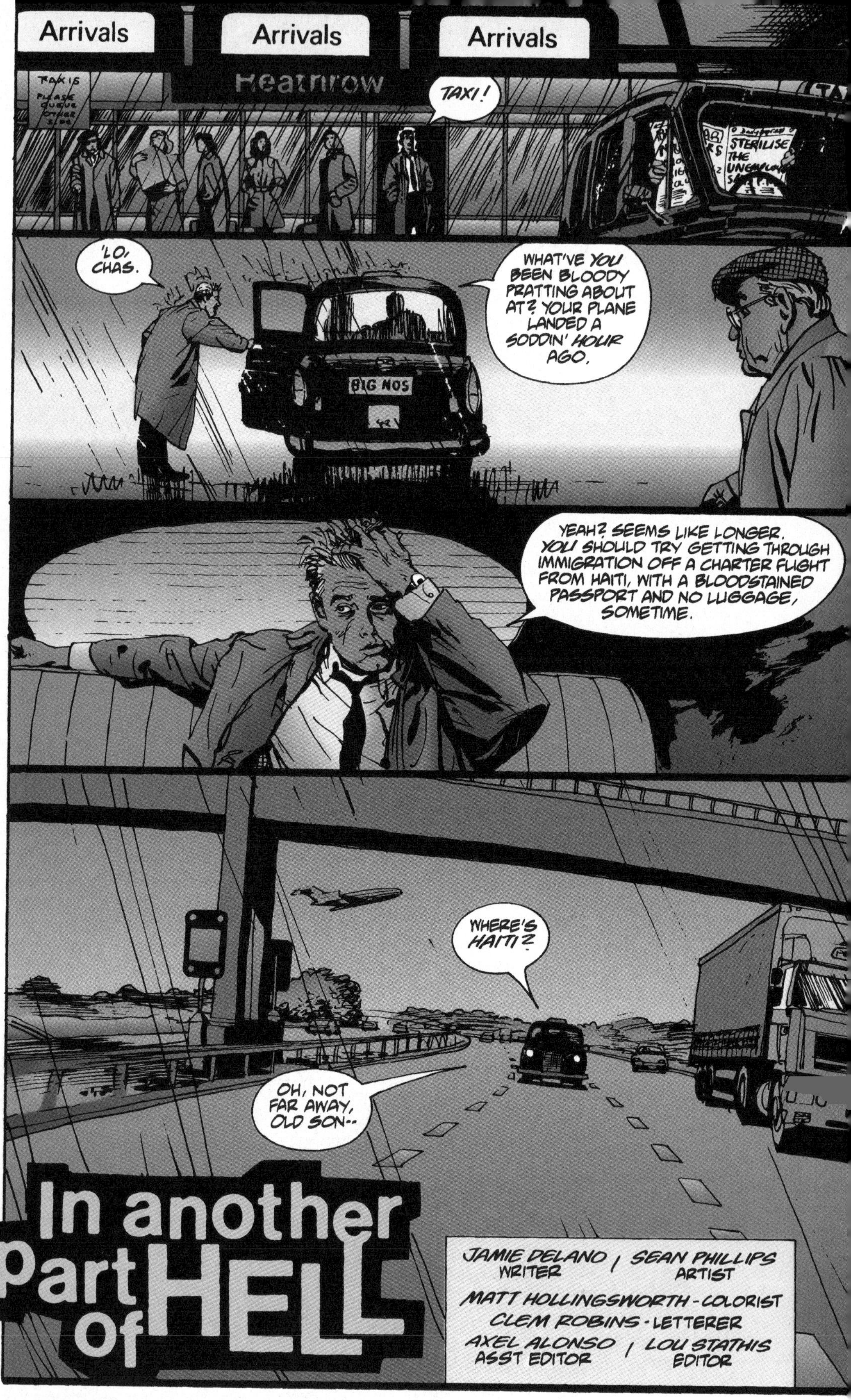

Arrivals
Arrivals
Arrivals
TAXIS PLEASE QUEUE OTHER SIDE
Heathrow
TAXI!
STERILISE THE
'LO, CHAS.
WHAT'VE YOU BEEN BLOODY PRATTING ABOUT AT? YOUR PLANE LANDED A SODDIN' HOUR AGO.
BIG NOS
YEAH? SEEMS LIKE LONGER. YOU SHOULD TRY GETTING THROUGH IMMIGRATION OFF A CHARTER FLIGHT FROM HAITI, WITH A BLOODSTAINED PASSPORT AND NO LUGGAGE, SOMETIME.
WHERE'S HAITI?
OH, NOT FAR AWAY, OLD SON--
In another Part of HELL
JAMIE DELANO / SEAN PHILLIPS
WRITER ARTIST
MATT HOLLINGSWORTH - COLORIST
CLEM ROBINS - LETTERER
AXEL ALONSO / LOU STATHIS
ASST EDITOR EDITOR

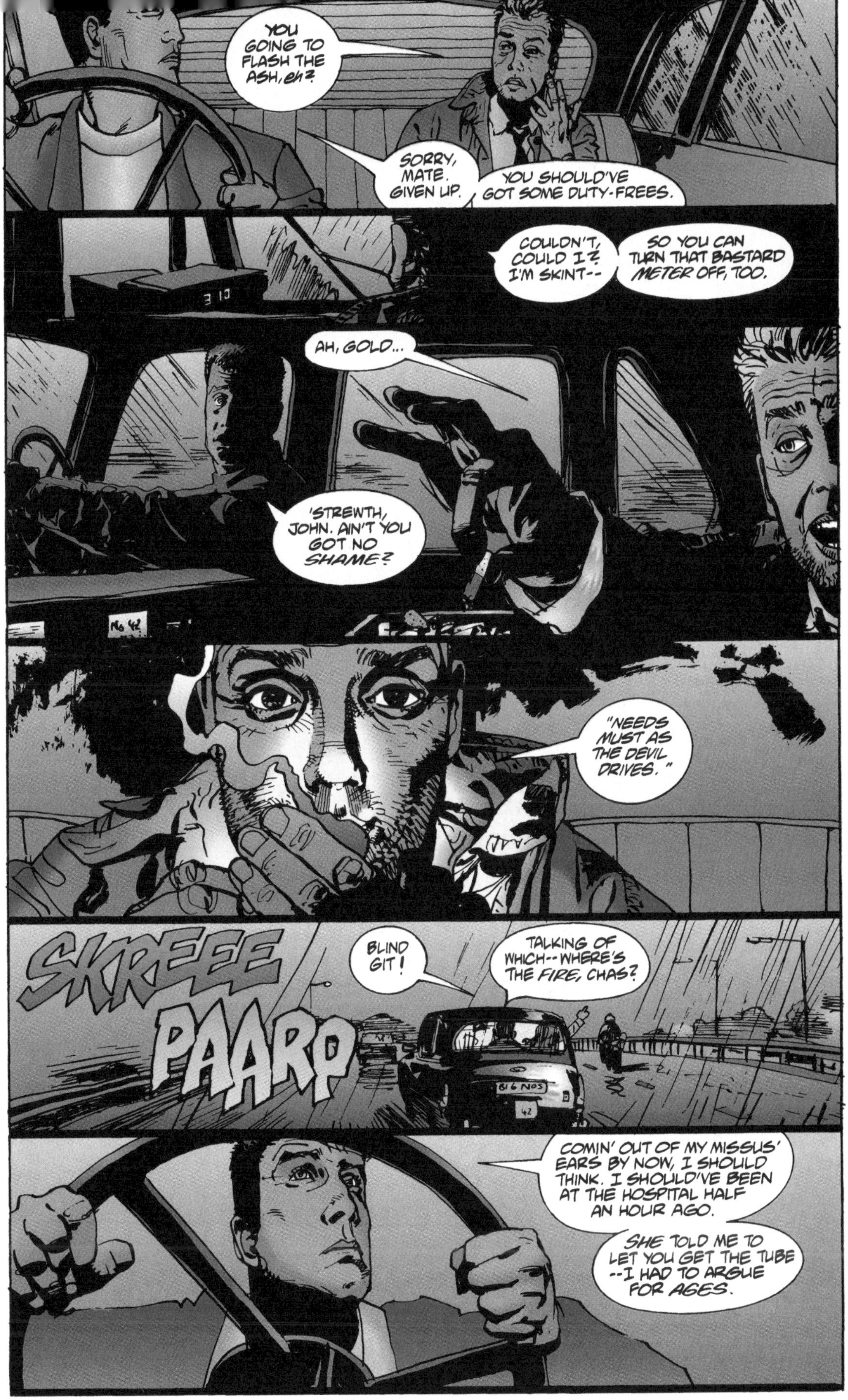
YOU GOING TO FLASH THE ASH, EH?
SORRY, MATE. GIVEN UP.
YOU SHOULD'VE GOT SOME DUTY-FREES.
COULDN'T, COULD I? I'M SKINT--
SO YOU CAN TURN THAT BASTARD METER OFF, TOO.
AH, GOLD...
'STREWTH, JOHN. AIN'T YOU GOT NO SHAME?
"NEEDS MUST AS THE DEVIL DRIVES."
SKREEE
PAARP
BLIND GIT!
TALKING OF WHICH--WHERE'S THE FIRE, CHAS?
COMIN' OUT OF MY MISSUS' EARS BY NOW, I SHOULD THINK. I SHOULD'VE BEEN AT THE HOSPITAL HALF AN HOUR AGO.
SHE TOLD ME TO LET YOU GET THE TUBE --I HAD TO ARGUE FOR AGES.

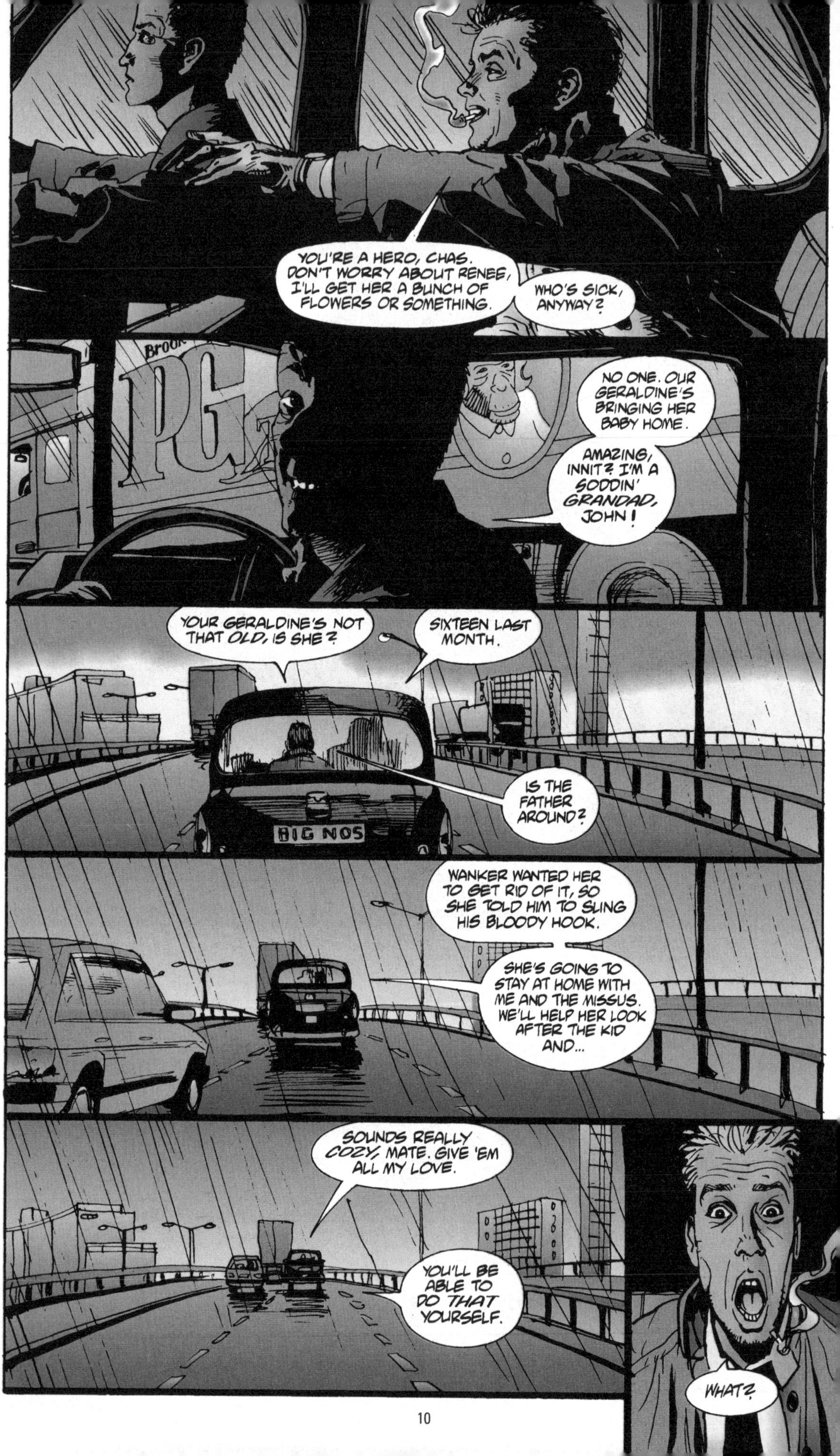
YOU'RE A HERO, CHAS. DON'T WORRY ABOUT RENEE, I'LL GET HER A BUNCH OF FLOWERS OR SOMETHING.
WHO'S SICK, ANYWAY?
NO ONE. OUR GERALDINE'S BRINGING HER BABY HOME.
AMAZING, INNIT? I'M A SODDIN' GRANDAD, JOHN!
YOUR GERALDINE'S NOT THAT OLD, IS SHE?
SIXTEEN LAST MONTH.
BIG NOS
IS THE FATHER AROUND?
WANKER WANTED HER TO GET RID OF IT, SO SHE TOLD HIM TO SLING HIS BLOODY HOOK.
SHE'S GOING TO STAY AT HOME WITH ME AND THE MISSUS. WE'LL HELP HER LOOK AFTER THE KID AND...
SOUNDS REALLY COZY, MATE. GIVE 'EM ALL MY LOVE.
YOU'LL BE ABLE TO DO THAT YOURSELF.
WHAT?

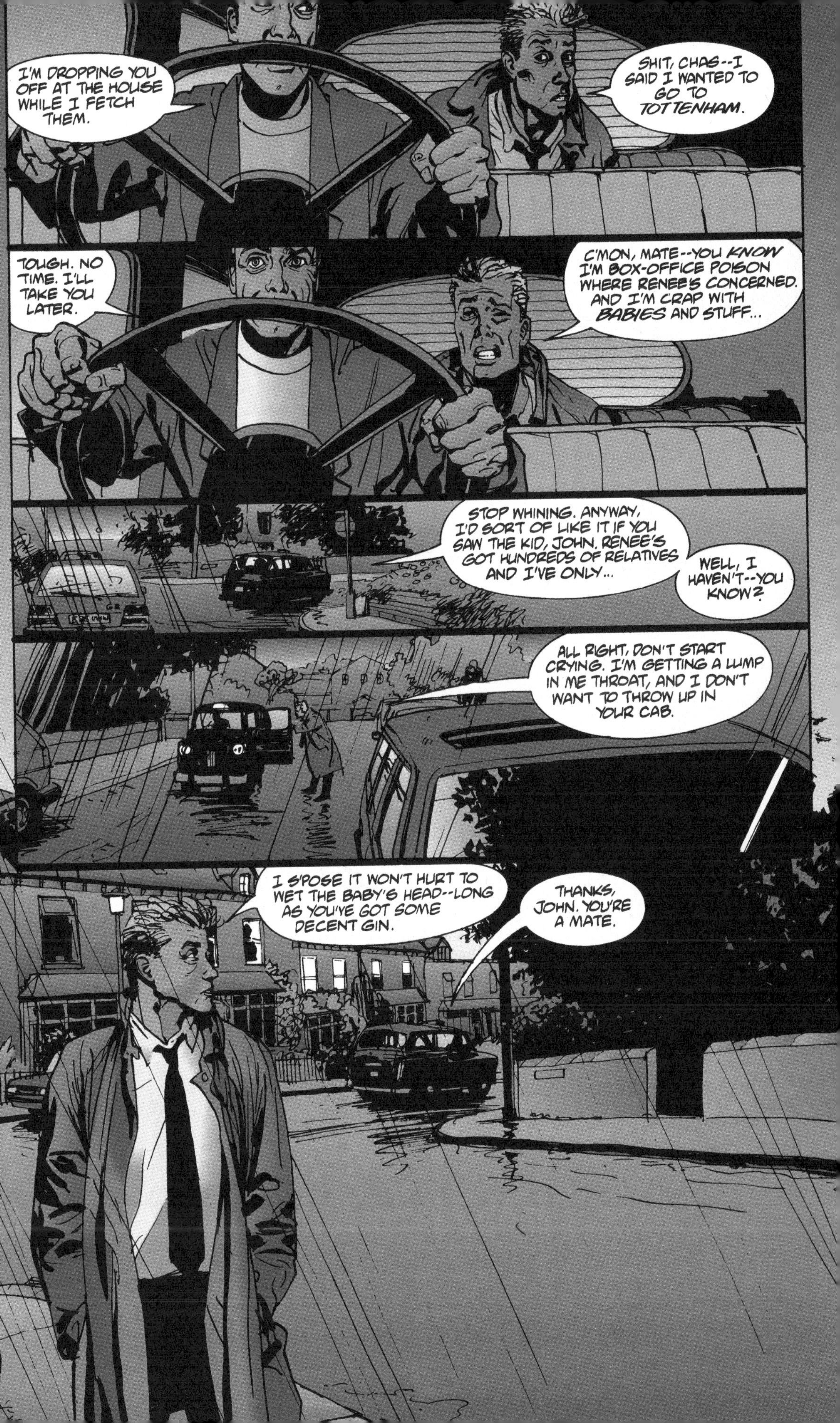

I'M DROPPING YOU OFF AT THE HOUSE WHILE I FETCH THEM.
SHIT, CHAS--I SAID I WANTED TO GO TO TOTTENHAM.
TOUGH. NO TIME. I'LL TAKE YOU LATER.
C'MON, MATE--YOU KNOW I'M BOX-OFFICE POISON WHERE RENEE'S CONCERNED. AND I'M CRAP WITH BABIES AND STUFF...
STOP WHINING. ANYWAY, I'D SORT OF LIKE IT IF YOU SAW THE KID, JOHN. RENEE'S GOT HUNDREDS OF RELATIVES AND I'VE ONLY...
WELL, I HAVEN'T--YOU KNOW?
ALL RIGHT, DON'T START CRYING. I'M GETTING A LUMP IN ME THROAT, AND I DON'T WANT TO THROW UP IN YOUR CAB.
I S'POSE IT WON'T HURT TO WET THE BABY'S HEAD--LONG AS YOU'VE GOT SOME DECENT GIN.
THANKS, JOHN. YOU'RE A MATE.

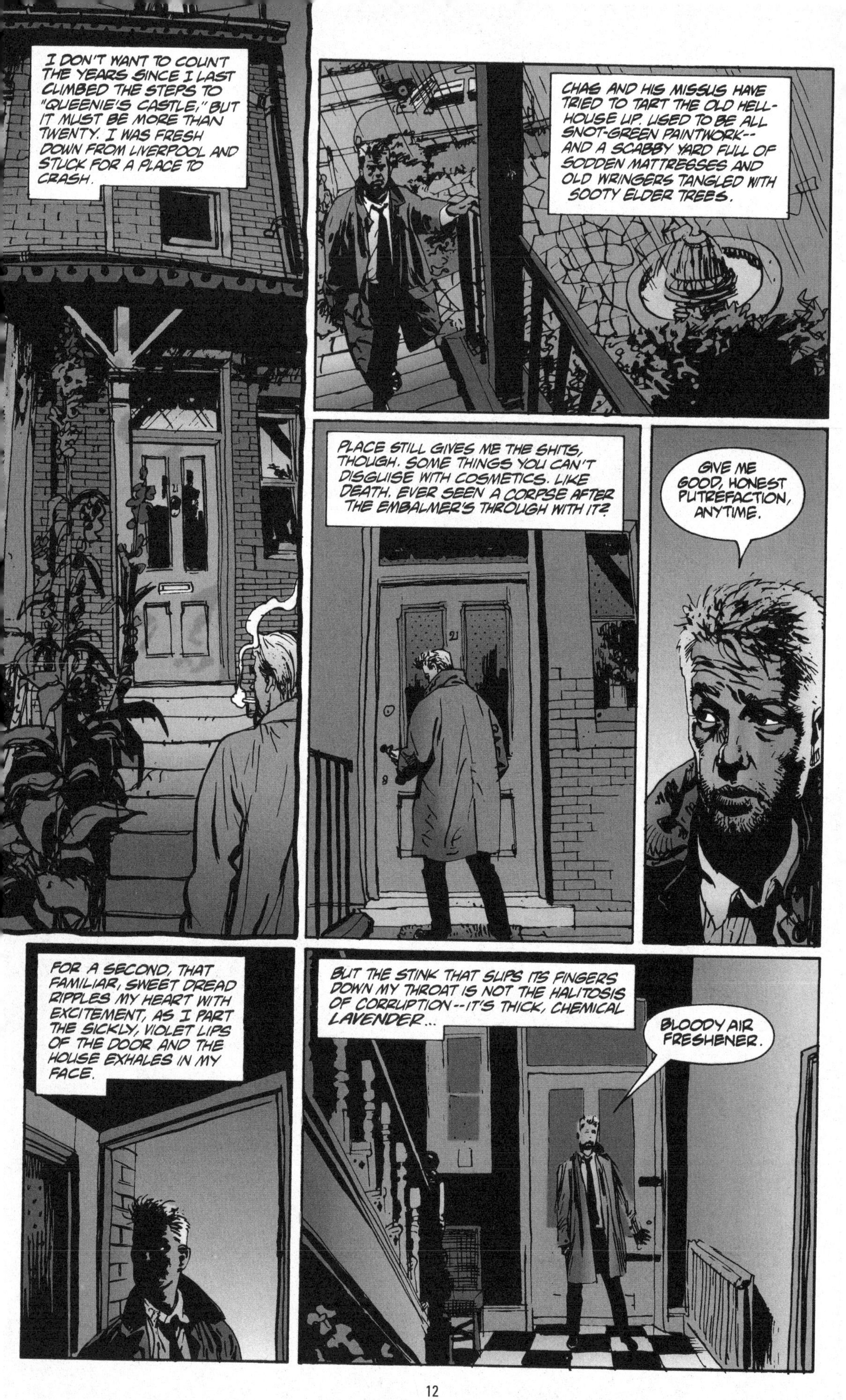
I DON'T WANT TO COUNT THE YEARS SINCE I LAST CLIMBED THE STEPS TO "QUEENIE'S CASTLE," BUT IT MUST BE MORE THAN TWENTY. I WAS FRESH DOWN FROM LIVERPOOL AND STUCK FOR A PLACE TO CRASH.
CHAS AND HIS MISSUS HAVE TRIED TO TART THE OLD HELL-HOUSE UP. USED TO BE ALL SNOT-GREEN PAINTWORK-- AND A SCABBY YARD FULL OF SODDEN MATTRESSES AND OLD WRINGERS TANGLED WITH SOOTY ELDER TREES.
PLACE STILL GIVES ME THE SHITS, THOUGH. SOME THINGS YOU CAN'T DISGUISE WITH COSMETICS. LIKE DEATH. EVER SEEN A CORPSE AFTER THE EMBALMER'S THROUGH WITH IT?
GIVE ME GOOD, HONEST PUTREFACTION, ANYTIME.
FOR A SECOND, THAT FAMILIAR, SWEET DREAD RIPPLES MY HEART WITH EXCITEMENT, AS I PART THE SICKLY, VIOLET LIPS OF THE DOOR AND THE HOUSE EXHALES IN MY FACE.
BUT THE STINK THAT SLIPS ITS FINGERS DOWN MY THROAT IS NOT THE HALITOSIS OF CORRUPTION--IT'S THICK, CHEMICAL LAVENDER...
BLOODY AIR FRESHENER.

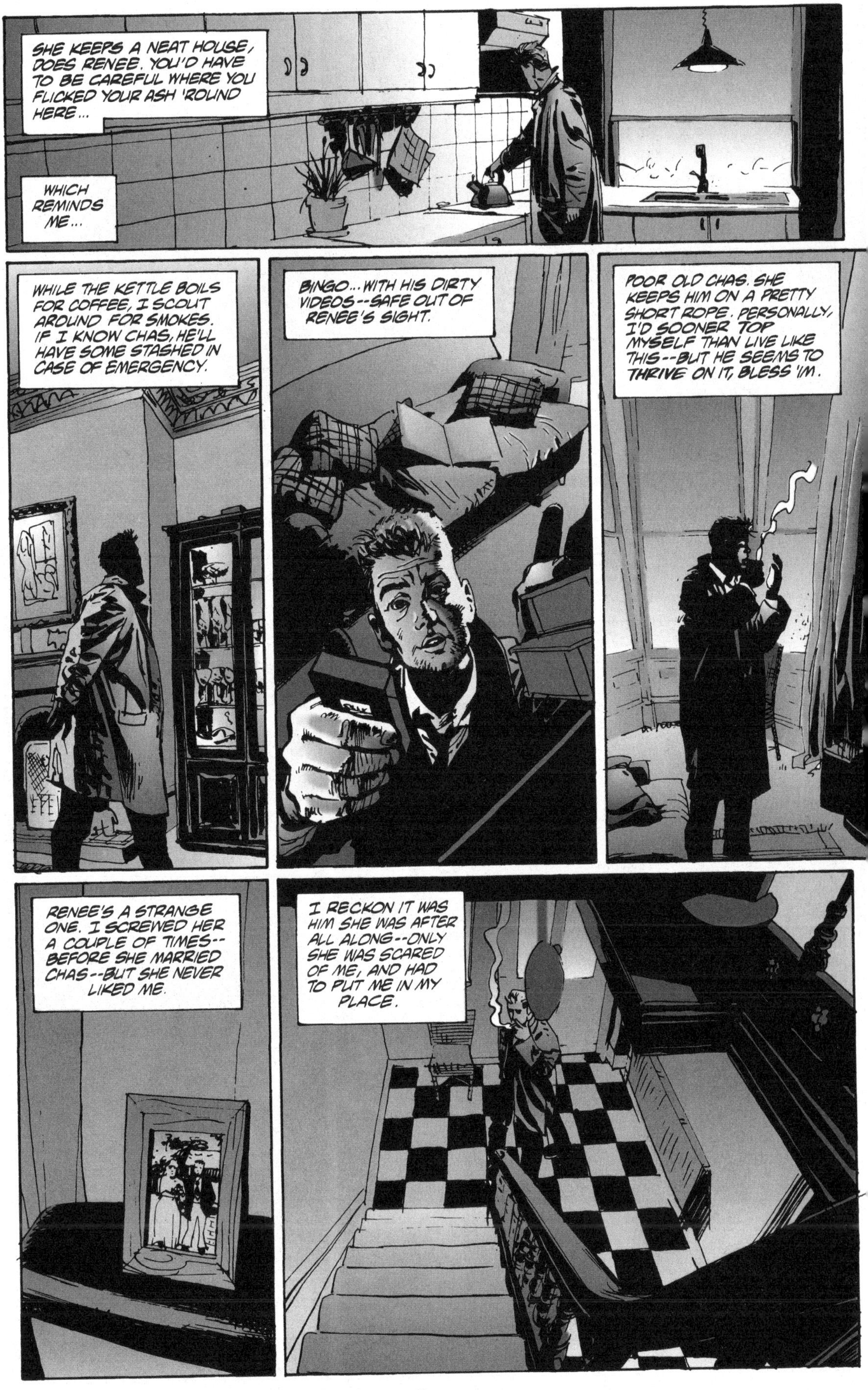
SHE KEEPS A NEAT HOUSE, DOES RENEE. YOU'D HAVE TO BE CAREFUL WHERE YOU FLICKED YOUR ASH 'ROUND HERE...
WHICH REMINDS ME...
WHILE THE KETTLE BOILS FOR COFFEE, I SCOUT AROUND FOR SMOKES. IF I KNOW CHAS, HE'LL HAVE SOME STASHED IN CASE OF EMERGENCY.
BINGO... WITH HIS DIRTY VIDEOS--SAFE OUT OF RENEE'S SIGHT.
POOR OLD CHAS. SHE KEEPS HIM ON A PRETTY SHORT ROPE. PERSONALLY, I'D SOONER TOP MYSELF THAN LIVE LIKE THIS--BUT HE SEEMS TO THRIVE ON IT, BLESS 'IM.
RENEE'S A STRANGE ONE. I SCREWED HER A COUPLE OF TIMES--BEFORE SHE MARRIED CHAS--BUT SHE NEVER LIKED ME.
I RECKON IT WAS HIM SHE WAS AFTER ALL ALONG--ONLY SHE WAS SCARED OF ME, AND HAD TO PUT ME IN MY PLACE.

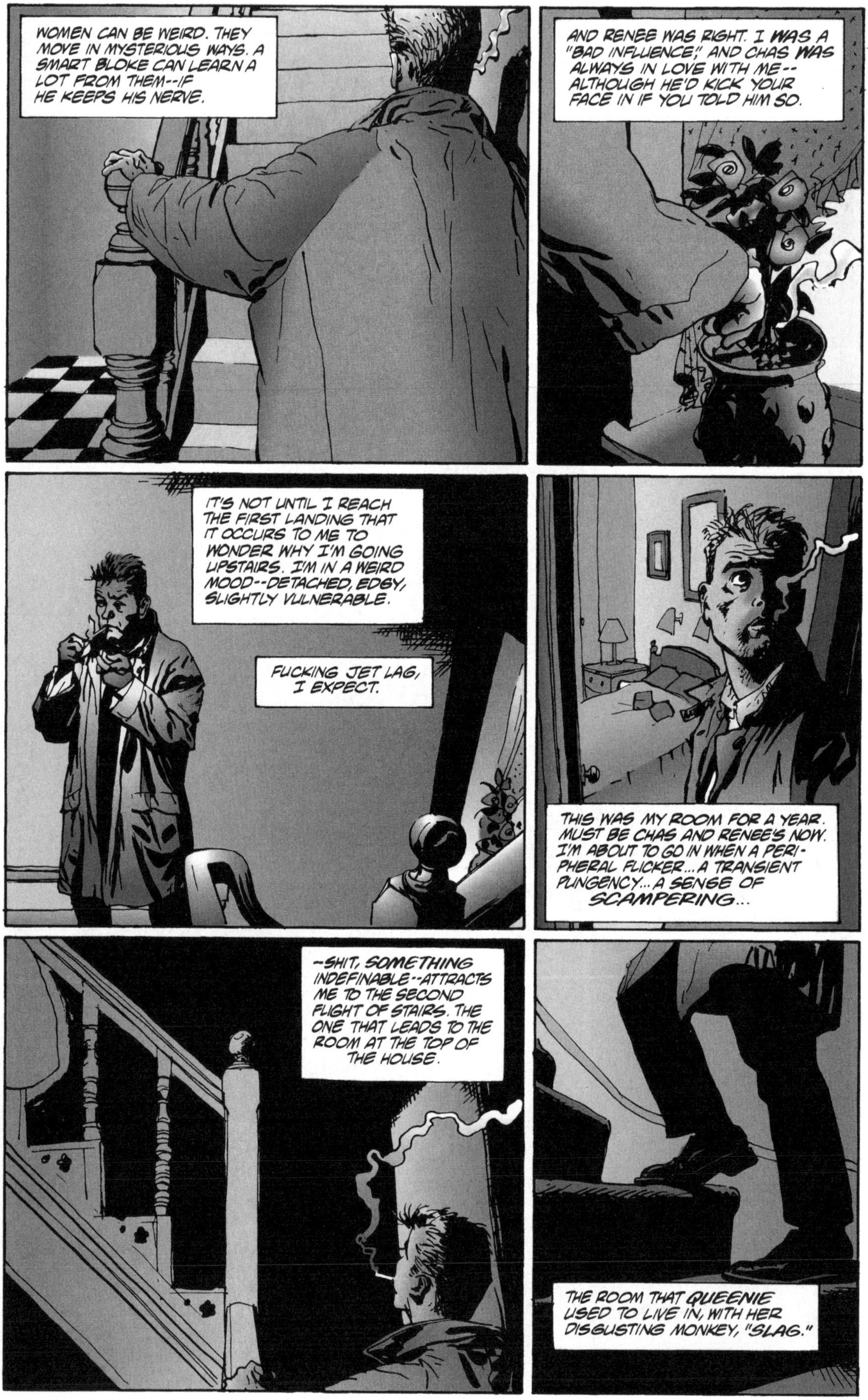
WOMEN CAN BE WEIRD. THEY MOVE IN MYSTERIOUS WAYS. A SMART BLOKE CAN LEARN A LOT FROM THEM--IF HE KEEPS HIS NERVE.
AND RENEE WAS RIGHT. I WAS A "BAD INFLUENCE," AND CHAS WAS ALWAYS IN LOVE WITH ME-- ALTHOUGH HE'D KICK YOUR FACE IN IF YOU TOLD HIM SO.
IT'S NOT UNTIL I REACH THE FIRST LANDING THAT IT OCCURS TO ME TO WONDER WHY I'M GOING UPSTAIRS. I'M IN A WEIRD MOOD--DETACHED, EDGY, SLIGHTLY VULNERABLE.
FUCKING JET LAG, I EXPECT.
THIS WAS MY ROOM FOR A YEAR. MUST BE CHAS AND RENEE'S NOW. I'M ABOUT TO GO IN WHEN A PERI-PHERAL FLICKER... A TRANSIENT PUNGENCY... A SENSE OF SCAMPERING...
--SHIT, SOMETHING INDEFINABLE--ATTRACTS ME TO THE SECOND FLIGHT OF STAIRS. THE ONE THAT LEADS TO THE ROOM AT THE TOP OF THE HOUSE.
THE ROOM THAT QUEENIE USED TO LIVE IN, WITH HER DISGUSTING MONKEY, "SLAG."

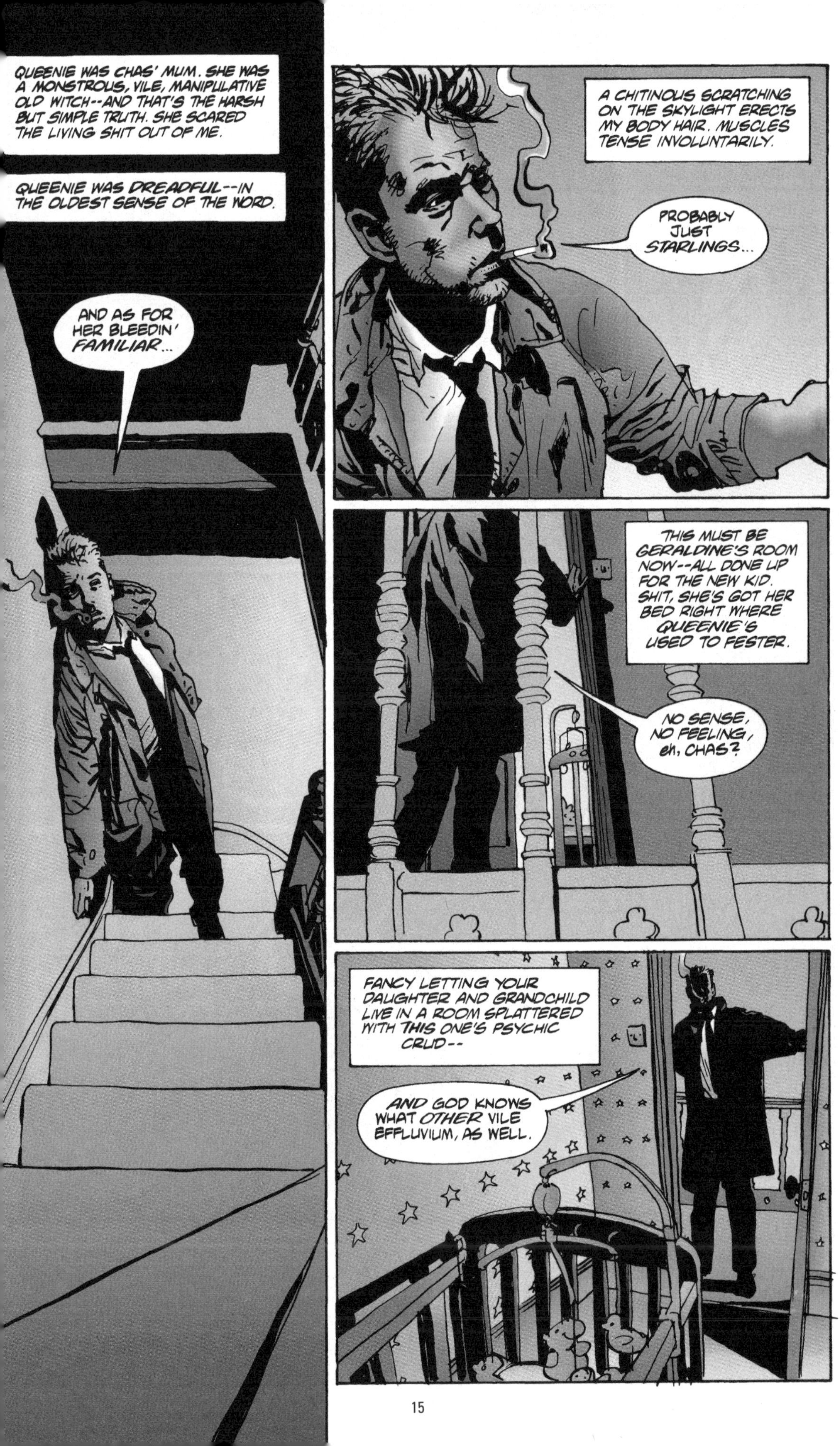
QUEENIE WAS CHAS' MUM. SHE WAS A MONSTROUS, VILE, MANIPULATIVE OLD WITCH--AND THAT'S THE HARSH BUT SIMPLE TRUTH. SHE SCARED THE LIVING SHIT OUT OF ME.
QUEENIE WAS DREADFUL--IN THE OLDEST SENSE OF THE WORD.
AND AS FOR HER BLEEDIN' FAMILIAR...
A CHITINOUS SCRATCHING ON THE SKYLIGHT ERECTS MY BODY HAIR. MUSCLES TENSE INVOLUNTARILY.
PROBABLY JUST STARLINGS...
THIS MUST BE GERALDINE'S ROOM NOW--ALL DONE UP FOR THE NEW KID. SHIT, SHE'S GOT HER BED RIGHT WHERE QUEENIE'S USED TO FESTER.
NO SENSE, NO FEELING, eh, CHAS?
FANCY LETTING YOUR DAUGHTER AND GRANDCHILD LIVE IN A ROOM SPLATTERED WITH THIS ONE'S PSYCHIC CRUD--
AND GOD KNOWS WHAT OTHER VILE EFFLUVIUM, AS WELL.

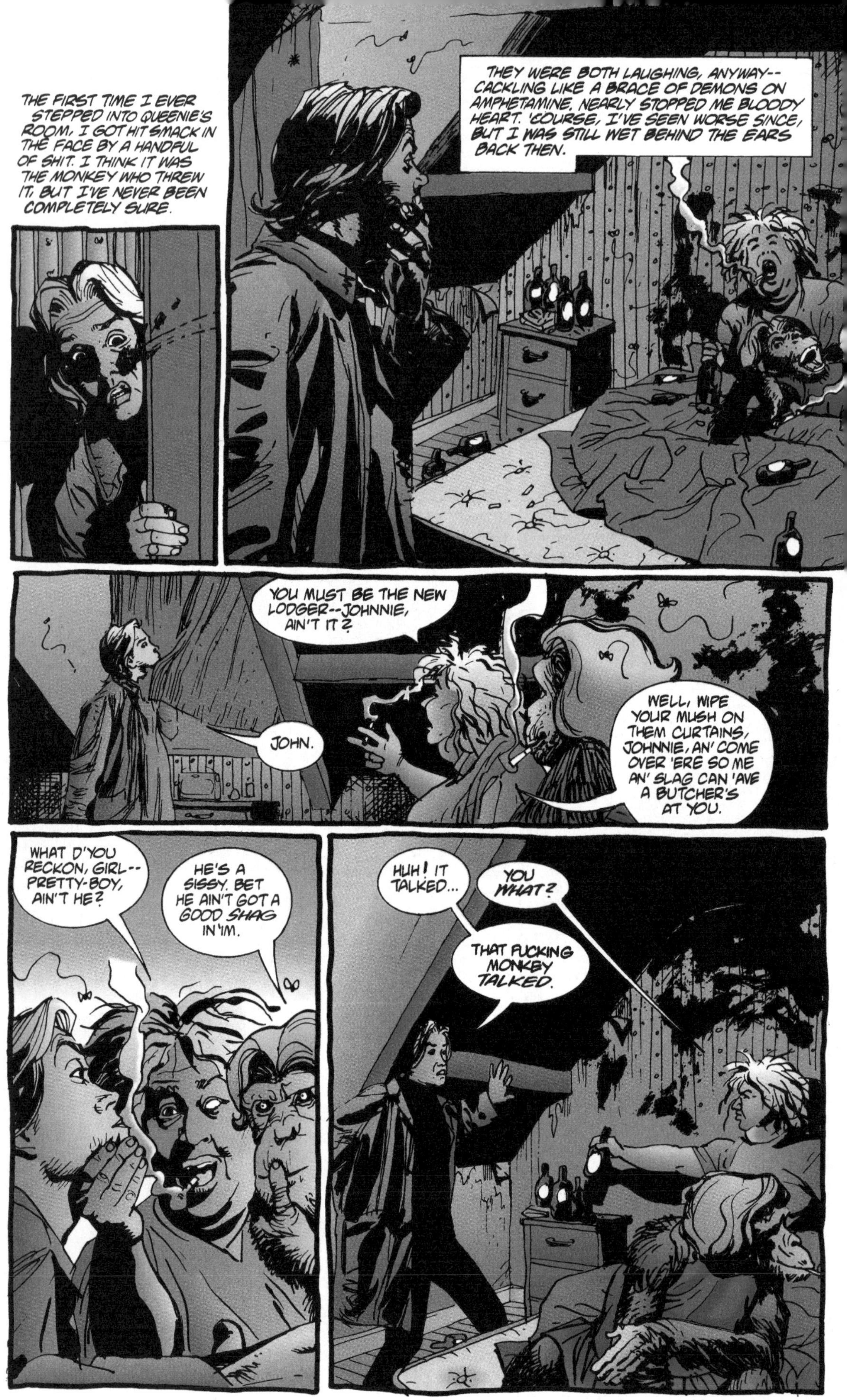
THE FIRST TIME I EVER STEPPED INTO QUEENIE'S ROOM, I GOT HIT SMACK IN THE FACE BY A HANDFUL OF SHIT. I THINK IT WAS THE MONKEY WHO THREW IT, BUT I'VE NEVER BEEN COMPLETELY SURE.
THEY WERE BOTH LAUGHING, ANYWAY--CACKLING LIKE A BRACE OF DEMONS ON AMPHETAMINE. NEARLY STOPPED ME BLOODY HEART. 'COURSE, I'VE SEEN WORSE SINCE, BUT I WAS STILL WET BEHIND THE EARS BACK THEN.
YOU MUST BE THE NEW LODGER--JOHNNIE, AIN'T IT?
JOHN.
WELL, WIPE YOUR MUSH ON THEM CURTAINS, JOHNNIE, AN' COME OVER 'ERE SO ME AN' SLAG CAN 'AVE A BUTCHER'S AT YOU.
WHAT D'YOU RECKON, GIRL--PRETTY-BOY, AIN'T HE?
HE'S A SISSY. BET HE AIN'T GOT A GOOD SHAG IN 'IM.
HUH! IT TALKED...
YOU WHAT?
THAT FUCKING MONKEY TALKED.

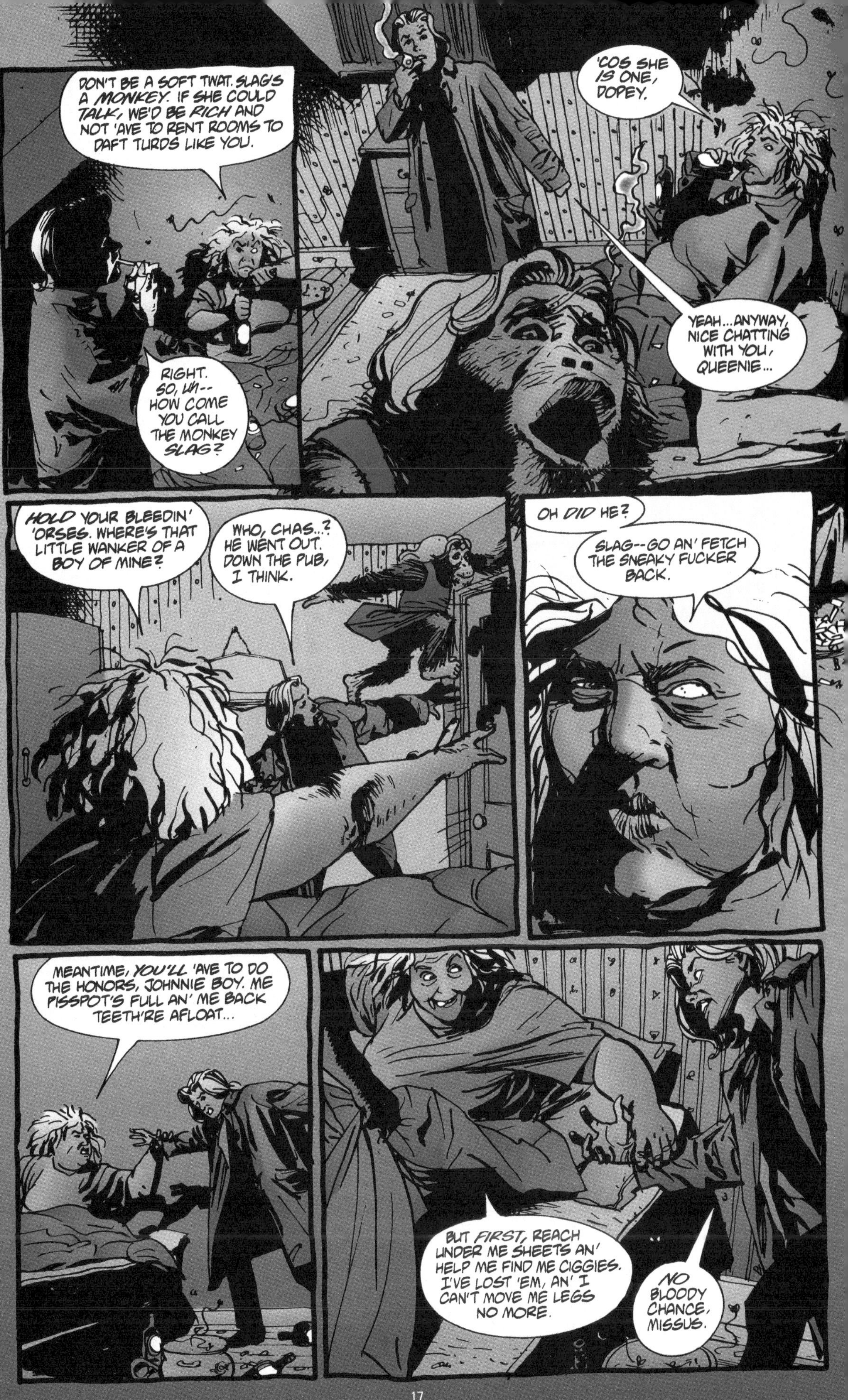
DON'T BE A SOFT TWAT. SLAG'S A MONKEY. IF SHE COULD TALK, WE'D BE RICH AND NOT 'AVE TO RENT ROOMS TO DAFT TURDS LIKE YOU.
RIGHT. SO, UH-- HOW COME YOU CALL THE MONKEY SLAG?
'COS SHE IS ONE, DOPEY.
YEAH...ANYWAY, NICE CHATTING WITH YOU, QUEENIE...
HOLD YOUR BLEEDIN' 'ORSES. WHERE'S THAT LITTLE WANKER OF A BOY OF MINE?
WHO, CHAS...? HE WENT OUT. DOWN THE PUB, I THINK.
OH DID HE?
SLAG--GO AN' FETCH THE SNEAKY FUCKER BACK.
MEANTIME, YOU'LL 'AVE TO DO THE HONORS, JOHNNIE BOY. ME PISSPOT'S FULL AN' ME BACK TEETH'RE AFLOAT...
BUT FIRST, REACH UNDER ME SHEETS AN' HELP ME FIND ME CIGGIES. I'VE LOST 'EM, AN' I CAN'T MOVE ME LEGS NO MORE.
NO BLOODY CHANCE, MISSUS.

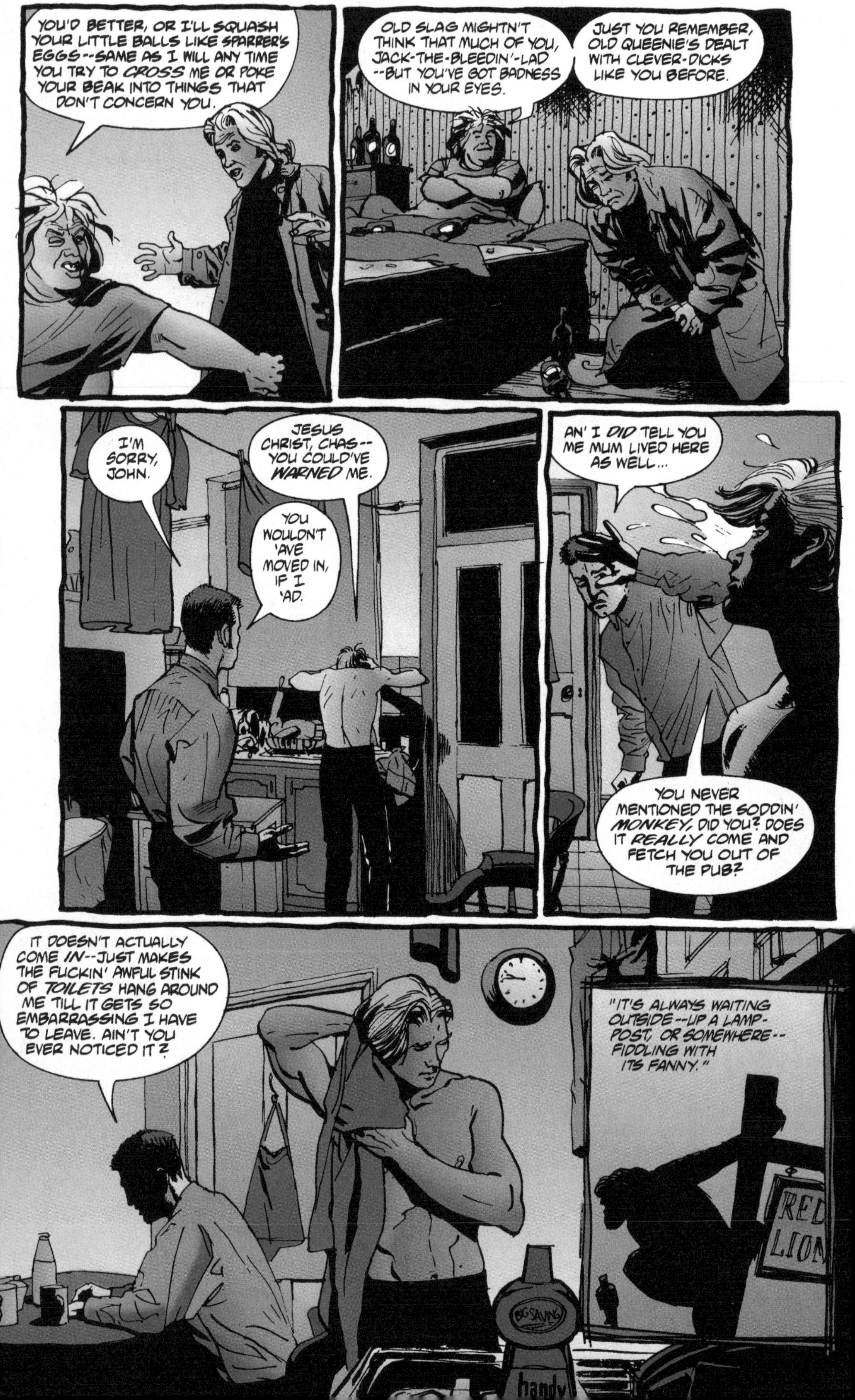
YOU'D BETTER, OR I'LL SQUASH YOUR LITTLE BALLS LIKE SPARRER'S EGGS--SAME AS I WILL ANY TIME YOU TRY TO *CROSS* ME OR POKE YOUR BEAK INTO THINGS THAT DON'T CONCERN YOU.
OLD SLAG MIGHTN'T THINK THAT MUCH OF YOU, JACK-THE-BLEEDIN'-LAD --BUT YOU'VE GOT BADNESS IN YOUR EYES.
JUST YOU REMEMBER, OLD QUEENIE'S DEALT WITH CLEVER-DICKS LIKE YOU BEFORE.
I'M SORRY, JOHN.
JESUS CHRIST, CHAS-- YOU COULD'VE *WARNED* ME.
YOU WOULDN'T 'AVE MOVED IN, IF I 'AD.
AN' I *DID* TELL YOU ME MUM LIVED HERE AS WELL...
YOU NEVER MENTIONED THE SODDIN' *MONKEY*, DID YOU? DOES IT *REALLY* COME AND FETCH YOU OUT OF THE PUB?
IT DOESN'T ACTUALLY COME *IN*--JUST MAKES THE FUCKIN' AWFUL STINK OF *TOILETS* HANG AROUND ME TILL IT GETS SO EMBARRASSING I HAVE TO LEAVE. AIN'T YOU EVER NOTICED IT?
"IT'S ALWAYS WAITING OUTSIDE--UP A LAMP-POST, OR SOMEWHERE--FIDDLING WITH ITS FANNY."
RED LION
BIG SAVING
handy

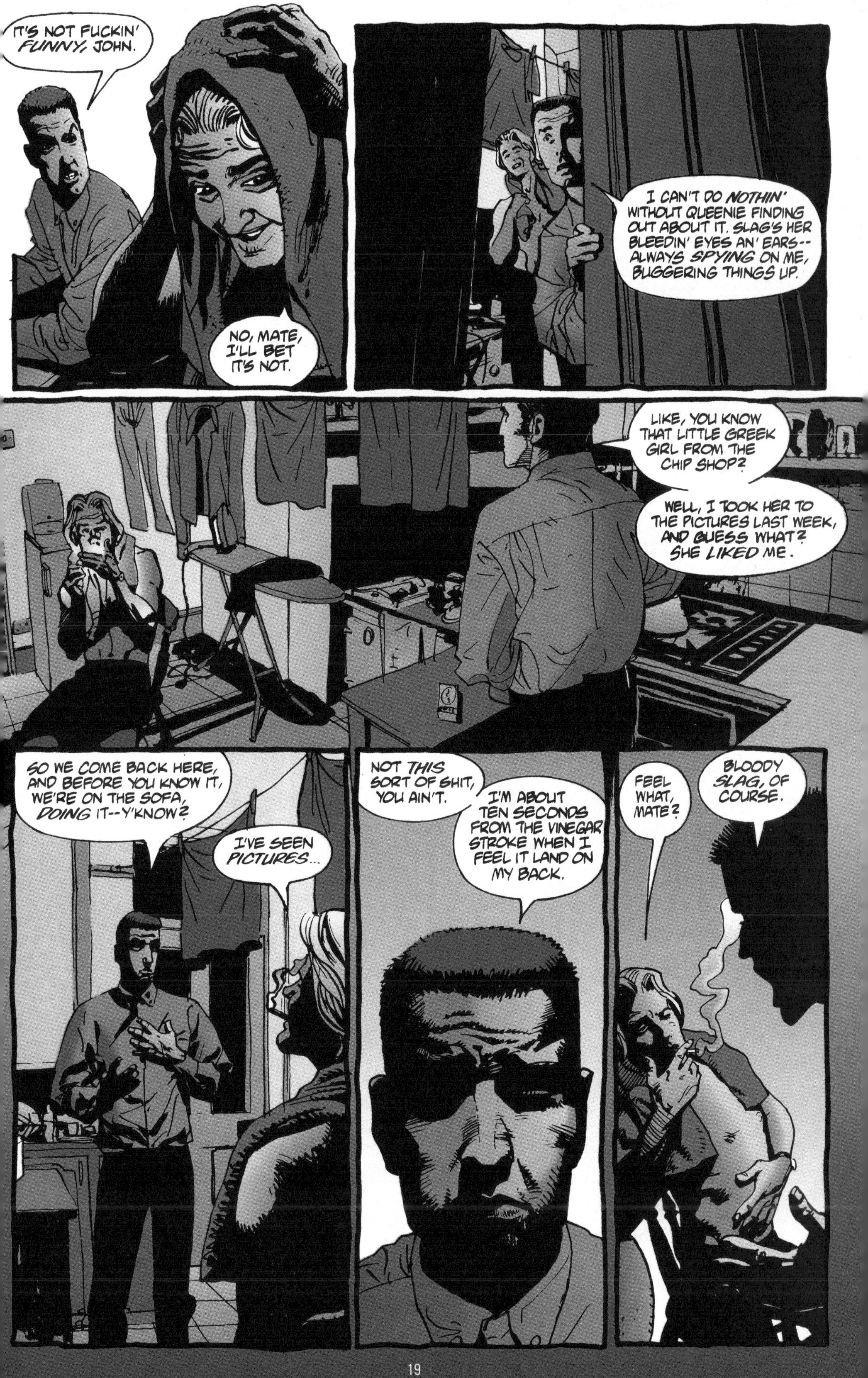
IT'S NOT FUCKIN' FUNNY, JOHN.
NO, MATE, I'LL BET IT'S NOT.
I CAN'T DO NOTHIN' WITHOUT QUEENIE FINDING OUT ABOUT IT. SLAG'S HER BLEEDIN' EYES AN' EARS-- ALWAYS SPYING ON ME, BUGGERING THINGS UP.
LIKE, YOU KNOW THAT LITTLE GREEK GIRL FROM THE CHIP SHOP?
WELL, I TOOK HER TO THE PICTURES LAST WEEK, AND GUESS WHAT? SHE LIKED ME.
SO WE COME BACK HERE, AND BEFORE YOU KNOW IT, WE'RE ON THE SOFA, DOING IT--Y'KNOW?
I'VE SEEN PICTURES...
NOT THIS SORT OF SHIT, YOU AIN'T.
I'M ABOUT TEN SECONDS FROM THE VINEGAR STROKE WHEN I FEEL IT LAND ON MY BACK.
FEEL WHAT, MATE?
BLOODY SLAG, OF COURSE.

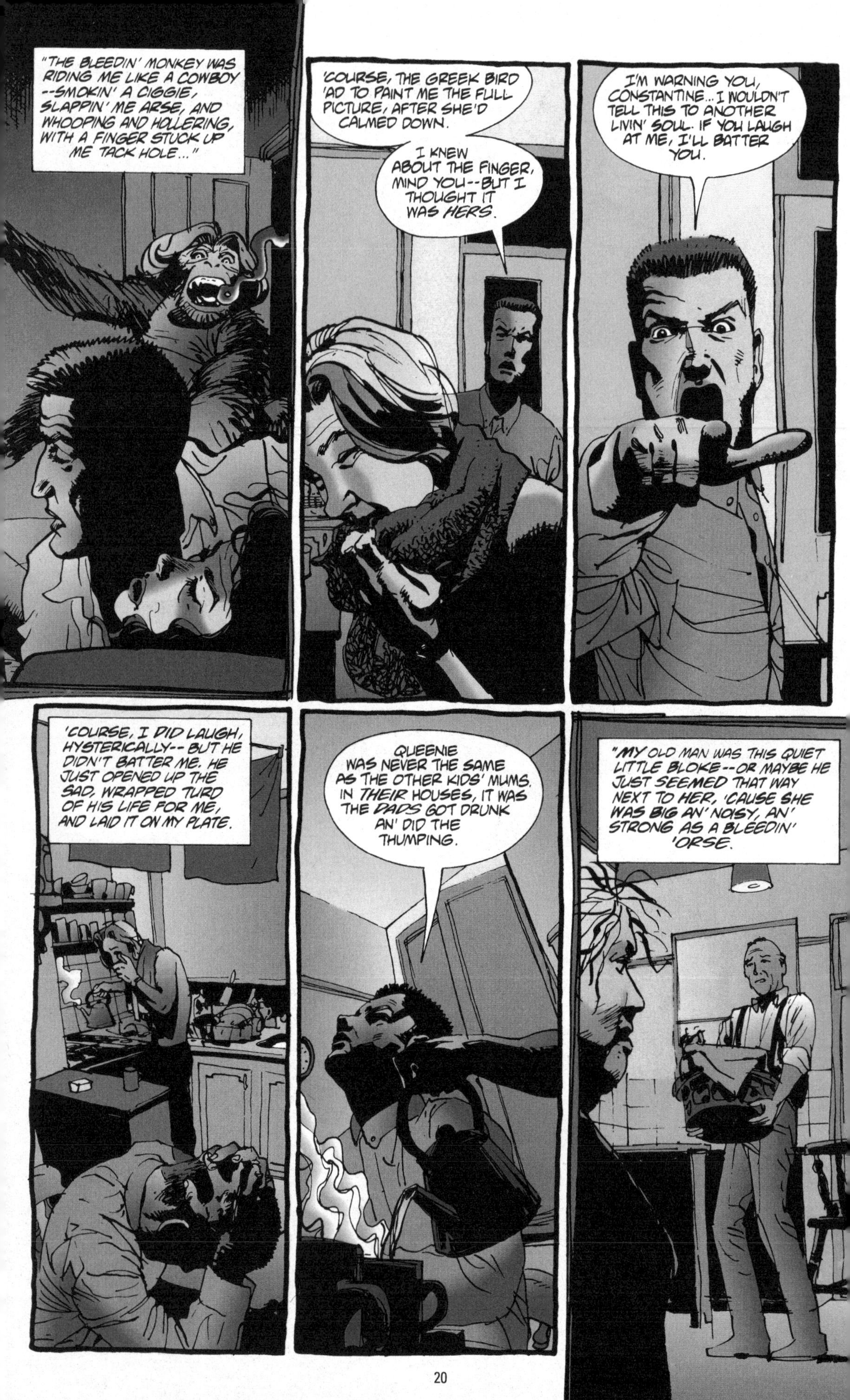
"THE BLEEDIN' MONKEY WAS RIDING ME LIKE A COWBOY --SMOKIN' A CIGGIE, SLAPPIN' ME ARSE, AND WHOOPING AND HOLLERING, WITH A FINGER STUCK UP ME TACK HOLE..."
'COURSE, THE GREEK BIRD 'AD TO PAINT ME THE FULL PICTURE, AFTER SHE'D CALMED DOWN.
I KNEW ABOUT THE FINGER, MIND YOU--BUT I THOUGHT IT WAS HERS.
I'M WARNING YOU, CONSTANTINE... I WOULDN'T TELL THIS TO ANOTHER LIVIN' SOUL. IF YOU LAUGH AT ME, I'LL BATTER YOU.
'COURSE, I DID LAUGH, HYSTERICALLY-- BUT HE DIDN'T BATTER ME. HE JUST OPENED UP THE SAD, WRAPPED TURD OF HIS LIFE FOR ME, AND LAID IT ON MY PLATE.
QUEENIE WAS NEVER THE SAME AS THE OTHER KIDS' MUMS. IN THEIR HOUSES, IT WAS THE DADS GOT DRUNK AN' DID THE THUMPING.
"MY OLD MAN WAS THIS QUIET LITTLE BLOKE--OR MAYBE HE JUST SEEMED THAT WAY NEXT TO HER, 'CAUSE SHE WAS BIG AN' NOISY, AN' STRONG AS A BLEEDIN' 'ORSE.

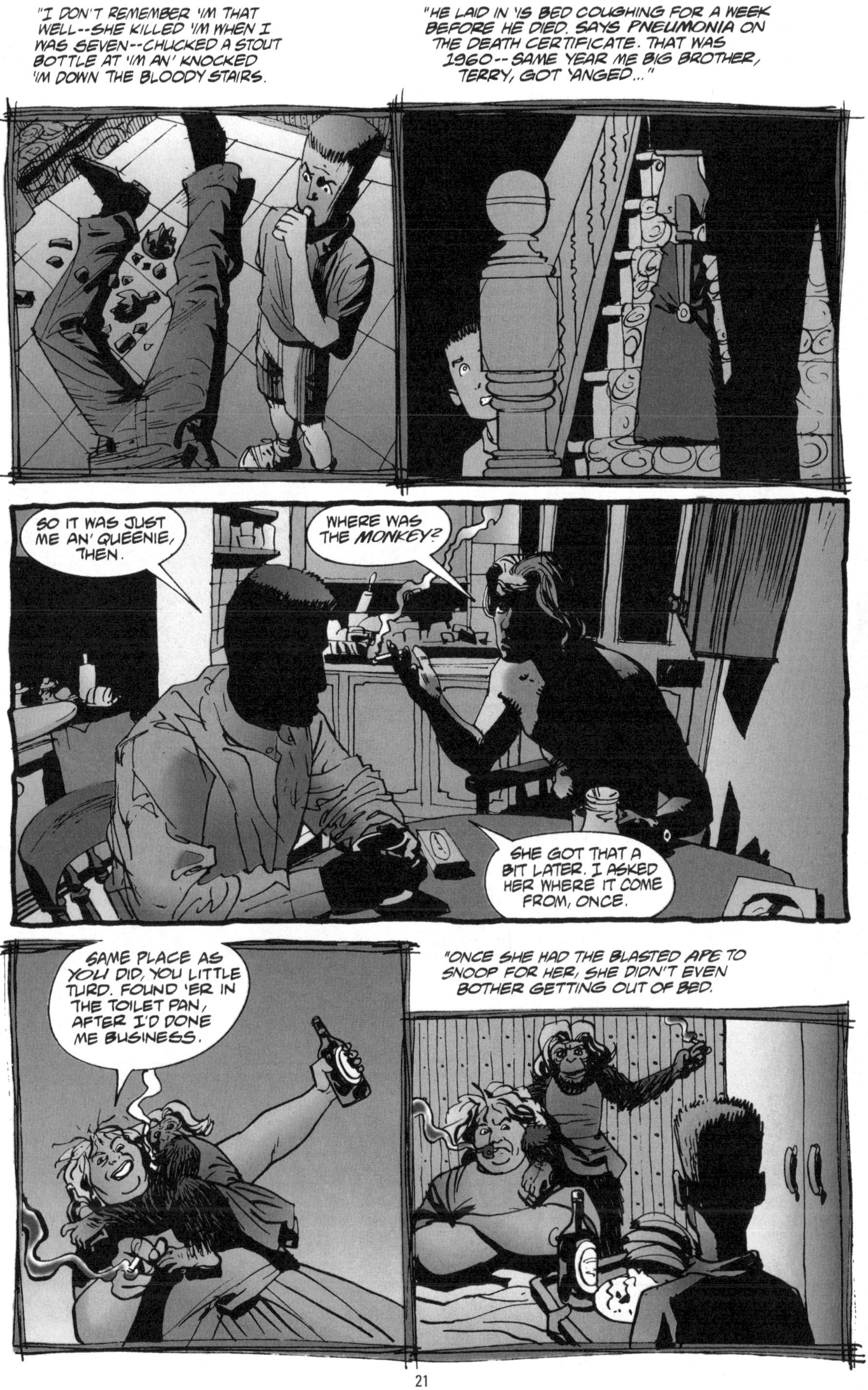
"I DON'T REMEMBER 'IM THAT WELL--SHE KILLED 'IM WHEN I WAS SEVEN--CHUCKED A STOUT BOTTLE AT 'IM AN' KNOCKED 'IM DOWN THE BLOODY STAIRS.
"HE LAID IN 'IS BED COUGHING FOR A WEEK BEFORE HE DIED. SAYS PNEUMONIA ON THE DEATH CERTIFICATE. THAT WAS 1960--SAME YEAR ME BIG BROTHER, TERRY, GOT 'ANGED..."
SO IT WAS JUST ME AN' QUEENIE, THEN.
WHERE WAS THE MONKEY?
SHE GOT THAT A BIT LATER. I ASKED HER WHERE IT COME FROM, ONCE.
SAME PLACE AS YOU DID, YOU LITTLE TURD. FOUND 'ER IN THE TOILET PAN, AFTER I'D DONE ME BUSINESS.
"ONCE SHE HAD THE BLASTED APE TO SNOOP FOR HER, SHE DIDN'T EVEN BOTHER GETTING OUT OF BED.

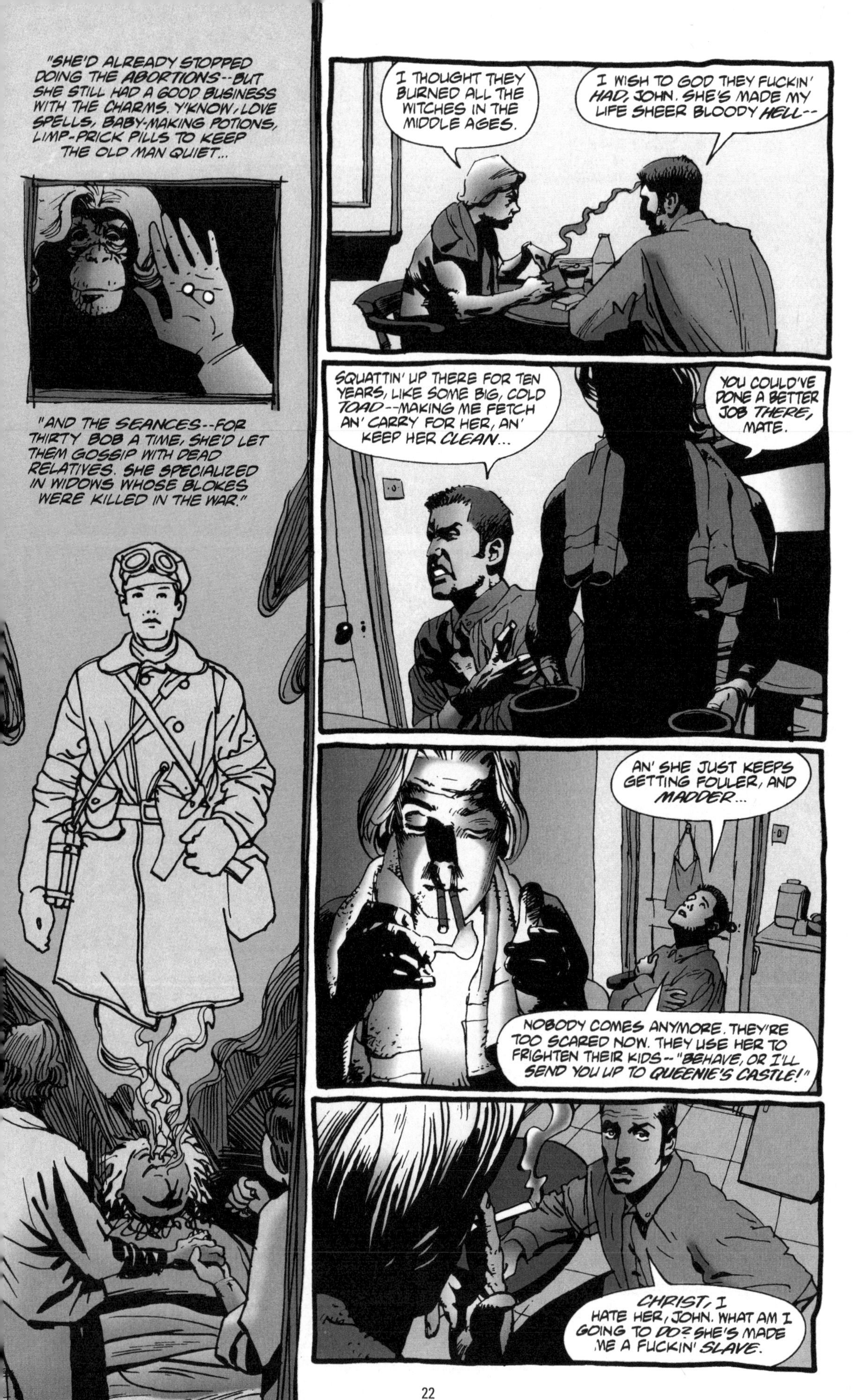
"SHE'D ALREADY STOPPED DOING THE ABORTIONS--BUT SHE STILL HAD A GOOD BUSINESS WITH THE CHARMS. Y'KNOW, LOVE SPELLS, BABY-MAKING POTIONS, LIMP-PRICK PILLS TO KEEP THE OLD MAN QUIET...
"AND THE SEANCES--FOR THIRTY BOB A TIME, SHE'D LET THEM GOSSIP WITH DEAD RELATIVES. SHE SPECIALIZED IN WIDOWS WHOSE BLOKES WERE KILLED IN THE WAR."
I THOUGHT THEY BURNED ALL THE WITCHES IN THE MIDDLE AGES.
I WISH TO GOD THEY FUCKIN' HAD, JOHN. SHE'S MADE MY LIFE SHEER BLOODY HELL--
SQUATTIN' UP THERE FOR TEN YEARS, LIKE SOME BIG, COLD TOAD--MAKING ME FETCH AN' CARRY FOR HER, AN' KEEP HER CLEAN...
YOU COULD'VE DONE A BETTER JOB THERE, MATE.
AN' SHE JUST KEEPS GETTING FOULER, AND MADDER...
NOBODY COMES ANYMORE. THEY'RE TOO SCARED NOW. THEY USE HER TO FRIGHTEN THEIR KIDS--"BEHAVE, OR I'LL SEND YOU UP TO QUEENIE'S CASTLE!"
CHRIST, I HATE HER, JOHN. WHAT AM I GOING TO DO? SHE'S MADE ME A FUCKIN' SLAVE.

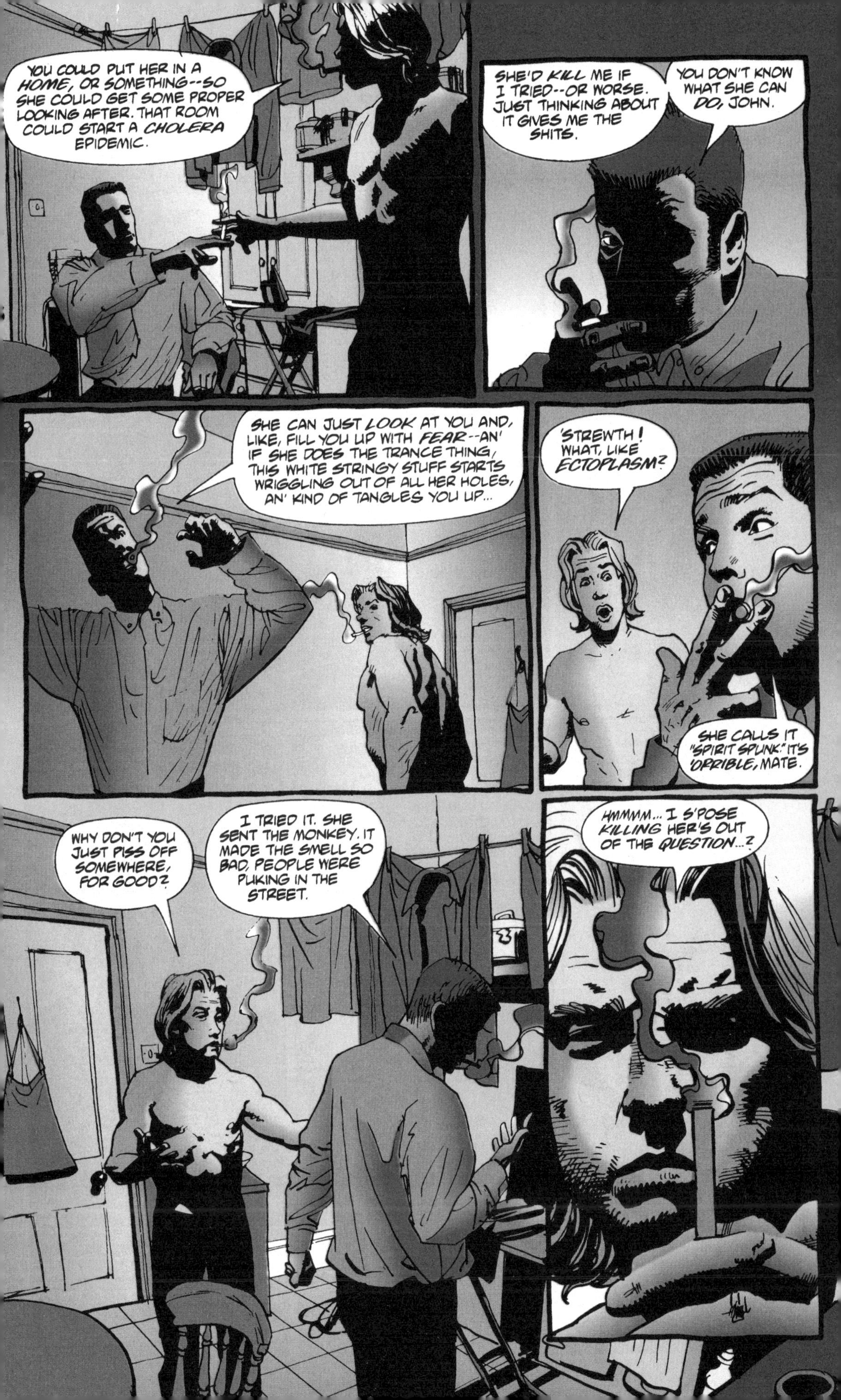

YOU COULD PUT HER IN A HOME, OR SOMETHING--SO SHE COULD GET SOME PROPER LOOKING AFTER. THAT ROOM COULD START A CHOLERA EPIDEMIC.
SHE'D KILL ME IF I TRIED--OR WORSE. JUST THINKING ABOUT IT GIVES ME THE SHITS.
YOU DON'T KNOW WHAT SHE CAN DO, JOHN.
SHE CAN JUST LOOK AT YOU AND, LIKE, FILL YOU UP WITH FEAR--AN' IF SHE DOES THE TRANCE THING, THIS WHITE STRINGY STUFF STARTS WRIGGLING OUT OF ALL HER HOLES, AN' KIND OF TANGLES YOU UP...
'STREWTH! WHAT, LIKE ECTOPLASM?
SHE CALLS IT "SPIRIT SPUNK." IT'S 'ORRIBLE, MATE.
WHY DON'T YOU JUST PISS OFF SOMEWHERE, FOR GOOD?
I TRIED IT. SHE SENT THE MONKEY. IT MADE THE SMELL SO BAD, PEOPLE WERE PUKING IN THE STREET.
HMMMM... I S'POSE KILLING HER'S OUT OF THE QUESTION...?

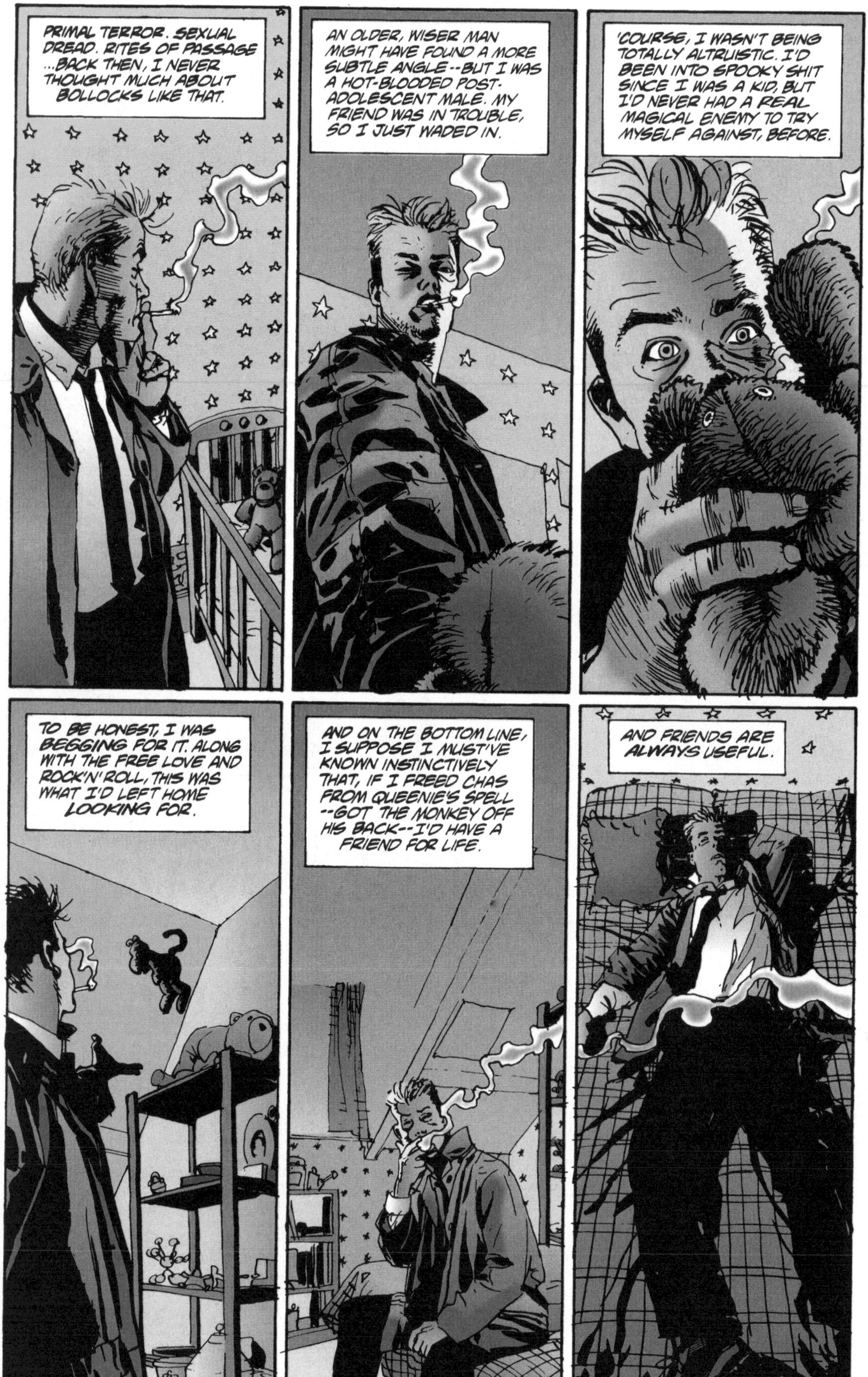
PRIMAL TERROR. SEXUAL DREAD. RITES OF PASSAGE ...BACK THEN, I NEVER THOUGHT MUCH ABOUT BOLLOCKS LIKE THAT.
AN OLDER, WISER MAN MIGHT HAVE FOUND A MORE SUBTLE ANGLE--BUT I WAS A HOT-BLOODED POST-ADOLESCENT MALE. MY FRIEND WAS IN TROUBLE, SO I JUST WADED IN.
'COURSE, I WASN'T BEING TOTALLY ALTRUISTIC. I'D BEEN INTO SPOOKY SHIT SINCE I WAS A KID, BUT I'D NEVER HAD A REAL MAGICAL ENEMY TO TRY MYSELF AGAINST, BEFORE.
TO BE HONEST, I WAS BEGGING FOR IT. ALONG WITH THE FREE LOVE AND ROCK'N' ROLL, THIS WAS WHAT I'D LEFT HOME LOOKING FOR.
AND ON THE BOTTOM LINE, I SUPPOSE I MUST'VE KNOWN INSTINCTIVELY THAT, IF I FREED CHAS FROM QUEENIE'S SPELL --GOT THE MONKEY OFF HIS BACK--I'D HAVE A FRIEND FOR LIFE.
AND FRIENDS ARE ALWAYS USEFUL.

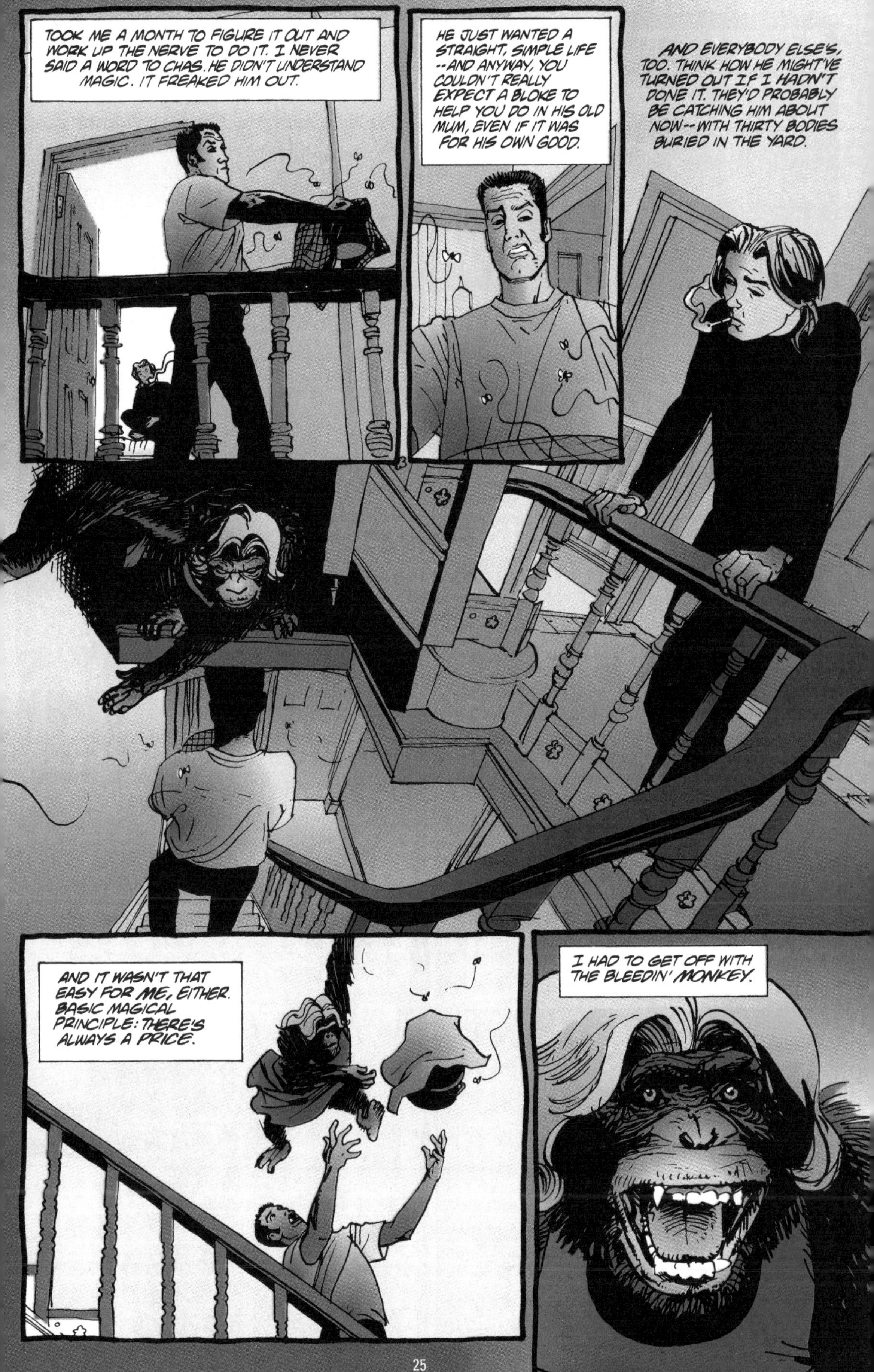

TOOK ME A MONTH TO FIGURE IT OUT AND WORK UP THE NERVE TO DO IT. I NEVER SAID A WORD TO CHAS. HE DIDN'T UNDERSTAND MAGIC. IT FREAKED HIM OUT.
HE JUST WANTED A STRAIGHT, SIMPLE LIFE --AND ANYWAY, YOU COULDN'T REALLY EXPECT A BLOKE TO HELP YOU DO IN HIS OLD MUM, EVEN IF IT WAS FOR HIS OWN GOOD.
AND EVERYBODY ELSE'S, TOO. THINK HOW HE MIGHT'VE TURNED OUT IF I HADN'T DONE IT. THEY'D PROBABLY BE CATCHING HIM ABOUT NOW--WITH THIRTY BODIES BURIED IN THE YARD.
AND IT WASN'T THAT EASY FOR ME, EITHER. BASIC MAGICAL PRINCIPLE: THERE'S ALWAYS A PRICE.
I HAD TO GET OFF WITH THE BLEEDIN' MONKEY.

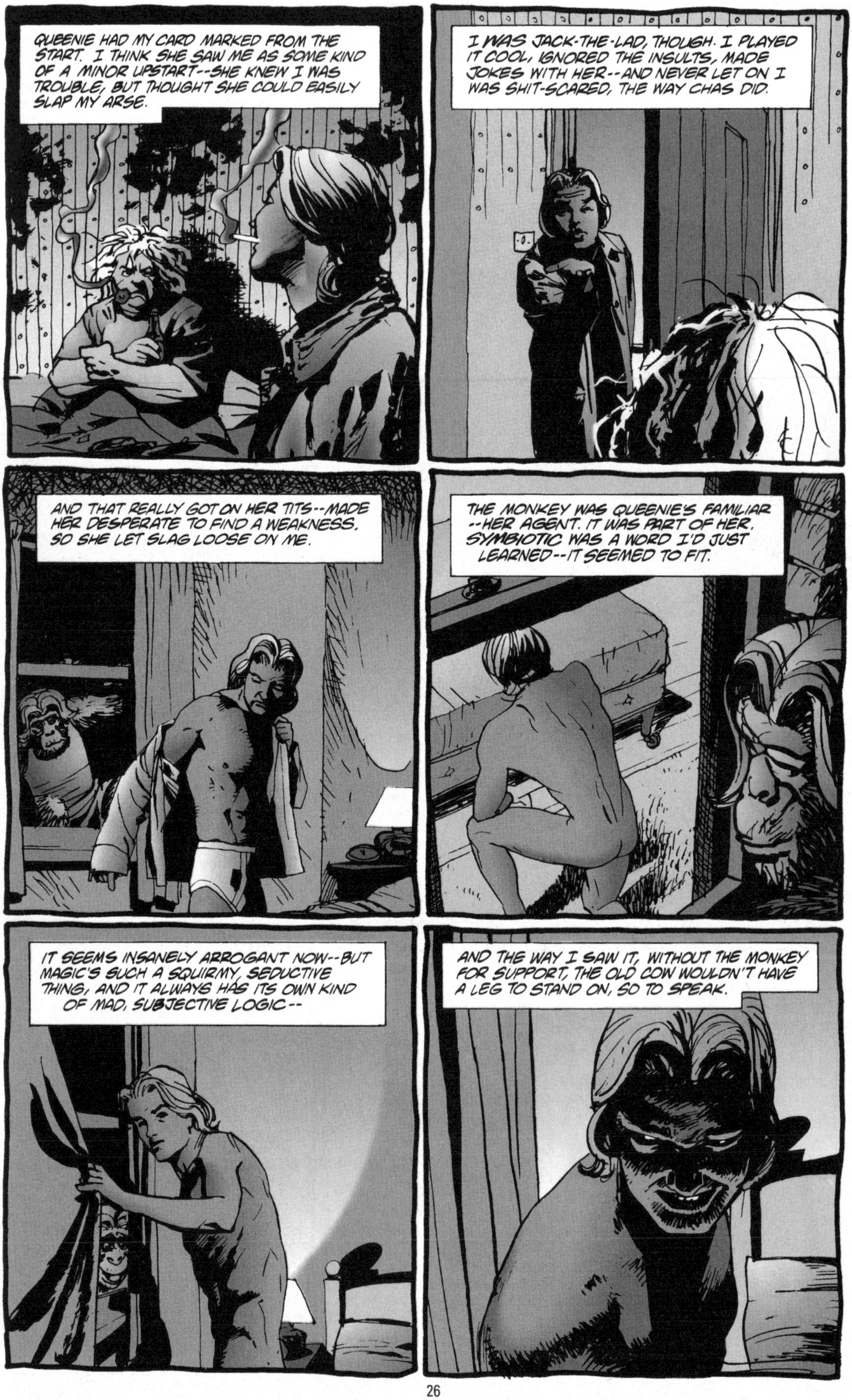
QUEENIE HAD MY CARD MARKED FROM THE START. I THINK SHE SAW ME AS SOME KIND OF A MINOR UPSTART--SHE KNEW I WAS TROUBLE, BUT THOUGHT SHE COULD EASILY SLAP MY ARSE.
I WAS JACK-THE-LAD, THOUGH. I PLAYED IT COOL, IGNORED THE INSULTS, MADE JOKES WITH HER--AND NEVER LET ON I WAS SHIT-SCARED, THE WAY CHAS DID.
AND THAT REALLY GOT ON HER TITS--MADE HER DESPERATE TO FIND A WEAKNESS. SO SHE LET SLAG LOOSE ON ME.
THE MONKEY WAS QUEENIE'S FAMILIAR --HER AGENT. IT WAS PART OF HER. SYMBIOTIC WAS A WORD I'D JUST LEARNED--IT SEEMED TO FIT.
IT SEEMS INSANELY ARROGANT NOW--BUT MAGIC'S SUCH A SQUIRMY, SEDUCTIVE THING, AND IT ALWAYS HAS ITS OWN KIND OF MAD, SUBJECTIVE LOGIC--
AND THE WAY I SAW IT, WITHOUT THE MONKEY FOR SUPPORT, THE OLD COW WOULDN'T HAVE A LEG TO STAND ON, SO TO SPEAK.

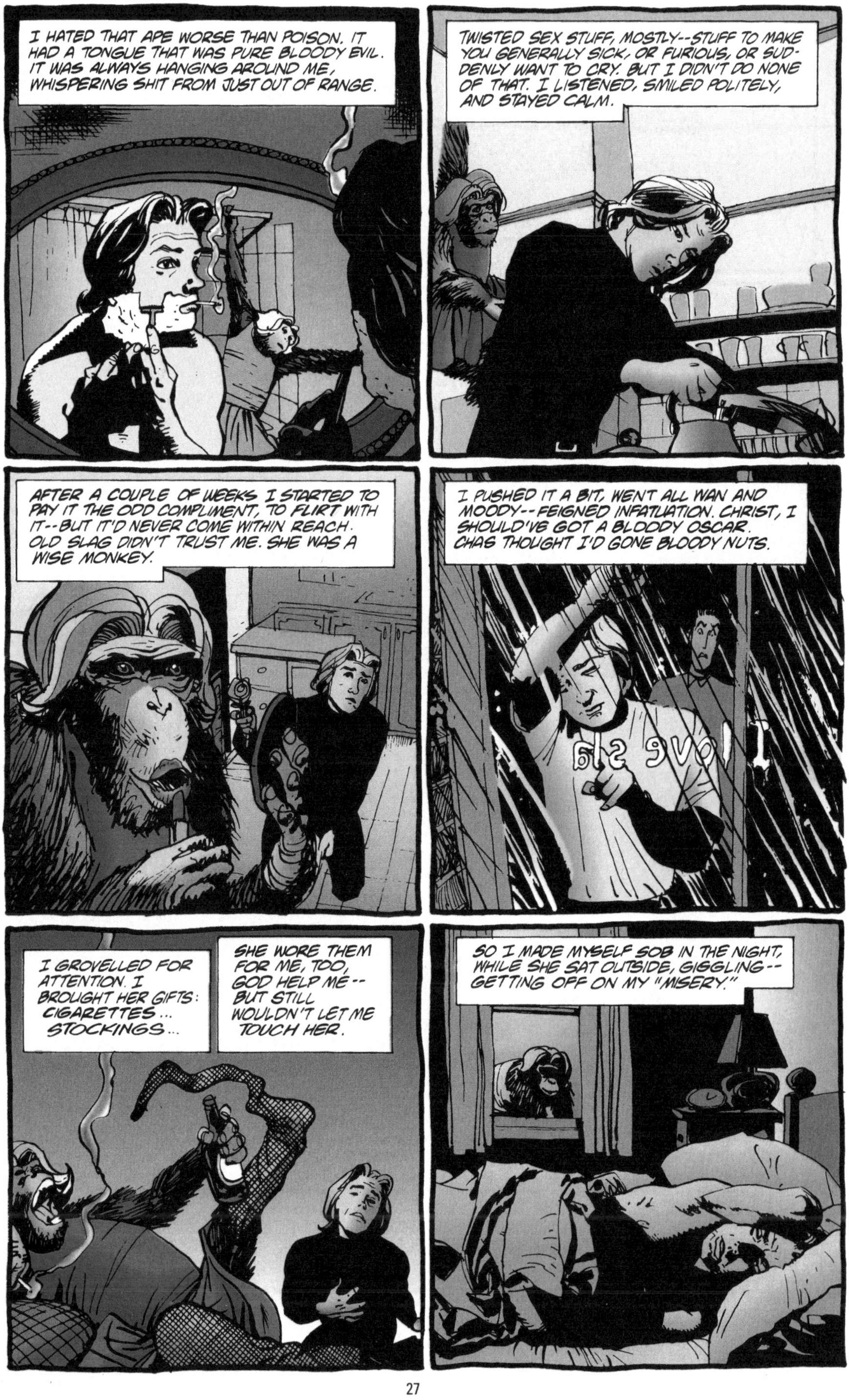
I HATED THAT APE WORSE THAN POISON. IT HAD A TONGUE THAT WAS PURE BLOODY EVIL. IT WAS ALWAYS HANGING AROUND ME, WHISPERING SHIT FROM JUST OUT OF RANGE.
TWISTED SEX STUFF, MOSTLY--STUFF TO MAKE YOU GENERALLY SICK, OR FURIOUS, OR SUDDENLY WANT TO CRY. BUT I DIDN'T DO NONE OF THAT. I LISTENED, SMILED POLITELY, AND STAYED CALM.
AFTER A COUPLE OF WEEKS I STARTED TO PAY IT THE ODD COMPLIMENT, TO FLIRT WITH IT--BUT IT'D NEVER COME WITHIN REACH. OLD SLAG DIDN'T TRUST ME. SHE WAS A WISE MONKEY.
I PUSHED IT A BIT, WENT ALL WAN AND MOODY--FEIGNED INFATUATION. CHRIST, I SHOULD'VE GOT A BLOODY OSCAR. CHAS THOUGHT I'D GONE BLOODY NUTS.
I GROVELLED FOR ATTENTION. I BROUGHT HER GIFTS: CIGARETTES... STOCKINGS...
SHE WORE THEM FOR ME, TOO, GOD HELP ME--BUT STILL WOULDN'T LET ME TOUCH HER.
SO I MADE MYSELF SOB IN THE NIGHT, WHILE SHE SAT OUTSIDE, GIGGLING--GETTING OFF ON MY "MISERY."

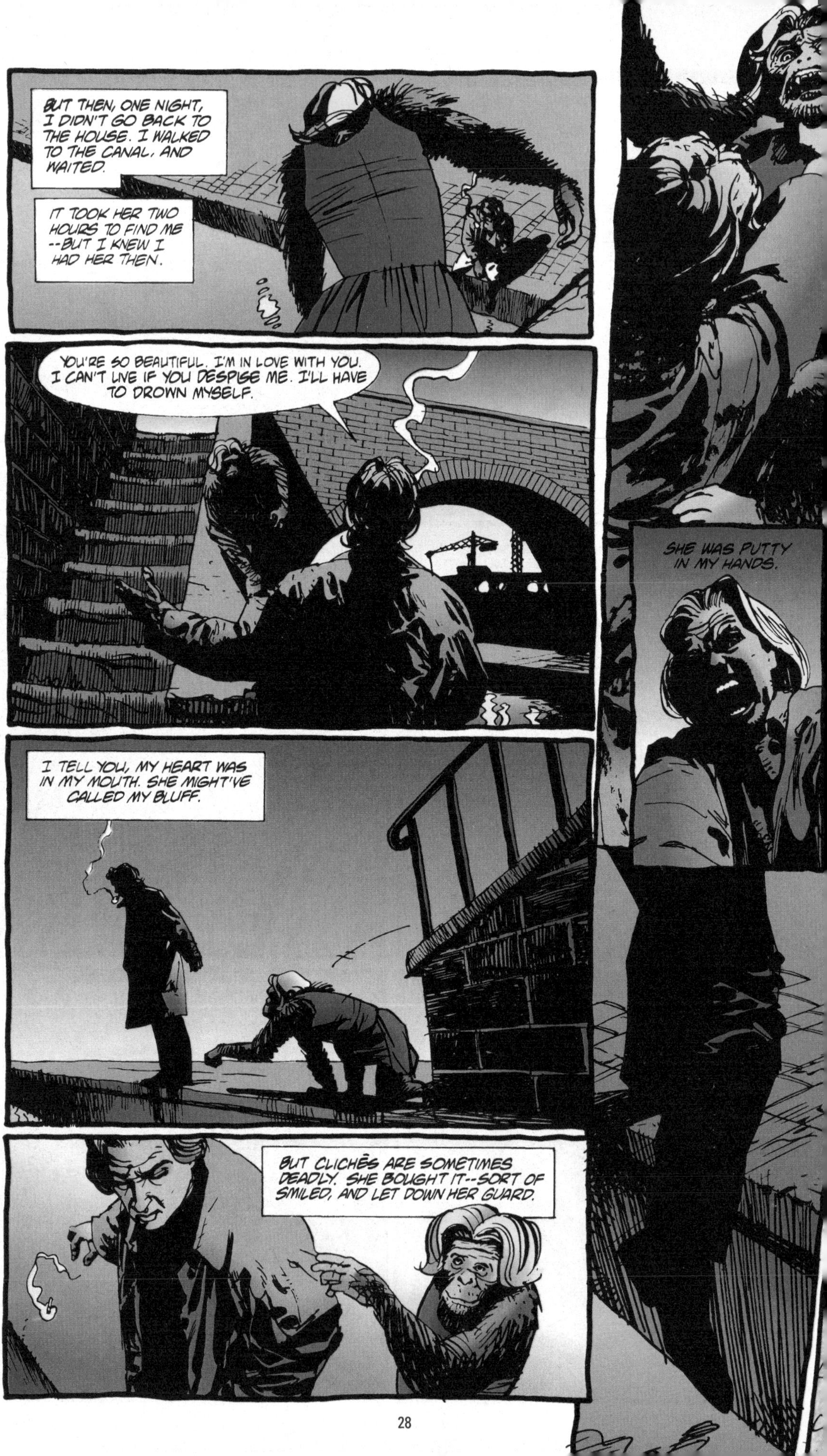
BUT THEN, ONE NIGHT, I DIDN'T GO BACK TO THE HOUSE. I WALKED TO THE CANAL, AND WAITED.
IT TOOK HER TWO HOURS TO FIND ME --BUT I KNEW I HAD HER THEN.
YOU'RE SO BEAUTIFUL. I'M IN LOVE WITH YOU. I CAN'T LIVE IF YOU DESPISE ME. I'LL HAVE TO DROWN MYSELF.
I TELL YOU, MY HEART WAS IN MY MOUTH. SHE MIGHT'VE CALLED MY BLUFF.
BUT CLICHÉS ARE SOMETIMES DEADLY. SHE BOUGHT IT--SORT OF SMILED, AND LET DOWN HER GUARD.
SHE WAS PUTTY IN MY HANDS.

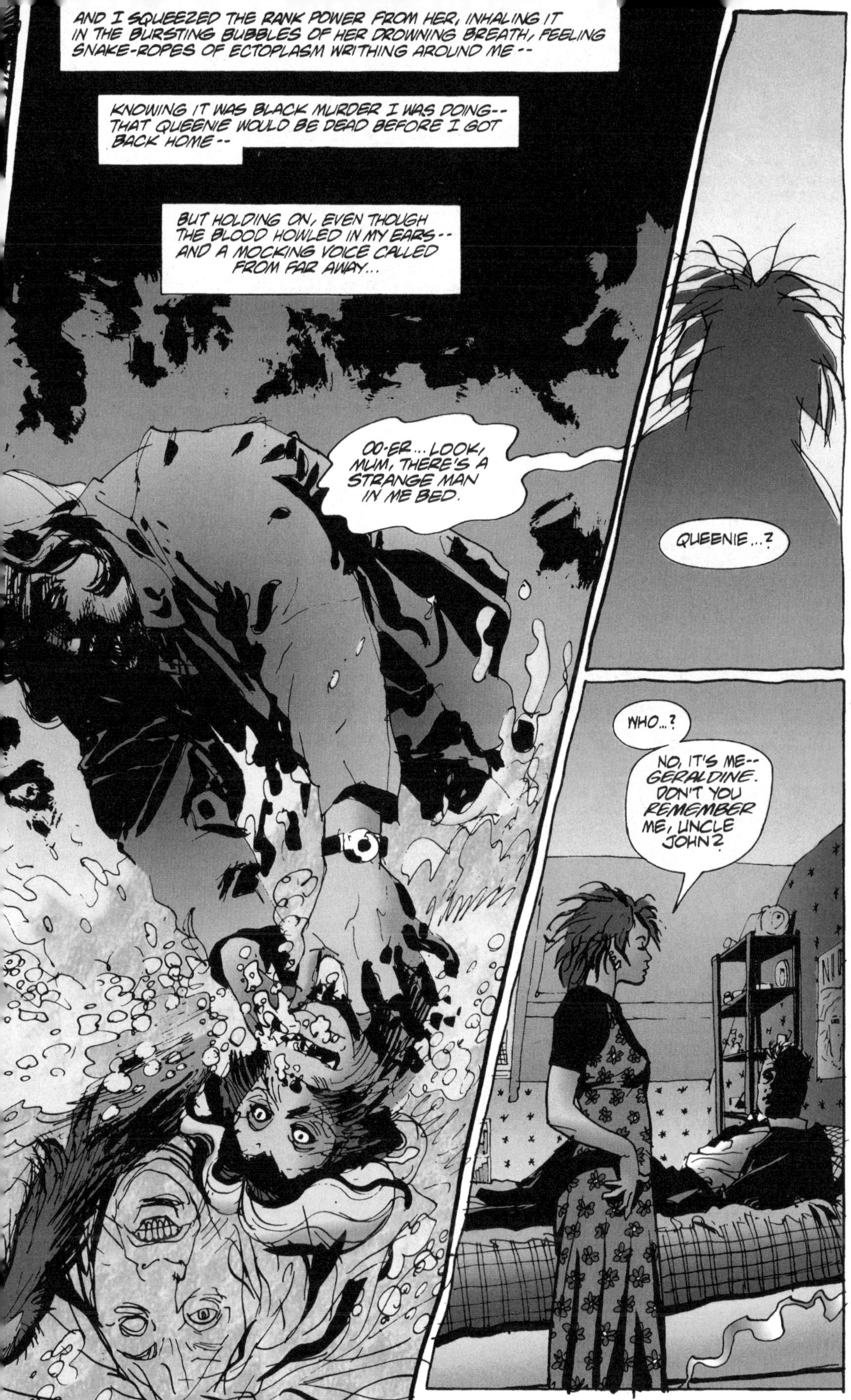
AND I SQUEEZED THE RANK POWER FROM HER, INHALING IT IN THE BURSTING BUBBLES OF HER DROWNING BREATH, FEELING SNAKE-ROPES OF ECTOPLASM WRITHING AROUND ME--
KNOWING IT WAS BLACK MURDER I WAS DOING--THAT QUEENIE WOULD BE DEAD BEFORE I GOT BACK HOME--
BUT HOLDING ON, EVEN THOUGH THE BLOOD HOWLED IN MY EARS--AND A MOCKING VOICE CALLED FROM FAR AWAY...
OO-ER... LOOK, MUM, THERE'S A STRANGE MAN IN ME BED.
QUEENIE...?
WHO...?
NO, IT'S ME--GERALDINE. DON'T YOU REMEMBER ME, UNCLE JOHN?

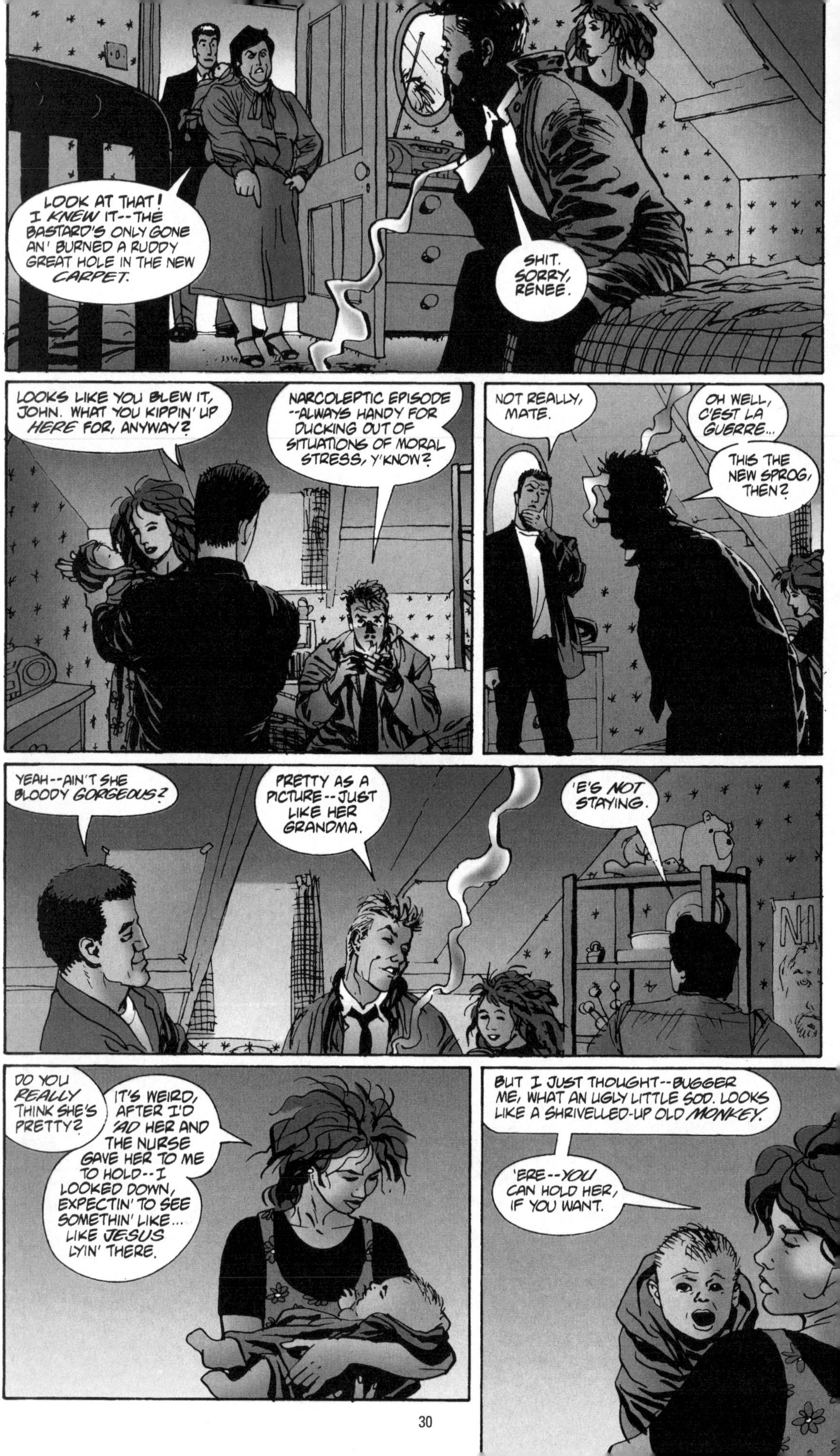
LOOK AT THAT! I KNEW IT--THE BASTARD'S ONLY GONE AN' BURNED A RUDDY GREAT HOLE IN THE NEW CARPET.
SHIT. SORRY, RENEE.
LOOKS LIKE YOU BLEW IT, JOHN. WHAT YOU KIPPIN' UP HERE FOR, ANYWAY?
NARCOLEPTIC EPISODE --ALWAYS HANDY FOR DUCKING OUT OF SITUATIONS OF MORAL STRESS, Y'KNOW?
NOT REALLY, MATE.
OH WELL, C'EST LA GUERRE...
THIS THE NEW SPROG, THEN?
YEAH--AIN'T SHE BLOODY GORGEOUS?
PRETTY AS A PICTURE--JUST LIKE HER GRANDMA.
'E'S NOT STAYING.
DO YOU REALLY THINK SHE'S PRETTY?
IT'S WEIRD, AFTER I'D 'AD HER AND THE NURSE GAVE HER TO ME TO HOLD--I LOOKED DOWN, EXPECTIN' TO SEE SOMETHIN' LIKE... LIKE JESUS LYIN' THERE.
BUT I JUST THOUGHT--BUGGER ME, WHAT AN UGLY LITTLE SOD. LOOKS LIKE A SHRIVELLED-UP OLD MONKEY.
'ERE--YOU CAN HOLD HER, IF YOU WANT.

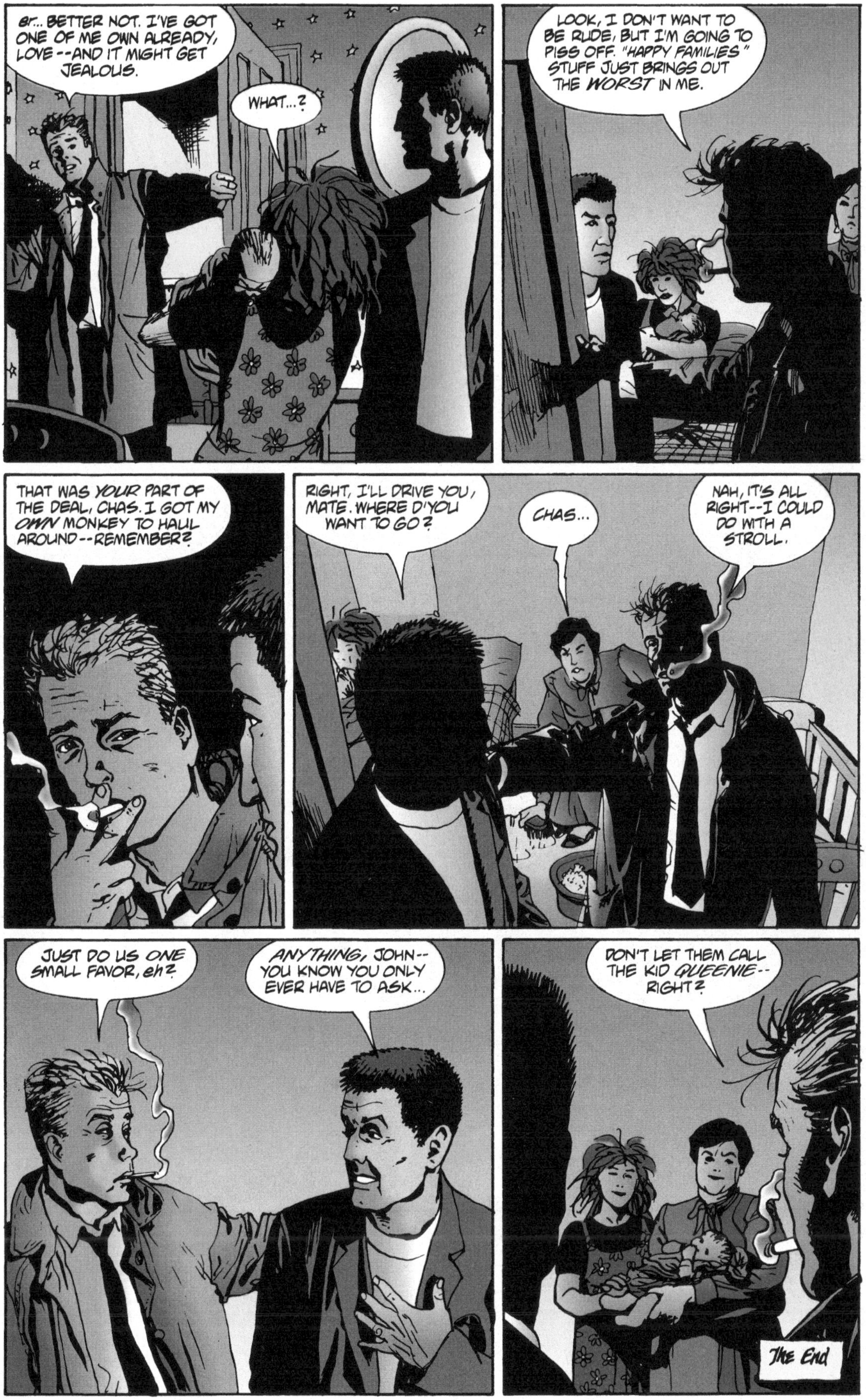
er... BETTER NOT. I'VE GOT ONE OF ME OWN ALREADY, LOVE--AND IT MIGHT GET JEALOUS.
WHAT...?
LOOK, I DON'T WANT TO BE RUDE, BUT I'M GOING TO PISS OFF. "HAPPY FAMILIES" STUFF JUST BRINGS OUT THE WORST IN ME.
THAT WAS YOUR PART OF THE DEAL, CHAS. I GOT MY OWN MONKEY TO HAUL AROUND--REMEMBER?
RIGHT, I'LL DRIVE YOU, MATE. WHERE D'YOU WANT TO GO?
CHAS...
NAH, IT'S ALL RIGHT--I COULD DO WITH A STROLL.
JUST DO US ONE SMALL FAVOR, eh?
ANYTHING, JOHN--YOU KNOW YOU ONLY EVER HAVE TO ASK...
DON'T LET THEM CALL THE KID QUEENIE--RIGHT?
The End

JOHN CONSTANTINE
HELLBLAZER
Sean '94
EDDIE CAMPBELL • SEAN PHILLIPS

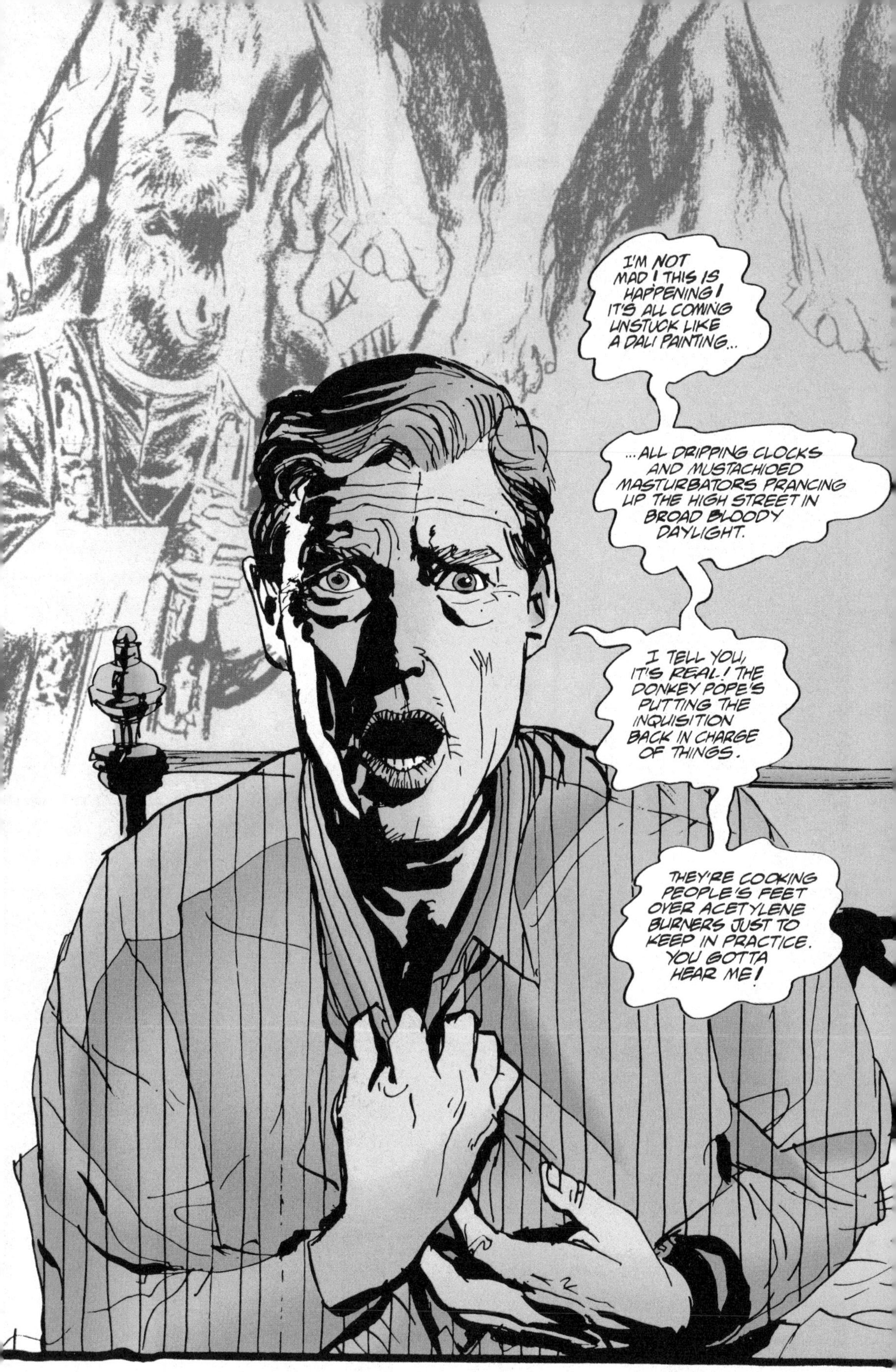

I'M NOT MAD! THIS IS HAPPENING! IT'S ALL COMING UNSTUCK LIKE A DALI PAINTING...
...ALL DRIPPING CLOCKS AND MUSTACHIOED MASTURBATORS PRANCING UP THE HIGH STREET IN BROAD BLOODY DAYLIGHT.
I TELL YOU, IT'S REAL! THE DONKEY POPE'S PUTTING THE INQUISITION BACK IN CHARGE OF THINGS.
THEY'RE COOKING PEOPLE'S FEET OVER ACETYLENE BURNERS JUST TO KEEP IN PRACTICE. YOU GOTTA HEAR ME!

JOHN CONSTANTINE
HELLBLAZER
Sean '94
EDDIE CAMPBELL • SEAN PHILLIPS

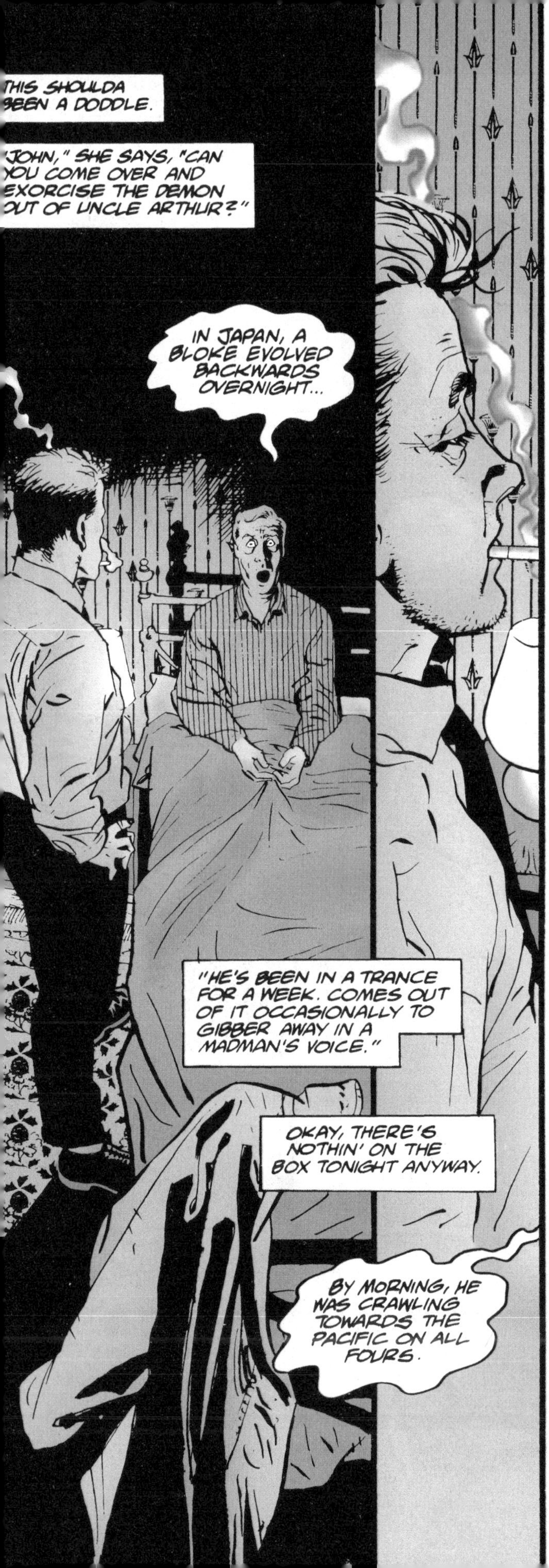
THIS SHOULDA BEEN A DODDLE.
"JOHN," SHE SAYS, "CAN YOU COME OVER AND EXORCISE THE DEMON OUT OF UNCLE ARTHUR?"
IN JAPAN, A BLOKE EVOLVED BACKWARDS OVERNIGHT...
"HE'S BEEN IN A TRANCE FOR A WEEK. COMES OUT OF IT OCCASIONALLY TO GIBBER AWAY IN A MADMAN'S VOICE."
OKAY, THERE'S NOTHIN' ON THE BOX TONIGHT ANYWAY.
BY MORNING, HE WAS CRAWLING TOWARDS THE PACIFIC ON ALL FOURS.

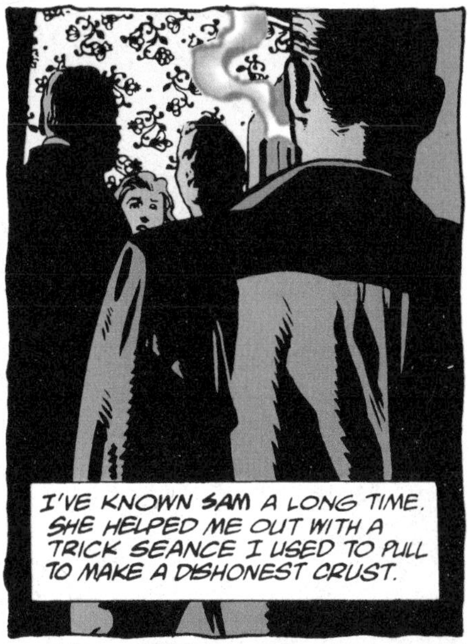
I'VE KNOWN SAM A LONG TIME. SHE HELPED ME OUT WITH A TRICK SEANCE I USED TO PULL TO MAKE A DISHONEST CRUST.

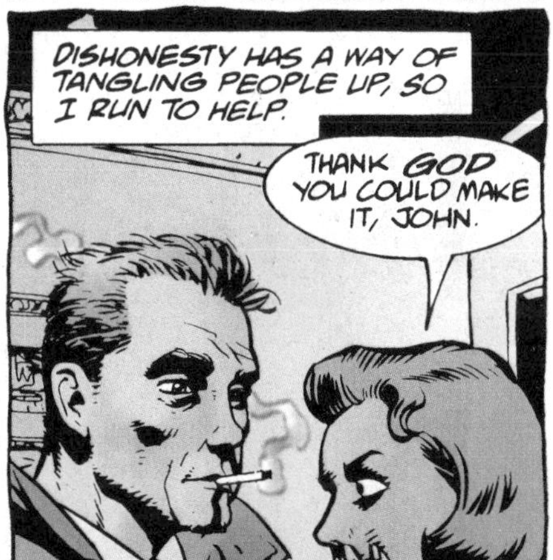
DISHONESTY HAS A WAY OF TANGLING PEOPLE UP, SO I RUN TO HELP.
THANK GOD YOU COULD MAKE IT, JOHN.

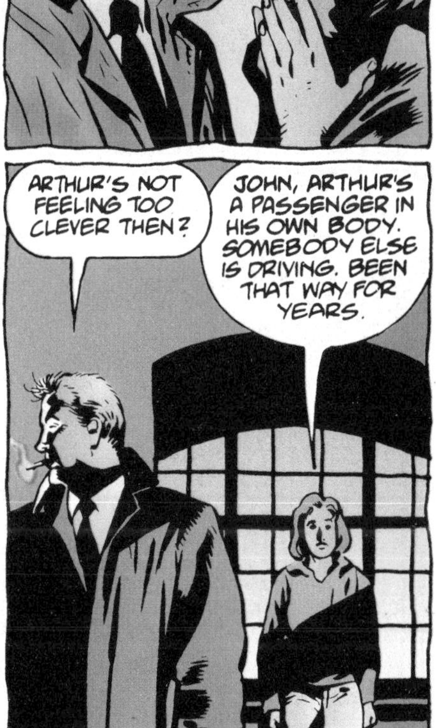
ARTHUR'S NOT FEELING TOO CLEVER THEN?
JOHN, ARTHUR'S A PASSENGER IN HIS OWN BODY. SOMEBODY ELSE IS DRIVING. BEEN THAT WAY FOR YEARS.

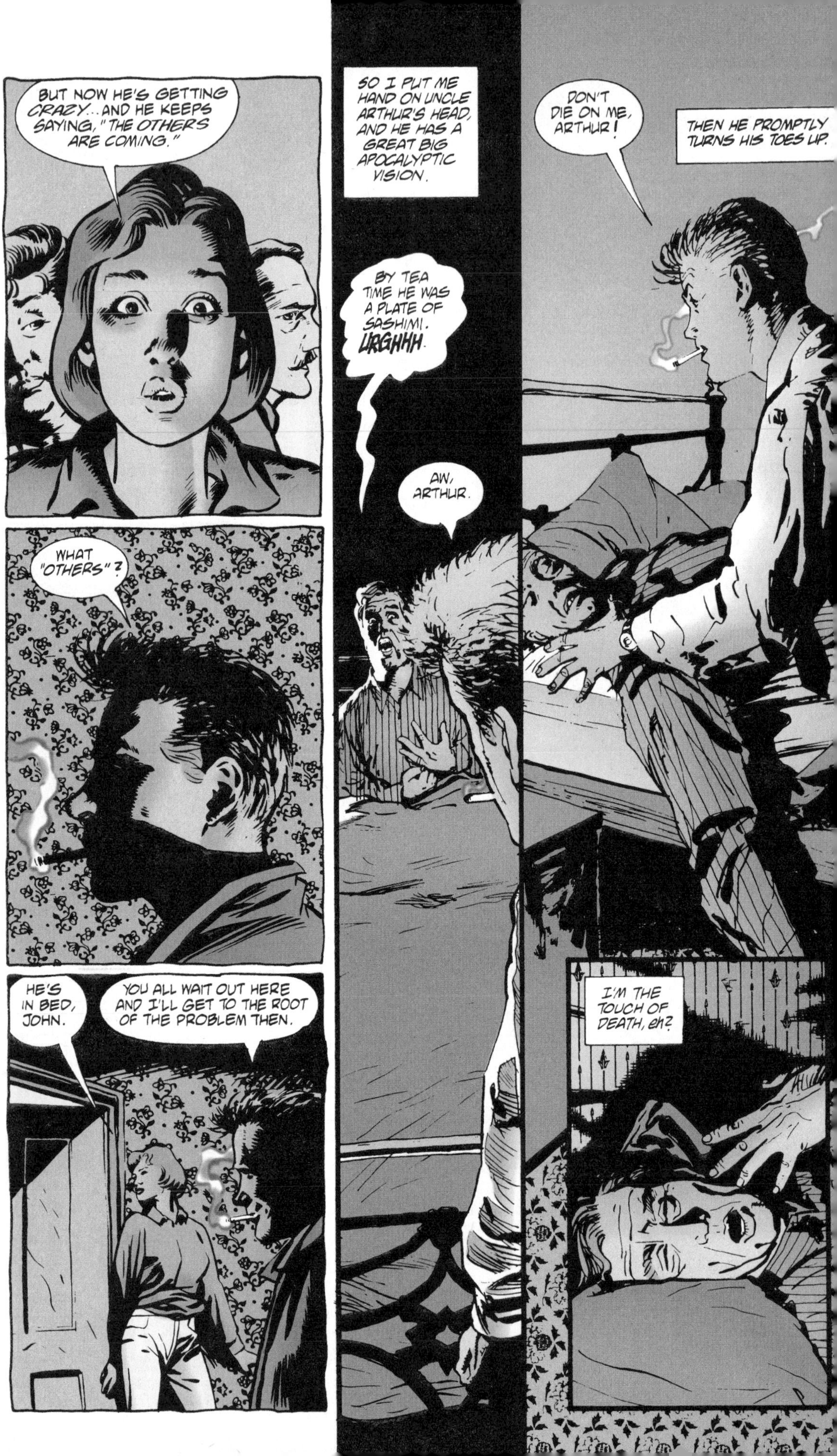
BUT NOW HE'S GETTING CRAZY... AND HE KEEPS SAYING, "THE OTHERS ARE COMING."
WHAT "OTHERS"?
HE'S IN BED, JOHN.
YOU ALL WAIT OUT HERE AND I'LL GET TO THE ROOT OF THE PROBLEM THEN.
SO I PUT ME HAND ON UNCLE ARTHUR'S HEAD, AND HE HAS A GREAT BIG APOCALYPTIC VISION.
DON'T DIE ON ME, ARTHUR!
THEN HE PROMPTLY TURNS HIS TOES UP.
BY TEA TIME HE WAS A PLATE OF SASHIMI. URGHHH.
AW, ARTHUR.
I'M THE TOUCH OF DEATH, eh?

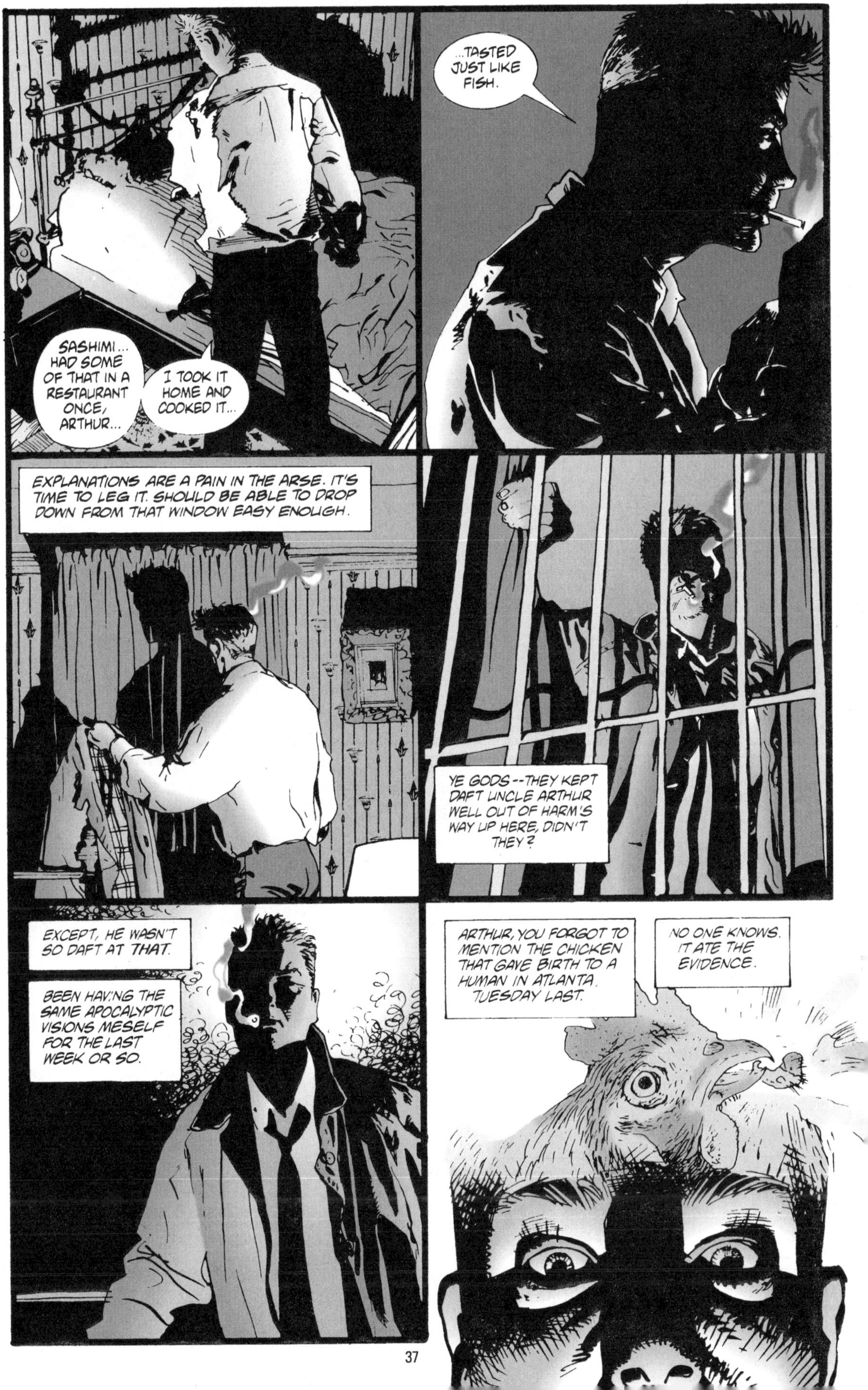
SASHIMI... HAD SOME OF THAT IN A RESTAURANT ONCE, ARTHUR...
I TOOK IT HOME AND COOKED IT...
...TASTED JUST LIKE FISH.
EXPLANATIONS ARE A PAIN IN THE ARSE. IT'S TIME TO LEG IT. SHOULD BE ABLE TO DROP DOWN FROM THAT WINDOW EASY ENOUGH.
YE GODS--THEY KEPT DAFT UNCLE ARTHUR WELL OUT OF HARM'S WAY UP HERE, DIDN'T THEY?
EXCEPT, HE WASN'T SO DAFT AT THAT.
BEEN HAVING THE SAME APOCALYPTIC VISIONS MESELF FOR THE LAST WEEK OR SO.
ARTHUR, YOU FORGOT TO MENTION THE CHICKEN THAT GAVE BIRTH TO A HUMAN IN ATLANTA, TUESDAY LAST.
NO ONE KNOWS. IT ATE THE EVIDENCE.

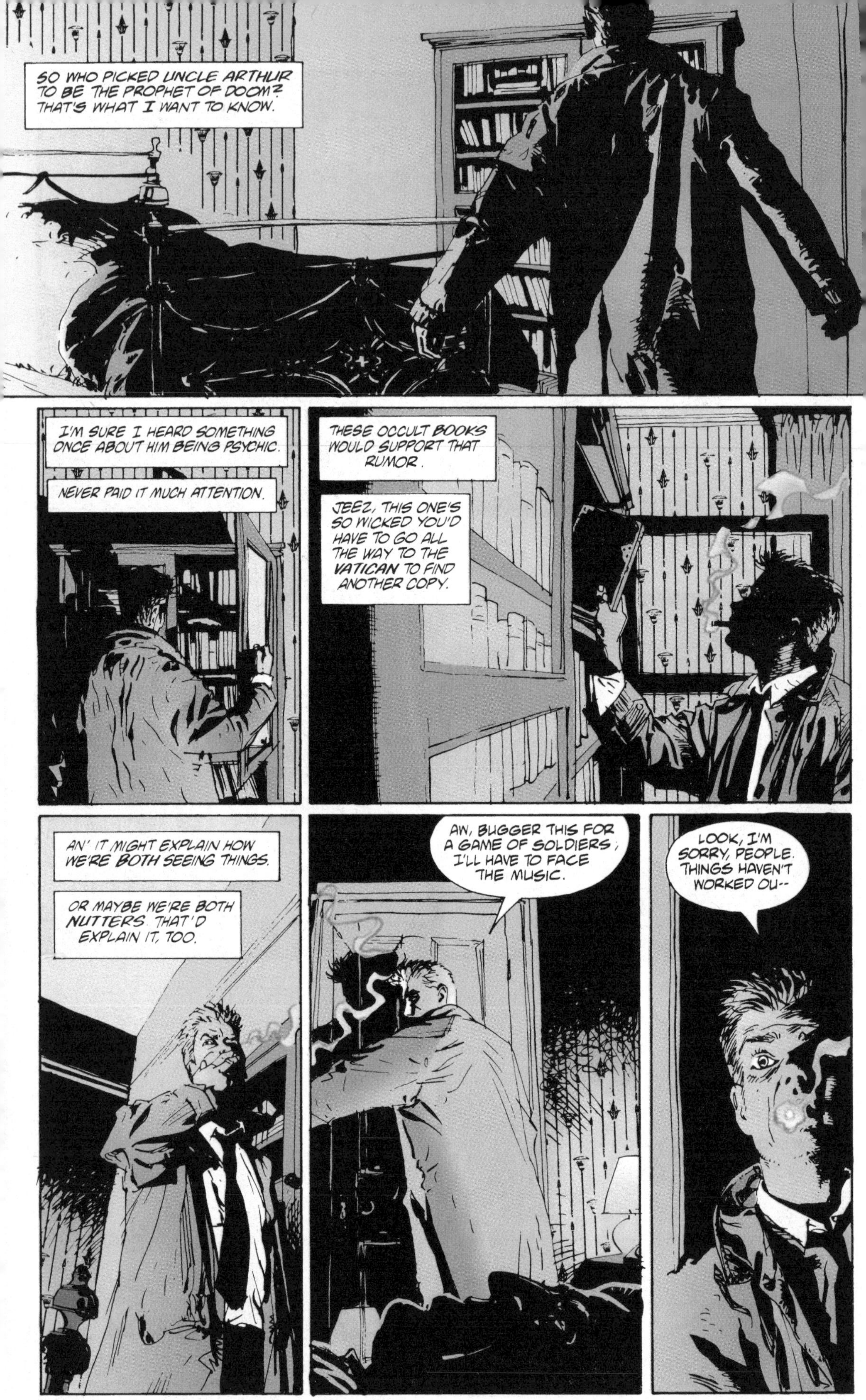
SO WHO PICKED UNCLE ARTHUR TO BE THE PROPHET OF DOOM? THAT'S WHAT I WANT TO KNOW.
I'M SURE I HEARD SOMETHING ONCE ABOUT HIM BEING PSYCHIC.
NEVER PAID IT MUCH ATTENTION.
THESE OCCULT BOOKS WOULD SUPPORT THAT RUMOR.
JEEZ, THIS ONE'S SO WICKED YOU'D HAVE TO GO ALL THE WAY TO THE VATICAN TO FIND ANOTHER COPY.
AN' IT MIGHT EXPLAIN HOW WE'RE BOTH SEEING THINGS.
OR MAYBE WE'RE BOTH NUTTERS. THAT'D EXPLAIN IT, TOO.
AW, BUGGER THIS FOR A GAME OF SOLDIERS; I'LL HAVE TO FACE THE MUSIC.
LOOK, I'M SORRY, PEOPLE. THINGS HAVEN'T WORKED OU--

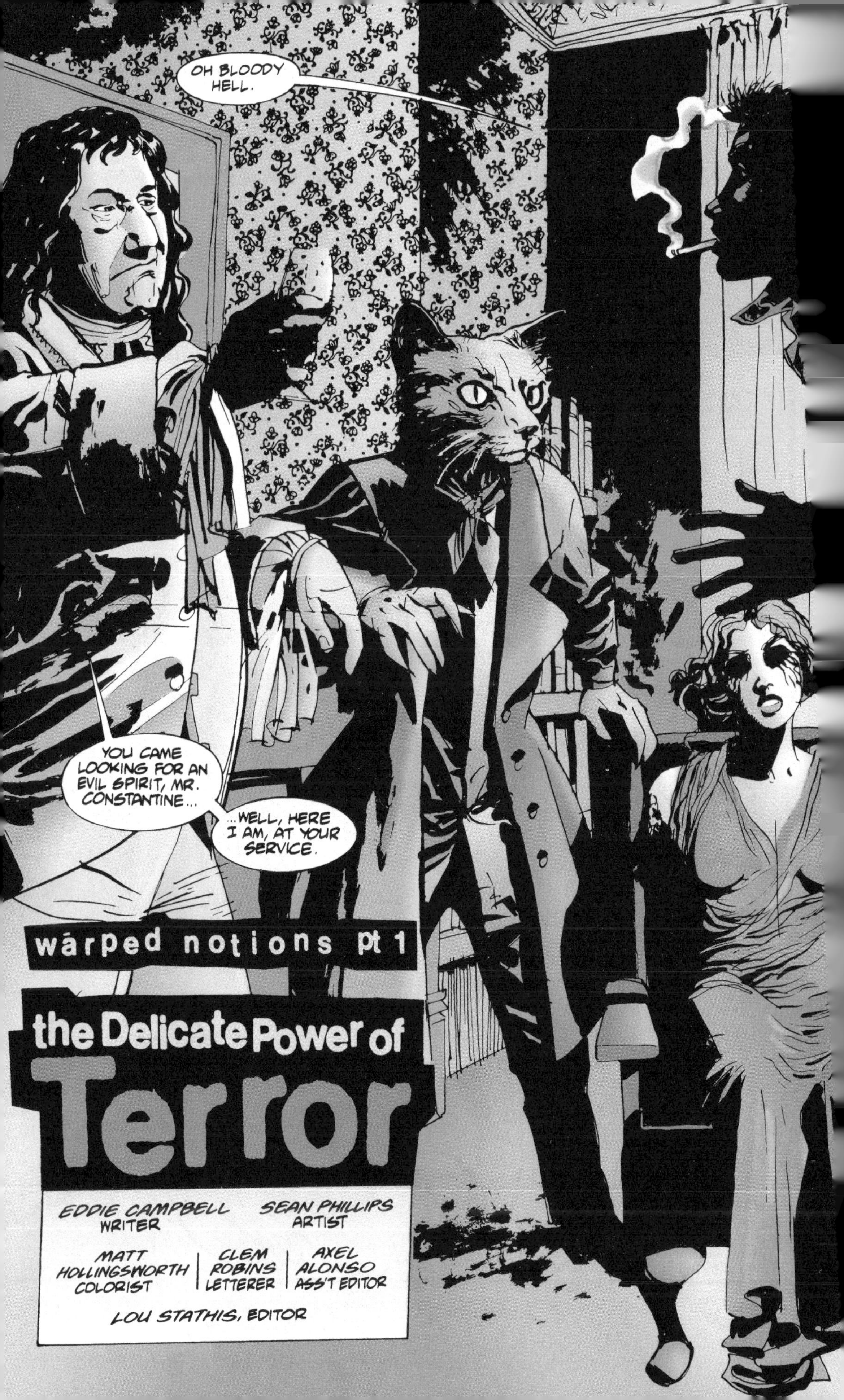

OH BLOODY HELL.
YOU CAME LOOKING FOR AN EVIL SPIRIT, MR. CONSTANTINE...
...WELL, HERE I AM, AT YOUR SERVICE.
warped notions pt 1
the Delicate Power of Terror
EDDIE CAMPBELL WRITER
SEAN PHILLIPS ARTIST
MATT HOLLINGSWORTH COLORIST
CLEM ROBINS LETTERER
AXEL ALONSO ASS'T EDITOR
LOU STATHIS, EDITOR

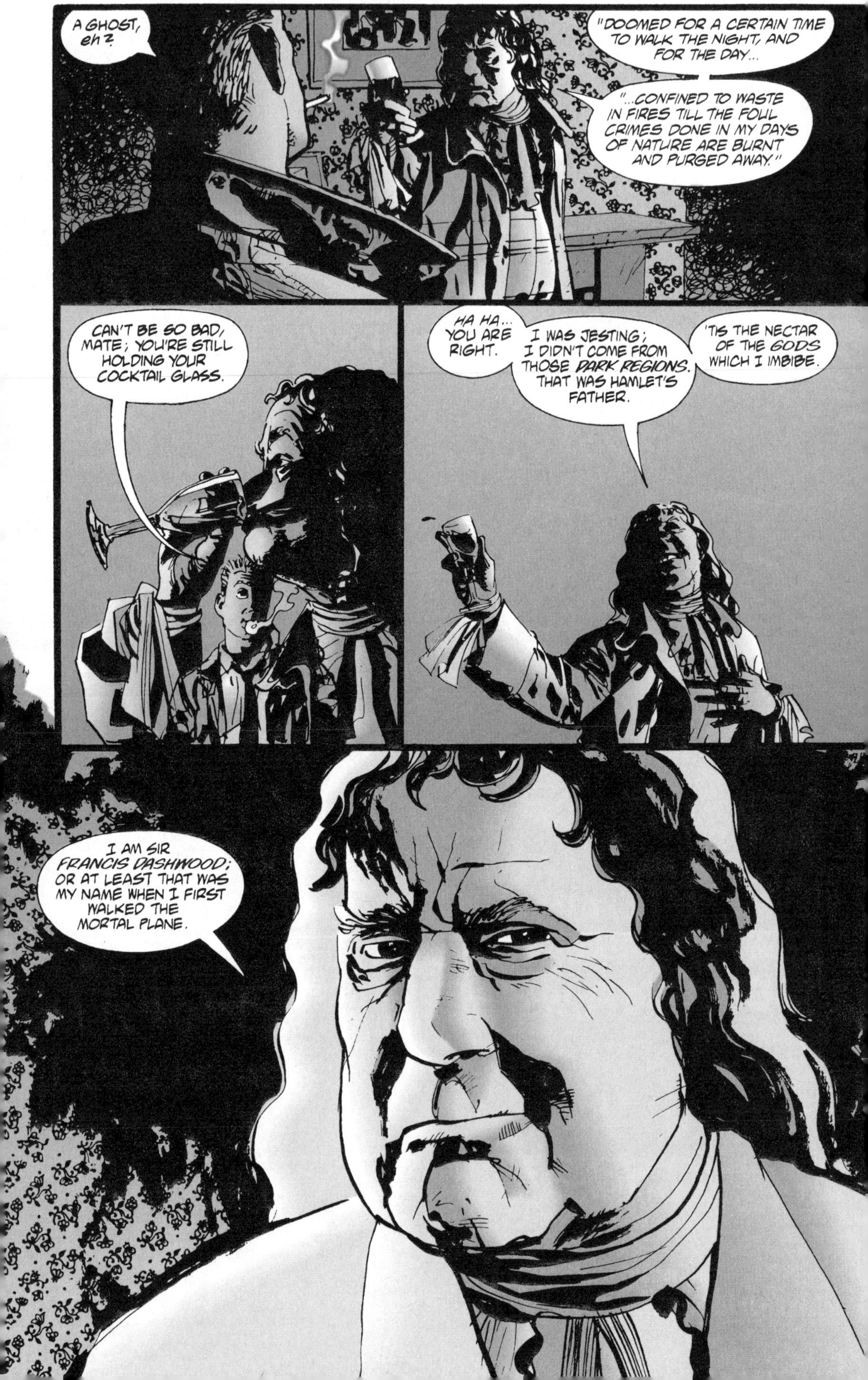
A GHOST, eh?
"DOOMED FOR A CERTAIN TIME TO WALK THE NIGHT, AND FOR THE DAY...
"...CONFINED TO WASTE IN FIRES TILL THE FOUL CRIMES DONE IN MY DAYS OF NATURE ARE BURNT AND PURGED AWAY."
CAN'T BE SO BAD, MATE; YOU'RE STILL HOLDING YOUR COCKTAIL GLASS.
HA HA... YOU ARE RIGHT.
I WAS JESTING; I DIDN'T COME FROM THOSE DARK REGIONS. THAT WAS HAMLET'S FATHER.
'TIS THE NECTAR OF THE GODS WHICH I IMBIBE.
I AM SIR FRANCIS DASHWOOD; OR AT LEAST THAT WAS MY NAME WHEN I FIRST WALKED THE MORTAL PLANE.

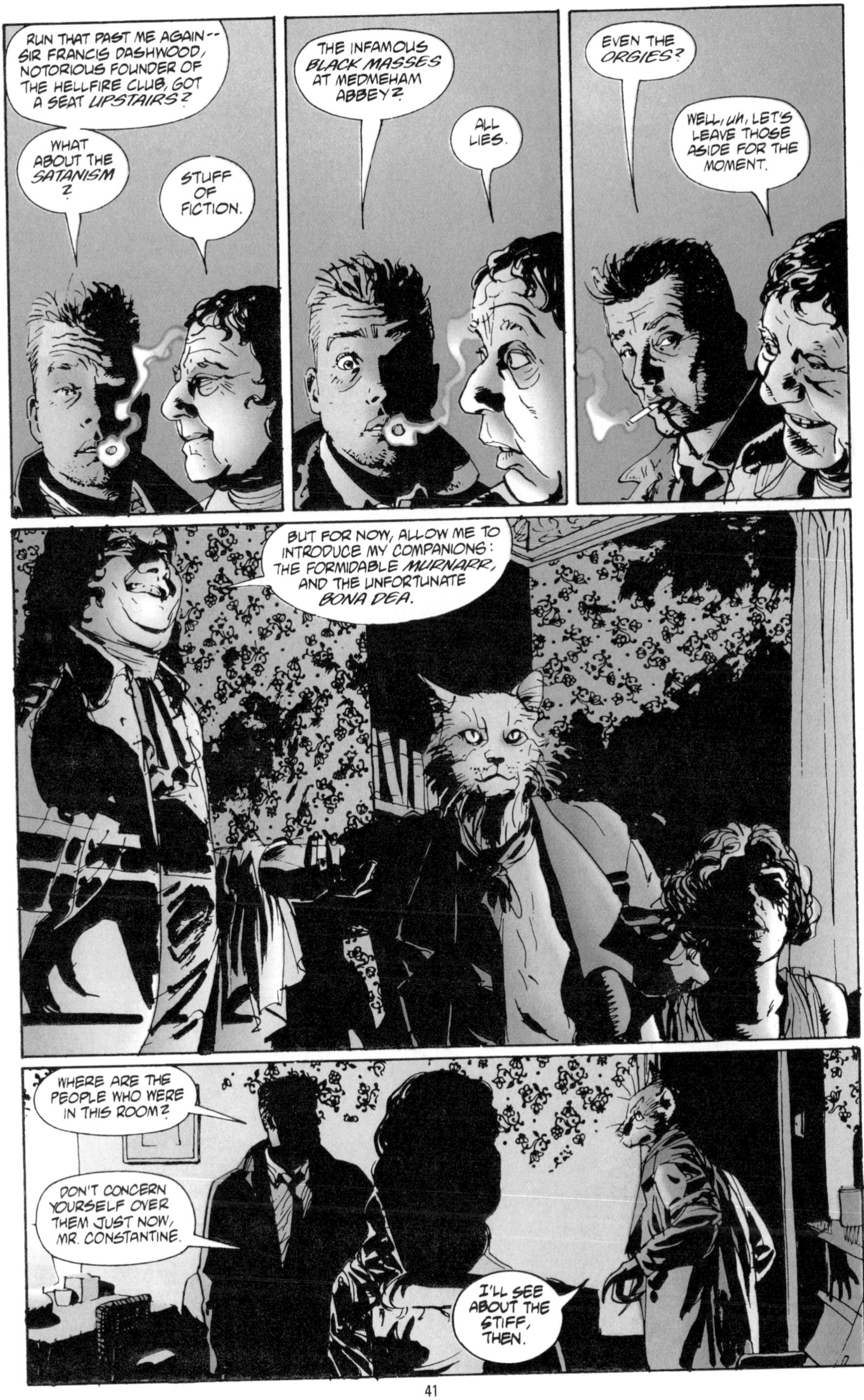
RUN THAT PAST ME AGAIN-- SIR FRANCIS DASHWOOD, NOTORIOUS FOUNDER OF THE HELLFIRE CLUB, GOT A SEAT UPSTAIRS?
WHAT ABOUT THE SATANISM?
STUFF OF FICTION.
THE INFAMOUS BLACK MASSES AT MEDMEHAM ABBEY?
ALL LIES.
EVEN THE ORGIES?
WELL, UH, LET'S LEAVE THOSE ASIDE FOR THE MOMENT.
BUT FOR NOW, ALLOW ME TO INTRODUCE MY COMPANIONS: THE FORMIDABLE MURNARR, AND THE UNFORTUNATE BONA DEA.
WHERE ARE THE PEOPLE WHO WERE IN THIS ROOM?
DON'T CONCERN YOURSELF OVER THEM JUST NOW, MR. CONSTANTINE.
I'LL SEE ABOUT THE STIFF, THEN.

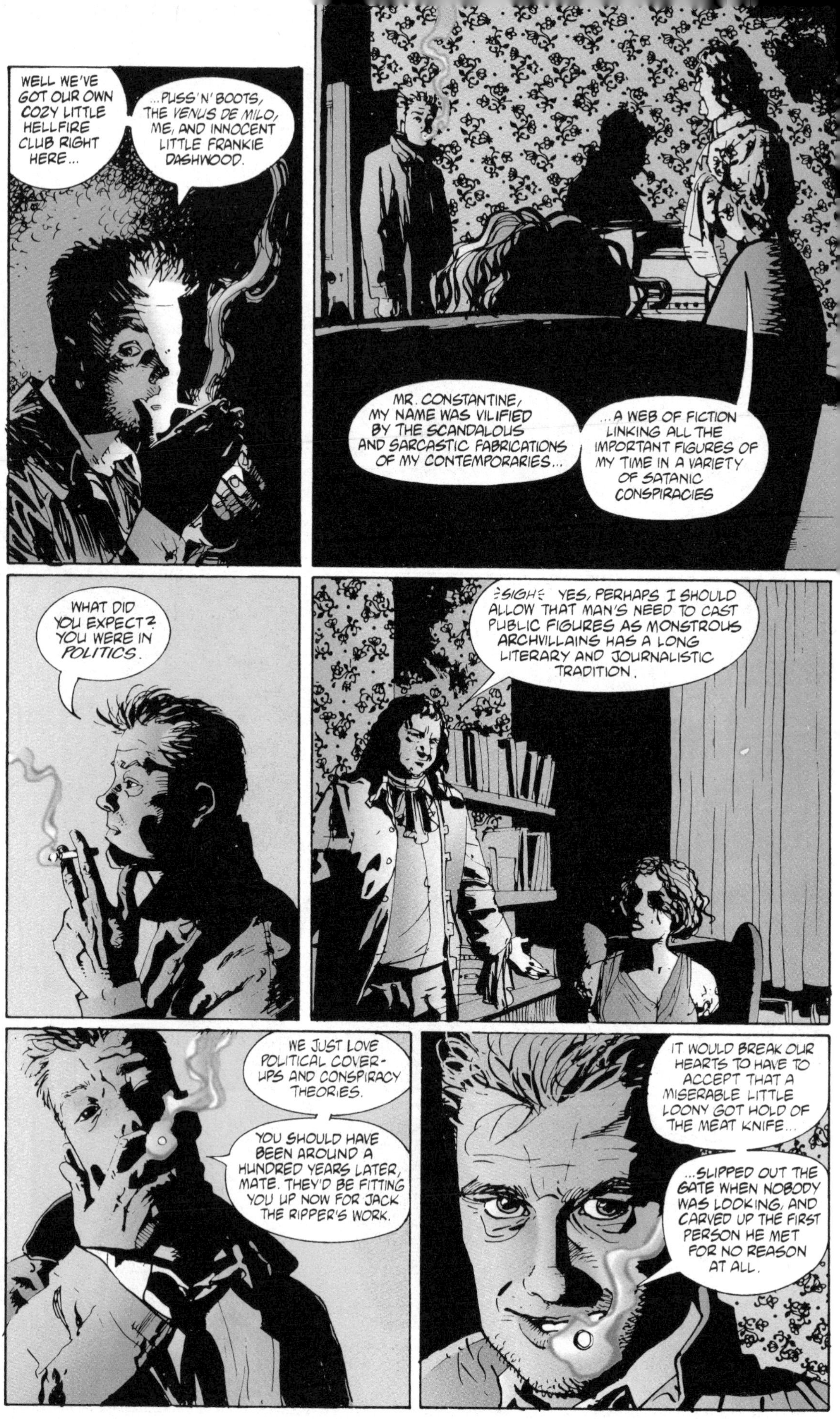
WELL WE'VE GOT OUR OWN COZY LITTLE HELLFIRE CLUB RIGHT HERE...
...PUSS 'N' BOOTS, THE VENUS DE MILO, ME, AND INNOCENT LITTLE FRANKIE DASHWOOD.
MR. CONSTANTINE, MY NAME WAS VILIFIED BY THE SCANDALOUS AND SARCASTIC FABRICATIONS OF MY CONTEMPORARIES...
...A WEB OF FICTION LINKING ALL THE IMPORTANT FIGURES OF MY TIME IN A VARIETY OF SATANIC CONSPIRACIES
WHAT DID YOU EXPECT? YOU WERE IN POLITICS.
SIGH YES, PERHAPS I SHOULD ALLOW THAT MAN'S NEED TO CAST PUBLIC FIGURES AS MONSTROUS ARCHVILLAINS HAS A LONG LITERARY AND JOURNALISTIC TRADITION.
WE JUST LOVE POLITICAL COVER-UPS AND CONSPIRACY THEORIES.
YOU SHOULD HAVE BEEN AROUND A HUNDRED YEARS LATER, MATE. THEY'D BE FITTING YOU UP NOW FOR JACK THE RIPPER'S WORK.
IT WOULD BREAK OUR HEARTS TO HAVE TO ACCEPT THAT A MISERABLE LITTLE LOONY GOT HOLD OF THE MEAT KNIFE...
...SLIPPED OUT THE GATE WHEN NOBODY WAS LOOKING, AND CARVED UP THE FIRST PERSON HE MET FOR NO REASON AT ALL.

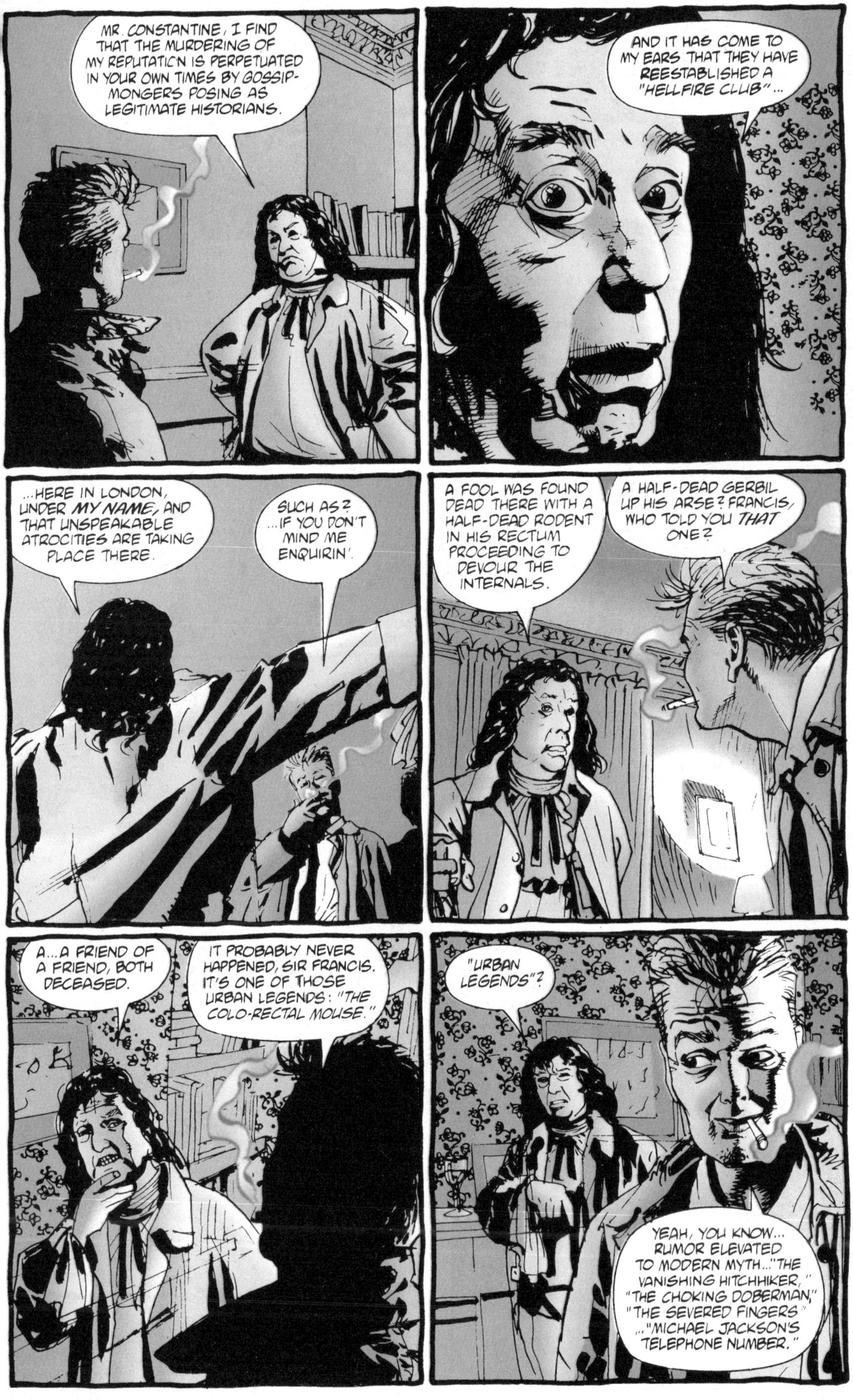
MR. CONSTANTINE, I FIND THAT THE MURDERING OF MY REPUTATION IS PERPETUATED IN YOUR OWN TIMES BY GOSSIP-MONGERS POSING AS LEGITIMATE HISTORIANS.
AND IT HAS COME TO MY EARS THAT THEY HAVE REESTABLISHED A "HELLFIRE CLUB"...
...HERE IN LONDON, UNDER *MY NAME,* AND THAT UNSPEAKABLE ATROCITIES ARE TAKING PLACE THERE.
SUCH AS? ...IF YOU DON'T MIND ME ENQUIRIN'.
A FOOL WAS FOUND DEAD THERE WITH A HALF-DEAD RODENT IN HIS RECTUM PROCEEDING TO DEVOUR THE INTERNALS.
A HALF-DEAD GERBIL UP HIS ARSE? FRANCIS, WHO TOLD YOU *THAT* ONE?
A...A FRIEND OF A FRIEND, BOTH DECEASED.
IT PROBABLY NEVER HAPPENED, SIR FRANCIS. IT'S ONE OF THOSE URBAN LEGENDS: "THE COLO-RECTAL MOUSE."
"URBAN LEGENDS"?
YEAH, YOU KNOW... RUMOR ELEVATED TO MODERN MYTH..."THE VANISHING HITCHHIKER," "THE CHOKING DOBERMAN," "THE SEVERED FINGERS" ..."MICHAEL JACKSON'S TELEPHONE NUMBER."

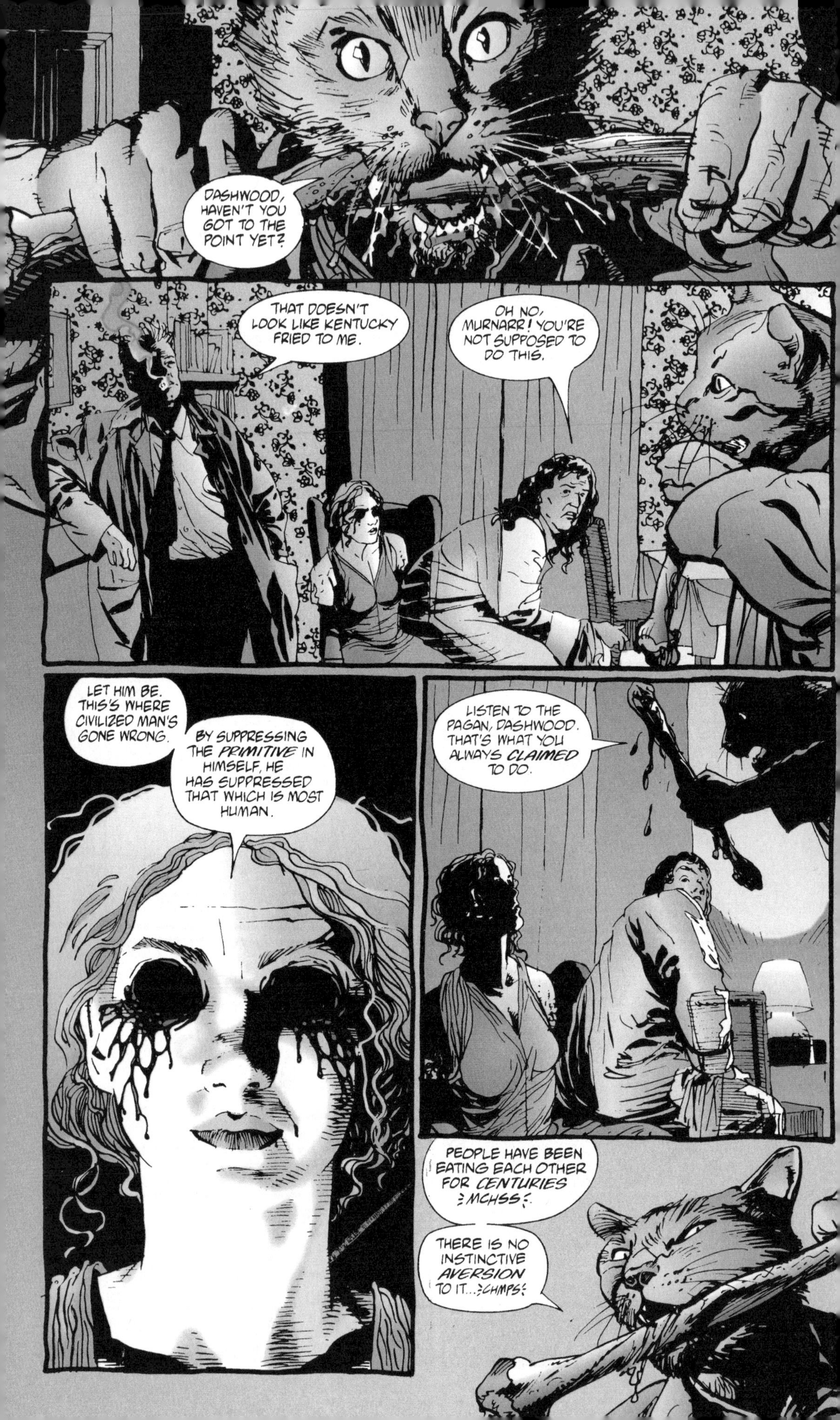
DASHWOOD, HAVEN'T YOU GOT TO THE POINT YET?
THAT DOESN'T LOOK LIKE KENTUCKY FRIED TO ME.
OH NO, MURNARR! YOU'RE NOT SUPPOSED TO DO THIS.
LET HIM BE. THIS'S WHERE CIVILIZED MAN'S GONE WRONG.
BY SUPPRESSING THE *PRIMITIVE* IN HIMSELF, HE HAS SUPPRESSED THAT WHICH IS MOST HUMAN.
LISTEN TO THE PAGAN, DASHWOOD. THAT'S WHAT YOU ALWAYS *CLAIMED* TO DO.
PEOPLE HAVE BEEN EATING EACH OTHER FOR *CENTURIES* MCHSS
THERE IS NO INSTINCTIVE *AVERSION* TO IT... CHMPS

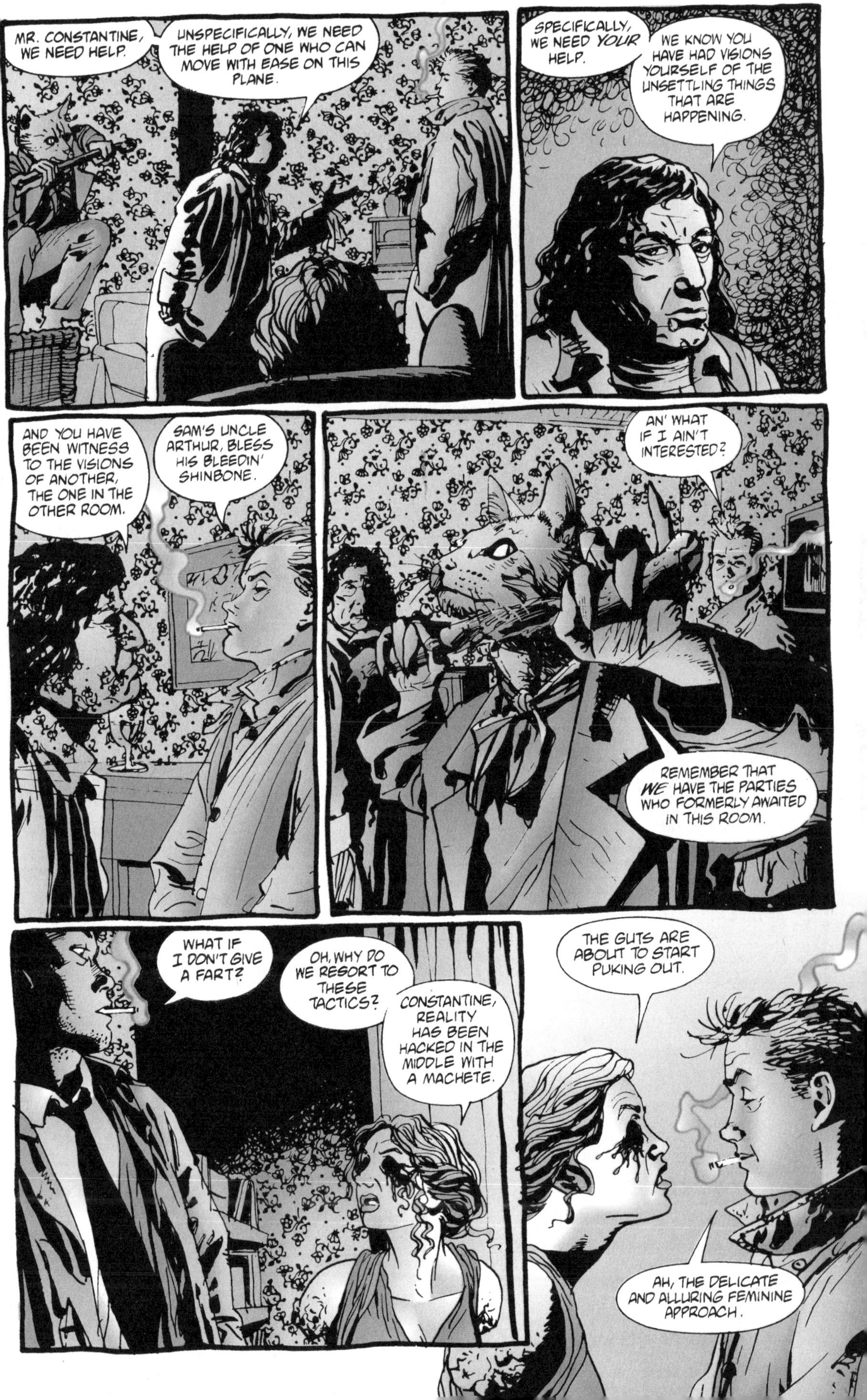
MR. CONSTANTINE, WE NEED HELP.
UNSPECIFICALLY, WE NEED THE HELP OF ONE WHO CAN MOVE WITH EASE ON THIS PLANE.
SPECIFICALLY, WE NEED YOUR HELP.
WE KNOW YOU HAVE HAD VISIONS YOURSELF OF THE UNSETTLING THINGS THAT ARE HAPPENING.
AND YOU HAVE BEEN WITNESS TO THE VISIONS OF ANOTHER, THE ONE IN THE OTHER ROOM.
SAM'S UNCLE ARTHUR, BLESS HIS BLEEDIN' SHINBONE.
AN' WHAT IF I AIN'T INTERESTED?
REMEMBER THAT WE HAVE THE PARTIES WHO FORMERLY AWAITED IN THIS ROOM.
WHAT IF I DON'T GIVE A FART?
OH, WHY DO WE RESORT TO THESE TACTICS?
CONSTANTINE, REALITY HAS BEEN HACKED IN THE MIDDLE WITH A MACHETE.
THE GUTS ARE ABOUT TO START PUKING OUT.
AH, THE DELICATE AND ALLURING FEMININE APPROACH.

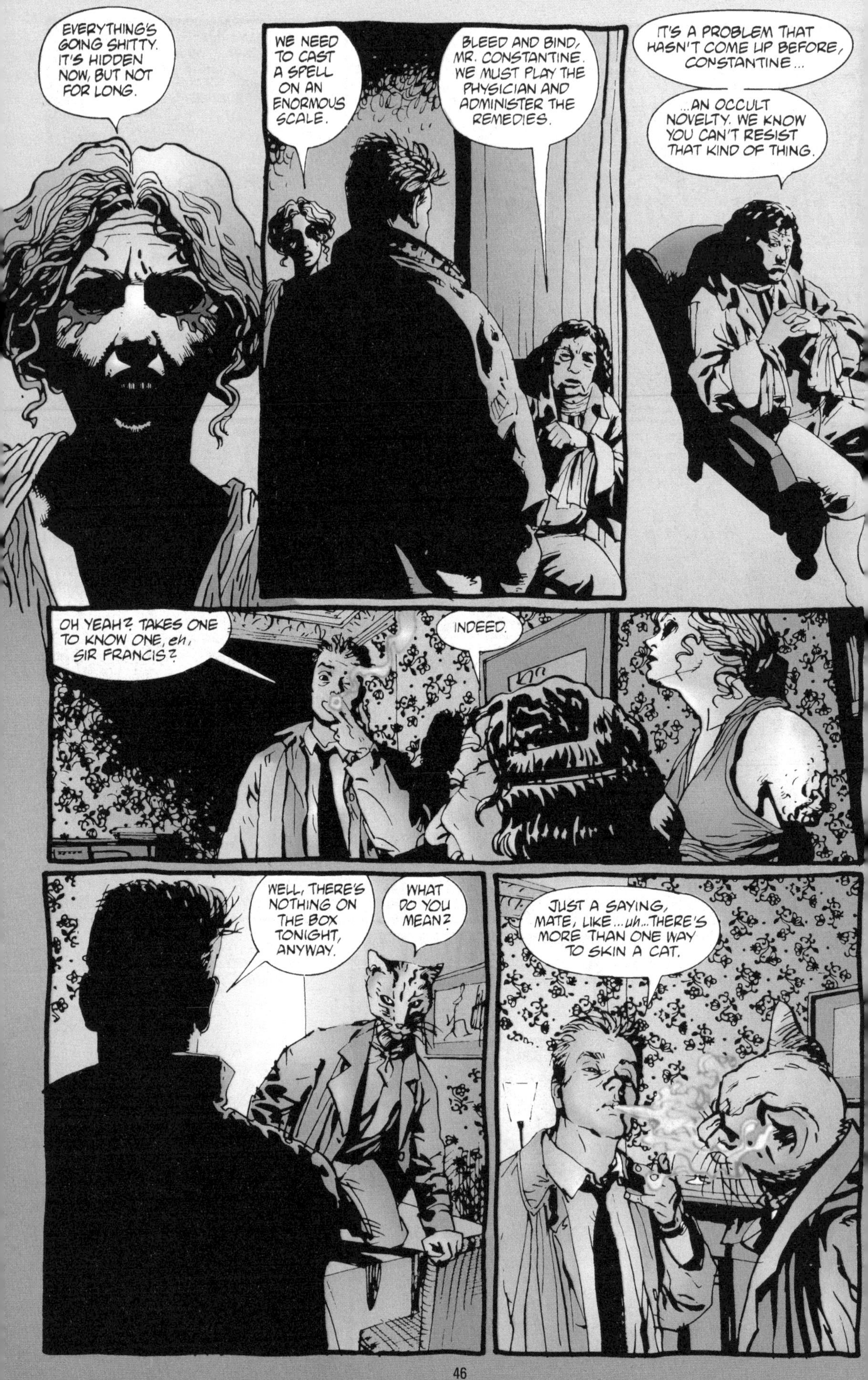
EVERYTHING'S GOING SHITTY. IT'S HIDDEN NOW, BUT NOT FOR LONG.
WE NEED TO CAST A SPELL ON AN ENORMOUS SCALE.
BLEED AND BIND, MR. CONSTANTINE. WE MUST PLAY THE PHYSICIAN AND ADMINISTER THE REMEDIES.
IT'S A PROBLEM THAT HASN'T COME UP BEFORE, CONSTANTINE...
...AN OCCULT NOVELTY. WE KNOW YOU CAN'T RESIST THAT KIND OF THING.
OH YEAH? TAKES ONE TO KNOW ONE, eh, SIR FRANCIS?
INDEED.
WELL, THERE'S NOTHING ON THE BOX TONIGHT, ANYWAY.
WHAT DO YOU MEAN?
JUST A SAYING, MATE, LIKE...uh...THERE'S MORE THAN ONE WAY TO SKIN A CAT.

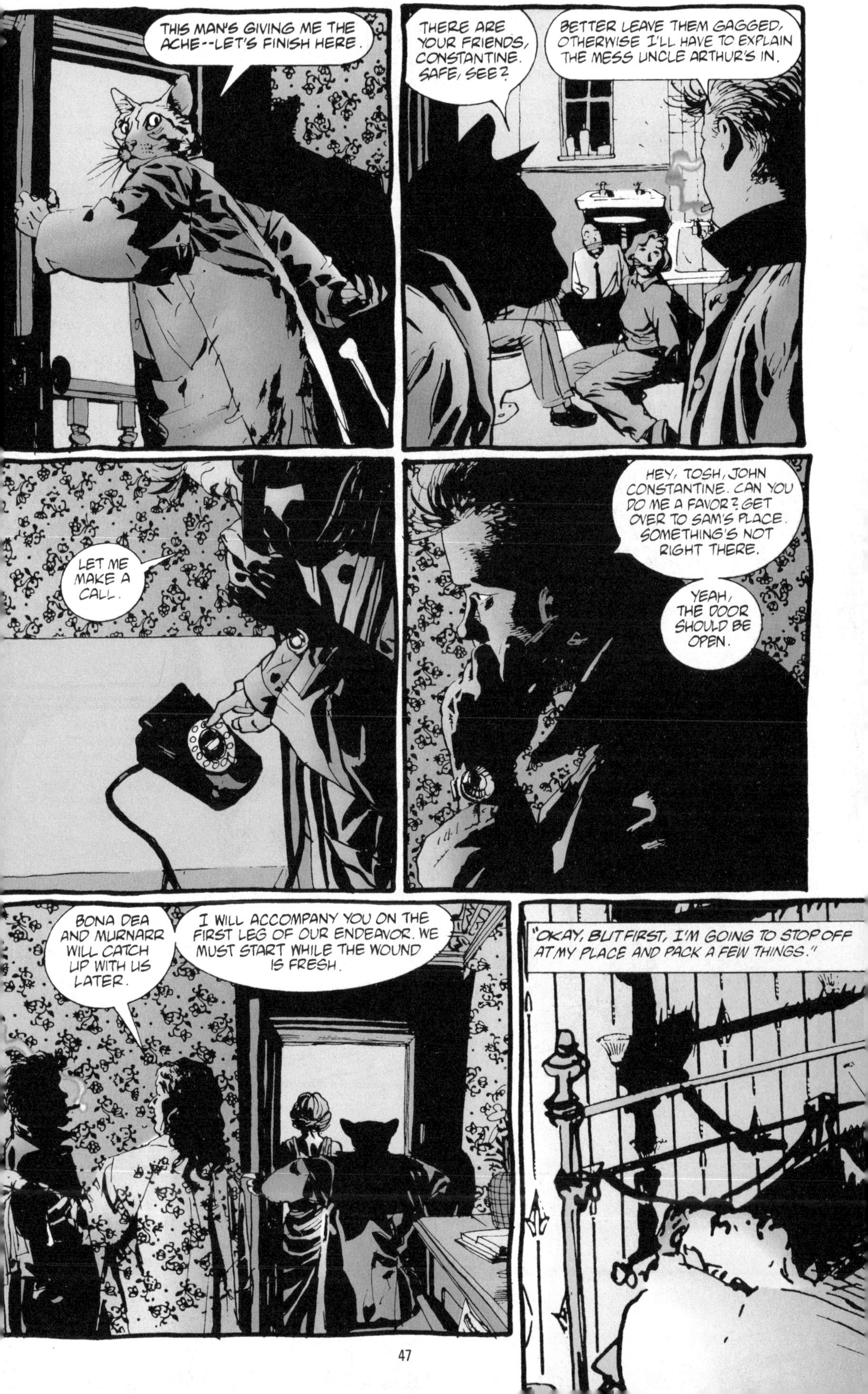

THIS MAN'S GIVING ME THE ACHE--LET'S FINISH HERE.
THERE ARE YOUR FRIENDS, CONSTANTINE. SAFE, SEE?
BETTER LEAVE THEM GAGGED, OTHERWISE I'LL HAVE TO EXPLAIN THE MESS UNCLE ARTHUR'S IN.
LET ME MAKE A CALL.
HEY, TOSH, JOHN CONSTANTINE. CAN YOU DO ME A FAVOR? GET OVER TO SAM'S PLACE. SOMETHING'S NOT RIGHT THERE.
YEAH, THE DOOR SHOULD BE OPEN.
BONA DEA AND MURNARR WILL CATCH UP WITH US LATER.
I WILL ACCOMPANY YOU ON THE FIRST LEG OF OUR ENDEAVOR. WE MUST START WHILE THE WOUND IS FRESH.
"OKAY, BUT FIRST, I'M GOING TO STOP OFF AT MY PLACE AND PACK A FEW THINGS."

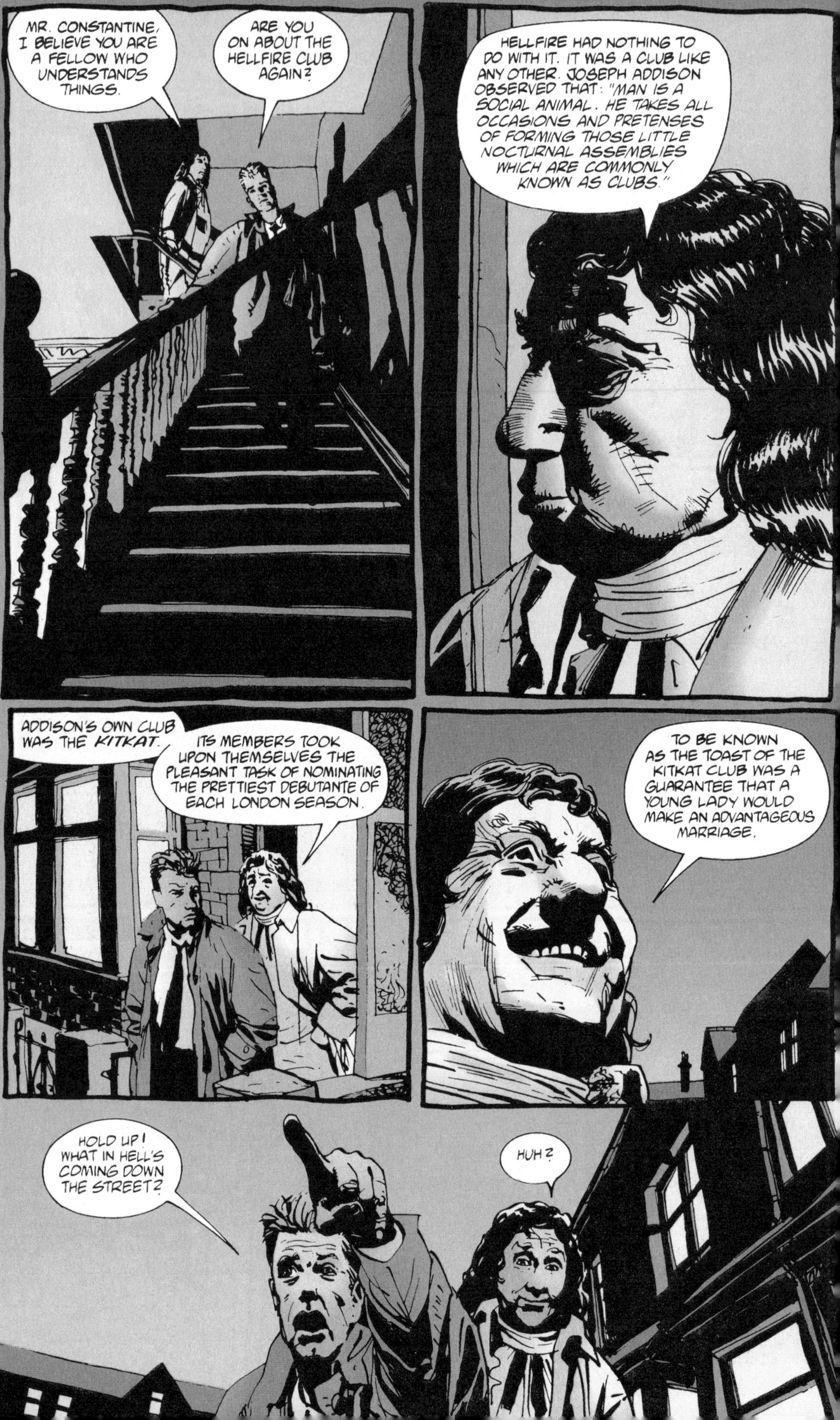
MR. CONSTANTINE, I BELIEVE YOU ARE A FELLOW WHO UNDERSTANDS THINGS.
ARE YOU ON ABOUT THE HELLFIRE CLUB AGAIN?
HELLFIRE HAD NOTHING TO DO WITH IT. IT WAS A CLUB LIKE ANY OTHER. JOSEPH ADDISON OBSERVED THAT: "MAN IS A SOCIAL ANIMAL. HE TAKES ALL OCCASIONS AND PRETENSES OF FORMING THOSE LITTLE NOCTURNAL ASSEMBLIES WHICH ARE COMMONLY KNOWN AS CLUBS."
ADDISON'S OWN CLUB WAS THE *KITKAT*.
ITS MEMBERS TOOK UPON THEMSELVES THE PLEASANT TASK OF NOMINATING THE PRETTIEST DEBUTANTE OF EACH LONDON SEASON.
TO BE KNOWN AS THE TOAST OF THE KITKAT CLUB WAS A GUARANTEE THAT A YOUNG LADY WOULD MAKE AN ADVANTAGEOUS MARRIAGE.
HOLD UP! WHAT IN HELL'S COMING DOWN THE STREET?
HUH?

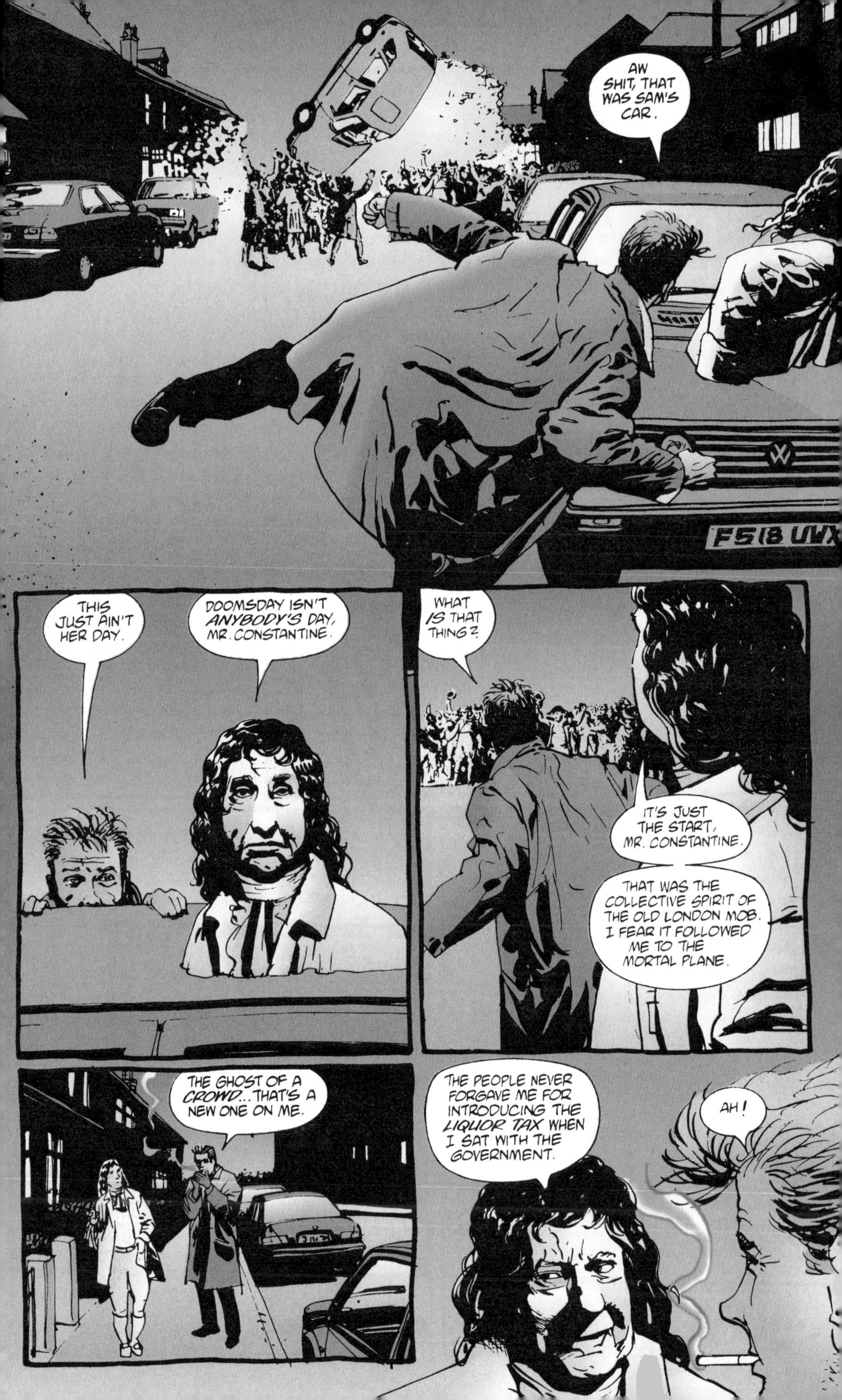

AW SHIT, THAT WAS SAM'S CAR.
F518 UWX
THIS JUST AIN'T HER DAY.
DOOMSDAY ISN'T *ANYBODY'S* DAY, MR. CONSTANTINE.
WHAT *IS* THAT THING?
IT'S JUST THE START, MR. CONSTANTINE.
THAT WAS THE COLLECTIVE SPIRIT OF THE OLD LONDON MOB. I FEAR IT FOLLOWED ME TO THE MORTAL PLANE.
THE GHOST OF A *CROWD*... THAT'S A NEW ONE ON ME.
THE PEOPLE NEVER FORGAVE ME FOR INTRODUCING THE *LIQUOR TAX* WHEN I SAT WITH THE GOVERNMENT.
AH!

THERE ARE OTHER DANGERS I CANNOT *BEGIN* TO WARN YOU OF.

ALL THE DOORS AND GATES THAT KEPT EVERYTHING IN ITS PLACE HAVE BEEN FLUNG OPEN.

UNREASON HAS BEEN LET LOOSE LIKE A MAD DOG.

WE MUST HIE AWAY FROM HERE.

RIGHT. I'M TAKING THE TUBE THEN.

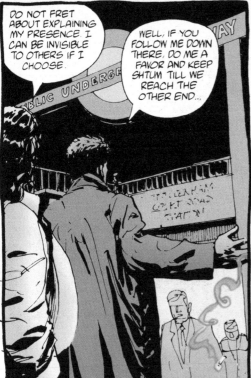

DO NOT FRET ABOUT EXPLAINING MY PRESENCE. I CAN BE INVISIBLE TO OTHERS IF I CHOOSE.

WELL, IF YOU FOLLOW ME DOWN THERE, DO ME A FAVOR AND KEEP SHTUM TILL WE REACH THE OTHER END...

IF I'M HEARD TALKING TO MESELF, I'LL BE FINISHING MY MONOLOG IN THE NUT HOUSE.

MAYBE I'LL EVEN BE THE NEXT LOONY TO GET HOLD OF THE MEAT KNIFE...

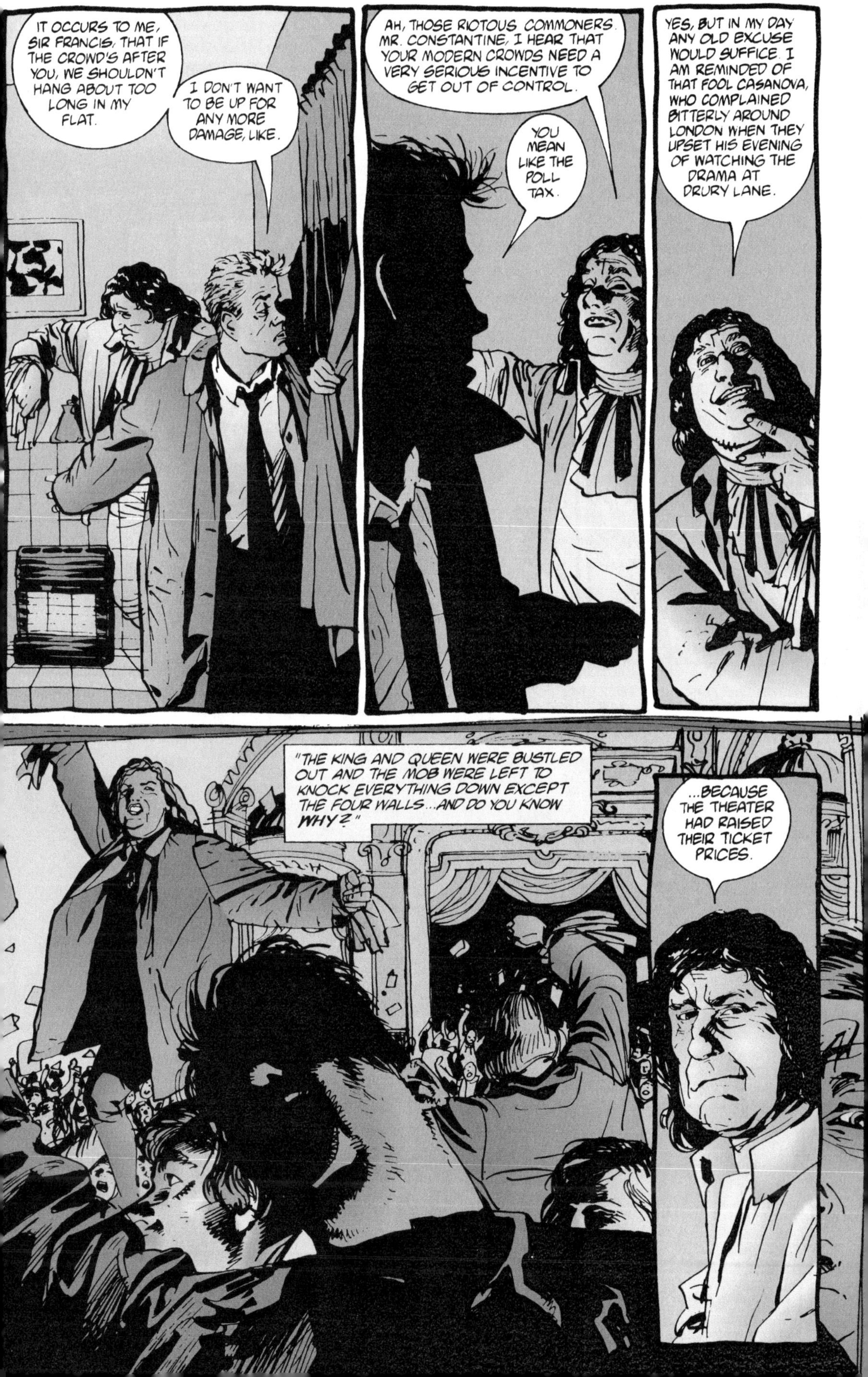
IT OCCURS TO ME, SIR FRANCIS, THAT IF THE CROWD'S AFTER YOU, WE SHOULDN'T HANG ABOUT TOO LONG IN MY FLAT.
I DON'T WANT TO BE UP FOR ANY MORE DAMAGE, LIKE.
AH, THOSE RIOTOUS COMMONERS. MR. CONSTANTINE, I HEAR THAT YOUR MODERN CROWDS NEED A VERY SERIOUS INCENTIVE TO GET OUT OF CONTROL.
YOU MEAN LIKE THE POLL TAX.
YES, BUT IN MY DAY ANY OLD EXCUSE WOULD SUFFICE. I AM REMINDED OF THAT FOOL CASANOVA, WHO COMPLAINED BITTERLY AROUND LONDON WHEN THEY UPSET HIS EVENING OF WATCHING THE DRAMA AT DRURY LANE.
"THE KING AND QUEEN WERE BUSTLED OUT AND THE MOB WERE LEFT TO KNOCK EVERYTHING DOWN EXCEPT THE FOUR WALLS...AND DO YOU KNOW WHY?"
...BECAUSE THE THEATER HAD RAISED THEIR TICKET PRICES.

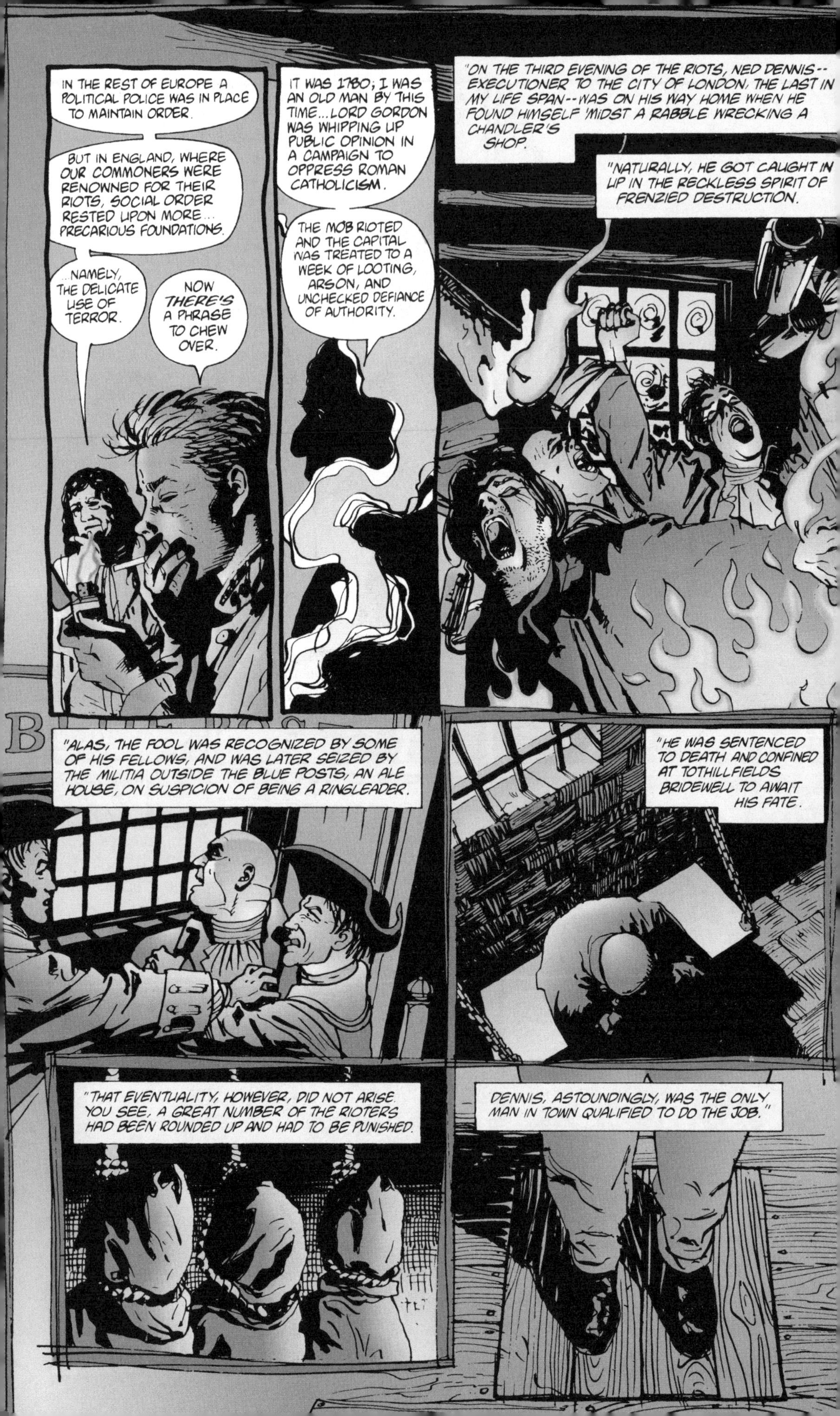
IN THE REST OF EUROPE A POLITICAL POLICE WAS IN PLACE TO MAINTAIN ORDER.
BUT IN ENGLAND, WHERE OUR COMMONERS WERE RENOWNED FOR THEIR RIOTS, SOCIAL ORDER RESTED UPON MORE... PRECARIOUS FOUNDATIONS.
...NAMELY, THE DELICATE USE OF TERROR.
NOW THERE'S A PHRASE TO CHEW OVER.
IT WAS 1780; I WAS AN OLD MAN BY THIS TIME... LORD GORDON WAS WHIPPING UP PUBLIC OPINION IN A CAMPAIGN TO OPPRESS ROMAN CATHOLICISM.
THE MOB RIOTED AND THE CAPITAL WAS TREATED TO A WEEK OF LOOTING, ARSON, AND UNCHECKED DEFIANCE OF AUTHORITY.
"ON THE THIRD EVENING OF THE RIOTS, NED DENNIS-- EXECUTIONER TO THE CITY OF LONDON, THE LAST IN MY LIFE SPAN--WAS ON HIS WAY HOME WHEN HE FOUND HIMSELF 'MIDST A RABBLE WRECKING A CHANDLER'S SHOP.
"NATURALLY, HE GOT CAUGHT IN UP IN THE RECKLESS SPIRIT OF FRENZIED DESTRUCTION.
"ALAS, THE FOOL WAS RECOGNIZED BY SOME OF HIS FELLOWS, AND WAS LATER SEIZED BY THE MILITIA OUTSIDE THE BLUE POSTS, AN ALE HOUSE, ON SUSPICION OF BEING A RINGLEADER.
"HE WAS SENTENCED TO DEATH AND CONFINED AT TOTHILLFIELDS BRIDEWELL TO AWAIT HIS FATE.
"THAT EVENTUALITY, HOWEVER, DID NOT ARISE. YOU SEE, A GREAT NUMBER OF THE RIOTERS HAD BEEN ROUNDED UP AND HAD TO BE PUNISHED.
DENNIS, ASTOUNDINGLY, WAS THE ONLY MAN IN TOWN QUALIFIED TO DO THE JOB."

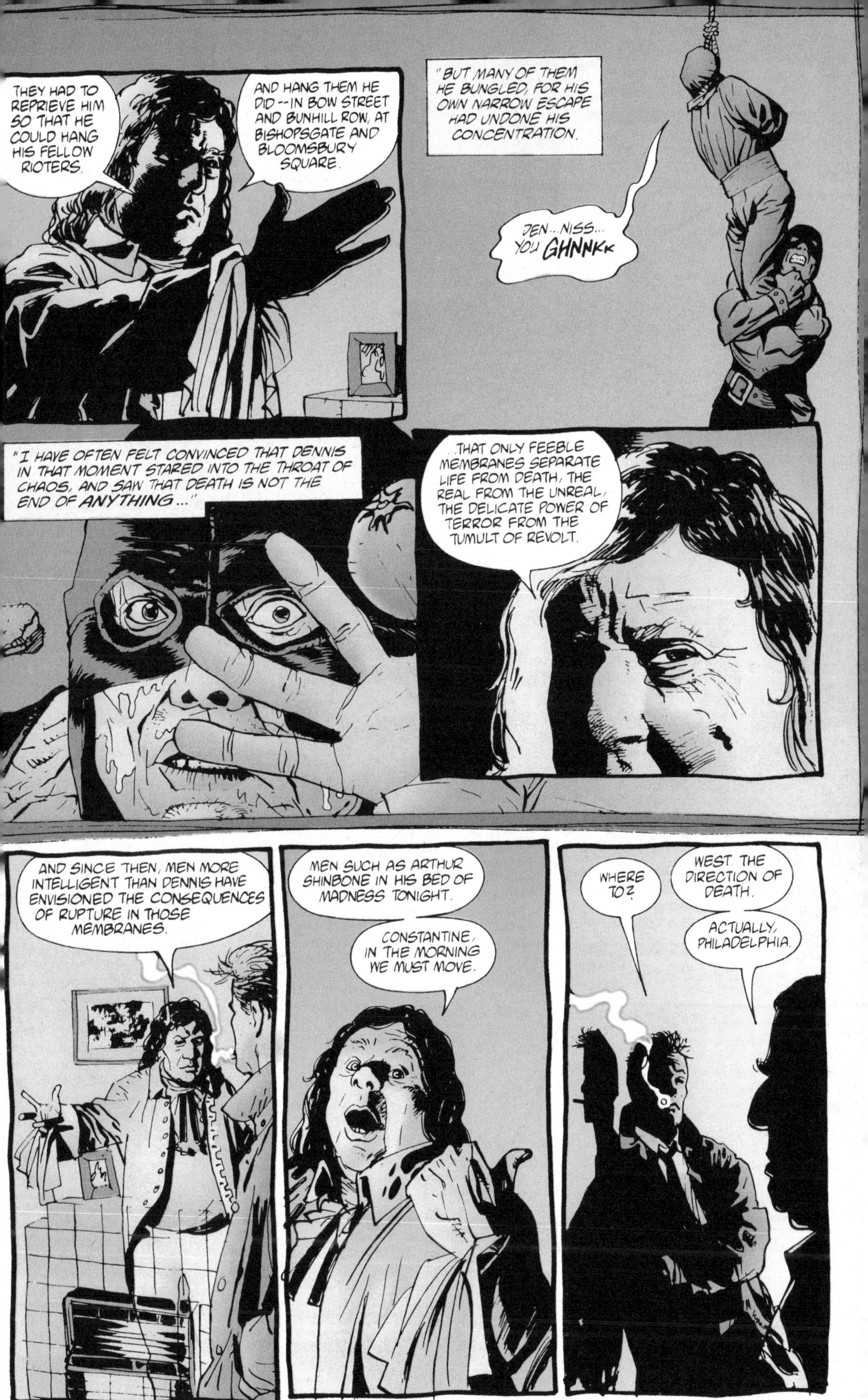
THEY HAD TO REPRIEVE HIM SO THAT HE COULD HANG HIS FELLOW RIOTERS.
AND HANG THEM HE DID--IN BOW STREET AND BUNHILL ROW, AT BISHOPSGATE AND BLOOMSBURY SQUARE.
"BUT MANY OF THEM HE BUNGLED, FOR HIS OWN NARROW ESCAPE HAD UNDONE HIS CONCENTRATION.
DEN...NISS... YOU GHNNKK
"I HAVE OFTEN FELT CONVINCED THAT DENNIS IN THAT MOMENT STARED INTO THE THROAT OF CHAOS, AND SAW THAT DEATH IS NOT THE END OF ANYTHING..."
...THAT ONLY FEEBLE MEMBRANES SEPARATE LIFE FROM DEATH, THE REAL FROM THE UNREAL, THE DELICATE POWER OF TERROR FROM THE TUMULT OF REVOLT.
AND SINCE THEN, MEN MORE INTELLIGENT THAN DENNIS HAVE ENVISIONED THE CONSEQUENCES OF RUPTURE IN THOSE MEMBRANES.
MEN SUCH AS ARTHUR SHINBONE IN HIS BED OF MADNESS TONIGHT.
CONSTANTINE, IN THE MORNING WE MUST MOVE.
WHERE TO?
WEST. THE DIRECTION OF DEATH.
ACTUALLY, PHILADELPHIA.

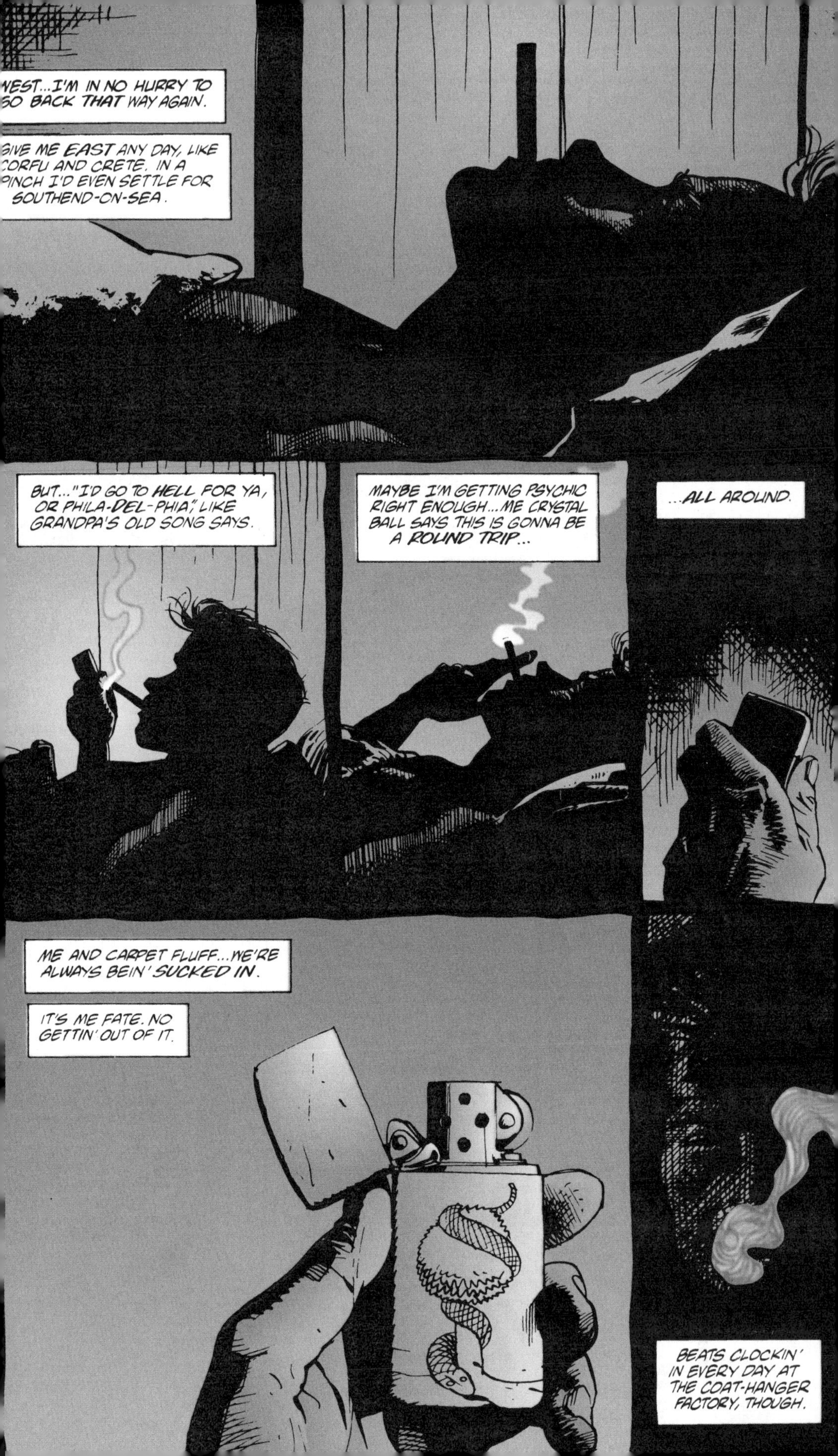
WEST...I'M IN NO HURRY TO GO BACK THAT WAY AGAIN.
GIVE ME EAST ANY DAY, LIKE CORFU AND CRETE. IN A PINCH I'D EVEN SETTLE FOR SOUTHEND-ON-SEA.
BUT..."I'D GO TO HELL FOR YA, OR PHILA-DEL-PHIA," LIKE GRANDPA'S OLD SONG SAYS.
MAYBE I'M GETTING PSYCHIC RIGHT ENOUGH...ME CRYSTAL BALL SAYS THIS IS GONNA BE A ROUND TRIP...
...ALL AROUND.
ME AND CARPET FLUFF...WE'RE ALWAYS BEIN' SUCKED IN.
IT'S ME FATE. NO GETTIN' OUT OF IT.
BEATS CLOCKIN' IN EVERY DAY AT THE COAT-HANGER FACTORY, THOUGH.

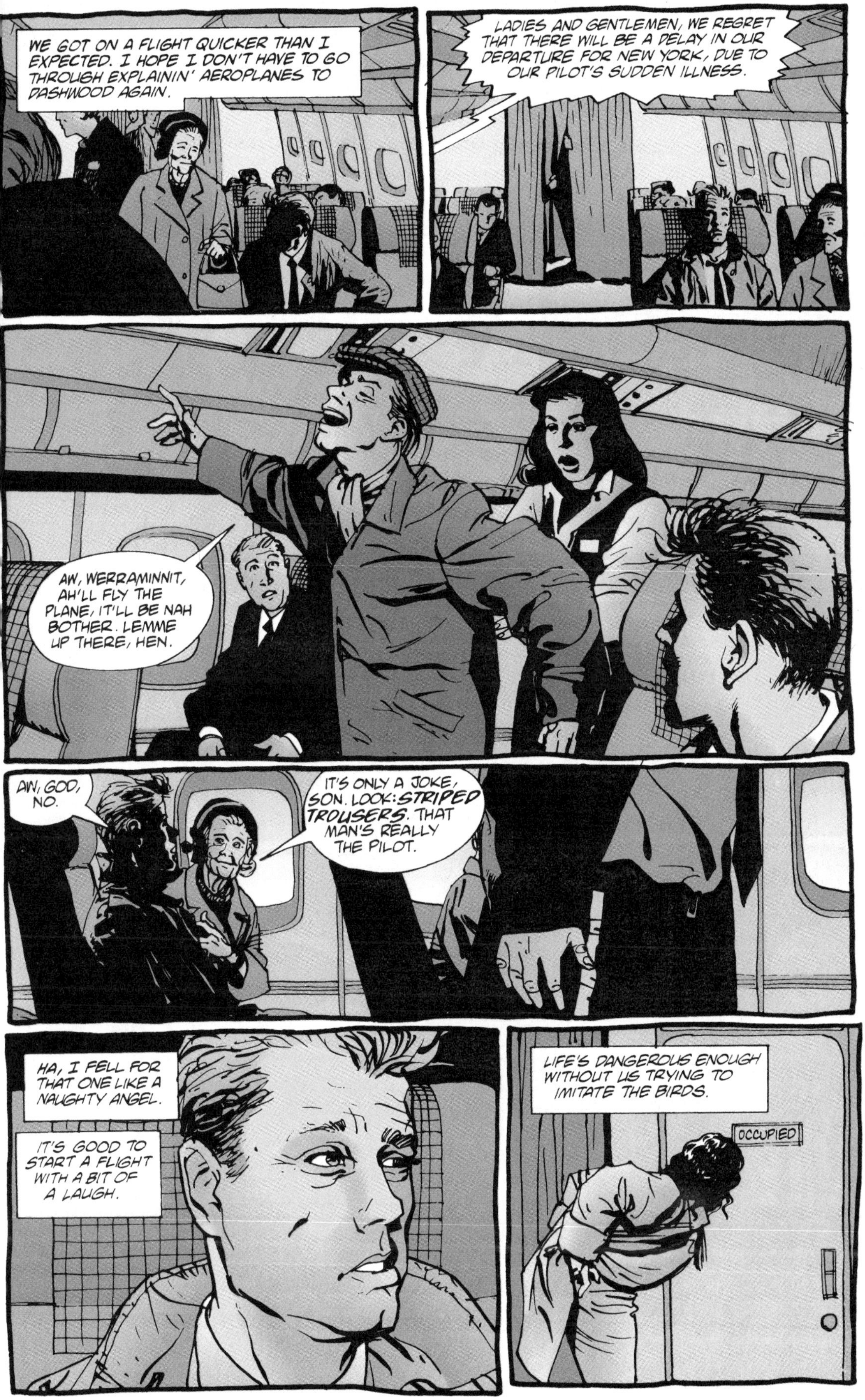

WE GOT ON A FLIGHT QUICKER THAN I EXPECTED. I HOPE I DON'T HAVE TO GO THROUGH EXPLAININ' AEROPLANES TO DASHWOOD AGAIN.
LADIES AND GENTLEMEN, WE REGRET THAT THERE WILL BE A DELAY IN OUR DEPARTURE FOR NEW YORK, DUE TO OUR PILOT'S SUDDEN ILLNESS.
AW, WERRAMINNIT, AH'LL FLY THE PLANE, IT'LL BE NAH BOTHER. LEMME UP THERE, HEN.
AW, GOD, NO.
IT'S ONLY A JOKE, SON. LOOK: STRIPED TROUSERS. THAT MAN'S REALLY THE PILOT.
HA, I FELL FOR THAT ONE LIKE A NAUGHTY ANGEL.
IT'S GOOD TO START A FLIGHT WITH A BIT OF A LAUGH.
LIFE'S DANGEROUS ENOUGH WITHOUT US TRYING TO IMITATE THE BIRDS.
OCCUPIED

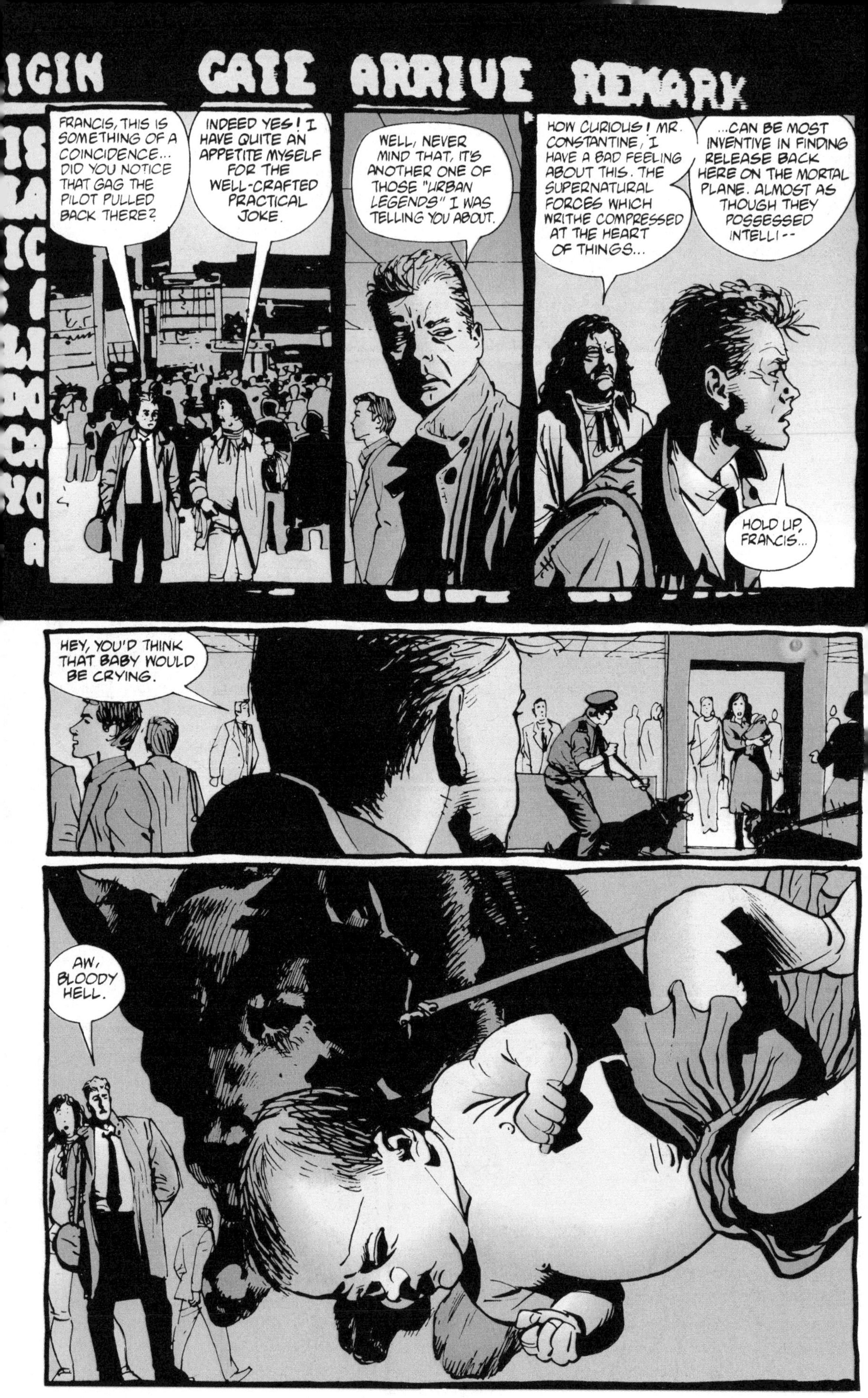
IGIN GATE ARRIVE REMARK
FRANCIS, THIS IS SOMETHING OF A COINCIDENCE... DID YOU NOTICE THAT GAG THE PILOT PULLED BACK THERE?
INDEED YES! I HAVE QUITE AN APPETITE MYSELF FOR THE WELL-CRAFTED PRACTICAL JOKE.
WELL, NEVER MIND THAT, IT'S ANOTHER ONE OF THOSE "URBAN LEGENDS" I WAS TELLING YOU ABOUT.
HOW CURIOUS! MR. CONSTANTINE, I HAVE A BAD FEELING ABOUT THIS. THE SUPERNATURAL FORCES WHICH WRITHE COMPRESSED AT THE HEART OF THINGS...
...CAN BE MOST INVENTIVE IN FINDING RELEASE BACK HERE ON THE MORTAL PLANE. ALMOST AS THOUGH THEY POSSESSED INTELLI--
HOLD UP, FRANCIS...
HEY, YOU'D THINK THAT BABY WOULD BE CRYING.
AW, BLOODY HELL.

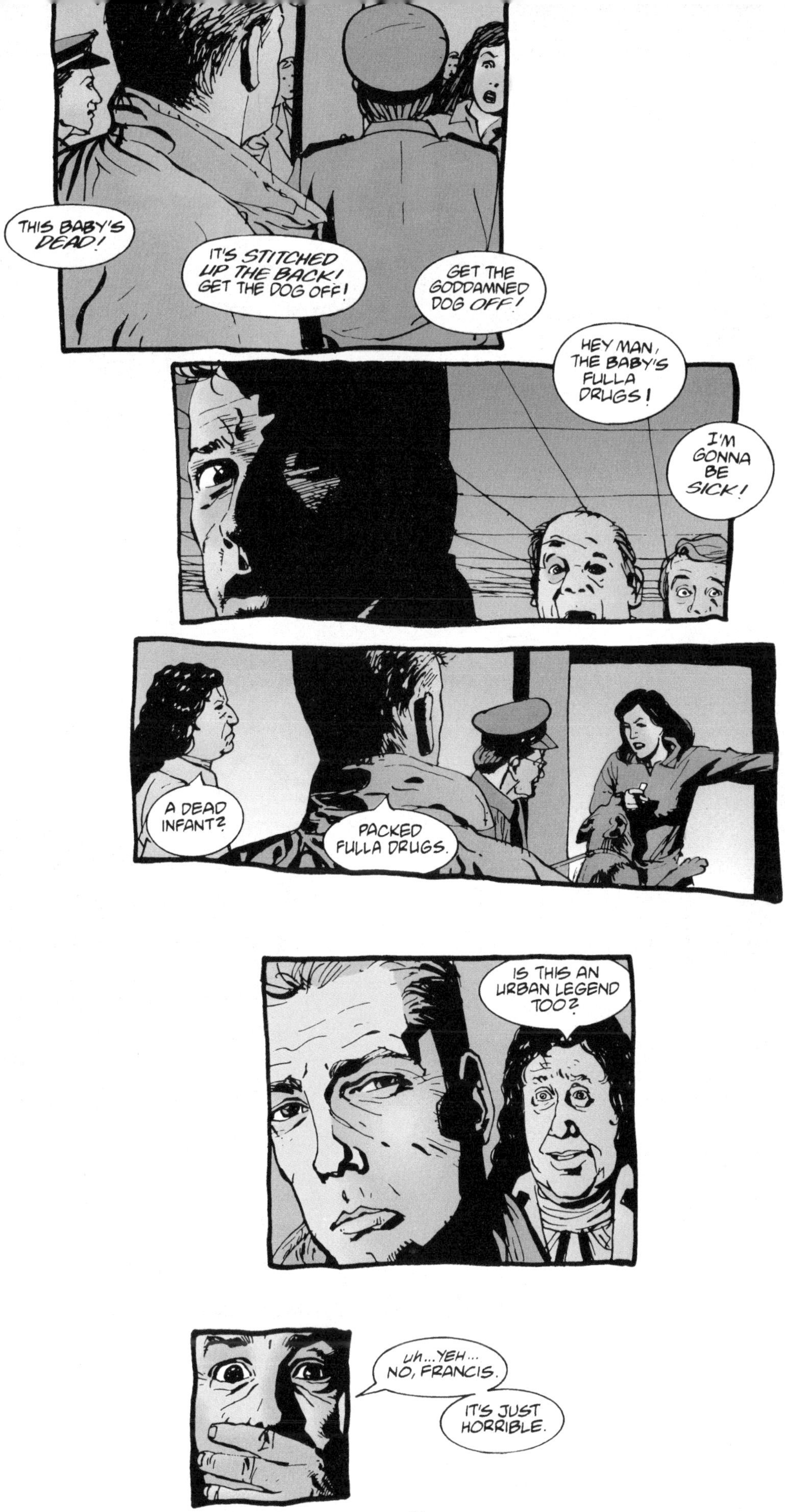
THIS BABY'S DEAD!
IT'S STITCHED UP THE BACK! GET THE DOG OFF!
GET THE GODDAMNED DOG OFF!
HEY MAN, THE BABY'S FULLA DRUGS!
I'M GONNA BE SICK!
A DEAD INFANT?
PACKED FULLA DRUGS.
IS THIS AN URBAN LEGEND TOO?
uh...YEH... NO, FRANCIS.
IT'S JUST HORRIBLE.

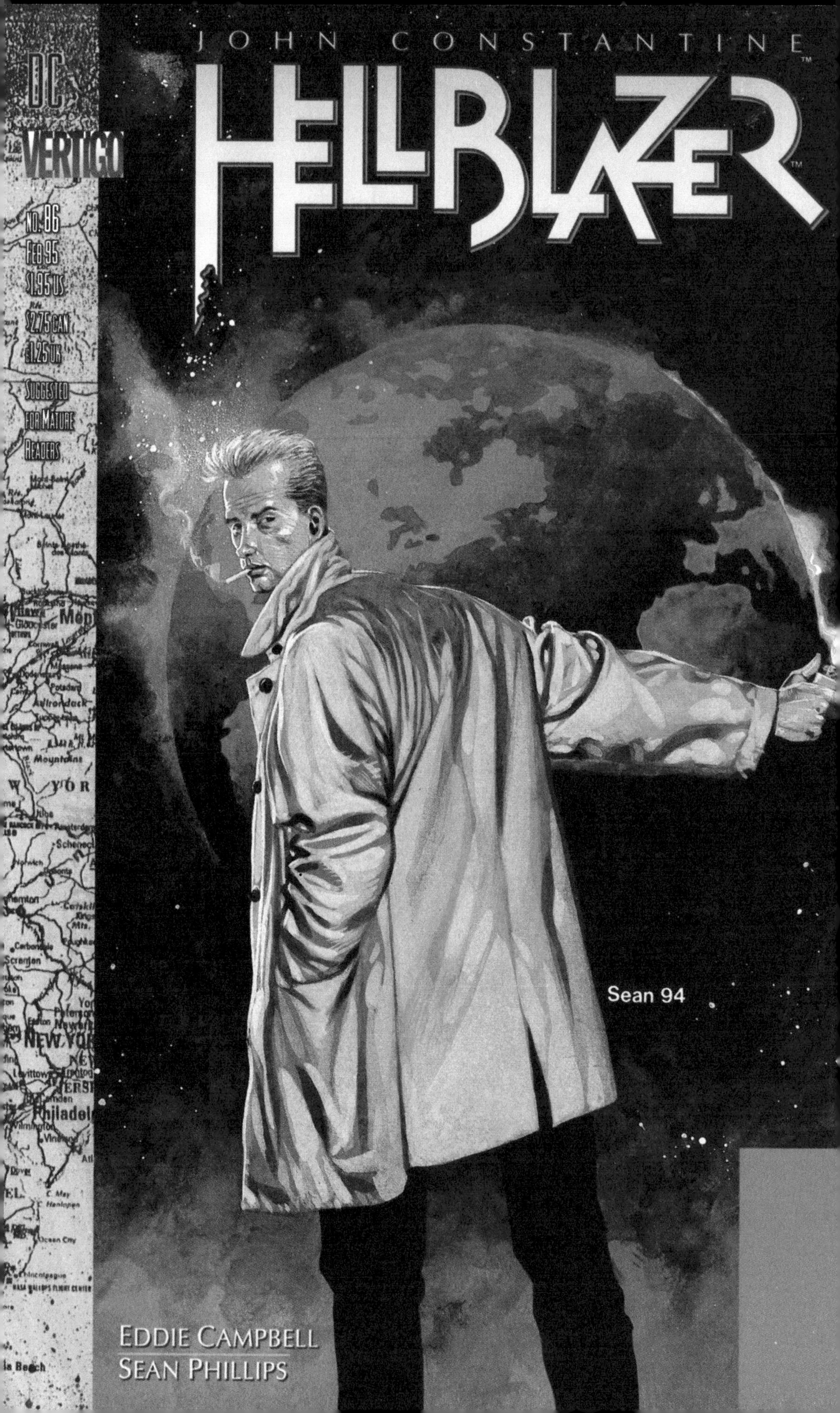

JOHN CONSTANTINE
HELLBLAZER™
DC
VERTIGO
No. 86
Feb 95
$1.95 US
$2.75 CAN
£1.25 UK
SUGGESTED FOR MATURE READERS
Sean 94
EDDIE CAMPBELL
SEAN PHILLIPS

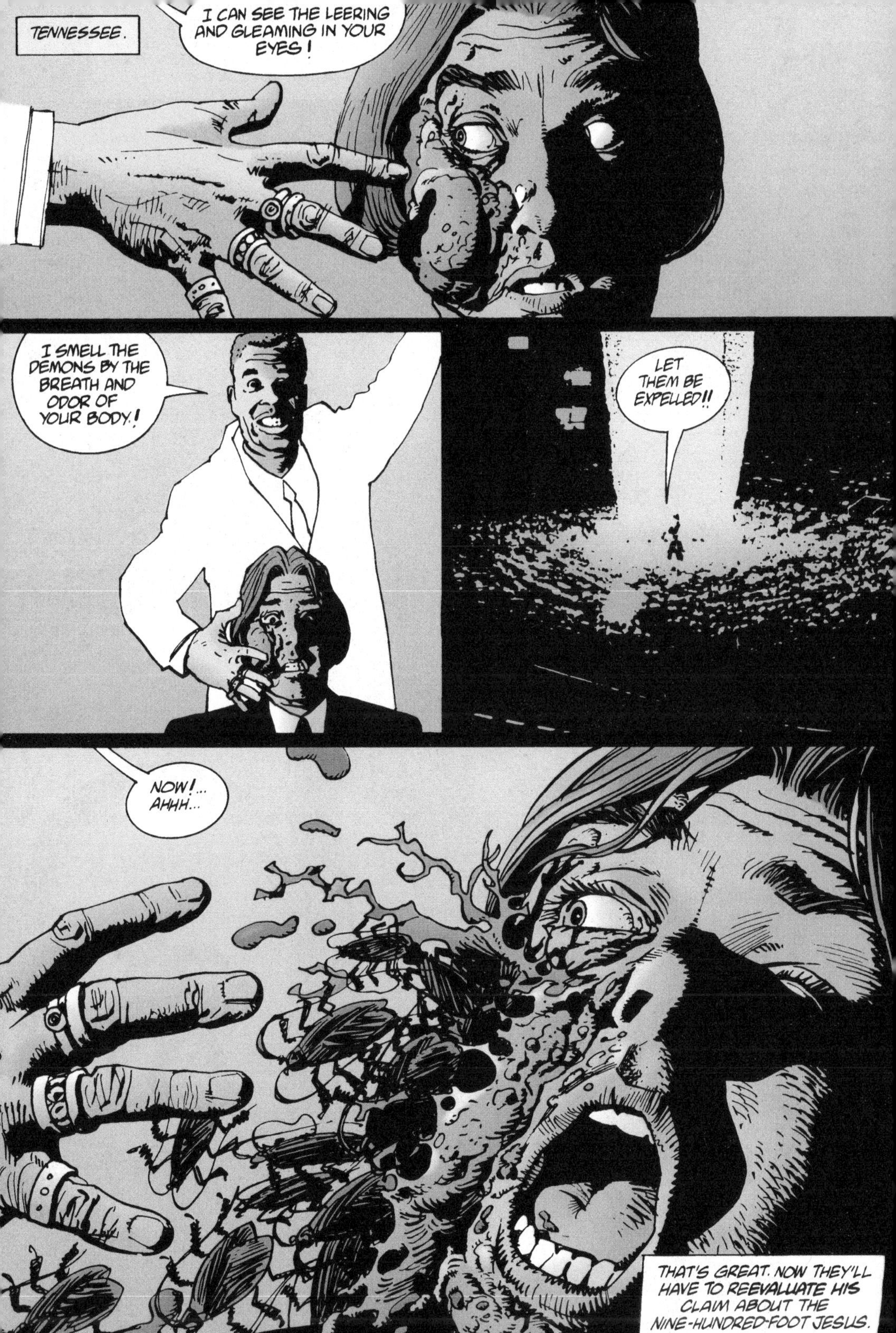
TENNESSEE.
I CAN SEE THE LEERING AND GLEAMING IN YOUR EYES!
I SMELL THE DEMONS BY THE BREATH AND ODOR OF YOUR BODY!
LET THEM BE EXPELLED!!
NOW!... AHHH...
THAT'S GREAT. NOW THEY'LL HAVE TO REEVALUATE HIS CLAIM ABOUT THE NINE-HUNDRED-FOOT JESUS.

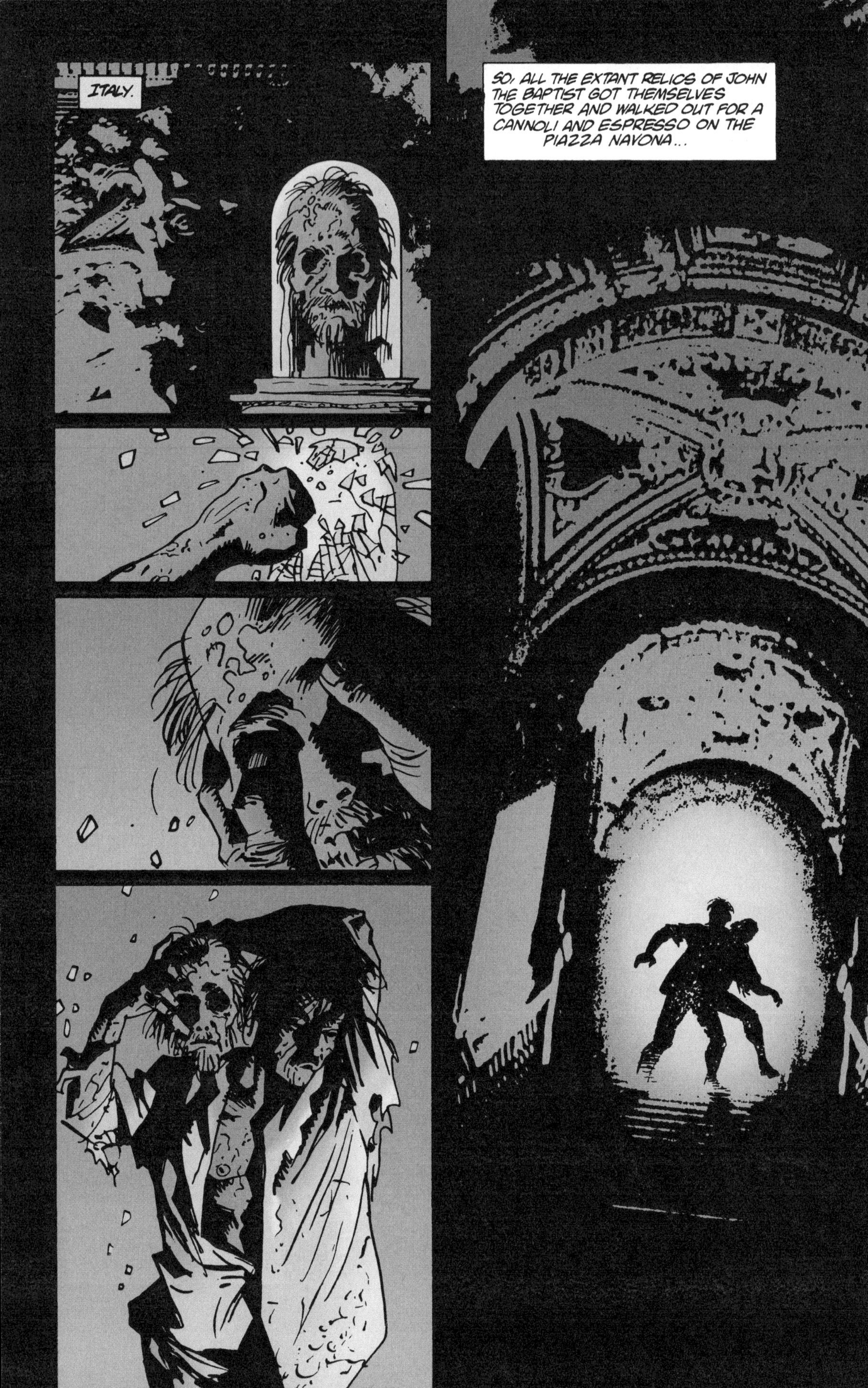
ITALY.
SO, ALL THE EXTANT RELICS OF JOHN THE BAPTIST GOT THEMSELVES TOGETHER AND WALKED OUT FOR A CANNOLI AND ESPRESSO ON THE PIAZZA NAVONA...

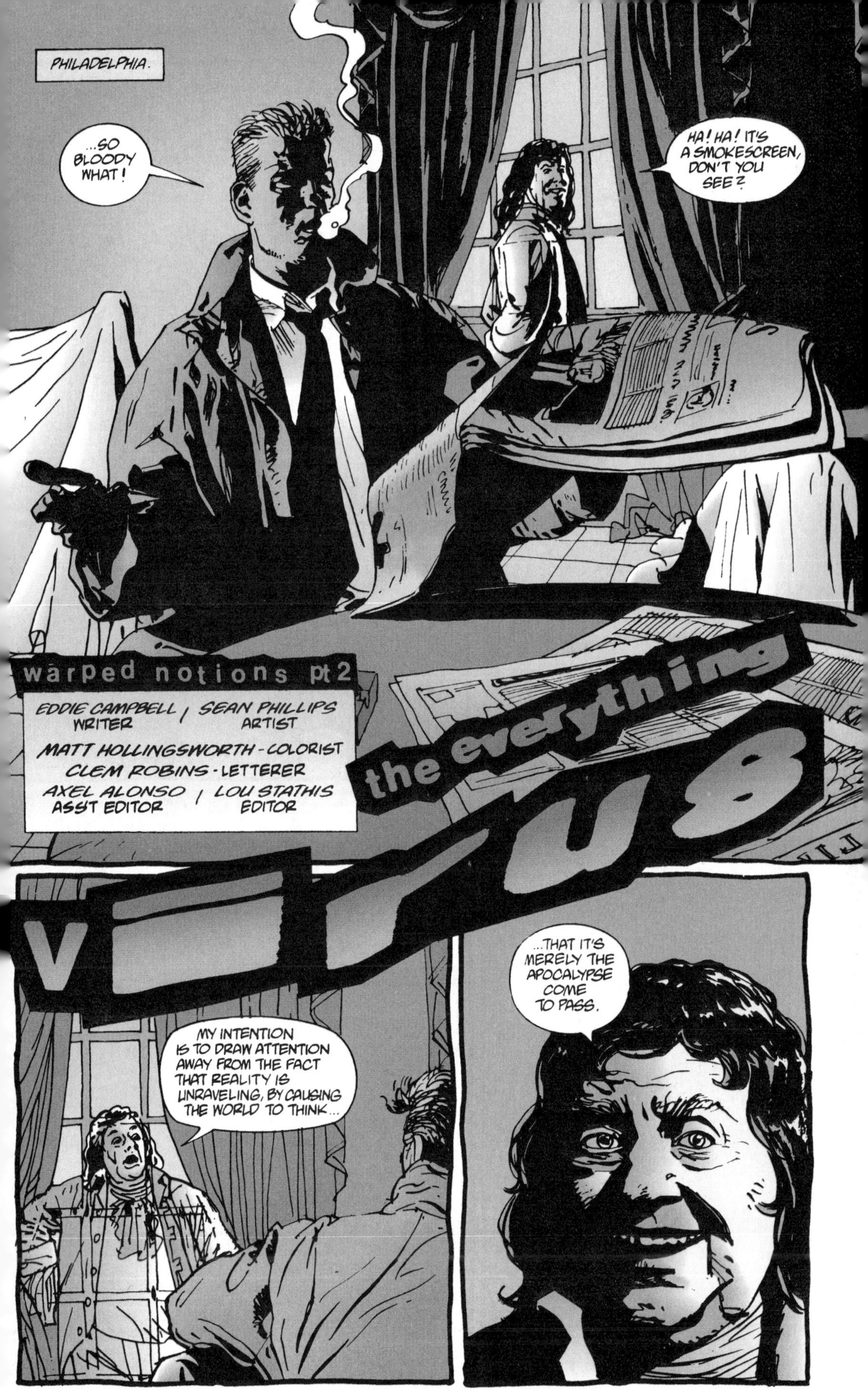

PHILADELPHIA.
...SO BLOODY WHAT!
HA! HA! IT'S A SMOKESCREEN, DON'T YOU SEE?
warped notions pt2
EDDIE CAMPBELL WRITER / SEAN PHILLIPS ARTIST
MATT HOLLINGSWORTH - COLORIST
CLEM ROBINS - LETTERER
AXEL ALONSO ASS'T EDITOR / LOU STATHIS EDITOR
the everything VIRUS
MY INTENTION IS TO DRAW ATTENTION AWAY FROM THE FACT THAT REALITY IS UNRAVELING, BY CAUSING THE WORLD TO THINK...
...THAT IT'S MERELY THE APOCALYPSE COME TO PASS.

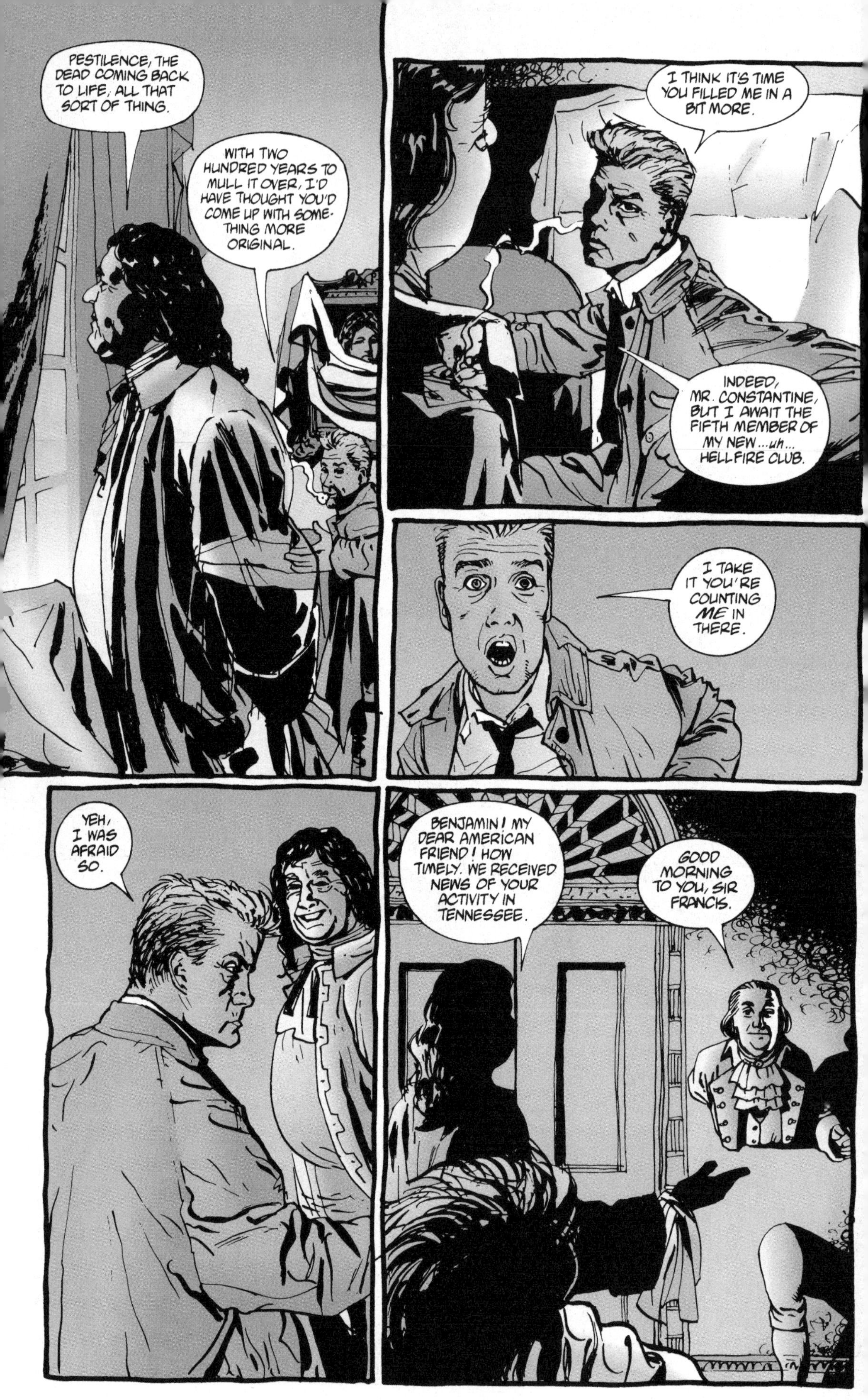
PESTILENCE, THE DEAD COMING BACK TO LIFE, ALL THAT SORT OF THING.
WITH TWO HUNDRED YEARS TO MULL IT OVER, I'D HAVE THOUGHT YOU'D COME UP WITH SOME-THING MORE ORIGINAL.
I THINK IT'S TIME YOU FILLED ME IN A BIT MORE.
INDEED, MR. CONSTANTINE, BUT I AWAIT THE FIFTH MEMBER OF MY NEW ...uh... HELLFIRE CLUB.
I TAKE IT YOU'RE COUNTING ME IN THERE.
YEH, I WAS AFRAID SO.
BENJAMIN! MY DEAR AMERICAN FRIEND! HOW TIMELY. WE RECEIVED NEWS OF YOUR ACTIVITY IN TENNESSEE.
GOOD MORNING TO YOU, SIR FRANCIS.

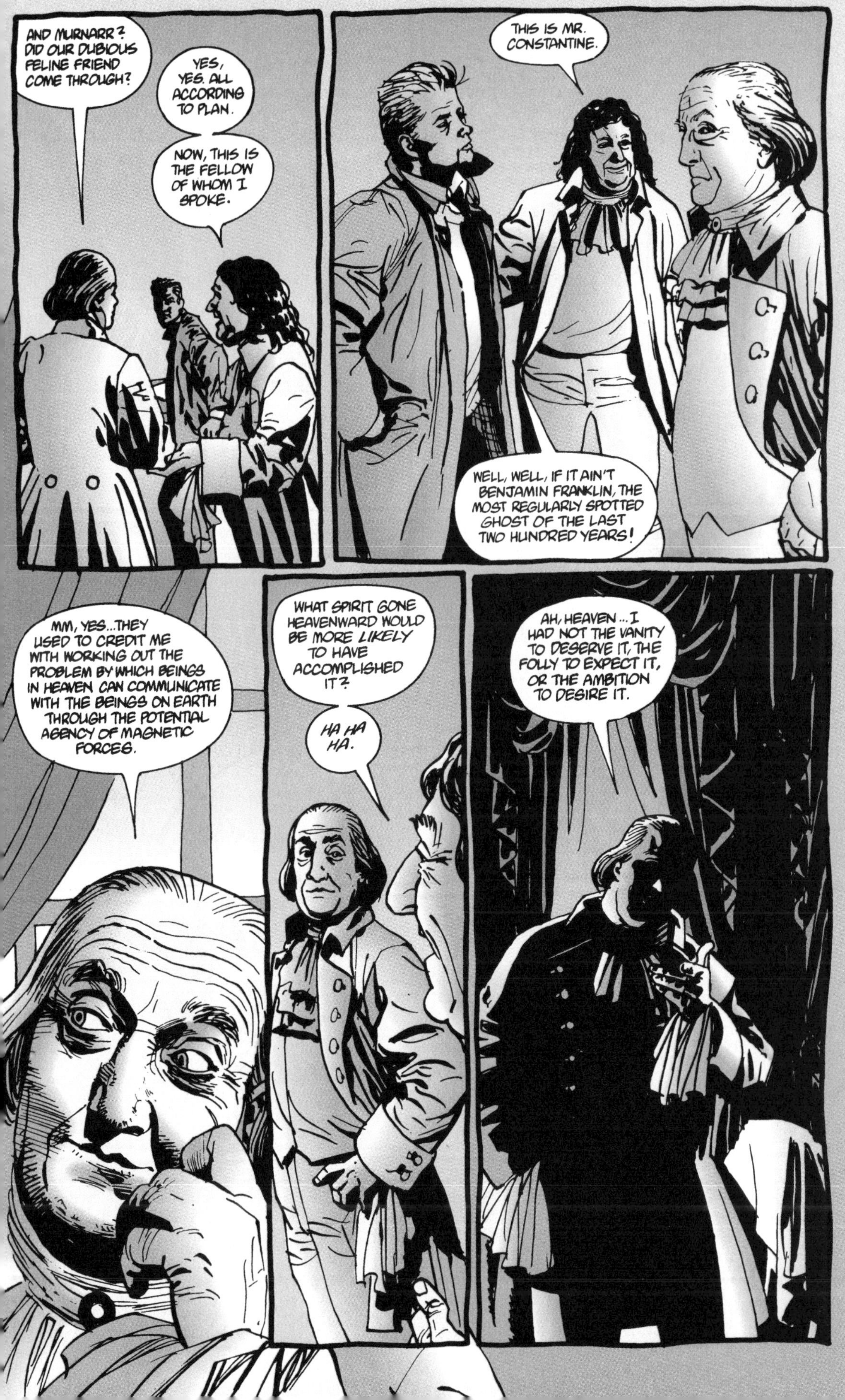
AND MURNARR? DID OUR DUBIOUS FELINE FRIEND COME THROUGH?
YES, YES. ALL ACCORDING TO PLAN.
NOW, THIS IS THE FELLOW OF WHOM I SPOKE.
THIS IS MR. CONSTANTINE.
WELL, WELL, IF IT AIN'T BENJAMIN FRANKLIN, THE MOST REGULARLY SPOTTED GHOST OF THE LAST TWO HUNDRED YEARS!
MM, YES...THEY USED TO CREDIT ME WITH WORKING OUT THE PROBLEM BY WHICH BEINGS IN HEAVEN CAN COMMUNICATE WITH THE BEINGS ON EARTH THROUGH THE POTENTIAL AGENCY OF MAGNETIC FORCES.
WHAT SPIRIT GONE HEAVENWARD WOULD BE MORE *LIKELY* TO HAVE ACCOMPLISHED IT?
HA HA HA.
AH, HEAVEN... I HAD NOT THE VANITY TO DESERVE IT, THE FOLLY TO EXPECT IT, OR THE AMBITION TO DESIRE IT.

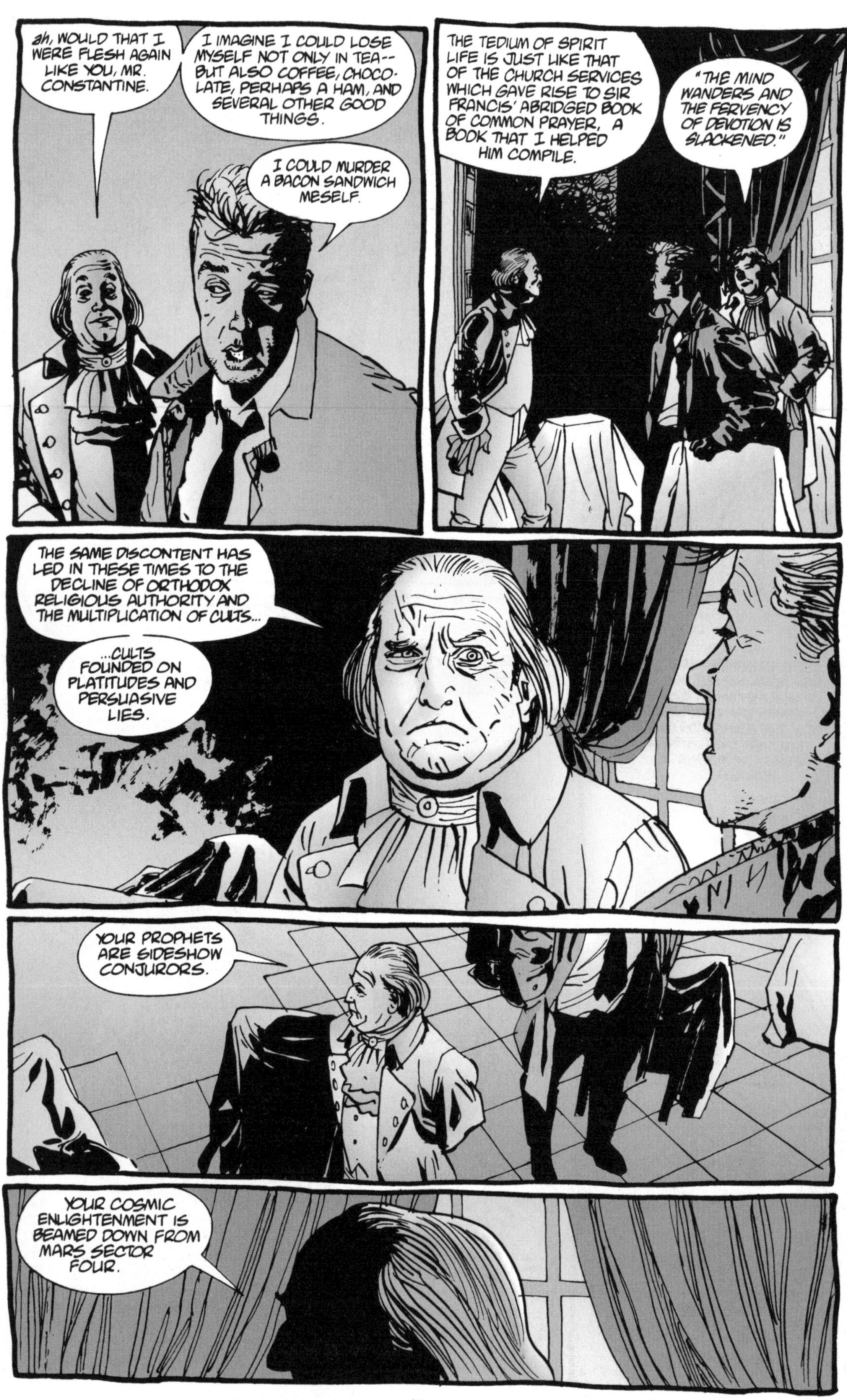
ah, WOULD THAT I WERE FLESH AGAIN LIKE YOU, MR. CONSTANTINE.
I IMAGINE I COULD LOSE MYSELF NOT ONLY IN TEA-- BUT ALSO COFFEE, CHOCOLATE, PERHAPS A HAM, AND SEVERAL OTHER GOOD THINGS.
I COULD MURDER A BACON SANDWICH MESELF.
THE TEDIUM OF SPIRIT LIFE IS JUST LIKE THAT OF THE CHURCH SERVICES WHICH GAVE RISE TO SIR FRANCIS' ABRIDGED BOOK OF COMMON PRAYER, A BOOK THAT I HELPED HIM COMPILE.
"THE MIND WANDERS AND THE FERVENCY OF DEVOTION IS SLACKENED."
THE SAME DISCONTENT HAS LED IN THESE TIMES TO THE DECLINE OF ORTHODOX RELIGIOUS AUTHORITY AND THE MULTIPLICATION OF CULTS...
...CULTS FOUNDED ON PLATITUDES AND PERSUASIVE LIES.
YOUR PROPHETS ARE SIDESHOW CONJURORS.
YOUR COSMIC ENLIGHTENMENT IS BEAMED DOWN FROM MARS SECTOR FOUR.

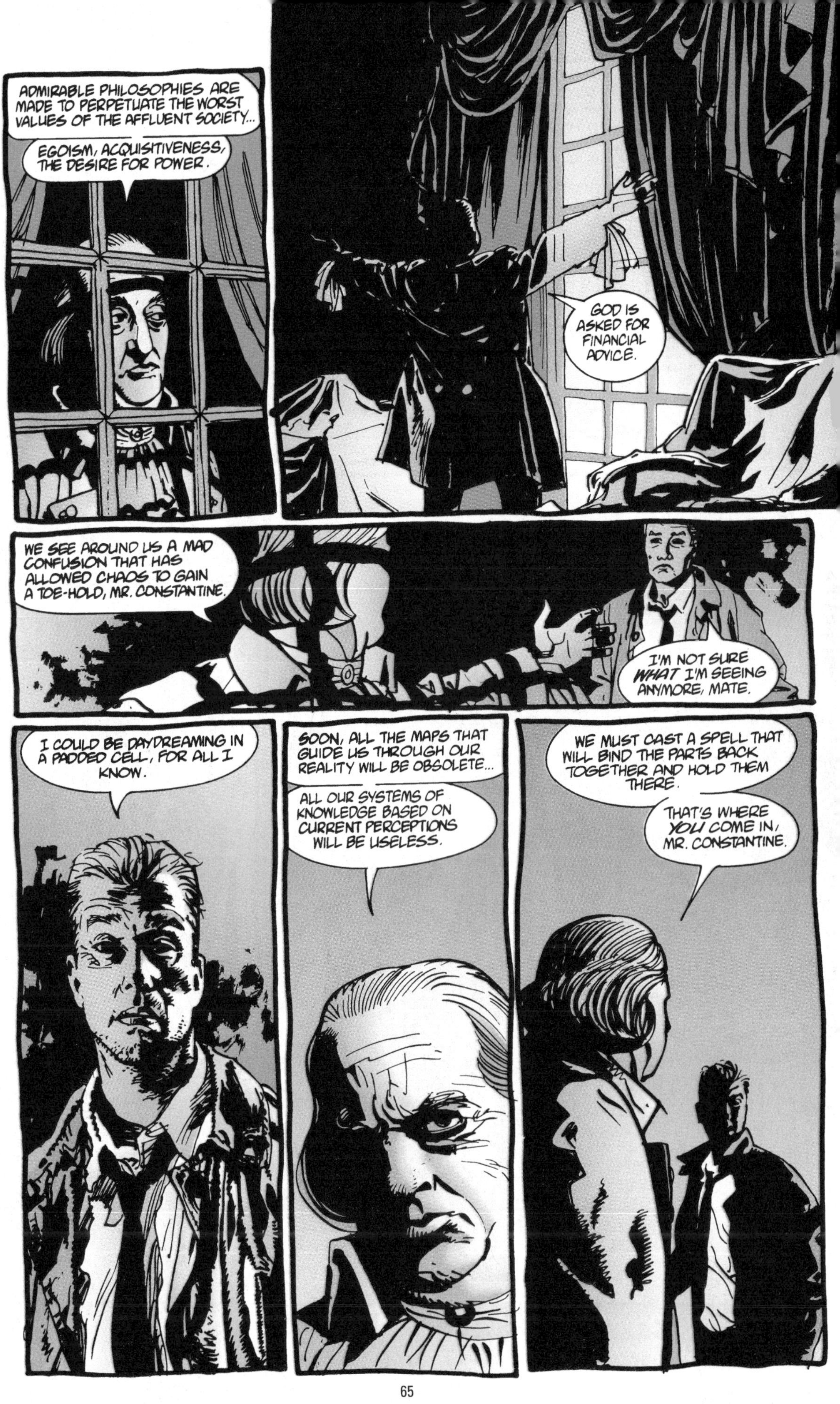
ADMIRABLE PHILOSOPHIES ARE MADE TO PERPETUATE THE WORST VALUES OF THE AFFLUENT SOCIETY...
EGOISM, ACQUISITIVENESS, THE DESIRE FOR POWER.
GOD IS ASKED FOR FINANCIAL ADVICE.
WE SEE AROUND US A MAD CONFUSION THAT HAS ALLOWED CHAOS TO GAIN A TOE-HOLD, MR. CONSTANTINE.
I'M NOT SURE WHAT I'M SEEING ANYMORE, MATE.
I COULD BE DAYDREAMING IN A PADDED CELL, FOR ALL I KNOW.
SOON, ALL THE MAPS THAT GUIDE US THROUGH OUR REALITY WILL BE OBSOLETE...
ALL OUR SYSTEMS OF KNOWLEDGE BASED ON CURRENT PERCEPTIONS WILL BE USELESS.
WE MUST CAST A SPELL THAT WILL BIND THE PARTS BACK TOGETHER AND HOLD THEM THERE.
THAT'S WHERE YOU COME IN, MR. CONSTANTINE.

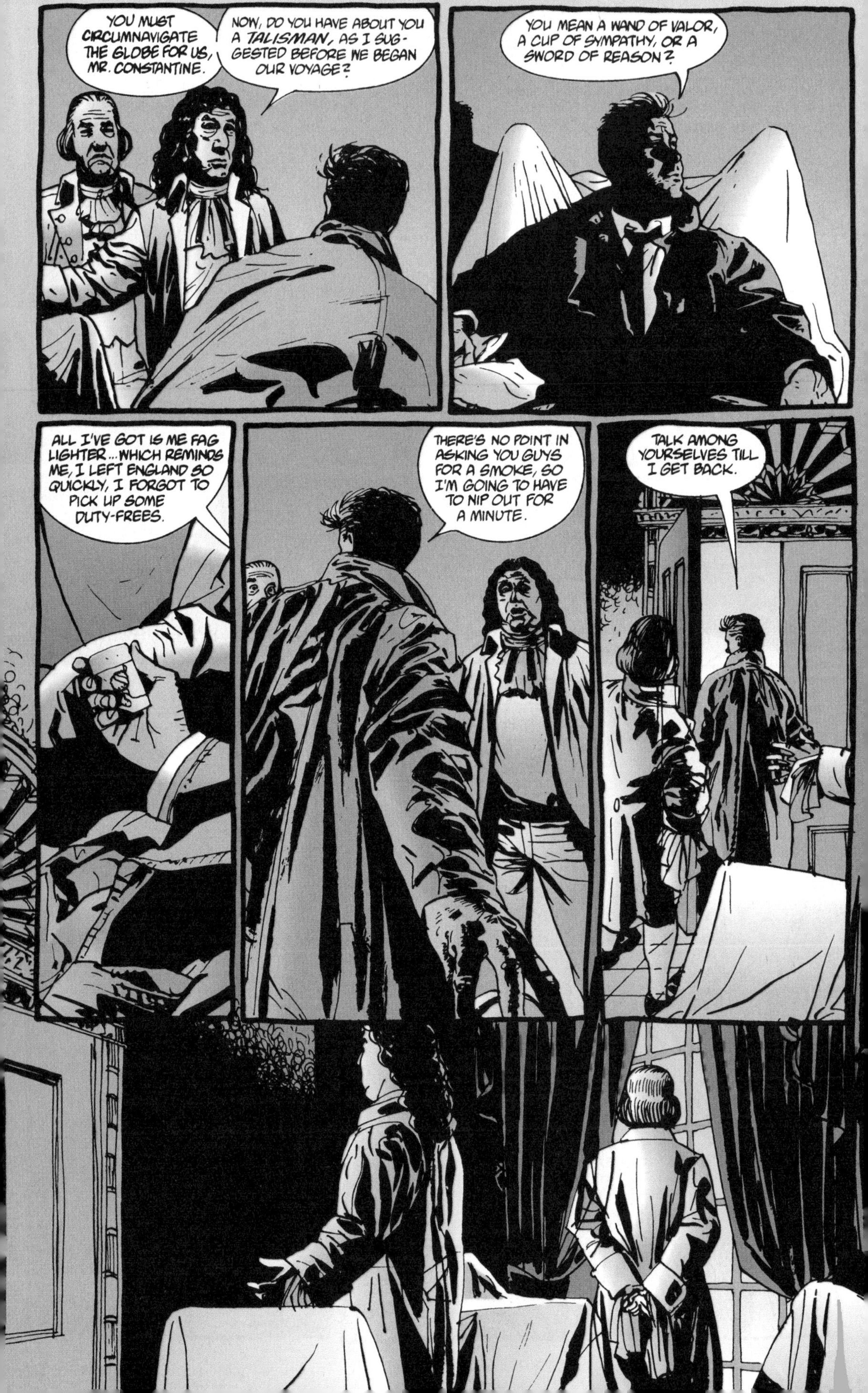
YOU MUST CIRCUMNAVIGATE THE GLOBE FOR US, MR. CONSTANTINE.
NOW, DO YOU HAVE ABOUT YOU A *TALISMAN*, AS I SUGGESTED BEFORE WE BEGAN OUR VOYAGE?
YOU MEAN A WAND OF VALOR, A CUP OF SYMPATHY, OR A SWORD OF REASON?
ALL I'VE GOT IS ME FAG LIGHTER... WHICH REMINDS ME, I LEFT ENGLAND SO QUICKLY, I FORGOT TO PICK UP SOME DUTY-FREES.
THERE'S NO POINT IN ASKING YOU GUYS FOR A SMOKE, SO I'M GOING TO HAVE TO NIP OUT FOR A MINUTE.
TALK AMONG YOURSELVES TILL I GET BACK.

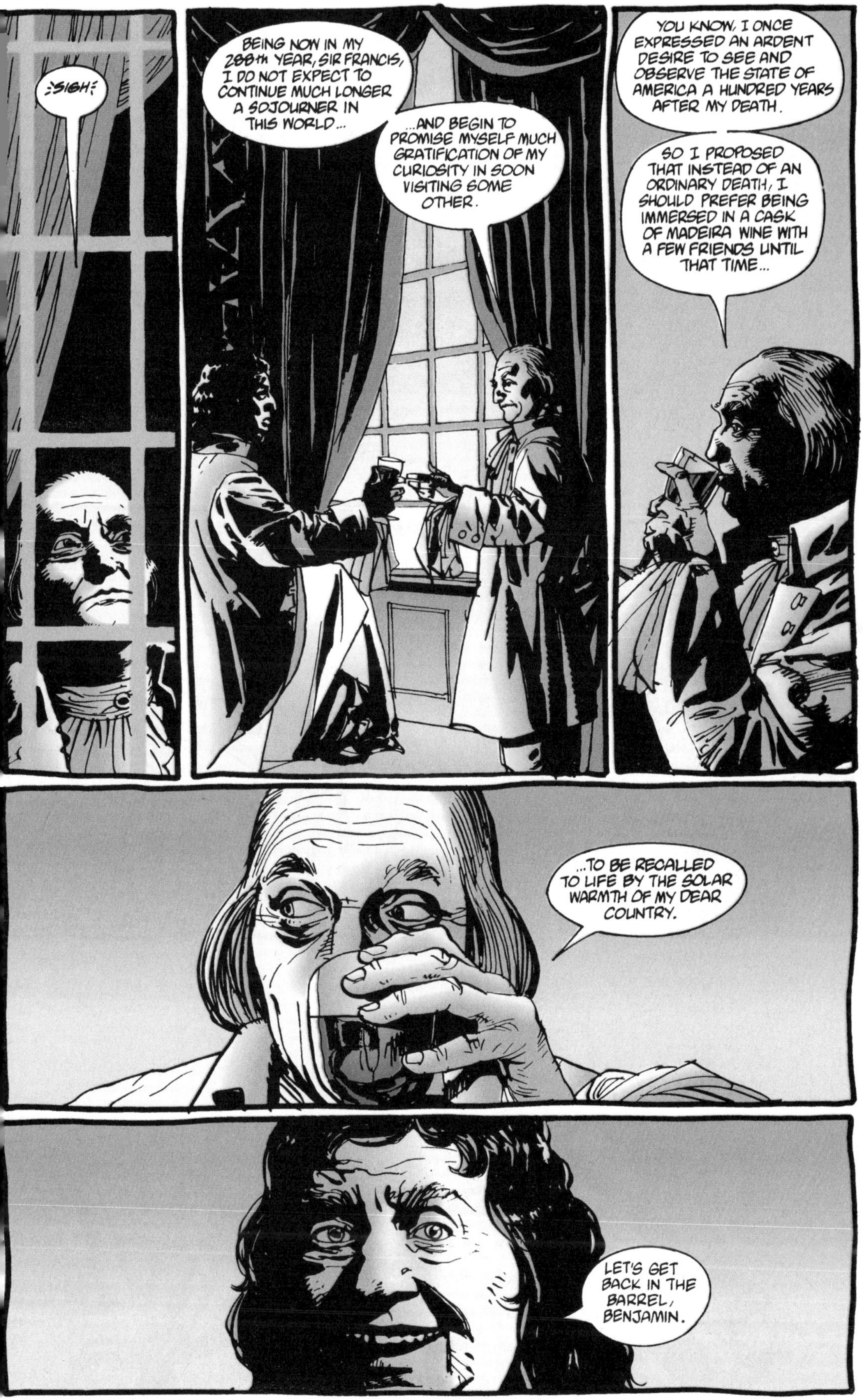
:SIGH:
BEING NOW IN MY 288th YEAR, SIR FRANCIS, I DO NOT EXPECT TO CONTINUE MUCH LONGER A SOJOURNER IN THIS WORLD...
...AND BEGIN TO PROMISE MYSELF MUCH GRATIFICATION OF MY CURIOSITY IN SOON VISITING SOME OTHER.
YOU KNOW, I ONCE EXPRESSED AN ARDENT DESIRE TO SEE AND OBSERVE THE STATE OF AMERICA A HUNDRED YEARS AFTER MY DEATH.
SO I PROPOSED THAT INSTEAD OF AN ORDINARY DEATH, I SHOULD PREFER BEING IMMERSED IN A CASK OF MADEIRA WINE WITH A FEW FRIENDS UNTIL THAT TIME...
...TO BE RECALLED TO LIFE BY THE SOLAR WARMTH OF MY DEAR COUNTRY.
LET'S GET BACK IN THE BARREL, BENJAMIN.

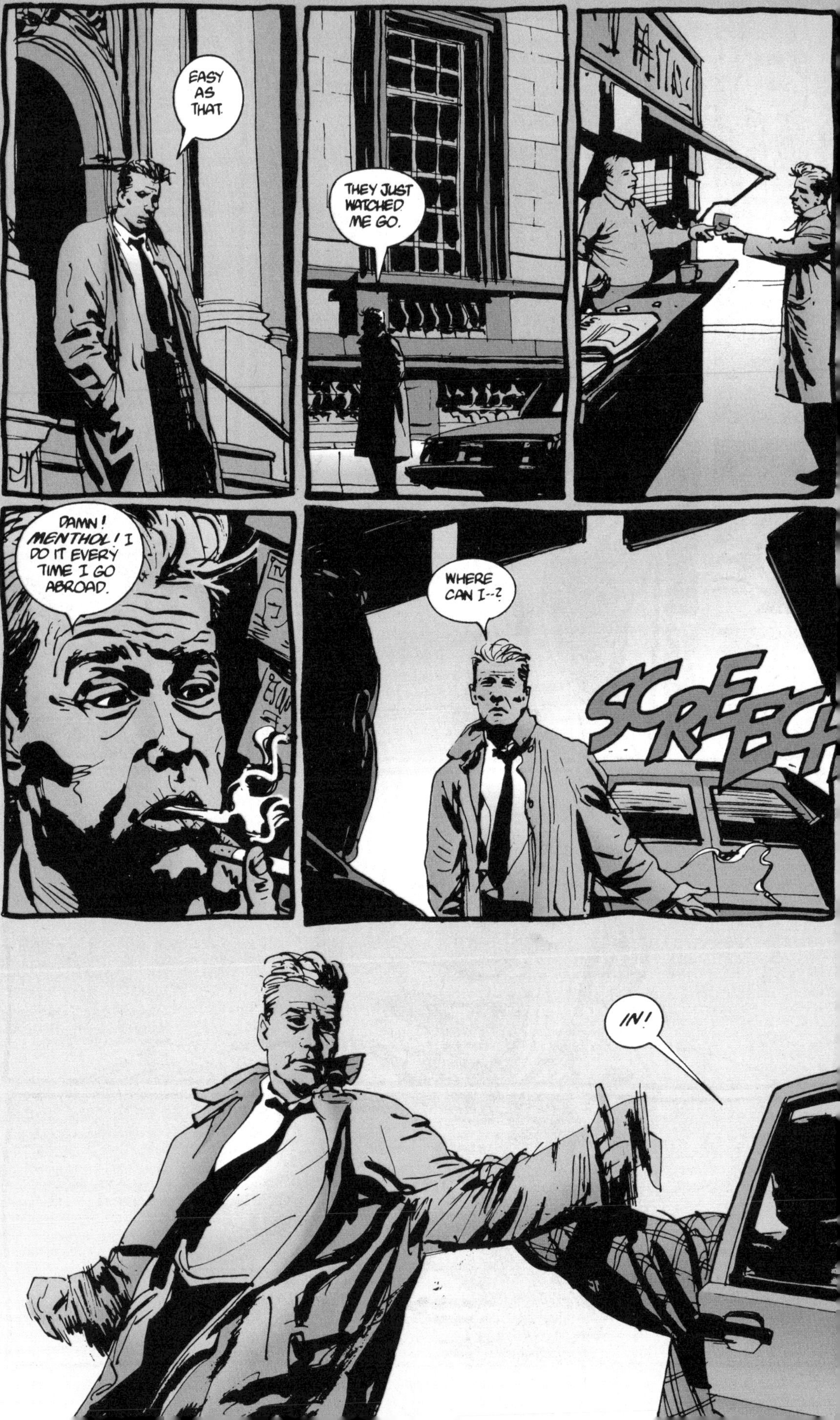
EASY AS THAT.
THEY JUST WATCHED ME GO.
DAMN! MENTHOL! I DO IT EVERY TIME I GO ABROAD.
WHERE CAN I--?
SCREECH
IN!

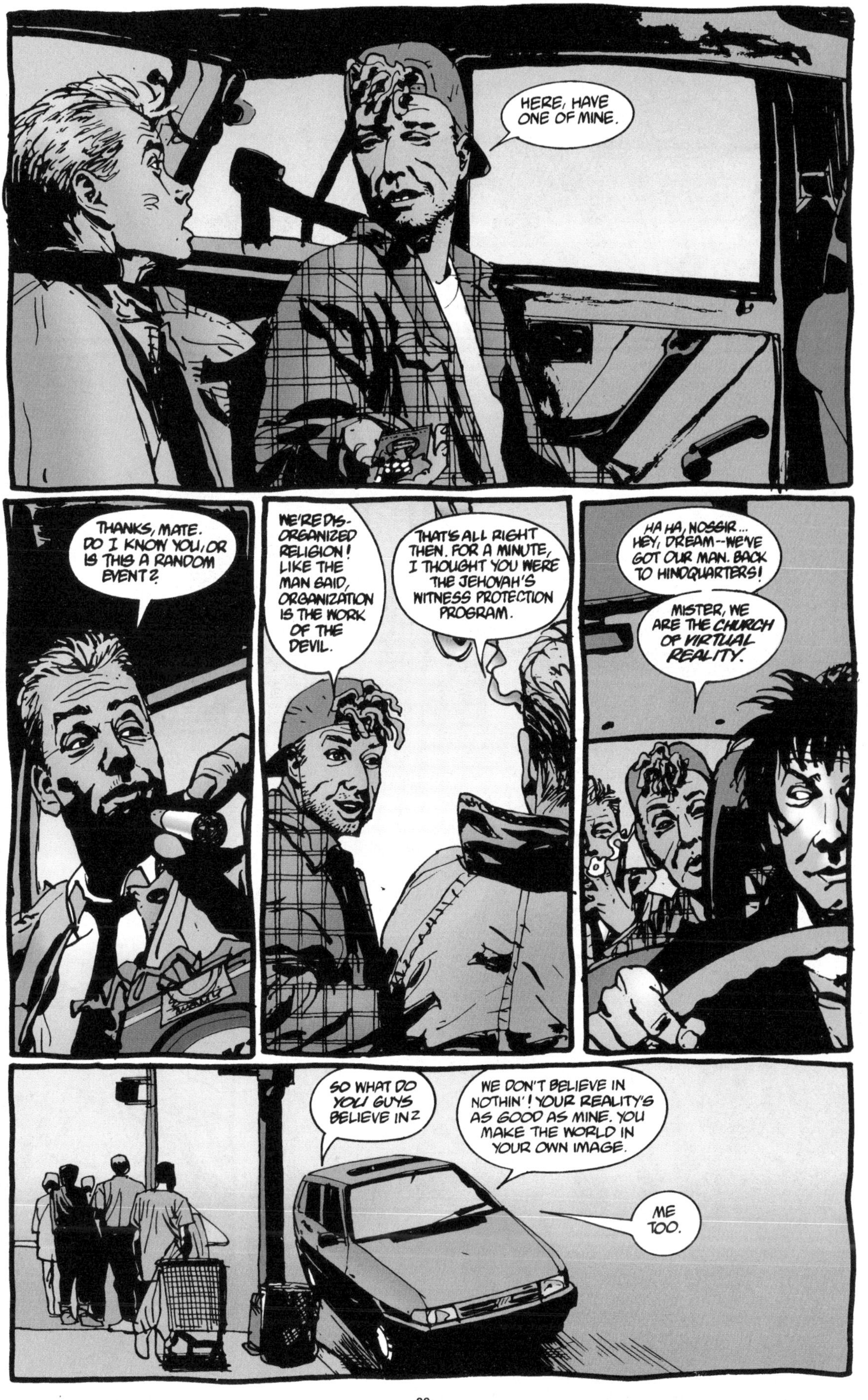

HERE, HAVE ONE OF MINE.
THANKS, MATE. DO I KNOW YOU, OR IS THIS A RANDOM EVENT?
WE'RE DIS-ORGANIZED RELIGION! LIKE THE MAN SAID, ORGANIZATION IS THE WORK OF THE DEVIL.
THAT'S ALL RIGHT THEN. FOR A MINUTE, I THOUGHT YOU WERE THE JEHOVAH'S WITNESS PROTECTION PROGRAM.
HA HA, NOSSIR... HEY, DREAM--WE'VE GOT OUR MAN. BACK TO HINDQUARTERS!
MISTER, WE ARE THE CHURCH OF VIRTUAL REALITY.
SO WHAT DO YOU GUYS BELIEVE IN?
WE DON'T BELIEVE IN NOTHIN'! YOUR REALITY'S AS GOOD AS MINE. YOU MAKE THE WORLD IN YOUR OWN IMAGE.
ME TOO.

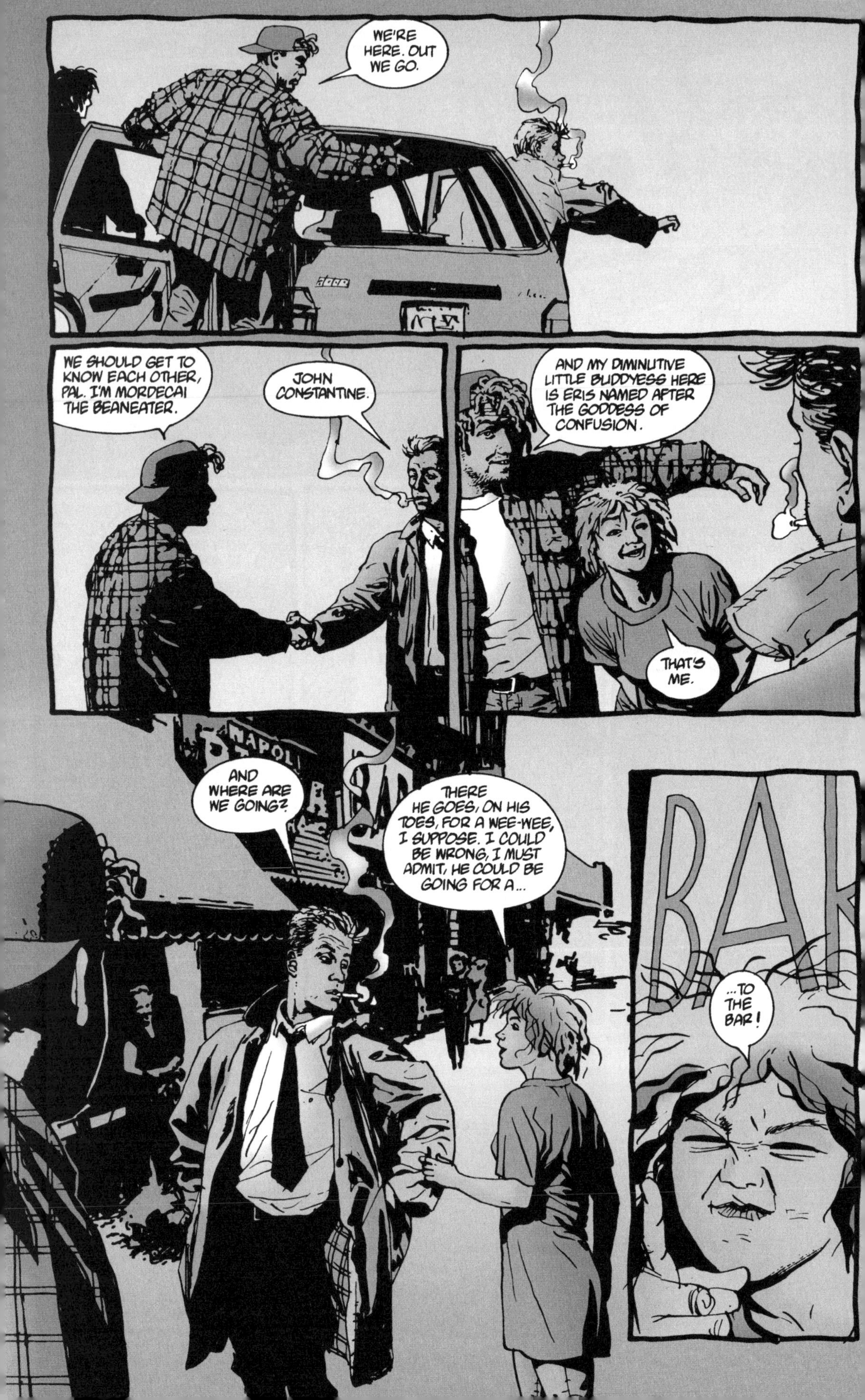
WE'RE HERE. OUT WE GO.
WE SHOULD GET TO KNOW EACH OTHER, PAL. I'M MORDECAI THE BEANEATER.
JOHN CONSTANTINE.
AND MY DIMINUTIVE LITTLE BUDDYESS HERE IS ERIS NAMED AFTER THE GODDESS OF CONFUSION.
THAT'S ME.
NAPOLI
BAR
AND WHERE ARE WE GOING?
THERE HE GOES, ON HIS TOES, FOR A WEE-WEE, I SUPPOSE. I COULD BE WRONG, I MUST ADMIT, HE COULD BE GOING FOR A...
BAR
...TO THE BAR!

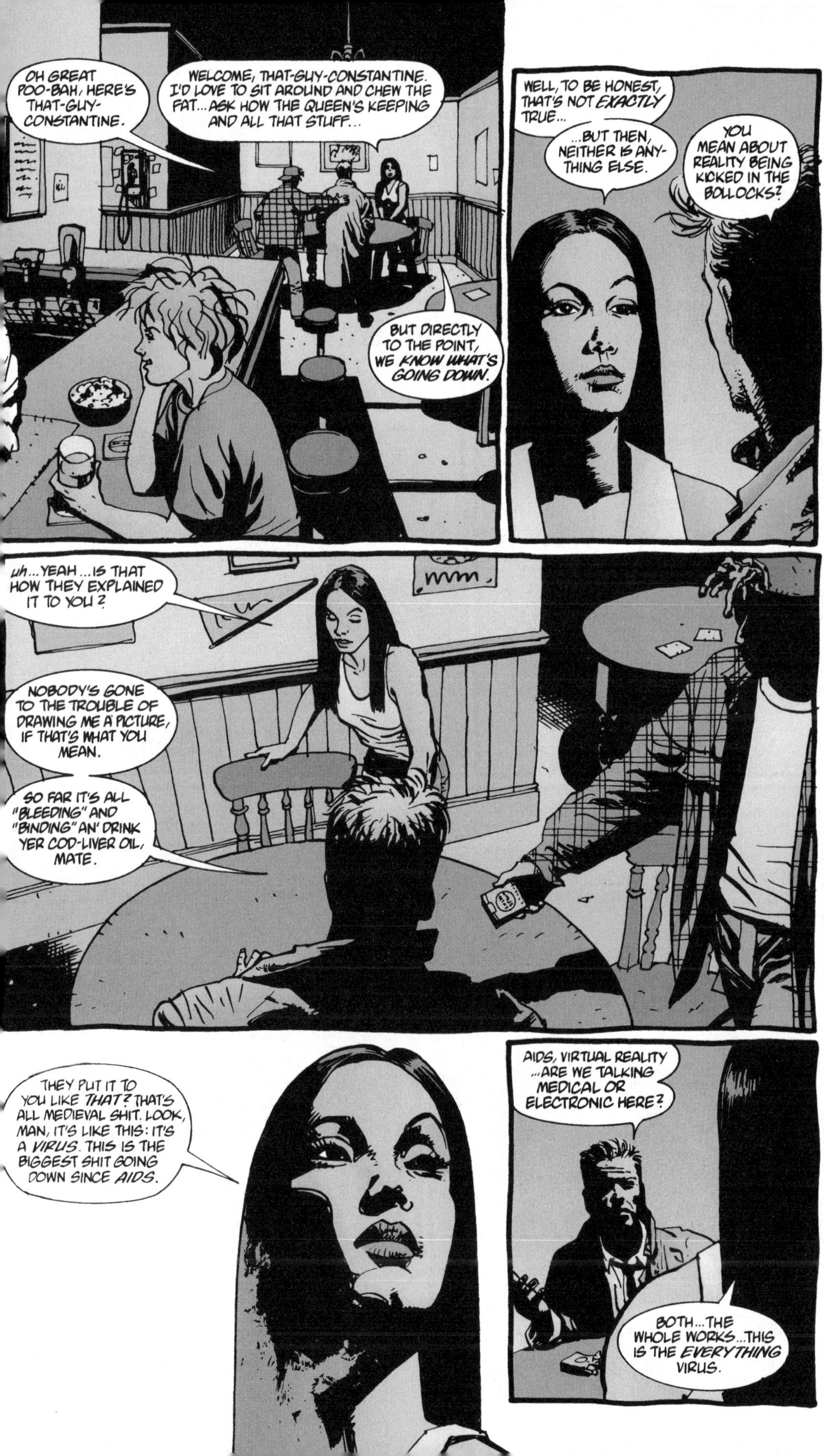
OH GREAT POO-BAH, HERE'S THAT-GUY-CONSTANTINE.
WELCOME, THAT-GUY-CONSTANTINE. I'D LOVE TO SIT AROUND AND CHEW THE FAT... ASK HOW THE QUEEN'S KEEPING AND ALL THAT STUFF...
BUT DIRECTLY TO THE POINT, WE *KNOW WHAT'S GOING DOWN.*
WELL, TO BE HONEST, THAT'S NOT *EXACTLY* TRUE...
...BUT THEN, NEITHER IS ANYTHING ELSE.
YOU MEAN ABOUT REALITY BEING KICKED IN THE BOLLOCKS?
uh... YEAH ... IS THAT HOW THEY EXPLAINED IT TO YOU?
NOBODY'S GONE TO THE TROUBLE OF DRAWING ME A PICTURE, IF THAT'S WHAT YOU MEAN.
SO FAR IT'S ALL "BLEEDING" AND "BINDING" AN' DRINK YER COD-LIVER OIL, MATE.
THEY PUT IT TO YOU LIKE *THAT?* THAT'S ALL MEDIEVAL SHIT. LOOK, MAN, IT'S LIKE THIS: IT'S A *VIRUS*. THIS IS THE BIGGEST SHIT GOING DOWN SINCE *AIDS*.
AIDS, VIRTUAL REALITY ...ARE WE TALKING MEDICAL OR ELECTRONIC HERE?
BOTH... THE WHOLE WORKS... THIS IS THE *EVERYTHING* VIRUS.

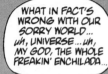

WHAT IN FACT'S WRONG WITH OUR SORRY WORLD... *uh,* UNIVERSE... *uh,* MY GOD, THE WHOLE FREAKIN' ENCHILADA...

...IS THAT IT'S... NO, FORGET THAT... LOOK, IT'S LIKE THIS...

VIRUSES.

YEP, *VIRUSES.* THEY'RE BIOLOGICAL *PIRATES.* THEY INVADE LIVING CELLS AND EXPLOIT THE COMPLEX MACHINERY TO MAKE *MORE* VIRUSES.

AND ALMOST *ALL* OF THE CHEMICAL REACTIONS REQUIRED TO BRING ABOUT THIS ENDLESS CYCLE ARE PERFORMED BY THE CELLS THEY INVADE, RATHER THAN BY THE VIRUS ITSELF.

AND THE WEIRD THING IS, IT'S ALMOST A SENTIENT THING. WE'RE PLAYING FOOT-BALL, AND *IT* COMES ON PLAYING CHECKERS.

YEAH, ARSENAL'S BEEN DOIN' THAT ALL SEASON.

THIS IS SERIOUS, CONSTANTINE; WE DON'T JUST GET DEAD ...IT'S WORSE THAN THAT.

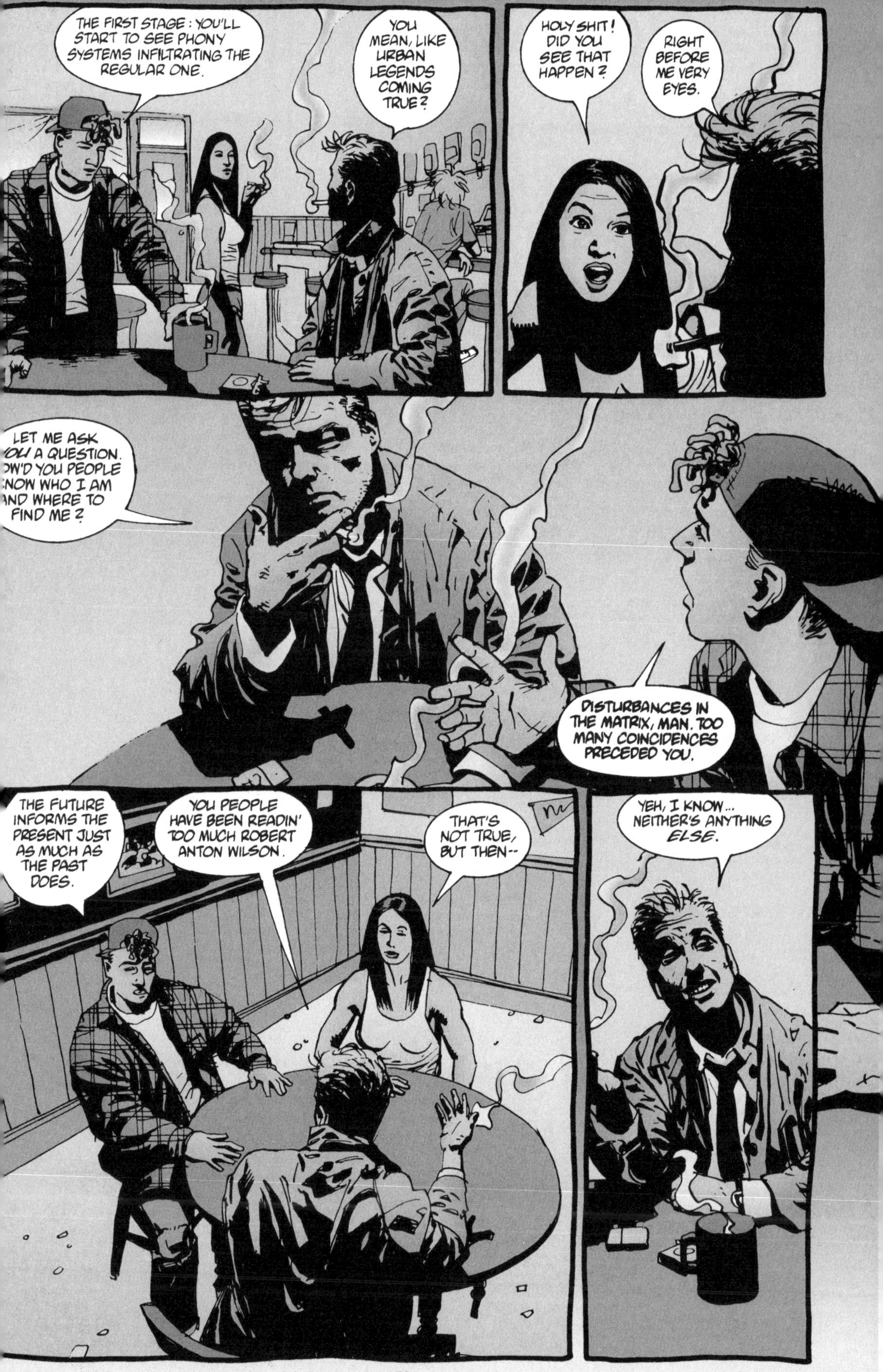
THE FIRST STAGE: YOU'LL START TO SEE PHONY SYSTEMS INFILTRATING THE REGULAR ONE.
YOU MEAN, LIKE URBAN LEGENDS COMING TRUE?
HOLY SHIT! DID YOU SEE THAT HAPPEN?
RIGHT BEFORE ME VERY EYES.
LET ME ASK YOU A QUESTION. HOW'D YOU PEOPLE KNOW WHO I AM AND WHERE TO FIND ME?
DISTURBANCES IN THE MATRIX, MAN. TOO MANY COINCIDENCES PRECEDED YOU.
THE FUTURE INFORMS THE PRESENT JUST AS MUCH AS THE PAST DOES.
YOU PEOPLE HAVE BEEN READIN' TOO MUCH ROBERT ANTON WILSON.
THAT'S NOT TRUE, BUT THEN--
YEH, I KNOW... NEITHER'S ANYTHING ELSE.

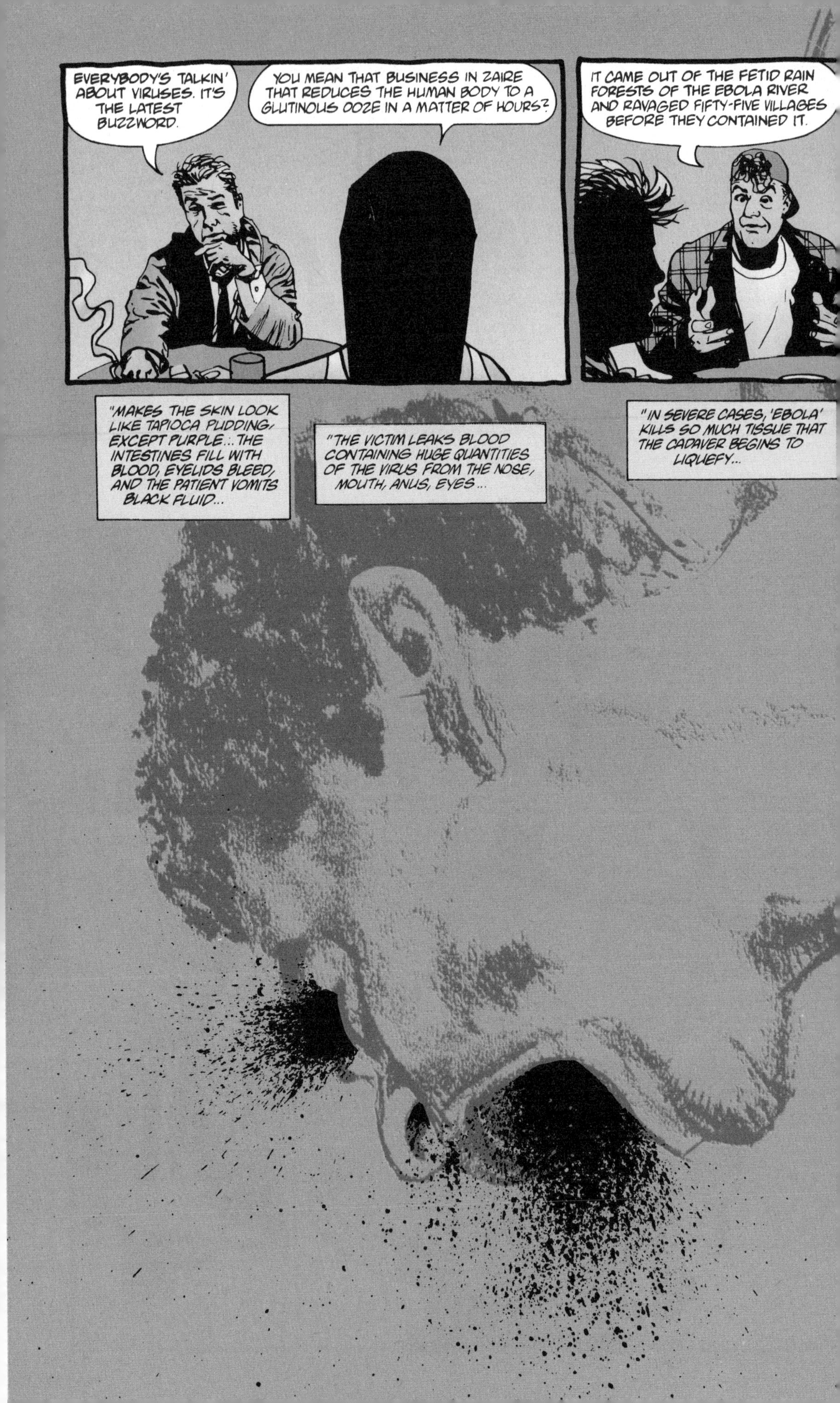
EVERYBODY'S TALKIN' ABOUT VIRUSES. IT'S THE LATEST BUZZWORD.
YOU MEAN THAT BUSINESS IN ZAIRE THAT REDUCES THE HUMAN BODY TO A GLUTINOUS OOZE IN A MATTER OF HOURS?
IT CAME OUT OF THE FETID RAIN FORESTS OF THE EBOLA RIVER AND RAVAGED FIFTY-FIVE VILLAGES BEFORE THEY CONTAINED IT.
"MAKES THE SKIN LOOK LIKE TAPIOCA PUDDING, EXCEPT PURPLE... THE INTESTINES FILL WITH BLOOD, EYELIDS BLEED, AND THE PATIENT VOMITS BLACK FLUID...
"THE VICTIM LEAKS BLOOD CONTAINING HUGE QUANTITIES OF THE VIRUS FROM THE NOSE, MOUTH, ANUS, EYES...
"IN SEVERE CASES, 'EBOLA' KILLS SO MUCH TISSUE THAT THE CADAVER BEGINS TO LIQUEFY...

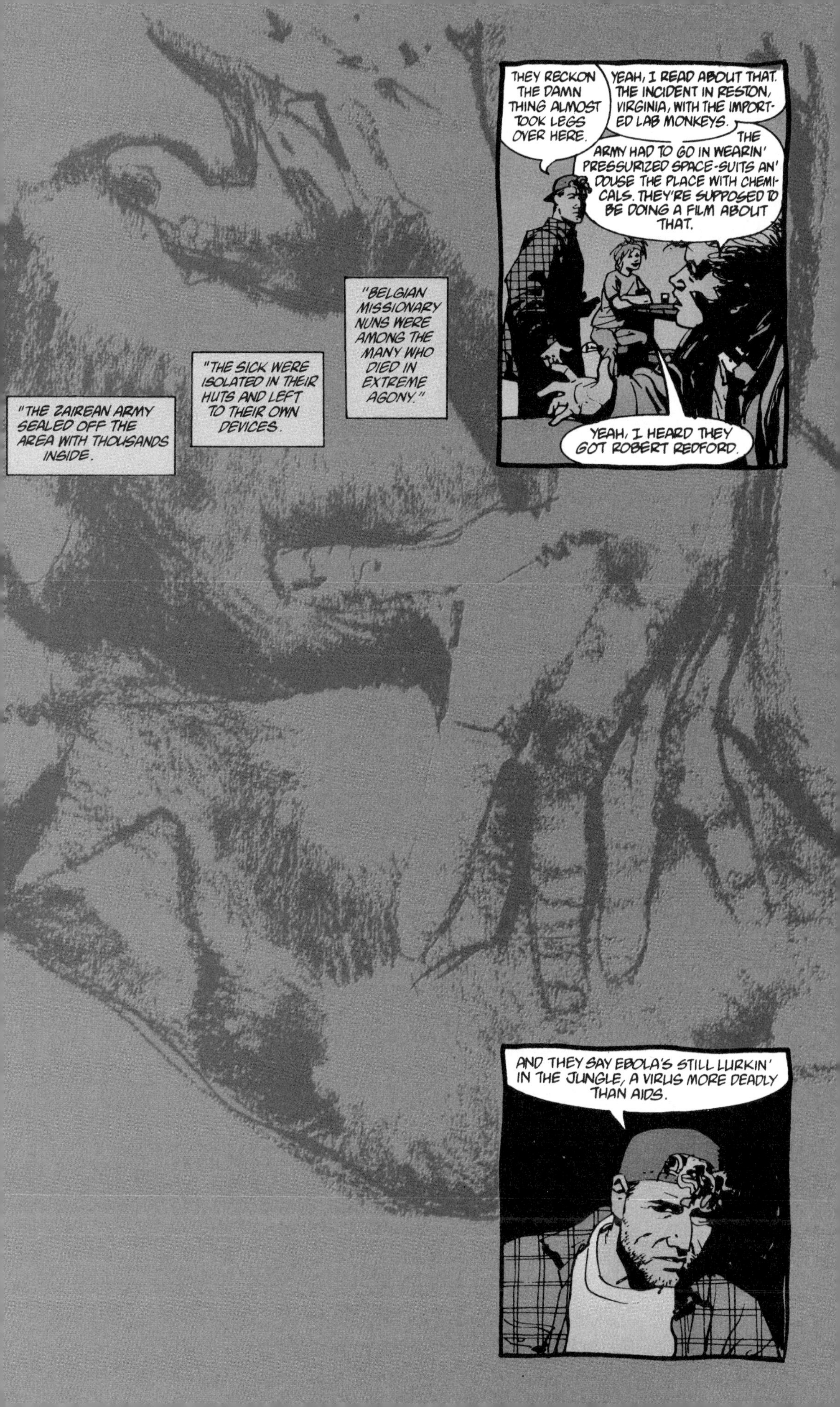

THEY RECKON THE DAMN THING ALMOST TOOK LEGS OVER HERE.
YEAH, I READ ABOUT THAT. THE INCIDENT IN RESTON, VIRGINIA, WITH THE IMPORTED LAB MONKEYS.
THE ARMY HAD TO GO IN WEARIN' PRESSURIZED SPACE-SUITS AN' DOUSE THE PLACE WITH CHEMICALS. THEY'RE SUPPOSED TO BE DOING A FILM ABOUT THAT.
YEAH, I HEARD THEY GOT ROBERT REDFORD.
"THE ZAIREAN ARMY SEALED OFF THE AREA WITH THOUSANDS INSIDE.
"THE SICK WERE ISOLATED IN THEIR HUTS AND LEFT TO THEIR OWN DEVICES.
"BELGIAN MISSIONARY NUNS WERE AMONG THE MANY WHO DIED IN EXTREME AGONY."
AND THEY SAY EBOLA'S STILL LURKIN' IN THE JUNGLE, A VIRUS MORE DEADLY THAN AIDS.

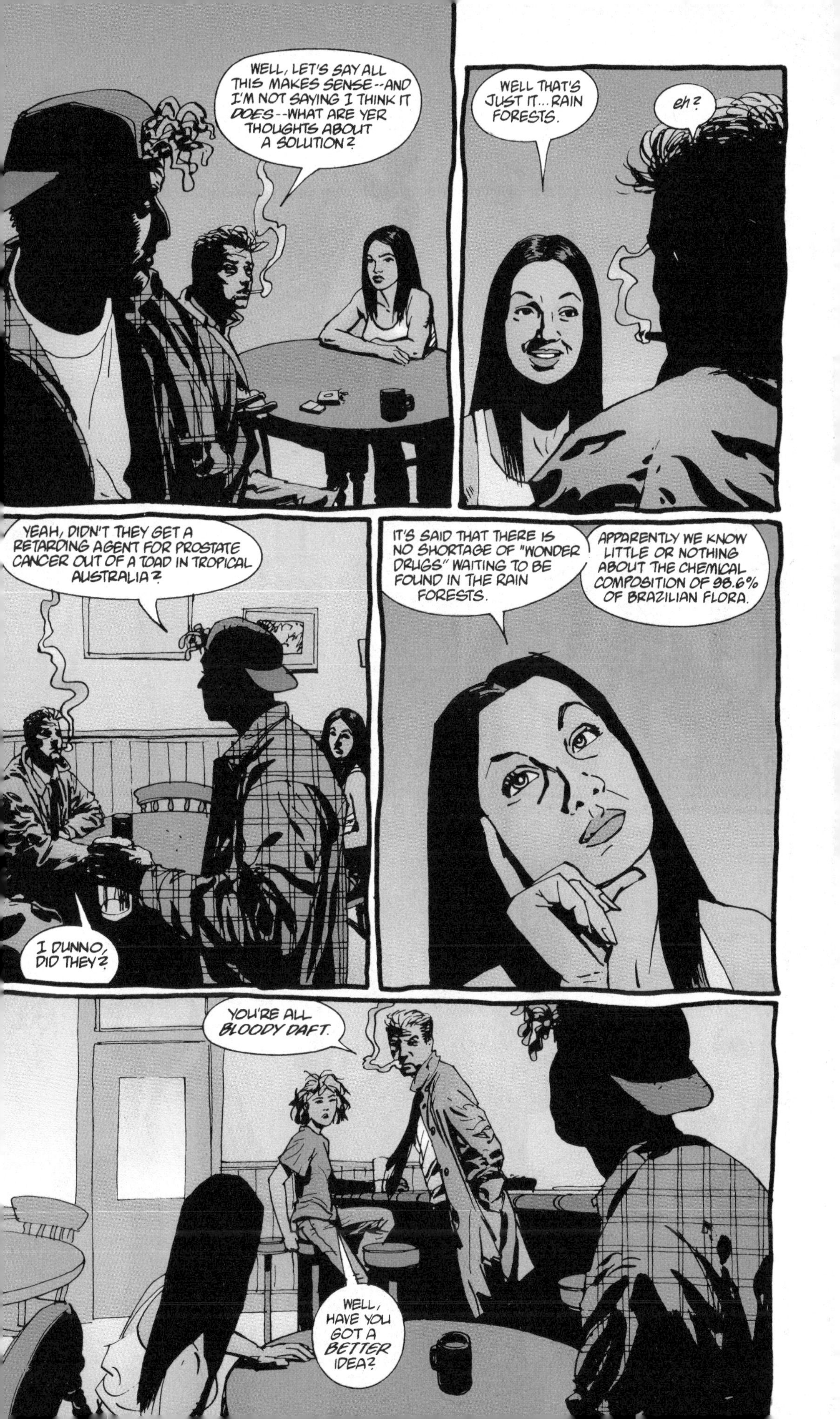
WELL, LET'S SAY ALL THIS MAKES SENSE--AND I'M NOT SAYING I THINK IT DOES--WHAT ARE YER THOUGHTS ABOUT A SOLUTION?
WELL THAT'S JUST IT... RAIN FORESTS.
eh?
YEAH, DIDN'T THEY GET A RETARDING AGENT FOR PROSTATE CANCER OUT OF A TOAD IN TROPICAL AUSTRALIA?
I DUNNO, DID THEY?
IT'S SAID THAT THERE IS NO SHORTAGE OF "WONDER DRUGS" WAITING TO BE FOUND IN THE RAIN FORESTS.
APPARENTLY WE KNOW LITTLE OR NOTHING ABOUT THE CHEMICAL COMPOSITION OF 98.6% OF BRAZILIAN FLORA.
YOU'RE ALL BLOODY DAFT.
WELL, HAVE YOU GOT A BETTER IDEA?

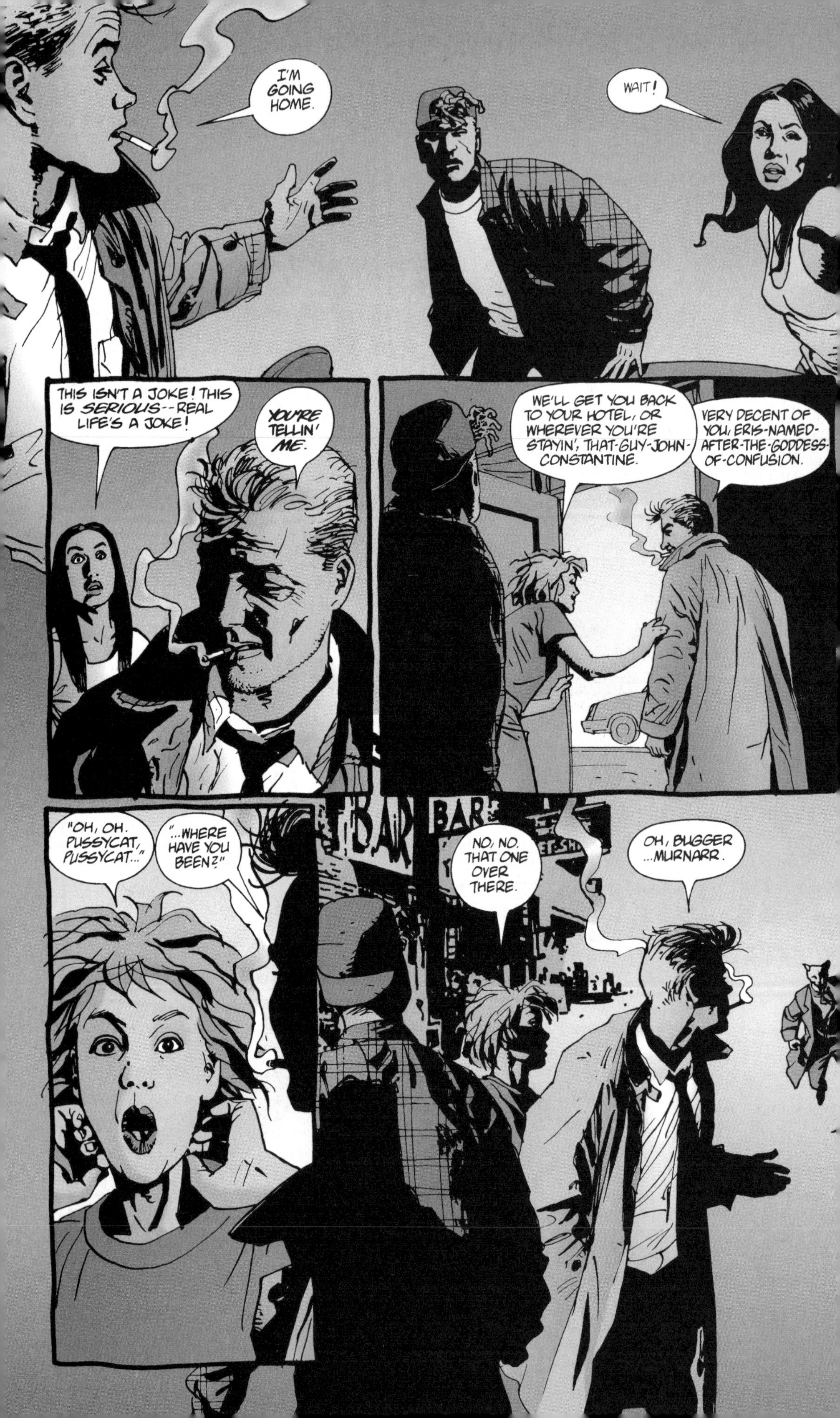
I'M GOING HOME.
WAIT!
THIS ISN'T A JOKE! THIS IS SERIOUS--REAL LIFE'S A JOKE!
YOU'RE TELLIN' ME.
WE'LL GET YOU BACK TO YOUR HOTEL, OR WHEREVER YOU'RE STAYIN', THAT-GUY-JOHN-CONSTANTINE.
VERY DECENT OF YOU, ERIS-NAMED-AFTER-THE-GODDESS-OF-CONFUSION.
"OH, OH. PUSSYCAT, PUSSYCAT..."
"...WHERE HAVE YOU BEEN?"
BAR
BAR
NO, NO. THAT ONE OVER THERE.
OH, BUGGER ...MURNARR.

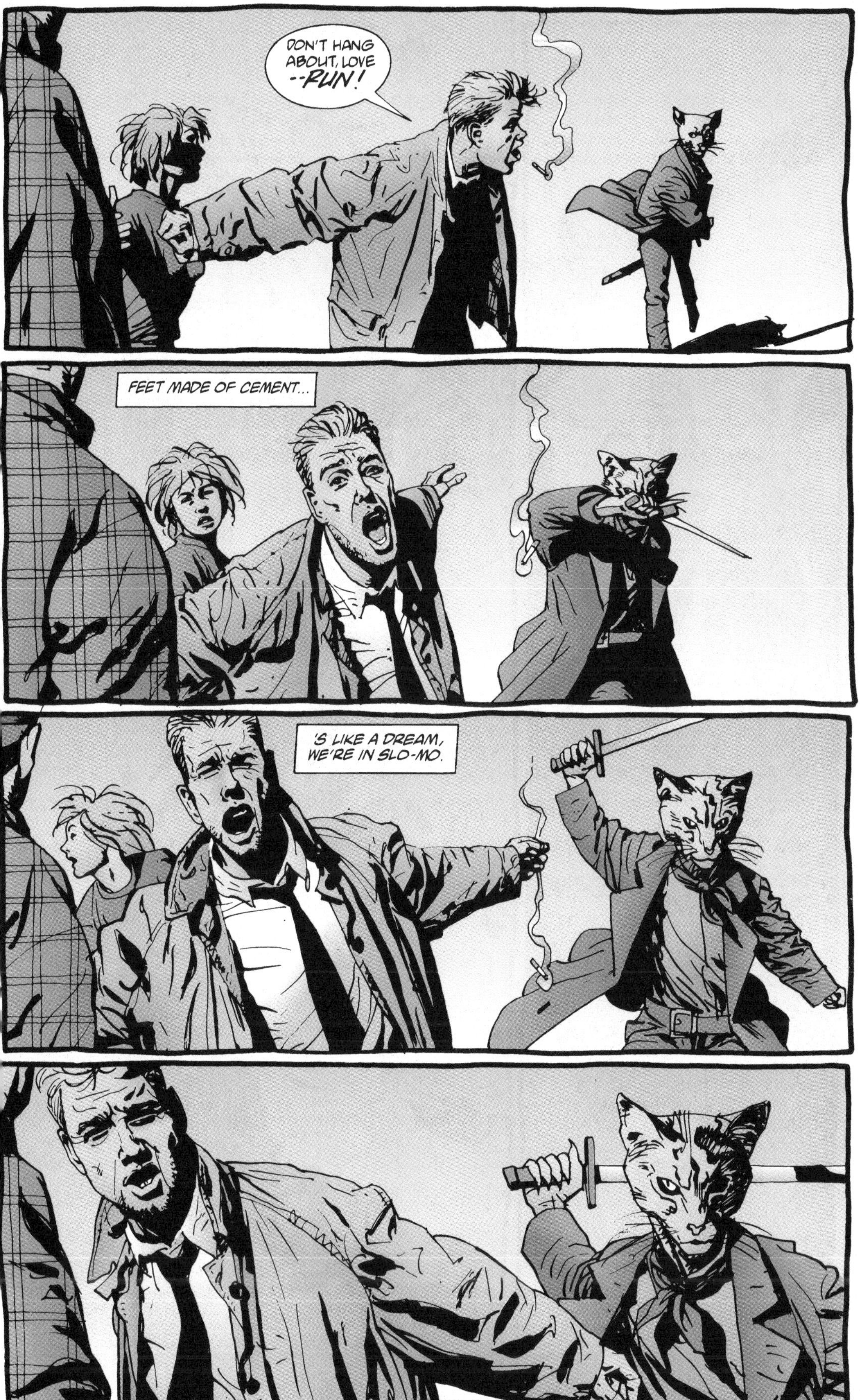
DON'T HANG ABOUT, LOVE --RUN!
FEET MADE OF CEMENT...
'S LIKE A DREAM, WE'RE IN SLO-MO.

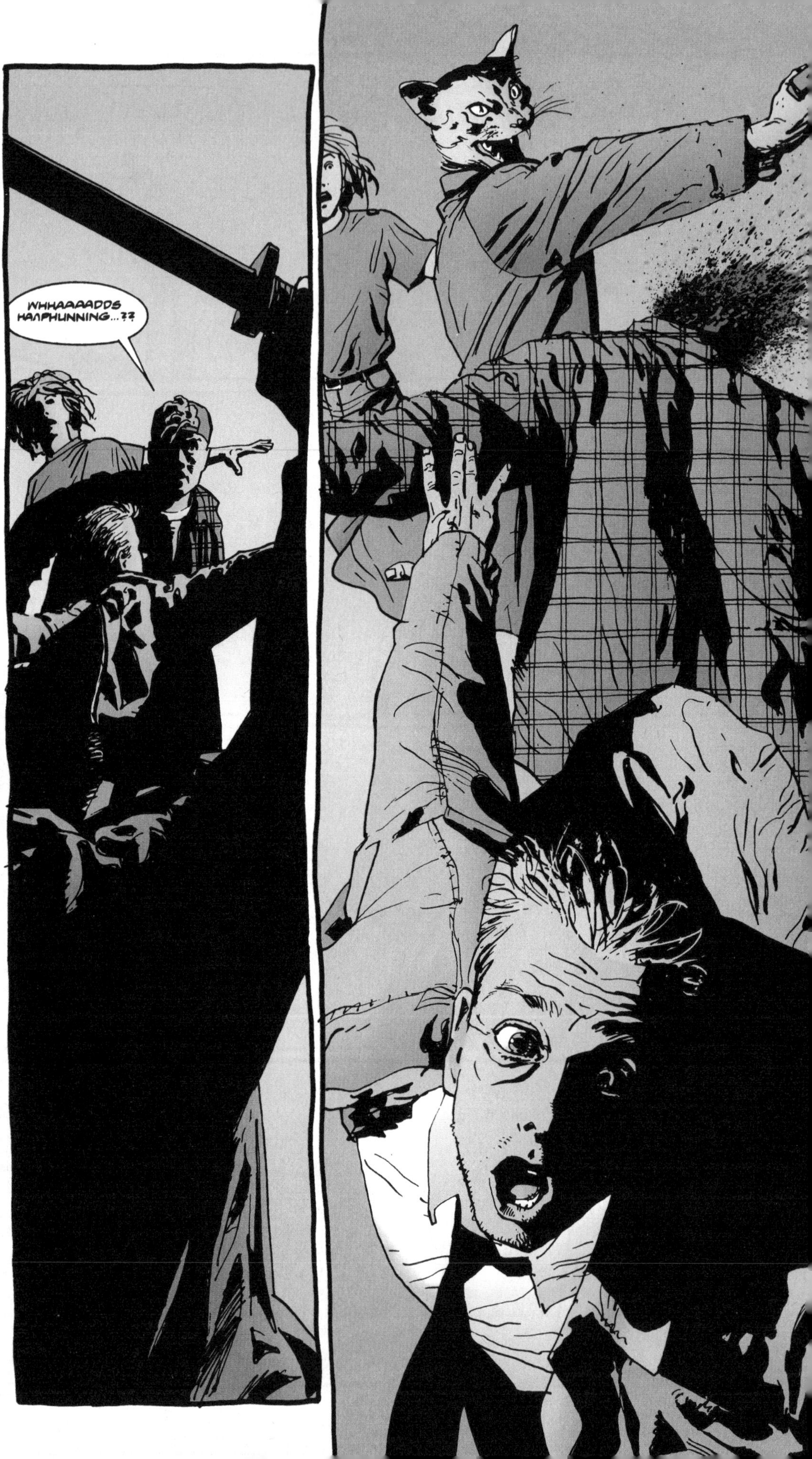
WHHAAAAADDS HAAPHUNNING...??

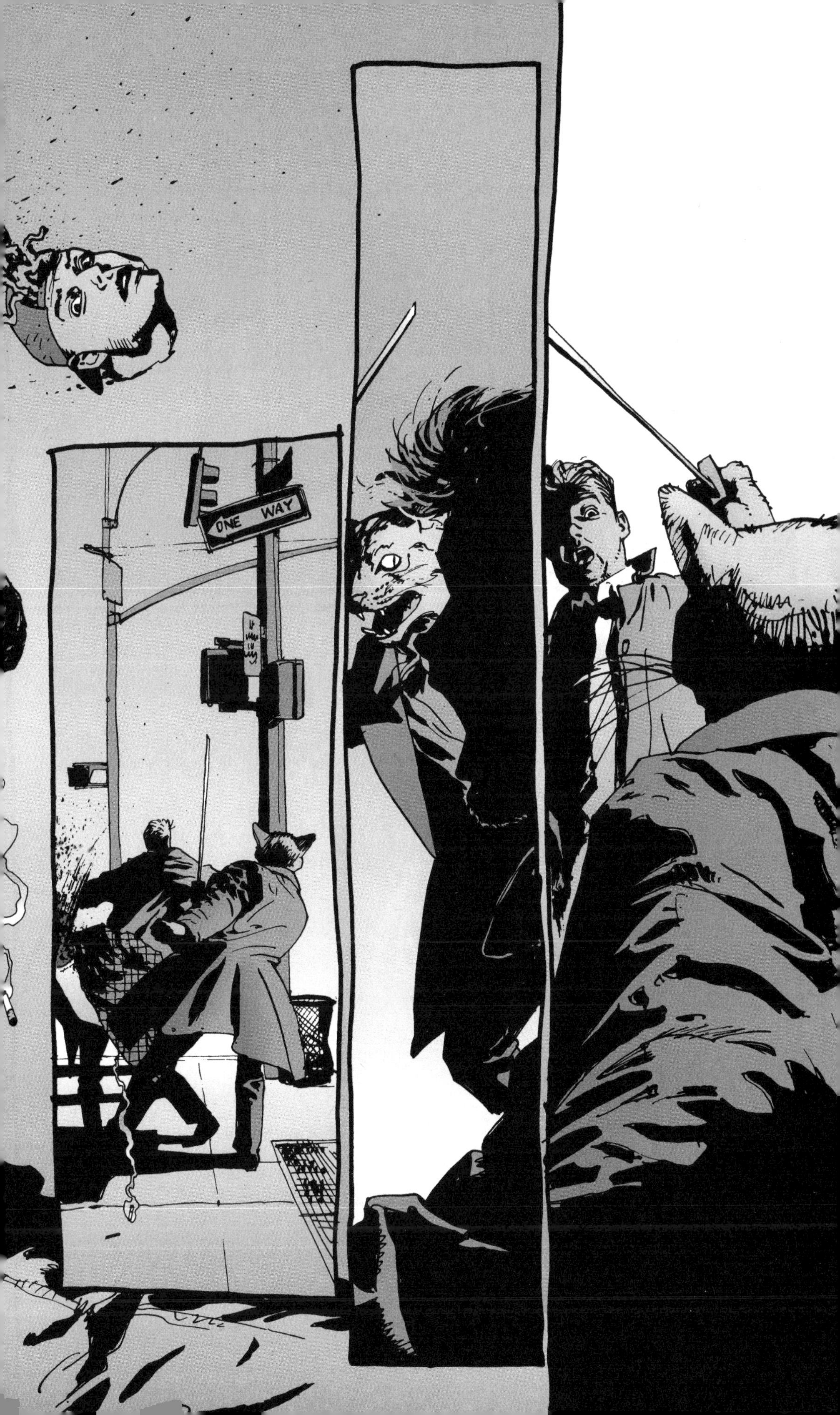
ONE WAY

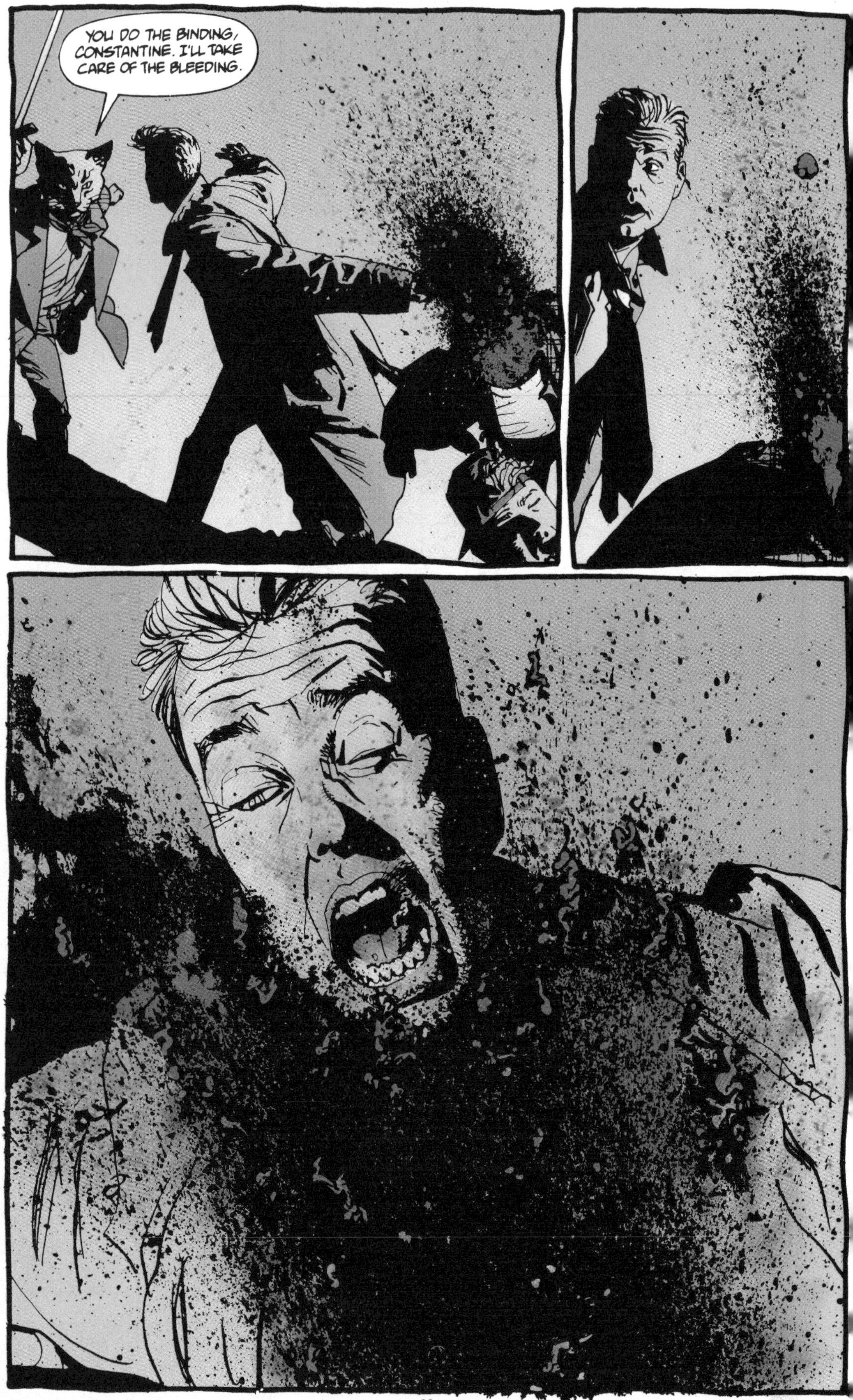
YOU DO THE BINDING, CONSTANTINE. I'LL TAKE CARE OF THE BLEEDING.

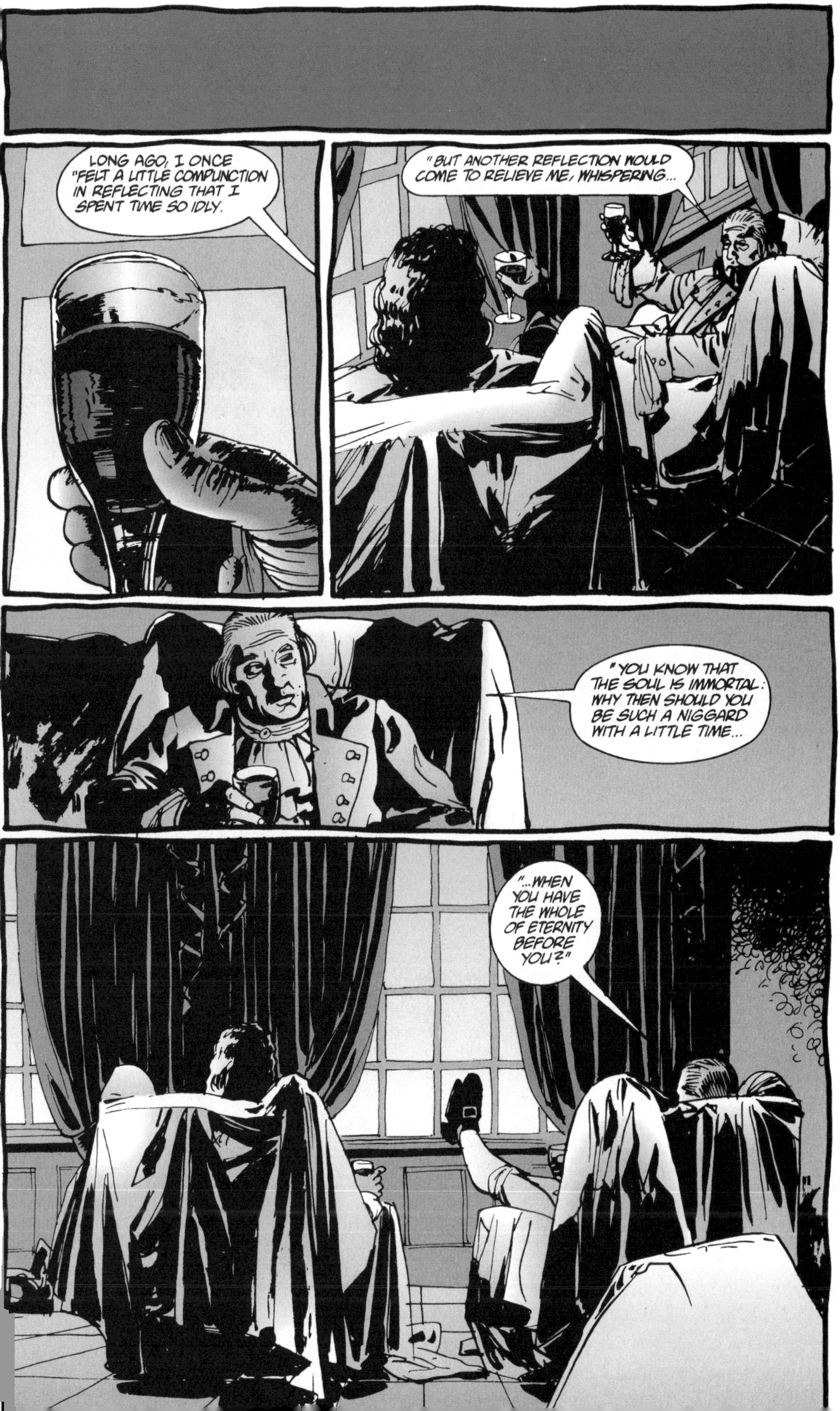
LONG AGO, I ONCE "FELT A LITTLE COMPUNCTION IN REFLECTING THAT I SPENT TIME SO IDLY.
"BUT ANOTHER REFLECTION WOULD COME TO RELIEVE ME, WHISPERING...
"YOU KNOW THAT THE SOUL IS IMMORTAL: WHY THEN SHOULD YOU BE SUCH A NIGGARD WITH A LITTLE TIME...
"...WHEN YOU HAVE THE WHOLE OF ETERNITY BEFORE YOU?"

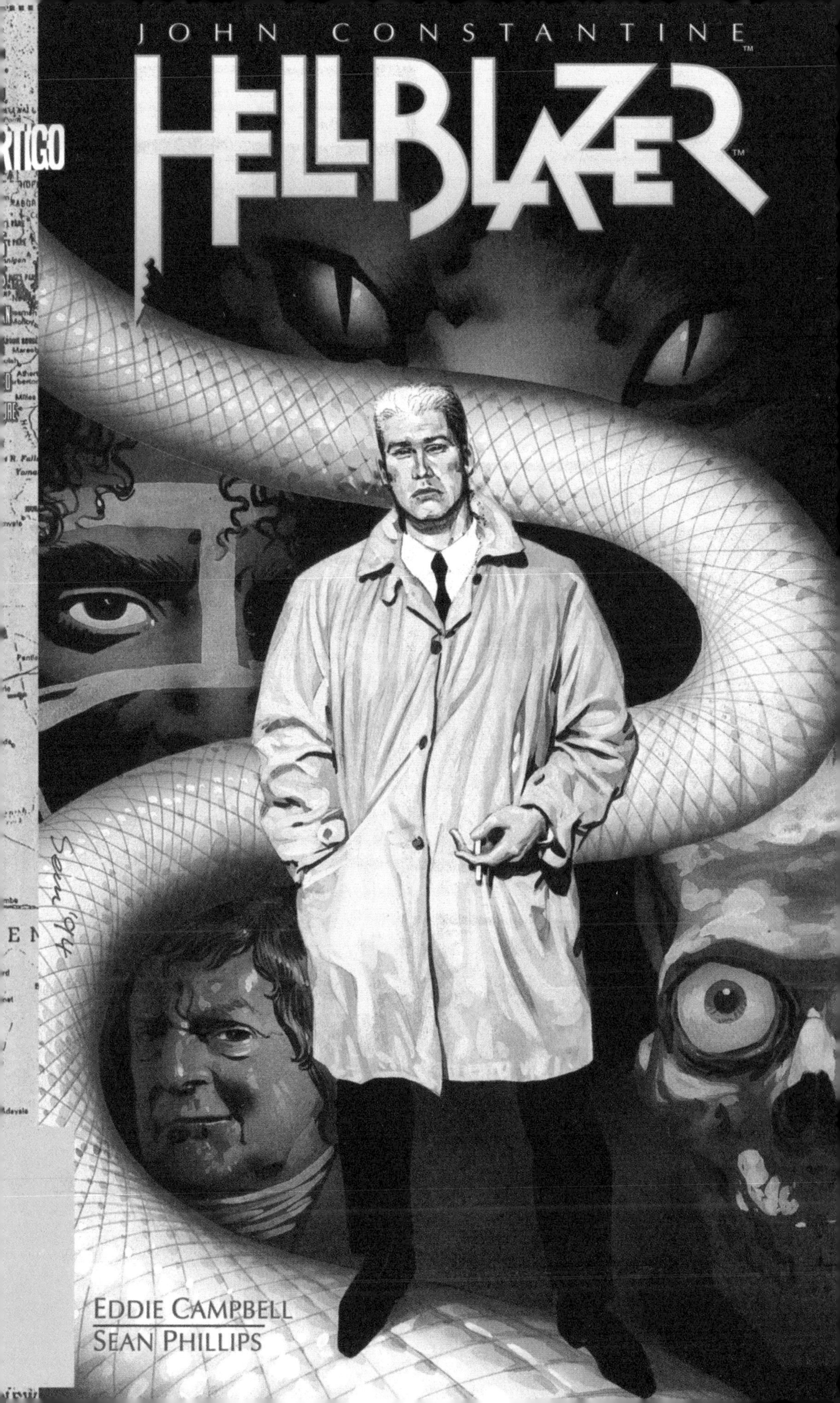
JOHN CONSTANTINE
HELLBLAZER
EDDIE CAMPBELL
SEAN PHILLIPS

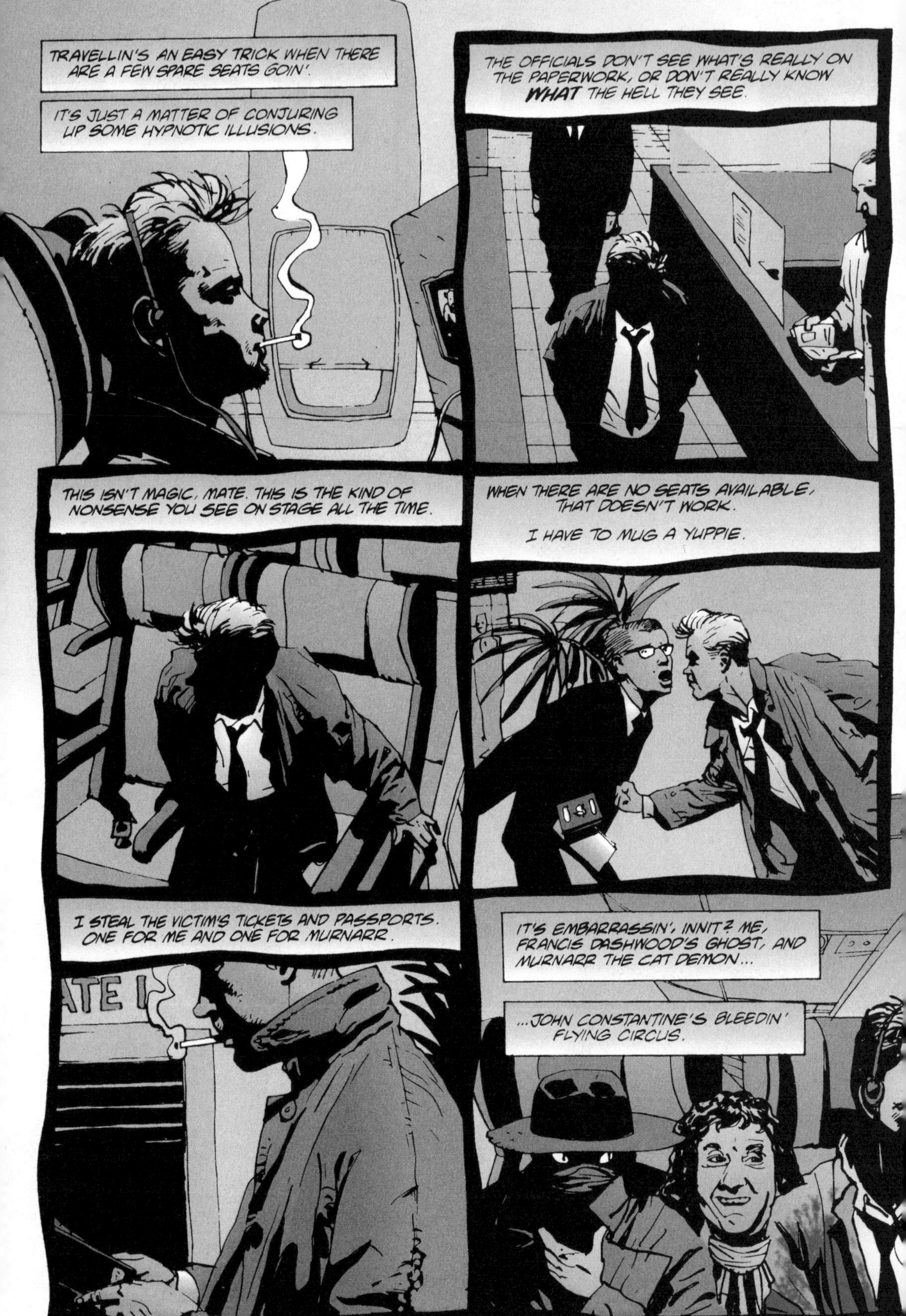
TRAVELLIN'S AN EASY TRICK WHEN THERE ARE A FEW SPARE SEATS GOIN'.
IT'S JUST A MATTER OF CONJURING UP SOME HYPNOTIC ILLUSIONS.
THE OFFICIALS DON'T SEE WHAT'S REALLY ON THE PAPERWORK, OR DON'T REALLY KNOW **WHAT** THE HELL THEY SEE.
THIS ISN'T MAGIC, MATE. THIS IS THE KIND OF NONSENSE YOU SEE ON STAGE ALL THE TIME.
WHEN THERE ARE NO SEATS AVAILABLE, THAT DOESN'T WORK.
I HAVE TO MUG A YUPPIE.
I STEAL THE VICTIM'S TICKETS AND PASSPORTS. ONE FOR ME AND ONE FOR MURNARR.
ATE I
IT'S EMBARRASSIN', INNIT? ME, FRANCIS DASHWOOD'S GHOST, AND MURNARR THE CAT DEMON...
...JOHN CONSTANTINE'S BLEEDIN' FLYING CIRCUS.

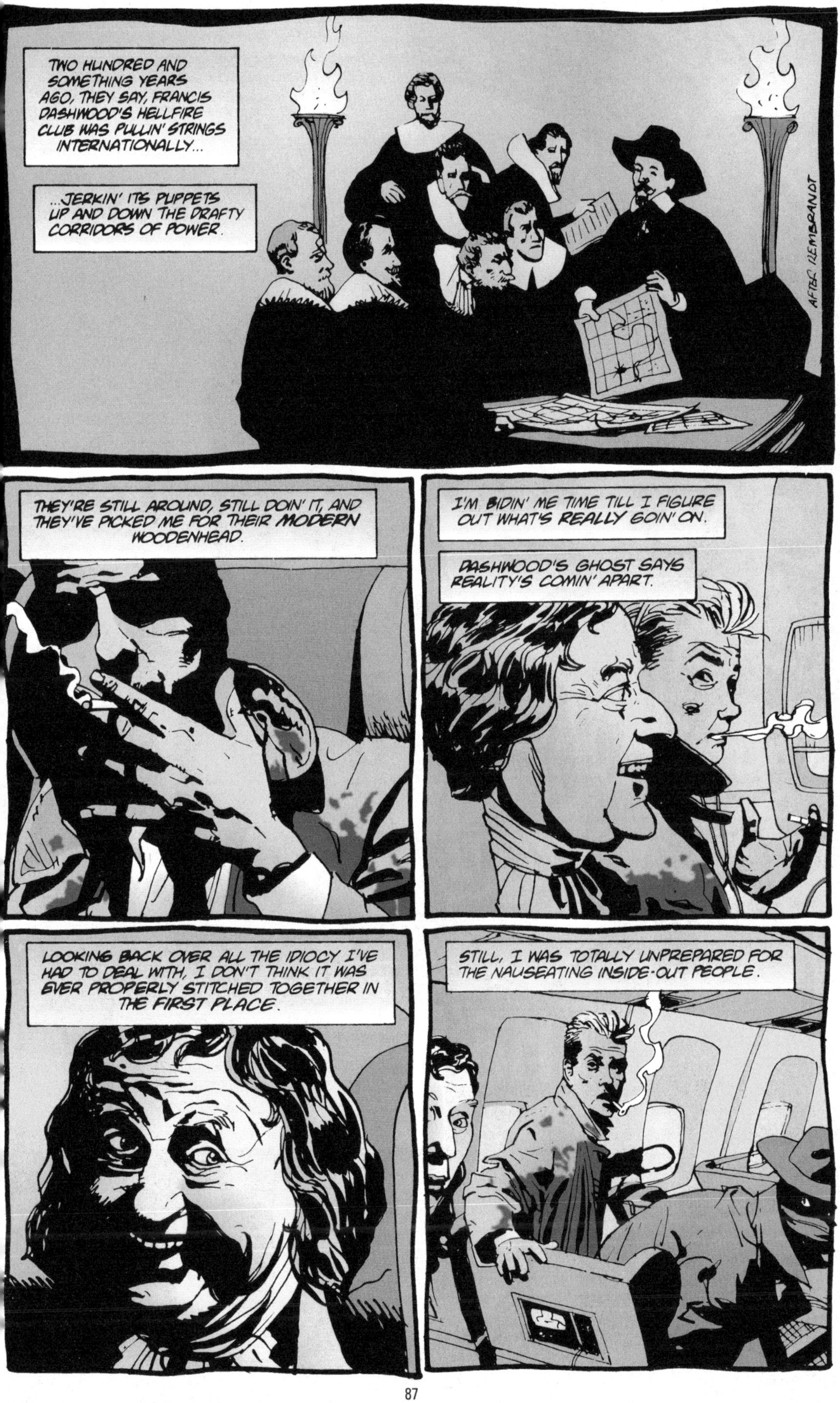
TWO HUNDRED AND SOMETHING YEARS AGO, THEY SAY, FRANCIS DASHWOOD'S HELLFIRE CLUB WAS PULLIN' STRINGS INTERNATIONALLY...
...JERKIN' ITS PUPPETS UP AND DOWN THE DRAFTY CORRIDORS OF POWER.
AFTER REMBRANDT
THEY'RE STILL AROUND, STILL DOIN' IT, AND THEY'VE PICKED ME FOR THEIR MODERN WOODENHEAD.
I'M BIDIN' ME TIME TILL I FIGURE OUT WHAT'S REALLY GOIN' ON.
DASHWOOD'S GHOST SAYS REALITY'S COMIN' APART.
LOOKING BACK OVER ALL THE IDIOCY I'VE HAD TO DEAL WITH, I DON'T THINK IT WAS EVER PROPERLY STITCHED TOGETHER IN THE FIRST PLACE.
STILL, I WAS TOTALLY UNPREPARED FOR THE NAUSEATING INSIDE-OUT PEOPLE.

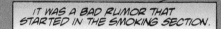

IT WAS A BAD RUMOR THAT
STARTED IN THE SMOKING SECTION.

WITHIN TWENTY MINUTES,
THE WHOLE PLANE WAS IN
AN UPROAR.

warped notions pt3

EDDIE CAMPBELL / SEAN PHILLIPS
WRITER   ARTIST

MATT HOLLINGSWORTH - COLORIST
CLEM ROBINS · LETTERER

AXEL ALONSO / LOU STATHIS
ASS'T EDITOR   EDITOR

the

shout

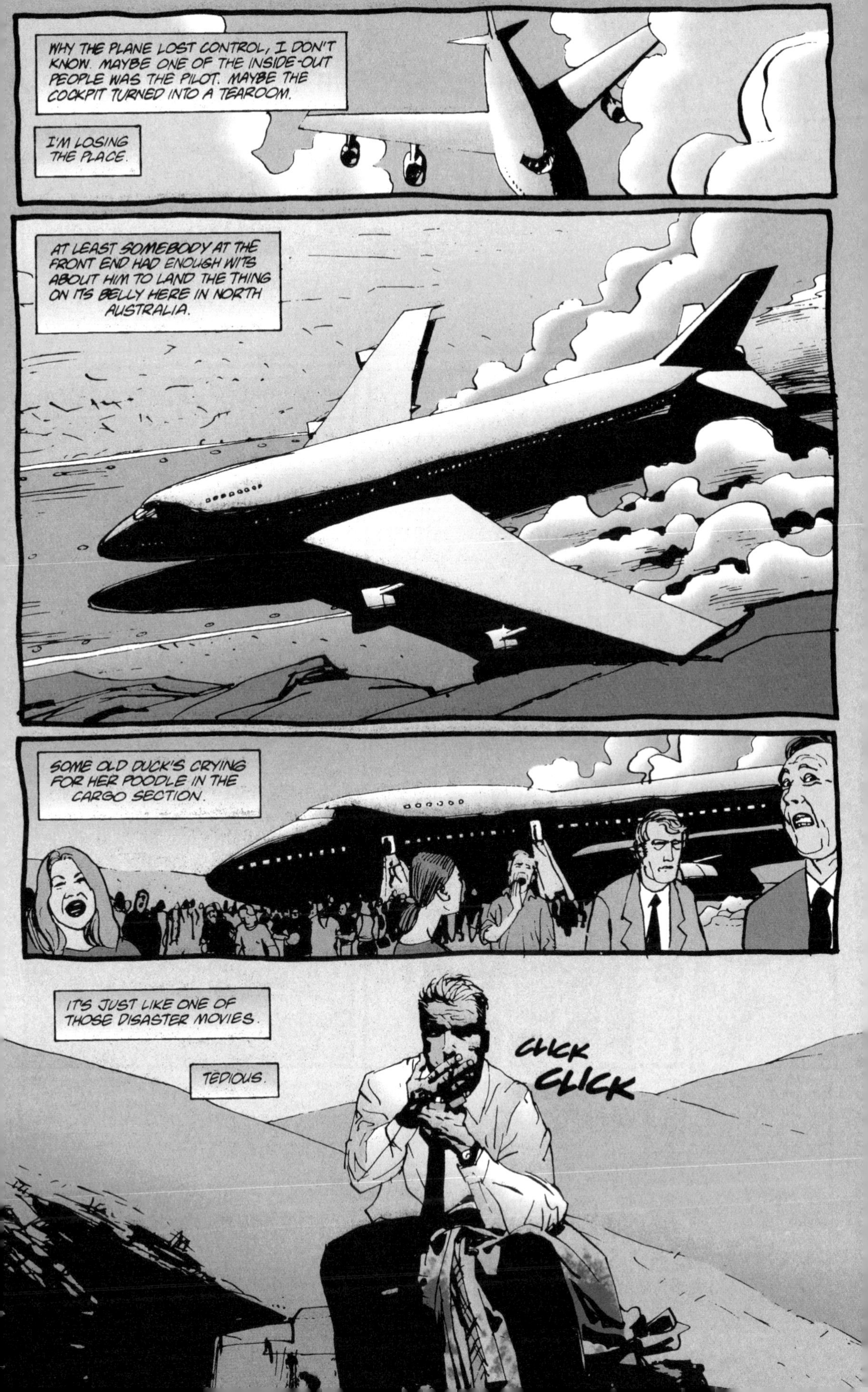
WHY THE PLANE LOST CONTROL, I DON'T KNOW. MAYBE ONE OF THE INSIDE-OUT PEOPLE WAS THE PILOT. MAYBE THE COCKPIT TURNED INTO A TEAROOM.
I'M LOSING THE PLACE.
AT LEAST SOMEBODY AT THE FRONT END HAD ENOUGH WITS ABOUT HIM TO LAND THE THING ON ITS BELLY HERE IN NORTH AUSTRALIA.
SOME OLD DUCK'S CRYING FOR HER POODLE IN THE CARGO SECTION.
IT'S JUST LIKE ONE OF THOSE DISASTER MOVIES.
TEDIOUS.
CLICK
CLICK

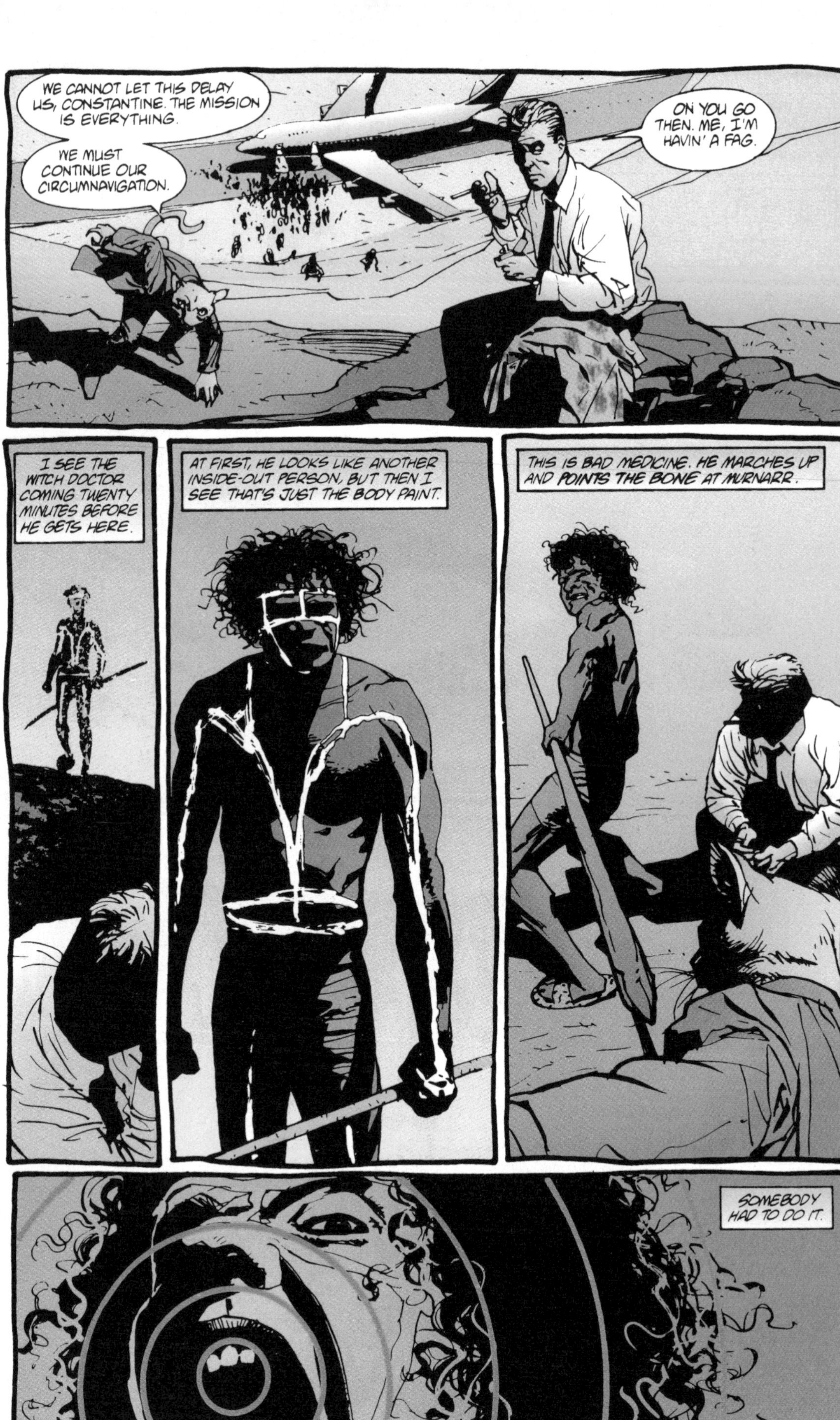
WE CANNOT LET THIS DELAY US, CONSTANTINE. THE MISSION IS EVERYTHING.
WE MUST CONTINUE OUR CIRCUMNAVIGATION.
ON YOU GO THEN. ME, I'M HAVIN' A FAG.
I SEE THE WITCH DOCTOR COMING TWENTY MINUTES BEFORE HE GETS HERE.
AT FIRST, HE LOOKS LIKE ANOTHER INSIDE-OUT PERSON, BUT THEN I SEE THAT'S JUST THE BODY PAINT.
THIS IS BAD MEDICINE. HE MARCHES UP AND POINTS THE BONE AT MURNARR.
SOMEBODY HAD TO DO IT.

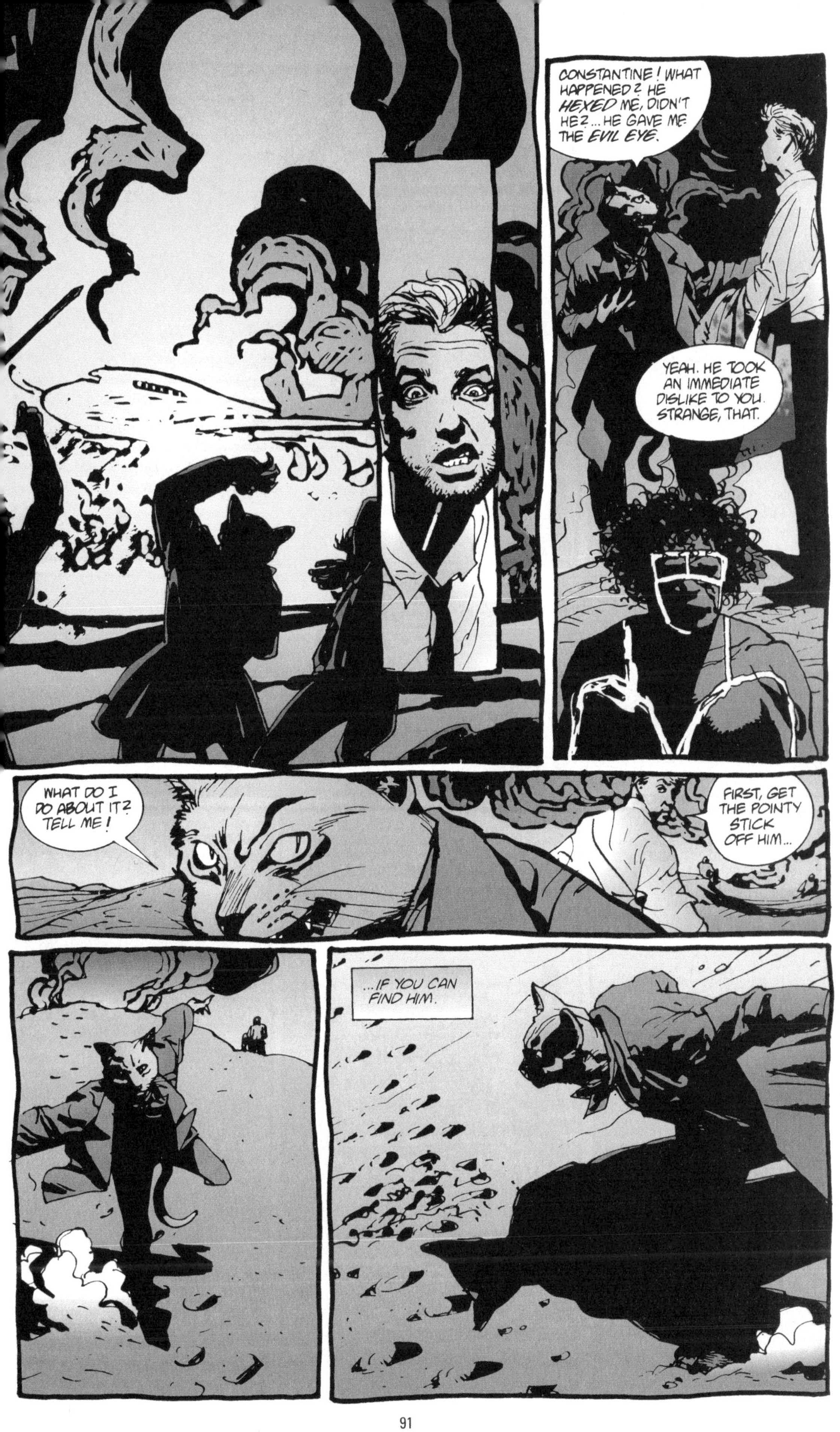
CONSTANTINE! WHAT HAPPENED? HE HEXED ME, DIDN'T HE? ... HE GAVE ME THE EVIL EYE.
YEAH. HE TOOK AN IMMEDIATE DISLIKE TO YOU. STRANGE, THAT.
WHAT DO I DO ABOUT IT? TELL ME!
FIRST, GET THE POINTY STICK OFF HIM...
...IF YOU CAN FIND HIM.

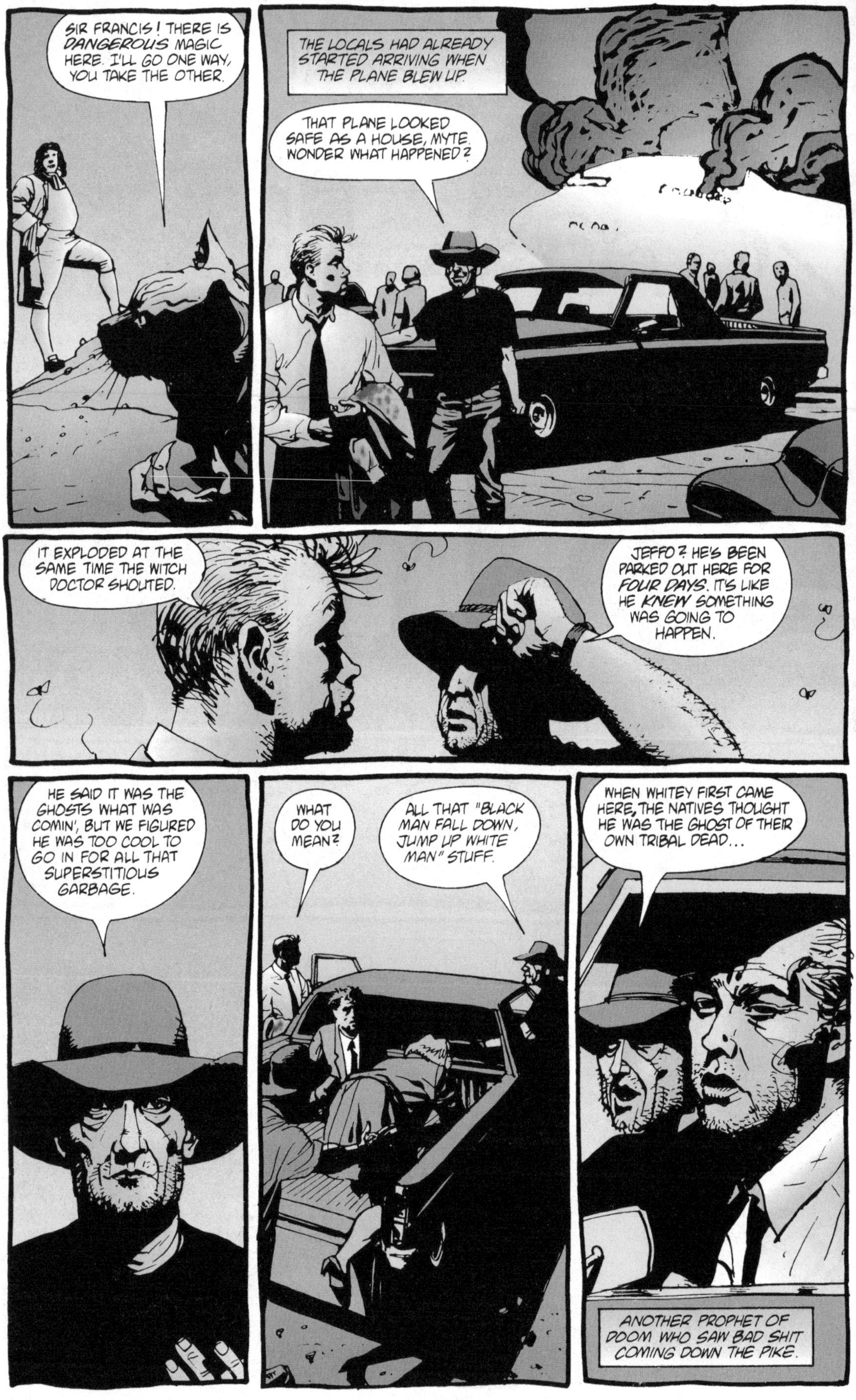
SIR FRANCIS! THERE IS DANGEROUS MAGIC HERE. I'LL GO ONE WAY, YOU TAKE THE OTHER.
THE LOCALS HAD ALREADY STARTED ARRIVING WHEN THE PLANE BLEW UP.
THAT PLANE LOOKED SAFE AS A HOUSE, MYTE. WONDER WHAT HAPPENED?
IT EXPLODED AT THE SAME TIME THE WITCH DOCTOR SHOUTED.
JEFFO? HE'S BEEN PARKED OUT HERE FOR FOUR DAYS. IT'S LIKE HE KNEW SOMETHING WAS GOING TO HAPPEN.
HE SAID IT WAS THE GHOSTS WHAT WAS COMIN', BUT WE FIGURED HE WAS TOO COOL TO GO IN FOR ALL THAT SUPERSTITIOUS GARBAGE.
WHAT DO YOU MEAN?
ALL THAT "BLACK MAN FALL DOWN, JUMP UP WHITE MAN" STUFF.
WHEN WHITEY FIRST CAME HERE, THE NATIVES THOUGHT HE WAS THE GHOST OF THEIR OWN TRIBAL DEAD...
ANOTHER PROPHET OF DOOM WHO SAW BAD SHIT COMING DOWN THE PIKE.

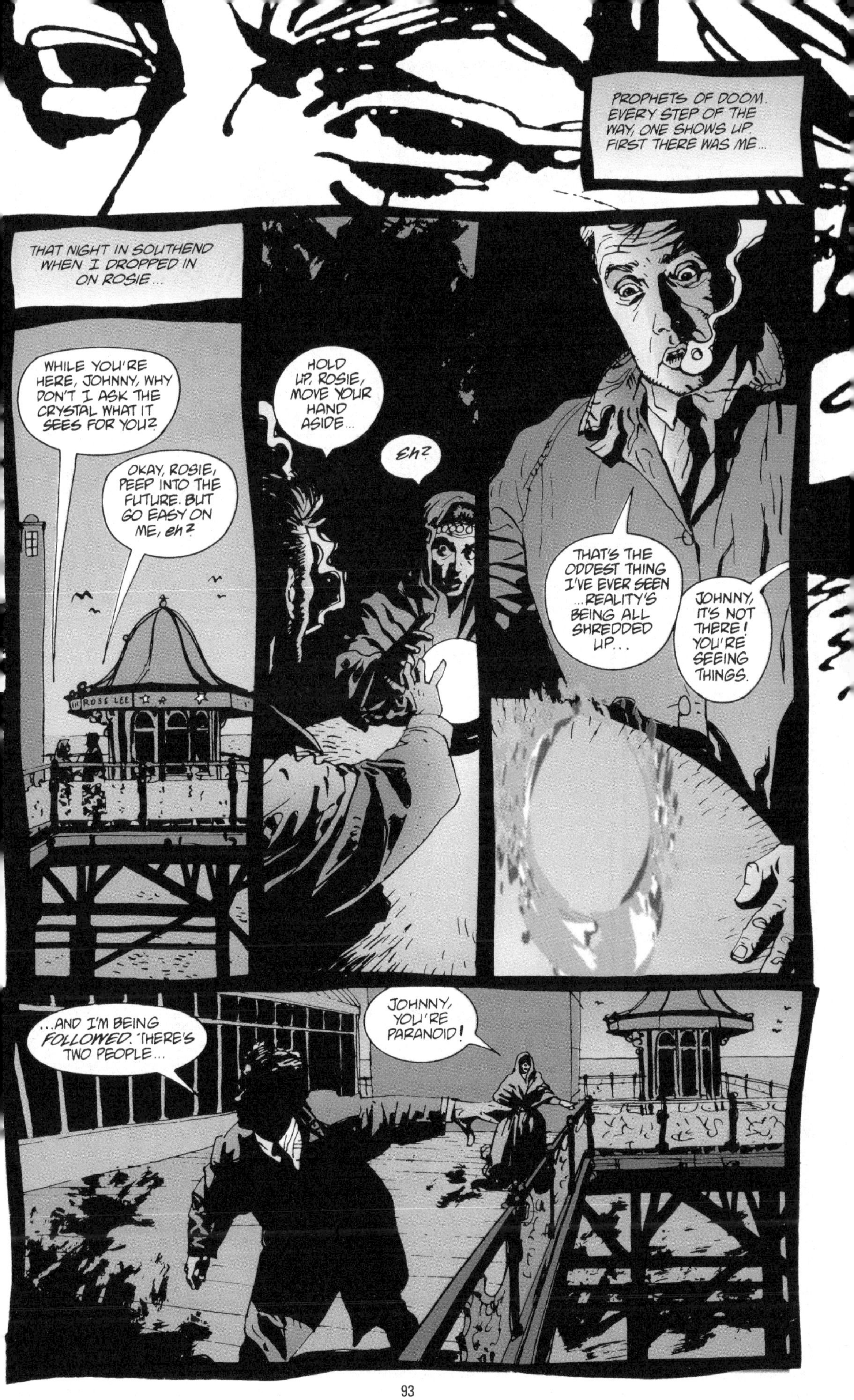
PROPHETS OF DOOM. EVERY STEP OF THE WAY, ONE SHOWS UP. FIRST THERE WAS ME...
THAT NIGHT IN SOUTHEND WHEN I DROPPED IN ON ROSIE...
WHILE YOU'RE HERE, JOHNNY, WHY DON'T I ASK THE CRYSTAL WHAT IT SEES FOR YOU?
OKAY, ROSIE, PEEP INTO THE FUTURE. BUT GO EASY ON ME, eh?
ROSE LEE
HOLD UP, ROSIE, MOVE YOUR HAND ASIDE...
eh?
THAT'S THE ODDEST THING I'VE EVER SEEN ...REALITY'S BEING ALL SHREDDED UP...
JOHNNY, IT'S NOT THERE! YOU'RE SEEING THINGS.
...AND I'M BEING FOLLOWED. THERE'S TWO PEOPLE...
JOHNNY, YOU'RE PARANOID!

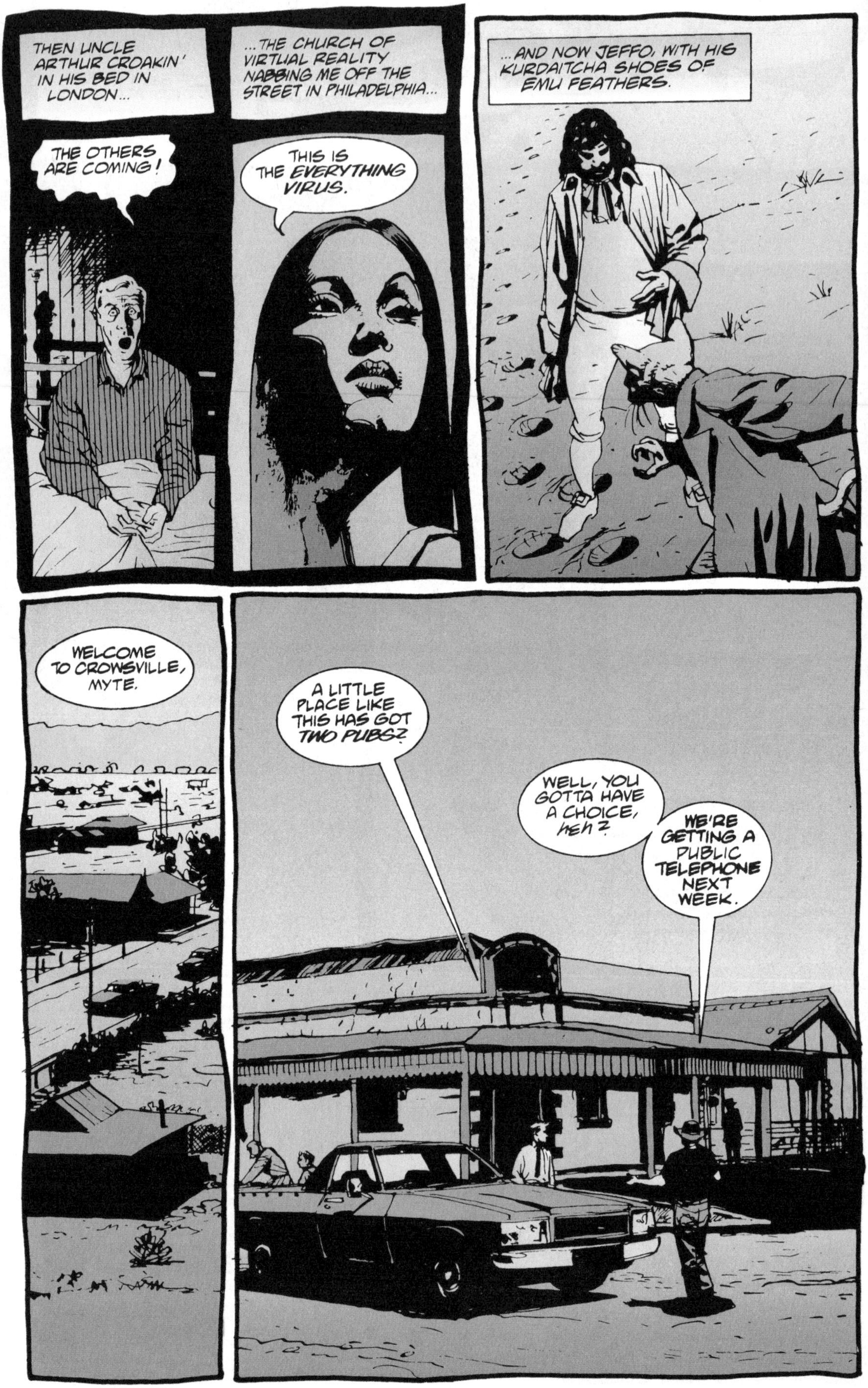
THEN UNCLE ARTHUR CROAKIN' IN HIS BED IN LONDON...
THE OTHERS ARE COMING!
...THE CHURCH OF VIRTUAL REALITY NABBING ME OFF THE STREET IN PHILADELPHIA...
THIS IS THE *EVERYTHING VIRUS.*
...AND NOW JEFFO, WITH HIS KURDAITCHA SHOES OF EMU FEATHERS.
WELCOME TO CROWSVILLE, MYTE.
A LITTLE PLACE LIKE THIS HAS GOT *TWO PUBS?*
WELL, YOU GOTTA HAVE A CHOICE, *heh?*
WE'RE GETTING A PUBLIC **TELEPHONE** NEXT WEEK.

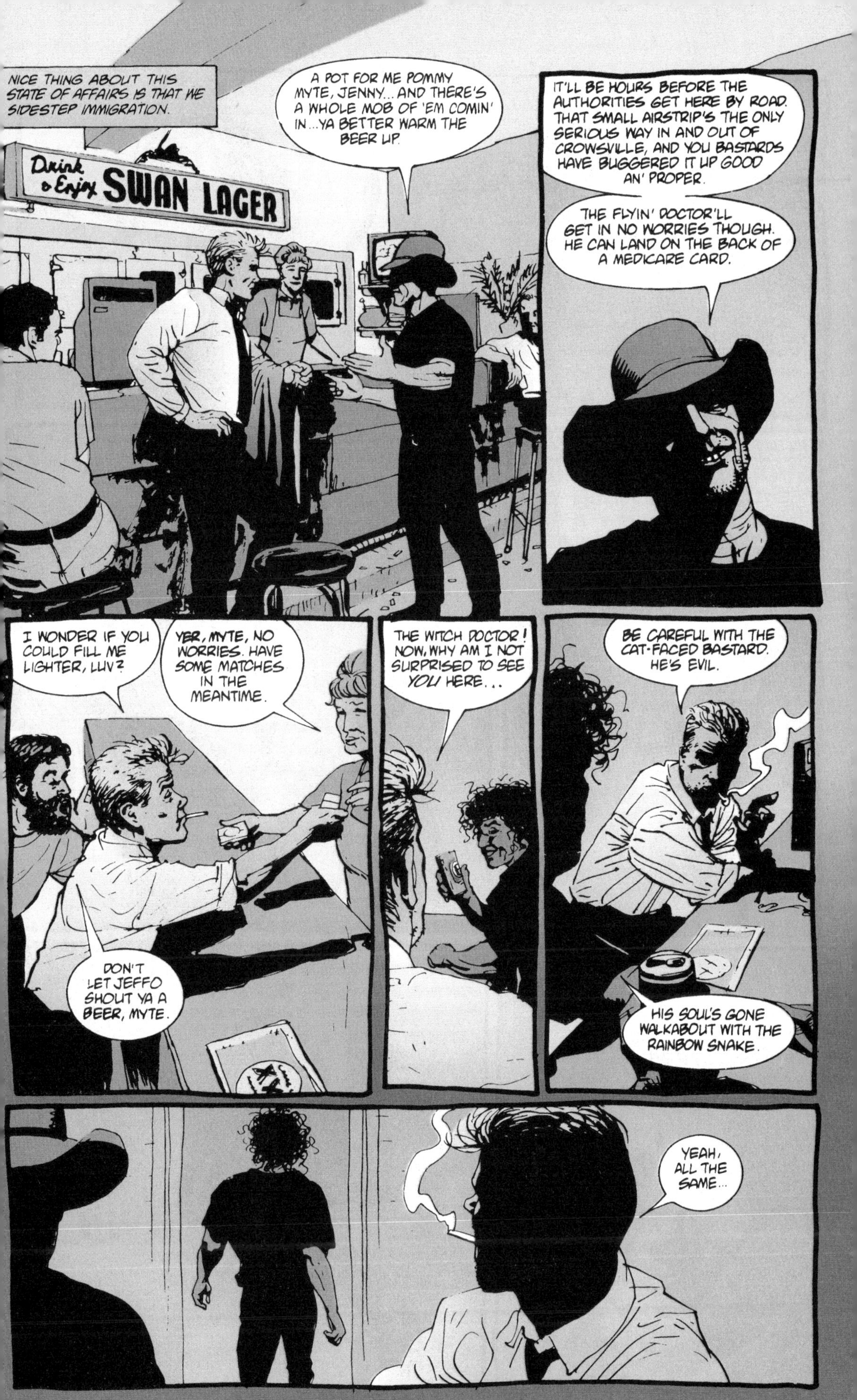
NICE THING ABOUT THIS STATE OF AFFAIRS IS THAT WE SIDESTEP IMMIGRATION.
A POT FOR ME POMMY MYTE, JENNY... AND THERE'S A WHOLE MOB OF 'EM COMIN' IN...YA BETTER WARM THE BEER UP.
Drink & Enjoy SWAN LAGER
IT'LL BE HOURS BEFORE THE AUTHORITIES GET HERE BY ROAD. THAT SMALL AIRSTRIP'S THE ONLY SERIOUS WAY IN AND OUT OF CROWSVILLE, AND YOU BASTARDS HAVE BUGGERED IT UP GOOD AN' PROPER.
THE FLYIN' DOCTOR'LL GET IN NO WORRIES THOUGH. HE CAN LAND ON THE BACK OF A MEDICARE CARD.
I WONDER IF YOU COULD FILL ME LIGHTER, LUV?
YER, MYTE, NO WORRIES. HAVE SOME MATCHES IN THE MEANTIME.
DON'T LET JEFFO SHOUT YA A BEER, MYTE.
THE WITCH DOCTOR! NOW, WHY AM I NOT SURPRISED TO SEE YOU HERE...
BE CAREFUL WITH THE CAT-FACED BASTARD. HE'S EVIL.
HIS SOUL'S GONE WALKABOUT WITH THE RAINBOW SNAKE.
YEAH, ALL THE SAME...

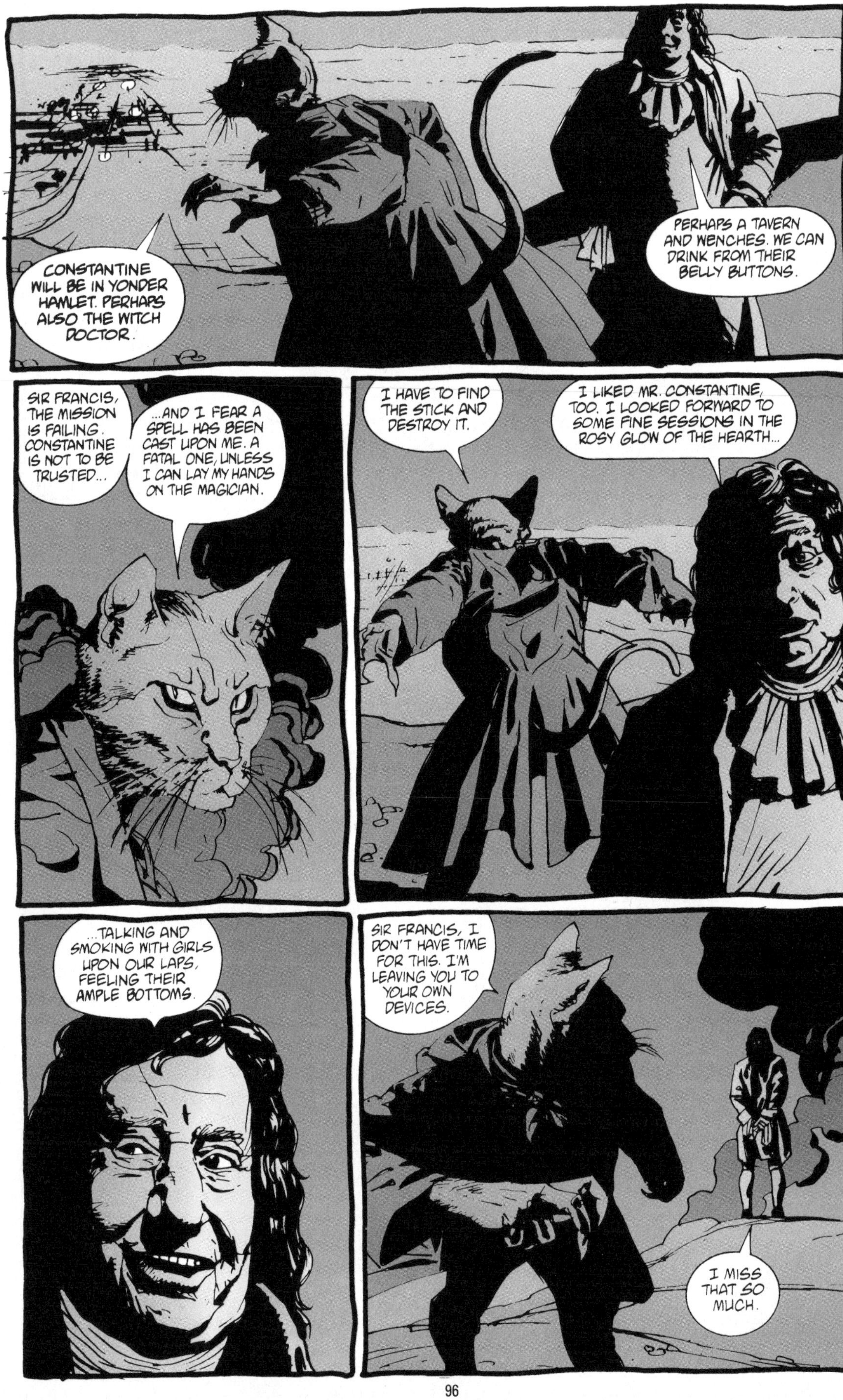
CONSTANTINE WILL BE IN YONDER HAMLET. PERHAPS ALSO THE WITCH DOCTOR.
PERHAPS A TAVERN AND WENCHES. WE CAN DRINK FROM THEIR BELLY BUTTONS.
SIR FRANCIS, THE MISSION IS FAILING. CONSTANTINE IS NOT TO BE TRUSTED...
...AND I FEAR A SPELL HAS BEEN CAST UPON ME. A FATAL ONE, UNLESS I CAN LAY MY HANDS ON THE MAGICIAN.
I HAVE TO FIND THE STICK AND DESTROY IT.
I LIKED MR. CONSTANTINE, TOO. I LOOKED FORWARD TO SOME FINE SESSIONS IN THE ROSY GLOW OF THE HEARTH...
...TALKING AND SMOKING WITH GIRLS UPON OUR LAPS, FEELING THEIR AMPLE BOTTOMS.
SIR FRANCIS, I DON'T HAVE TIME FOR THIS. I'M LEAVING YOU TO YOUR OWN DEVICES.
I MISS THAT SO MUCH.

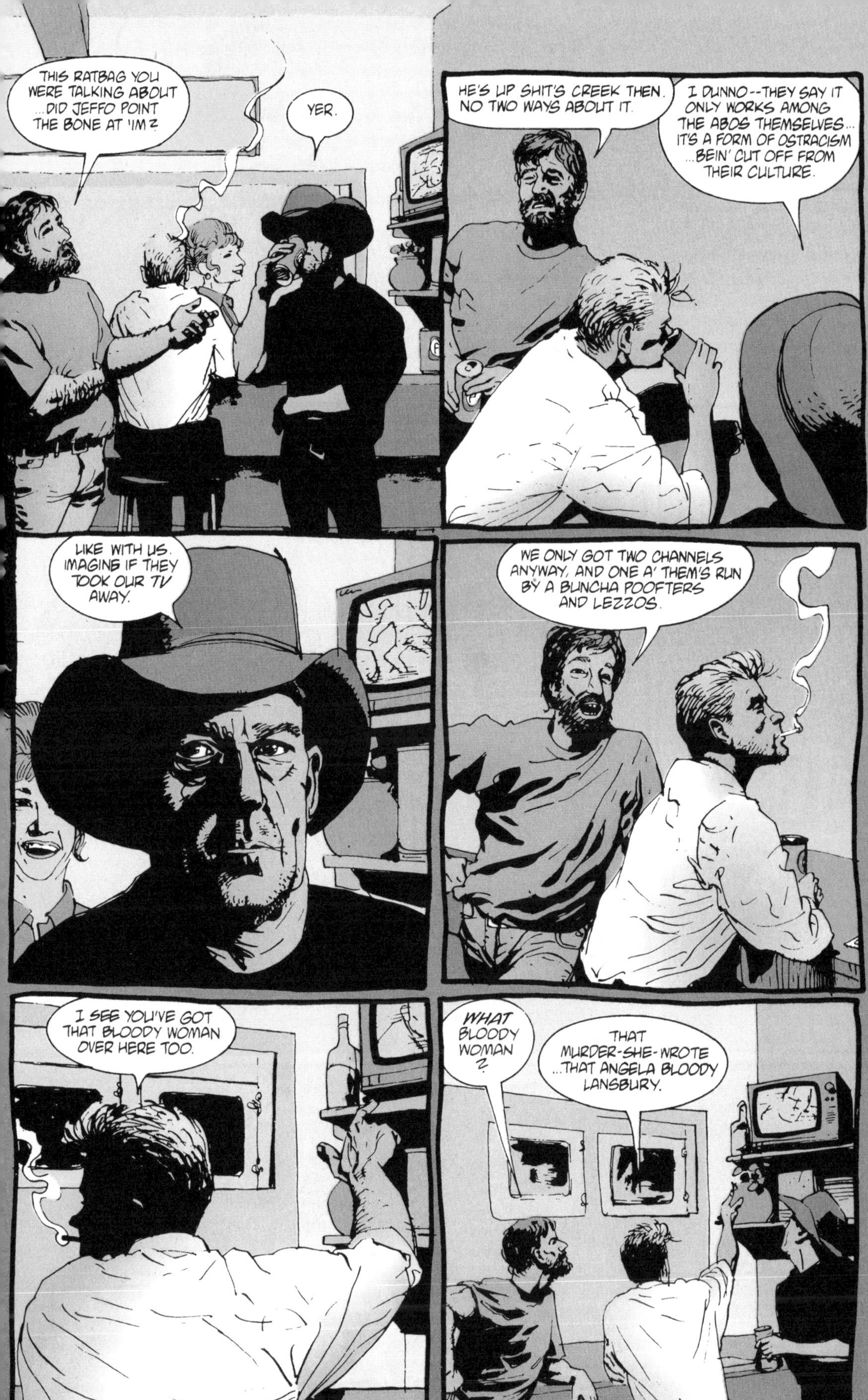

THIS RATBAG YOU WERE TALKING ABOUT ...DID JEFFO POINT THE BONE AT 'IM?
YER.
HE'S UP SHIT'S CREEK THEN. NO TWO WAYS ABOUT IT.
I DUNNO--THEY SAY IT ONLY WORKS AMONG THE ABOS THEMSELVES... IT'S A FORM OF OSTRACISM ...BEIN' CUT OFF FROM THEIR CULTURE.
LIKE WITH US. IMAGINE IF THEY TOOK OUR TV AWAY.
WE ONLY GOT TWO CHANNELS ANYWAY, AND ONE A' THEM'S RUN BY A BUNCHA POOFTERS AND LEZZOS.
I SEE YOU'VE GOT THAT BLOODY WOMAN OVER HERE TOO.
WHAT BLOODY WOMAN?
THAT MURDER-SHE-WROTE ...THAT ANGELA BLOODY LANSBURY.

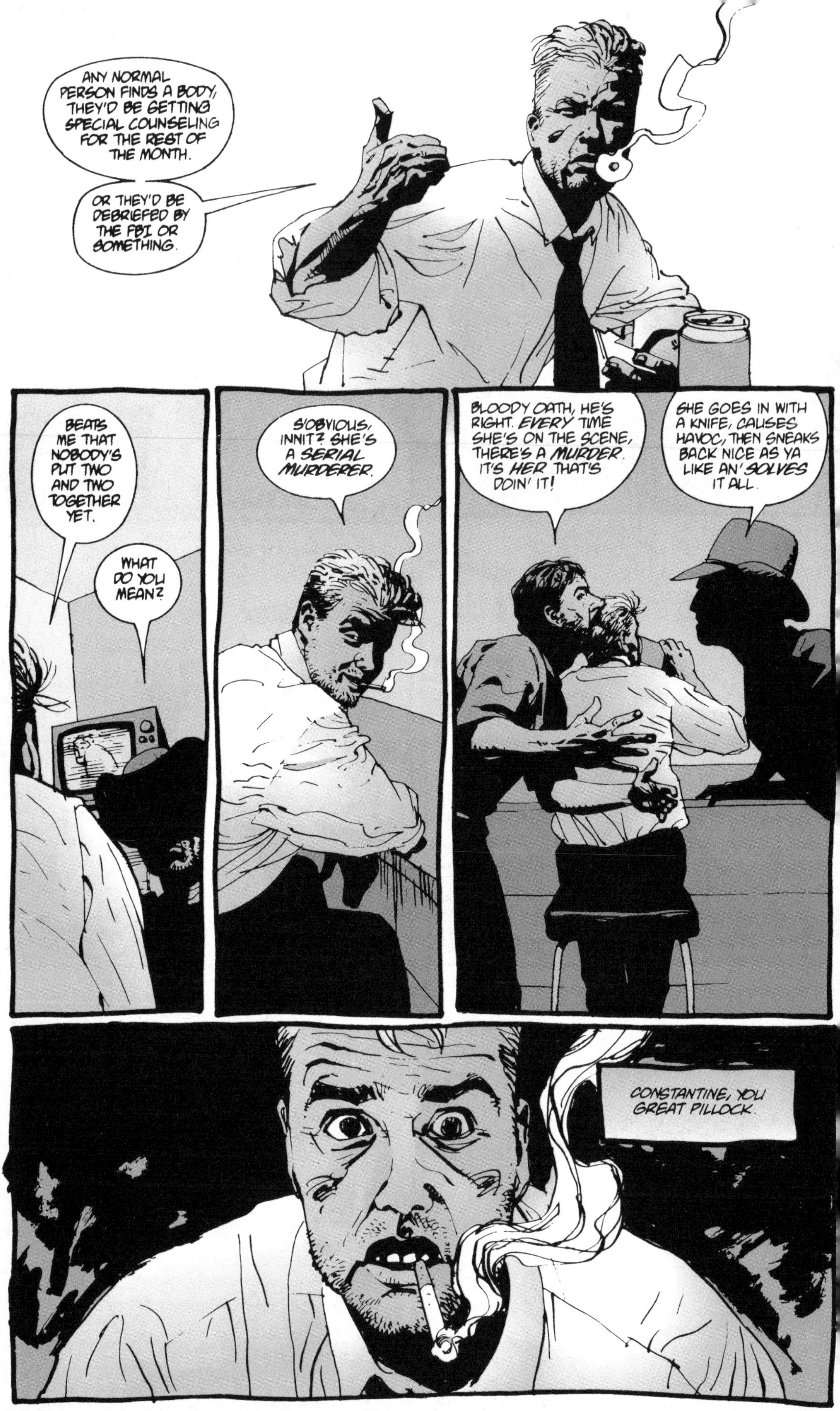
ANY NORMAL PERSON FINDS A BODY, THEY'D BE GETTING SPECIAL COUNSELING FOR THE REST OF THE MONTH.
OR THEY'D BE DEBRIEFED BY THE FBI OR SOMETHING.
BEATS ME THAT NOBODY'S PUT TWO AND TWO TOGETHER YET.
WHAT DO YOU MEAN?
S'OBVIOUS, INNIT? SHE'S A SERIAL MURDERER.
BLOODY OATH, HE'S RIGHT. EVERY TIME SHE'S ON THE SCENE, THERE'S A MURDER. IT'S HER THAT'S DOIN' IT!
SHE GOES IN WITH A KNIFE, CAUSES HAVOC, THEN SNEAKS BACK NICE AS YA LIKE AN' SOLVES IT ALL.
CONSTANTINE, YOU GREAT PILLOCK.

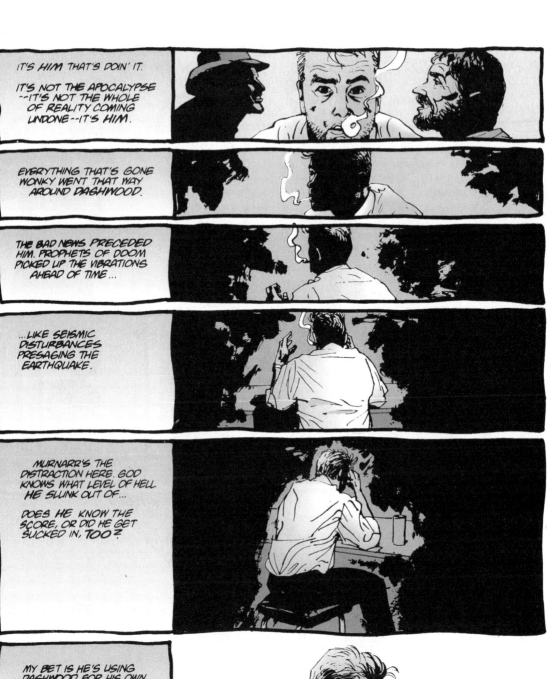

IT'S *HIM* THAT'S DOIN' IT.

IT'S NOT THE APOCALYPSE --IT'S NOT THE WHOLE OF REALITY COMING UNDONE--IT'S *HIM*.

EVERYTHING THAT'S GONE WONKY WENT THAT WAY AROUND *DASHWOOD*.

THE BAD NEWS PRECEDED HIM. PROPHETS OF DOOM PICKED UP THE VIBRATIONS AHEAD OF TIME...

...LIKE SEISMIC DISTURBANCES PRESAGING THE EARTHQUAKE.

MURNARR'S THE DISTRACTION HERE. GOD KNOWS WHAT LEVEL OF HELL HE SLUNK OUT OF...

DOES HE KNOW THE SCORE, OR DID HE GET SUCKED IN, *TOO*?

MY BET IS HE'S USING *DASHWOOD* FOR HIS OWN ENDS. HE'S ALWAYS THE ONE PUTTING THE SHOW BACK ON COURSE.

GOTTA THINK, MAN.

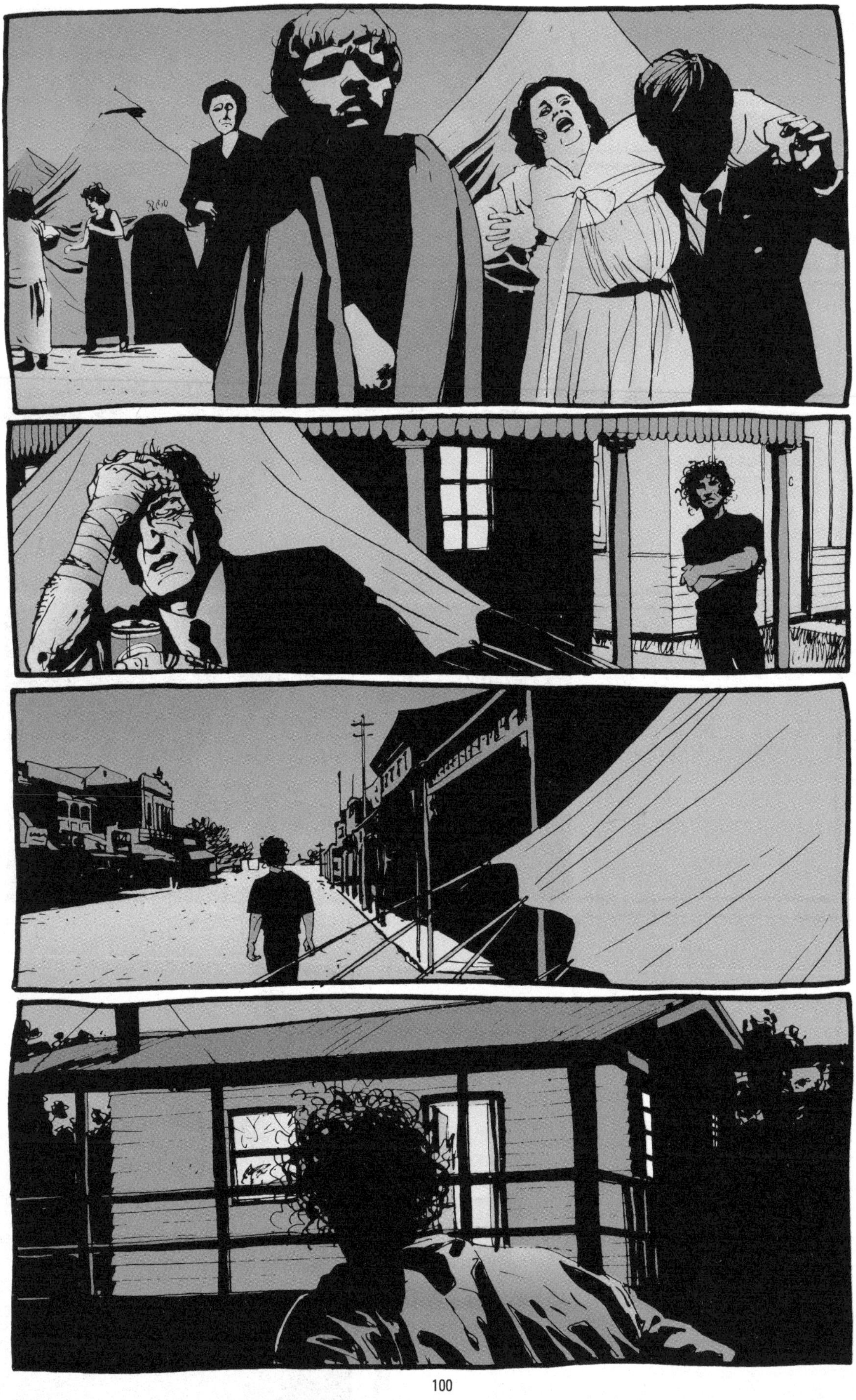

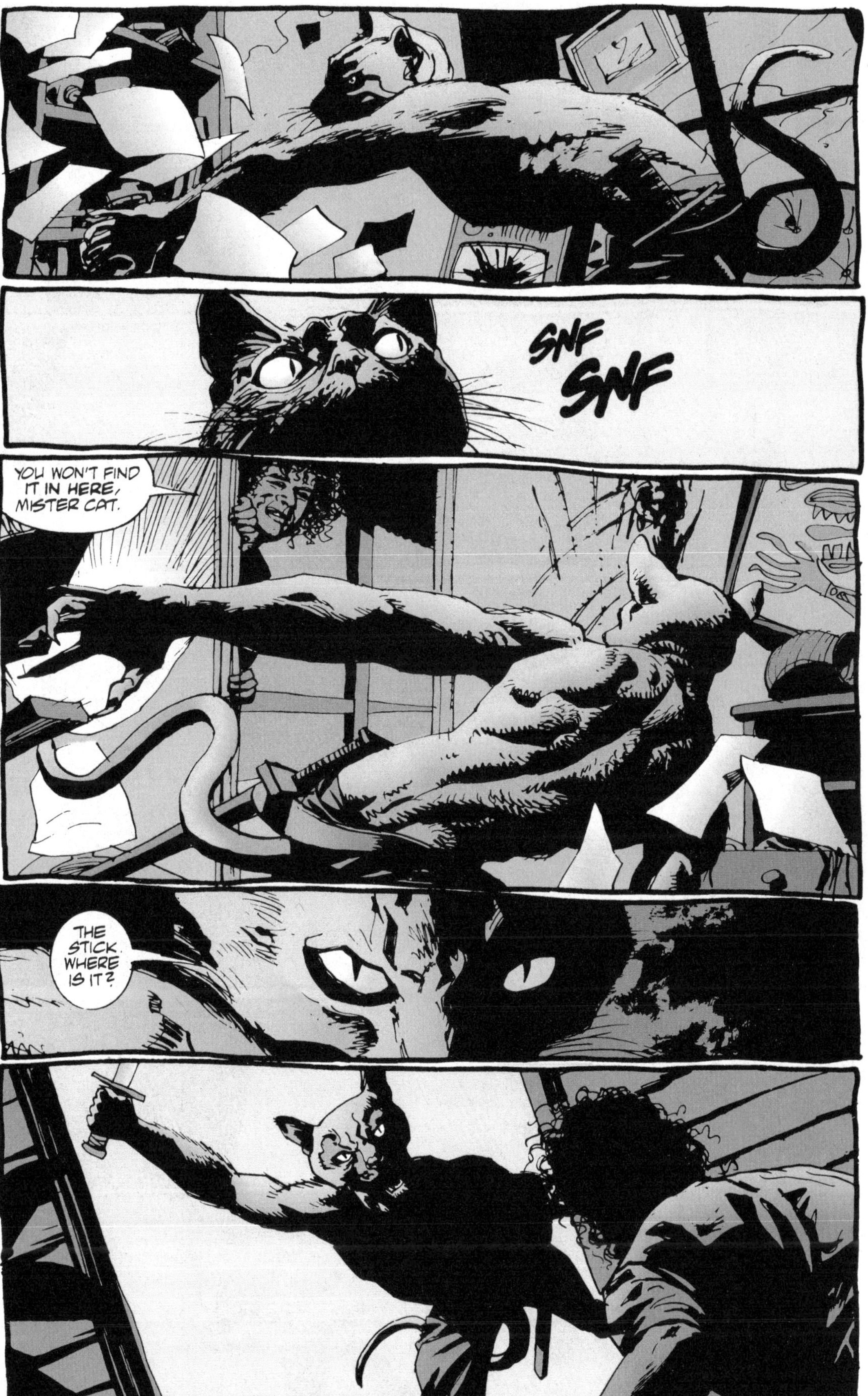
SNF
SNF
YOU WON'T FIND IT IN HERE, MISTER CAT.
THE STICK. WHERE IS IT?

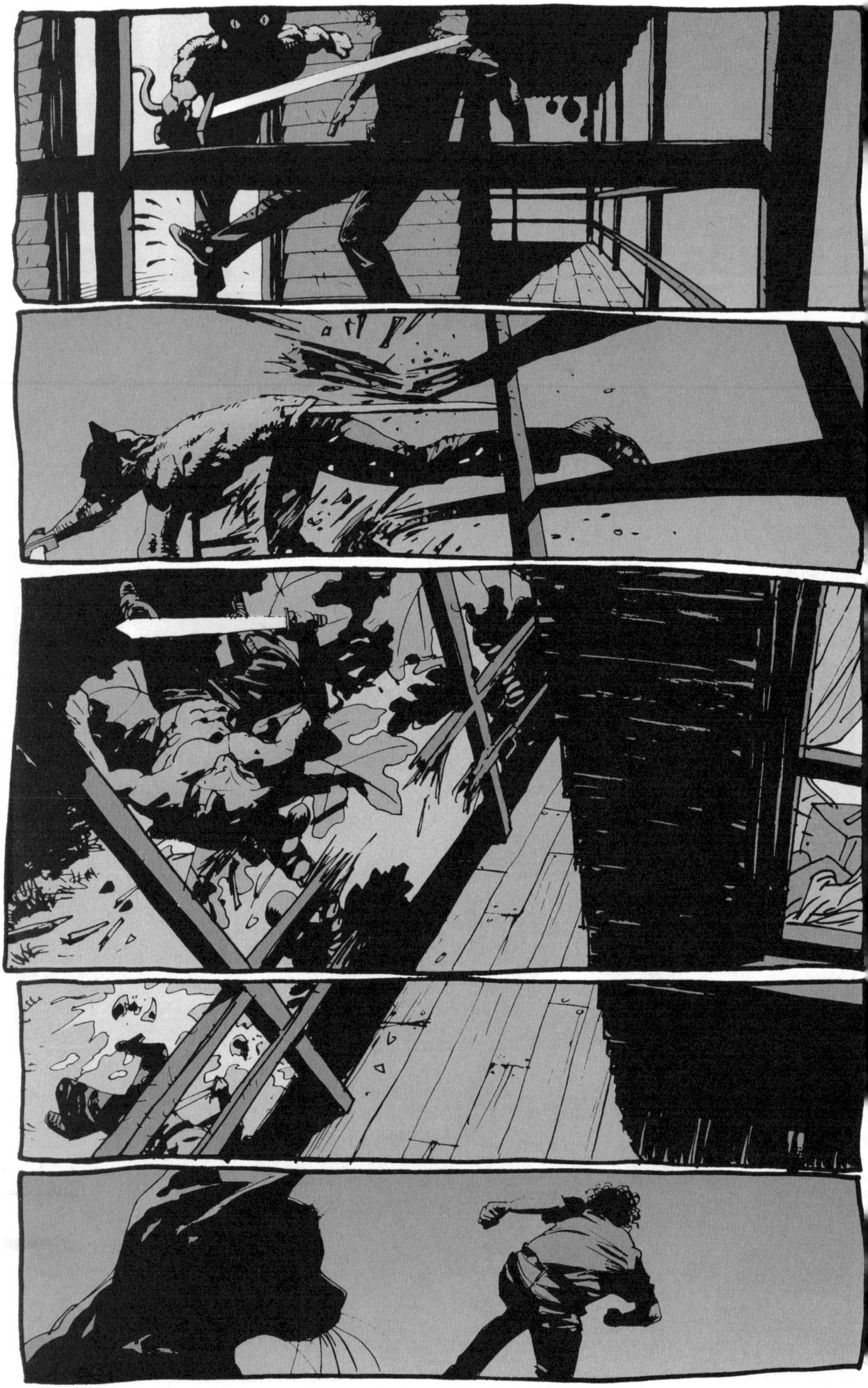

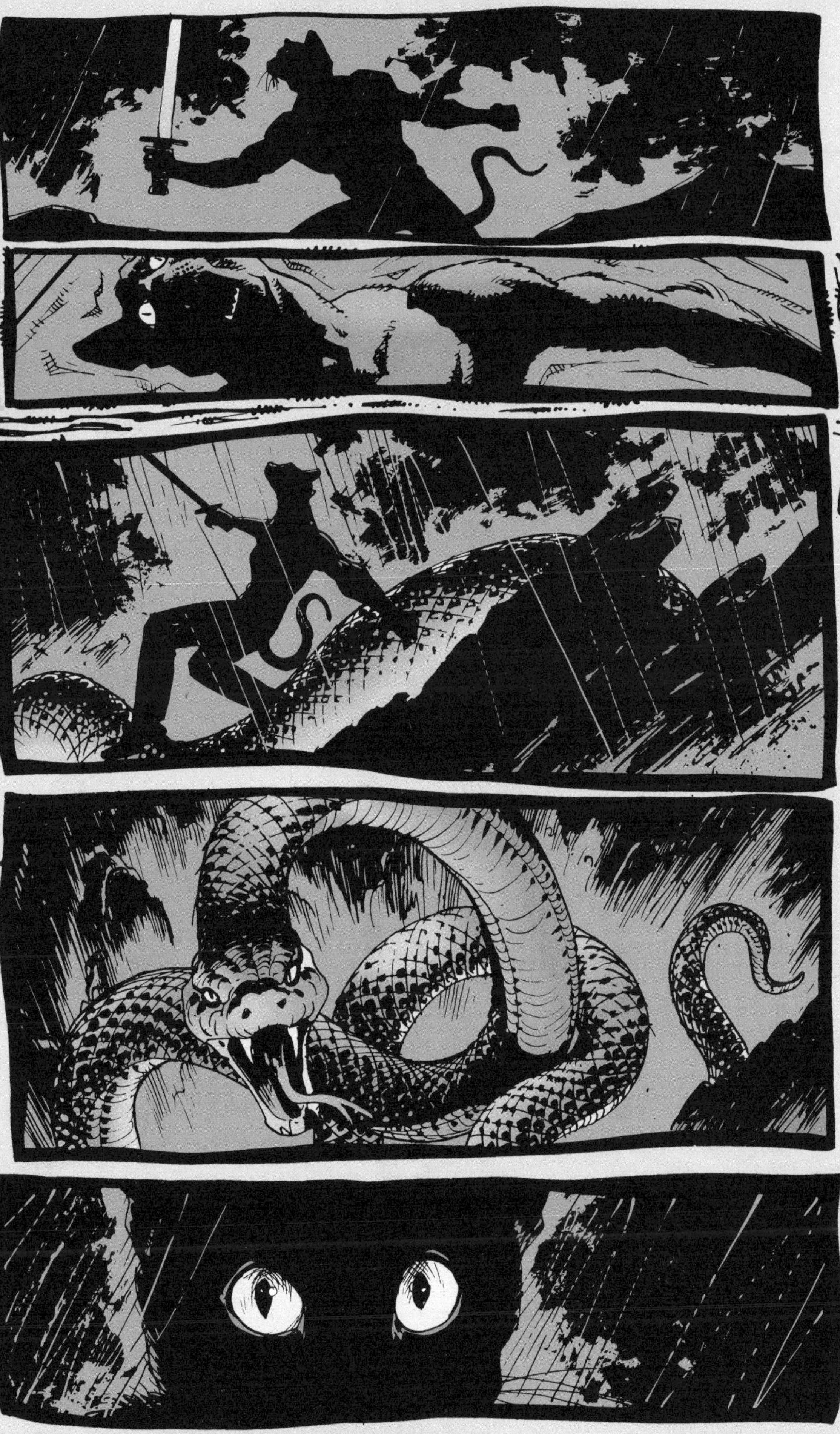

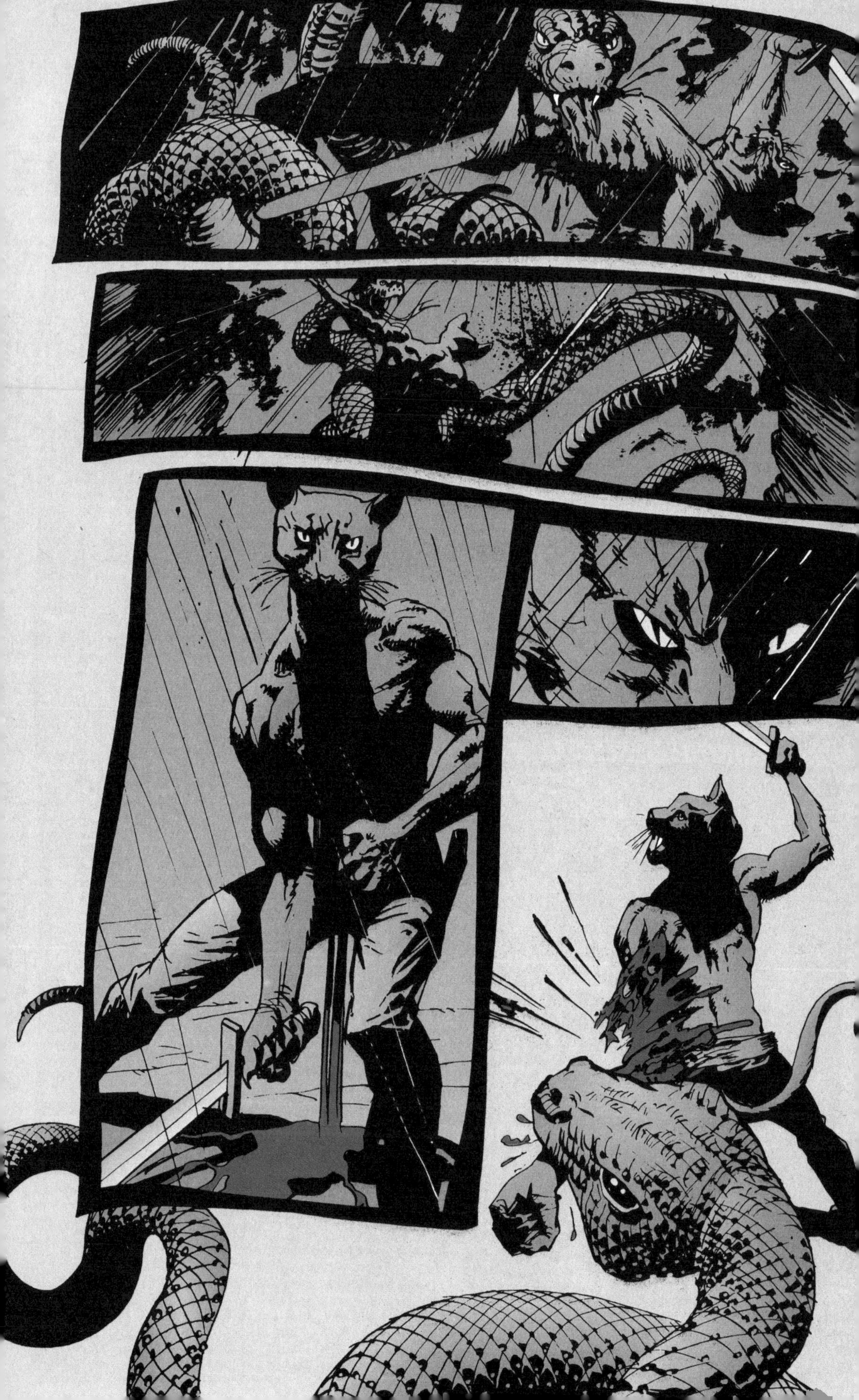

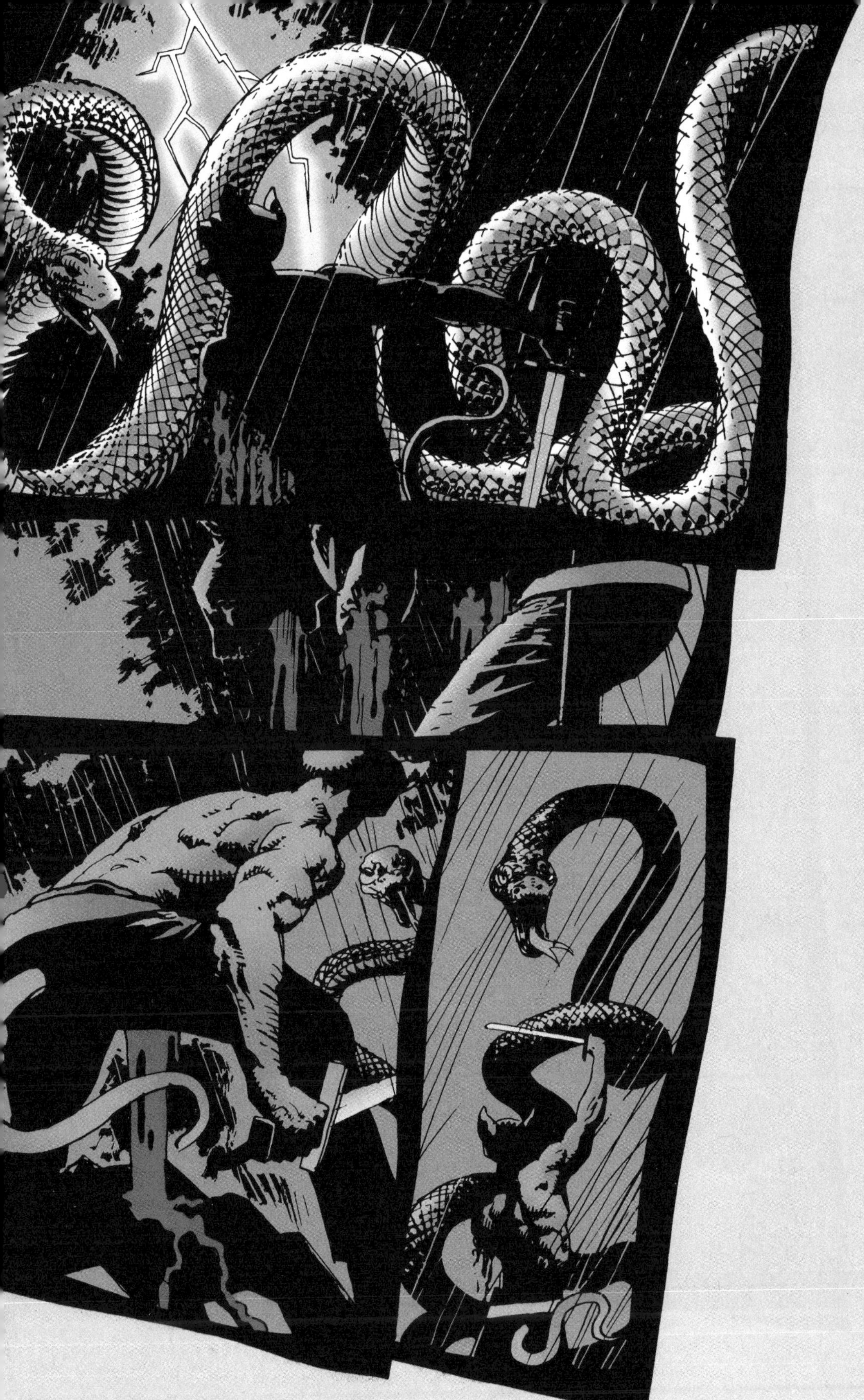

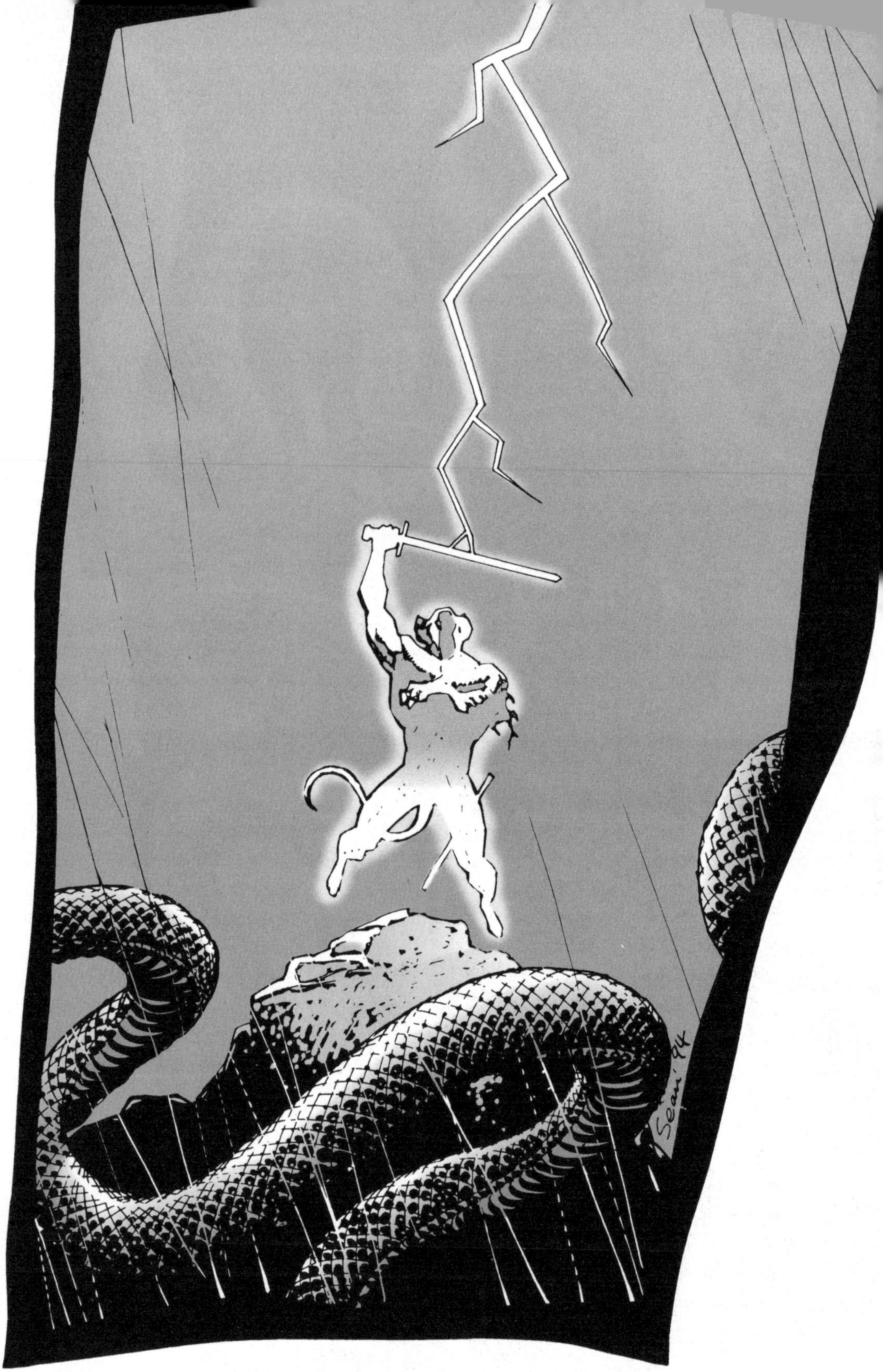
Sean '94

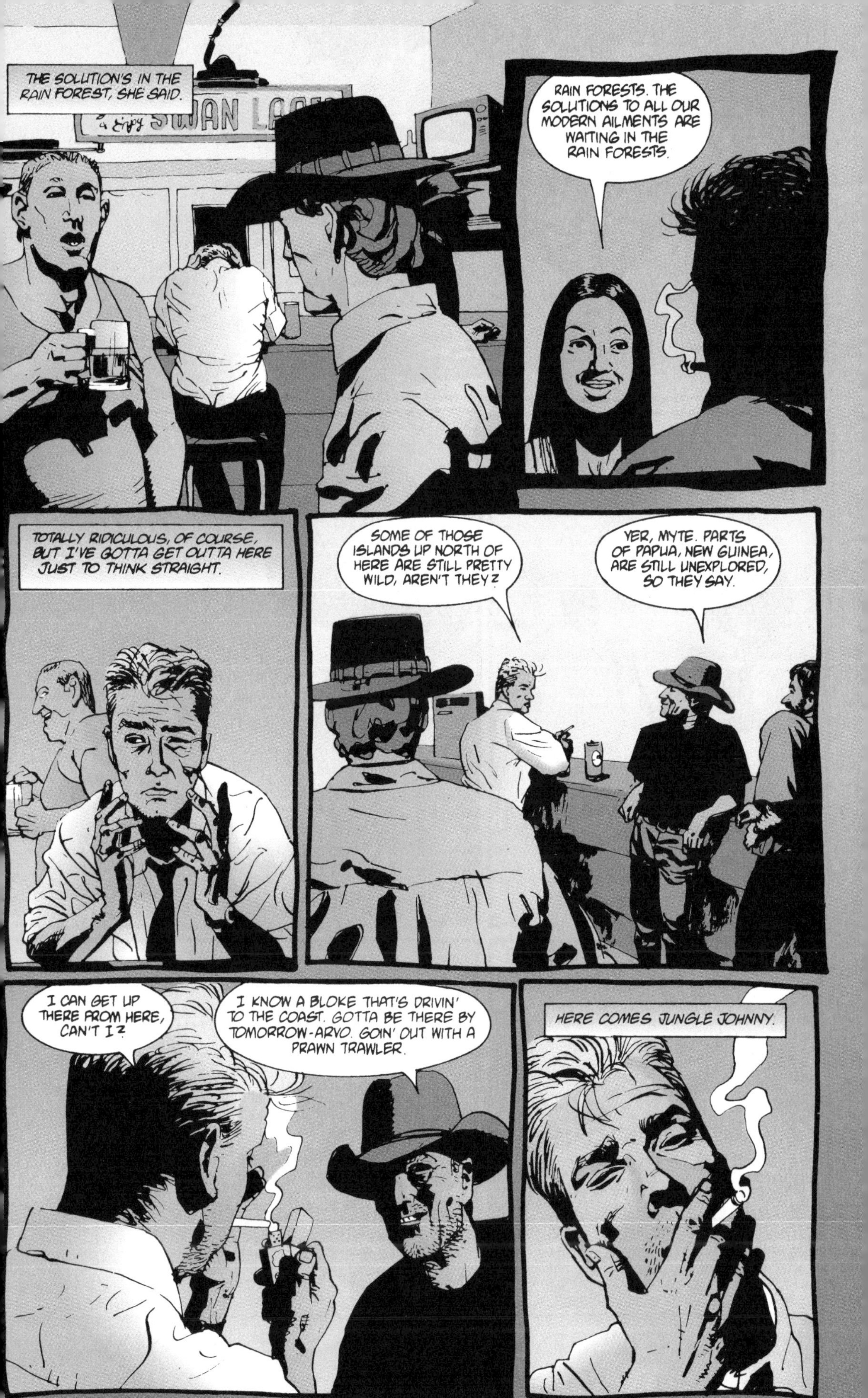
THE SOLUTION'S IN THE RAIN FOREST, SHE SAID.
SWAN LA
RAIN FORESTS. THE SOLUTIONS TO ALL OUR MODERN AILMENTS ARE WAITING IN THE RAIN FORESTS.
TOTALLY RIDICULOUS, OF COURSE, BUT I'VE GOTTA GET OUTTA HERE JUST TO THINK STRAIGHT.
SOME OF THOSE ISLANDS UP NORTH OF HERE ARE STILL PRETTY WILD, AREN'T THEY?
YER, MYTE. PARTS OF PAPUA, NEW GUINEA, ARE STILL UNEXPLORED, SO THEY SAY.
I CAN GET UP THERE FROM HERE, CAN'T I?
I KNOW A BLOKE THAT'S DRIVIN' TO THE COAST. GOTTA BE THERE BY TOMORROW-ARVO. GOIN' OUT WITH A PRAWN TRAWLER.
HERE COMES JUNGLE JOHNNY.

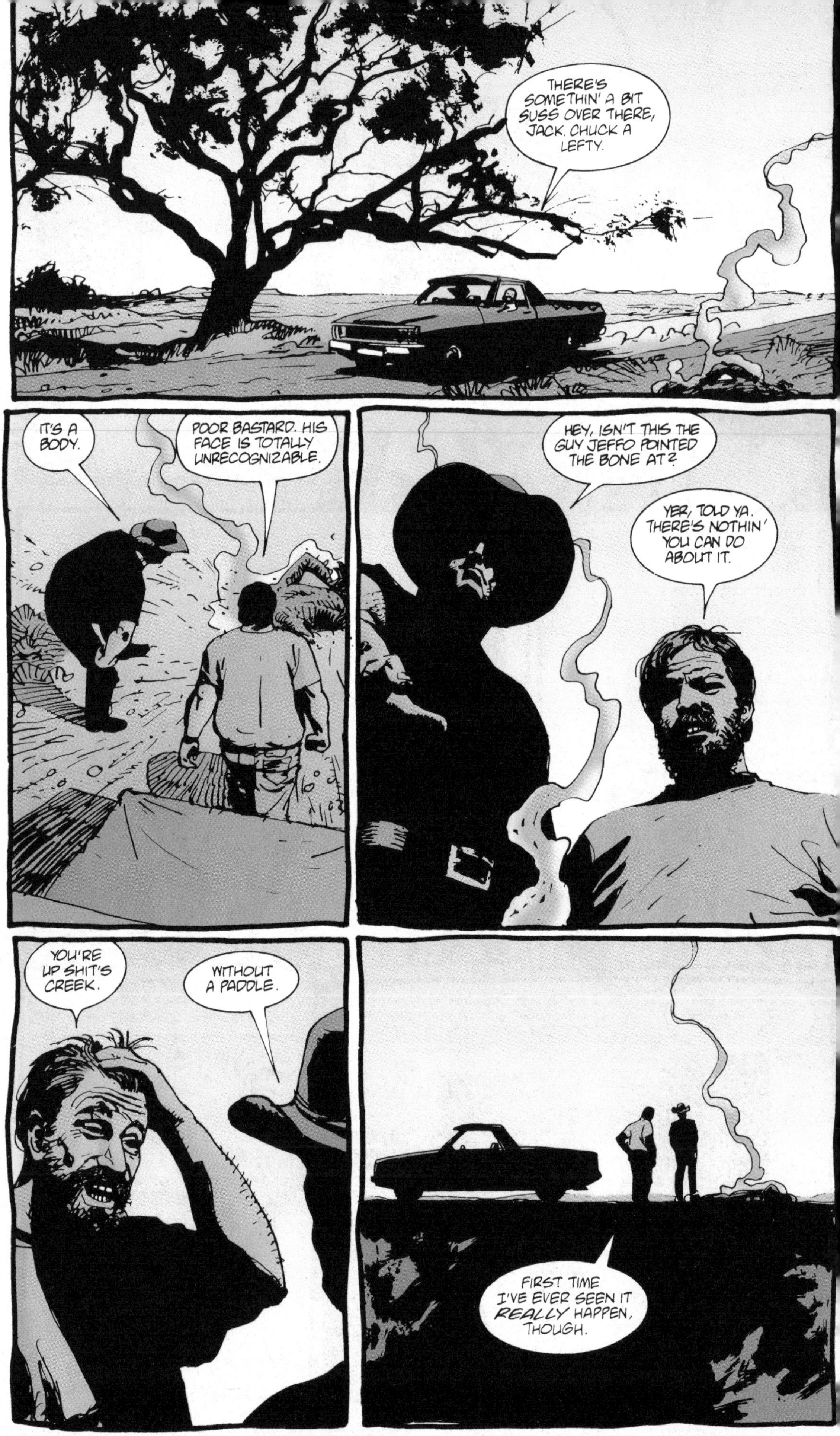
THERE'S SOMETHIN' A BIT SUSS OVER THERE, JACK. CHUCK A LEFTY.
IT'S A BODY.
POOR BASTARD. HIS FACE IS TOTALLY UNRECOGNIZABLE.
HEY, ISN'T THIS THE GUY JEFFO POINTED THE BONE AT?
YER, TOLD YA. THERE'S NOTHIN' YOU CAN DO ABOUT IT.
YOU'RE UP SHIT'S CREEK.
WITHOUT A PADDLE.
FIRST TIME I'VE EVER SEEN IT *REALLY* HAPPEN, THOUGH.

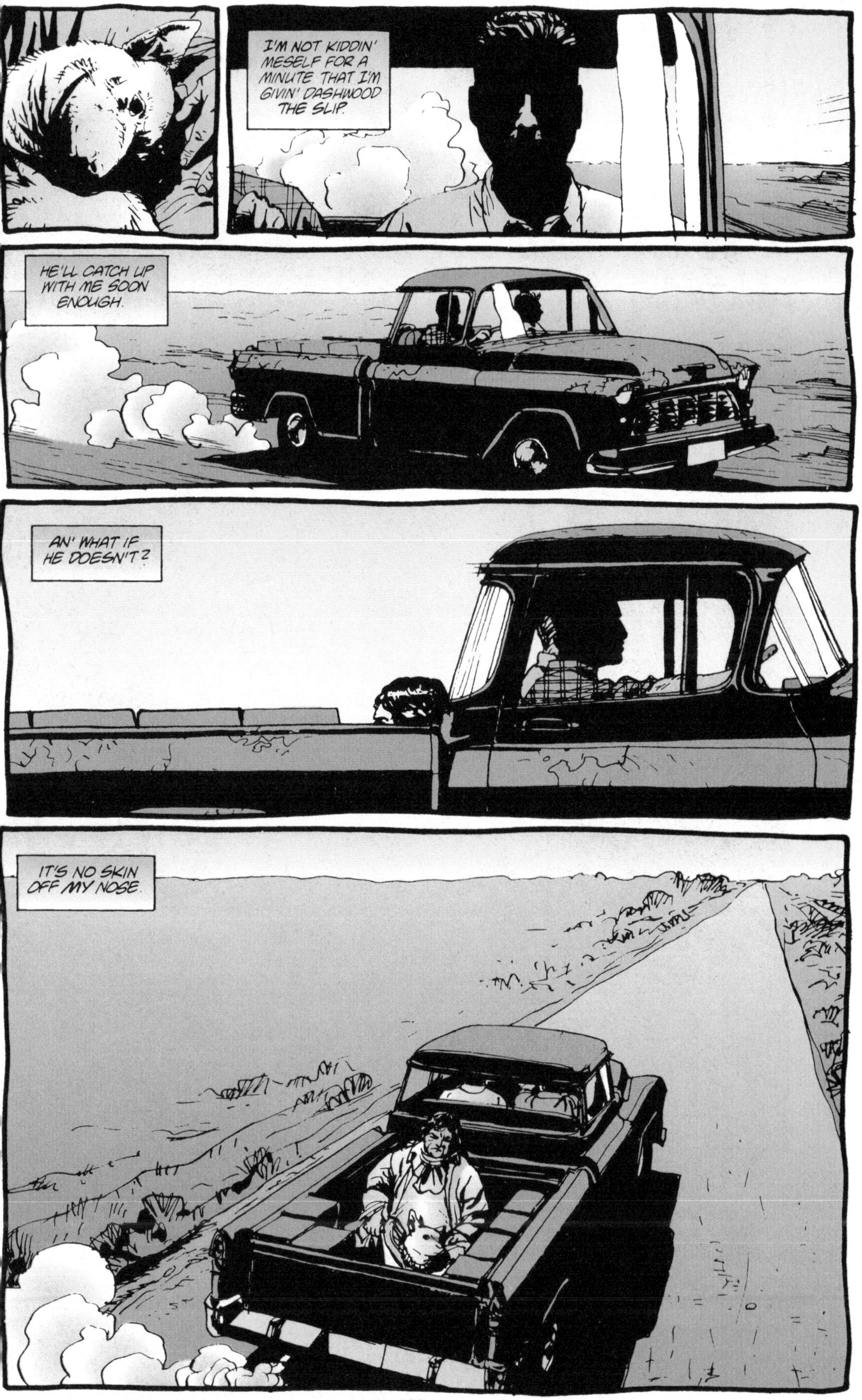
I'M NOT KIDDIN' MESELF FOR A MINUTE THAT I'M GIVIN' DASHWOOD THE SLIP.
HE'LL CATCH UP WITH ME SOON ENOUGH.
AN' WHAT IF HE DOESN'T?
IT'S NO SKIN OFF MY NOSE.

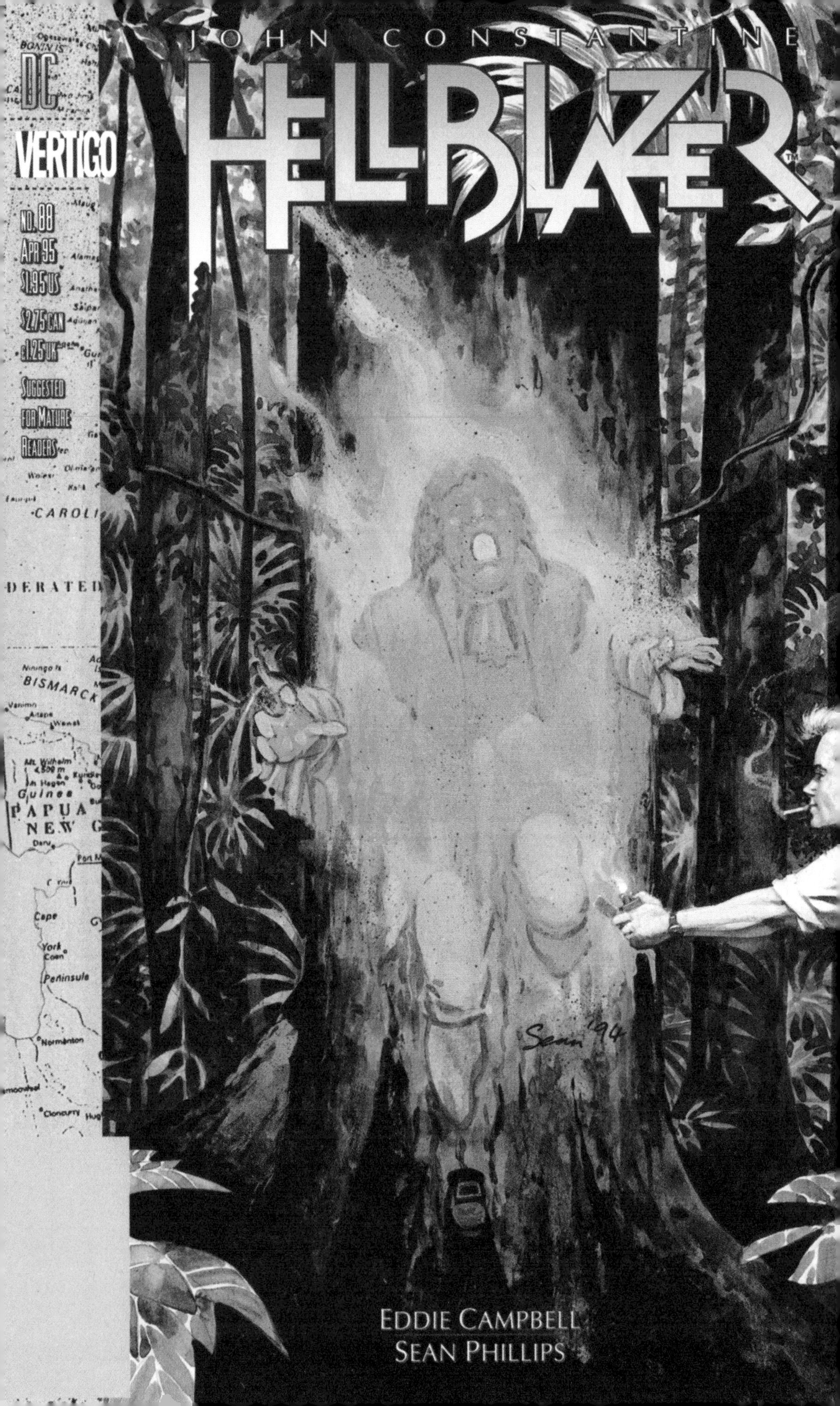

JOHN CONSTANTINE
HELLBLAZER
DC
VERTIGO
NO. 88
APR 95
$1.95 US
$2.75 CAN
£1.25 UK
SUGGESTED FOR MATURE READERS
Sean '94
EDDIE CAMPBELL
SEAN PHILLIPS

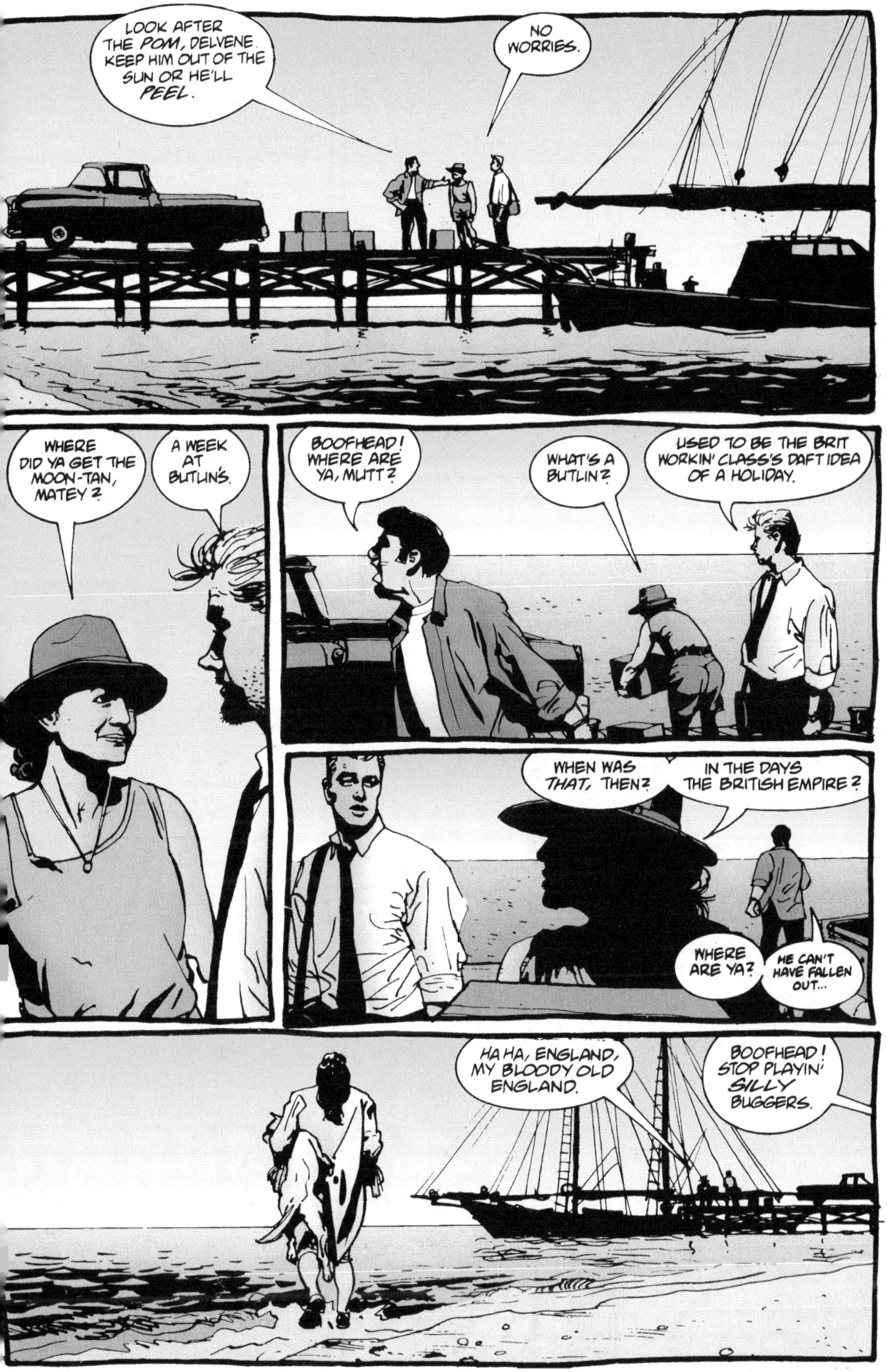
LOOK AFTER THE POM, DELVENE. KEEP HIM OUT OF THE SUN OR HE'LL PEEL.
NO WORRIES.
WHERE DID YA GET THE MOON-TAN, MATEY?
A WEEK AT BUTLIN'S.
BOOFHEAD! WHERE ARE YA, MUTT?
WHAT'S A BUTLIN?
USED TO BE THE BRIT WORKIN' CLASS'S DAFT IDEA OF A HOLIDAY.
WHEN WAS THAT, THEN?
IN THE DAYS THE BRITISH EMPIRE?
WHERE ARE YA?
HE CAN'T HAVE FALLEN OUT...
HA HA, ENGLAND, MY BLOODY OLD ENGLAND.
BOOFHEAD! STOP PLAYIN' SILLY BUGGERS.

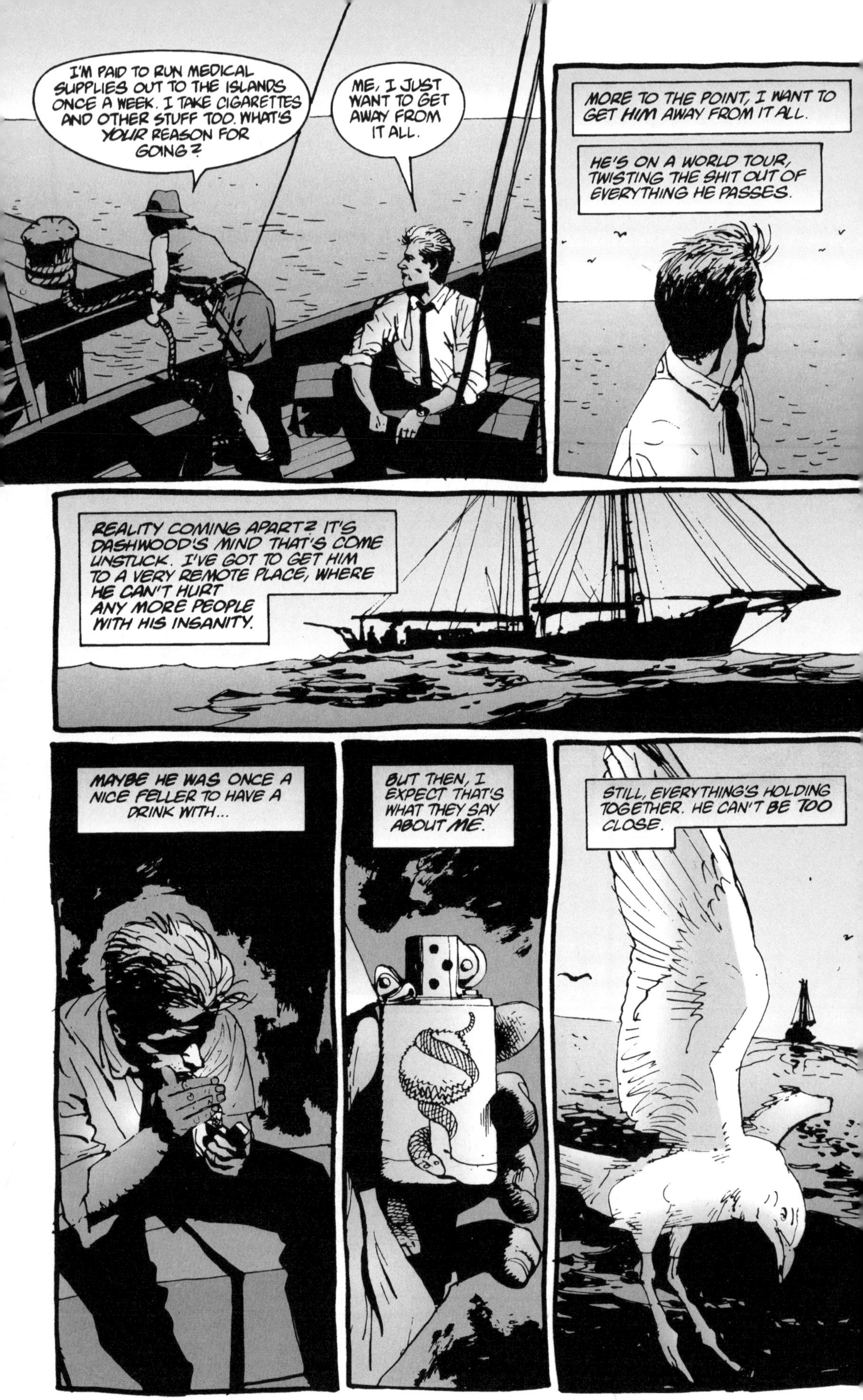
I'M PAID TO RUN MEDICAL SUPPLIES OUT TO THE ISLANDS ONCE A WEEK. I TAKE CIGARETTES AND OTHER STUFF TOO. WHAT'S YOUR REASON FOR GOING?
ME, I JUST WANT TO GET AWAY FROM IT ALL.
MORE TO THE POINT, I WANT TO GET HIM AWAY FROM IT ALL.
HE'S ON A WORLD TOUR, TWISTING THE SHIT OUT OF EVERYTHING HE PASSES.
REALITY COMING APART? IT'S DASHWOOD'S MIND THAT'S COME UNSTUCK. I'VE GOT TO GET HIM TO A VERY REMOTE PLACE, WHERE HE CAN'T HURT ANY MORE PEOPLE WITH HIS INSANITY.
MAYBE HE WAS ONCE A NICE FELLER TO HAVE A DRINK WITH...
BUT THEN, I EXPECT THAT'S WHAT THEY SAY ABOUT ME.
STILL, EVERYTHING'S HOLDING TOGETHER. HE CAN'T BE TOO CLOSE.

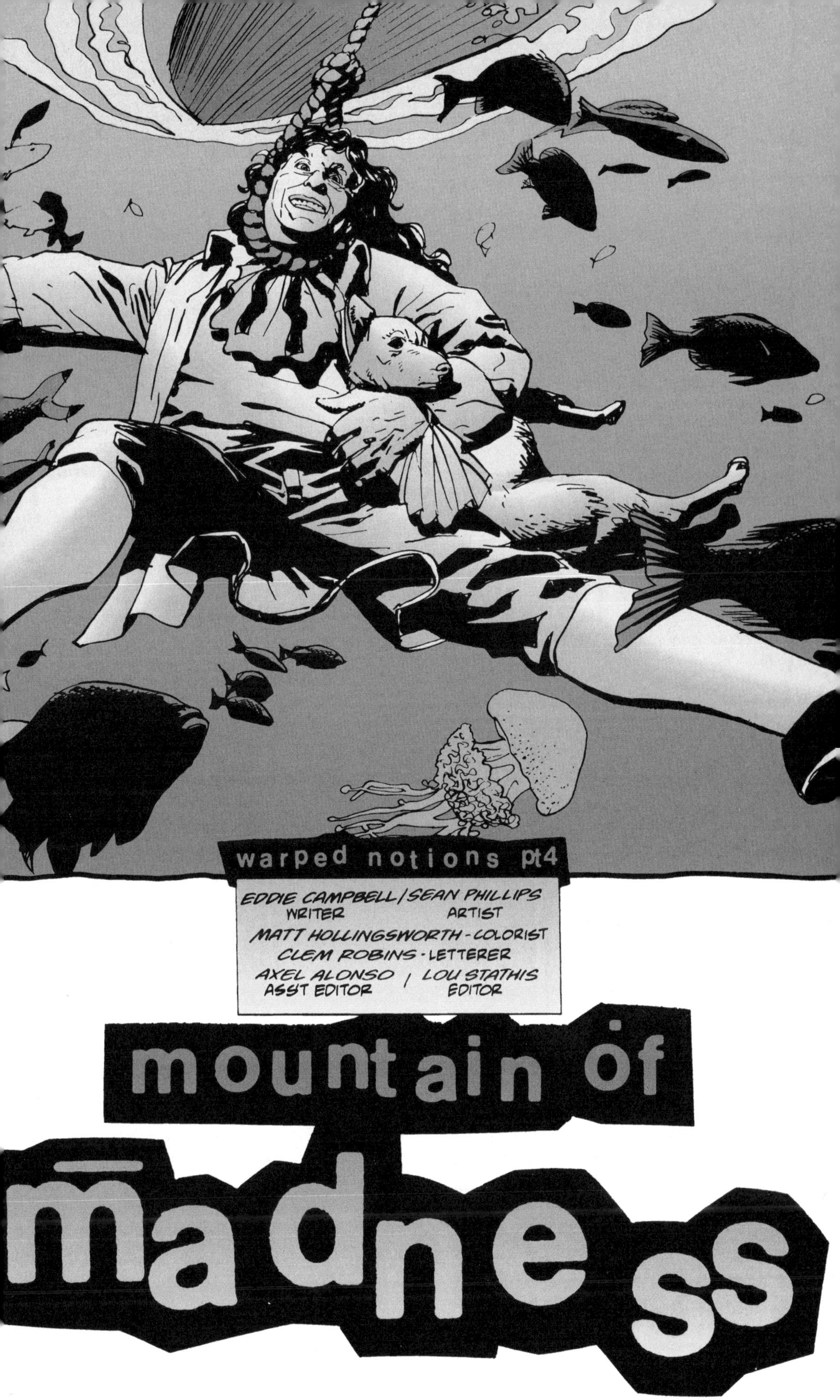
warped notions pt4

EDDIE CAMPBELL / SEAN PHILLIPS
WRITER / ARTIST
MATT HOLLINGSWORTH - COLORIST
CLEM ROBINS - LETTERER
AXEL ALONSO / LOU STATHIS
ASS'T EDITOR / EDITOR

mountain of madness

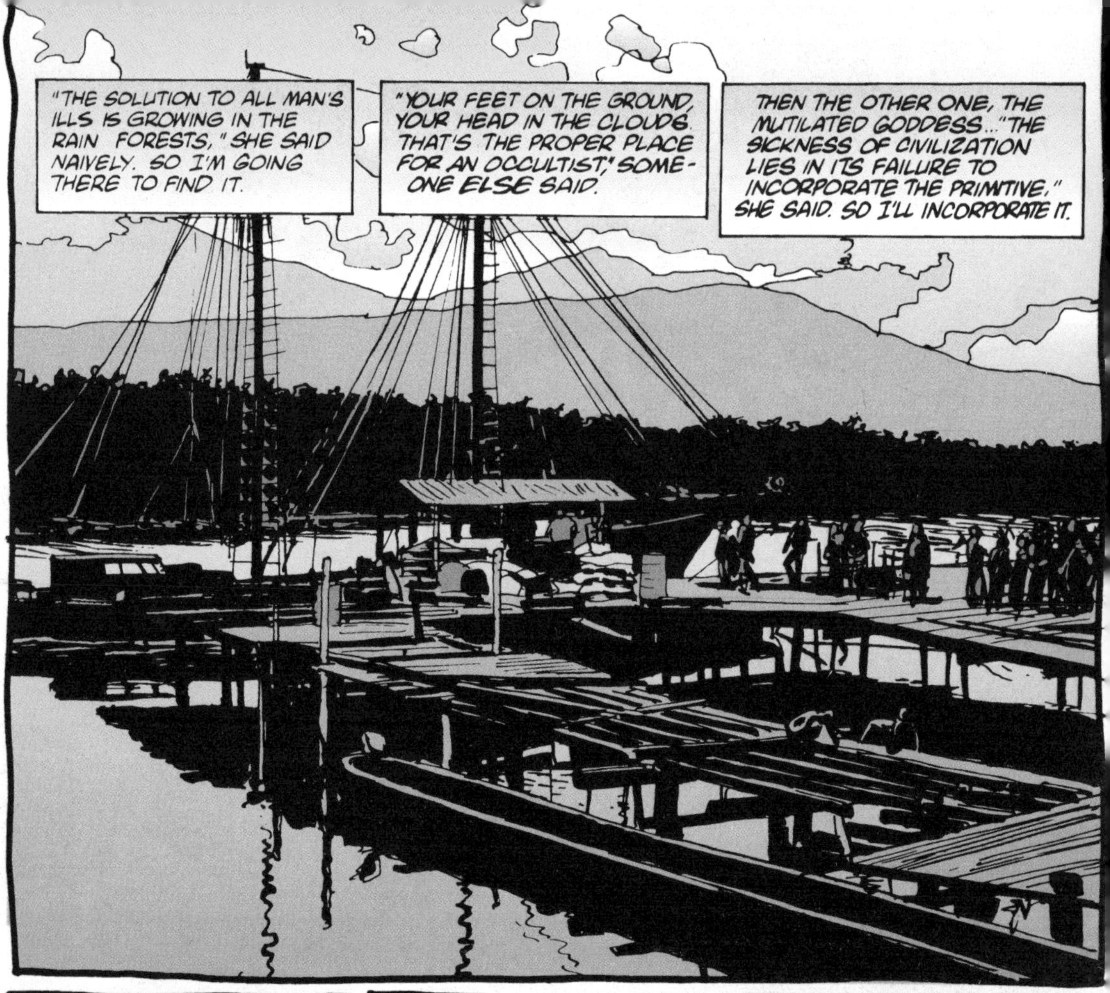
"THE SOLUTION TO ALL MAN'S ILLS IS GROWING IN THE RAIN FORESTS," SHE SAID NAIVELY. SO I'M GOING THERE TO FIND IT.
"YOUR FEET ON THE GROUND, YOUR HEAD IN THE CLOUDS. THAT'S THE PROPER PLACE FOR AN OCCULTIST," SOME-ONE ELSE SAID.
THEN THE OTHER ONE, THE MUTILATED GODDESS..."THE SICKNESS OF CIVILIZATION LIES IN ITS FAILURE TO INCORPORATE THE PRIMITIVE," SHE SAID. SO I'LL INCORPORATE IT.

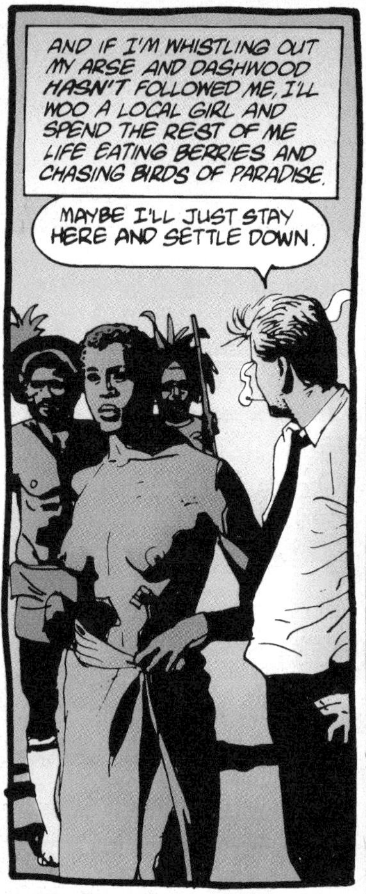
AND IF I'M WHISTLING OUT MY ARSE AND DASHWOOD HASN'T FOLLOWED ME, I'LL WOO A LOCAL GIRL AND SPEND THE REST OF ME LIFE EATING BERRIES AND CHASING BIRDS OF PARADISE.
MAYBE I'LL JUST STAY HERE AND SETTLE DOWN.

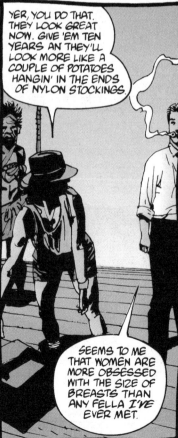

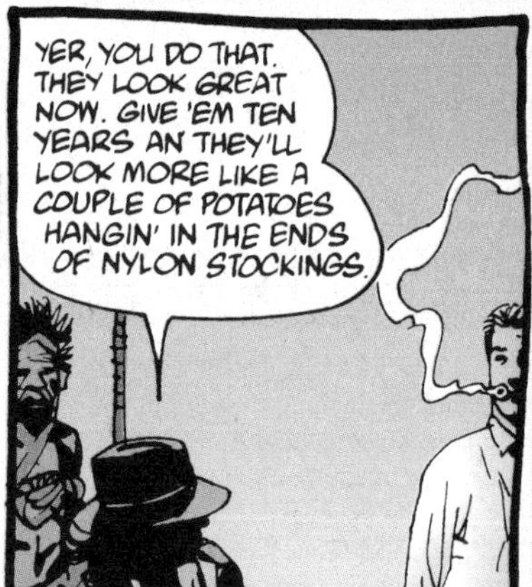
YER, YOU DO THAT. THEY LOOK GREAT NOW. GIVE 'EM TEN YEARS AN THEY'LL LOOK MORE LIKE A COUPLE OF POTATOES HANGIN' IN THE ENDS OF NYLON STOCKINGS.
SEEMS TO ME THAT WOMEN ARE MORE OBSESSED WITH THE SIZE OF BREASTS THAN ANY FELLA I'VE EVER MET.

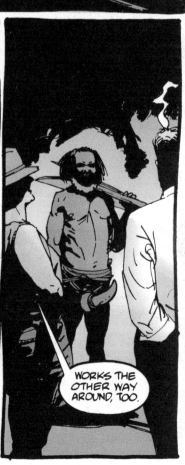

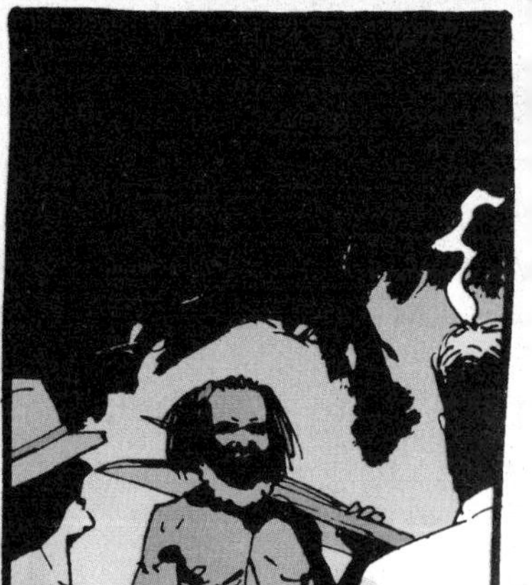
WORKS THE OTHER WAY AROUND, TOO.

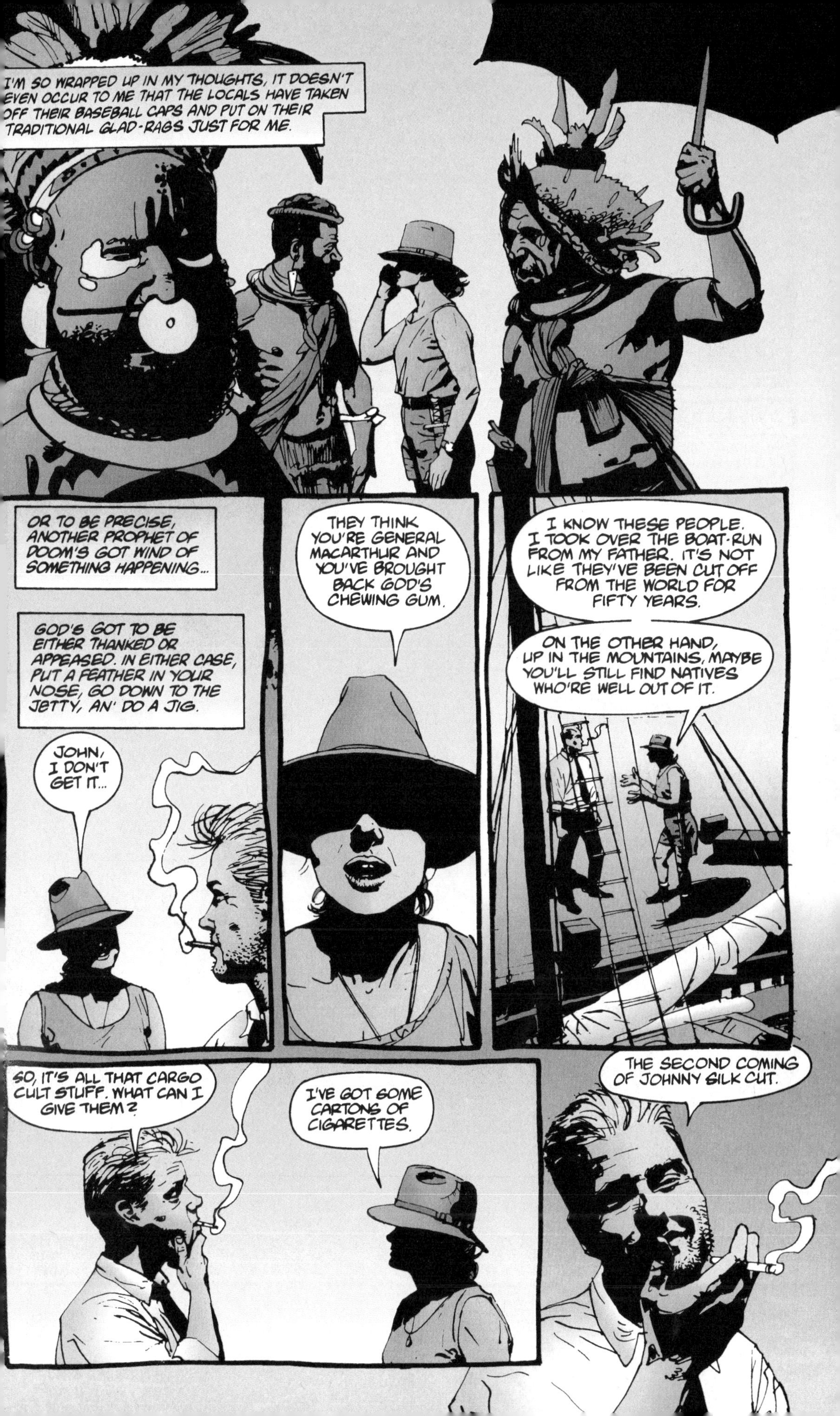
I'M SO WRAPPED UP IN MY THOUGHTS, IT DOESN'T EVEN OCCUR TO ME THAT THE LOCALS HAVE TAKEN OFF THEIR BASEBALL CAPS AND PUT ON THEIR TRADITIONAL GLAD-RAGS JUST FOR ME.
OR TO BE PRECISE, ANOTHER PROPHET OF DOOM'S GOT WIND OF SOMETHING HAPPENING...
GOD'S GOT TO BE EITHER THANKED OR APPEASED. IN EITHER CASE, PUT A FEATHER IN YOUR NOSE, GO DOWN TO THE JETTY, AN' DO A JIG.
JOHN, I DON'T GET IT...
THEY THINK YOU'RE GENERAL MACARTHUR AND YOU'VE BROUGHT BACK GOD'S CHEWING GUM.
I KNOW THESE PEOPLE. I TOOK OVER THE BOAT-RUN FROM MY FATHER. IT'S NOT LIKE THEY'VE BEEN CUT OFF FROM THE WORLD FOR FIFTY YEARS.
ON THE OTHER HAND, UP IN THE MOUNTAINS, MAYBE YOU'LL STILL FIND NATIVES WHO'RE WELL OUT OF IT.
SO, IT'S ALL THAT CARGO CULT STUFF. WHAT CAN I GIVE THEM?
I'VE GOT SOME CARTONS OF CIGARETTES.
THE SECOND COMING OF JOHNNY SILK CUT.

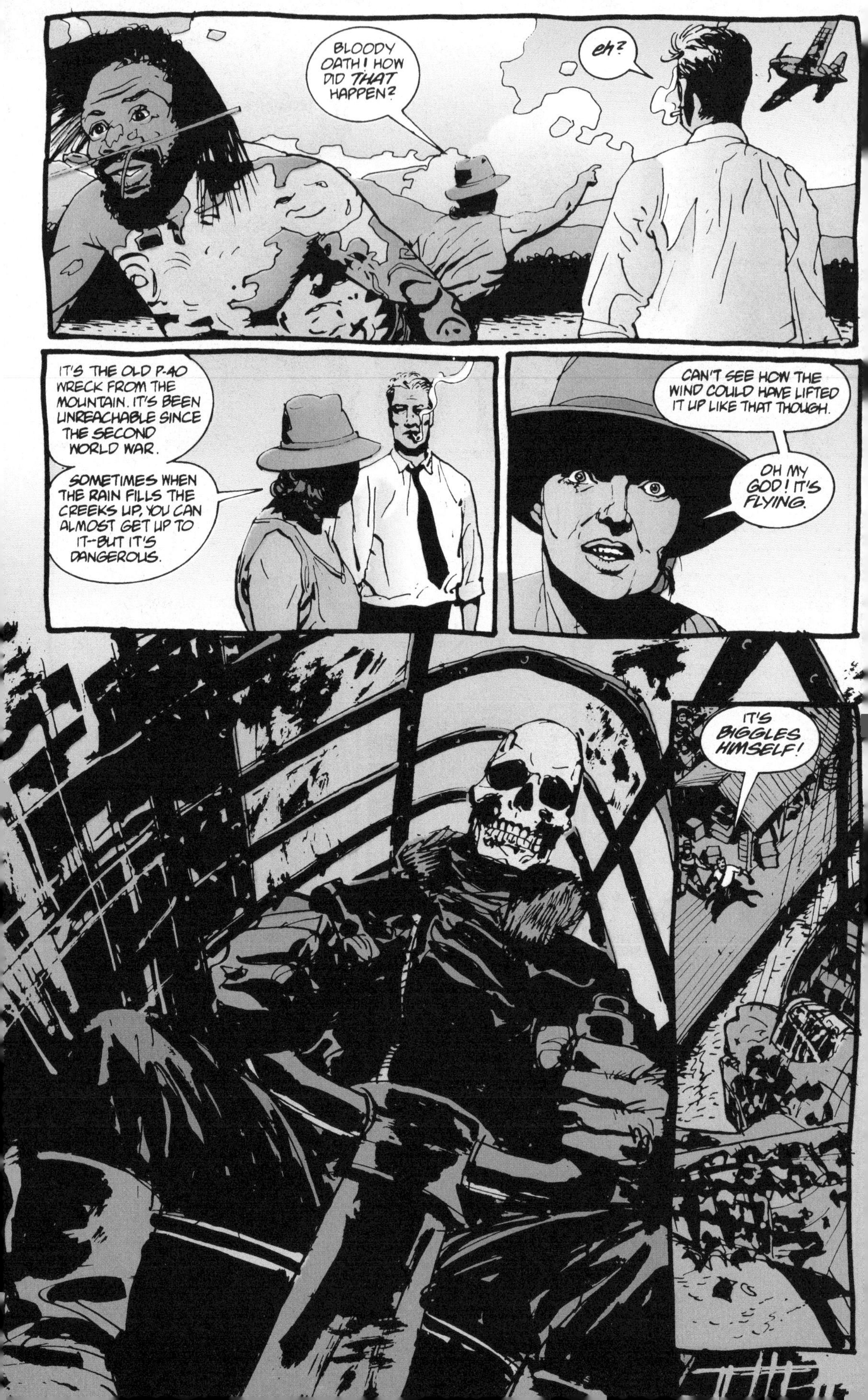
BLOODY OATH! HOW DID THAT HAPPEN?
eh?
IT'S THE OLD P-40 WRECK FROM THE MOUNTAIN. IT'S BEEN UNREACHABLE SINCE THE SECOND WORLD WAR.
SOMETIMES WHEN THE RAIN FILLS THE CREEKS UP, YOU CAN ALMOST GET UP TO IT--BUT IT'S DANGEROUS.
CAN'T SEE HOW THE WIND COULD HAVE LIFTED IT UP LIKE THAT THOUGH.
OH MY GOD! IT'S FLYING.
IT'S BIGGLES HIMSELF!

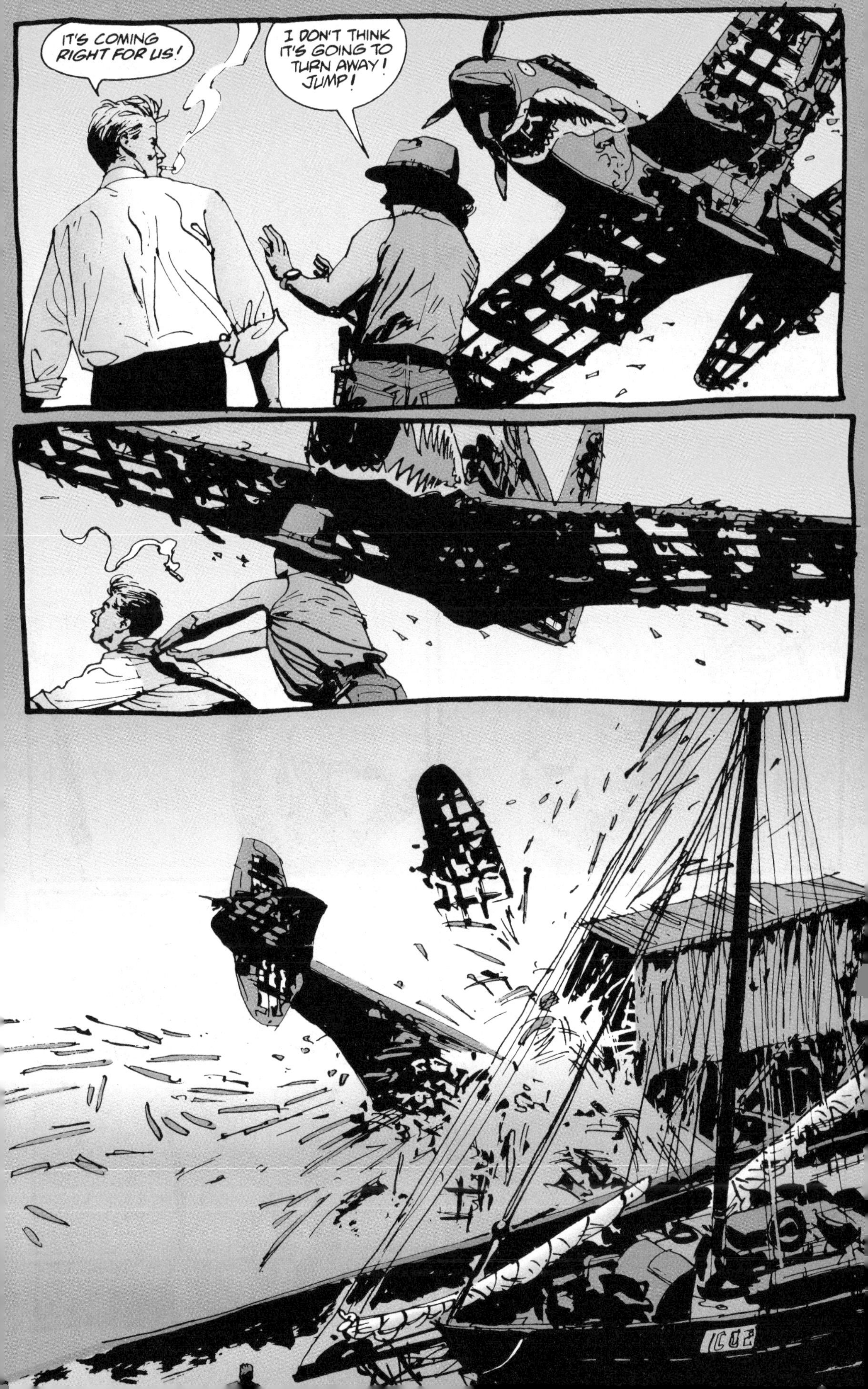
IT'S COMING RIGHT FOR US!
I DON'T THINK IT'S GOING TO TURN AWAY! JUMP!

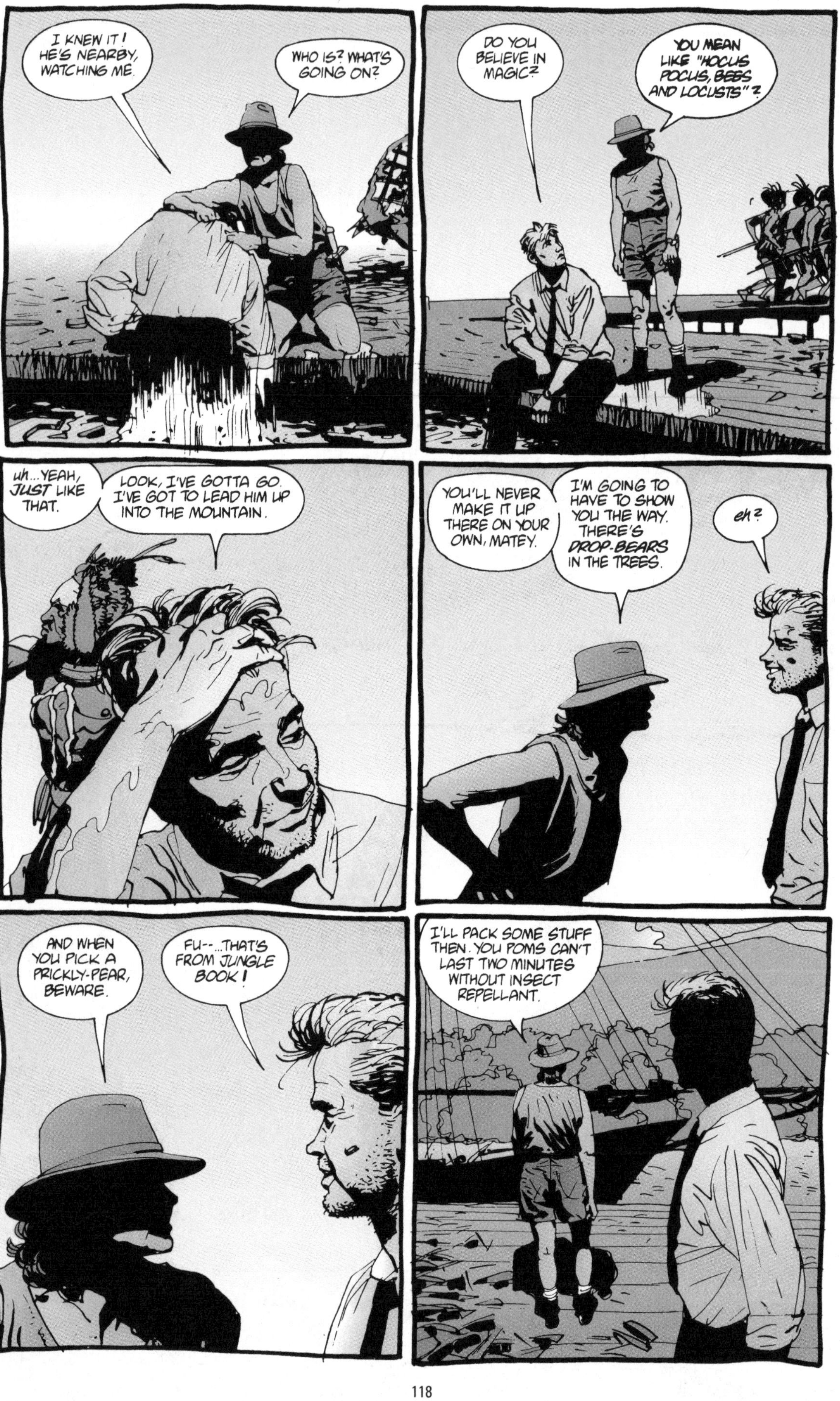
I KNEW IT! HE'S NEARBY, WATCHING ME.
WHO IS? WHAT'S GOING ON?
DO YOU BELIEVE IN MAGIC?
YOU MEAN LIKE "HOCUS POCUS, BEES AND LOCUSTS"?
uh...YEAH, JUST LIKE THAT.
LOOK, I'VE GOTTA GO. I'VE GOT TO LEAD HIM UP INTO THE MOUNTAIN.
YOU'LL NEVER MAKE IT UP THERE ON YOUR OWN, MATEY.
I'M GOING TO HAVE TO SHOW YOU THE WAY. THERE'S DROP-BEARS IN THE TREES.
eh?
AND WHEN YOU PICK A PRICKLY-PEAR, BEWARE.
FU--...THAT'S FROM JUNGLE BOOK!
I'LL PACK SOME STUFF THEN. YOU POMS CAN'T LAST TWO MINUTES WITHOUT INSECT REPELLANT.

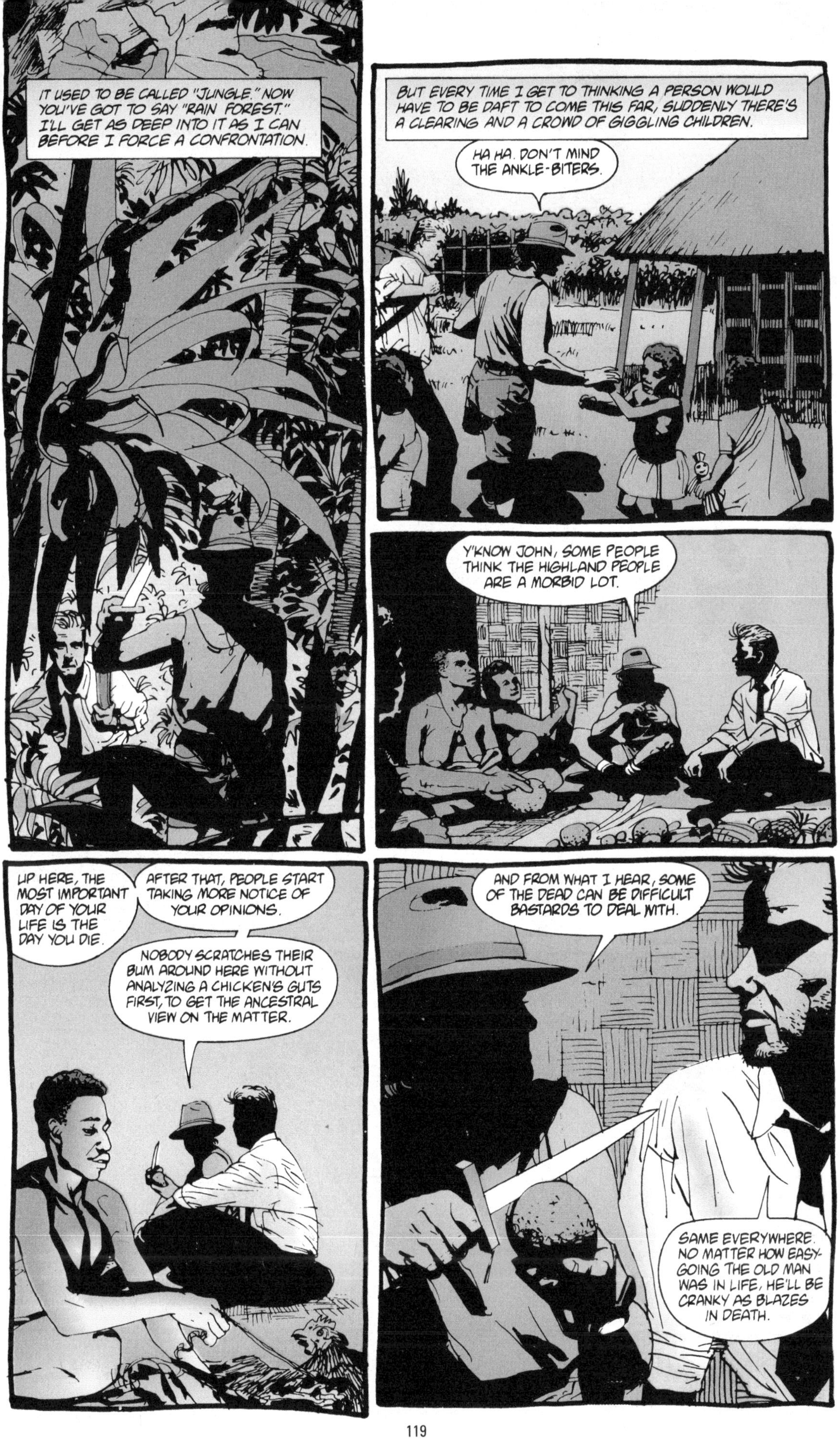
IT USED TO BE CALLED "JUNGLE." NOW YOU'VE GOT TO SAY "RAIN FOREST." I'LL GET AS DEEP INTO IT AS I CAN BEFORE I FORCE A CONFRONTATION.
BUT EVERY TIME I GET TO THINKING A PERSON WOULD HAVE TO BE DAFT TO COME THIS FAR, SUDDENLY THERE'S A CLEARING AND A CROWD OF GIGGLING CHILDREN.
HA HA. DON'T MIND THE ANKLE-BITERS.
Y'KNOW JOHN, SOME PEOPLE THINK THE HIGHLAND PEOPLE ARE A MORBID LOT.
UP HERE, THE MOST IMPORTANT DAY OF YOUR LIFE IS THE DAY YOU DIE.
AFTER THAT, PEOPLE START TAKING MORE NOTICE OF YOUR OPINIONS.
NOBODY SCRATCHES THEIR BUM AROUND HERE WITHOUT ANALYZING A CHICKEN'S GUTS FIRST, TO GET THE ANCESTRAL VIEW ON THE MATTER.
AND FROM WHAT I HEAR, SOME OF THE DEAD CAN BE DIFFICULT BASTARDS TO DEAL WITH.
SAME EVERYWHERE. NO MATTER HOW EASY-GOING THE OLD MAN WAS IN LIFE, HE'LL BE CRANKY AS BLAZES IN DEATH.

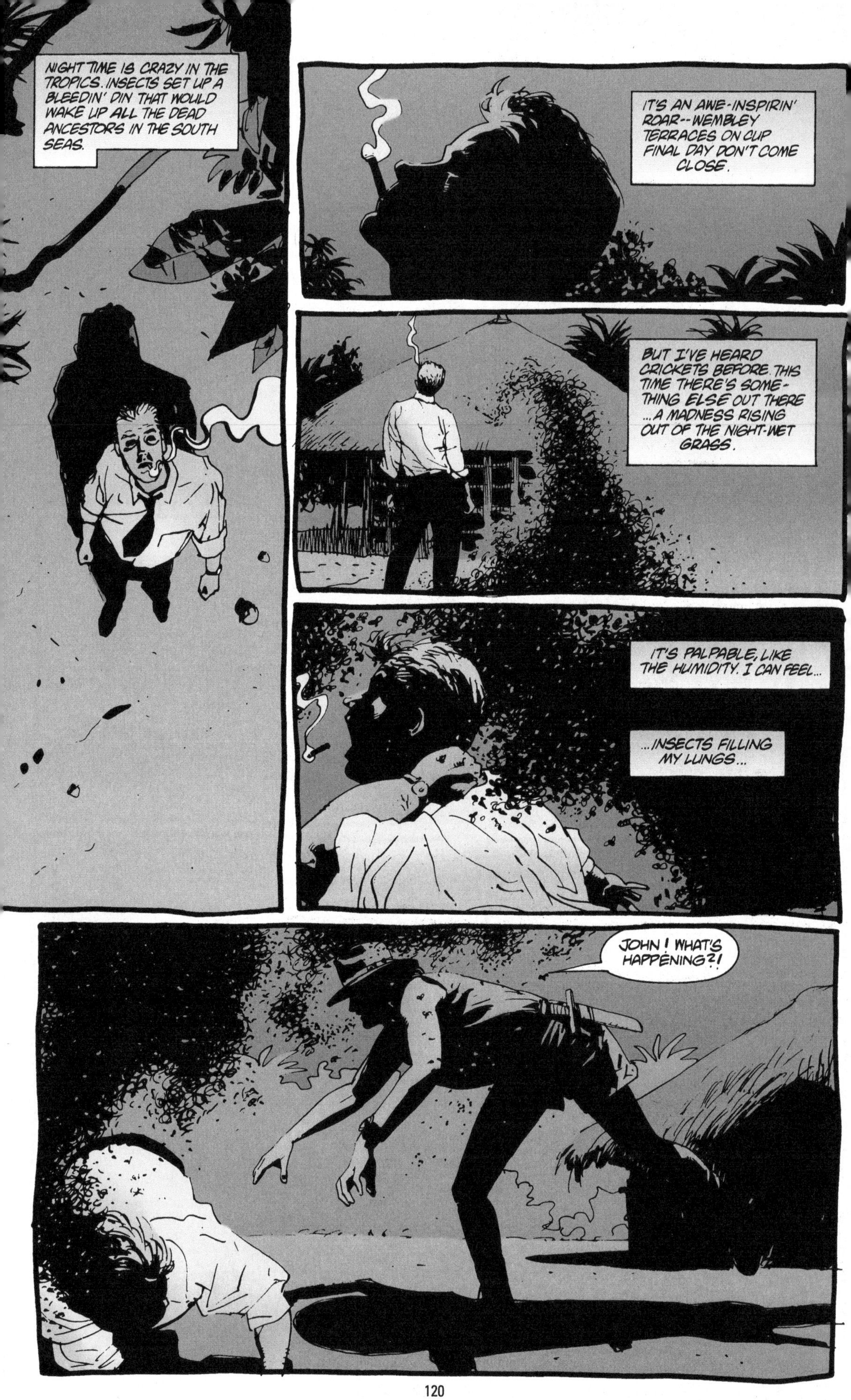
NIGHT TIME IS CRAZY IN THE TROPICS. INSECTS SET UP A BLEEDIN' DIN THAT WOULD WAKE UP ALL THE DEAD ANCESTORS IN THE SOUTH SEAS.
IT'S AN AWE-INSPIRIN' ROAR--WEMBLEY TERRACES ON CUP FINAL DAY DON'T COME CLOSE.
BUT I'VE HEARD CRICKETS BEFORE. THIS TIME THERE'S SOME-THING ELSE OUT THERE ...A MADNESS RISING OUT OF THE NIGHT-WET GRASS.
IT'S PALPABLE, LIKE THE HUMIDITY. I CAN FEEL...
...INSECTS FILLING MY LUNGS...
JOHN! WHAT'S HAPPENING?!

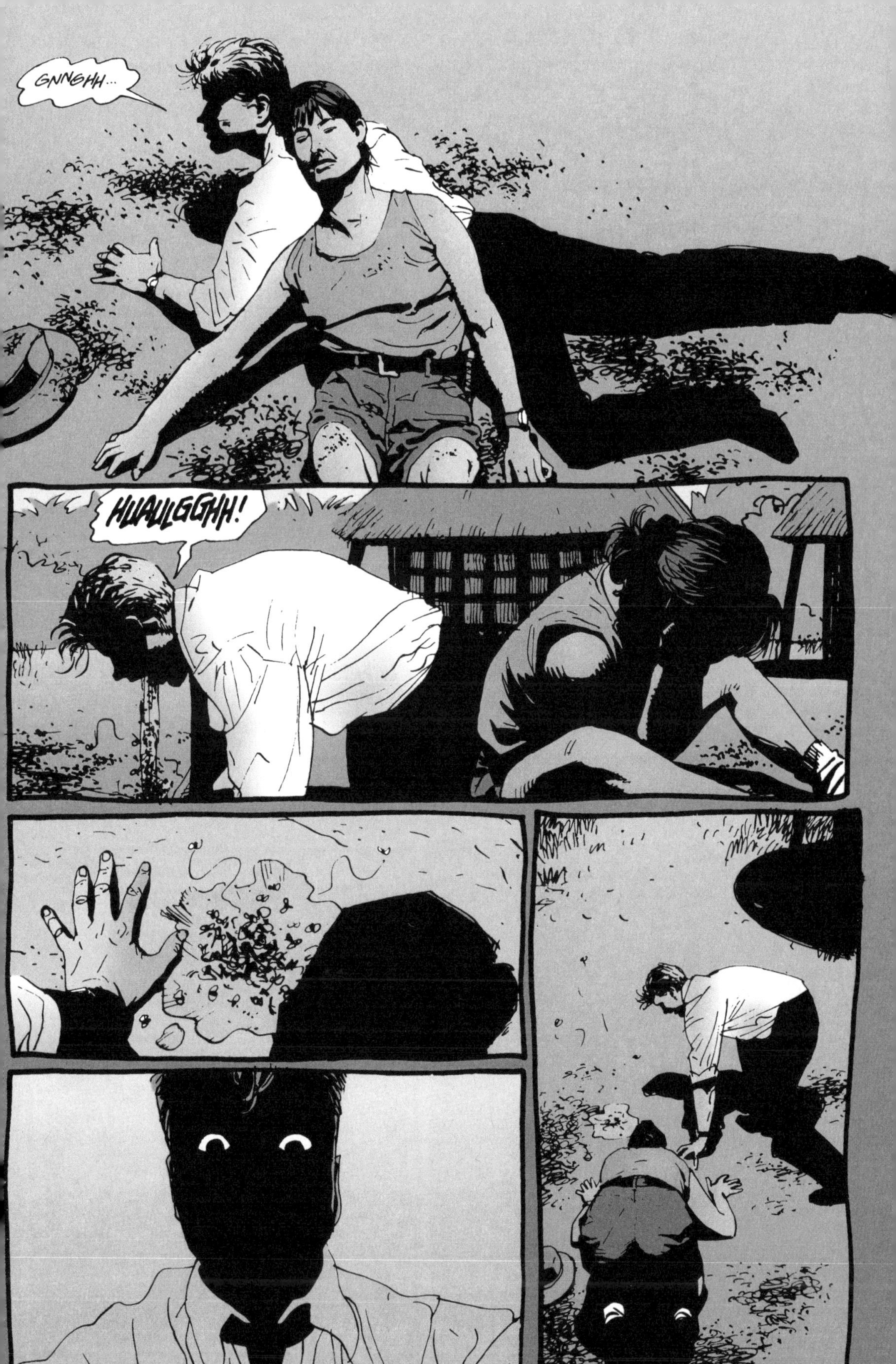
GNNGHH...
HUAULGGHH!

THE PLACE IS DESERTED, JOHN.

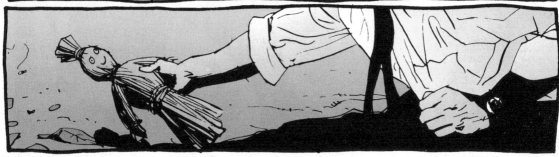

WHAT'S THROUGH THERE--THE VILLAGERS?

NONE THAT ARE STILL LIVING.

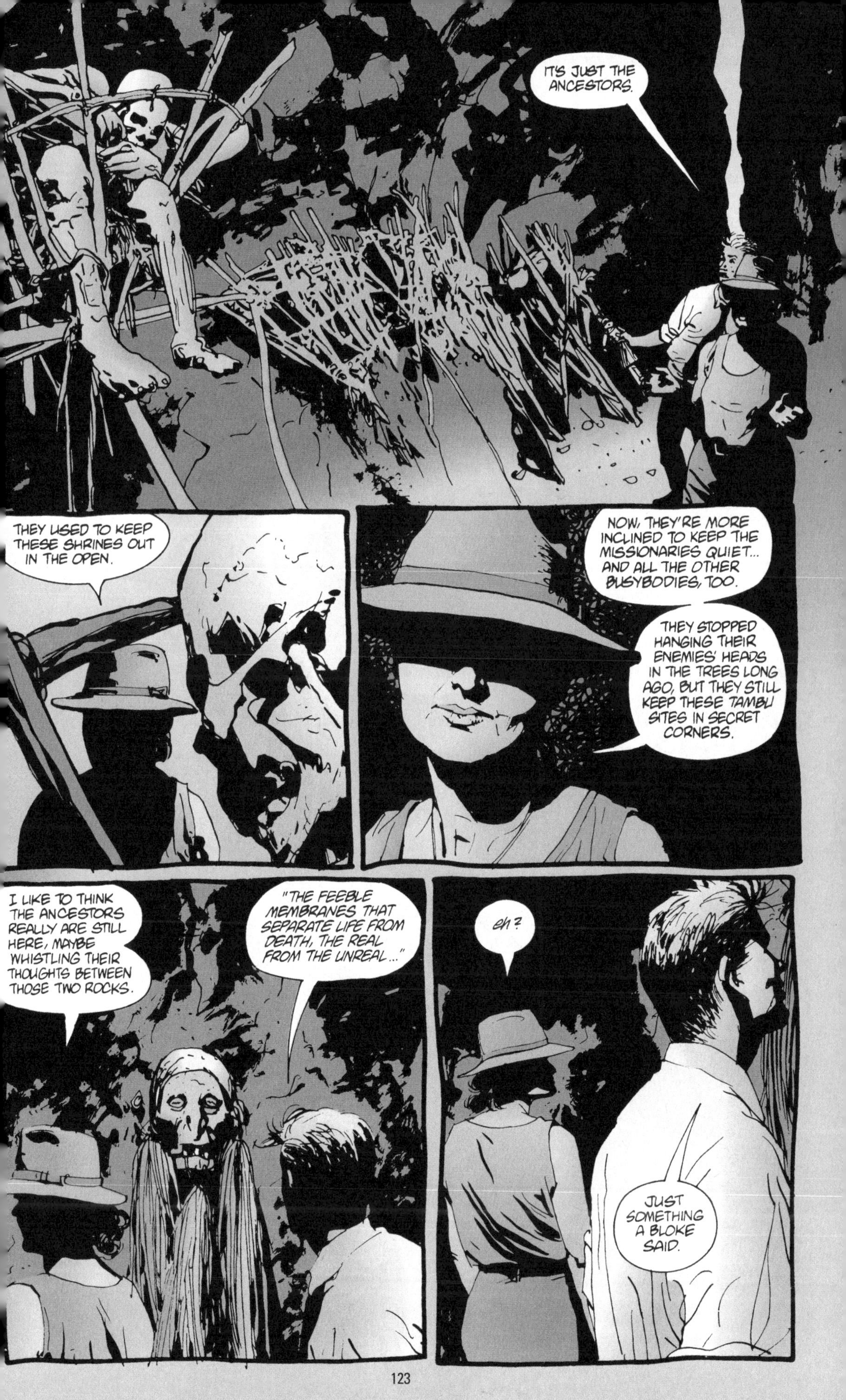
IT'S JUST THE ANCESTORS.
THEY USED TO KEEP THESE SHRINES OUT IN THE OPEN.
NOW, THEY'RE MORE INCLINED TO KEEP THE MISSIONARIES QUIET... AND ALL THE OTHER BUSYBODIES, TOO.
THEY STOPPED HANGING THEIR ENEMIES' HEADS IN THE TREES LONG AGO, BUT THEY STILL KEEP THESE TAMBU SITES IN SECRET CORNERS.
I LIKE TO THINK THE ANCESTORS REALLY ARE STILL HERE, MAYBE WHISTLING THEIR THOUGHTS BETWEEN THOSE TWO ROCKS.
"THE FEEBLE MEMBRANES THAT SEPARATE LIFE FROM DEATH, THE REAL FROM THE UNREAL..."
eh?
JUST SOMETHING A BLOKE SAID.

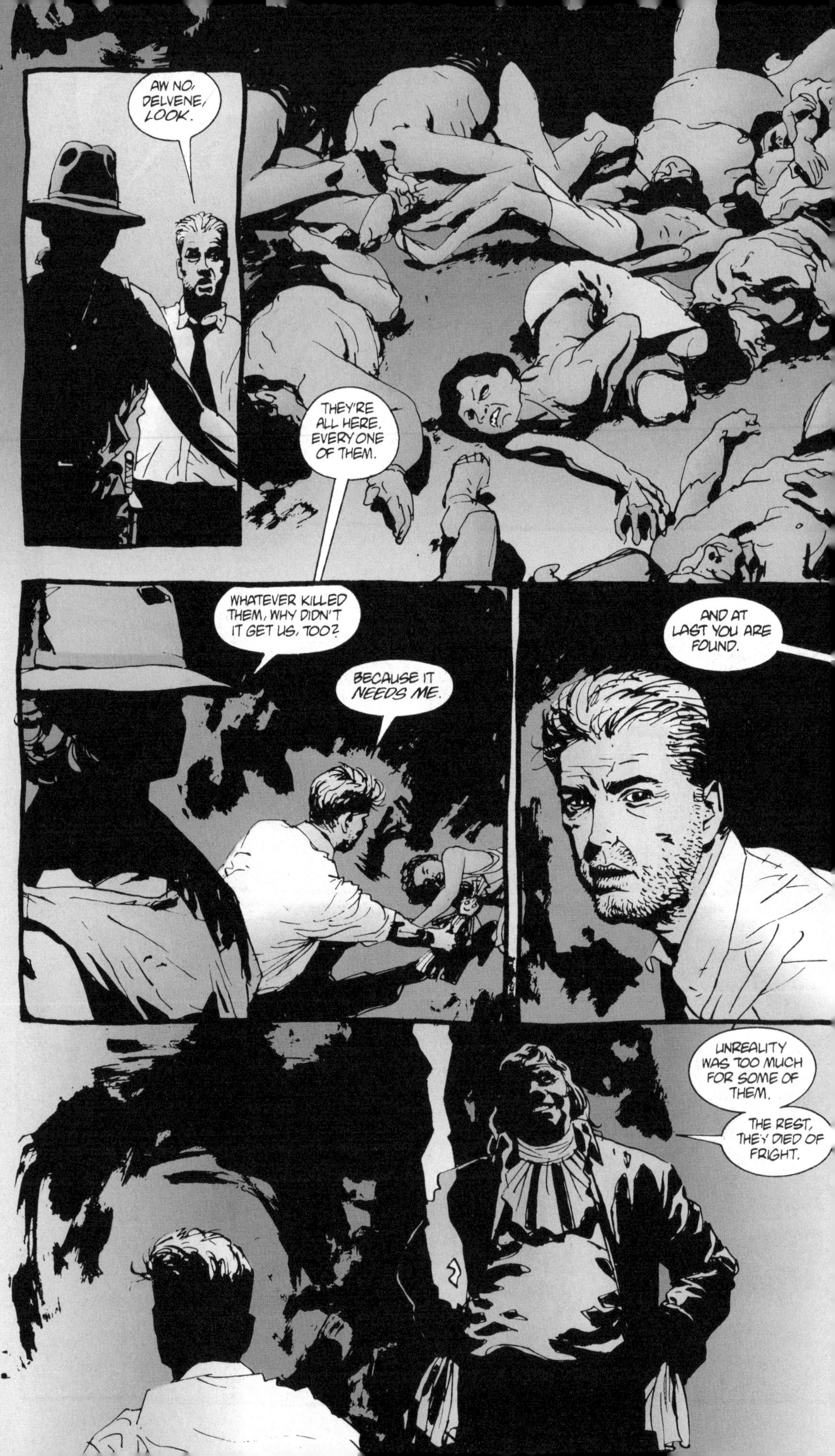
AW NO, DELVENE, LOOK.
THEY'RE ALL HERE. EVERY ONE OF THEM.
WHATEVER KILLED THEM, WHY DIDN'T IT GET US, TOO?
BECAUSE IT NEEDS ME.
AND AT LAST YOU ARE FOUND.
UNREALITY WAS TOO MUCH FOR SOME OF THEM.
THE REST, THEY DIED OF FRIGHT.

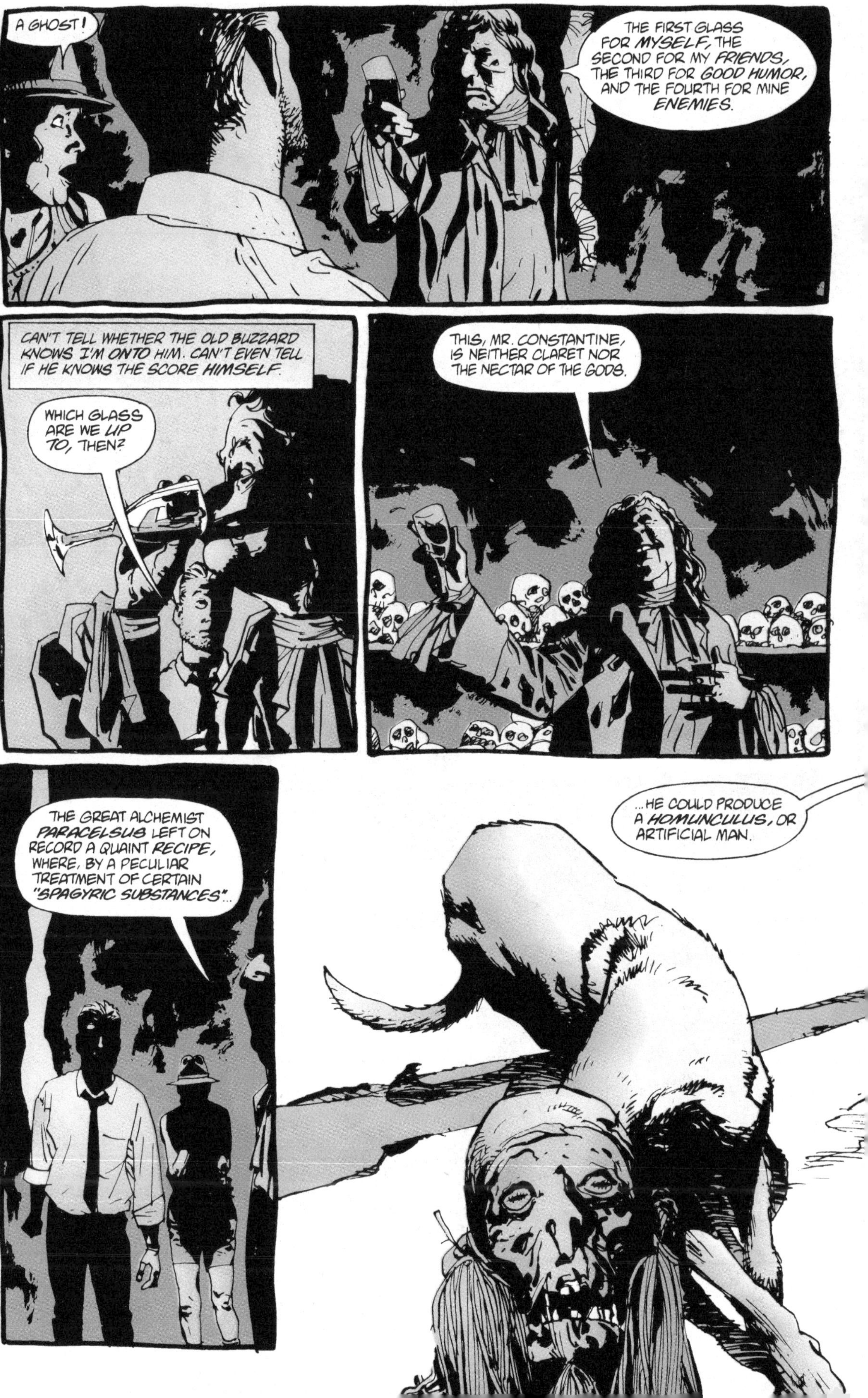
A GHOST!
THE FIRST GLASS FOR MYSELF, THE SECOND FOR MY FRIENDS, THE THIRD FOR GOOD HUMOR, AND THE FOURTH FOR MINE ENEMIES.
CAN'T TELL WHETHER THE OLD BUZZARD KNOWS I'M ONTO HIM. CAN'T EVEN TELL IF HE KNOWS THE SCORE HIMSELF.
WHICH GLASS ARE WE UP TO, THEN?
THIS, MR. CONSTANTINE, IS NEITHER CLARET NOR THE NECTAR OF THE GODS.
THE GREAT ALCHEMIST PARACELSUS LEFT ON RECORD A QUAINT RECIPE, WHERE, BY A PECULIAR TREATMENT OF CERTAIN "SPAGYRIC SUBSTANCES"...
...HE COULD PRODUCE A HOMUNCULUS, OR ARTIFICIAL MAN.

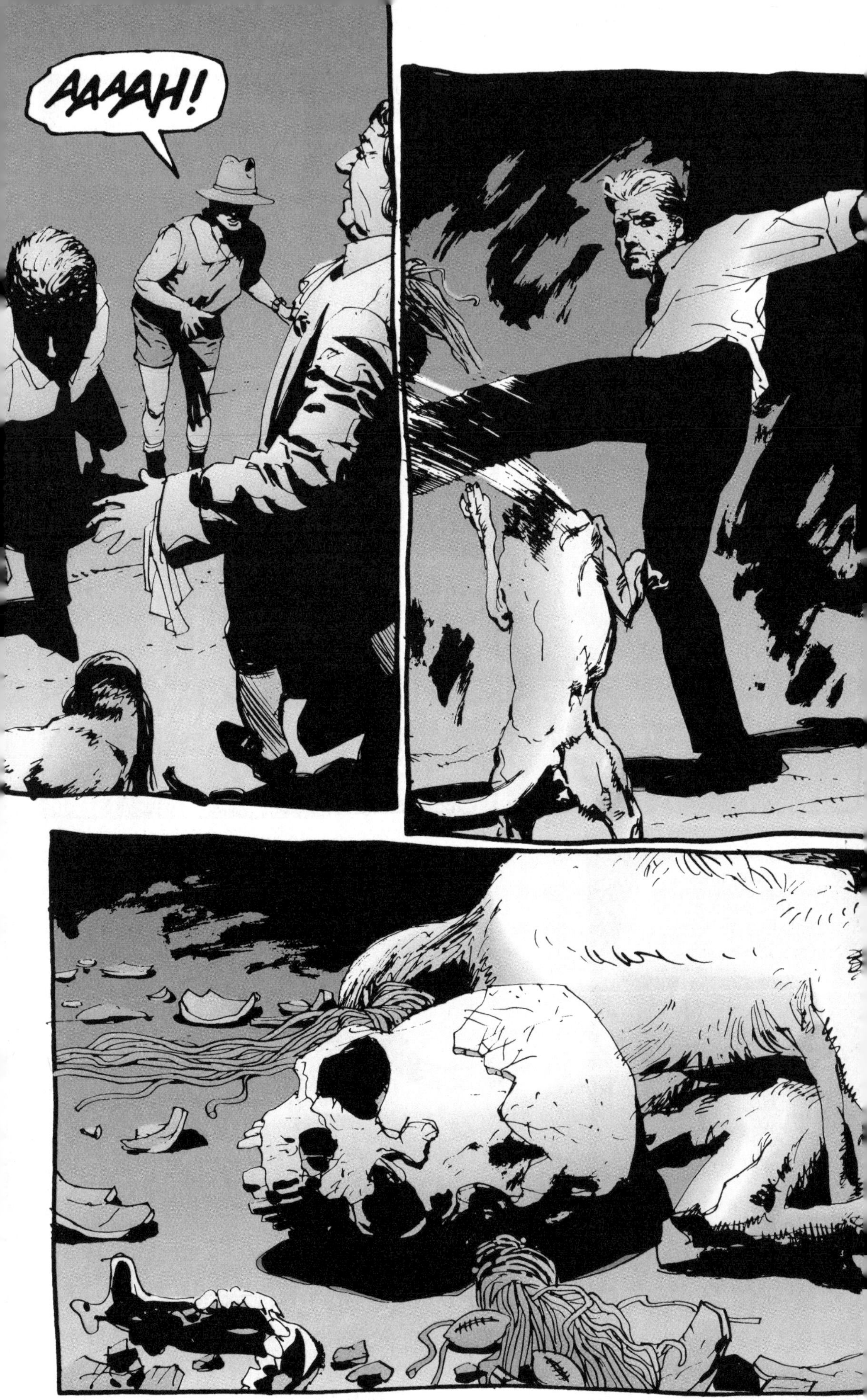
AAAAH!

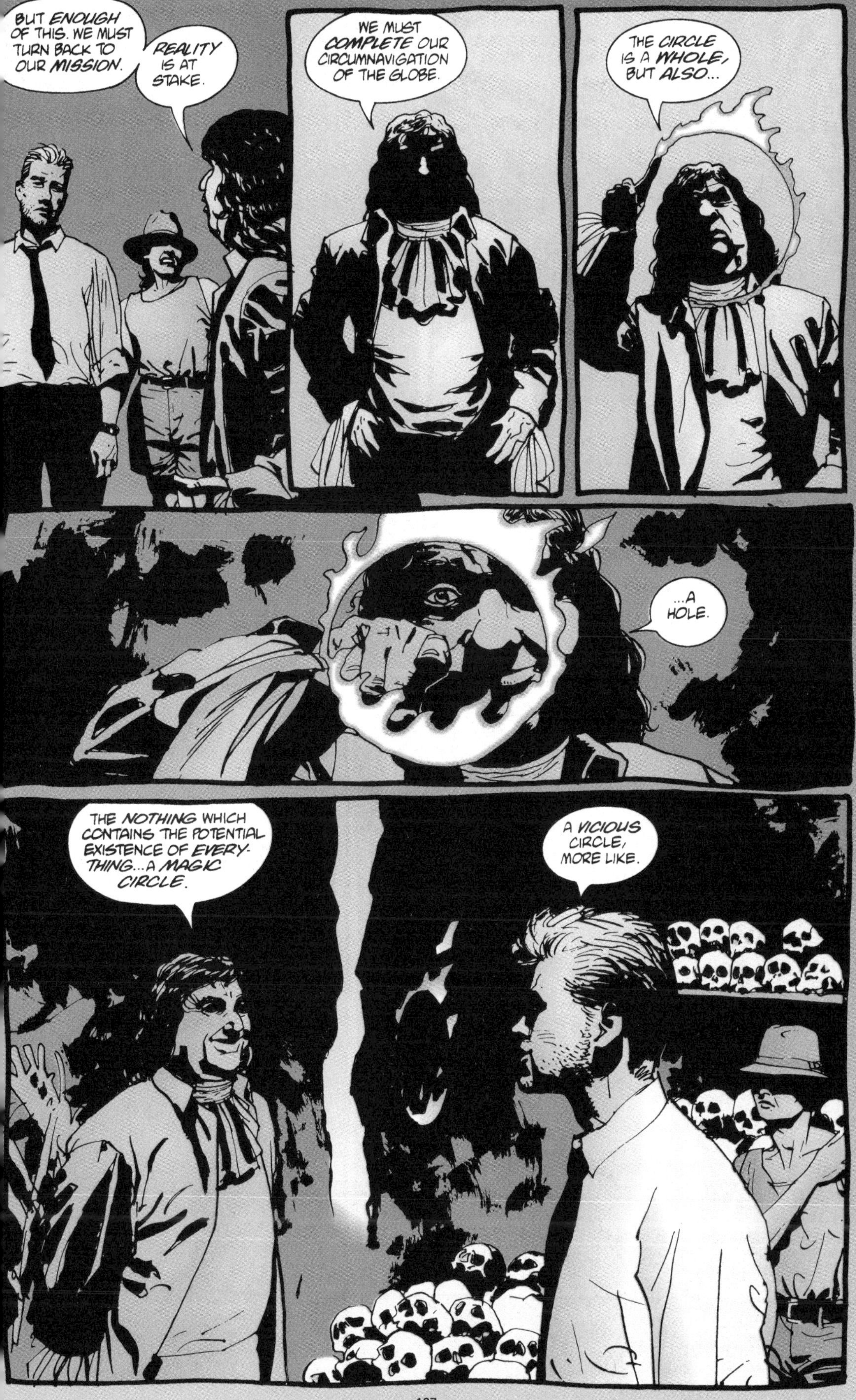
BUT ENOUGH OF THIS. WE MUST TURN BACK TO OUR MISSION.
REALITY IS AT STAKE.
WE MUST COMPLETE OUR CIRCUMNAVIGATION OF THE GLOBE.
THE CIRCLE IS A WHOLE, BUT ALSO...
...A HOLE.
THE NOTHING WHICH CONTAINS THE POTENTIAL EXISTENCE OF EVERY-THING...A MAGIC CIRCLE.
A VICIOUS CIRCLE, MORE LIKE.

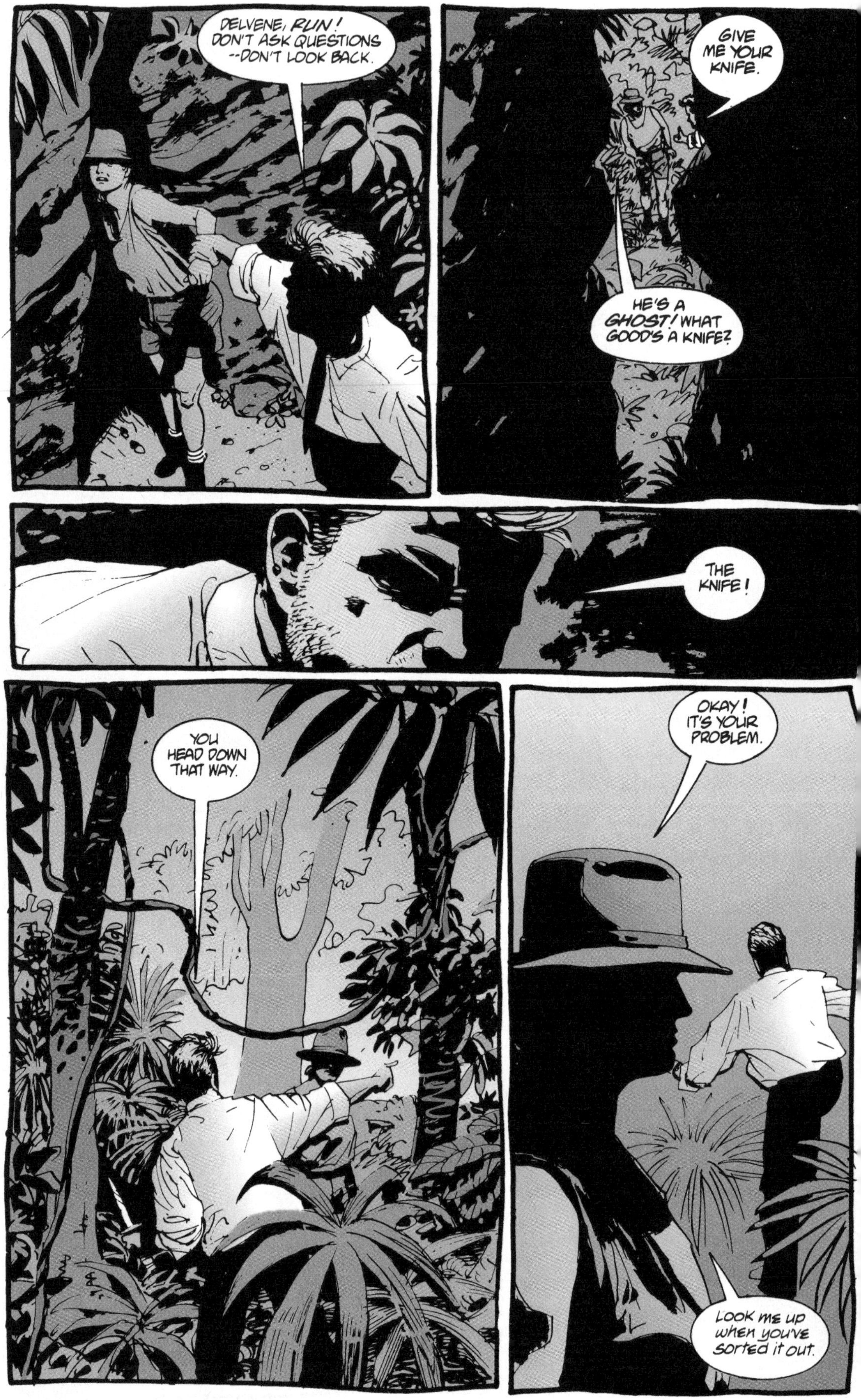
DELVENE, RUN! DON'T ASK QUESTIONS --DON'T LOOK BACK.
GIVE ME YOUR KNIFE.
HE'S A GHOST! WHAT GOOD'S A KNIFE?
THE KNIFE!
YOU HEAD DOWN THAT WAY.
OKAY! IT'S YOUR PROBLEM.
Look me up when you've sorted it out.

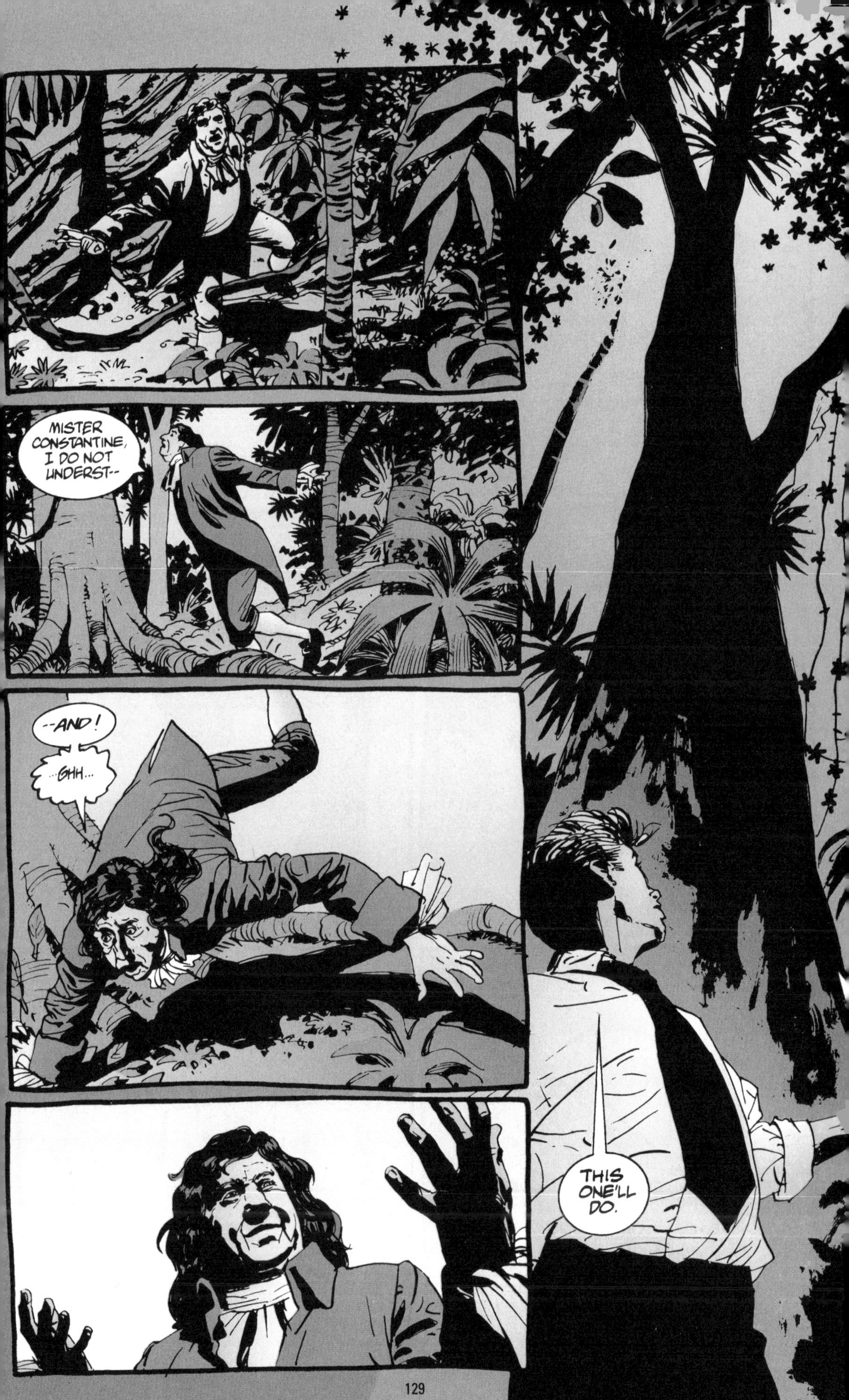
MISTER CONSTANTINE, I DO NOT UNDERST--
--AND!
...GHH...
THIS ONE'LL DO.

CONSTANTINE!

GOTTA WORK FAST.

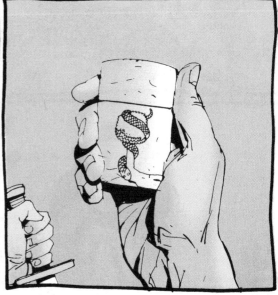

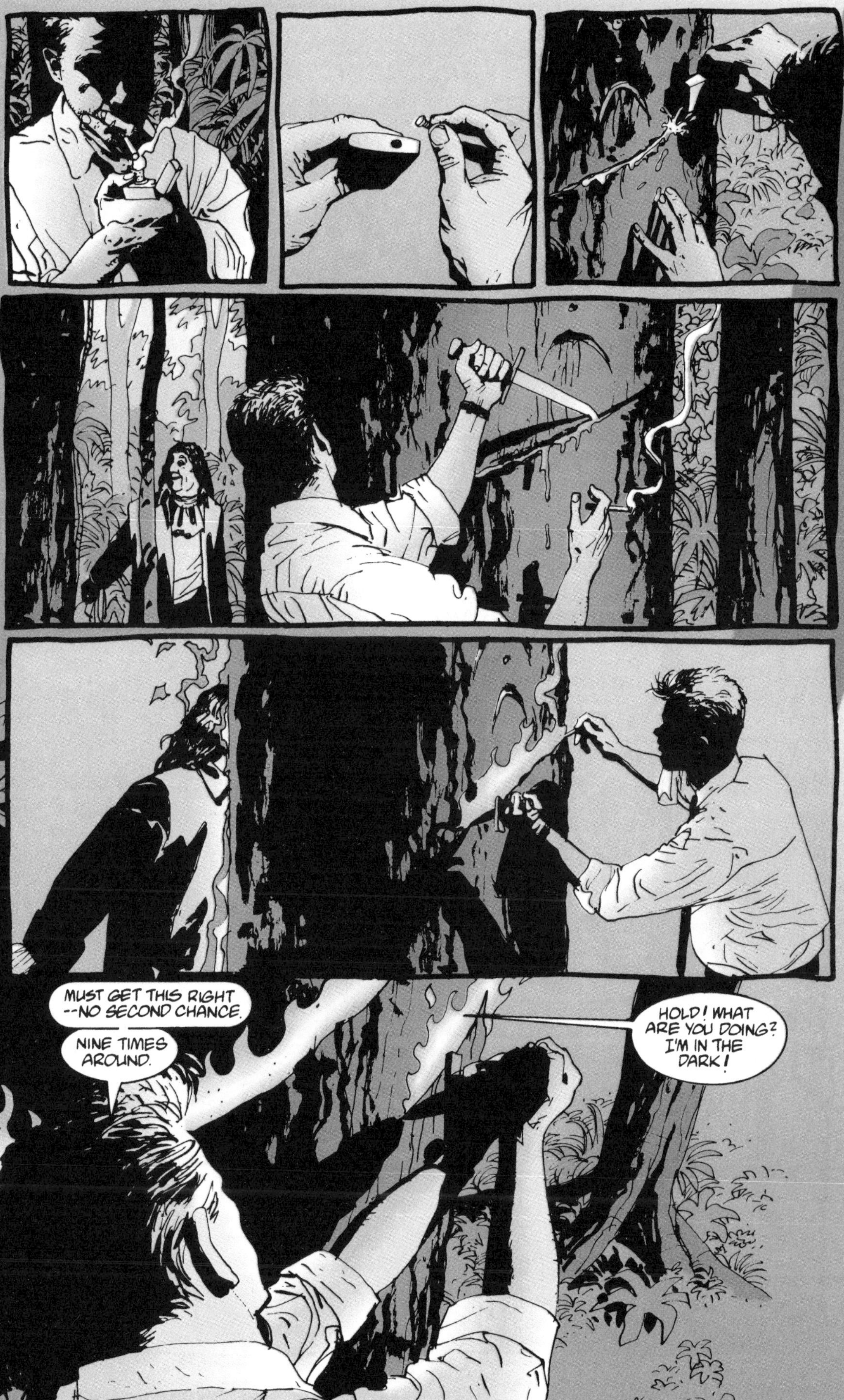
MUST GET THIS RIGHT --NO SECOND CHANCE.
NINE TIMES AROUND.
HOLD! WHAT ARE YOU DOING? I'M IN THE DARK!

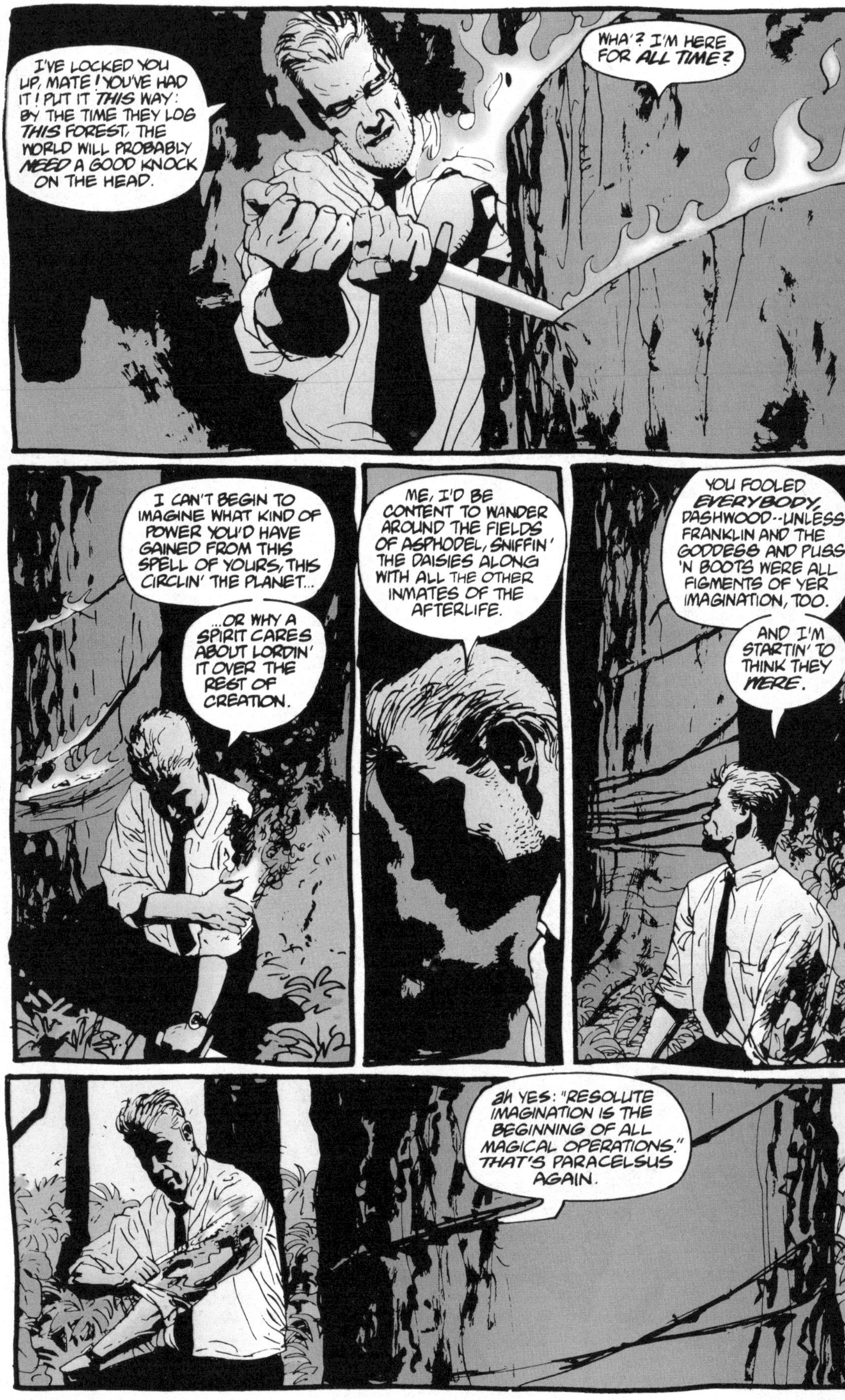
I'VE LOCKED YOU UP, MATE! YOU'VE HAD IT! PUT IT THIS WAY: BY THE TIME THEY LOG THIS FOREST, THE WORLD WILL PROBABLY NEED A GOOD KNOCK ON THE HEAD.
WHA'? I'M HERE FOR ALL TIME?
I CAN'T BEGIN TO IMAGINE WHAT KIND OF POWER YOU'D HAVE GAINED FROM THIS SPELL OF YOURS, THIS CIRCLIN' THE PLANET...
...OR WHY A SPIRIT CARES ABOUT LORDIN' IT OVER THE REST OF CREATION.
ME, I'D BE CONTENT TO WANDER AROUND THE FIELDS OF ASPHODEL, SNIFFIN' THE DAISIES ALONG WITH ALL THE OTHER INMATES OF THE AFTERLIFE.
YOU FOOLED EVERYBODY, DASHWOOD--UNLESS FRANKLIN AND THE GODDESS AND PUSS 'N BOOTS WERE ALL FIGMENTS OF YER IMAGINATION, TOO.
AND I'M STARTIN' TO THINK THEY WERE.
AH YES: "RESOLUTE IMAGINATION IS THE BEGINNING OF ALL MAGICAL OPERATIONS." THAT'S PARACELSUS AGAIN.

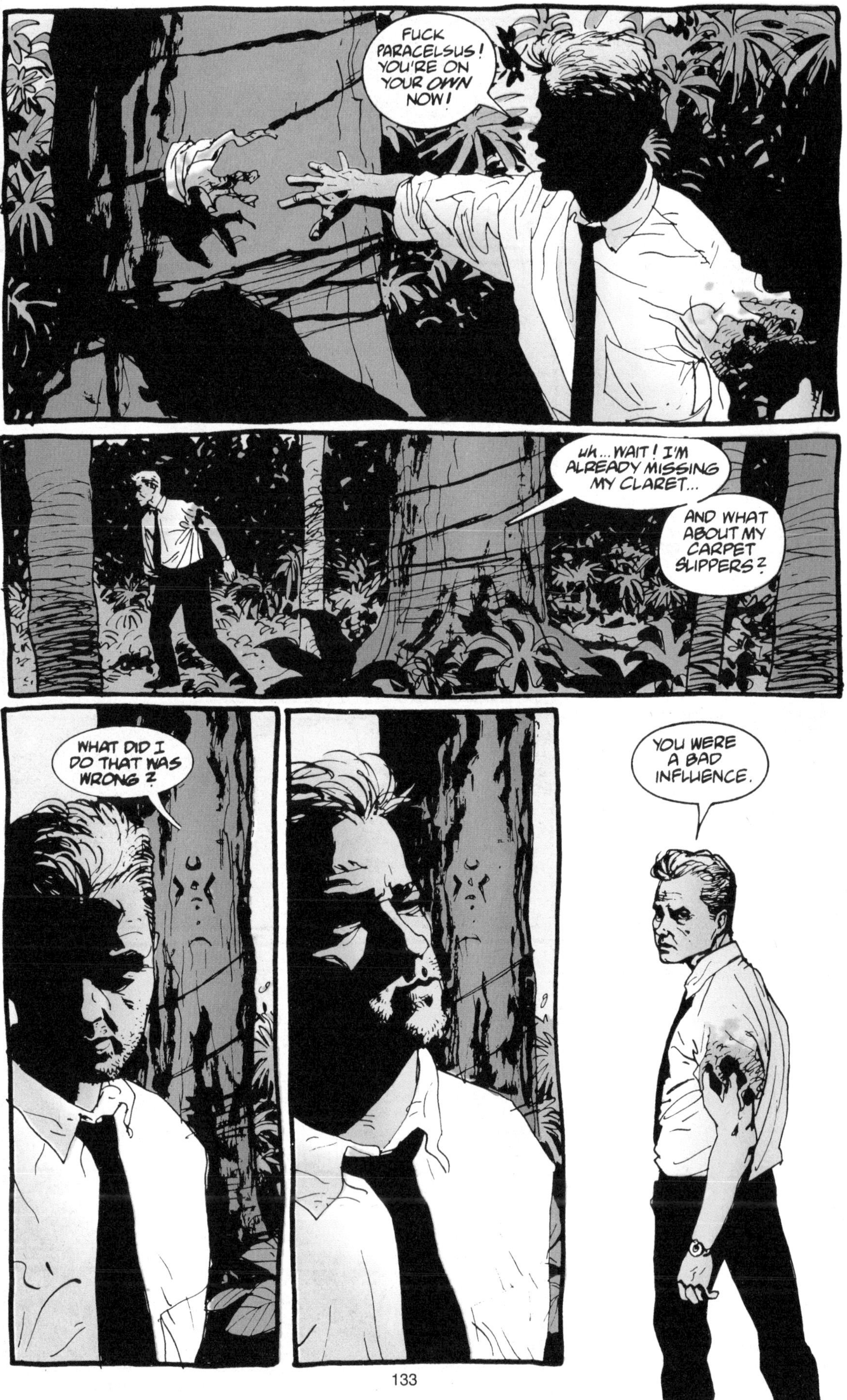
FUCK PARACELSUS! YOU'RE ON YOUR OWN NOW!
uh... WAIT! I'M ALREADY MISSING MY CLARET...
AND WHAT ABOUT MY CARPET SLIPPERS?
WHAT DID I DO THAT WAS WRONG?
YOU WERE A BAD INFLUENCE.

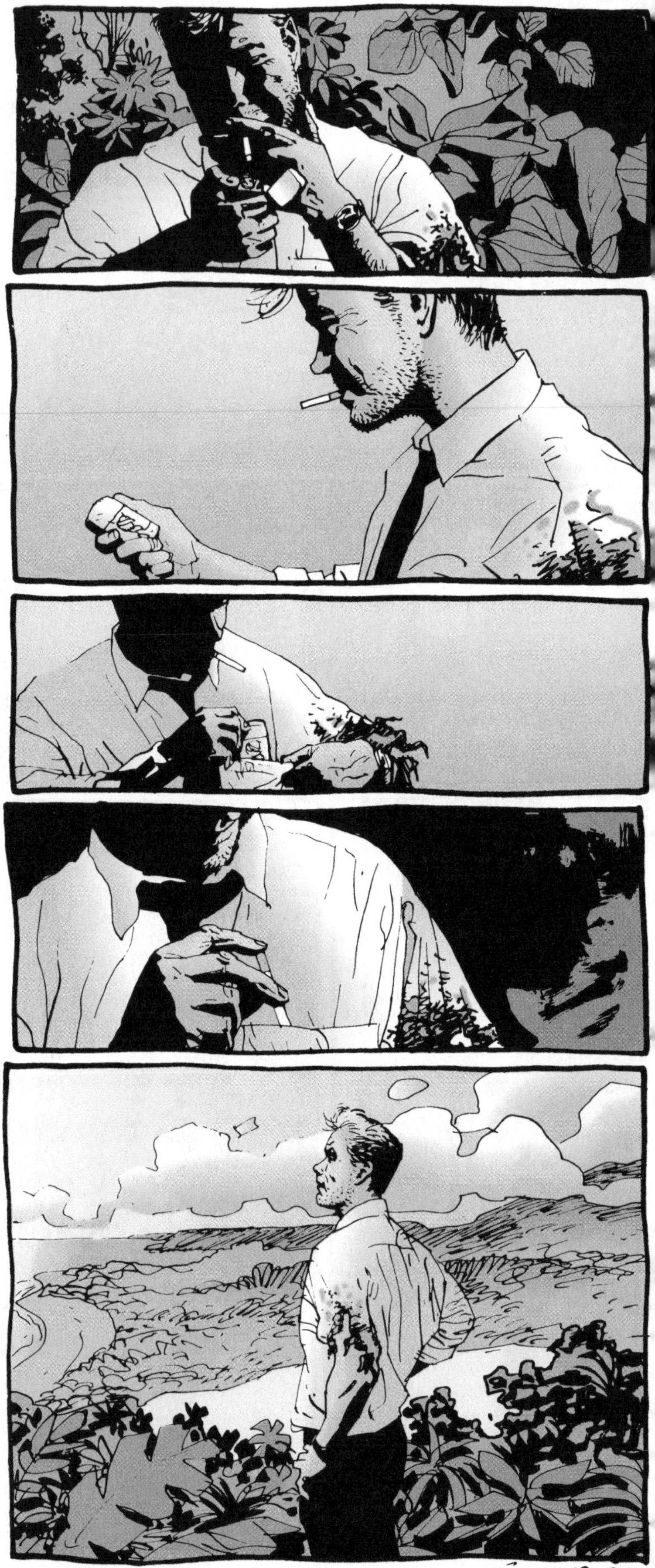
I ALWAYS FIGURED IF I GOT THROUGH LIFE WITHOUT ADDING ANY MORE BOLLOCKS TO THE WORLD'S SUM TOTAL OF BOLLOCKS...
...THEN I COULD HOLD ME HEAD HIGH AND SAY I WASN'T PART OF IT.
NOW I'VE GONE AND DONE WHAT ALL THE SELF-RIGHTEOUS FAT BASTARDS ARE DOING--
TAKEN OUR MADNESS AND DUMPED IT WHERE IT ISN'T WANTED.
ONE MORE REASON WHY I CAN'T LOOK AT MESELF IN THE MIRROR IN THE MORNIN'.
the end
Sean 12-94

JOHN CONSTANTINE
HELLBLAZER
Sean '94
PAUL JENKINS
SEAN PHILLIPS

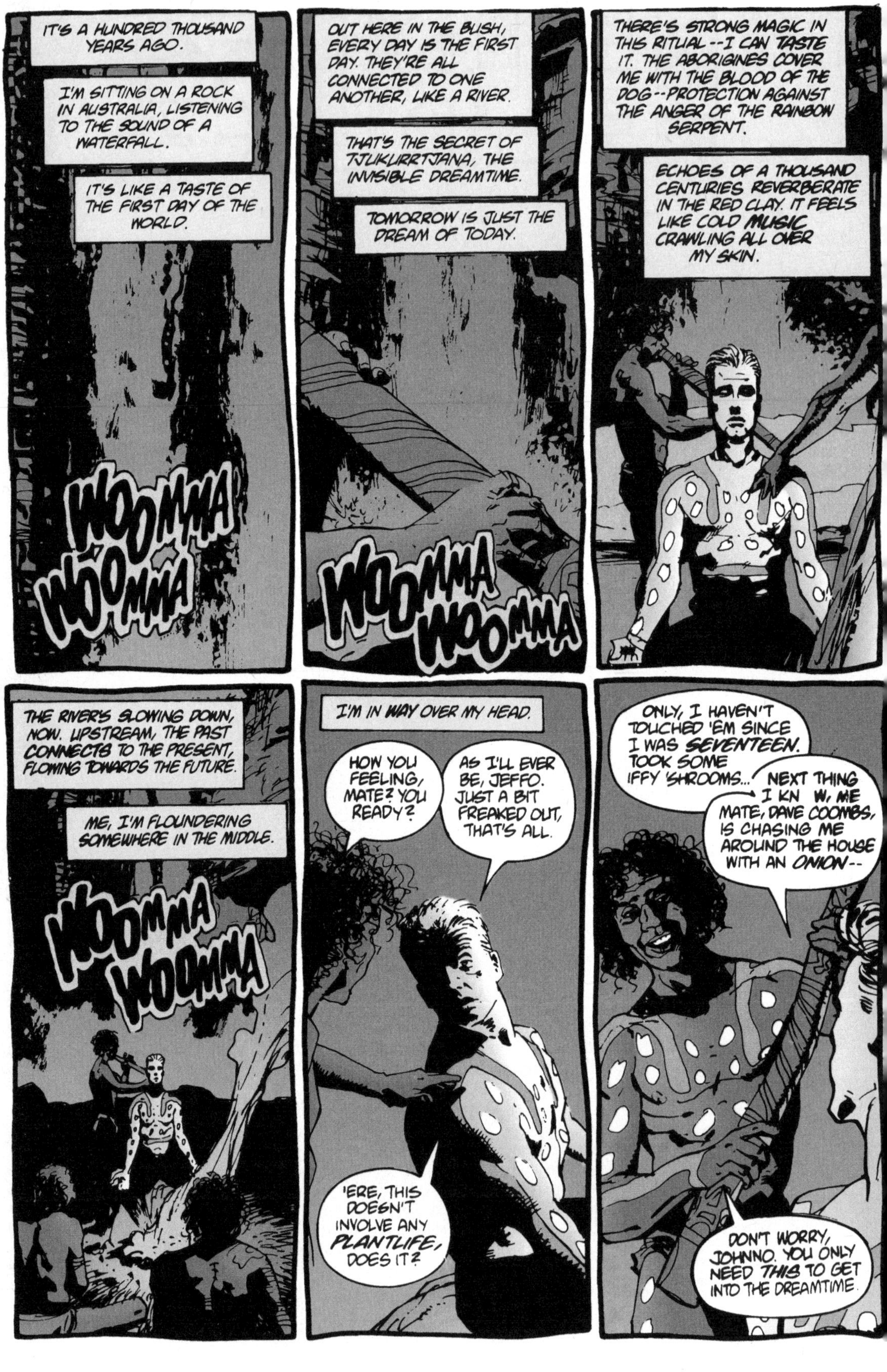
IT'S A HUNDRED THOUSAND YEARS AGO.
I'M SITTING ON A ROCK IN AUSTRALIA, LISTENING TO THE SOUND OF A WATERFALL.
IT'S LIKE A TASTE OF THE FIRST DAY OF THE WORLD.
WOOMMA WOOMMA
OUT HERE IN THE BUSH, EVERY DAY IS THE FIRST DAY. THEY'RE ALL CONNECTED TO ONE ANOTHER, LIKE A RIVER.
THAT'S THE SECRET OF TJUKURRTJANA, THE INVISIBLE DREAMTIME.
TOMORROW IS JUST THE DREAM OF TODAY.
WOOMMA WOOMMA
THERE'S STRONG MAGIC IN THIS RITUAL --I CAN TASTE IT. THE ABORIGINES COVER ME WITH THE BLOOD OF THE DOG--PROTECTION AGAINST THE ANGER OF THE RAINBOW SERPENT.
ECHOES OF A THOUSAND CENTURIES REVERBERATE IN THE RED CLAY. IT FEELS LIKE COLD MUSIC CRAWLING ALL OVER MY SKIN.
THE RIVER'S SLOWING DOWN, NOW. UPSTREAM, THE PAST CONNECTS TO THE PRESENT, FLOWING TOWARDS THE FUTURE.
ME, I'M FLOUNDERING SOMEWHERE IN THE MIDDLE.
WOOMMA WOOMMA
I'M IN WAY OVER MY HEAD.
HOW YOU FEELING, MATE? YOU READY?
AS I'LL EVER BE, JEFFO. JUST A BIT FREAKED OUT, THAT'S ALL.
'ERE, THIS DOESN'T INVOLVE ANY PLANTLIFE, DOES IT?
ONLY, I HAVEN'T TOUCHED 'EM SINCE I WAS SEVENTEEN. TOOK SOME IFFY 'SHROOMS...
NEXT THING I KN W, ME MATE, DAVE COOMBS, IS CHASING ME AROUND THE HOUSE WITH AN ONION--
DON'T WORRY, JOHNNO. YOU ONLY NEED THIS TO GET INTO THE DREAMTIME.

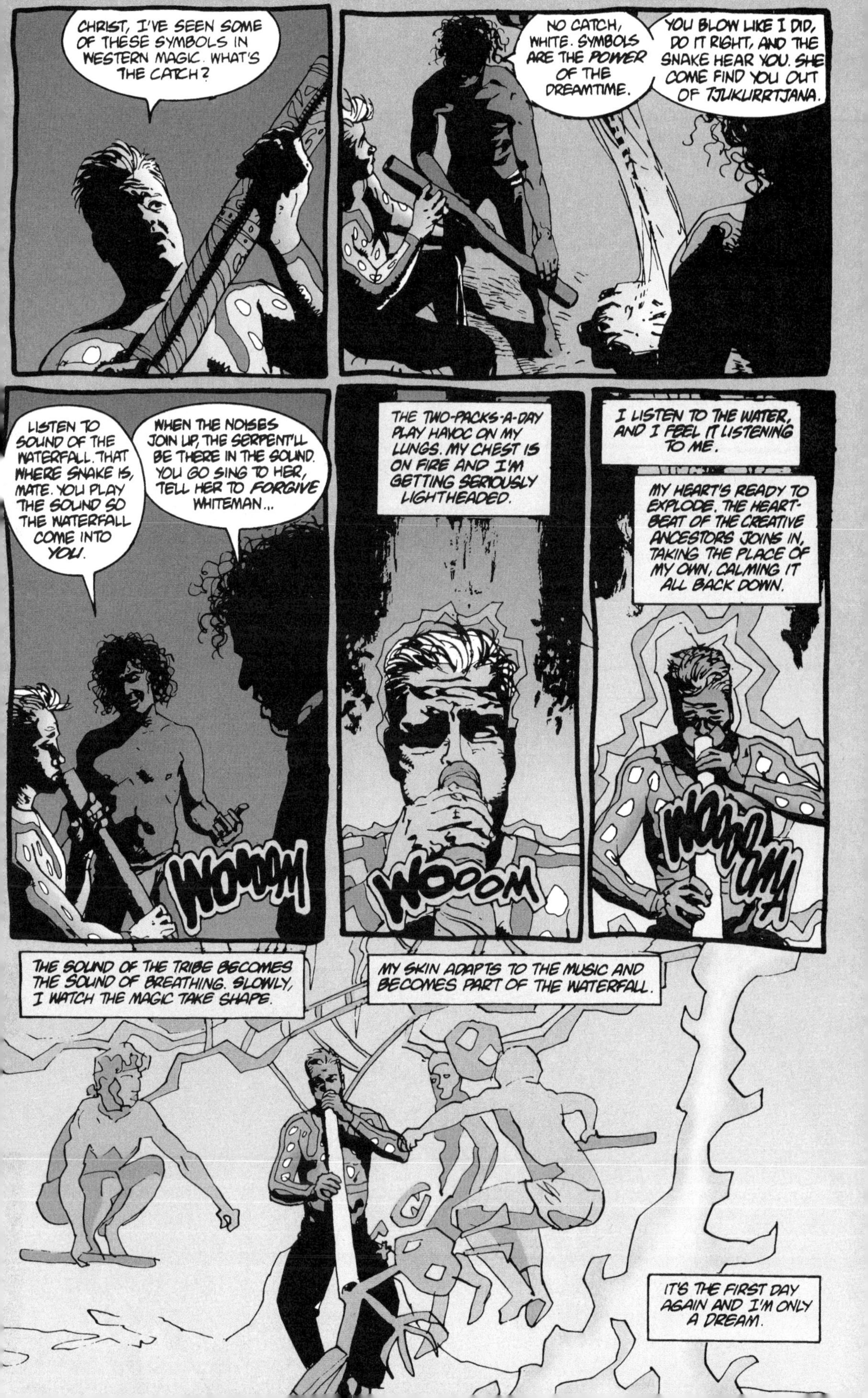
CHRIST, I'VE SEEN SOME OF THESE SYMBOLS IN WESTERN MAGIC. WHAT'S THE CATCH?
NO CATCH, WHITE. SYMBOLS ARE THE *POWER* OF THE DREAMTIME.
YOU BLOW LIKE I DID, DO IT RIGHT, AND THE SNAKE HEAR YOU. SHE COME FIND YOU OUT OF TJUKURRTJANA.
LISTEN TO SOUND OF THE WATERFALL. THAT WHERE SNAKE IS, MATE. YOU PLAY THE SOUND SO THE WATERFALL COME INTO *YOU*.
WHEN THE NOISES JOIN UP, THE SERPENT'LL BE THERE IN THE SOUND. YOU GO SING TO HER, TELL HER TO *FORGIVE* WHITEMAN...
WOOOOM
THE TWO-PACKS-A-DAY PLAY HAVOC ON MY LUNGS. MY CHEST IS ON FIRE AND I'M GETTING SERIOUSLY LIGHTHEADED.
WOOOM
I LISTEN TO THE WATER, AND I FEEL IT LISTENING TO ME.
MY HEART'S READY TO EXPLODE. THE HEART-BEAT OF THE CREATIVE ANCESTORS JOINS IN, TAKING THE PLACE OF MY OWN, CALMING IT ALL BACK DOWN.
THE SOUND OF THE TRIBE BECOMES THE SOUND OF BREATHING. SLOWLY, I WATCH THE MAGIC TAKE SHAPE.
MY SKIN ADAPTS TO THE MUSIC AND BECOMES PART OF THE WATERFALL.
IT'S THE FIRST DAY AGAIN AND I'M ONLY A DREAM.

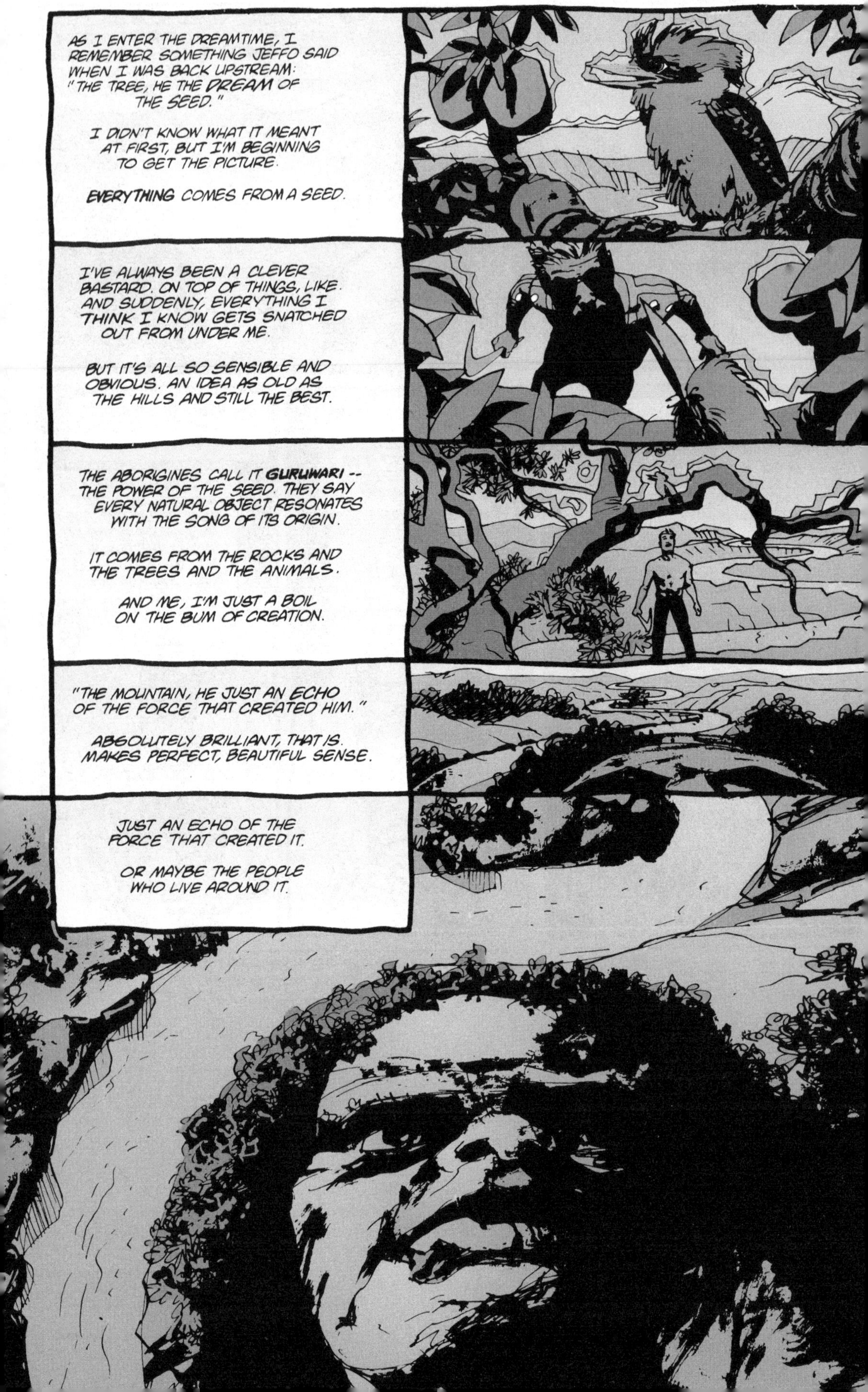
AS I ENTER THE DREAMTIME, I REMEMBER SOMETHING JEFFO SAID WHEN I WAS BACK UPSTREAM: "THE TREE, HE THE DREAM OF THE SEED."
I DIDN'T KNOW WHAT IT MEANT AT FIRST, BUT I'M BEGINNING TO GET THE PICTURE.
EVERYTHING COMES FROM A SEED.
I'VE ALWAYS BEEN A CLEVER BASTARD. ON TOP OF THINGS, LIKE. AND SUDDENLY, EVERYTHING I THINK I KNOW GETS SNATCHED OUT FROM UNDER ME.
BUT IT'S ALL SO SENSIBLE AND OBVIOUS. AN IDEA AS OLD AS THE HILLS AND STILL THE BEST.
THE ABORIGINES CALL IT GURUWARI -- THE POWER OF THE SEED. THEY SAY EVERY NATURAL OBJECT RESONATES WITH THE SONG OF ITS ORIGIN.
IT COMES FROM THE ROCKS AND THE TREES AND THE ANIMALS.
AND ME, I'M JUST A BOIL ON THE BUM OF CREATION.
"THE MOUNTAIN, HE JUST AN ECHO OF THE FORCE THAT CREATED HIM."
ABSOLUTELY BRILLIANT, THAT IS. MAKES PERFECT, BEAUTIFUL SENSE.
JUST AN ECHO OF THE FORCE THAT CREATED IT.
OR MAYBE THE PEOPLE WHO LIVE AROUND IT.

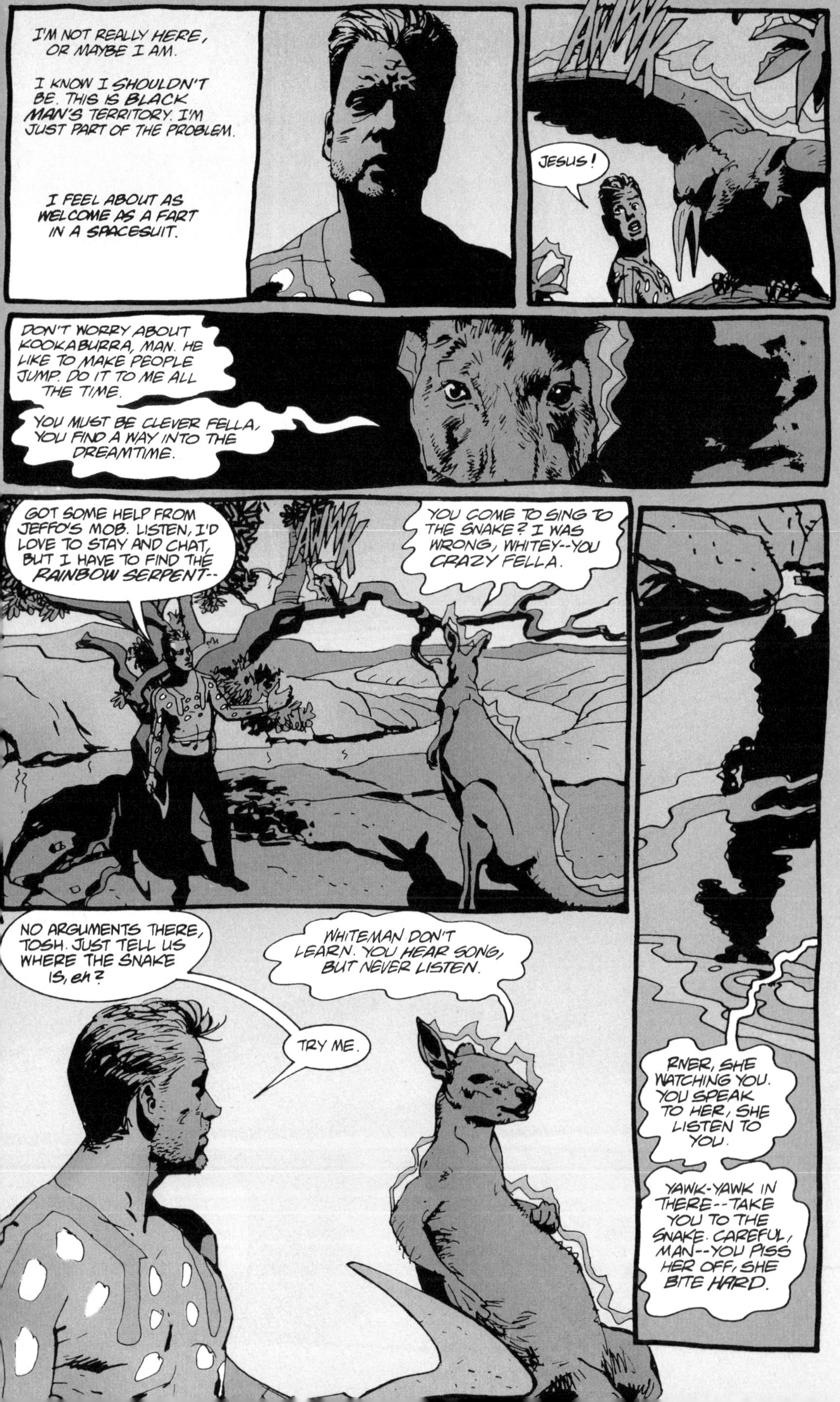
I'M NOT REALLY HERE, OR MAYBE I AM.
I KNOW I SHOULDN'T BE. THIS IS BLACK MAN'S TERRITORY. I'M JUST PART OF THE PROBLEM.
I FEEL ABOUT AS WELCOME AS A FART IN A SPACESUIT.
AWWK
JESUS!
DON'T WORRY ABOUT KOOKABURRA, MAN. HE LIKE TO MAKE PEOPLE JUMP. DO IT TO ME ALL THE TIME.
YOU MUST BE CLEVER FELLA, YOU FIND A WAY INTO THE DREAMTIME.
GOT SOME HELP FROM JEFFO'S MOB. LISTEN, I'D LOVE TO STAY AND CHAT, BUT I HAVE TO FIND THE RAINBOW SERPENT--
AWWK
YOU COME TO SING TO THE SNAKE? I WAS WRONG, WHITEY--YOU CRAZY FELLA.
NO ARGUMENTS THERE, TOSH. JUST TELL US WHERE THE SNAKE IS, eh?
WHITEMAN DON'T LEARN. YOU HEAR SONG, BUT NEVER LISTEN.
TRY ME.
RIVER, SHE WATCHING YOU. YOU SPEAK TO HER, SHE LISTEN TO YOU.
YAWK-YAWK IN THERE--TAKE YOU TO THE SNAKE. CAREFUL, MAN--YOU PISS HER OFF, SHE BITE HARD.

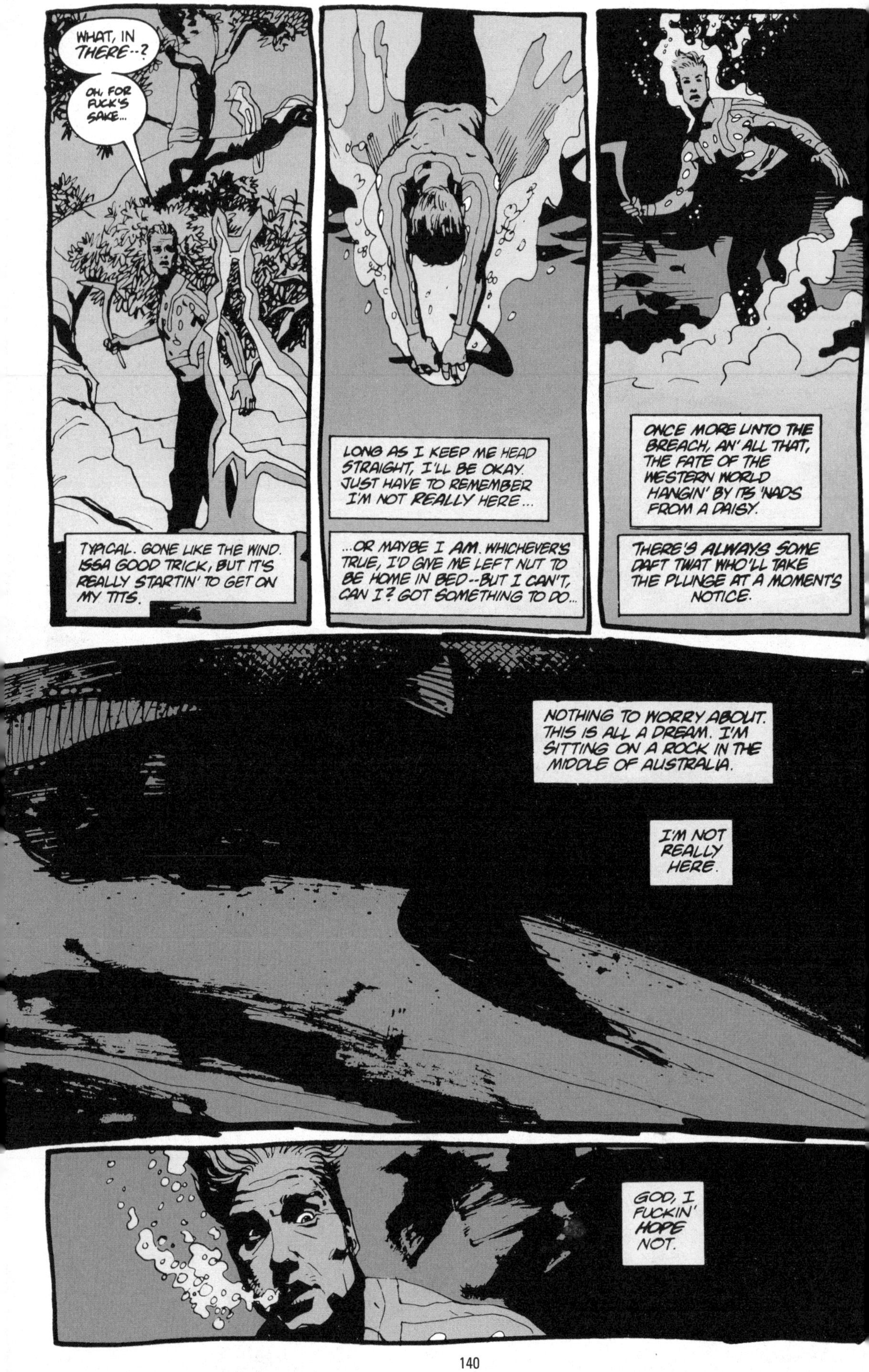
WHAT, IN THERE--?
OH, FOR FUCK'S SAKE...
TYPICAL. GONE LIKE THE WIND. ISSA GOOD TRICK, BUT IT'S REALLY STARTIN' TO GET ON MY TITS.
LONG AS I KEEP ME HEAD STRAIGHT, I'LL BE OKAY. JUST HAVE TO REMEMBER I'M NOT REALLY HERE...
...OR MAYBE I AM. WHICHEVER'S TRUE, I'D GIVE ME LEFT NUT TO BE HOME IN BED--BUT I CAN'T, CAN I? GOT SOMETHING TO DO...
ONCE MORE UNTO THE BREACH, AN' ALL THAT, THE FATE OF THE WESTERN WORLD HANGIN' BY ITS 'NADS FROM A DAISY.
THERE'S ALWAYS SOME DAFT TWAT WHO'LL TAKE THE PLUNGE AT A MOMENT'S NOTICE.
NOTHING TO WORRY ABOUT. THIS IS ALL A DREAM. I'M SITTING ON A ROCK IN THE MIDDLE OF AUSTRALIA.
I'M NOT REALLY HERE.
GOD, I FUCKIN' HOPE NOT.

dreamtime

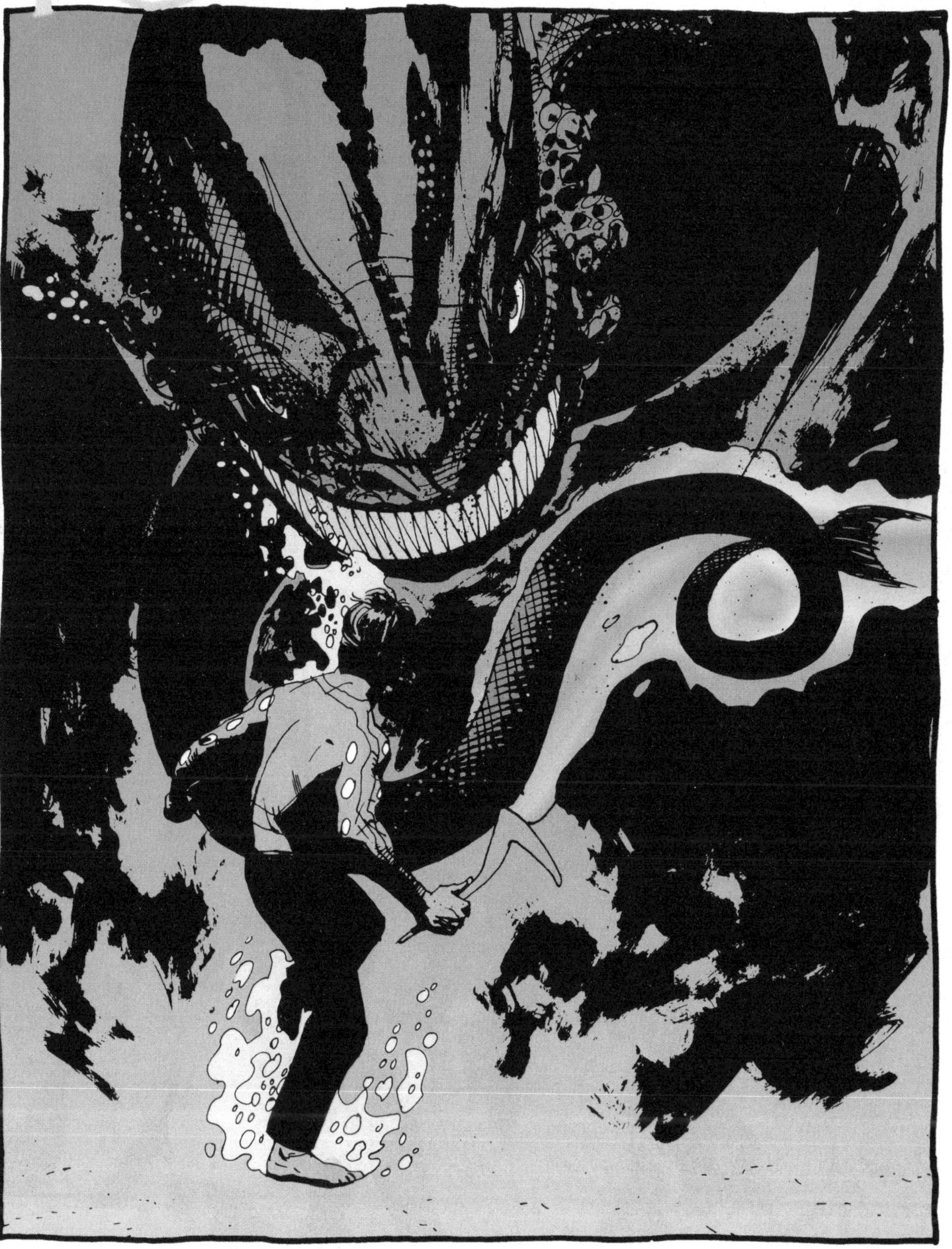

PAUL JENKINS WRITER · SEAN PHILLIPS ARTIST · MATT HOLLINGSWORTH COLORIST · CLEM ROBINS LETTERER · AXEL ALONSO ASST. EDITOR · LOU STATHIS EDITOR

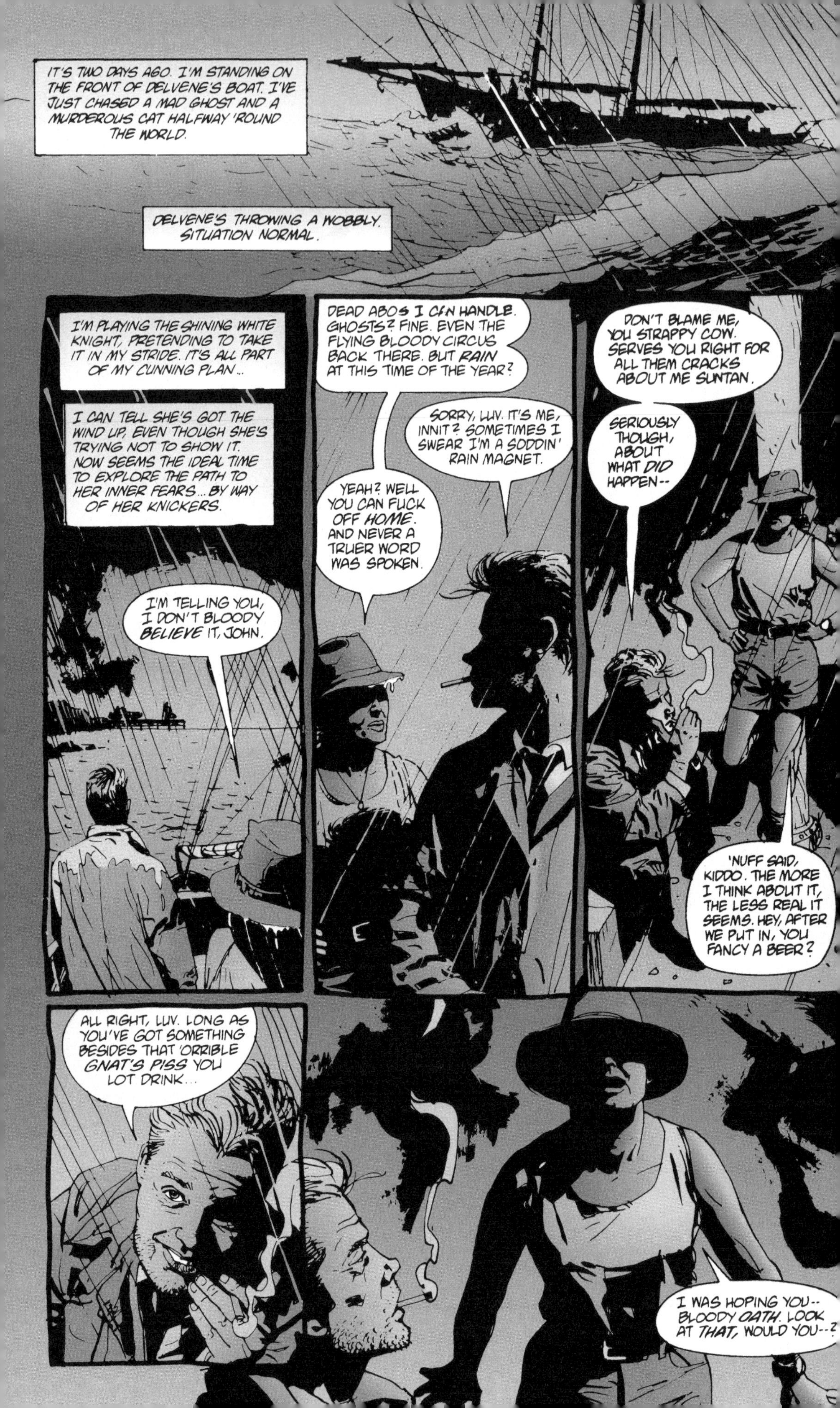
IT'S TWO DAYS AGO. I'M STANDING ON THE FRONT OF DELVENE'S BOAT. I'VE JUST CHASED A MAD GHOST AND A MURDEROUS CAT HALFWAY 'ROUND THE WORLD.
DELVENE'S THROWING A WOBBLY. SITUATION NORMAL.
I'M PLAYING THE SHINING WHITE KNIGHT, PRETENDING TO TAKE IT IN MY STRIDE. IT'S ALL PART OF MY CUNNING PLAN...
I CAN TELL SHE'S GOT THE WIND UP, EVEN THOUGH SHE'S TRYING NOT TO SHOW IT. NOW SEEMS THE IDEAL TIME TO EXPLORE THE PATH TO HER INNER FEARS... BY WAY OF HER KNICKERS.
I'M TELLING YOU, I DON'T BLOODY BELIEVE IT, JOHN.
DEAD ABOS I CAN HANDLE. GHOSTS? FINE. EVEN THE FLYING BLOODY CIRCUS BACK THERE. BUT RAIN AT THIS TIME OF THE YEAR?
SORRY, LUV. IT'S ME, INNIT? SOMETIMES I SWEAR I'M A SODDIN' RAIN MAGNET.
YEAH? WELL YOU CAN FUCK OFF HOME. AND NEVER A TRUER WORD WAS SPOKEN.
DON'T BLAME ME, YOU STRAPPY COW. SERVES YOU RIGHT FOR ALL THEM CRACKS ABOUT ME SUNTAN.
SERIOUSLY THOUGH, ABOUT WHAT DID HAPPEN--
'NUFF SAID, KIDDO. THE MORE I THINK ABOUT IT, THE LESS REAL IT SEEMS. HEY, AFTER WE PUT IN, YOU FANCY A BEER?
ALL RIGHT, LUV. LONG AS YOU'VE GOT SOMETHING BESIDES THAT 'ORRIBLE GNAT'S PISS YOU LOT DRINK...
I WAS HOPING YOU-- BLOODY OATH. LOOK AT THAT, WOULD YOU--?

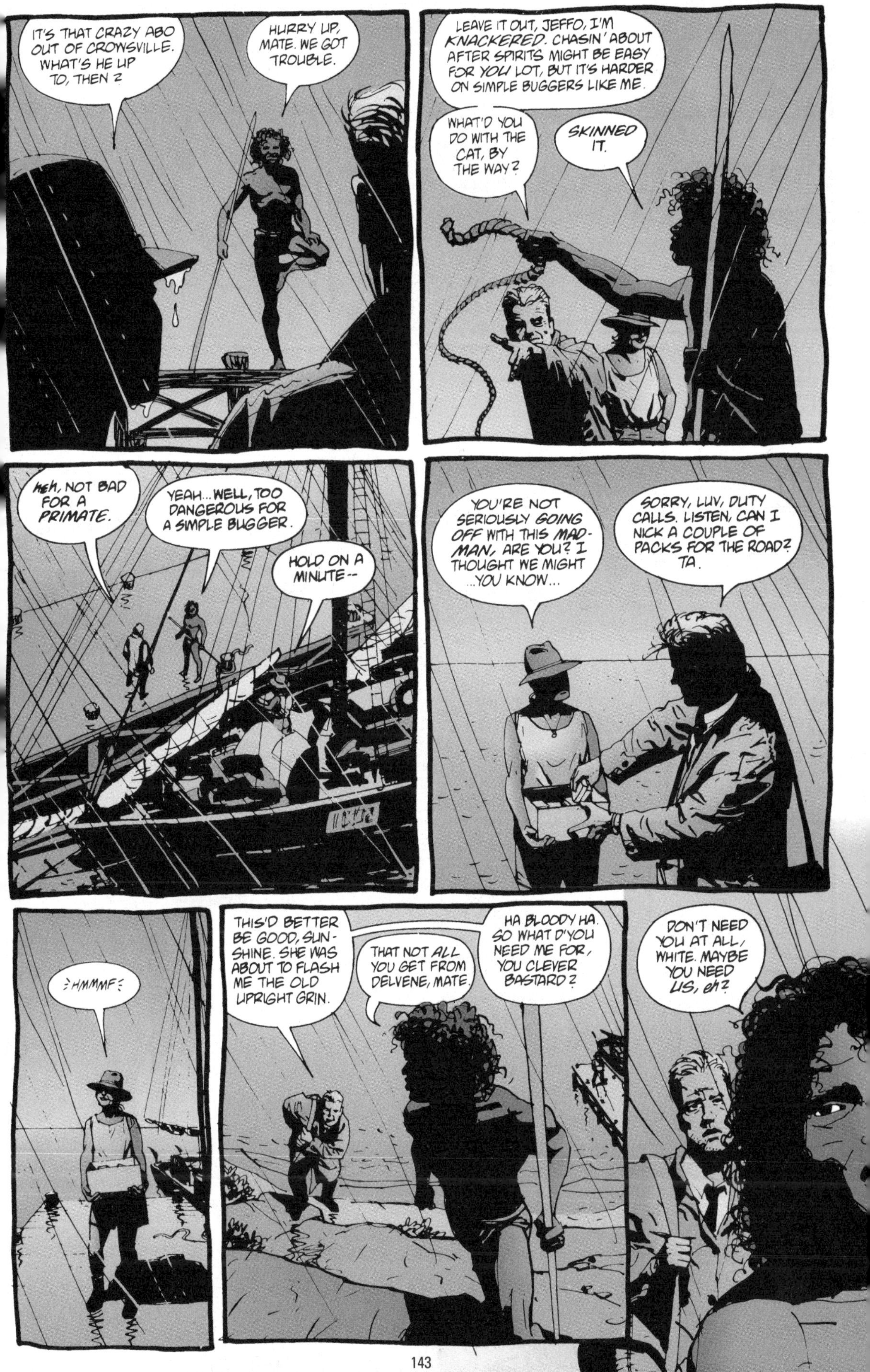
IT'S THAT CRAZY ABO OUT OF CROWSVILLE. WHAT'S HE UP TO, THEN ?
HURRY UP, MATE. WE GOT TROUBLE.
LEAVE IT OUT, JEFFO, I'M KNACKERED. CHASIN' ABOUT AFTER SPIRITS MIGHT BE EASY FOR YOU LOT, BUT IT'S HARDER ON SIMPLE BUGGERS LIKE ME.
WHAT'D YOU DO WITH THE CAT, BY THE WAY?
SKINNED IT.
HEH, NOT BAD FOR A PRIMATE.
YEAH... WELL, TOO DANGEROUS FOR A SIMPLE BUGGER.
HOLD ON A MINUTE--
YOU'RE NOT SERIOUSLY GOING OFF WITH THIS MAD-MAN, ARE YOU? I THOUGHT WE MIGHT ...YOU KNOW...
SORRY, LUV, DUTY CALLS. LISTEN, CAN I NICK A COUPLE OF PACKS FOR THE ROAD? TA.
HMMMF
THIS'D BETTER BE GOOD, SUN-SHINE. SHE WAS ABOUT TO FLASH ME THE OLD UPRIGHT GRIN.
THAT NOT ALL YOU GET FROM DELVENE, MATE.
HA BLOODY HA. SO WHAT D'YOU NEED ME FOR, YOU CLEVER BASTARD?
DON'T NEED YOU AT ALL, WHITE. MAYBE YOU NEED US, EH?

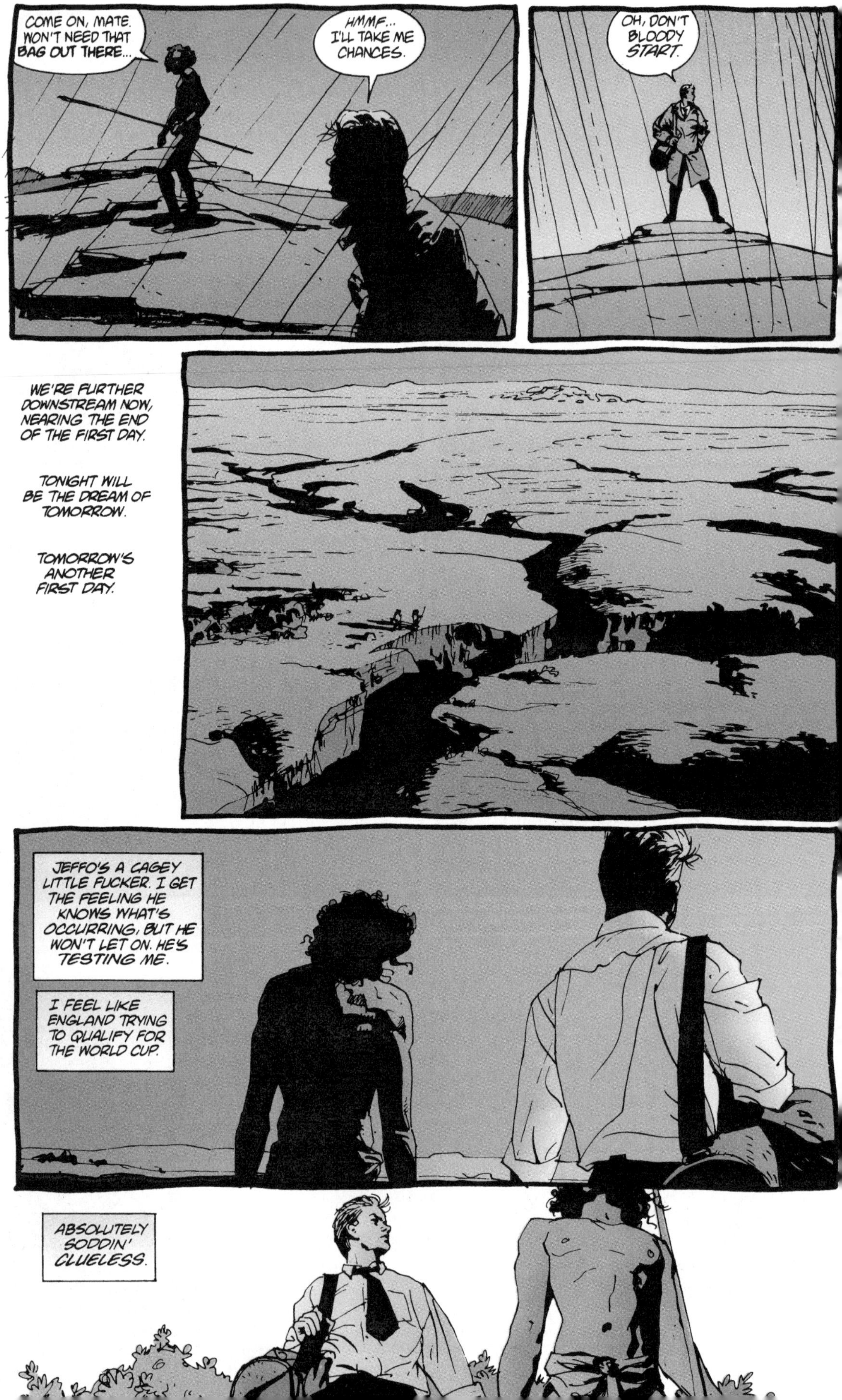
COME ON, MATE. WON'T NEED THAT BAG OUT THERE...
HMMF... I'LL TAKE ME CHANCES.
OH, DON'T BLOODY START.
WE'RE FURTHER DOWNSTREAM NOW, NEARING THE END OF THE FIRST DAY.
TONIGHT WILL BE THE DREAM OF TOMORROW.
TOMORROW'S ANOTHER FIRST DAY.
JEFFO'S A CAGEY LITTLE FUCKER. I GET THE FEELING HE KNOWS WHAT'S OCCURRING, BUT HE WON'T LET ON. HE'S TESTING ME.
I FEEL LIKE ENGLAND TRYING TO QUALIFY FOR THE WORLD CUP.
ABSOLUTELY SODDIN' CLUELESS.

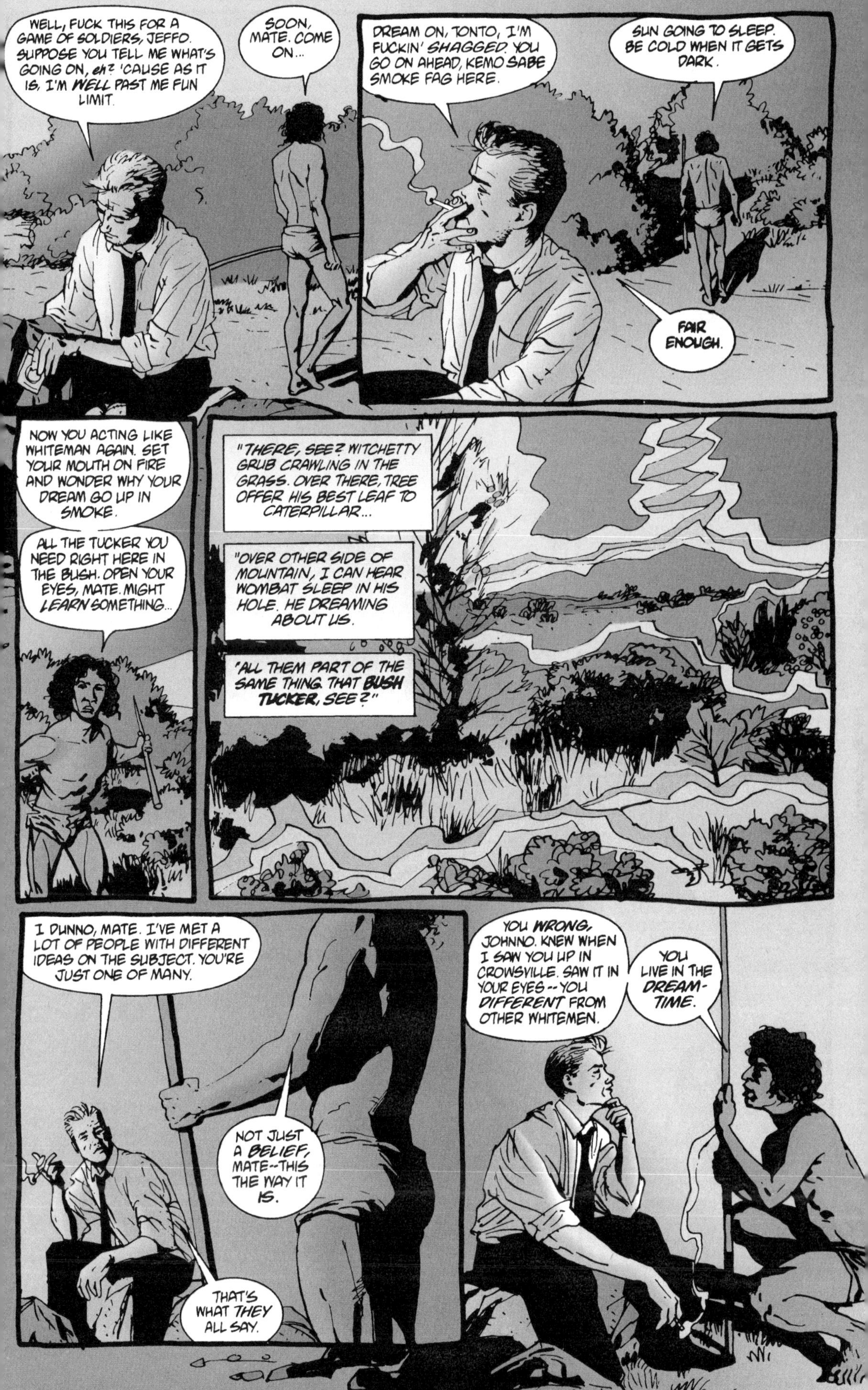

WELL, FUCK THIS FOR A GAME OF SOLDIERS, JEFFO. SUPPOSE YOU TELL ME WHAT'S GOING ON, eh? 'CAUSE AS IT IS, I'M WELL PAST ME FUN LIMIT.
SOON, MATE. COME ON...
DREAM ON, TONTO, I'M FUCKIN' SHAGGED. YOU GO ON AHEAD, KEMO SABE. SMOKE FAG HERE.
SUN GOING TO SLEEP. BE COLD WHEN IT GETS DARK.
FAIR ENOUGH.
NOW YOU ACTING LIKE WHITEMAN AGAIN. SET YOUR MOUTH ON FIRE AND WONDER WHY YOUR DREAM GO UP IN SMOKE.
ALL THE TUCKER YOU NEED RIGHT HERE IN THE BUSH. OPEN YOUR EYES, MATE. MIGHT LEARN SOMETHING...
"THERE, SEE? WITCHETTY GRUB CRAWLING IN THE GRASS. OVER THERE, TREE OFFER HIS BEST LEAF TO CATERPILLAR...
"OVER OTHER SIDE OF MOUNTAIN, I CAN HEAR WOMBAT SLEEP IN HIS HOLE. HE DREAMING ABOUT US.
"ALL THEM PART OF THE SAME THING. THAT BUSH TUCKER, SEE?"
I DUNNO, MATE. I'VE MET A LOT OF PEOPLE WITH DIFFERENT IDEAS ON THE SUBJECT. YOU'RE JUST ONE OF MANY.
NOT JUST A BELIEF, MATE--THIS THE WAY IT IS.
THAT'S WHAT THEY ALL SAY.
YOU WRONG, JOHNNO. KNEW WHEN I SAW YOU UP IN CROWSVILLE. SAW IT IN YOUR EYES--YOU DIFFERENT FROM OTHER WHITEMEN.
YOU LIVE IN THE DREAMTIME.

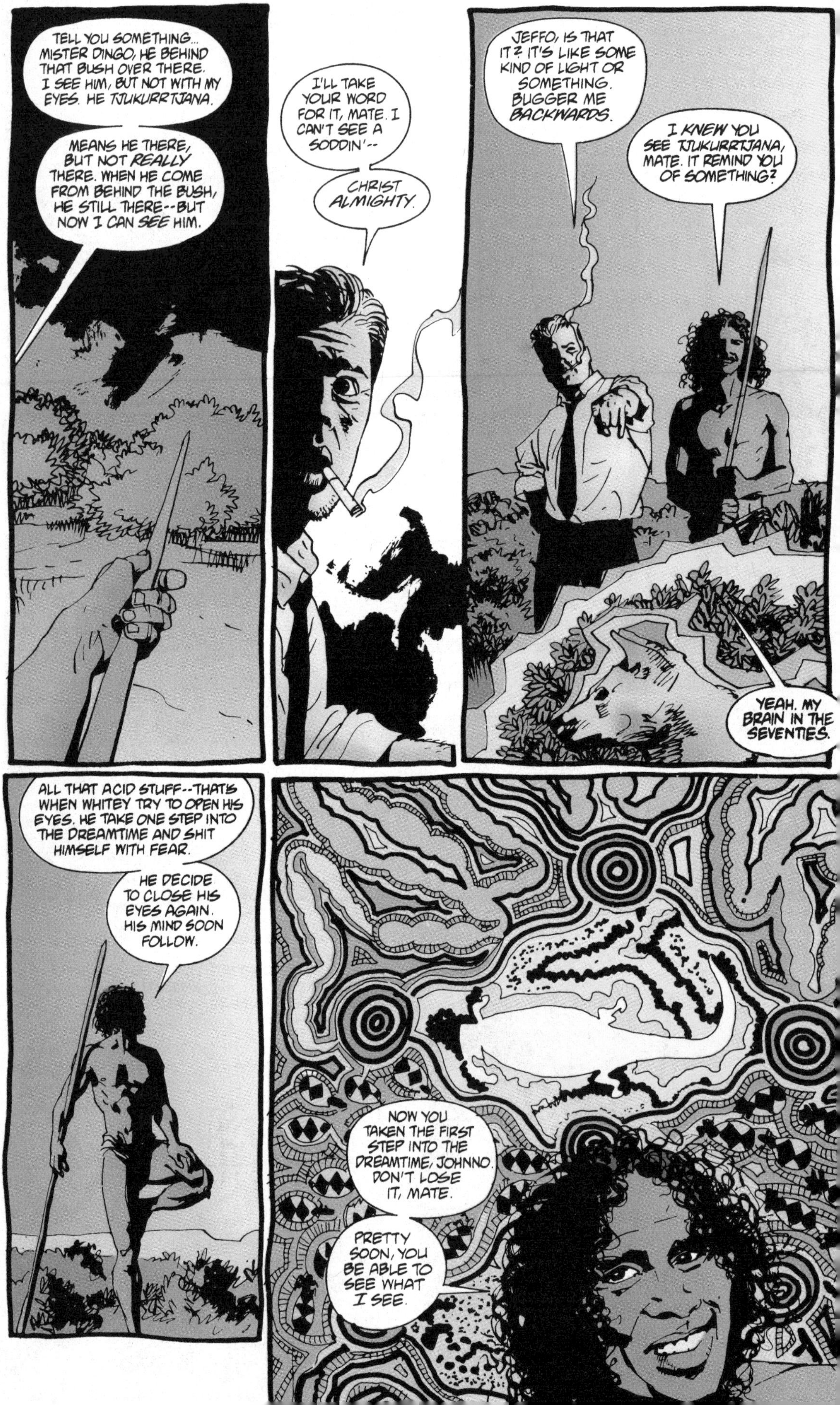
TELL YOU SOMETHING... MISTER DINGO, HE BEHIND THAT BUSH OVER THERE. I SEE HIM, BUT NOT WITH MY EYES. HE TJUKURRTJANA.
MEANS HE THERE, BUT NOT REALLY THERE. WHEN HE COME FROM BEHIND THE BUSH, HE STILL THERE--BUT NOW I CAN SEE HIM.
I'LL TAKE YOUR WORD FOR IT, MATE. I CAN'T SEE A SODDIN'--
CHRIST ALMIGHTY.
JEFFO, IS THAT IT? IT'S LIKE SOME KIND OF LIGHT OR SOMETHING. BUGGER ME BACKWARDS.
I KNEW YOU SEE TJUKURRTJANA, MATE. IT REMIND YOU OF SOMETHING?
YEAH. MY BRAIN IN THE SEVENTIES.
ALL THAT ACID STUFF--THAT'S WHEN WHITEY TRY TO OPEN HIS EYES. HE TAKE ONE STEP INTO THE DREAMTIME AND SHIT HIMSELF WITH FEAR.
HE DECIDE TO CLOSE HIS EYES AGAIN. HIS MIND SOON FOLLOW.
NOW YOU TAKEN THE FIRST STEP INTO THE DREAMTIME, JOHNNO. DON'T LOSE IT, MATE.
PRETTY SOON, YOU BE ABLE TO SEE WHAT I SEE.

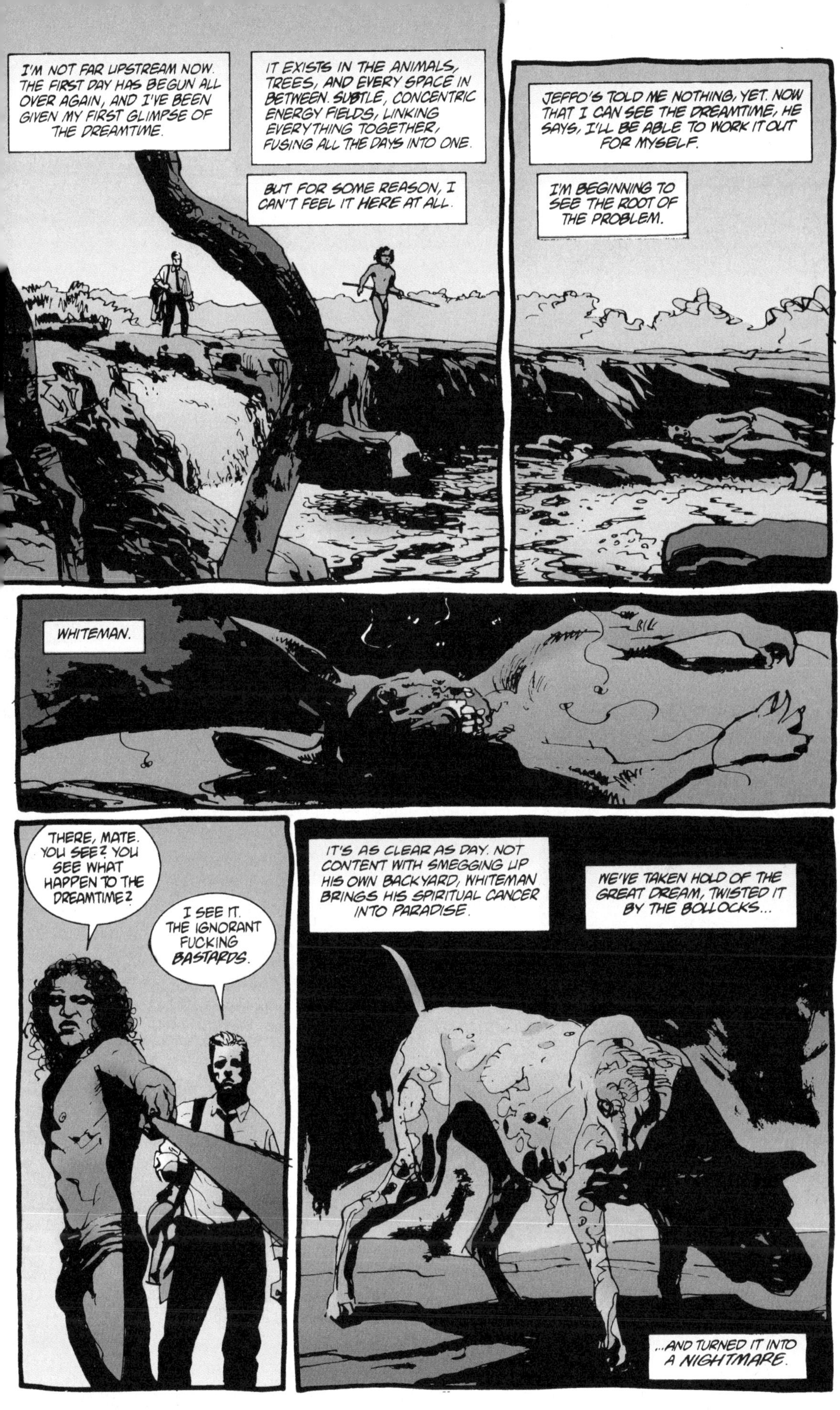

I'M NOT FAR UPSTREAM NOW. THE FIRST DAY HAS BEGUN ALL OVER AGAIN, AND I'VE BEEN GIVEN MY FIRST GLIMPSE OF THE DREAMTIME.
IT EXISTS IN THE ANIMALS, TREES, AND EVERY SPACE IN BETWEEN. SUBTLE, CONCENTRIC ENERGY FIELDS, LINKING EVERYTHING TOGETHER, FUSING ALL THE DAYS INTO ONE.
BUT FOR SOME REASON, I CAN'T FEEL IT HERE AT ALL.
JEFFO'S TOLD ME NOTHING, YET. NOW THAT I CAN SEE THE DREAMTIME, HE SAYS, I'LL BE ABLE TO WORK IT OUT FOR MYSELF.
I'M BEGINNING TO SEE THE ROOT OF THE PROBLEM.
WHITEMAN.
THERE, MATE. YOU SEE? YOU SEE WHAT HAPPEN TO THE DREAMTIME?
I SEE IT. THE IGNORANT FUCKING BASTARDS.
IT'S AS CLEAR AS DAY. NOT CONTENT WITH SMEGGING UP HIS OWN BACKYARD, WHITEMAN BRINGS HIS SPIRITUAL CANCER INTO PARADISE.
WE'VE TAKEN HOLD OF THE GREAT DREAM, TWISTED IT BY THE BOLLOCKS...
...AND TURNED IT INTO A NIGHTMARE.

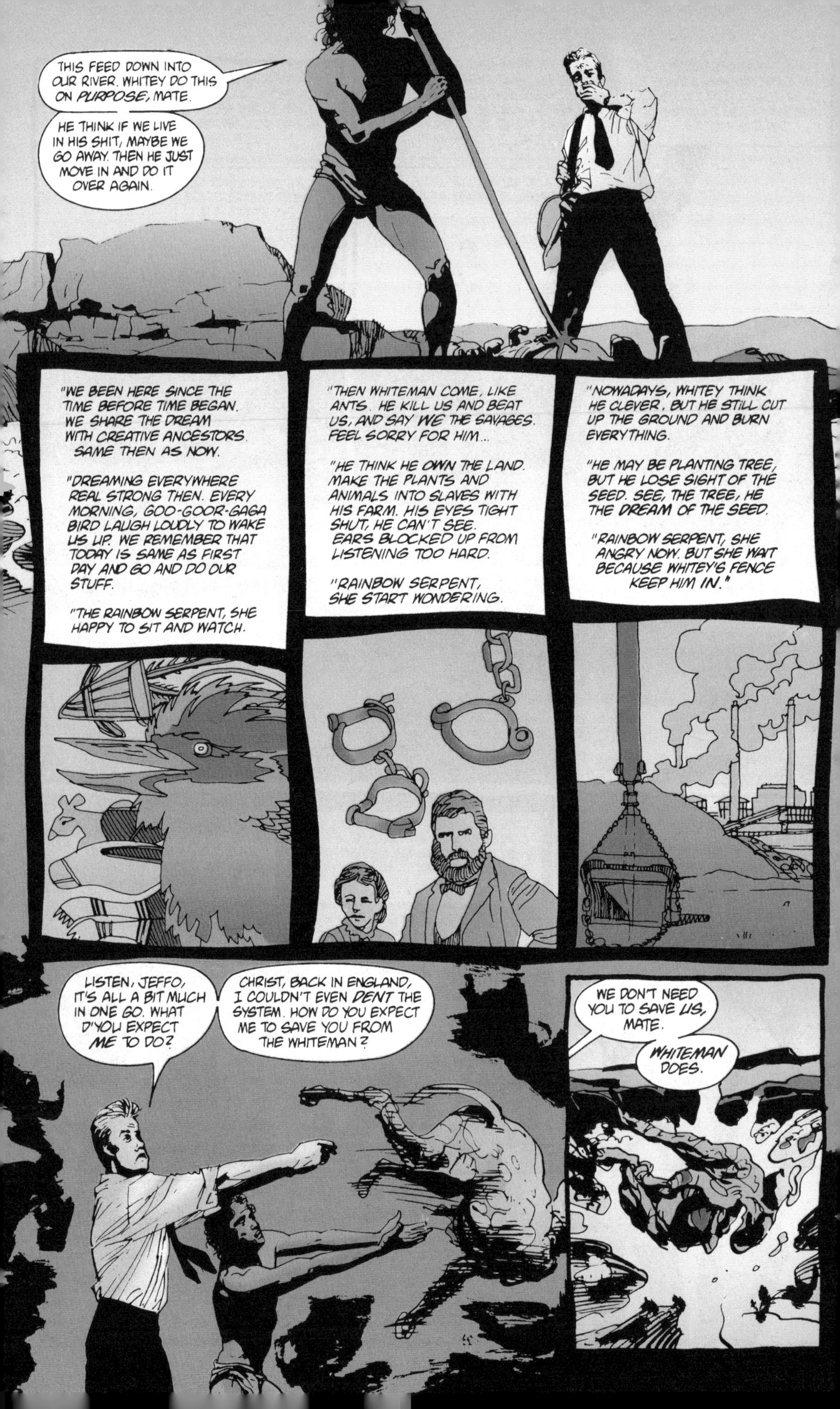
THIS FEED DOWN INTO OUR RIVER. WHITEY DO THIS ON PURPOSE, MATE.
HE THINK IF WE LIVE IN HIS SHIT, MAYBE WE GO AWAY. THEN HE JUST MOVE IN AND DO IT OVER AGAIN.
"WE BEEN HERE SINCE THE TIME BEFORE TIME BEGAN. WE SHARE THE DREAM WITH CREATIVE ANCESTORS. SAME THEN AS NOW.
"DREAMING EVERYWHERE REAL STRONG THEN. EVERY MORNING, GOO-GOOR-GAGA BIRD LAUGH LOUDLY TO WAKE US UP. WE REMEMBER THAT TODAY IS SAME AS FIRST DAY AND GO AND DO OUR STUFF.
"THE RAINBOW SERPENT, SHE HAPPY TO SIT AND WATCH.
"THEN WHITEMAN COME, LIKE ANTS. HE KILL US AND BEAT US, AND SAY WE THE SAVAGES. FEEL SORRY FOR HIM...
"HE THINK HE OWN THE LAND. MAKE THE PLANTS AND ANIMALS INTO SLAVES WITH HIS FARM. HIS EYES TIGHT SHUT, HE CAN'T SEE. EARS BLOCKED UP FROM LISTENING TOO HARD.
"RAINBOW SERPENT, SHE START WONDERING.
"NOWADAYS, WHITEY THINK HE CLEVER. BUT HE STILL CUT UP THE GROUND AND BURN EVERYTHING.
"HE MAY BE PLANTING TREE, BUT HE LOSE SIGHT OF THE SEED. SEE, THE TREE, HE THE DREAM OF THE SEED.
"RAINBOW SERPENT, SHE ANGRY NOW. BUT SHE WAIT BECAUSE WHITEY'S FENCE KEEP HIM IN."
LISTEN, JEFFO, IT'S ALL A BIT MUCH IN ONE GO. WHAT D'YOU EXPECT ME TO DO?
CHRIST, BACK IN ENGLAND, I COULDN'T EVEN DENT THE SYSTEM. HOW DO YOU EXPECT ME TO SAVE YOU FROM THE WHITEMAN?
WE DON'T NEED YOU TO SAVE US, MATE.
WHITEMAN DOES.

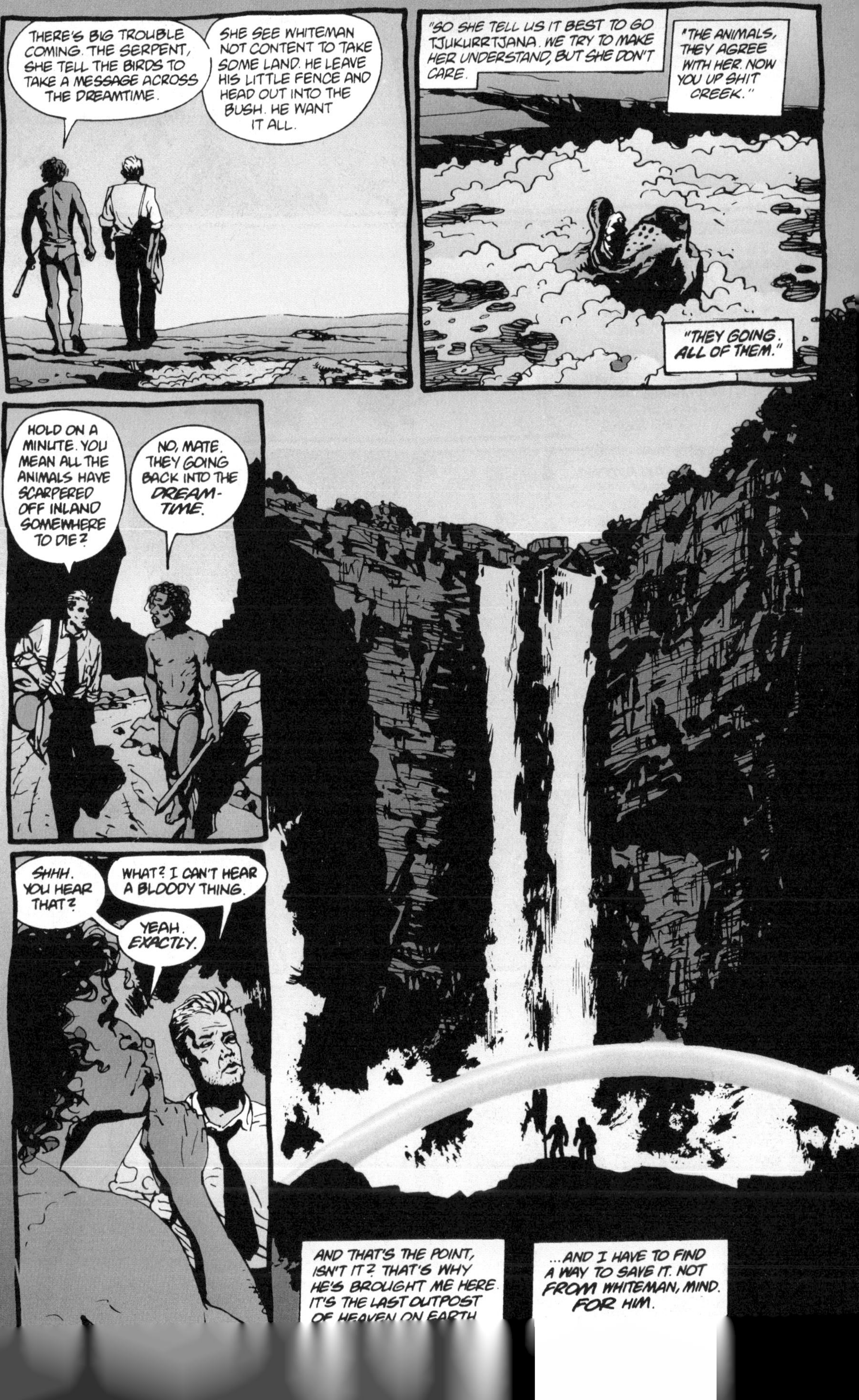
THERE'S BIG TROUBLE COMING. THE SERPENT, SHE TELL THE BIRDS TO TAKE A MESSAGE ACROSS THE DREAMTIME.
SHE SEE WHITEMAN NOT CONTENT TO TAKE SOME LAND. HE LEAVE HIS LITTLE FENCE AND HEAD OUT INTO THE BUSH. HE WANT IT ALL.
"SO SHE TELL US IT BEST TO GO TJUKURRTJANA. WE TRY TO MAKE HER UNDERSTAND, BUT SHE DON'T CARE.
"THE ANIMALS, THEY AGREE WITH HER. NOW YOU UP SHIT CREEK."
"THEY GOING. ALL OF THEM."
HOLD ON A MINUTE. YOU MEAN ALL THE ANIMALS HAVE SCARPERED OFF INLAND SOMEWHERE TO DIE?
NO, MATE. THEY GOING BACK INTO THE DREAM-TIME.
SHHH. YOU HEAR THAT?
WHAT? I CAN'T HEAR A BLOODY THING.
YEAH. EXACTLY.
AND THAT'S THE POINT, ISN'T IT? THAT'S WHY HE'S BROUGHT ME HERE. IT'S THE LAST OUTPOST OF HEAVEN ON EARTH
...AND I HAVE TO FIND A WAY TO SAVE IT. NOT FROM WHITEMAN, MIND. FOR HIM.

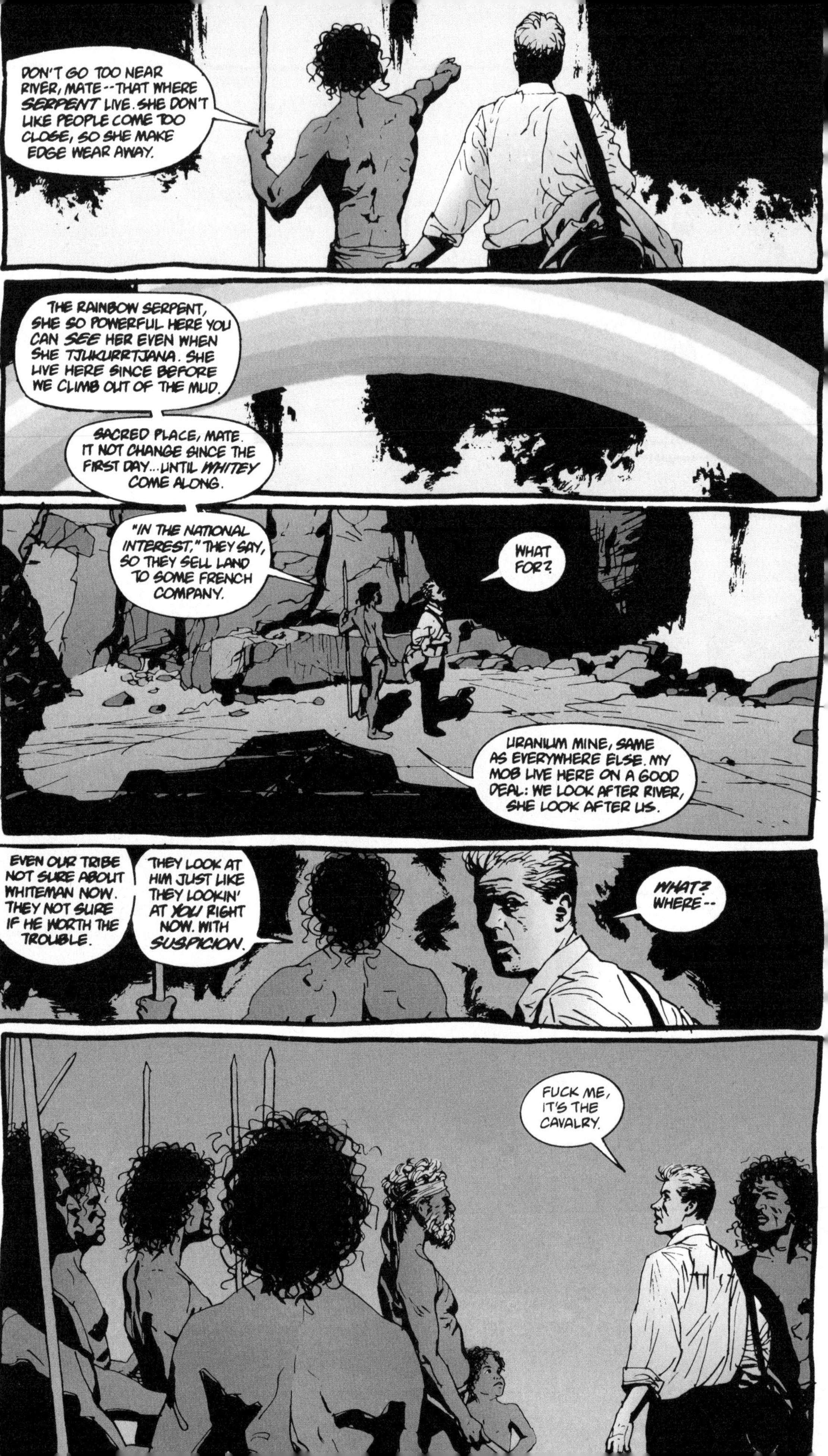
DON'T GO TOO NEAR RIVER, MATE--THAT WHERE SERPENT LIVE. SHE DON'T LIKE PEOPLE COME TOO CLOSE, SO SHE MAKE EDGE WEAR AWAY.
THE RAINBOW SERPENT, SHE SO POWERFUL HERE YOU CAN SEE HER EVEN WHEN SHE TJUKURRTJANA. SHE LIVE HERE SINCE BEFORE WE CLIMB OUT OF THE MUD.
SACRED PLACE, MATE. IT NOT CHANGE SINCE THE FIRST DAY...UNTIL WHITEY COME ALONG.
"IN THE NATIONAL INTEREST," THEY SAY, SO THEY SELL LAND TO SOME FRENCH COMPANY.
WHAT FOR?
URANIUM MINE, SAME AS EVERYWHERE ELSE. MY MOB LIVE HERE ON A GOOD DEAL: WE LOOK AFTER RIVER, SHE LOOK AFTER US.
EVEN OUR TRIBE NOT SURE ABOUT WHITEMAN NOW. THEY NOT SURE IF HE WORTH THE TROUBLE.
THEY LOOK AT HIM JUST LIKE THEY LOOKIN' AT YOU RIGHT NOW. WITH SUSPICION.
WHAT? WHERE--
FUCK ME, IT'S THE CAVALRY.

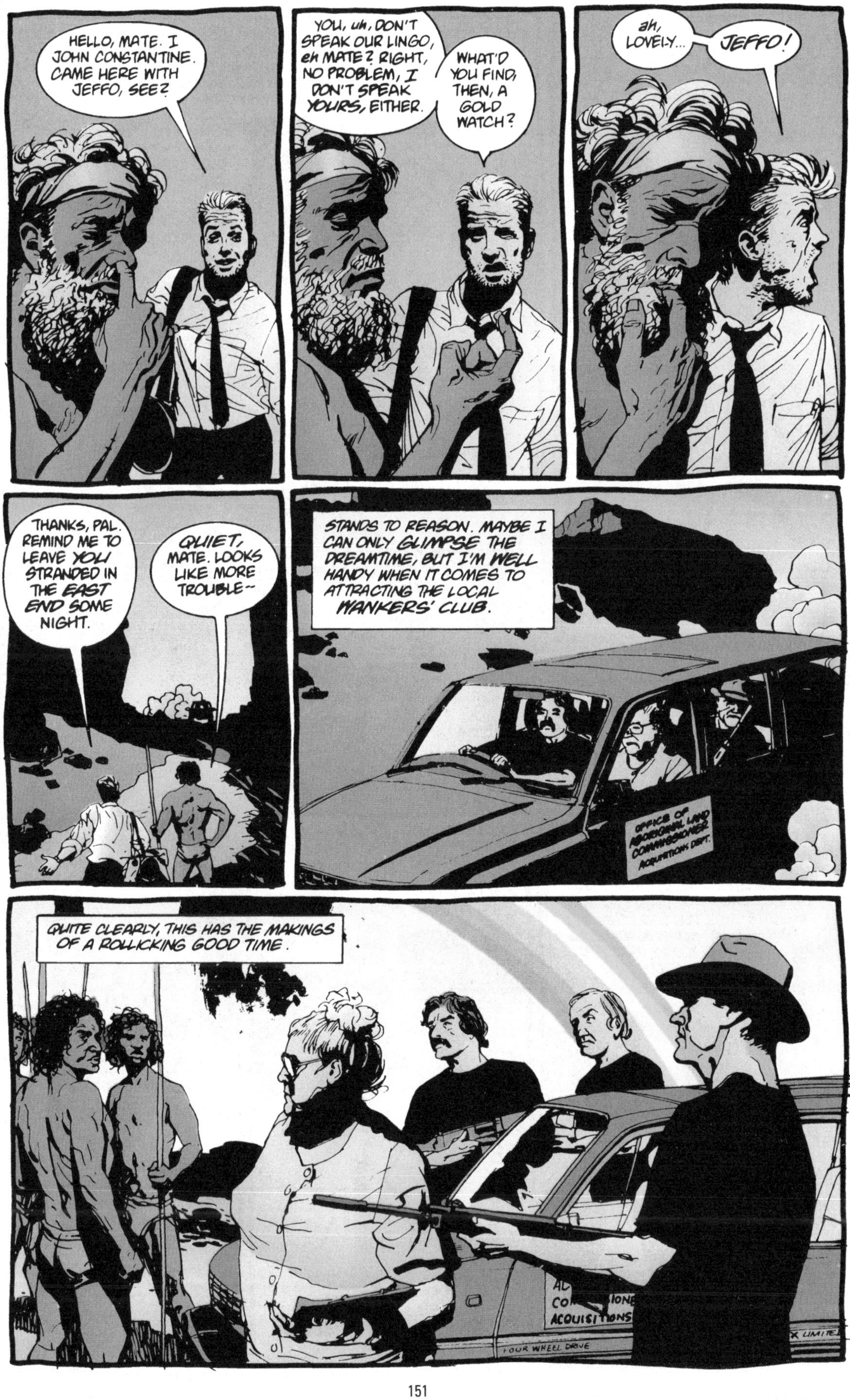

HELLO, MATE. I JOHN CONSTANTINE. CAME HERE WITH JEFFO, SEE?
YOU, uh, DON'T SPEAK OUR LINGO, eh MATE? RIGHT, NO PROBLEM, I DON'T SPEAK YOURS, EITHER.
WHAT'D YOU FIND, THEN, A GOLD WATCH?
ah, LOVELY...
JEFFO!
THANKS, PAL. REMIND ME TO LEAVE YOU STRANDED IN THE EAST END SOME NIGHT.
QUIET, MATE. LOOKS LIKE MORE TROUBLE--
STANDS TO REASON. MAYBE I CAN ONLY GLIMPSE THE DREAMTIME, BUT I'M WELL HANDY WHEN IT COMES TO ATTRACTING THE LOCAL WANKERS' CLUB.
OFFICE OF ABORIGINAL LAND COMMISSIONER ACQUISITIONS DEPT.
QUITE CLEARLY, THIS HAS THE MAKINGS OF A ROLLICKING GOOD TIME.
ACQUISITIONS
FOUR WHEEL DRIVE

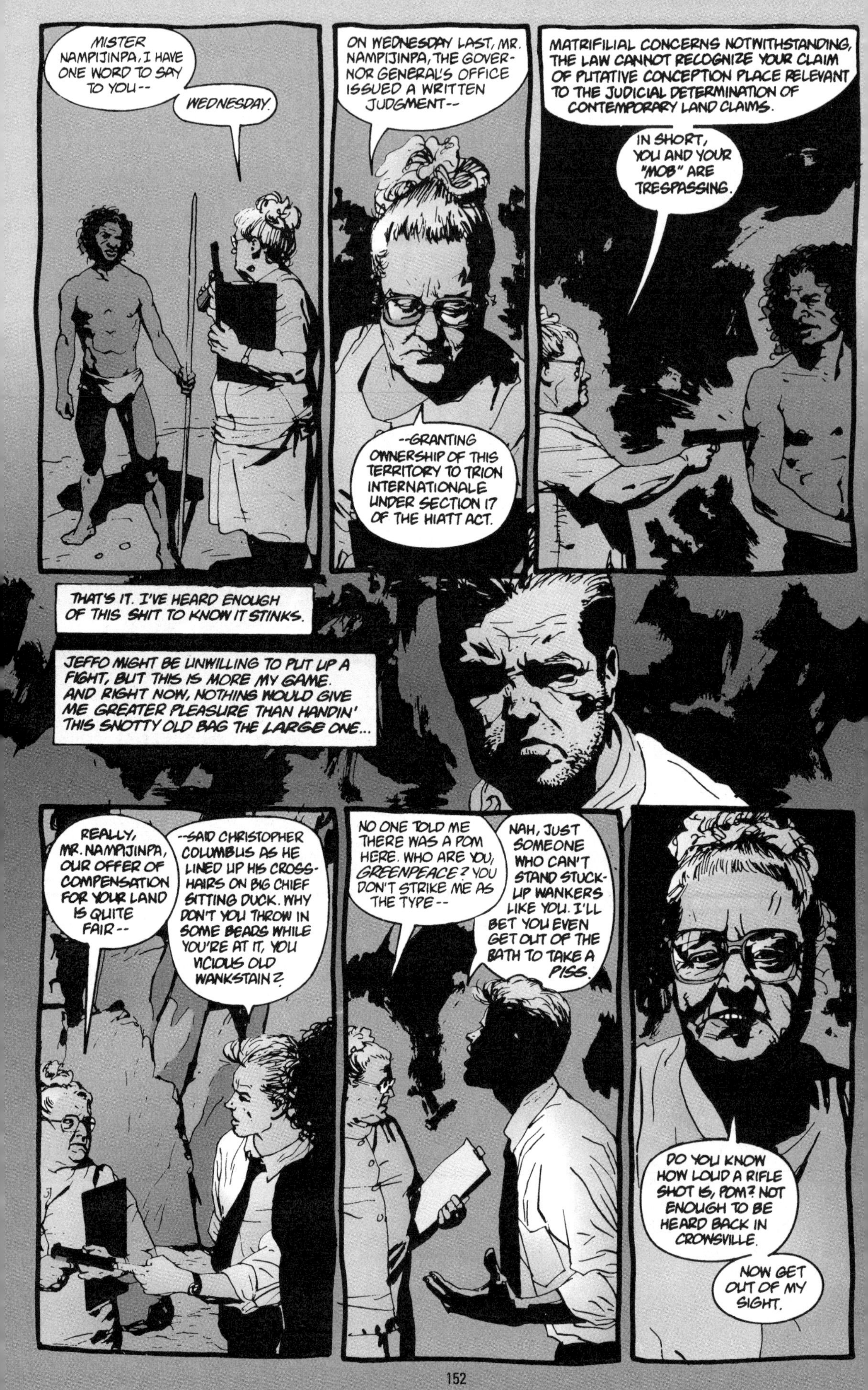

MISTER NAMPIJINPA, I HAVE ONE WORD TO SAY TO YOU--
WEDNESDAY.
ON WEDNESDAY LAST, MR. NAMPIJINPA, THE GOVERNOR GENERAL'S OFFICE ISSUED A WRITTEN JUDGMENT--
--GRANTING OWNERSHIP OF THIS TERRITORY TO TRION INTERNATIONALE UNDER SECTION 17 OF THE HIATT ACT.
MATRIFILIAL CONCERNS NOTWITHSTANDING, THE LAW CANNOT RECOGNIZE YOUR CLAIM OF PUTATIVE CONCEPTION PLACE RELEVANT TO THE JUDICIAL DETERMINATION OF CONTEMPORARY LAND CLAIMS.
IN SHORT, YOU AND YOUR "MOB" ARE TRESPASSING.
THAT'S IT. I'VE HEARD ENOUGH OF THIS SHIT TO KNOW IT STINKS.
JEFFO MIGHT BE UNWILLING TO PUT UP A FIGHT, BUT THIS IS MORE MY GAME. AND RIGHT NOW, NOTHING WOULD GIVE ME GREATER PLEASURE THAN HANDIN' THIS SNOTTY OLD BAG THE LARGE ONE...
REALLY, MR. NAMPIJINPA, OUR OFFER OF COMPENSATION FOR YOUR LAND IS QUITE FAIR--
--SAID CHRISTOPHER COLUMBUS AS HE LINED UP HIS CROSS-HAIRS ON BIG CHIEF SITTING DUCK. WHY DON'T YOU THROW IN SOME BEADS WHILE YOU'RE AT IT, YOU VICIOUS OLD WANKSTAIN?
NO ONE TOLD ME THERE WAS A POM HERE. WHO ARE YOU, GREENPEACE? YOU DON'T STRIKE ME AS THE TYPE--
NAH, JUST SOMEONE WHO CAN'T STAND STUCK-UP WANKERS LIKE YOU. I'LL BET YOU EVEN GET OUT OF THE BATH TO TAKE A PISS.
DO YOU KNOW HOW LOUD A RIFLE SHOT IS, POM? NOT ENOUGH TO BE HEARD BACK IN CROWSVILLE.
NOW GET OUT OF MY SIGHT.

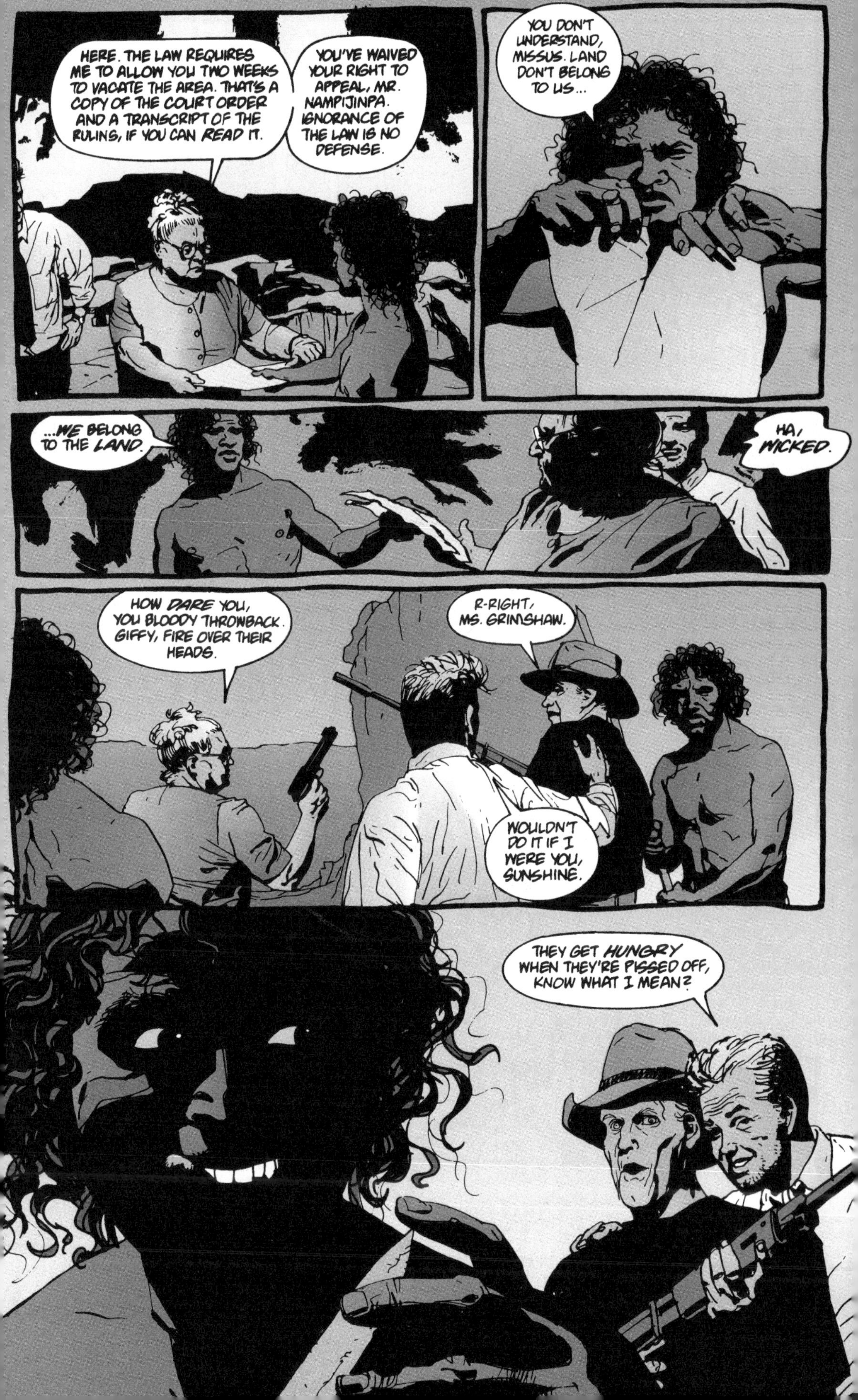
HERE. THE LAW REQUIRES ME TO ALLOW YOU TWO WEEKS TO VACATE THE AREA. THAT'S A COPY OF THE COURT ORDER AND A TRANSCRIPT OF THE RULINS, IF YOU CAN *READ* IT.
YOU'VE WAIVED YOUR RIGHT TO APPEAL, MR. NAMPIJINPA. IGNORANCE OF THE LAW IS NO DEFENSE.
YOU DON'T UNDERSTAND, MISSUS. LAND DON'T BELONG TO US...
...*WE* BELONG TO THE *LAND*.
HA, *WICKED*.
HOW *DARE* YOU, YOU BLOODY THROWBACK. GIFFY, FIRE OVER THEIR HEADS.
R-RIGHT, MS. GRIMSHAW.
WOULDN'T DO IT IF I WERE YOU, SUNSHINE.
THEY GET *HUNGRY* WHEN THEY'RE PISSED OFF, KNOW WHAT I MEAN?

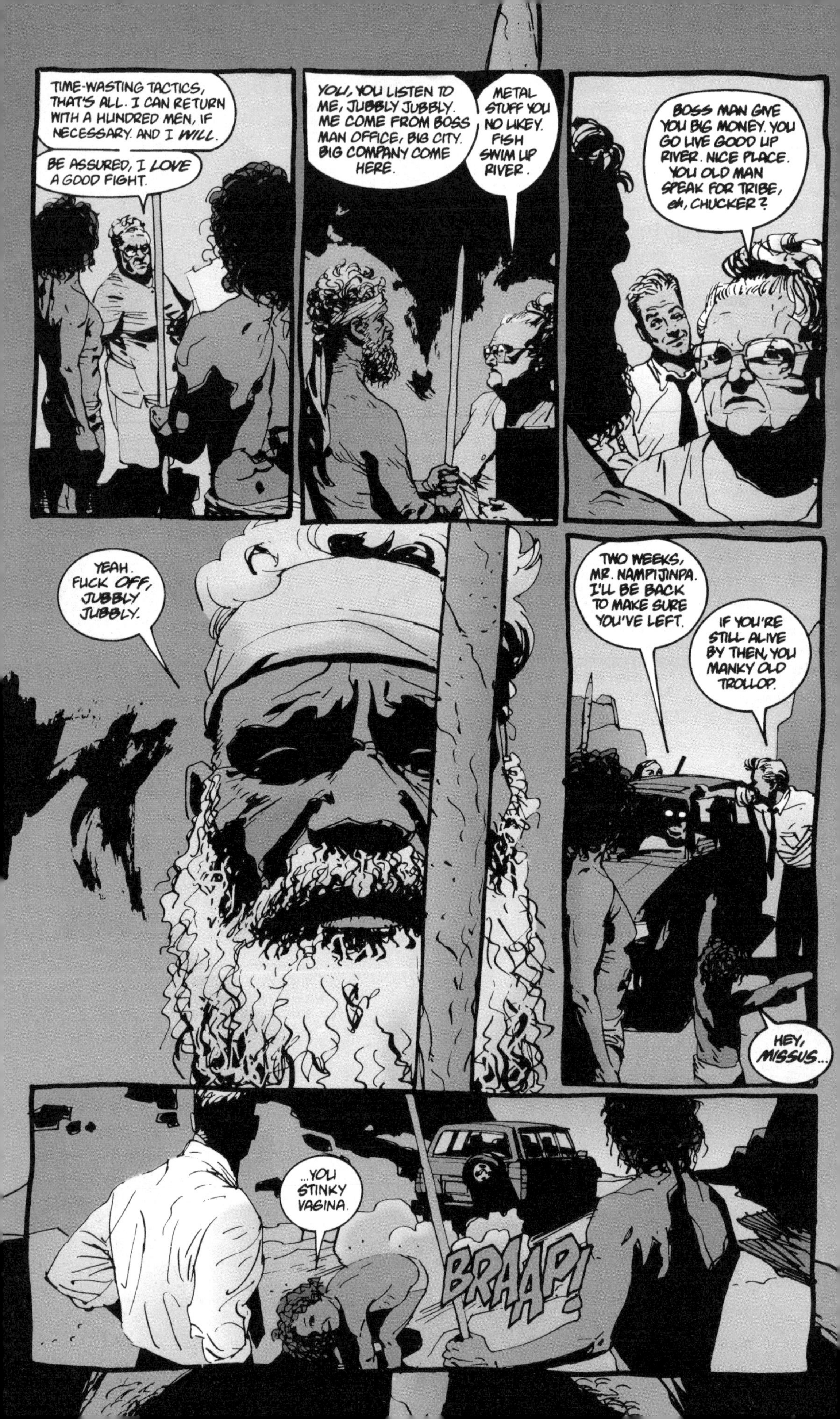
TIME-WASTING TACTICS, THAT'S ALL. I CAN RETURN WITH A HUNDRED MEN, IF NECESSARY. AND I WILL.
BE ASSURED, I LOVE A GOOD FIGHT.
YOU, YOU LISTEN TO ME, JUBBLY JUBBLY. ME COME FROM BOSS MAN OFFICE, BIG CITY. BIG COMPANY COME HERE.
METAL STUFF YOU NO LIKEY. FISH SWIM UP RIVER.
BOSS MAN GIVE YOU BIG MONEY. YOU GO LIVE GOOD UP RIVER. NICE PLACE. YOU OLD MAN SPEAK FOR TRIBE, eh, CHUCKER?
YEAH. FUCK OFF, JUBBLY JUBBLY.
TWO WEEKS, MR. NAMPIJINPA. I'LL BE BACK TO MAKE SURE YOU'VE LEFT.
IF YOU'RE STILL ALIVE BY THEN, YOU MANKY OLD TROLLOP.
HEY, MISSUS...
...YOU STINKY VAGINA.
BRAAP!

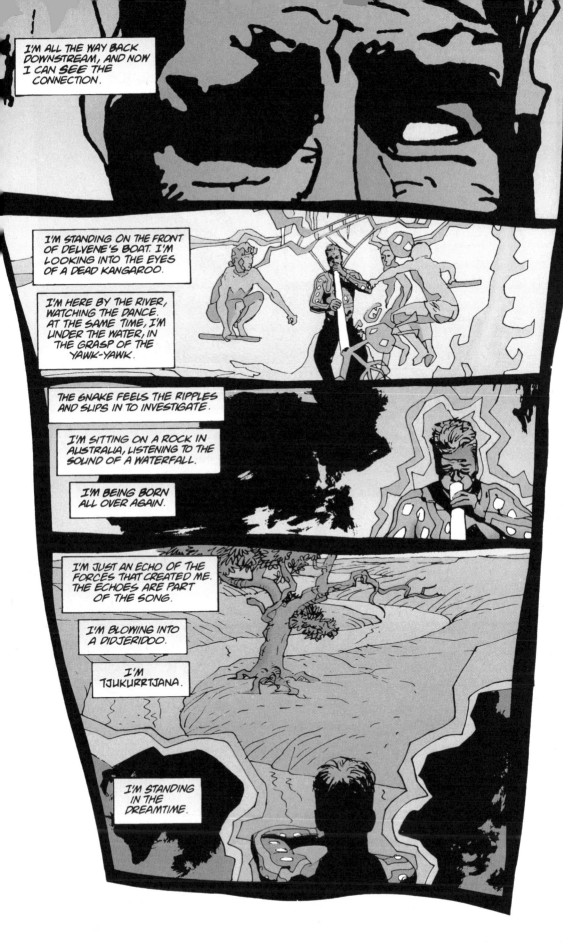

I'M ALL THE WAY BACK DOWNSTREAM, AND NOW I CAN SEE THE CONNECTION.

I'M STANDING ON THE FRONT OF DELVENE'S BOAT. I'M LOOKING INTO THE EYES OF A DEAD KANGAROO.

I'M HERE BY THE RIVER, WATCHING THE DANCE. AT THE SAME TIME, I'M UNDER THE WATER, IN THE GRASP OF THE YAWK-YAWK.

THE SNAKE FEELS THE RIPPLES AND SLIPS IN TO INVESTIGATE.

I'M SITTING ON A ROCK IN AUSTRALIA, LISTENING TO THE SOUND OF A WATERFALL.

I'M BEING BORN ALL OVER AGAIN.

I'M JUST AN ECHO OF THE FORCES THAT CREATED ME. THE ECHOES ARE PART OF THE SONG.

I'M BLOWING INTO A DIDJERIDOO.

I'M TJUKURRTJANA.

I'M STANDING IN THE DREAMTIME.

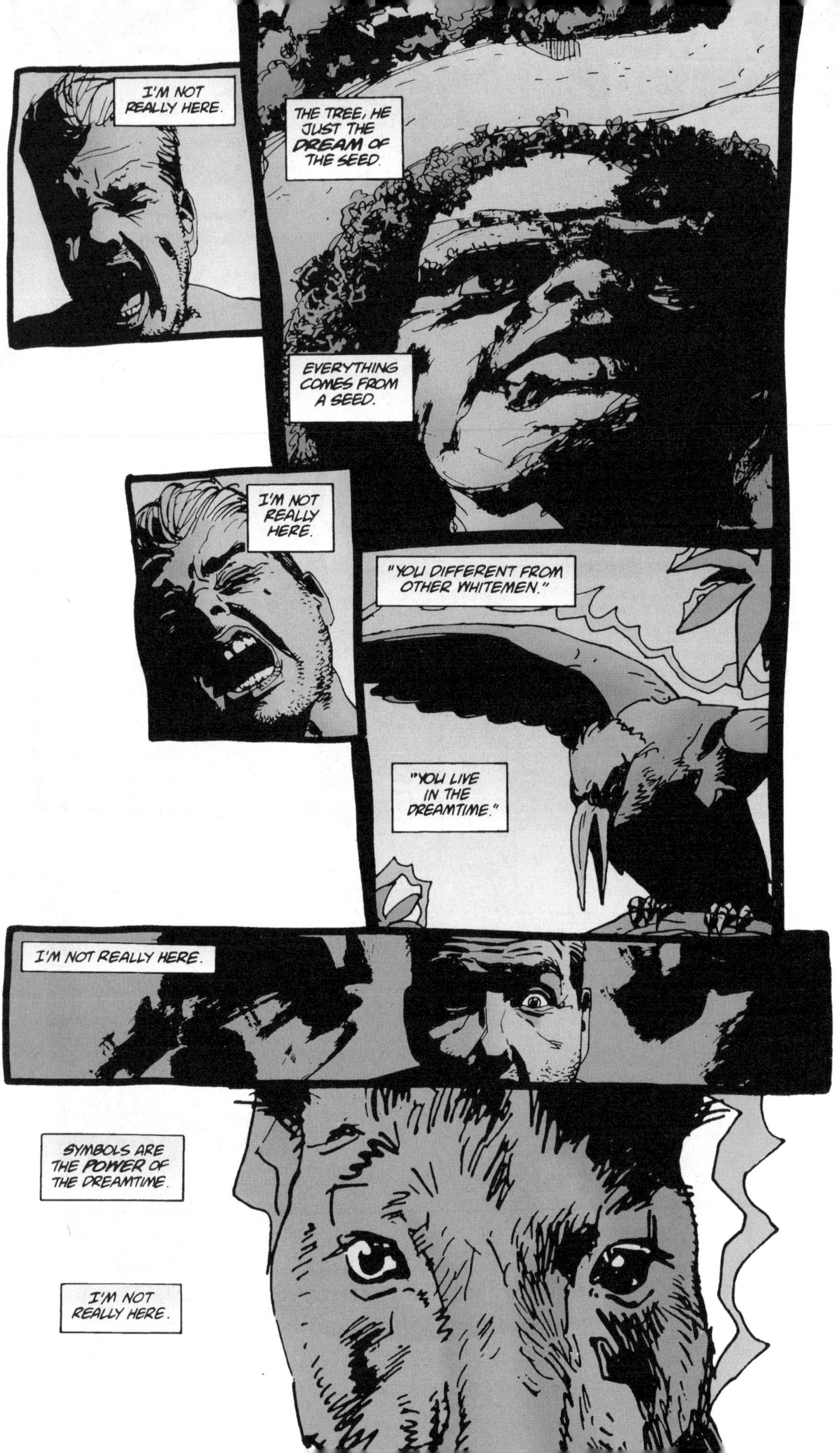
I'M NOT REALLY HERE.
THE TREE, HE JUST THE DREAM OF THE SEED.
EVERYTHING COMES FROM A SEED.
I'M NOT REALLY HERE.
"YOU DIFFERENT FROM OTHER WHITEMEN."
"YOU LIVE IN THE DREAMTIME."
I'M NOT REALLY HERE.
SYMBOLS ARE THE POWER OF THE DREAMTIME.
I'M NOT REALLY HERE.

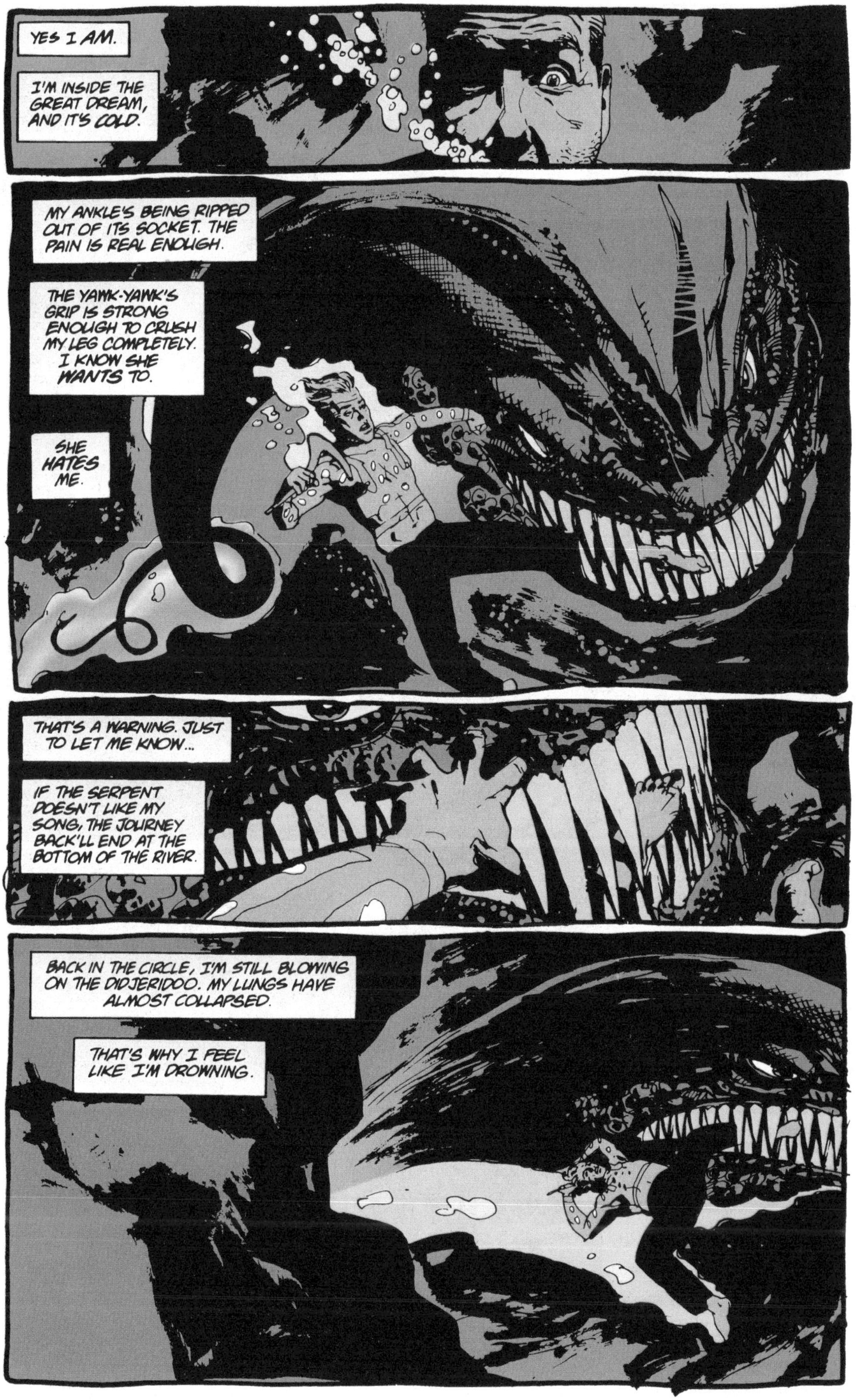
YES I AM.
I'M INSIDE THE GREAT DREAM, AND IT'S COLD.
MY ANKLE'S BEING RIPPED OUT OF ITS SOCKET. THE PAIN IS REAL ENOUGH.
THE YAWK-YAWK'S GRIP IS STRONG ENOUGH TO CRUSH MY LEG COMPLETELY. I KNOW SHE WANTS TO.
SHE HATES ME.
THAT'S A WARNING. JUST TO LET ME KNOW...
IF THE SERPENT DOESN'T LIKE MY SONG, THE JOURNEY BACK'LL END AT THE BOTTOM OF THE RIVER.
BACK IN THE CIRCLE, I'M STILL BLOWING ON THE DIDJERIDOO. MY LUNGS HAVE ALMOST COLLAPSED.
THAT'S WHY I FEEL LIKE I'M DROWNING.

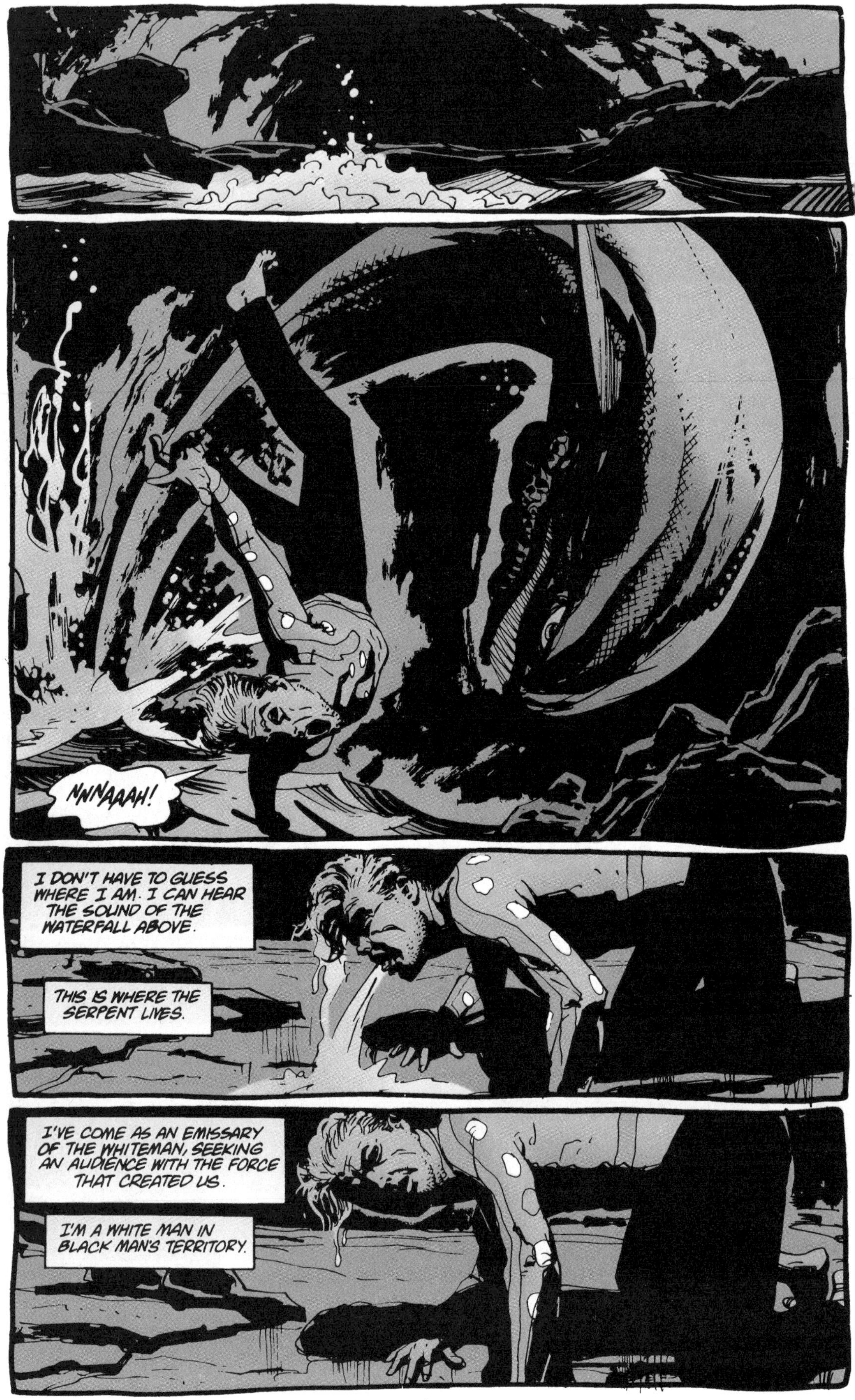
NNNAAAH!
I DON'T HAVE TO GUESS WHERE I AM. I CAN HEAR THE SOUND OF THE WATERFALL ABOVE.
THIS IS WHERE THE SERPENT LIVES.
I'VE COME AS AN EMISSARY OF THE WHITEMAN, SEEKING AN AUDIENCE WITH THE FORCE THAT CREATED US.
I'M A WHITE MAN IN BLACK MAN'S TERRITORY.

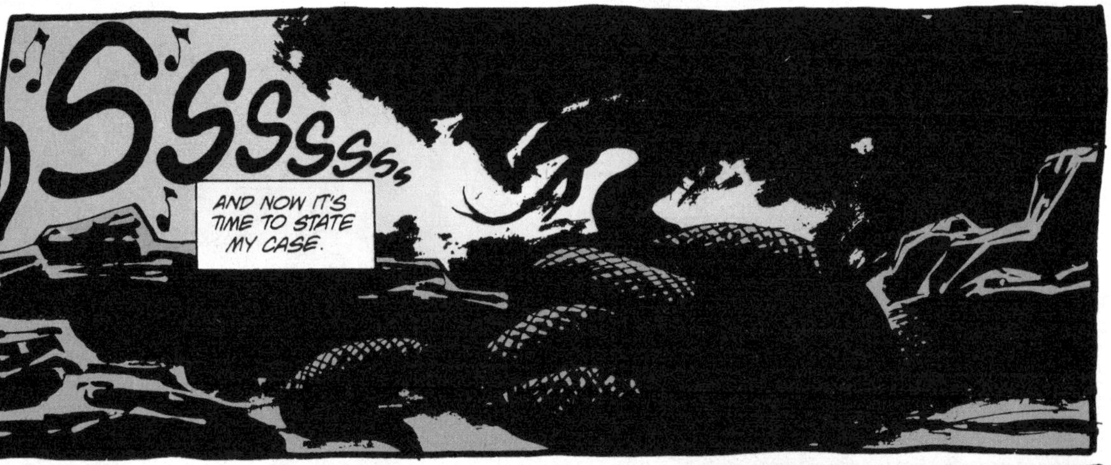
SSSSSSSs
AND NOW IT'S TIME TO STATE MY CASE.

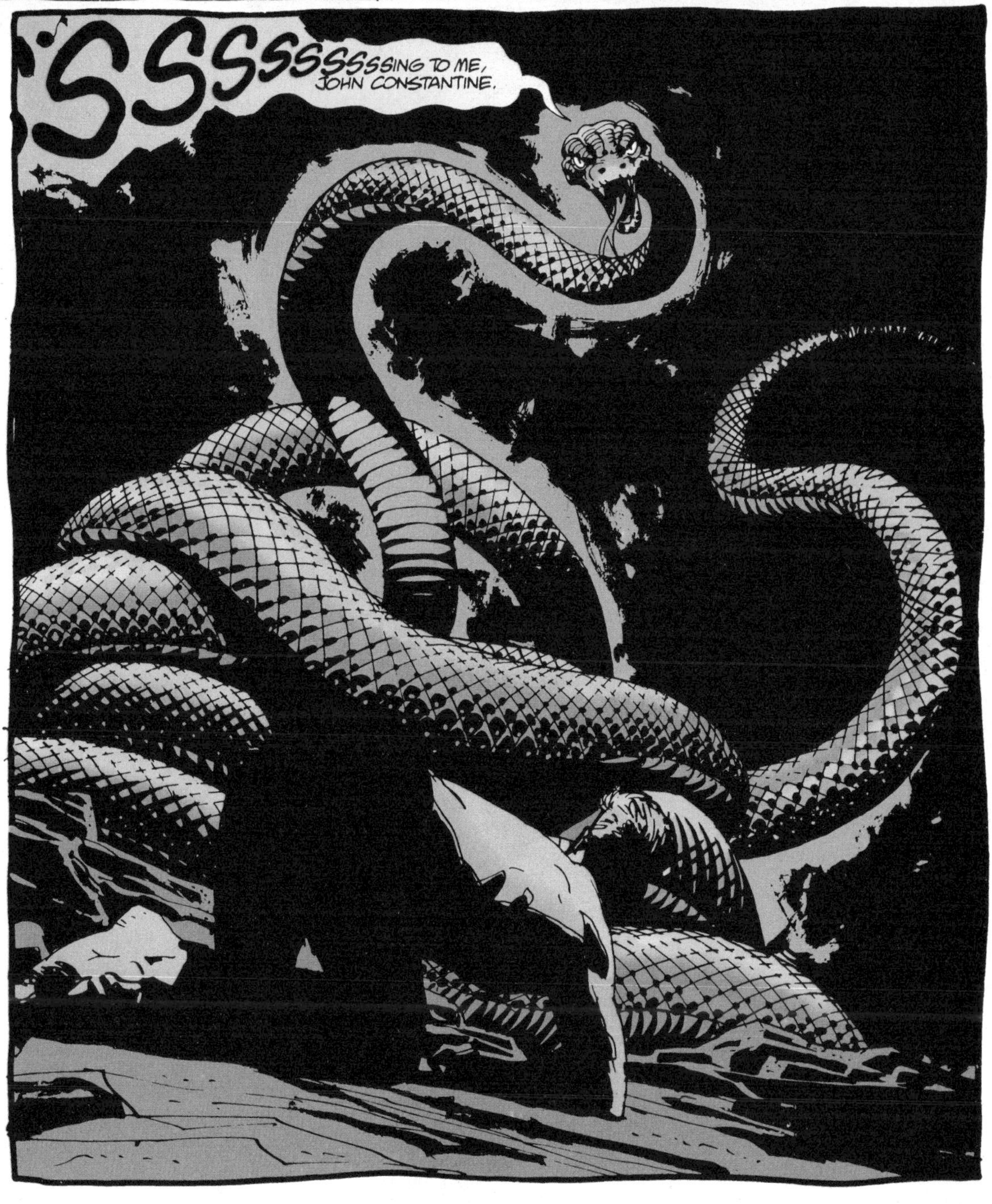
SSSSSSSSSSING TO ME, JOHN CONSTANTINE.

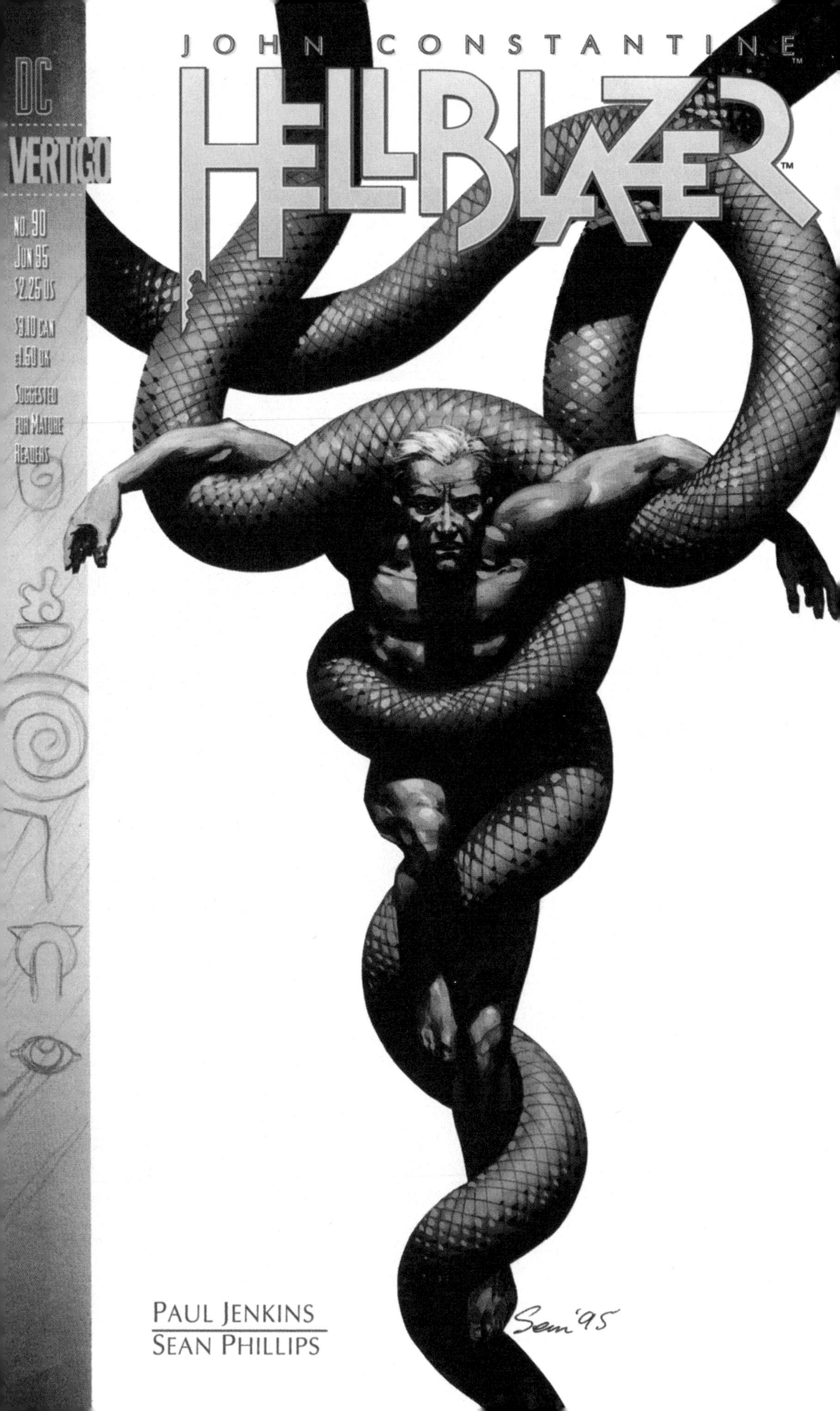
JOHN CONSTANTINE
HELLBLAZER™
DC
VERTIGO
NO. 90
JUN 95
$2.25 US
$3.10 CAN
£1.50 UK
SUGGESTED FOR MATURE READERS
PAUL JENKINS
SEAN PHILLIPS
Sean '95

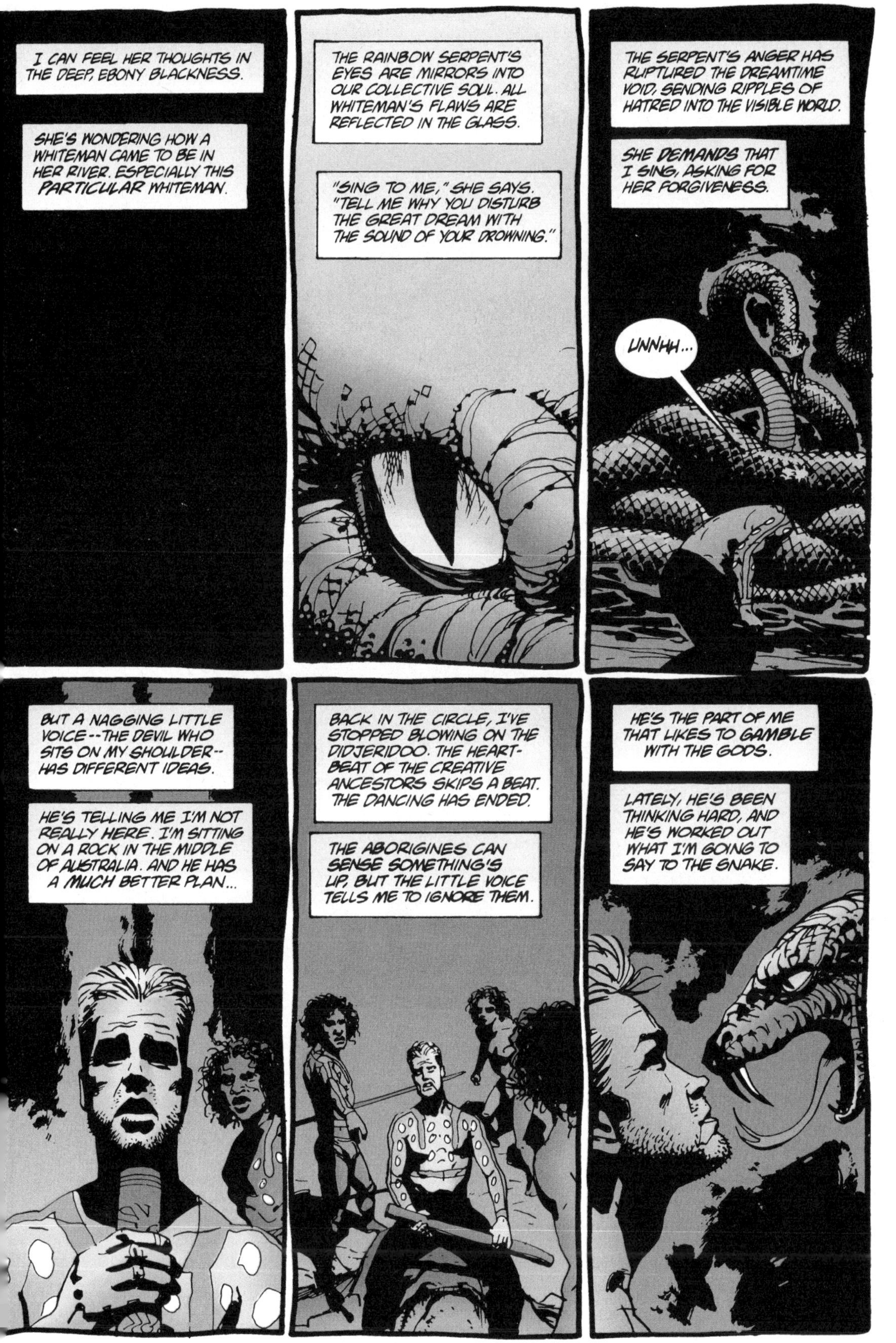

I CAN FEEL HER THOUGHTS IN THE DEEP, EBONY BLACKNESS.
SHE'S WONDERING HOW A WHITEMAN CAME TO BE IN HER RIVER. ESPECIALLY THIS PARTICULAR WHITEMAN.
THE RAINBOW SERPENT'S EYES ARE MIRRORS INTO OUR COLLECTIVE SOUL. ALL WHITEMAN'S FLAWS ARE REFLECTED IN THE GLASS.
"SING TO ME," SHE SAYS. "TELL ME WHY YOU DISTURB THE GREAT DREAM WITH THE SOUND OF YOUR DROWNING."
THE SERPENT'S ANGER HAS RUPTURED THE DREAMTIME VOID, SENDING RIPPLES OF HATRED INTO THE VISIBLE WORLD.
SHE DEMANDS THAT I SING, ASKING FOR HER FORGIVENESS.
UNNHH...
BUT A NAGGING LITTLE VOICE--THE DEVIL WHO SITS ON MY SHOULDER--HAS DIFFERENT IDEAS.
HE'S TELLING ME I'M NOT REALLY HERE. I'M SITTING ON A ROCK IN THE MIDDLE OF AUSTRALIA. AND HE HAS A MUCH BETTER PLAN...
BACK IN THE CIRCLE, I'VE STOPPED BLOWING ON THE DIDJERIDOO. THE HEART-BEAT OF THE CREATIVE ANCESTORS SKIPS A BEAT. THE DANCING HAS ENDED.
THE ABORIGINES CAN SENSE SOMETHING'S UP, BUT THE LITTLE VOICE TELLS ME TO IGNORE THEM.
HE'S THE PART OF ME THAT LIKES TO GAMBLE WITH THE GODS.
LATELY, HE'S BEEN THINKING HARD, AND HE'S WORKED OUT WHAT I'M GOING TO SAY TO THE SNAKE.

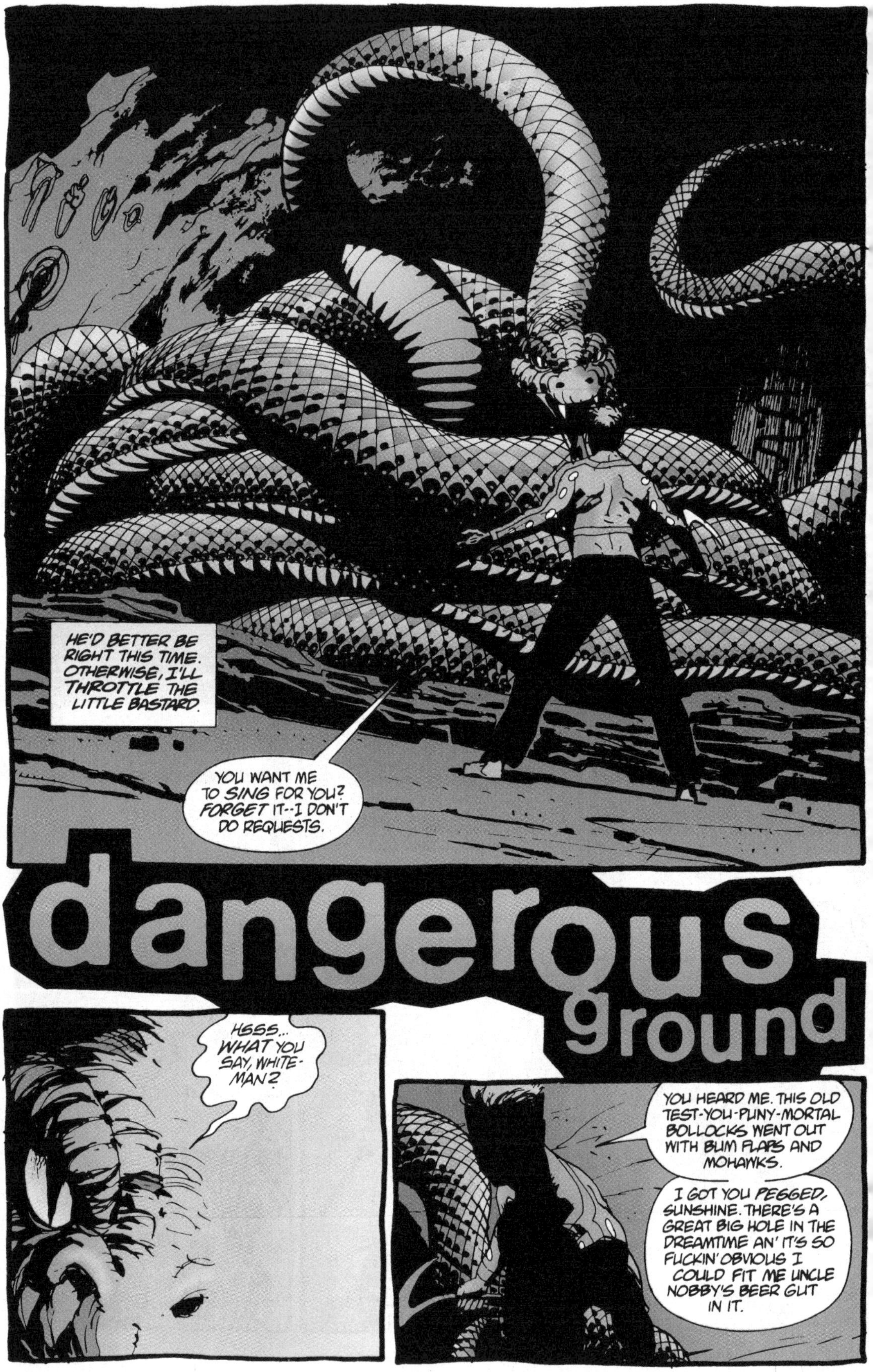
HE'D BETTER BE RIGHT THIS TIME. OTHERWISE, I'LL THROTTLE THE LITTLE BASTARD.
YOU WANT ME TO SING FOR YOU? FORGET IT--I DON'T DO REQUESTS.
dangerous ground
HSSS... WHAT YOU SAY, WHITE-MAN?
YOU HEARD ME. THIS OLD TEST-YOU-PUNY-MORTAL BOLLOCKS WENT OUT WITH BUM FLAPS AND MOHAWKS.
I GOT YOU PEGGED, SUNSHINE. THERE'S A GREAT BIG HOLE IN THE DREAMTIME AN' IT'S SO FUCKIN' OBVIOUS I COULD FIT ME UNCLE NOBBY'S BEER GUT IN IT.

PAUL JENKINS WRITER · SEAN PHILLIPS ARTIST · MATT HOLLINGSWORTH COLORIST · CLEM ROBINS LETTERER · AXEL ALONSO ASST. EDITOR · LOU STATHIS EDITOR

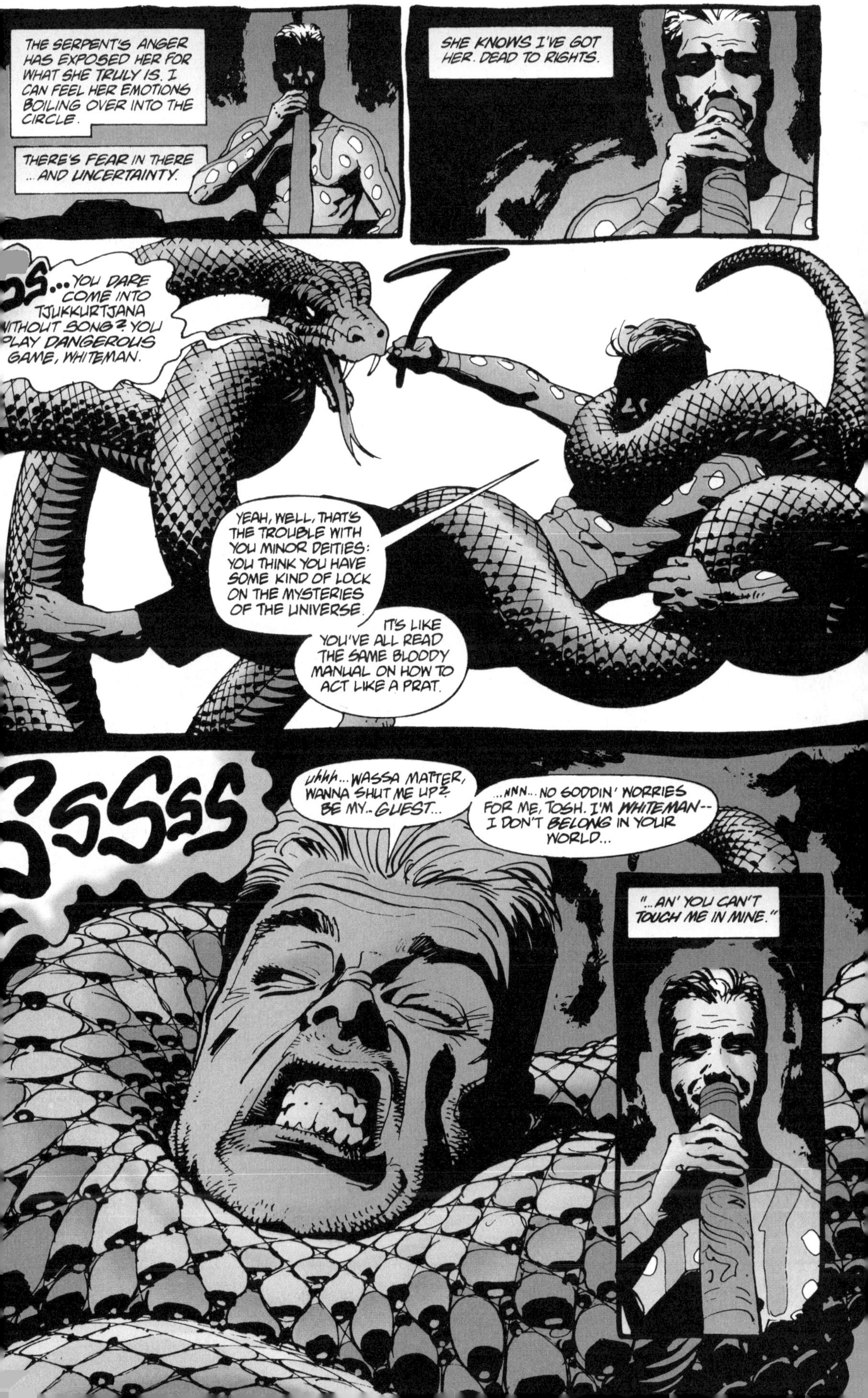
THE SERPENT'S ANGER HAS EXPOSED HER FOR WHAT SHE TRULY IS. I CAN FEEL HER EMOTIONS BOILING OVER INTO THE CIRCLE.
THERE'S FEAR IN THERE ... AND UNCERTAINTY.
SHE KNOWS I'VE GOT HER. DEAD TO RIGHTS.
SS... YOU DARE COME INTO TJUKKURTJANA WITHOUT SONG? YOU PLAY DANGEROUS GAME, WHITEMAN.
YEAH, WELL, THAT'S THE TROUBLE WITH YOU MINOR DEITIES: YOU THINK YOU HAVE SOME KIND OF LOCK ON THE MYSTERIES OF THE UNIVERSE.
IT'S LIKE YOU'VE ALL READ THE SAME BLOODY MANUAL ON HOW TO ACT LIKE A PRAT.
SSSSS
UHHH... WASSA MATTER, WANNA SHUT ME UP? BE MY.. GUEST...
...NNN... NO SODDIN' WORRIES FOR ME, TOSH. I'M WHITEMAN-- I DON'T BELONG IN YOUR WORLD...
"...AN' YOU CAN'T TOUCH ME IN MINE."

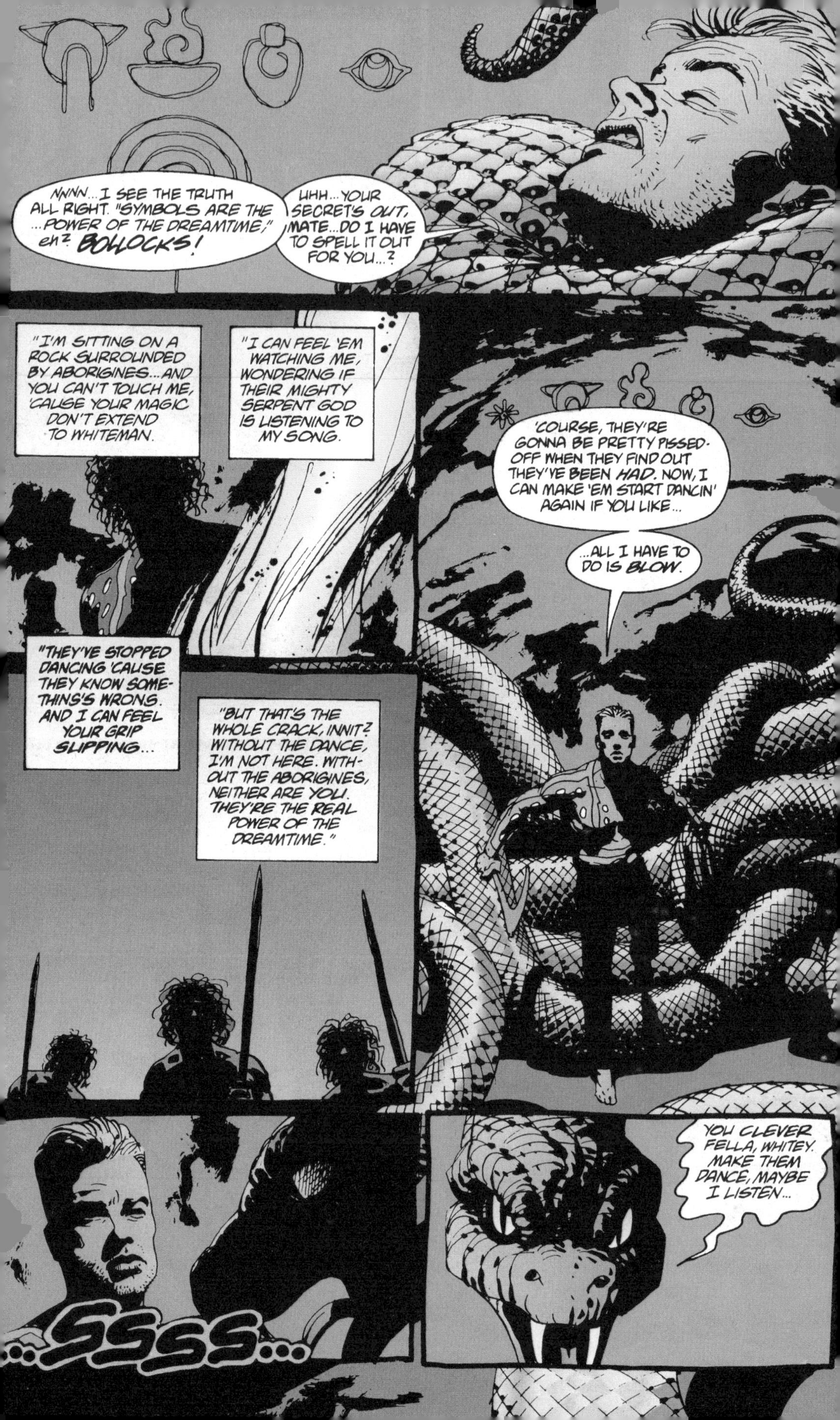
NNNN... I SEE THE TRUTH ALL RIGHT. "SYMBOLS ARE THE ...POWER OF THE DREAMTIME," eh? BOLLOCKS!
UHH... YOUR SECRET'S OUT, MATE...DO I HAVE TO SPELL IT OUT FOR YOU...?
"I'M SITTING ON A ROCK SURROUNDED BY ABORIGINES... AND YOU CAN'T TOUCH ME, 'CAUSE YOUR MAGIC DON'T EXTEND TO WHITEMAN.
"I CAN FEEL 'EM WATCHING ME, WONDERING IF THEIR MIGHTY SERPENT GOD IS LISTENING TO MY SONG.
"THEY'VE STOPPED DANCING 'CAUSE THEY KNOW SOME-THING'S WRONG. AND I CAN FEEL YOUR GRIP SLIPPING...
"BUT THAT'S THE WHOLE CRACK, INNIT? WITHOUT THE DANCE, I'M NOT HERE. WITH-OUT THE ABORIGINES, NEITHER ARE YOU. THEY'RE THE REAL POWER OF THE DREAMTIME."
'COURSE, THEY'RE GONNA BE PRETTY PISSED-OFF WHEN THEY FIND OUT THEY'VE BEEN HAD. NOW, I CAN MAKE 'EM START DANCIN' AGAIN IF YOU LIKE...
...ALL I HAVE TO DO IS BLOW.
...SSSSS...
YOU CLEVER FELLA, WHITEY. MAKE THEM DANCE, MAYBE I LISTEN...

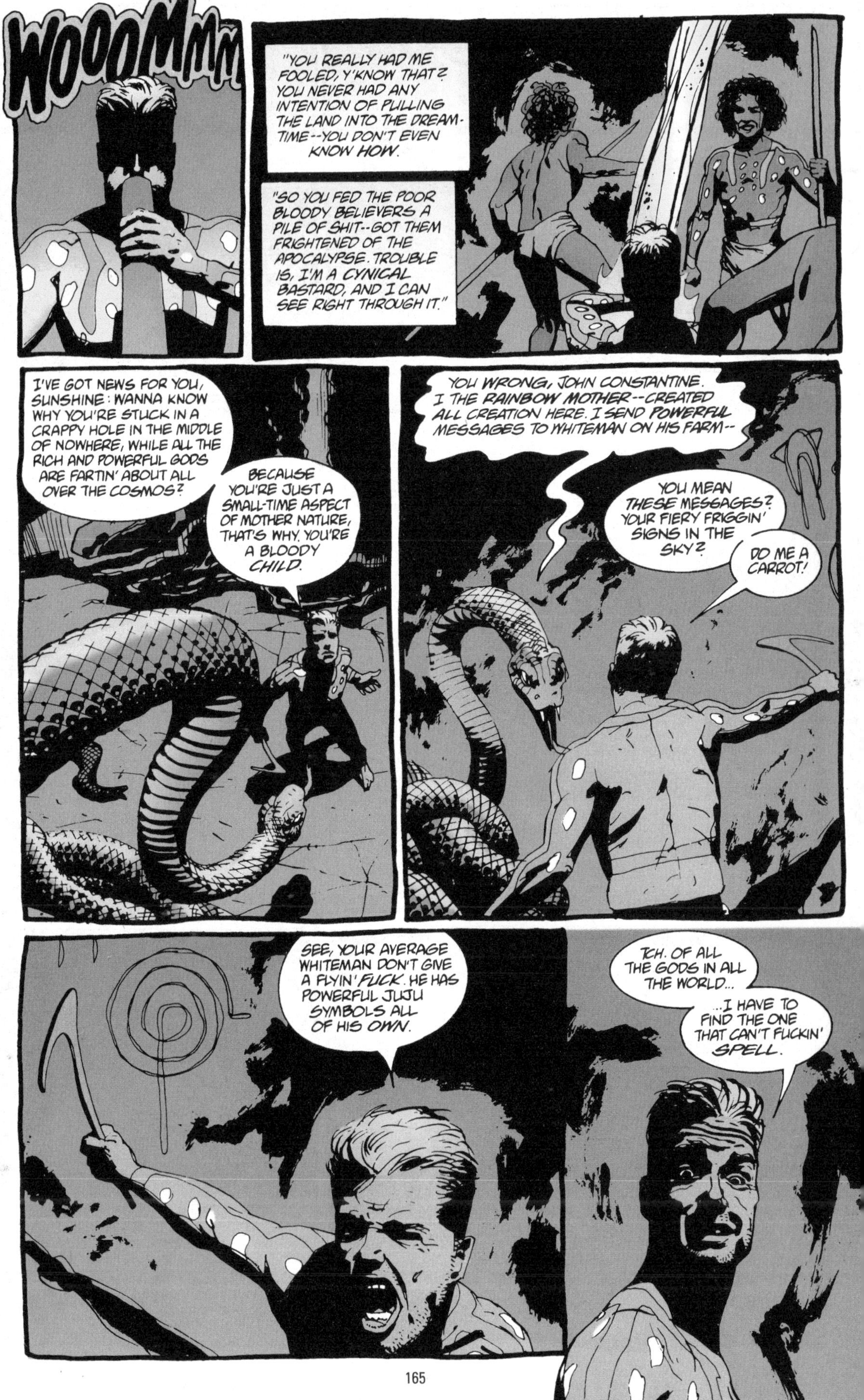
WOOOMMM
"YOU REALLY HAD ME FOOLED, Y'KNOW THAT? YOU NEVER HAD ANY INTENTION OF PULLING THE LAND INTO THE DREAM-TIME--YOU DON'T EVEN KNOW HOW.
"SO YOU FED THE POOR BLOODY BELIEVERS A PILE OF SHIT--GOT THEM FRIGHTENED OF THE APOCALYPSE. TROUBLE IS, I'M A CYNICAL BASTARD, AND I CAN SEE RIGHT THROUGH IT."
I'VE GOT NEWS FOR YOU, SUNSHINE: WANNA KNOW WHY YOU'RE STUCK IN A CRAPPY HOLE IN THE MIDDLE OF NOWHERE, WHILE ALL THE RICH AND POWERFUL GODS ARE FARTIN' ABOUT ALL OVER THE COSMOS?
BECAUSE YOU'RE JUST A SMALL-TIME ASPECT OF MOTHER NATURE, THAT'S WHY. YOU'RE A BLOODY CHILD.
YOU WRONG, JOHN CONSTANTINE. I THE RAINBOW MOTHER--CREATED ALL CREATION HERE. I SEND POWERFUL MESSAGES TO WHITEMAN ON HIS FARM--
YOU MEAN THESE MESSAGES? YOUR FIERY FRIGGIN' SIGNS IN THE SKY?
DO ME A CARROT!
SEE, YOUR AVERAGE WHITEMAN DON'T GIVE A FLYIN' FUCK. HE HAS POWERFUL JUJU SYMBOLS ALL OF HIS OWN.
TCH. OF ALL THE GODS IN ALL THE WORLD...
...I HAVE TO FIND THE ONE THAT CAN'T FUCKIN' SPELL.

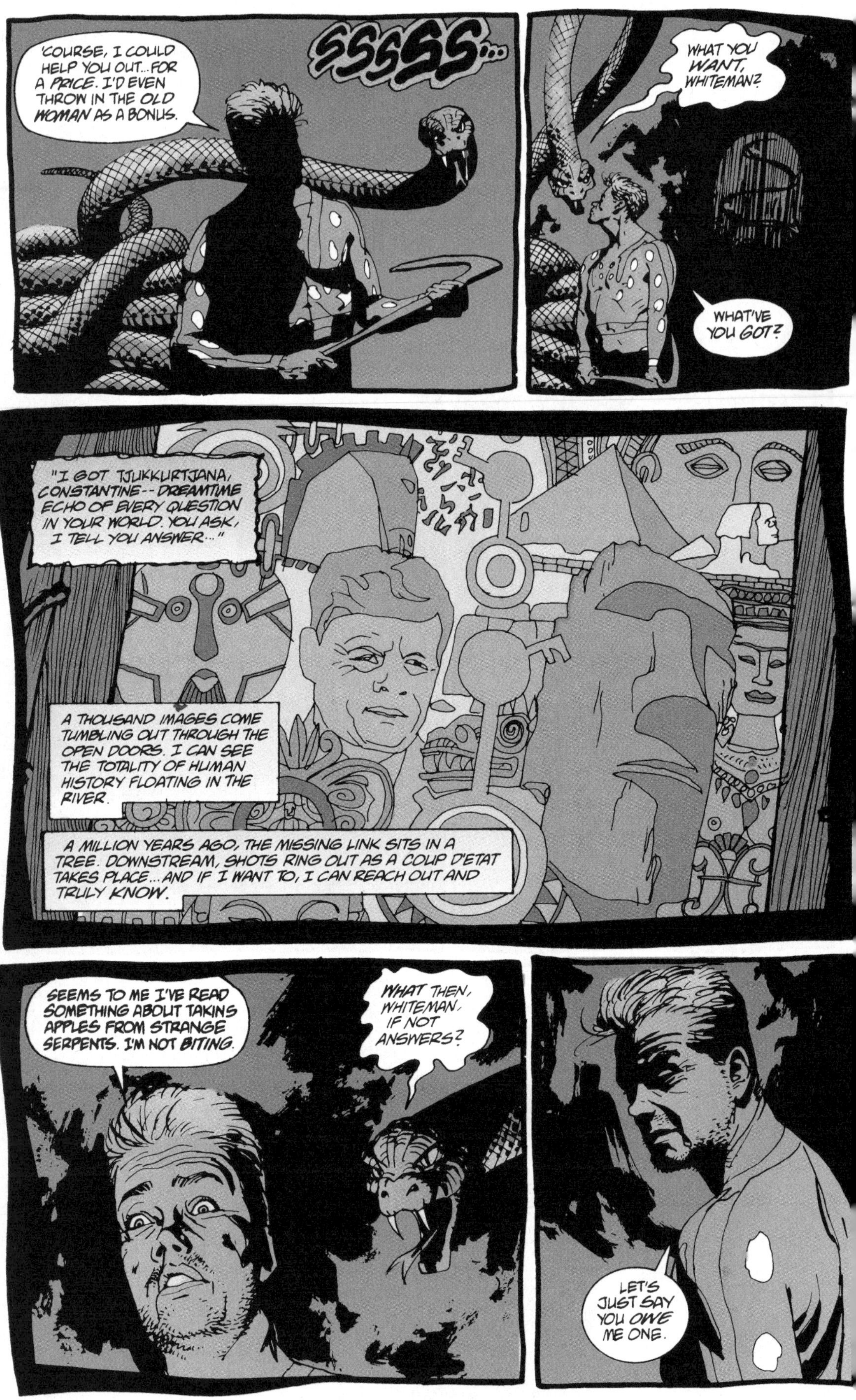
'COURSE, I COULD HELP YOU OUT... FOR A PRICE. I'D EVEN THROW IN THE OLD WOMAN AS A BONUS.
SSSSS...
WHAT YOU WANT, WHITEMAN?
WHAT'VE YOU GOT?
"I GOT TJUKKURTJANA, CONSTANTINE-- DREAMTIME ECHO OF EVERY QUESTION IN YOUR WORLD. YOU ASK, I TELL YOU ANSWER..."
A THOUSAND IMAGES COME TUMBLING OUT THROUGH THE OPEN DOORS. I CAN SEE THE TOTALITY OF HUMAN HISTORY FLOATING IN THE RIVER.
A MILLION YEARS AGO, THE MISSING LINK SITS IN A TREE. DOWNSTREAM, SHOTS RING OUT AS A COUP D'ETAT TAKES PLACE... AND IF I WANT TO, I CAN REACH OUT AND TRULY KNOW.
SEEMS TO ME I'VE READ SOMETHING ABOUT TAKING APPLES FROM STRANGE SERPENTS. I'M NOT BITING.
WHAT THEN, WHITEMAN, IF NOT ANSWERS?
LET'S JUST SAY YOU OWE ME ONE.

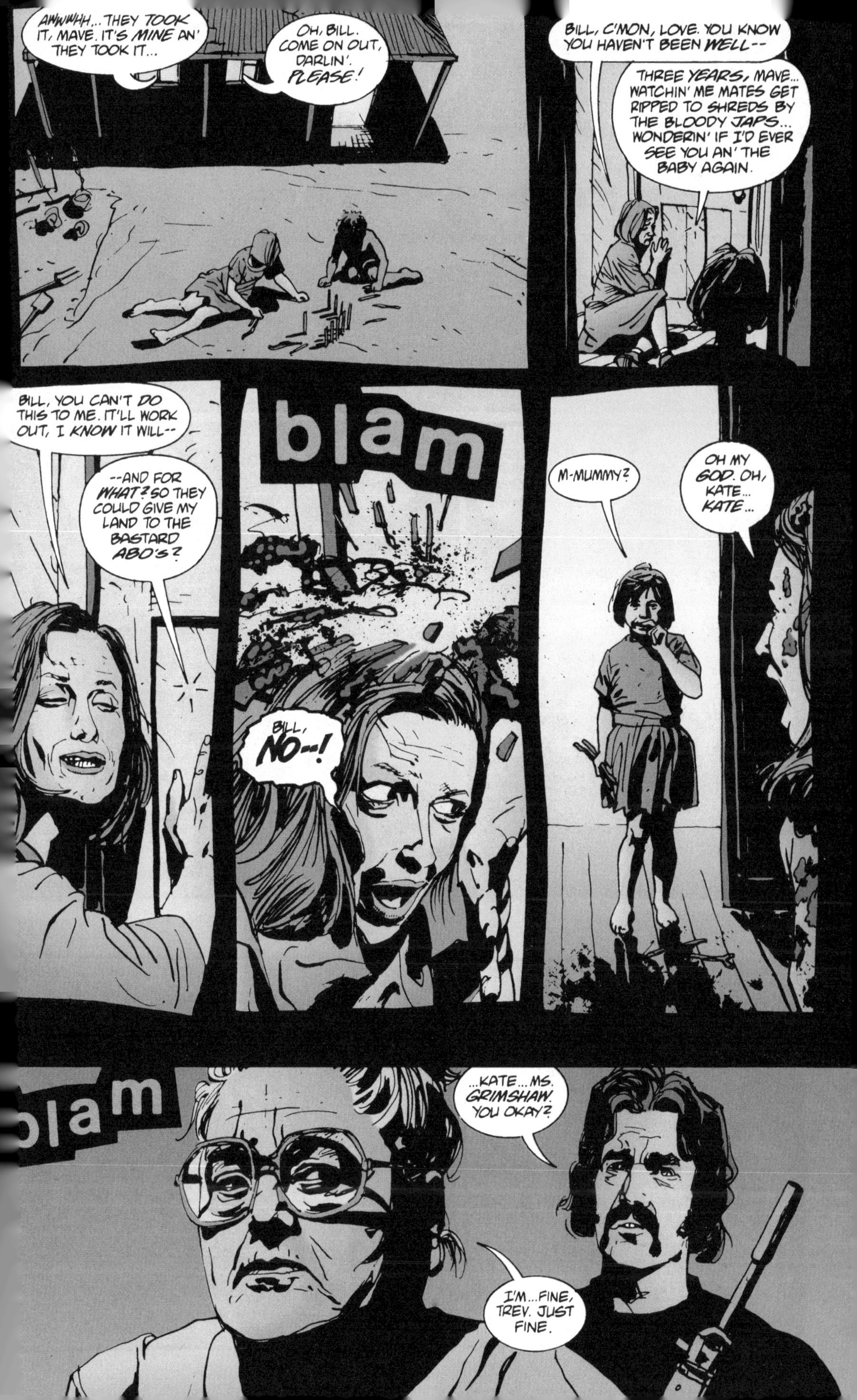
AWWWHH... THEY TOOK IT, MAVE. IT'S MINE AN' THEY TOOK IT...
OH, BILL. COME ON OUT, DARLIN'. PLEASE!
BILL, C'MON, LOVE. YOU KNOW YOU HAVEN'T BEEN WELL--
THREE YEARS, MAVE... WATCHIN' ME MATES GET RIPPED TO SHREDS BY THE BLOODY JAPS... WONDERIN' IF I'D EVER SEE YOU AN' THE BABY AGAIN.
BILL, YOU CAN'T DO THIS TO ME. IT'LL WORK OUT, I KNOW IT WILL--
--AND FOR WHAT? SO THEY COULD GIVE MY LAND TO THE BASTARD ABO'S?
blam
BILL, NO--!
M-MUMMY?
OH MY GOD. OH, KATE... KATE...
blam
...KATE... MS. GRIMSHAW. YOU OKAY?
I'M... FINE, TREV. JUST FINE.

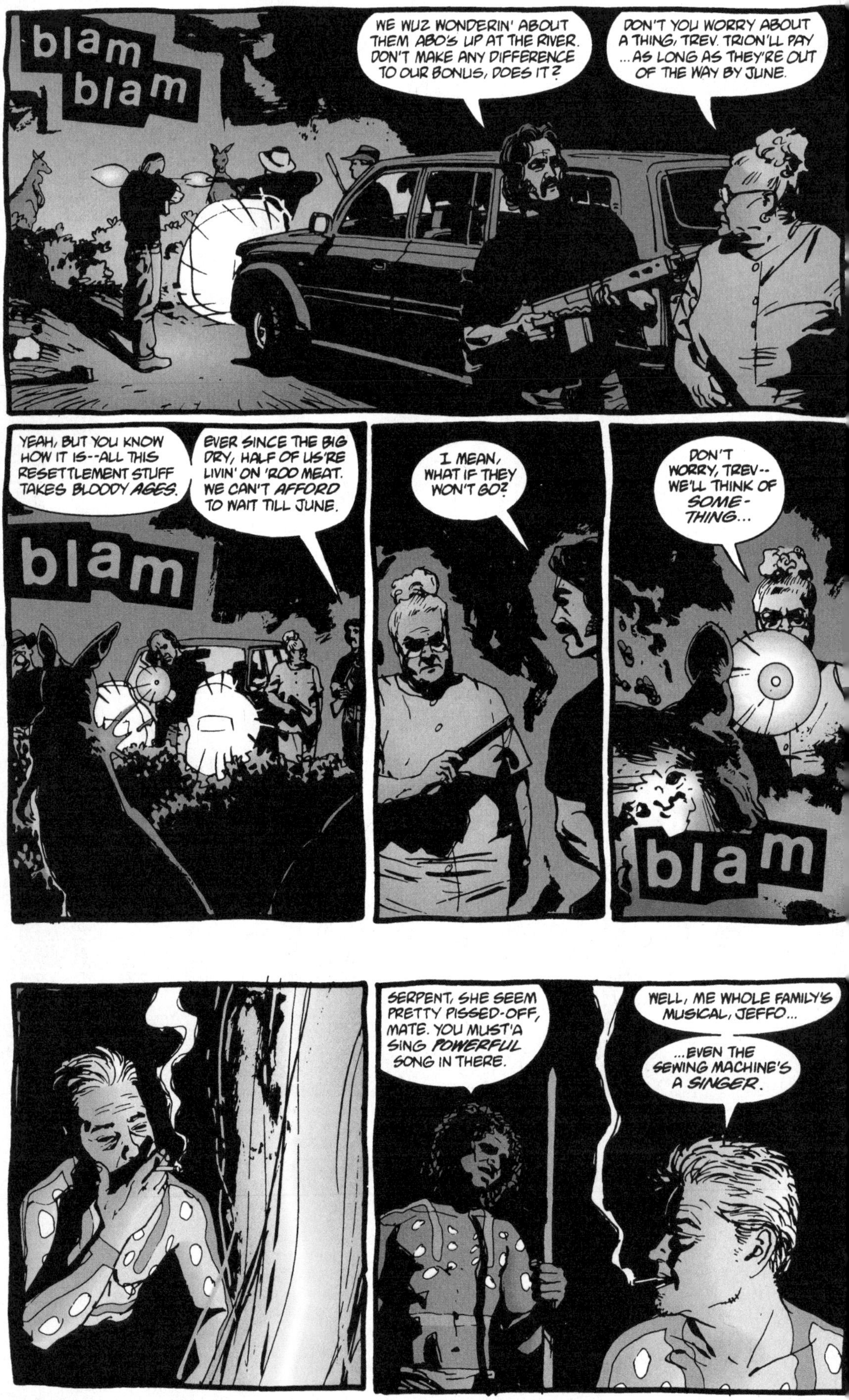
blam
blam
WE WUZ WONDERIN' ABOUT THEM ABO'S UP AT THE RIVER. DON'T MAKE ANY DIFFERENCE TO OUR BONUS, DOES IT?
DON'T YOU WORRY ABOUT A THING, TREV. TRION'LL PAY ...AS LONG AS THEY'RE OUT OF THE WAY BY JUNE.
YEAH, BUT YOU KNOW HOW IT IS--ALL THIS RESETTLEMENT STUFF TAKES BLOODY AGES.
EVER SINCE THE BIG DRY, HALF OF US'RE LIVIN' ON 'ROO MEAT. WE CAN'T AFFORD TO WAIT TILL JUNE.
blam
I MEAN, WHAT IF THEY WON'T GO?
DON'T WORRY, TREV-- WE'LL THINK OF SOME-THING...
blam
SERPENT, SHE SEEM PRETTY PISSED-OFF, MATE. YOU MUST'A SING POWERFUL SONG IN THERE.
WELL, ME WHOLE FAMILY'S MUSICAL, JEFFO...
...EVEN THE SEWING MACHINE'S A SINGER.

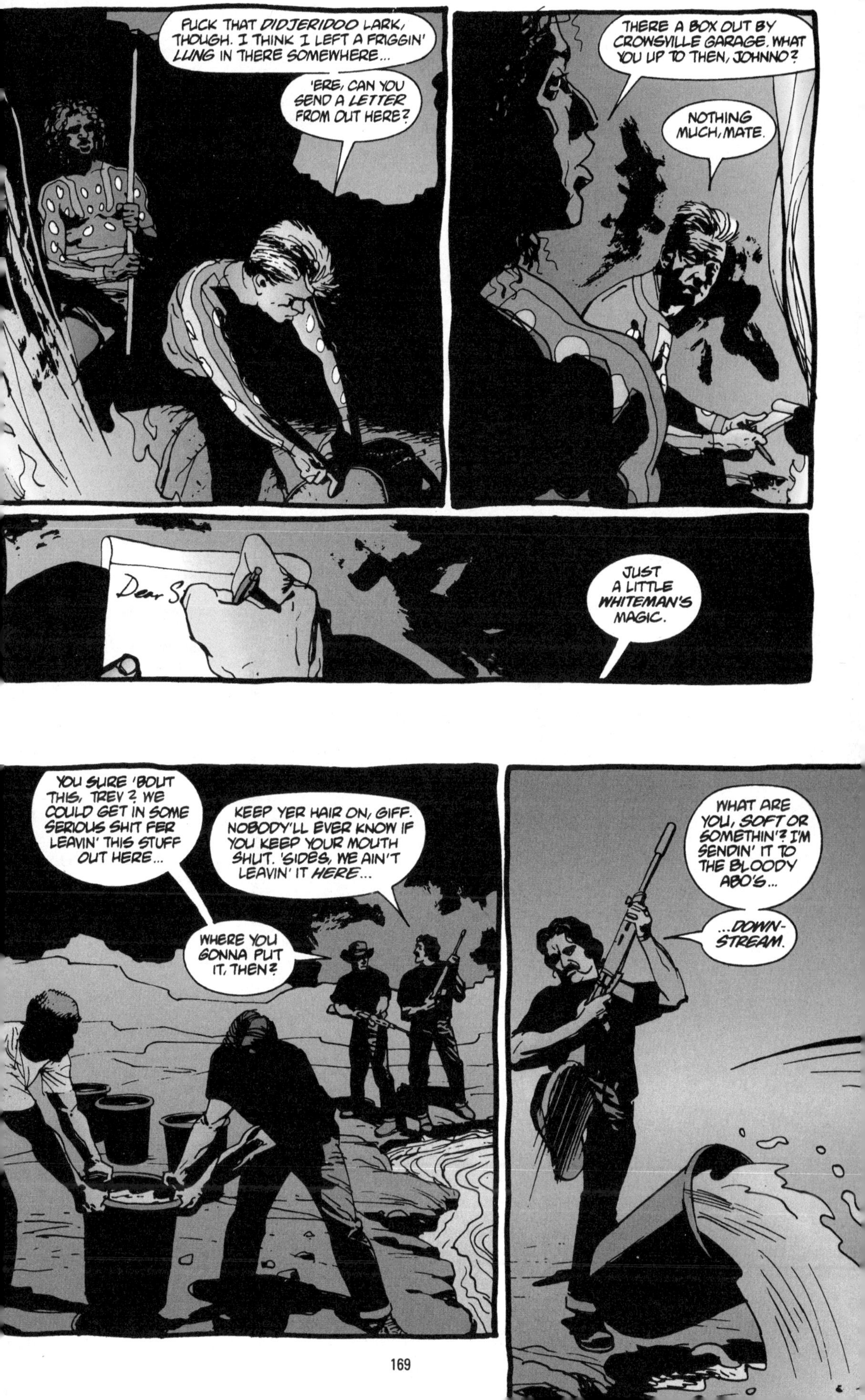
FUCK THAT DIDJERIDOO LARK, THOUGH. I THINK I LEFT A FRIGGIN' LUNG IN THERE SOMEWHERE...
'ERE, CAN YOU SEND A LETTER FROM OUT HERE?
THERE A BOX OUT BY CROWSVILLE GARAGE. WHAT YOU UP TO THEN, JOHNNO?
NOTHING MUCH, MATE.
Dear S
JUST A LITTLE WHITEMAN'S MAGIC.
YOU SURE 'BOUT THIS, TREV? WE COULD GET IN SOME SERIOUS SHIT FER LEAVIN' THIS STUFF OUT HERE...
KEEP YER HAIR ON, GIFF. NOBODY'LL EVER KNOW IF YOU KEEP YOUR MOUTH SHUT. 'SIDES, WE AIN'T LEAVIN' IT HERE...
WHERE YOU GONNA PUT IT, THEN?
WHAT ARE YOU, SOFT OR SOMETHIN'? I'M SENDIN' IT TO THE BLOODY ABO'S...
...DOWN-STREAM.

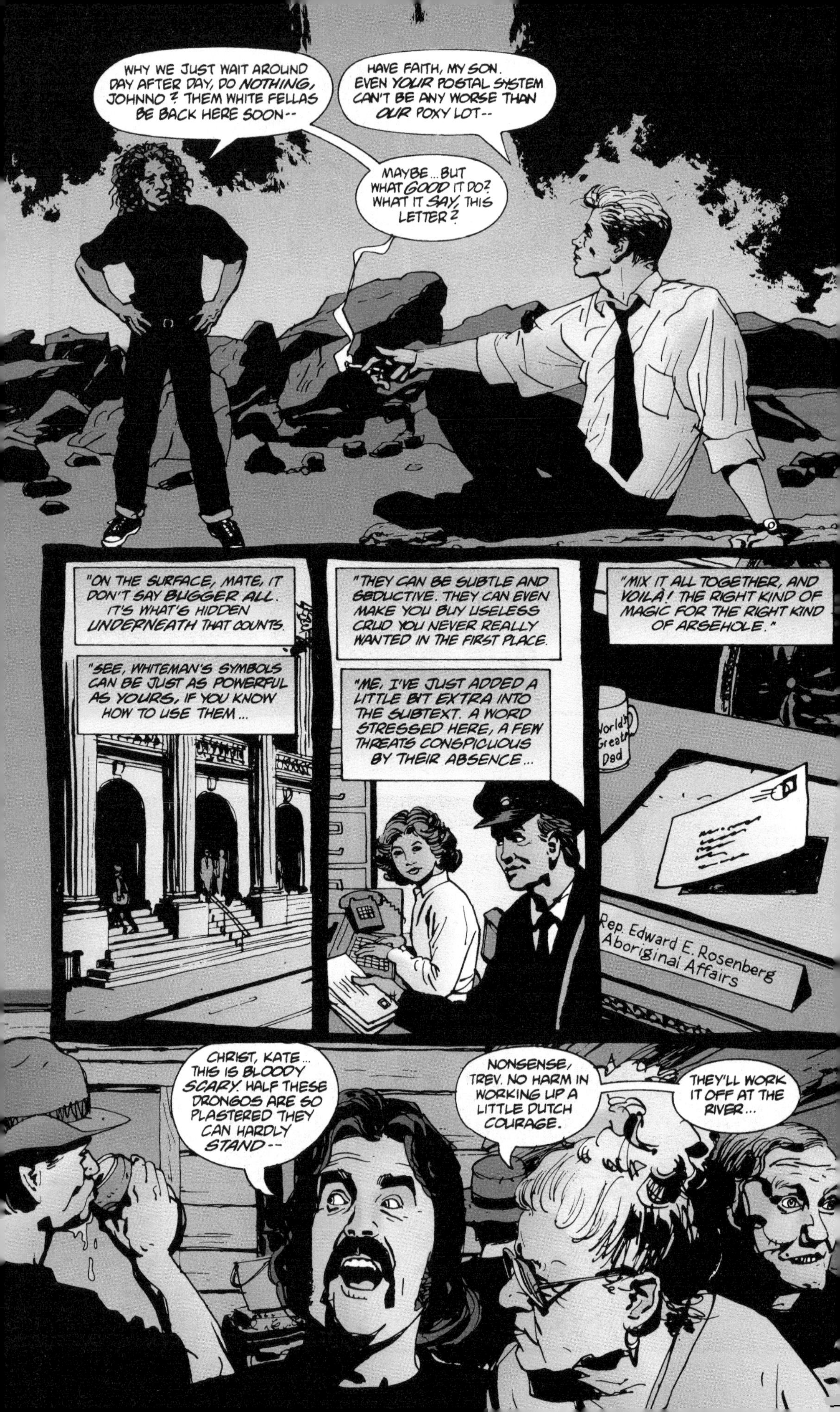
WHY WE JUST WAIT AROUND DAY AFTER DAY, DO NOTHING, JOHNNO? THEM WHITE FELLAS BE BACK HERE SOON--
HAVE FAITH, MY SON. EVEN YOUR POSTAL SYSTEM CAN'T BE ANY WORSE THAN OUR POXY LOT--
MAYBE... BUT WHAT GOOD IT DO? WHAT IT SAY, THIS LETTER?
"ON THE SURFACE, MATE, IT DON'T SAY BUGGER ALL. IT'S WHAT'S HIDDEN UNDERNEATH THAT COUNTS.
"SEE, WHITEMAN'S SYMBOLS CAN BE JUST AS POWERFUL AS YOURS, IF YOU KNOW HOW TO USE THEM...
"THEY CAN BE SUBTLE AND SEDUCTIVE. THEY CAN EVEN MAKE YOU BUY USELESS CRUD YOU NEVER REALLY WANTED IN THE FIRST PLACE.
"ME, I'VE JUST ADDED A LITTLE BIT EXTRA INTO THE SUBTEXT. A WORD STRESSED HERE, A FEW THREATS CONSPICUOUS BY THEIR ABSENCE...
"MIX IT ALL TOGETHER, AND VOILÀ! THE RIGHT KIND OF MAGIC FOR THE RIGHT KIND OF ARSEHOLE."
World's Greatest Dad
Rep. Edward E. Rosenberg
Aboriginai Affairs
CHRIST, KATE... THIS IS BLOODY SCARY. HALF THESE DRONGOS ARE SO PLASTERED THEY CAN HARDLY STAND--
NONSENSE, TREV. NO HARM IN WORKING UP A LITTLE DUTCH COURAGE.
THEY'LL WORK IT OFF AT THE RIVER...

SOME OF YOU'VE BEEN WONDERING WHEN YOU'RE GOING TO GET PAID. YOU'VE WAITED UNNECESSARILY FOR AN EXTRA TWO WEEKS --ALL THANKS TO THE STINKING BLOODY ABO'S DOWN AT THE RIVER.
LET ME ASSURE YOU, I'VE WAITED A LOT LONGER...
STILL, GOOD THINGS COME TO THOSE WHO WAIT. WE'VE BEEN AUTHORIZED TO USE EVERY METHOD AT OUR DISPOSAL TO TO RECLAIM THE LAND.
I ASSUME YOU KNOW WHAT THAT MEANS...
S'EASY, REALLY, JEFFO. IT'S JUST LIKE THE DREAM-TIME.
WHAT YOU SEE WITH YOUR EYES, THAT'S ONLY HALF THE STORY. THE REAL POWER'S HIDDEN UNDERNEATH, JUST OUT OF SIGHT.
"BUT WHITEMAN, HE'S AVOIDED IT SO LONG, HE'S FORGOTTEN. HE CAN'T SEE THE MAGIC, HE CAN ONLY FEEL THE EFFECTS.
"THE GLAMOUR CIRCUMVENTS HIS NORMAL REACTIONS. HE KNOWS HE'S BEING DECEIVED, BUT DOESN'T KNOW HOW TO FIGHT IT. THERE'S ONLY ONE THING HE CAN DO..."
JUST REMEMBER ONE THING: THAT CLEVER LITTLE POMMIE BASTARD IS MINE.
Land Acquisition
1701-B
Trion Inter
REJECTED
Kate Grimshaw
Kate Grimshaw

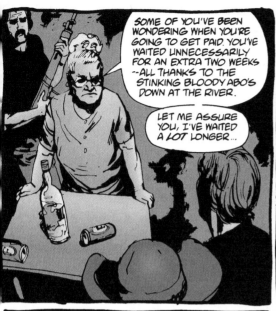

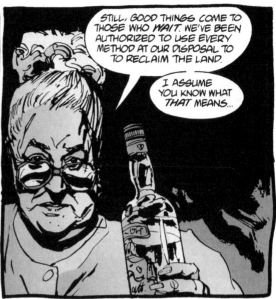

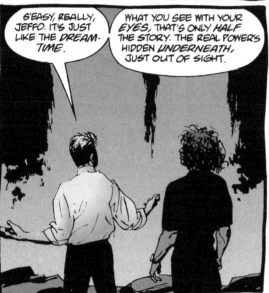

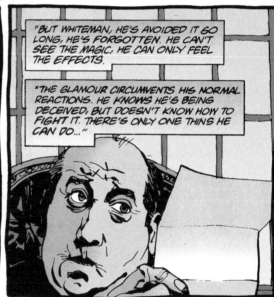

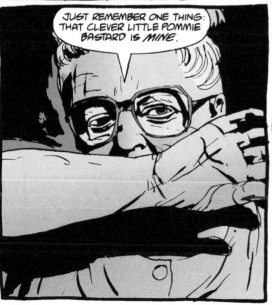

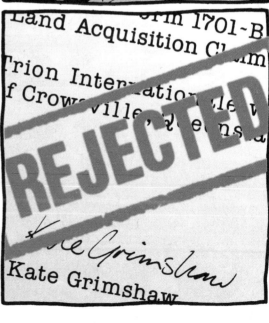

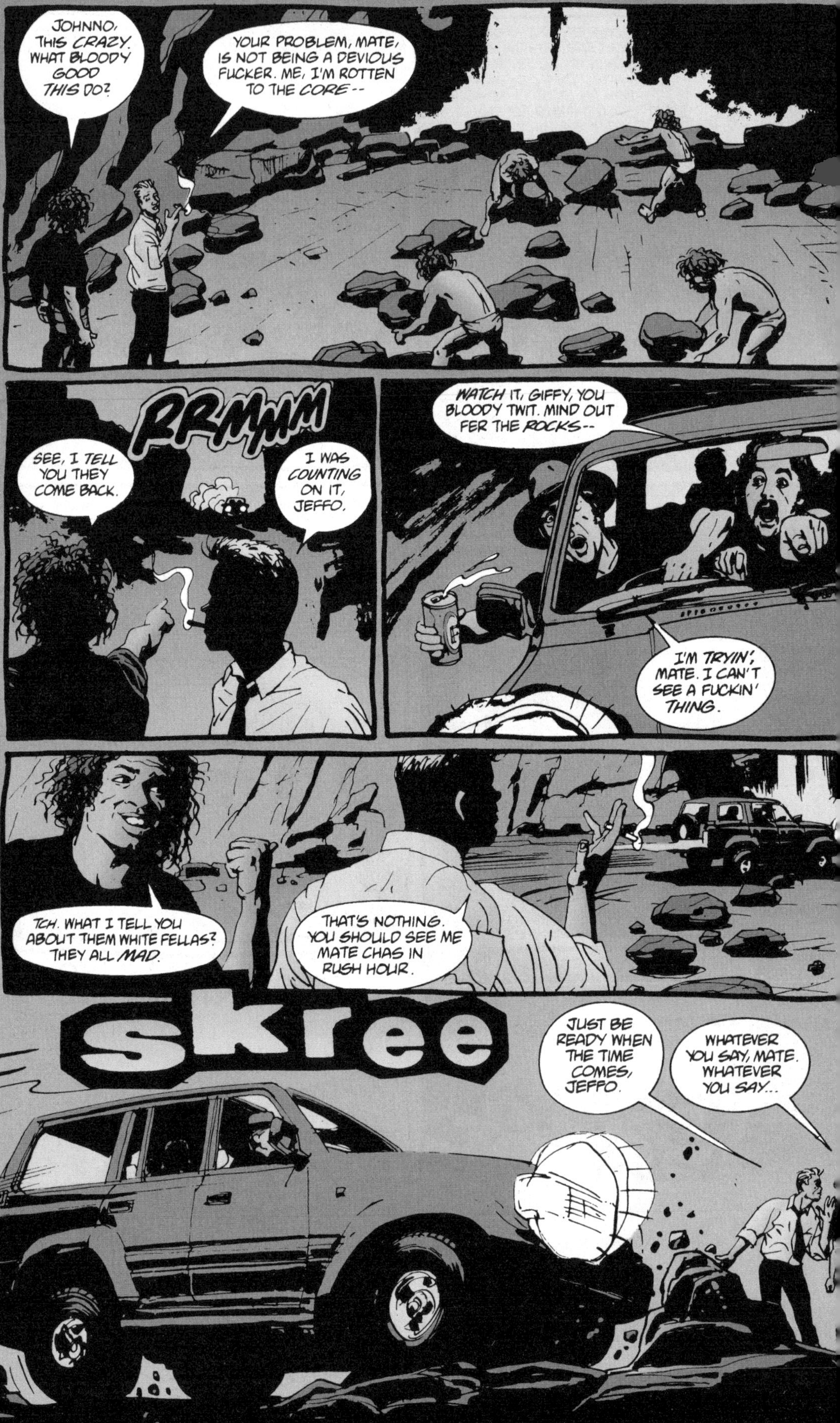
JOHNNO, THIS CRAZY. WHAT BLOODY GOOD THIS DO?
YOUR PROBLEM, MATE, IS NOT BEING A DEVIOUS FUCKER. ME, I'M ROTTEN TO THE CORE--
RRMMM
SEE, I TELL YOU THEY COME BACK.
I WAS COUNTING ON IT, JEFFO.
WATCH IT, GIFFY, YOU BLOODY TWIT. MIND OUT FER THE ROCKS--
I'M TRYIN', MATE. I CAN'T SEE A FUCKIN' THING.
TCH. WHAT I TELL YOU ABOUT THEM WHITE FELLAS? THEY ALL MAD.
THAT'S NOTHING. YOU SHOULD SEE ME MATE CHAS IN RUSH HOUR.
skree
JUST BE READY WHEN THE TIME COMES, JEFFO.
WHATEVER YOU SAY, MATE. WHATEVER YOU SAY...

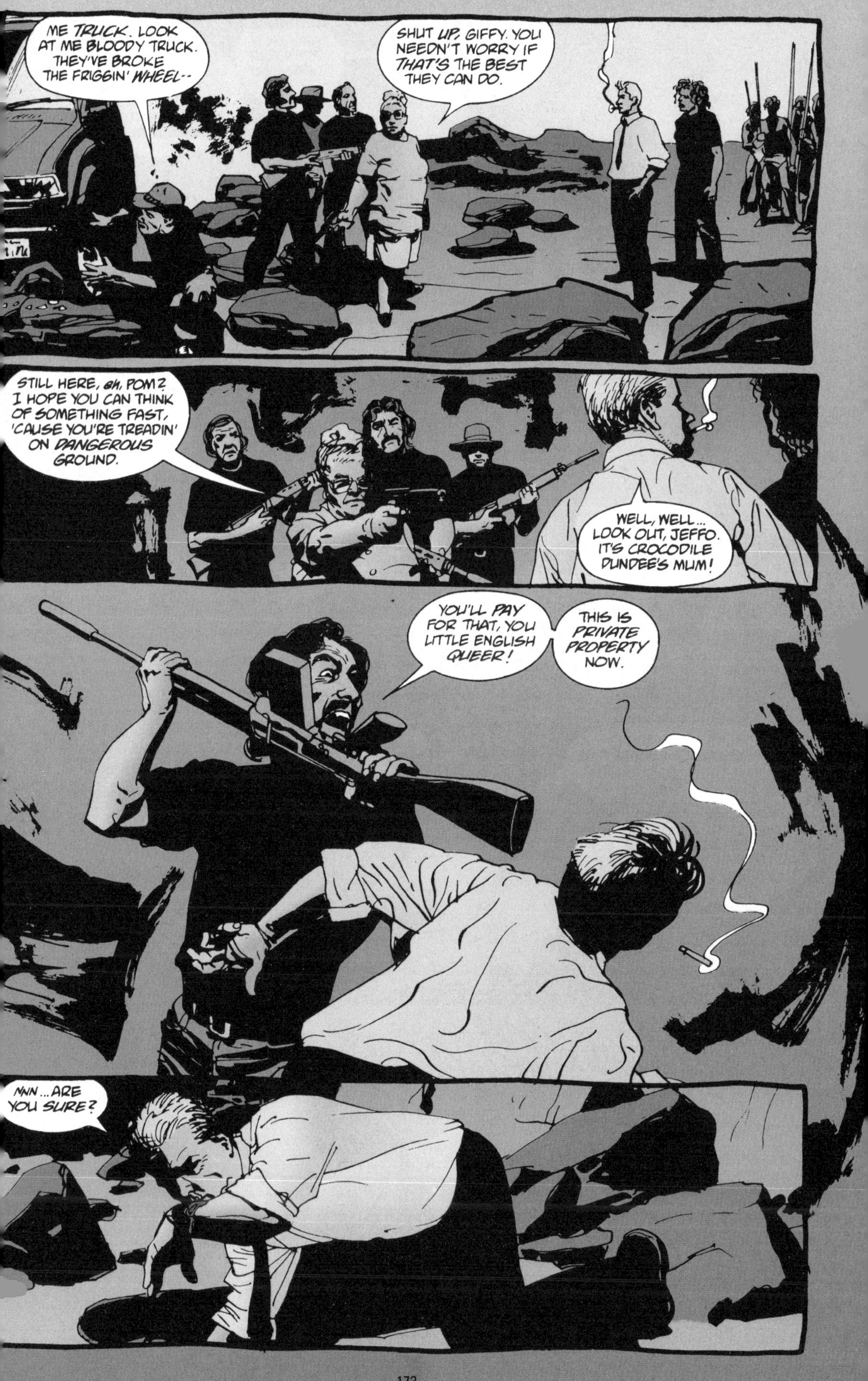

ME TRUCK. LOOK AT ME BLOODY TRUCK. THEY'VE BROKE THE FRIGGIN' WHEEL--
SHUT UP, GIFFY. YOU NEEDN'T WORRY IF THAT'S THE BEST THEY CAN DO.
STILL HERE, eh, POM? I HOPE YOU CAN THINK OF SOMETHING FAST, 'CAUSE YOU'RE TREADIN' ON DANGEROUS GROUND.
WELL, WELL... LOOK OUT, JEFFO. IT'S CROCODILE DUNDEE'S MUM!
YOU'LL PAY FOR THAT, YOU LITTLE ENGLISH QUEER!
THIS IS PRIVATE PROPERTY NOW.
NNN...ARE YOU SURE?

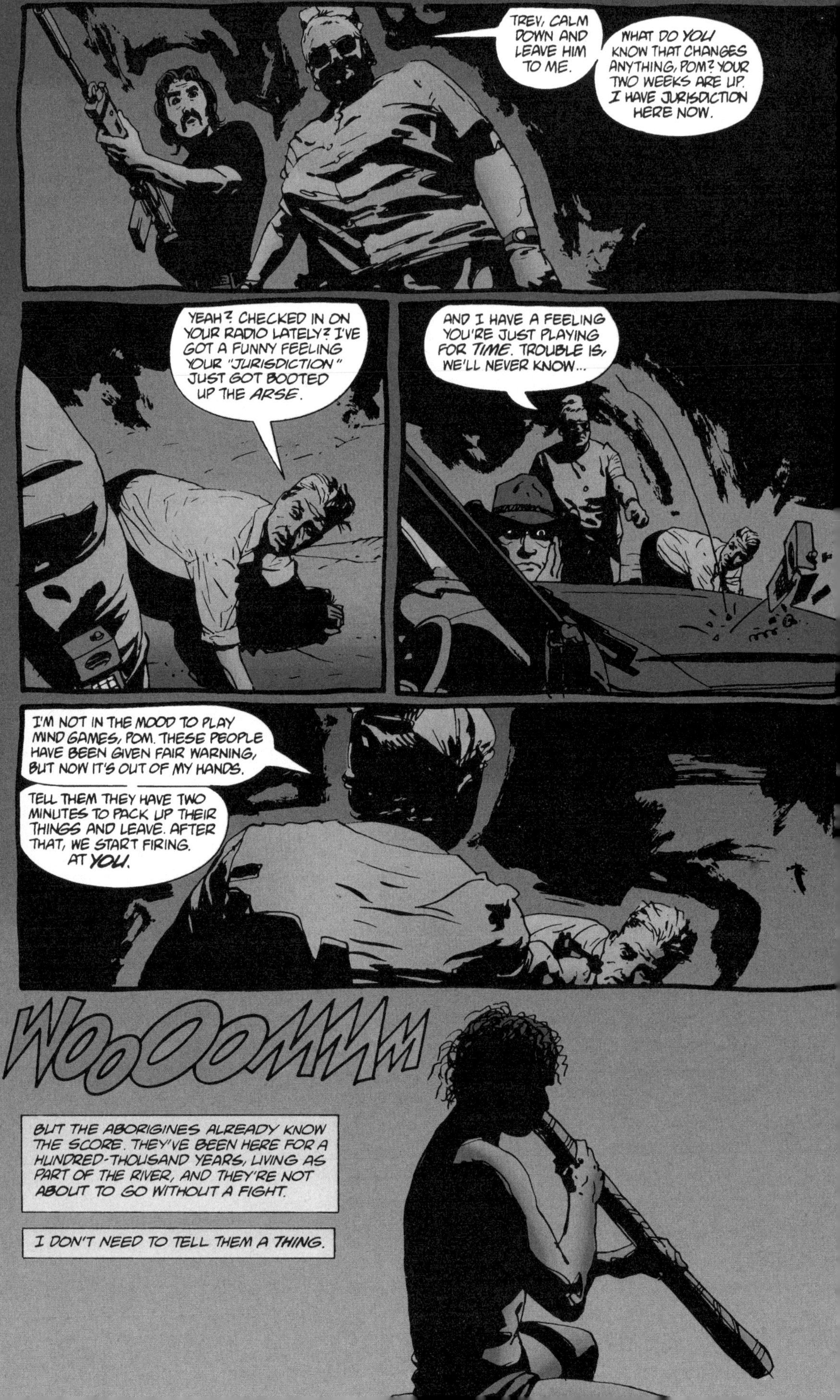
TREV, CALM DOWN AND LEAVE HIM TO ME.
WHAT DO YOU KNOW THAT CHANGES ANYTHING, POM? YOUR TWO WEEKS ARE UP. I HAVE JURISDICTION HERE NOW.
YEAH? CHECKED IN ON YOUR RADIO LATELY? I'VE GOT A FUNNY FEELING YOUR "JURISDICTION" JUST GOT BOOTED UP THE ARSE.
AND I HAVE A FEELING YOU'RE JUST PLAYING FOR TIME. TROUBLE IS, WE'LL NEVER KNOW...
I'M NOT IN THE MOOD TO PLAY MIND GAMES, POM. THESE PEOPLE HAVE BEEN GIVEN FAIR WARNING, BUT NOW IT'S OUT OF MY HANDS.
TELL THEM THEY HAVE TWO MINUTES TO PACK UP THEIR THINGS AND LEAVE. AFTER THAT, WE START FIRING. AT YOU.
WOOOOMMM
BUT THE ABORIGINES ALREADY KNOW THE SCORE. THEY'VE BEEN HERE FOR A HUNDRED-THOUSAND YEARS, LIVING AS PART OF THE RIVER, AND THEY'RE NOT ABOUT TO GO WITHOUT A FIGHT.
I DON'T NEED TO TELL THEM A THING.

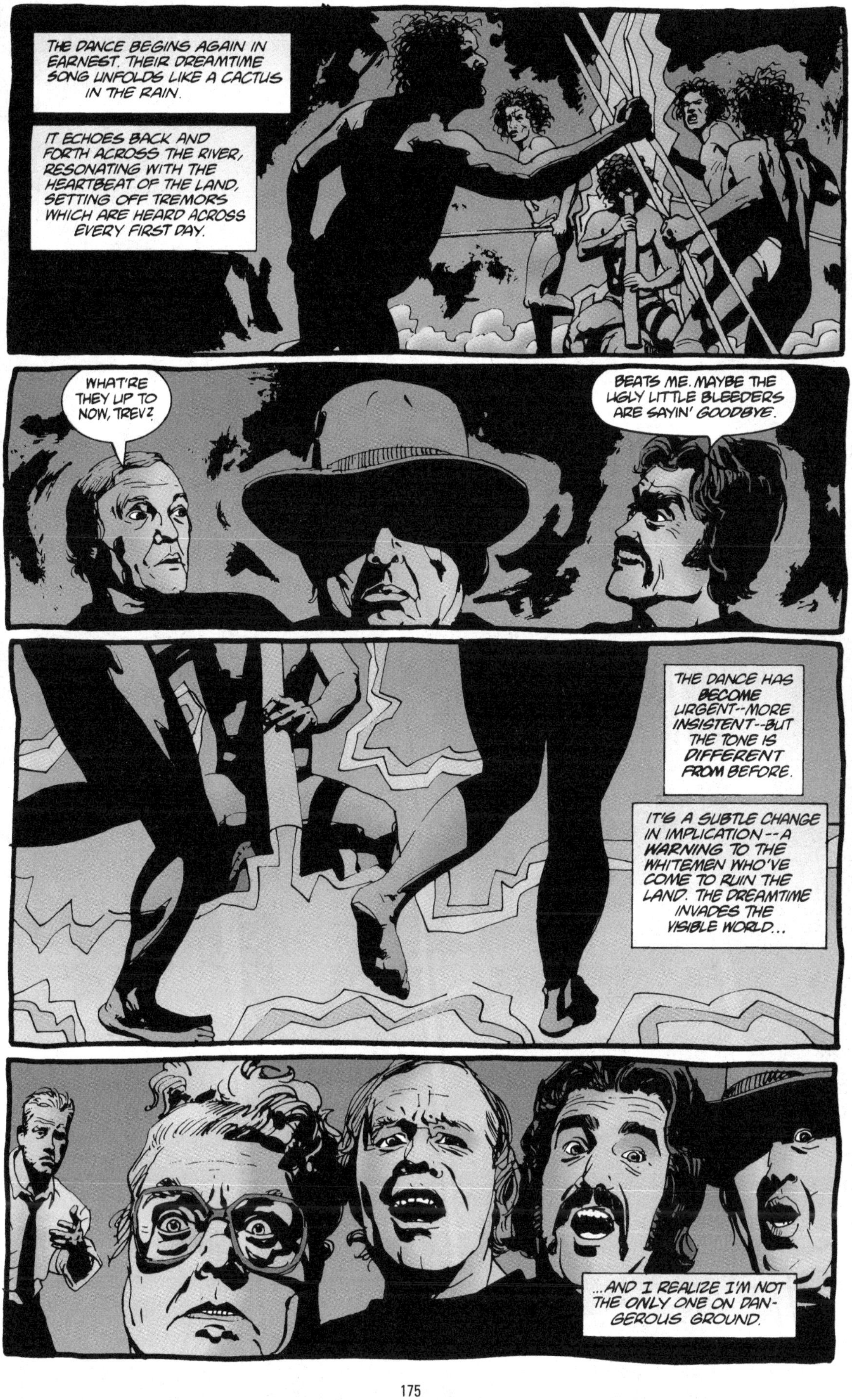
THE DANCE BEGINS AGAIN IN EARNEST. THEIR DREAMTIME SONG UNFOLDS LIKE A CACTUS IN THE RAIN.
IT ECHOES BACK AND FORTH ACROSS THE RIVER, RESONATING WITH THE HEARTBEAT OF THE LAND, SETTING OFF TREMORS WHICH ARE HEARD ACROSS EVERY FIRST DAY.
WHAT'RE THEY UP TO NOW, TREV?
BEATS ME. MAYBE THE UGLY LITTLE BLEEDERS ARE SAYIN' GOODBYE.
THE DANCE HAS BECOME URGENT--MORE INSISTENT--BUT THE TONE IS DIFFERENT FROM BEFORE.
IT'S A SUBTLE CHANGE IN IMPLICATION--A WARNING TO THE WHITEMEN WHO'VE COME TO RUIN THE LAND. THE DREAMTIME INVADES THE VISIBLE WORLD...
...AND I REALIZE I'M NOT THE ONLY ONE ON DAN-GEROUS GROUND.

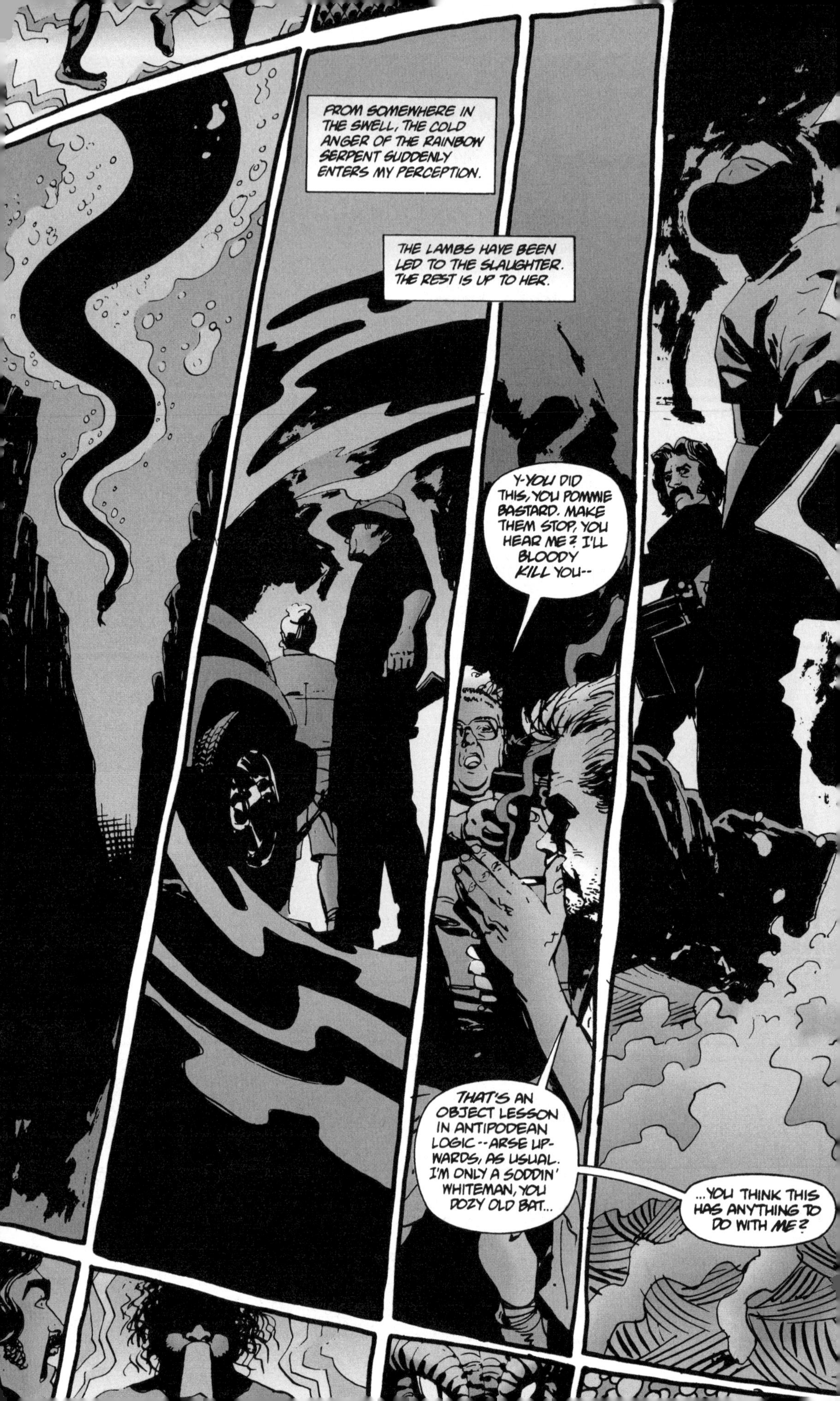
FROM SOMEWHERE IN THE SWELL, THE COLD ANGER OF THE RAINBOW SERPENT SUDDENLY ENTERS MY PERCEPTION.
THE LAMBS HAVE BEEN LED TO THE SLAUGHTER. THE REST IS UP TO HER.
Y-YOU DID THIS, YOU POMMIE BASTARD. MAKE THEM STOP, YOU HEAR ME? I'LL BLOODY KILL YOU--
THAT'S AN OBJECT LESSON IN ANTIPODEAN LOGIC--ARSE UPWARDS, AS USUAL. I'M ONLY A SODDIN' WHITEMAN, YOU DOZY OLD BAT...
...YOU THINK THIS HAS ANYTHING TO DO WITH ME?

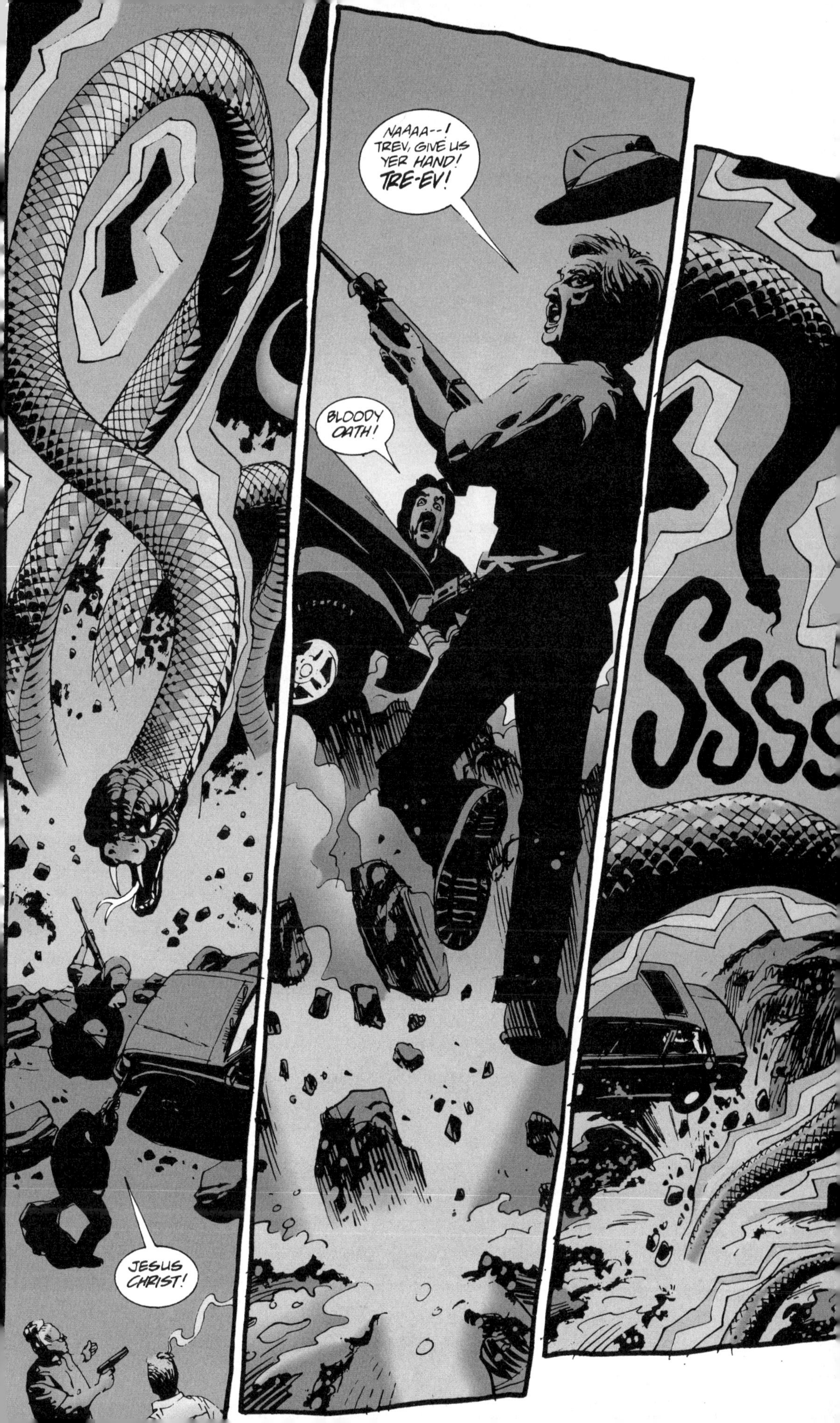
NAAAA--! TREV, GIVE US YER HAND! TRE-EV!
BLOODY OATH!
JESUS CHRIST!
SSSS

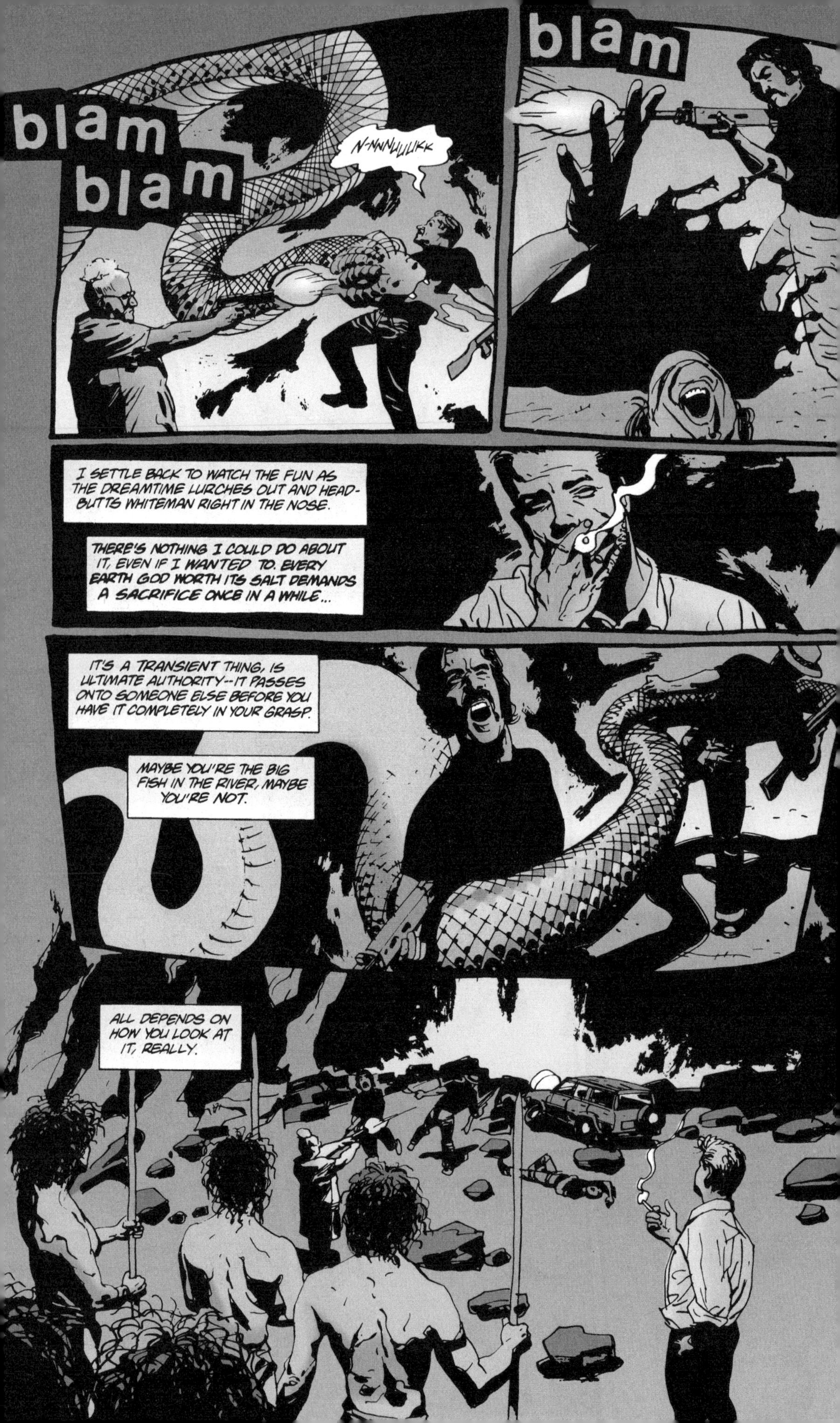

blam
blam
N-NNNUUUKK
blam
I SETTLE BACK TO WATCH THE FUN AS THE DREAMTIME LURCHES OUT AND HEAD-BUTTS WHITEMAN RIGHT IN THE NOSE.
THERE'S NOTHING I COULD DO ABOUT IT, EVEN IF I WANTED TO. EVERY EARTH GOD WORTH ITS SALT DEMANDS A SACRIFICE ONCE IN A WHILE...
IT'S A TRANSIENT THING, IS ULTIMATE AUTHORITY--IT PASSES ONTO SOMEONE ELSE BEFORE YOU HAVE IT COMPLETELY IN YOUR GRASP.
MAYBE YOU'RE THE BIG FISH IN THE RIVER, MAYBE YOU'RE NOT.
ALL DEPENDS ON HOW YOU LOOK AT IT, REALLY.

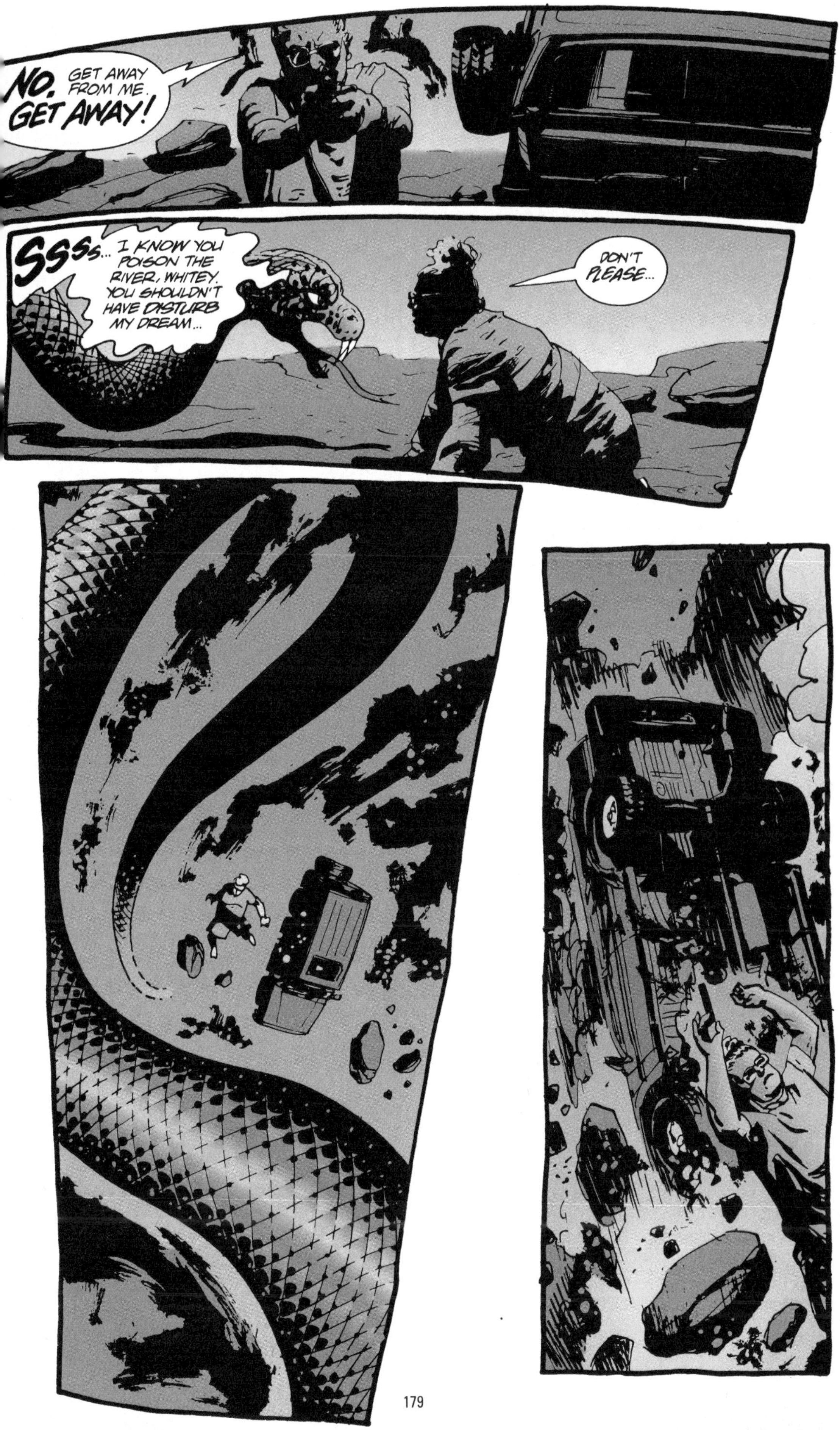
NO. GET AWAY FROM ME. GET AWAY!
Ssss... I KNOW YOU POISON THE RIVER, WHITEY. YOU SHOULDN'T HAVE DISTURB MY DREAM...
DON'T PLEASE...

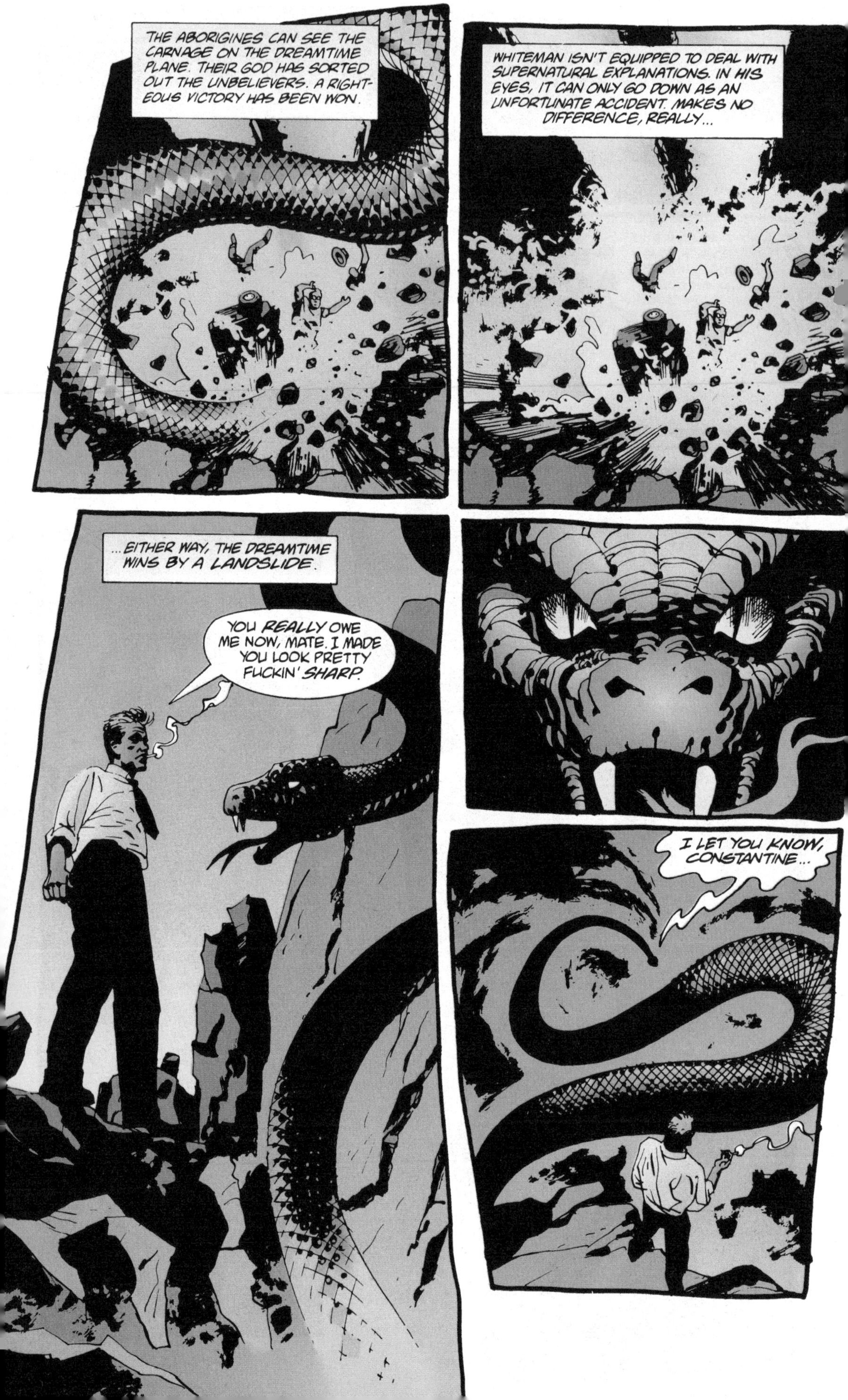
THE ABORIGINES CAN SEE THE CARNAGE ON THE DREAMTIME PLANE. THEIR GOD HAS SORTED OUT THE UNBELIEVERS. A RIGHTEOUS VICTORY HAS BEEN WON.
WHITEMAN ISN'T EQUIPPED TO DEAL WITH SUPERNATURAL EXPLANATIONS. IN HIS EYES, IT CAN ONLY GO DOWN AS AN UNFORTUNATE ACCIDENT. MAKES NO DIFFERENCE, REALLY...
...EITHER WAY, THE DREAMTIME WINS BY A LANDSLIDE.
YOU REALLY OWE ME NOW, MATE. I MADE YOU LOOK PRETTY FUCKIN' SHARP.
I LET YOU KNOW, CONSTANTINE...

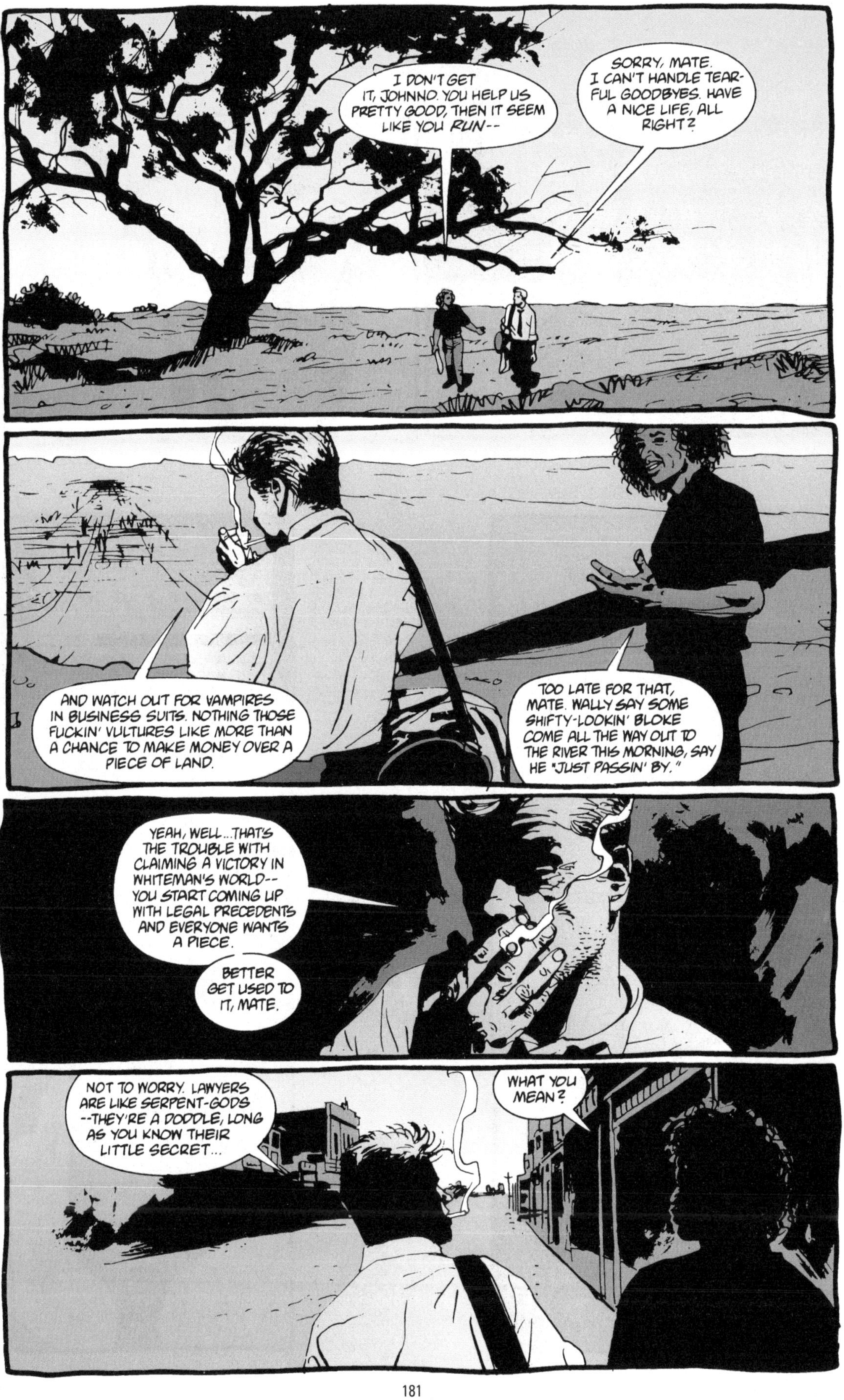
I DON'T GET IT, JOHNNO. YOU HELP US PRETTY GOOD, THEN IT SEEM LIKE YOU RUN--
SORRY, MATE. I CAN'T HANDLE TEAR-FUL GOODBYES. HAVE A NICE LIFE, ALL RIGHT?
AND WATCH OUT FOR VAMPIRES IN BUSINESS SUITS. NOTHING THOSE FUCKIN' VULTURES LIKE MORE THAN A CHANCE TO MAKE MONEY OVER A PIECE OF LAND.
TOO LATE FOR THAT, MATE. WALLY SAY SOME SHIFTY-LOOKIN' BLOKE COME ALL THE WAY OUT TO THE RIVER THIS MORNING, SAY HE "JUST PASSIN' BY."
YEAH, WELL...THAT'S THE TROUBLE WITH CLAIMING A VICTORY IN WHITEMAN'S WORLD--YOU START COMING UP WITH LEGAL PRECEDENTS AND EVERYONE WANTS A PIECE.
BETTER GET USED TO IT, MATE.
NOT TO WORRY. LAWYERS ARE LIKE SERPENT-GODS --THEY'RE A DODDLE, LONG AS YOU KNOW THEIR LITTLE SECRET...
WHAT YOU MEAN?

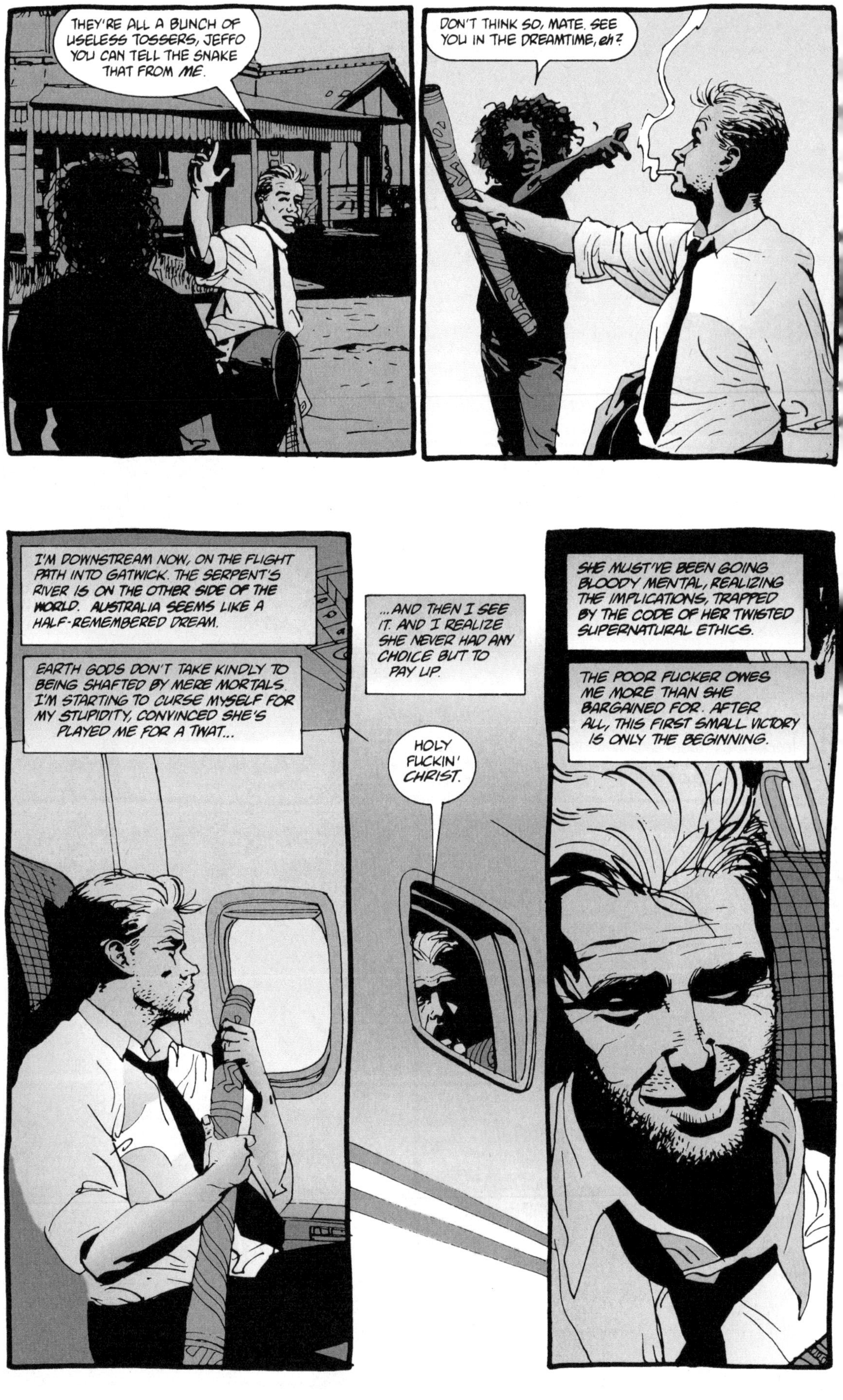
THEY'RE ALL A BUNCH OF USELESS TOSSERS, JEFFO YOU CAN TELL THE SNAKE THAT FROM ME.
DON'T THINK SO, MATE. SEE YOU IN THE DREAMTIME, eh?
I'M DOWNSTREAM NOW, ON THE FLIGHT PATH INTO GATWICK. THE SERPENT'S RIVER IS ON THE OTHER SIDE OF THE WORLD. AUSTRALIA SEEMS LIKE A HALF-REMEMBERED DREAM.
EARTH GODS DON'T TAKE KINDLY TO BEING SHAFTED BY MERE MORTALS. I'M STARTING TO CURSE MYSELF FOR MY STUPIDITY, CONVINCED SHE'S PLAYED ME FOR A TWAT...
...AND THEN I SEE IT. AND I REALIZE SHE NEVER HAD ANY CHOICE BUT TO PAY UP.
HOLY FUCKIN' CHRIST.
SHE MUST'VE BEEN GOING BLOODY MENTAL, REALIZING THE IMPLICATIONS, TRAPPED BY THE CODE OF HER TWISTED SUPERNATURAL ETHICS.
THE POOR FUCKER OWES ME MORE THAN SHE BARGAINED FOR. AFTER ALL, THIS FIRST SMALL VICTORY IS ONLY THE BEGINNING.

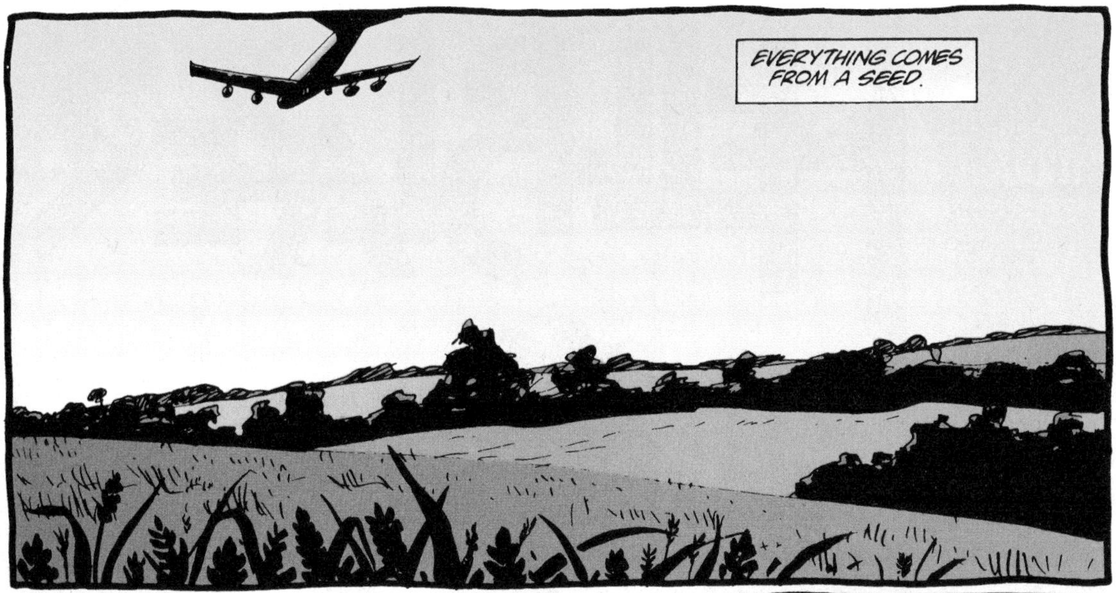
EVERYTHING COMES FROM A SEED.

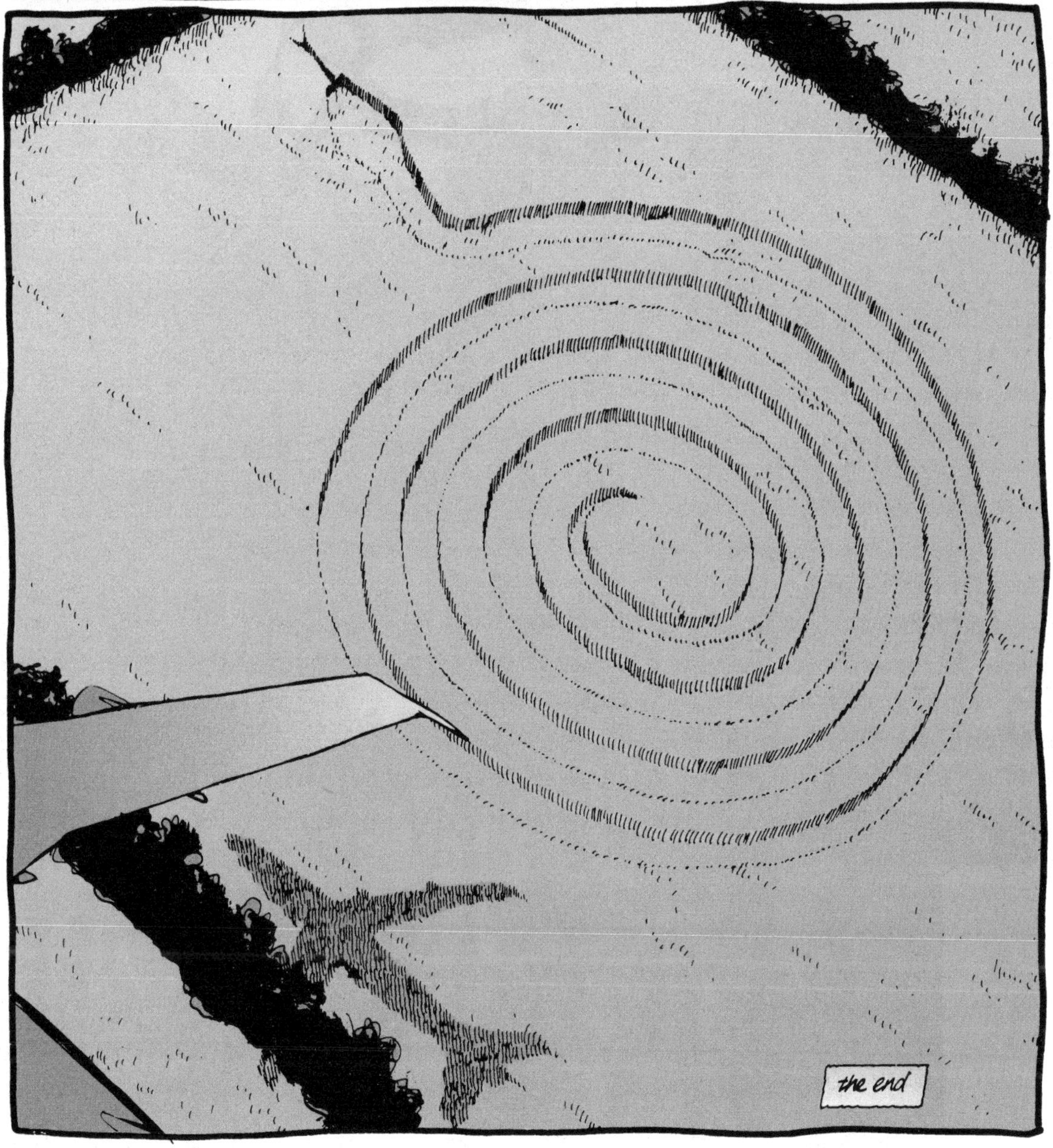
the end

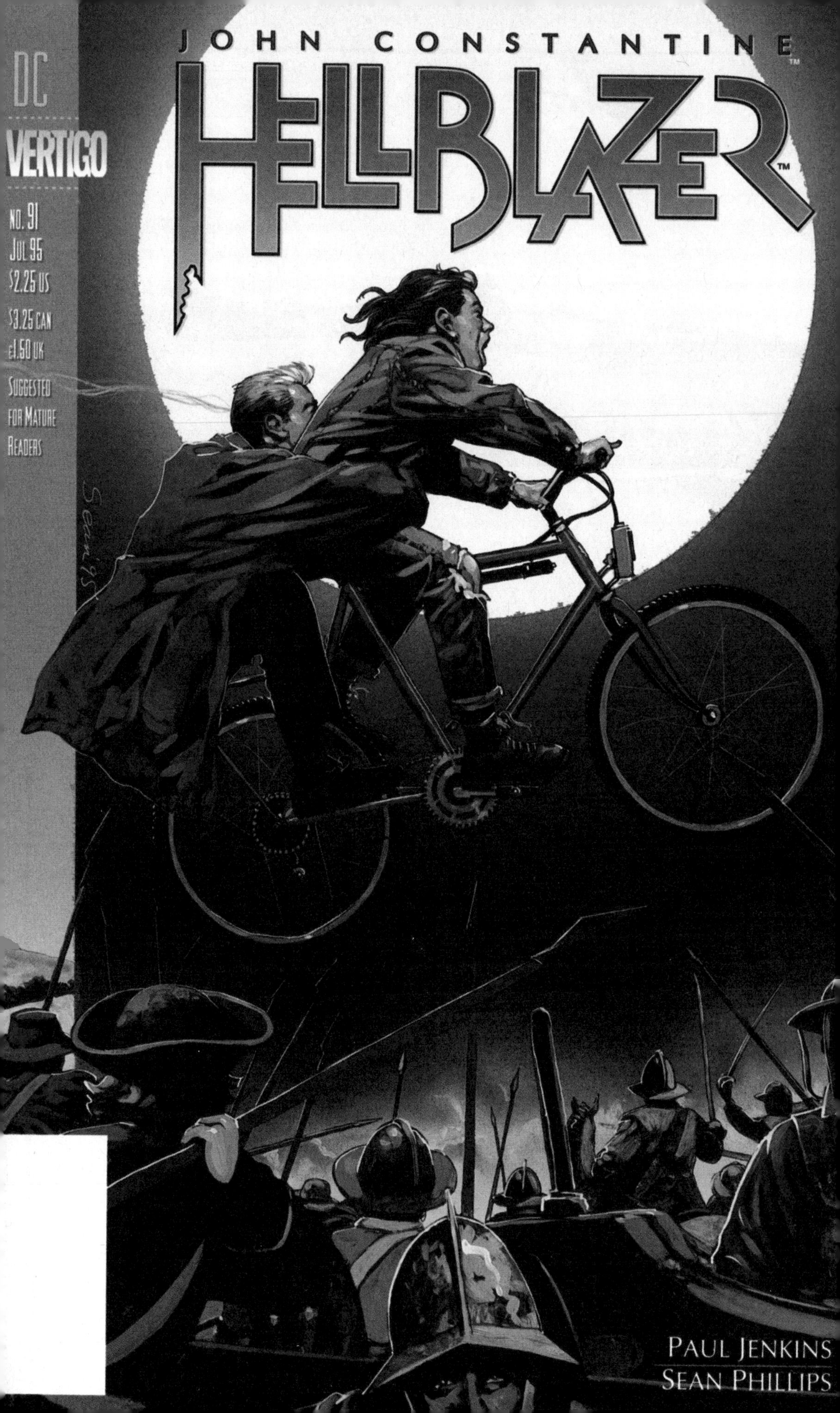

JOHN CONSTANTINE
HELLBLAZER
DC
VERTIGO
NO. 91
JUL 95
$2.25 US
$3.25 CAN
£1.50 UK
SUGGESTED FOR MATURE READERS
PAUL JENKINS
SEAN PHILLIPS

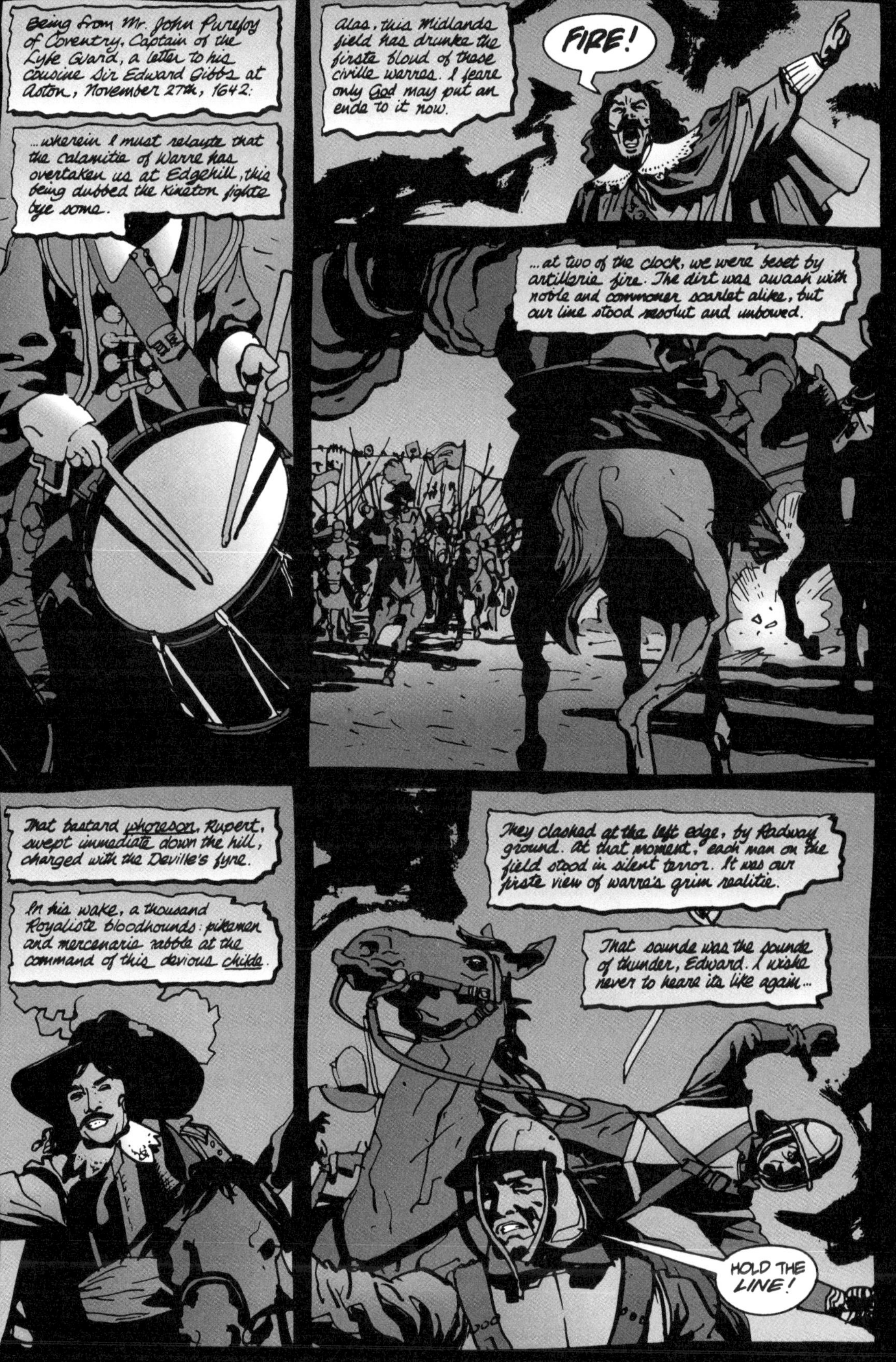
Being from Mr. John Purefoy of Coventry, Captain of the Lyfe Guard, a letter to his cousine Sir Edward Gibbs at Aston, November 27th, 1642:
...wherein I must relayte that the calamitie of Warre has overtaken us at Edgehill, this being dubbed the Kineton fighte bye some.
Alas, this Midlands field has drunke the firste bloud of these civille warres. I feare only God may put an ende to it now.
FIRE!
...at two of the clock, we were beset by artillerie fire. The dirt was awash with noble and commoner scarlet alike, but our line stood resolut and unbowed.
That bastard whoreson, Rupert, swept immediate down the hill, charged with the Deville's fyre.
In his wake, a thousand Royaliste bloodhounds: pikemen and mercenarie rabble at the command of this devious childe.
They clashed at the left edge, by Radway ground. At that moment, each man on the field stood in silent terror. It was our firste view of warre's grim realitie.
That sounde was the sounde of thunder, Edward. I wishe never to heare its like again...
HOLD THE LINE!

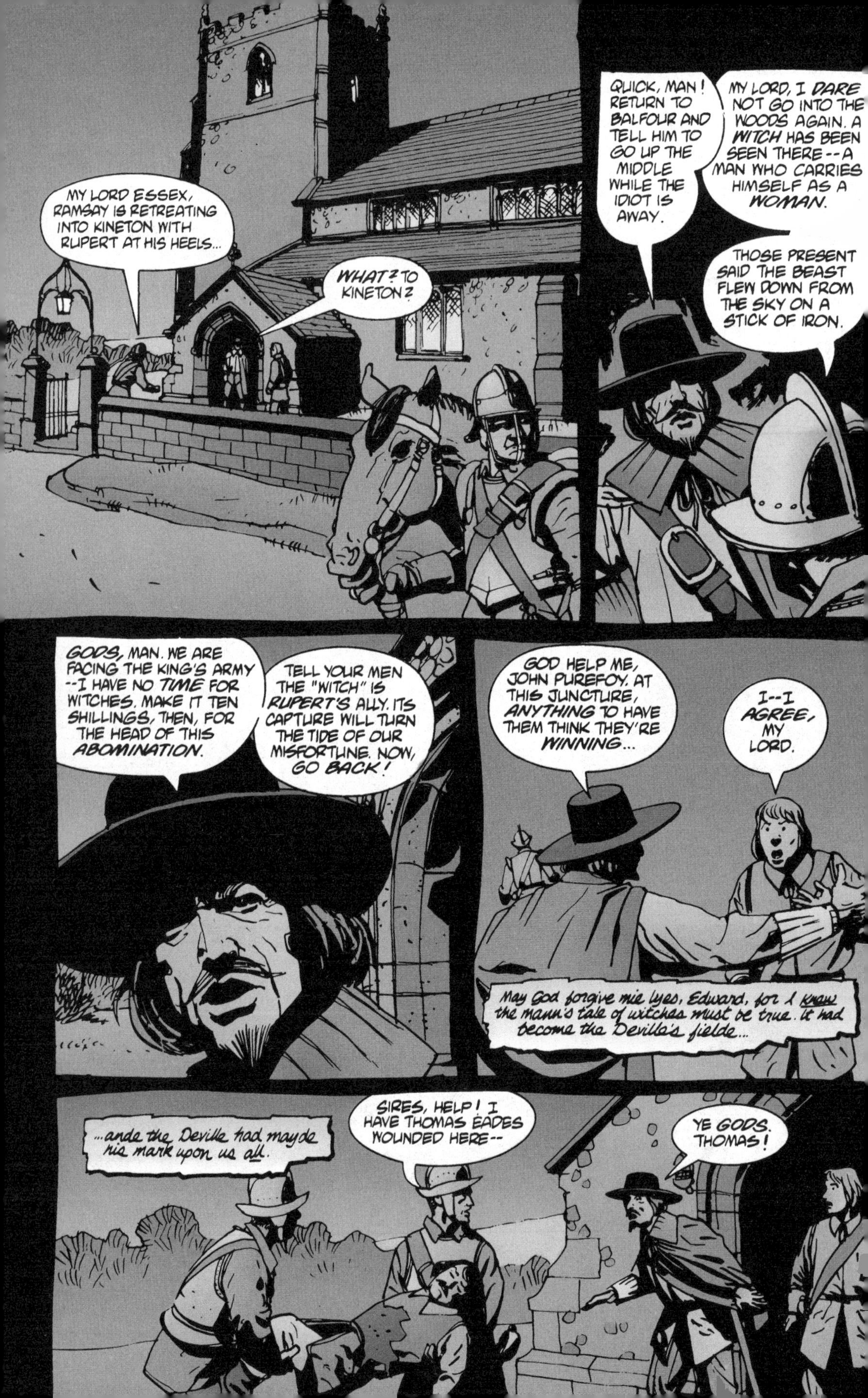

MY LORD ESSEX, RAMSAY IS RETREATING INTO KINETON WITH RUPERT AT HIS HEELS...
WHAT? TO KINETON?
QUICK, MAN! RETURN TO BALFOUR AND TELL HIM TO GO UP THE MIDDLE WHILE THE IDIOT IS AWAY.
MY LORD, I DARE NOT GO INTO THE WOODS AGAIN. A WITCH HAS BEEN SEEN THERE--A MAN WHO CARRIES HIMSELF AS A WOMAN.
THOSE PRESENT SAID THE BEAST FLEW DOWN FROM THE SKY ON A STICK OF IRON.
GODS, MAN. WE ARE FACING THE KING'S ARMY --I HAVE NO TIME FOR WITCHES. MAKE IT TEN SHILLINGS, THEN, FOR THE HEAD OF THIS ABOMINATION.
TELL YOUR MEN THE "WITCH" IS RUPERT'S ALLY. ITS CAPTURE WILL TURN THE TIDE OF OUR MISFORTUNE. NOW, GO BACK!
GOD HELP ME, JOHN PUREFOY. AT THIS JUNCTURE, ANYTHING TO HAVE THEM THINK THEY'RE WINNING...
I--I AGREE, MY LORD.
May God forgive mie lyes, Edward, for I knaw the mann's tale of witches must be true. It had become the Devilla's fielde...
...ande the Deville had mayde his mark upon us all.
SIRES, HELP! I HAVE THOMAS EADES WOUNDED HERE--
YE GODS. THOMAS!

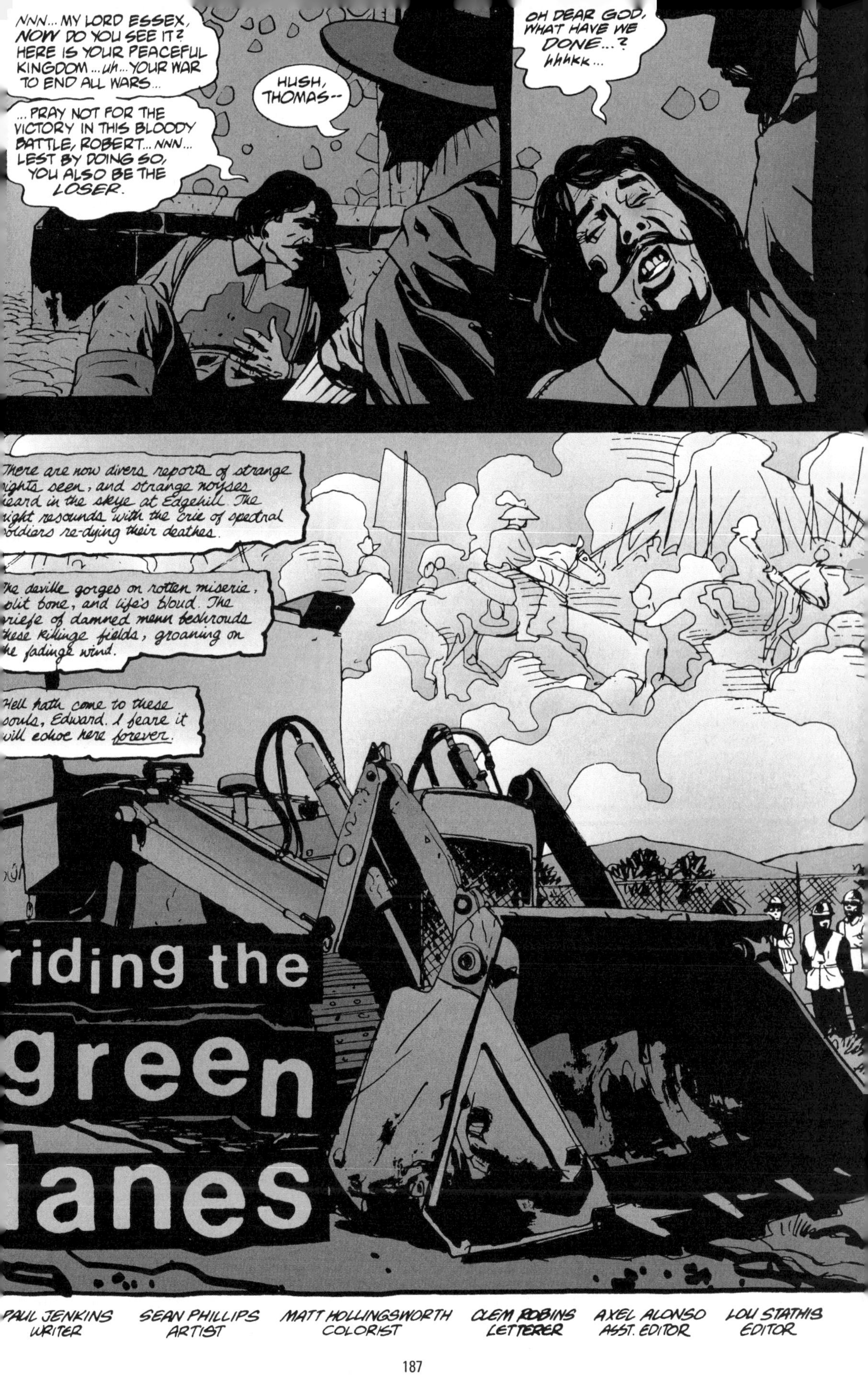

NNN... MY LORD ESSEX, NOW DO YOU SEE IT? HERE IS YOUR PEACEFUL KINGDOM ... uh ... YOUR WAR TO END ALL WARS...
... PRAY NOT FOR THE VICTORY IN THIS BLOODY BATTLE, ROBERT... NNN... LEST BY DOING SO, YOU ALSO BE THE LOSER.
HUSH, THOMAS--
OH DEAR GOD, WHAT HAVE WE DONE...? hhhkk...
There are now divers reports of strange ights seen, and strange noyses eard in the skye at Edgehill. The ight resounds with the crie of spectral oldiers re-dying their deathes.
he deville gorges on rotten miserie, plit bone, and life's bloud. The riefe of damned menn beshrouds these killinge fields, groaning on he fadinge wind.
Hell hath come to these souls, Edward. I feare it will echoe here forever.
riding the green lanes

PAUL JENKINS WRITER | SEAN PHILLIPS ARTIST | MATT HOLLINGSWORTH COLORIST | CLEM ROBINS LETTERER | AXEL ALONSO ASST. EDITOR | LOU STATHIS EDITOR

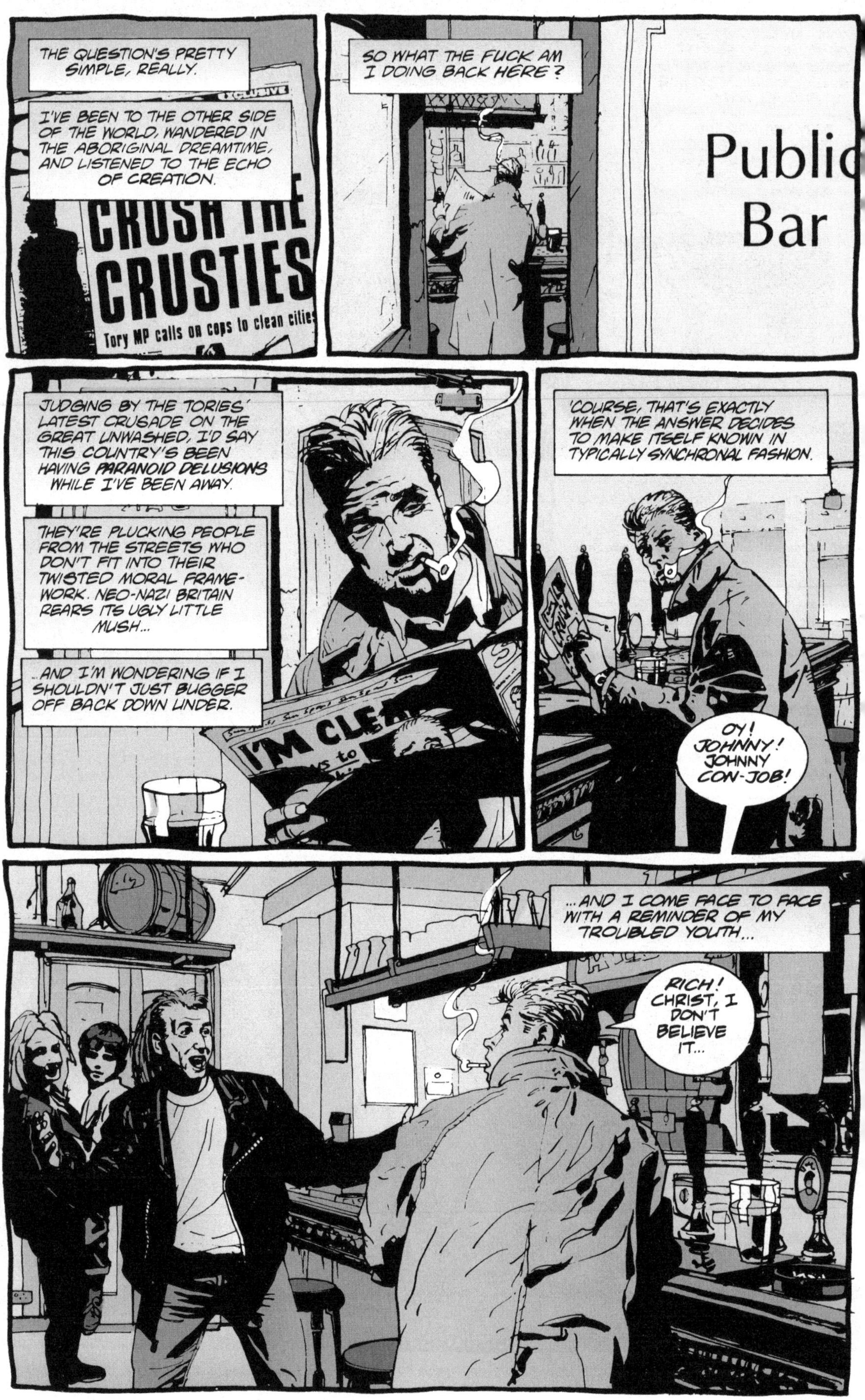
THE QUESTION'S PRETTY SIMPLE, REALLY.
I'VE BEEN TO THE OTHER SIDE OF THE WORLD, WANDERED IN THE ABORIGINAL DREAMTIME, AND LISTENED TO THE ECHO OF CREATION.
CRUSH THE CRUSTIES
Tory MP calls on cops to clean cities
SO WHAT THE FUCK AM I DOING BACK HERE?
Public Bar
JUDGING BY THE TORIES' LATEST CRUSADE ON THE GREAT UNWASHED, I'D SAY THIS COUNTRY'S BEEN HAVING PARANOID DELUSIONS WHILE I'VE BEEN AWAY.
THEY'RE PLUCKING PEOPLE FROM THE STREETS WHO DON'T FIT INTO THEIR TWISTED MORAL FRAME-WORK. NEO-NAZI BRITAIN REARS ITS UGLY LITTLE MUSH...
...AND I'M WONDERING IF I SHOULDN'T JUST BUGGER OFF BACK DOWN UNDER.
'COURSE, THAT'S EXACTLY WHEN THE ANSWER DECIDES TO MAKE ITSELF KNOWN IN TYPICALLY SYNCHRONAL FASHION.
OY! JOHNNY! JOHNNY CON-JOB!
...AND I COME FACE TO FACE WITH A REMINDER OF MY TROUBLED YOUTH...
RICH! CHRIST, I DON'T BELIEVE IT...

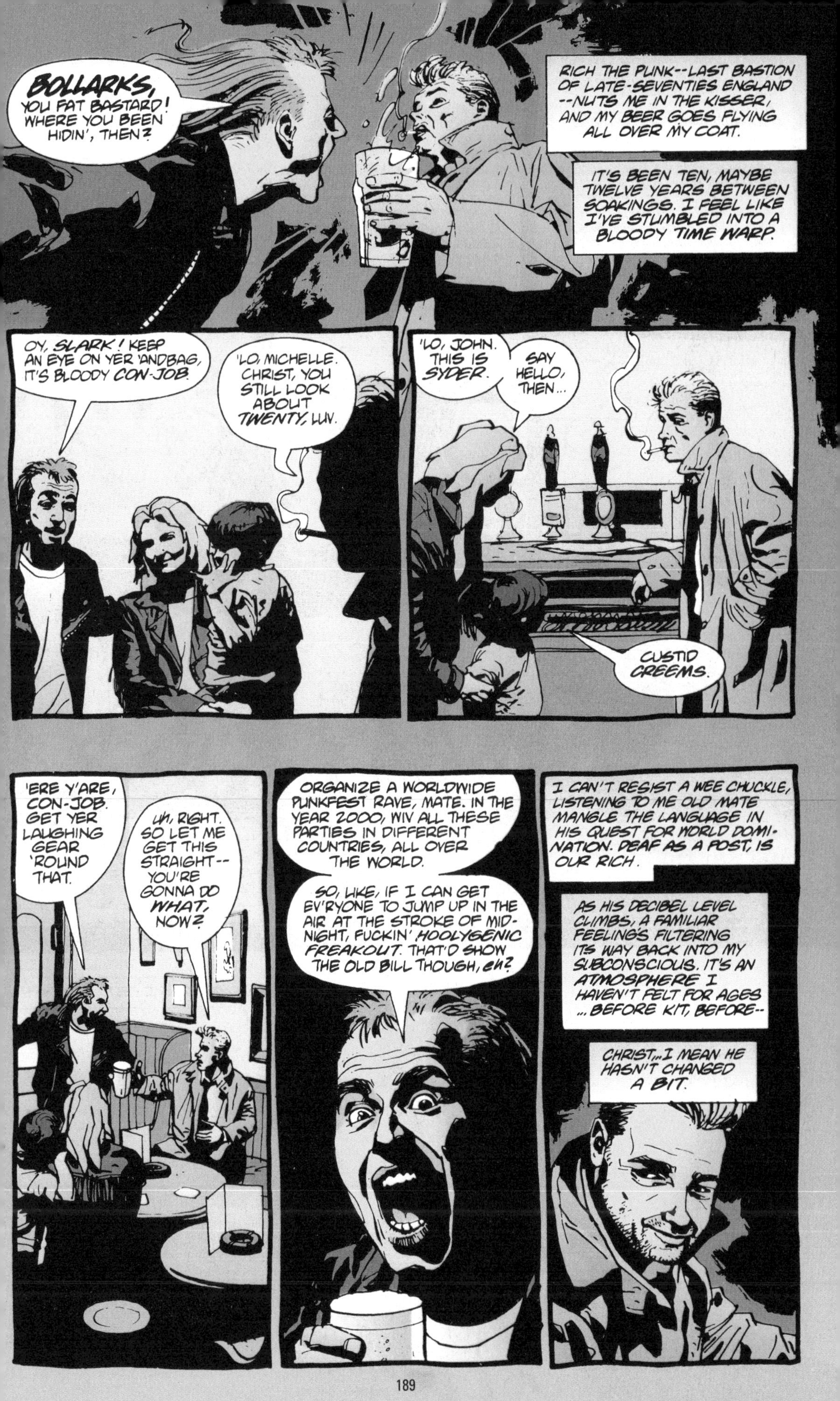

BOLLARKS, YOU FAT BASTARD! WHERE YOU BEEN HIDIN', THEN?
RICH THE PUNK--LAST BASTION OF LATE-SEVENTIES ENGLAND --NUTS ME IN THE KISSER, AND MY BEER GOES FLYING ALL OVER MY COAT.
IT'S BEEN TEN, MAYBE TWELVE YEARS BETWEEN SOAKINGS. I FEEL LIKE I'VE STUMBLED INTO A BLOODY TIME WARP.
OY, SLARK! KEEP AN EYE ON YER 'ANDBAG, IT'S BLOODY CON-JOB.
'LO, MICHELLE. CHRIST, YOU STILL LOOK ABOUT TWENTY, LUV.
'LO, JOHN. THIS IS SYDER.
SAY HELLO, THEN...
CUSTID CREEMS.
'ERE Y'ARE, CON-JOB. GET YER LAUGHING GEAR 'ROUND THAT.
UH, RIGHT. SO LET ME GET THIS STRAIGHT-- YOU'RE GONNA DO WHAT, NOW?
ORGANIZE A WORLDWIDE PUNKFEST RAVE, MATE. IN THE YEAR 2000, WIV ALL THESE PARTIES IN DIFFERENT COUNTRIES, ALL OVER THE WORLD.
SO, LIKE, IF I CAN GET EV'RYONE TO JUMP UP IN THE AIR AT THE STROKE OF MID-NIGHT, FUCKIN' HOOLYGENIC FREAKOUT. THAT'D SHOW THE OLD BILL THOUGH, EH?
I CAN'T RESIST A WEE CHUCKLE, LISTENING TO ME OLD MATE MANGLE THE LANGUAGE IN HIS QUEST FOR WORLD DOMI-NATION. DEAF AS A POST, IS OUR RICH.
AS HIS DECIBEL LEVEL CLIMBS, A FAMILIAR FEELING'S FILTERING ITS WAY BACK INTO MY SUBCONSCIOUS. IT'S AN ATMOSPHERE I HAVEN'T FELT FOR AGES ...BEFORE KIT, BEFORE--
CHRIST...I MEAN HE HASN'T CHANGED A BIT.

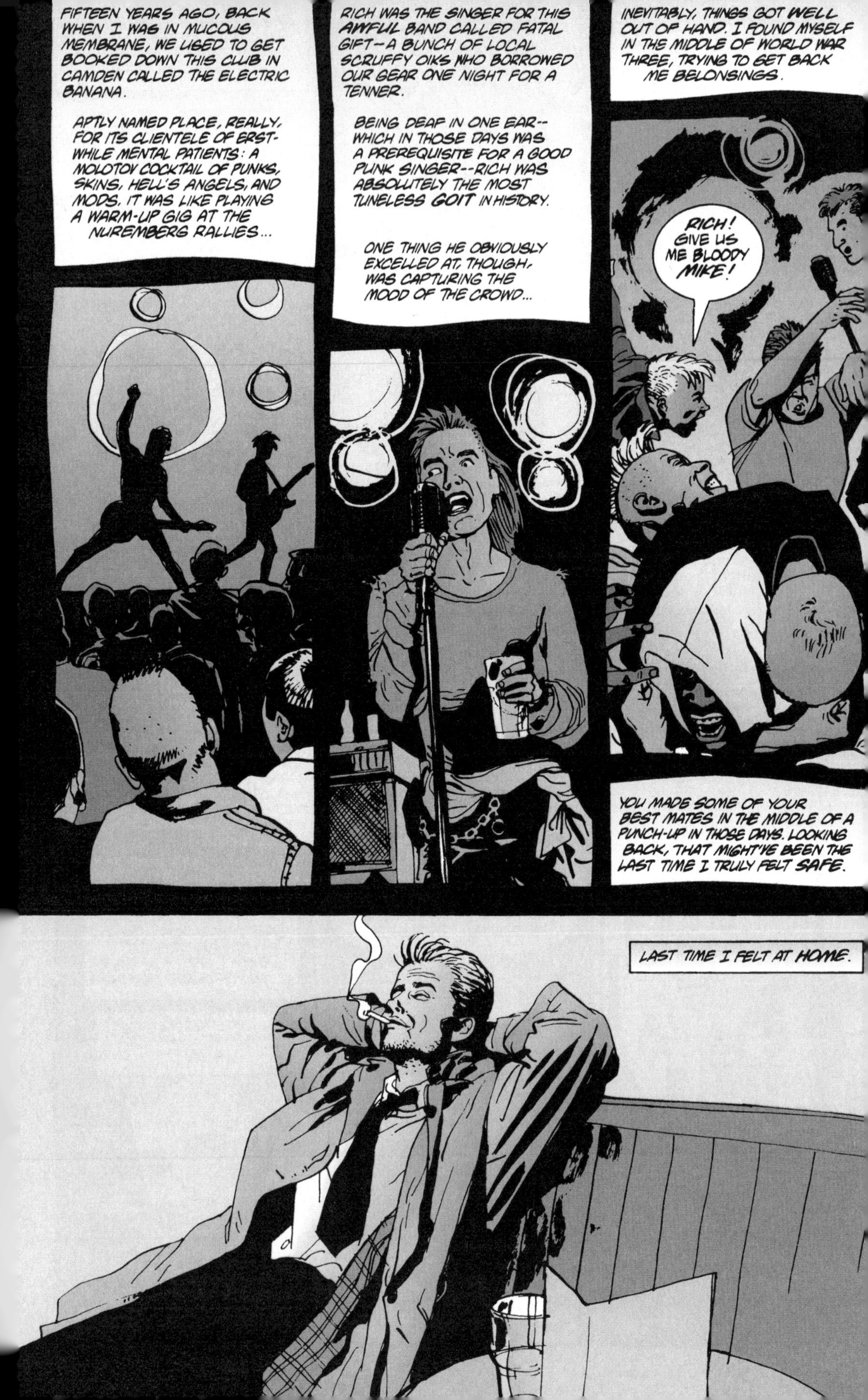

FIFTEEN YEARS AGO, BACK WHEN I WAS IN MUCOUS MEMBRANE, WE USED TO GET BOOKED DOWN THIS CLUB IN CAMDEN CALLED THE ELECTRIC BANANA.
APTLY NAMED PLACE, REALLY, FOR ITS CLIENTELE OF ERST-WHILE MENTAL PATIENTS: A MOLOTOV COCKTAIL OF PUNKS, SKINS, HELL'S ANGELS, AND MODS. IT WAS LIKE PLAYING A WARM-UP GIG AT THE NUREMBERG RALLIES...
RICH WAS THE SINGER FOR THIS AWFUL BAND CALLED FATAL GIFT--A BUNCH OF LOCAL SCRUFFY OIKS WHO BORROWED OUR GEAR ONE NIGHT FOR A TENNER.
BEING DEAF IN ONE EAR--WHICH IN THOSE DAYS WAS A PREREQUISITE FOR A GOOD PUNK SINGER--RICH WAS ABSOLUTELY THE MOST TUNELESS GOIT IN HISTORY.
ONE THING HE OBVIOUSLY EXCELLED AT, THOUGH, WAS CAPTURING THE MOOD OF THE CROWD...
INEVITABLY, THINGS GOT WELL OUT OF HAND. I FOUND MYSELF IN THE MIDDLE OF WORLD WAR THREE, TRYING TO GET BACK ME BELONGINGS.
RICH! GIVE US ME BLOODY MIKE!
YOU MADE SOME OF YOUR BEST MATES IN THE MIDDLE OF A PUNCH-UP IN THOSE DAYS. LOOKING BACK, THAT MIGHT'VE BEEN THE LAST TIME I TRULY FELT SAFE.
LAST TIME I FELT AT HOME.

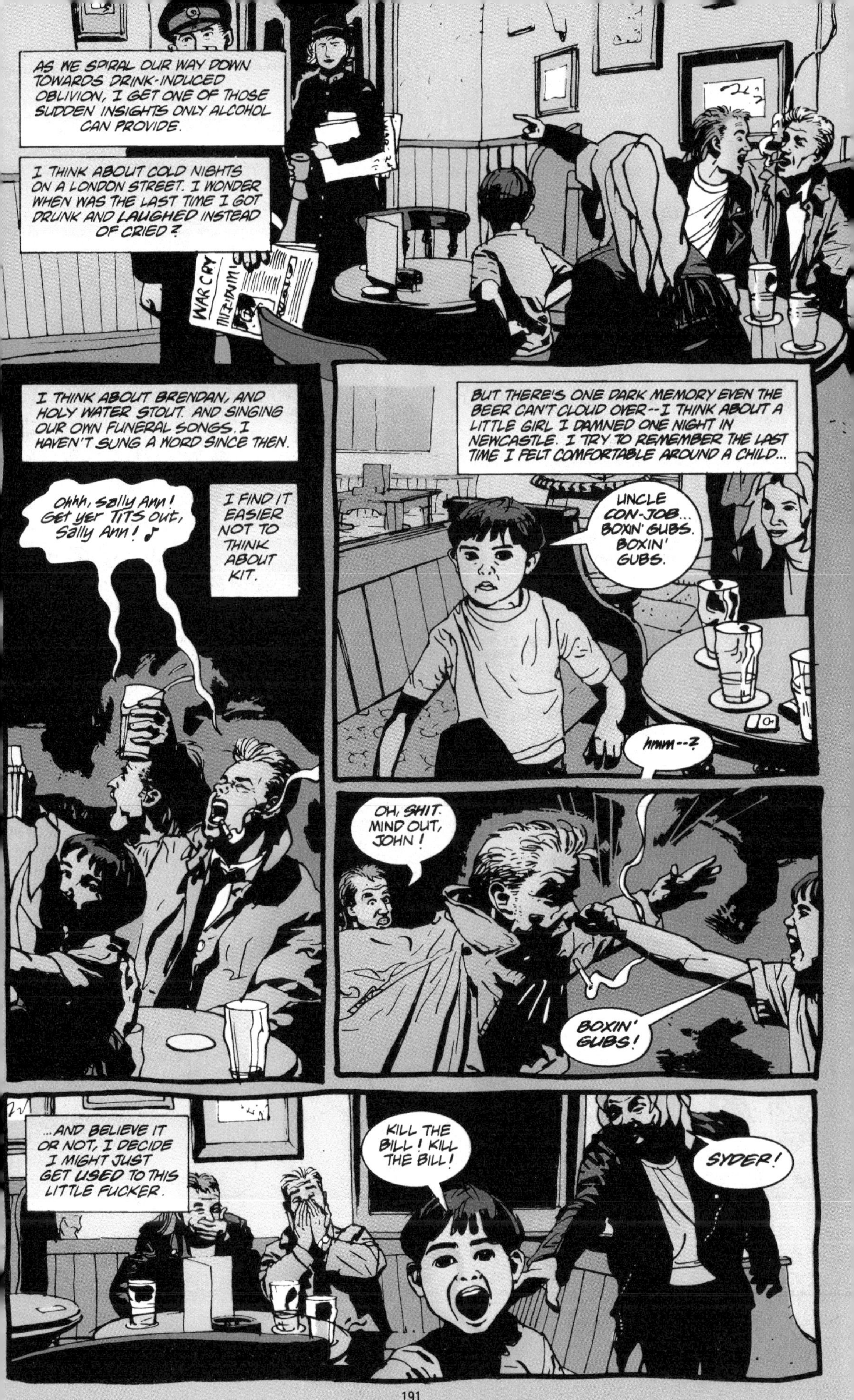
AS WE SPIRAL OUR WAY DOWN TOWARDS DRINK-INDUCED OBLIVION, I GET ONE OF THOSE SUDDEN INSIGHTS ONLY ALCOHOL CAN PROVIDE.
I THINK ABOUT COLD NIGHTS ON A LONDON STREET. I WONDER WHEN WAS THE LAST TIME I GOT DRUNK AND LAUGHED INSTEAD OF CRIED?
WAR CRY
I THINK ABOUT BRENDAN, AND HOLY WATER STOUT. AND SINGING OUR OWN FUNERAL SONGS. I HAVEN'T SUNG A WORD SINCE THEN.
Ohhh, Sally Ann! Get yer TITS out, Sally Ann! ♪
I FIND IT EASIER NOT TO THINK ABOUT KIT.
BUT THERE'S ONE DARK MEMORY EVEN THE BEER CAN'T CLOUD OVER--I THINK ABOUT A LITTLE GIRL I DAMNED ONE NIGHT IN NEWCASTLE. I TRY TO REMEMBER THE LAST TIME I FELT COMFORTABLE AROUND A CHILD...
UNCLE CON-JOB... BOXIN' GUBS. BOXIN' GUBS.
hmm--?
OH, SHIT. MIND OUT, JOHN!
BOXIN' GUBS!
...AND BELIEVE IT OR NOT, I DECIDE I MIGHT JUST GET USED TO THIS LITTLE FUCKER.
KILL THE BILL! KILL THE BILL!
SYDER!

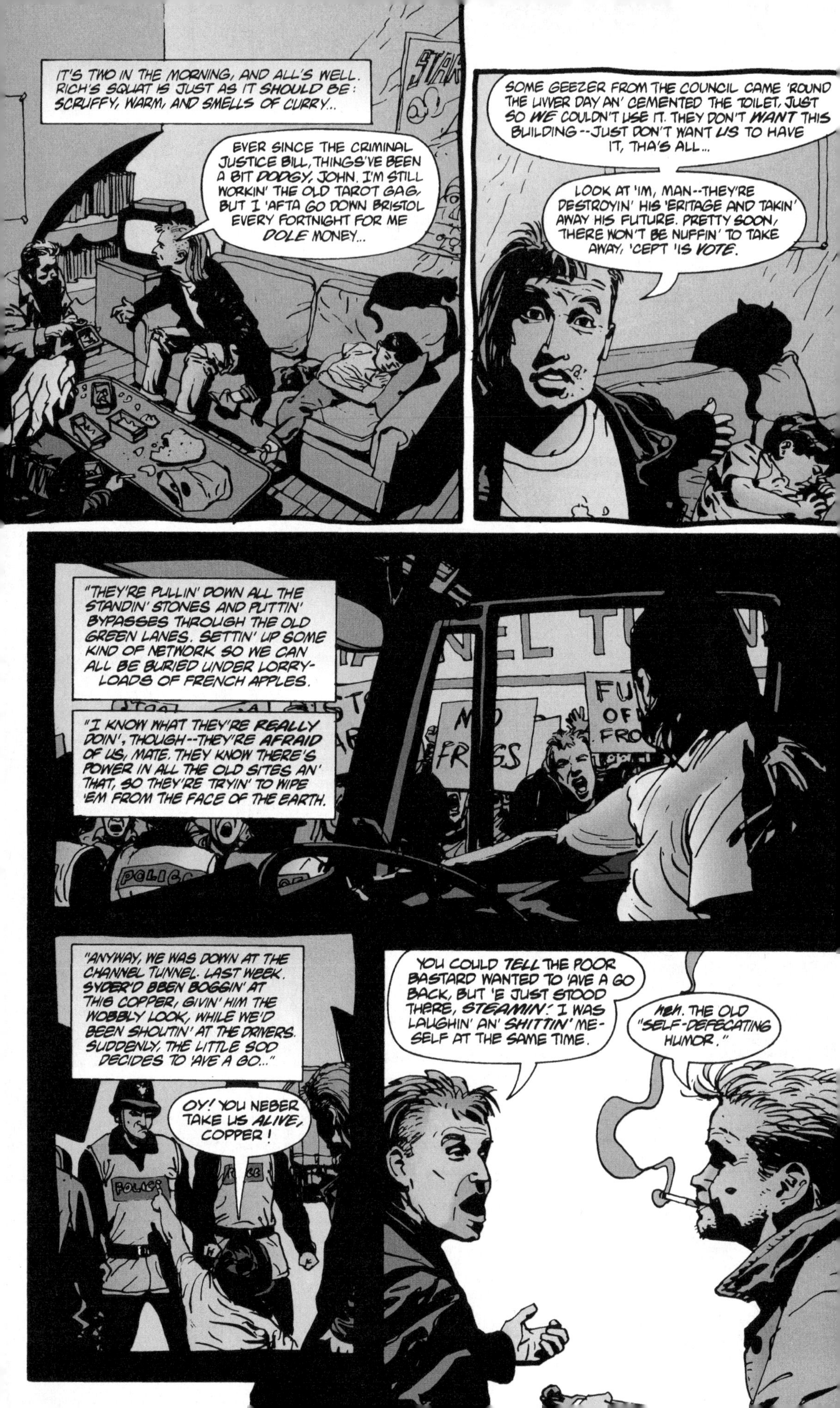
IT'S TWO IN THE MORNING, AND ALL'S WELL. RICH'S SQUAT IS JUST AS IT SHOULD BE: SCRUFFY, WARM, AND SMELLS OF CURRY...
EVER SINCE THE CRIMINAL JUSTICE BILL, THINGS'VE BEEN A BIT DODGY, JOHN. I'M STILL WORKIN' THE OLD TAROT GAG, BUT I 'AFTA GO DOWN BRISTOL EVERY FORTNIGHT FOR ME DOLE MONEY...
SOME GEEZER FROM THE COUNCIL CAME 'ROUND THE UVVER DAY AN' CEMENTED THE TOILET, JUST SO WE COULDN'T USE IT. THEY DON'T WANT THIS BUILDING--JUST DON'T WANT US TO HAVE IT, THA'S ALL...
LOOK AT 'IM, MAN--THEY'RE DESTROYIN' HIS 'ERITAGE AND TAKIN' AWAY HIS FUTURE. PRETTY SOON, THERE WON'T BE NUFFIN' TO TAKE AWAY, 'CEPT 'IS VOTE.
"THEY'RE PULLIN' DOWN ALL THE STANDIN' STONES AND PUTTIN' BYPASSES THROUGH THE OLD GREEN LANES. SETTIN' UP SOME KIND OF NETWORK SO WE CAN ALL BE BURIED UNDER LORRY-LOADS OF FRENCH APPLES.
"I KNOW WHAT THEY'RE REALLY DOIN', THOUGH--THEY'RE AFRAID OF US, MATE. THEY KNOW THERE'S POWER IN ALL THE OLD SITES AN' THAT, SO THEY'RE TRYIN' TO WIPE 'EM FROM THE FACE OF THE EARTH.
"ANYWAY, WE WAS DOWN AT THE CHANNEL TUNNEL. LAST WEEK. SYDER'D BEEN BOGGIN' AT THIS COPPER, GIVIN' HIM THE WOBBLY LOOK, WHILE WE'D BEEN SHOUTIN' AT THE DRIVERS. SUDDENLY, THE LITTLE SOD DECIDES TO 'AVE A GO..."
OY! YOU NEBER TAKE US ALIVE, COPPER!
YOU COULD TELL THE POOR BASTARD WANTED TO 'AVE A GO BACK, BUT 'E JUST STOOD THERE, STEAMIN'. I WAS LAUGHIN' AN' SHITTIN' ME-SELF AT THE SAME TIME.
HEH. THE OLD "SELF-DEFECATING HUMOR."

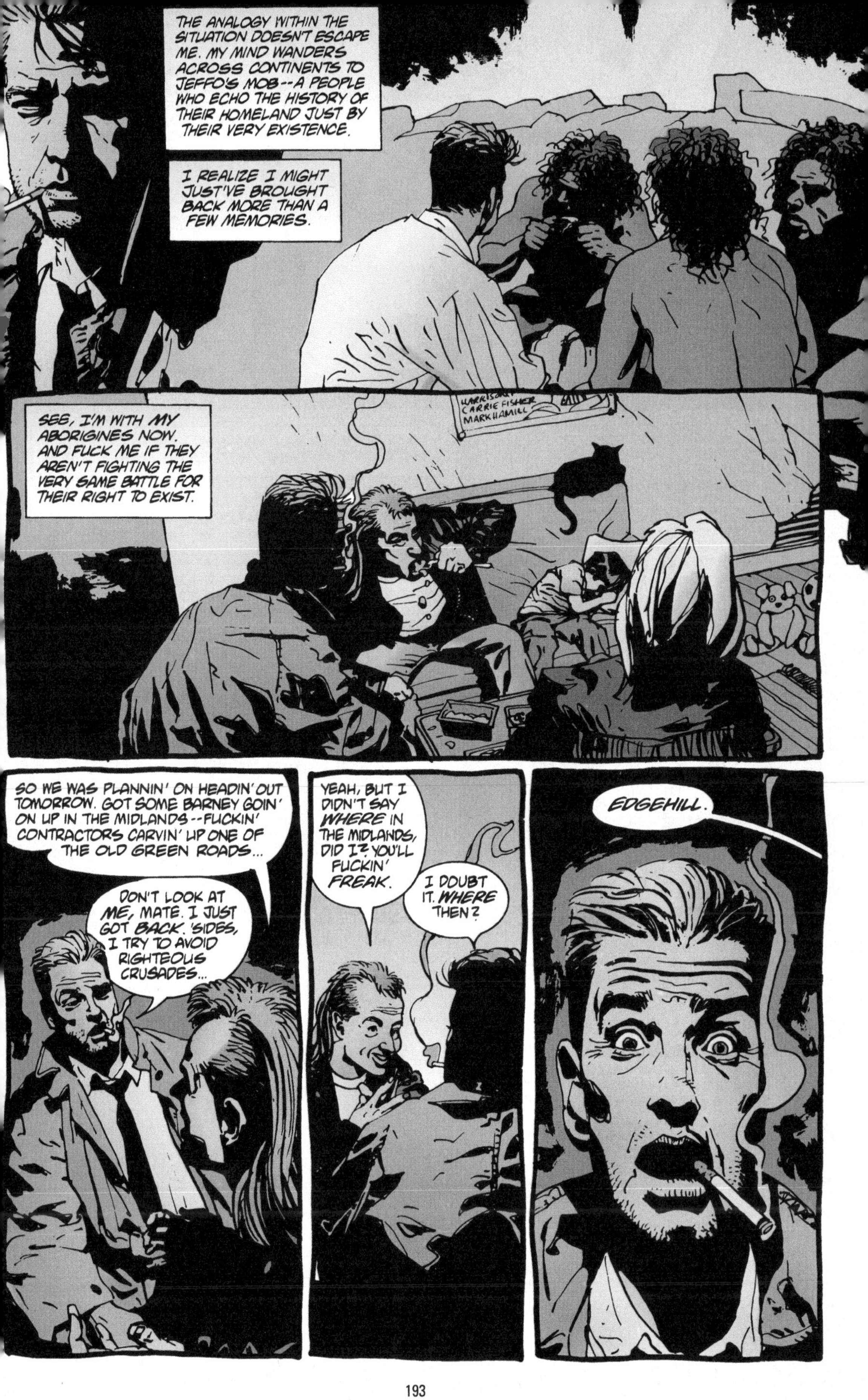
THE ANALOGY WITHIN THE SITUATION DOESN'T ESCAPE ME. MY MIND WANDERS ACROSS CONTINENTS TO JEFFO'S MOB--A PEOPLE WHO ECHO THE HISTORY OF THEIR HOMELAND JUST BY THEIR VERY EXISTENCE.
I REALIZE I MIGHT JUST'VE BROUGHT BACK MORE THAN A FEW MEMORIES.
SEE, I'M WITH MY ABORIGINES NOW. AND FUCK ME IF THEY AREN'T FIGHTING THE VERY SAME BATTLE FOR THEIR RIGHT TO EXIST.
CARRIE FISHER
MARK HAMILL
SO WE WAS PLANNIN' ON HEADIN' OUT TOMORROW. GOT SOME BARNEY GOIN' ON UP IN THE MIDLANDS--FUCKIN' CONTRACTORS CARVIN' UP ONE OF THE OLD GREEN ROADS...
DON'T LOOK AT ME, MATE. I JUST GOT BACK. 'SIDES, I TRY TO AVOID RIGHTEOUS CRUSADES...
YEAH, BUT I DIDN'T SAY WHERE IN THE MIDLANDS, DID I? YOU'LL FUCKIN' FREAK.
I DOUBT IT. WHERE THEN?
EDGEHILL.

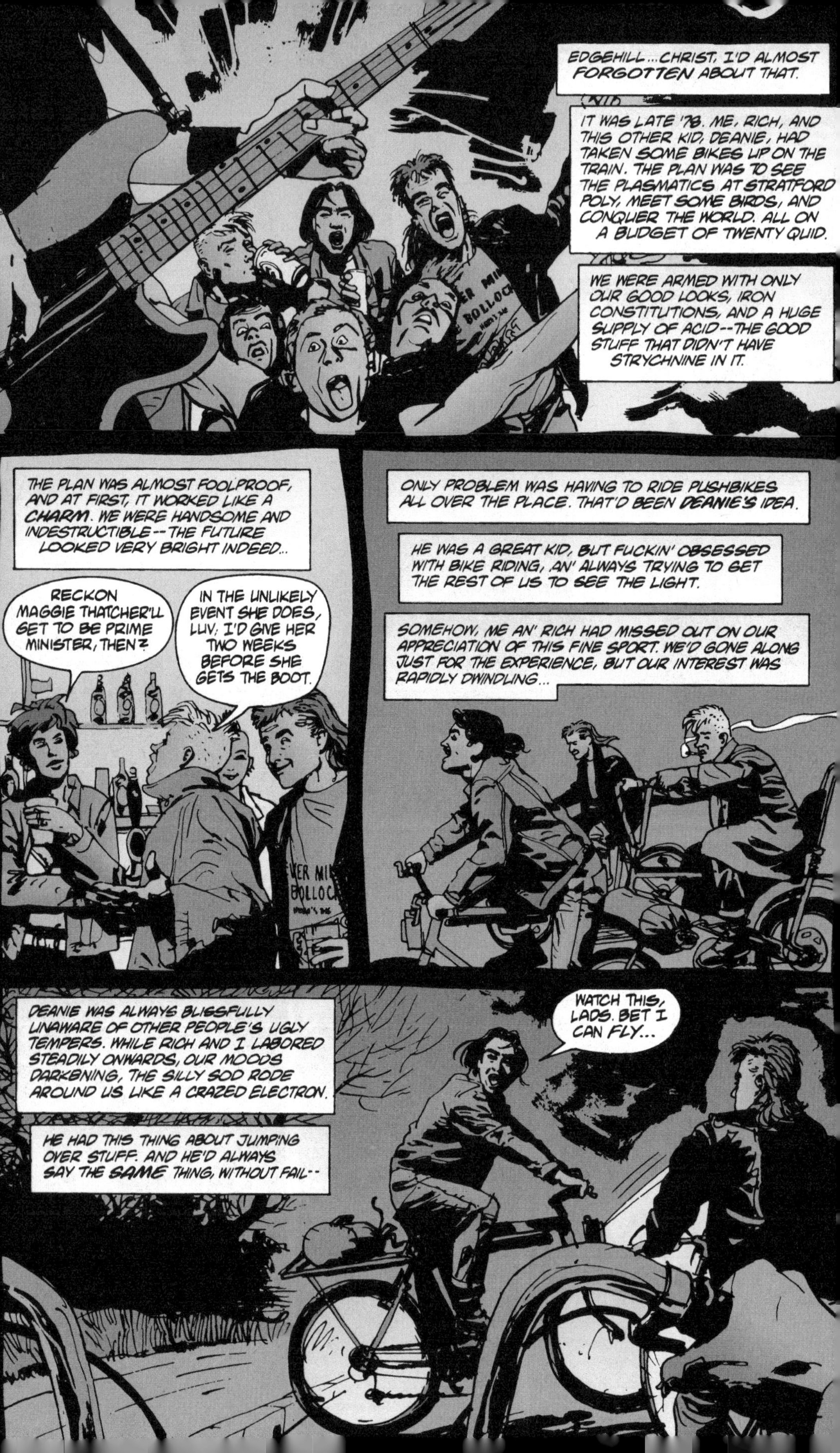
EDGEHILL...CHRIST, I'D ALMOST FORGOTTEN ABOUT THAT.
IT WAS LATE '78. ME, RICH, AND THIS OTHER KID, DEANIE, HAD TAKEN SOME BIKES UP ON THE TRAIN. THE PLAN WAS TO SEE THE PLASMATICS AT STRATFORD POLY, MEET SOME BIRDS, AND CONQUER THE WORLD. ALL ON A BUDGET OF TWENTY QUID.
WE WERE ARMED WITH ONLY OUR GOOD LOOKS, IRON CONSTITUTIONS, AND A HUGE SUPPLY OF ACID--THE GOOD STUFF THAT DIDN'T HAVE STRYCHNINE IN IT.
THE PLAN WAS ALMOST FOOLPROOF, AND AT FIRST, IT WORKED LIKE A CHARM. WE WERE HANDSOME AND INDESTRUCTIBLE--THE FUTURE LOOKED VERY BRIGHT INDEED...
RECKON MAGGIE THATCHER'LL GET TO BE PRIME MINISTER, THEN?
IN THE UNLIKELY EVENT SHE DOES, LUV, I'D GIVE HER TWO WEEKS BEFORE SHE GETS THE BOOT.
ONLY PROBLEM WAS HAVING TO RIDE PUSHBIKES ALL OVER THE PLACE. THAT'D BEEN DEANIE'S IDEA.
HE WAS A GREAT KID, BUT FUCKIN' OBSESSED WITH BIKE RIDING, AN' ALWAYS TRYING TO GET THE REST OF US TO SEE THE LIGHT.
SOMEHOW, ME AN' RICH HAD MISSED OUT ON OUR APPRECIATION OF THIS FINE SPORT. WE'D GONE ALONG JUST FOR THE EXPERIENCE, BUT OUR INTEREST WAS RAPIDLY DWINDLING...
DEANIE WAS ALWAYS BLISSFULLY UNAWARE OF OTHER PEOPLE'S UGLY TEMPERS. WHILE RICH AND I LABORED STEADILY ONWARDS, OUR MOODS DARKENING, THE SILLY SOD RODE AROUND US LIKE A CRAZED ELECTRON.
HE HAD THIS THING ABOUT JUMPING OVER STUFF. AND HE'D ALWAYS SAY THE SAME THING, WITHOUT FAIL--
WATCH THIS, LADS. BET I CAN FLY...

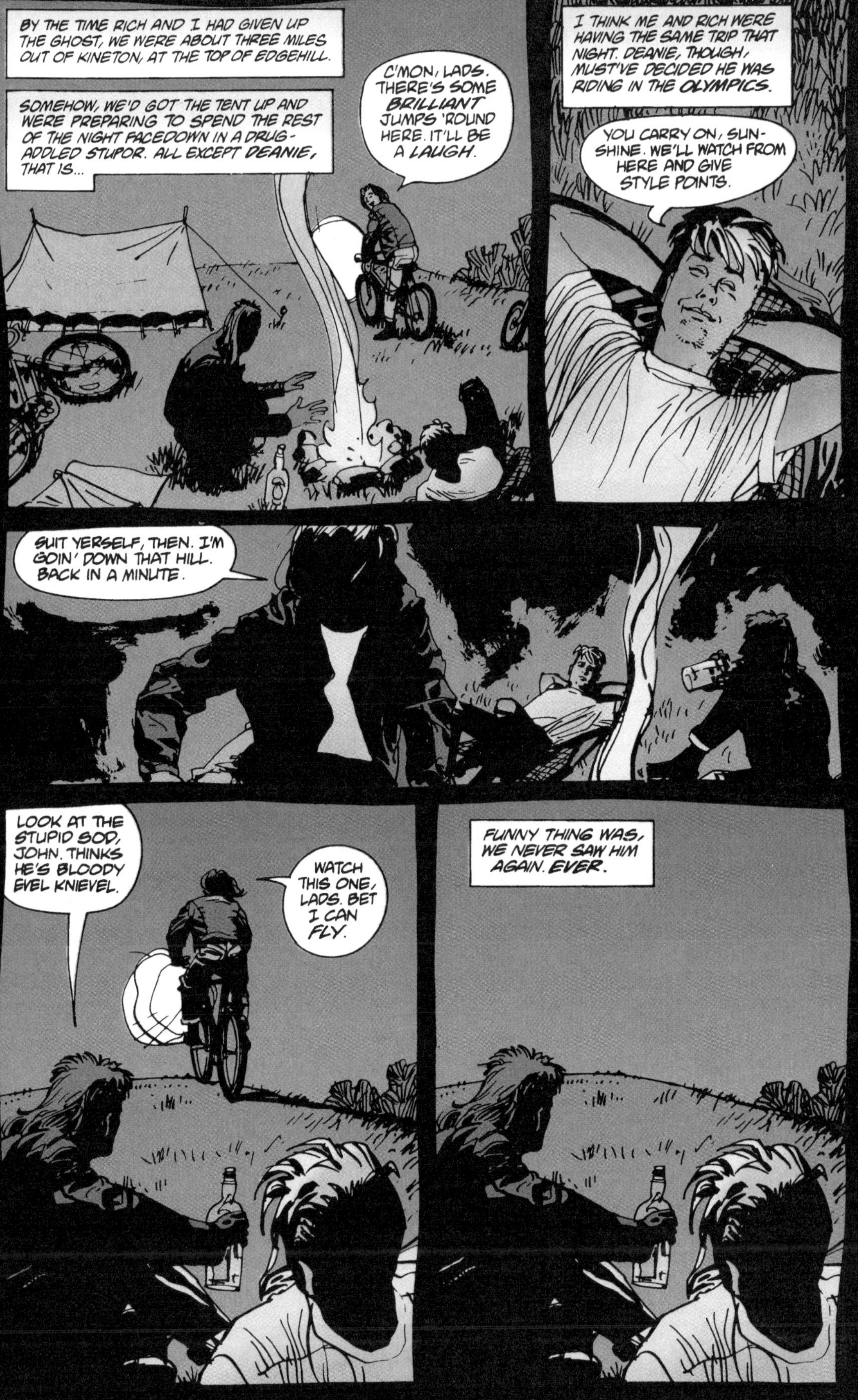
BY THE TIME RICH AND I HAD GIVEN UP THE GHOST, WE WERE ABOUT THREE MILES OUT OF KINETON, AT THE TOP OF EDGEHILL.
SOMEHOW, WE'D GOT THE TENT UP AND WERE PREPARING TO SPEND THE REST OF THE NIGHT FACEDOWN IN A DRUG-ADDLED STUPOR. ALL EXCEPT DEANIE, THAT IS...
C'MON, LADS. THERE'S SOME BRILLIANT JUMPS 'ROUND HERE. IT'LL BE A LAUGH.
I THINK ME AND RICH WERE HAVING THE SAME TRIP THAT NIGHT. DEANIE, THOUGH, MUST'VE DECIDED HE WAS RIDING IN THE OLYMPICS.
YOU CARRY ON, SUN-SHINE. WE'LL WATCH FROM HERE AND GIVE STYLE POINTS.
SUIT YERSELF, THEN. I'M GOIN' DOWN THAT HILL. BACK IN A MINUTE.
LOOK AT THE STUPID SOD, JOHN. THINKS HE'S BLOODY EVEL KNIEVEL.
WATCH THIS ONE, LADS. BET I CAN FLY.
FUNNY THING WAS, WE NEVER SAW HIM AGAIN. EVER.

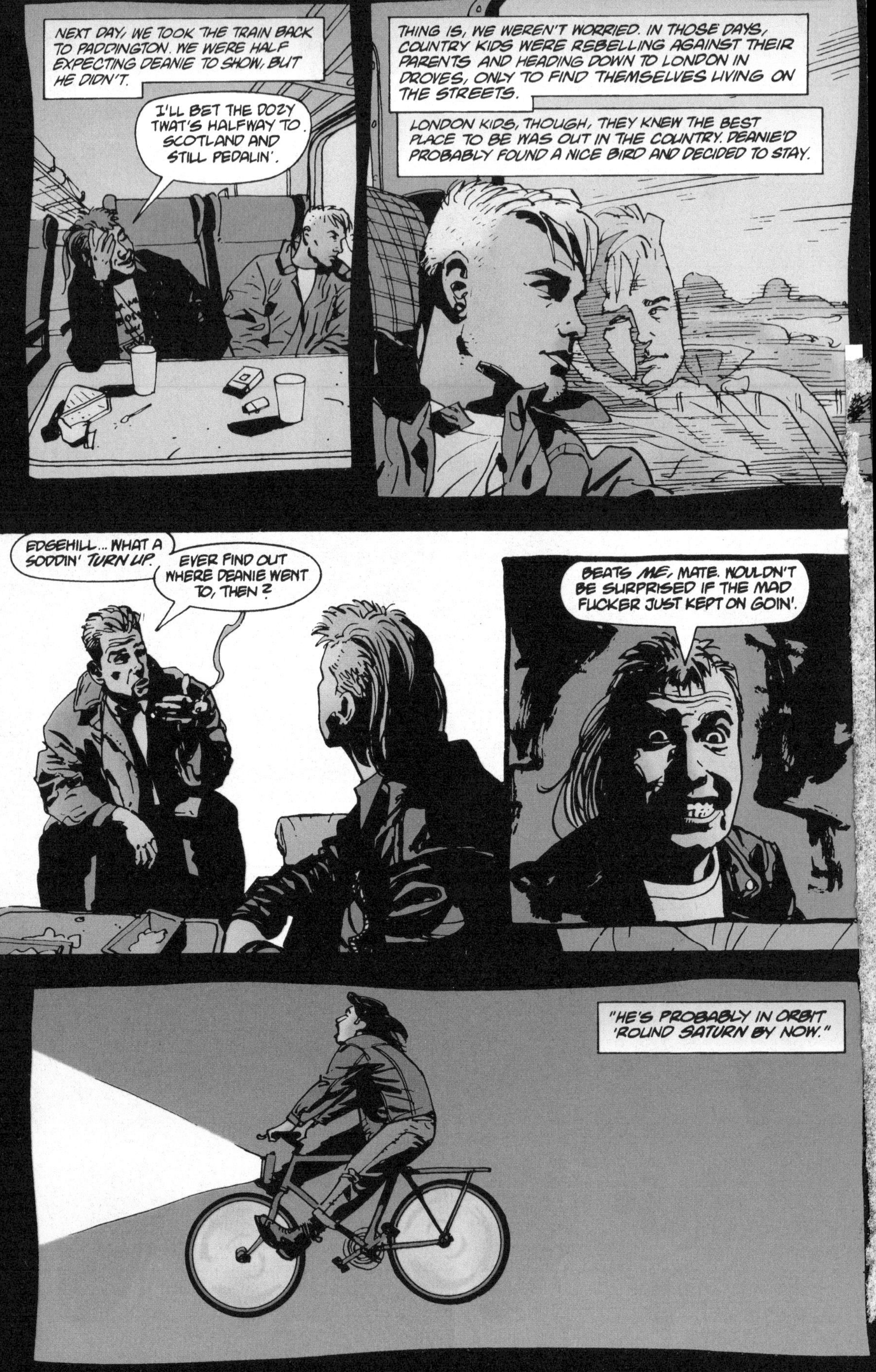
NEXT DAY, WE TOOK THE TRAIN BACK TO PADDINGTON. WE WERE HALF EXPECTING DEANIE TO SHOW, BUT HE DIDN'T.
I'LL BET THE DOZY TWAT'S HALFWAY TO SCOTLAND AND STILL PEDALIN'.
THING IS, WE WEREN'T WORRIED. IN THOSE DAYS, COUNTRY KIDS WERE REBELLING AGAINST THEIR PARENTS AND HEADING DOWN TO LONDON IN DROVES, ONLY TO FIND THEMSELVES LIVING ON THE STREETS.
LONDON KIDS, THOUGH, THEY KNEW THE BEST PLACE TO BE WAS OUT IN THE COUNTRY. DEANIE'D PROBABLY FOUND A NICE BIRD AND DECIDED TO STAY.
EDGEHILL... WHAT A SODDIN' *TURN UP*.
EVER FIND OUT WHERE DEANIE WENT TO, THEN?
BEATS *ME*, MATE. WOULDN'T BE SURPRISED IF THE MAD FUCKER JUST KEPT ON GOIN'.
"HE'S PROBABLY IN ORBIT 'ROUND SATURN BY NOW."

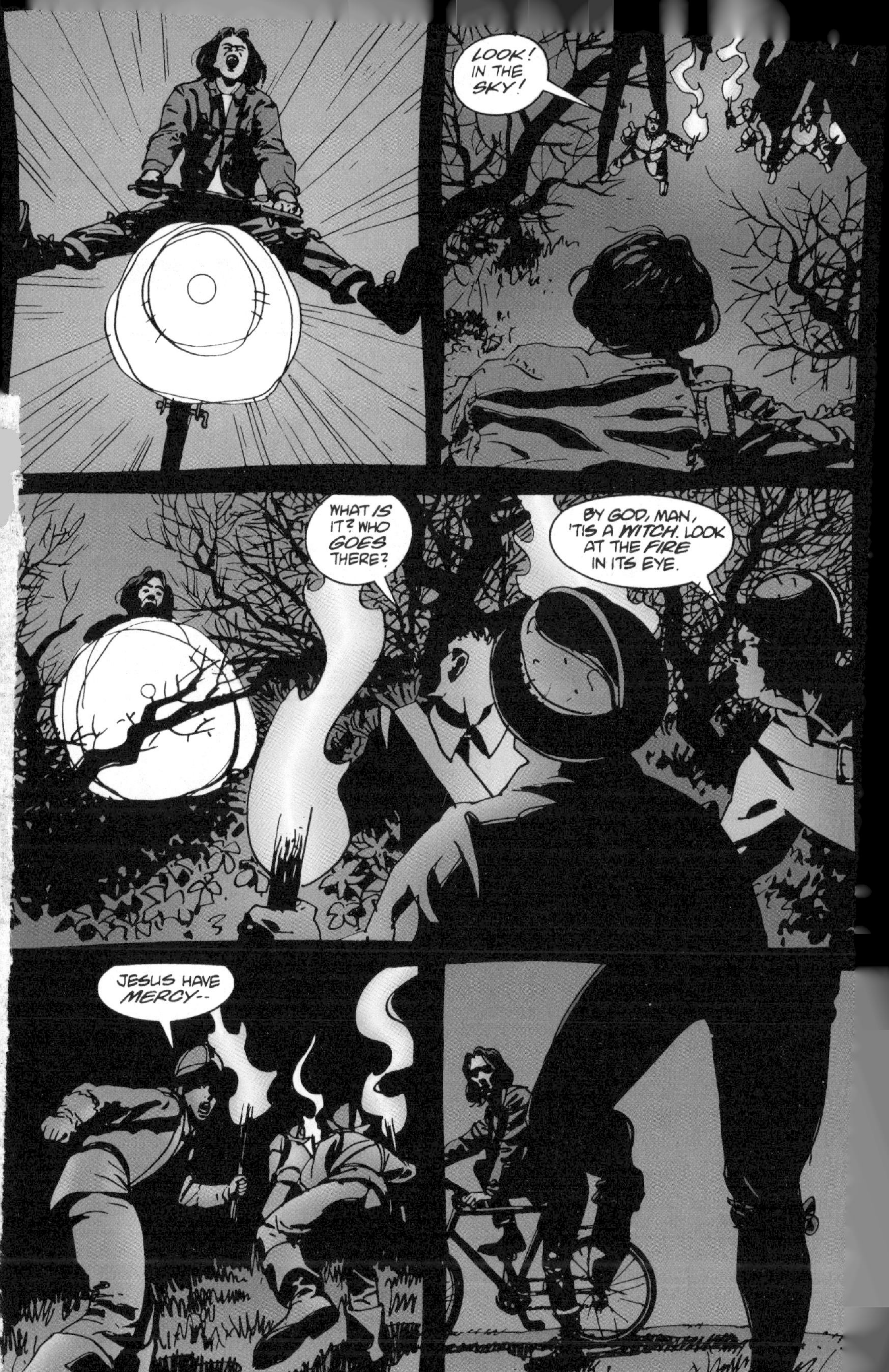

LOOK! IN THE SKY!
WHAT IS IT? WHO GOES THERE?
BY GOD, MAN, 'TIS A WITCH. LOOK AT THE FIRE IN ITS EYE.
JESUS HAVE MERCY--

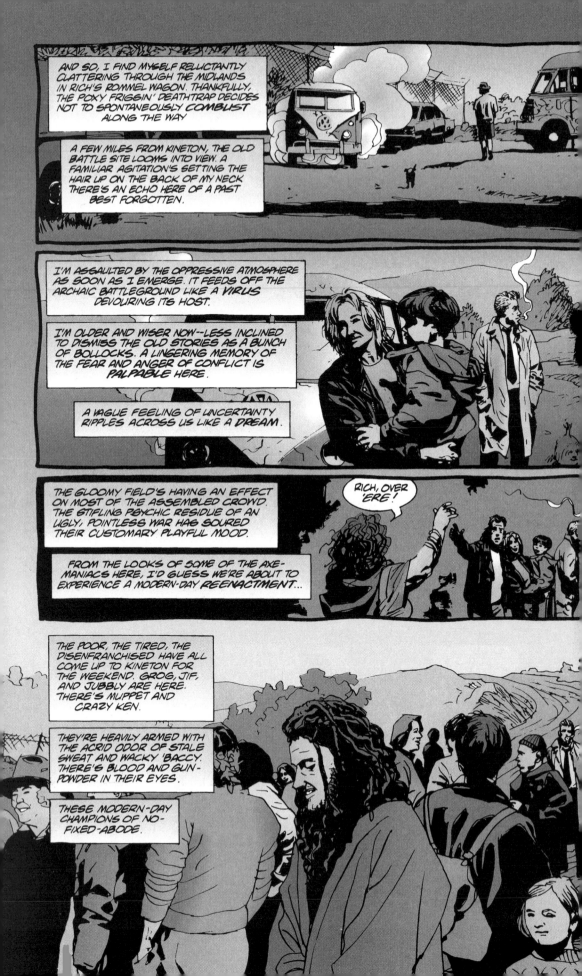

AND SO, I FIND MYSELF RELUCTANTLY CLATTERING THROUGH THE MIDLANDS IN RICH'S ROMMEL WAGON. THANKFULLY, THE POXY FRIGGIN' DEATHTRAP DECIDES NOT TO SPONTANEOUSLY *COMBUST* ALONG THE WAY

A FEW MILES FROM KINETON, THE OLD BATTLE SITE LOOMS INTO VIEW. A FAMILIAR AGITATION'S SETTING THE HAIR UP ON THE BACK OF MY NECK THERE'S AN ECHO HERE OF A PAST BEST FORGOTTEN.

I'M ASSAULTED BY THE OPPRESSIVE ATMOSPHERE AS SOON AS I EMERGE. IT FEEDS OFF THE ARCHAIC BATTLEGROUND LIKE A *VIRUS* DEVOURING ITS HOST.

I'M OLDER AND WISER NOW--LESS INCLINED TO DISMISS THE OLD STORIES AS A BUNCH OF BOLLOCKS. A LINGERING MEMORY OF THE FEAR AND ANGER OF CONFLICT IS *PALPABLE* HERE.

A VAGUE FEELING OF UNCERTAINTY RIPPLES ACROSS US LIKE A *DREAM.*

THE GLOOMY FIELD'S HAVING AN EFFECT ON MOST OF THE ASSEMBLED CROWD. THE STIFLING PSYCHIC RESIDUE OF AN UGLY, POINTLESS WAR HAS SOURED THEIR CUSTOMARY PLAYFUL MOOD.

FROM THE LOOKS OF SOME OF THE AXE-MANIACS HERE, I'D GUESS WE'RE ABOUT TO EXPERIENCE A MODERN-DAY *REENACTMENT...*

RICH, OVER 'ERE!

THE POOR, THE TIRED, THE DISENFRANCHISED HAVE ALL COME UP TO KINETON FOR THE WEEKEND. GROG, JIF, AND JUBBLY ARE HERE. THERE'S MUPPET AND CRAZY KEN.

THEY'RE HEAVILY ARMED WITH THE ACRID ODOR OF STALE SWEAT AND WACKY 'BACCY. THERE'S BLOOD AND GUN-POWDER IN THEIR EYES.

THESE MODERN-DAY CHAMPIONS OF NO-FIXED-ABODE.

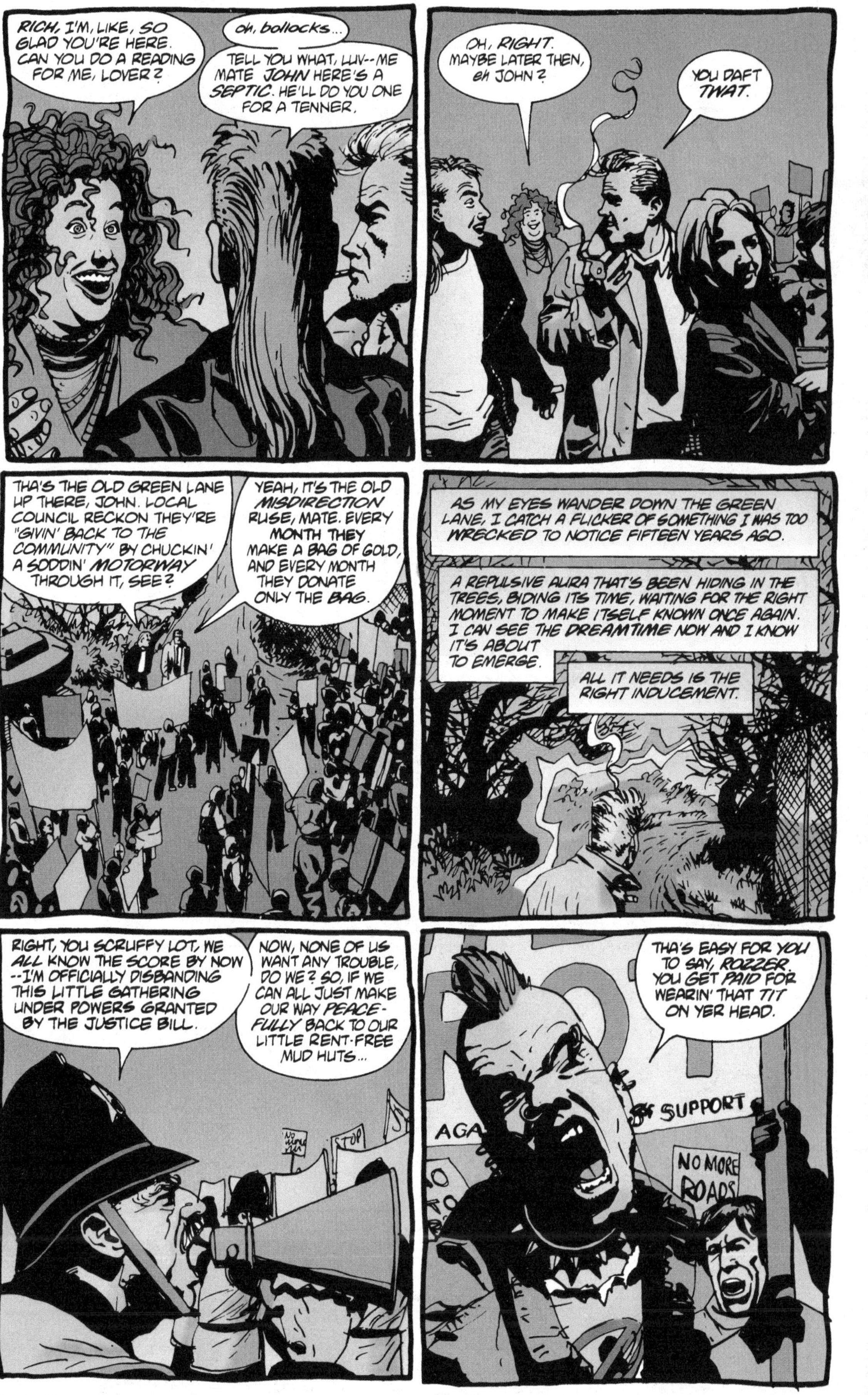
RICH, I'M, LIKE, SO GLAD YOU'RE HERE. CAN YOU DO A READING FOR ME, LOVER?
oh, bollocks...
TELL YOU WHAT, LUV--ME MATE JOHN HERE'S A SEPTIC. HE'LL DO YOU ONE FOR A TENNER.
OH, RIGHT. MAYBE LATER THEN, eh JOHN?
YOU DAFT TWAT.
THA'S THE OLD GREEN LANE UP THERE, JOHN. LOCAL COUNCIL RECKON THEY'RE "GIVIN' BACK TO THE COMMUNITY" BY CHUCKIN' A SODDIN' MOTORWAY THROUGH IT, SEE?
YEAH, IT'S THE OLD MISDIRECTION RUSE, MATE. EVERY MONTH THEY MAKE A BAG OF GOLD, AND EVERY MONTH THEY DONATE ONLY THE BAG.
AS MY EYES WANDER DOWN THE GREEN LANE, I CATCH A FLICKER OF SOMETHING I WAS TOO WRECKED TO NOTICE FIFTEEN YEARS AGO.
A REPULSIVE AURA THAT'S BEEN HIDING IN THE TREES, BIDING ITS TIME, WAITING FOR THE RIGHT MOMENT TO MAKE ITSELF KNOWN ONCE AGAIN. I CAN SEE THE DREAMTIME NOW AND I KNOW IT'S ABOUT TO EMERGE.
ALL IT NEEDS IS THE RIGHT INDUCEMENT.
RIGHT, YOU SCRUFFY LOT, WE ALL KNOW THE SCORE BY NOW --I'M OFFICIALLY DISBANDING THIS LITTLE GATHERING UNDER POWERS GRANTED BY THE JUSTICE BILL.
NOW, NONE OF US WANT ANY TROUBLE, DO WE? SO, IF WE CAN ALL JUST MAKE OUR WAY PEACEFULLY BACK TO OUR LITTLE RENT-FREE MUD HUTS...
STOP
THA'S EASY FOR YOU TO SAY, ROZZER. YOU GET PAID FOR WEARIN' THAT TIT ON YER HEAD.
AGA
SUPPORT
NO MORE ROADS

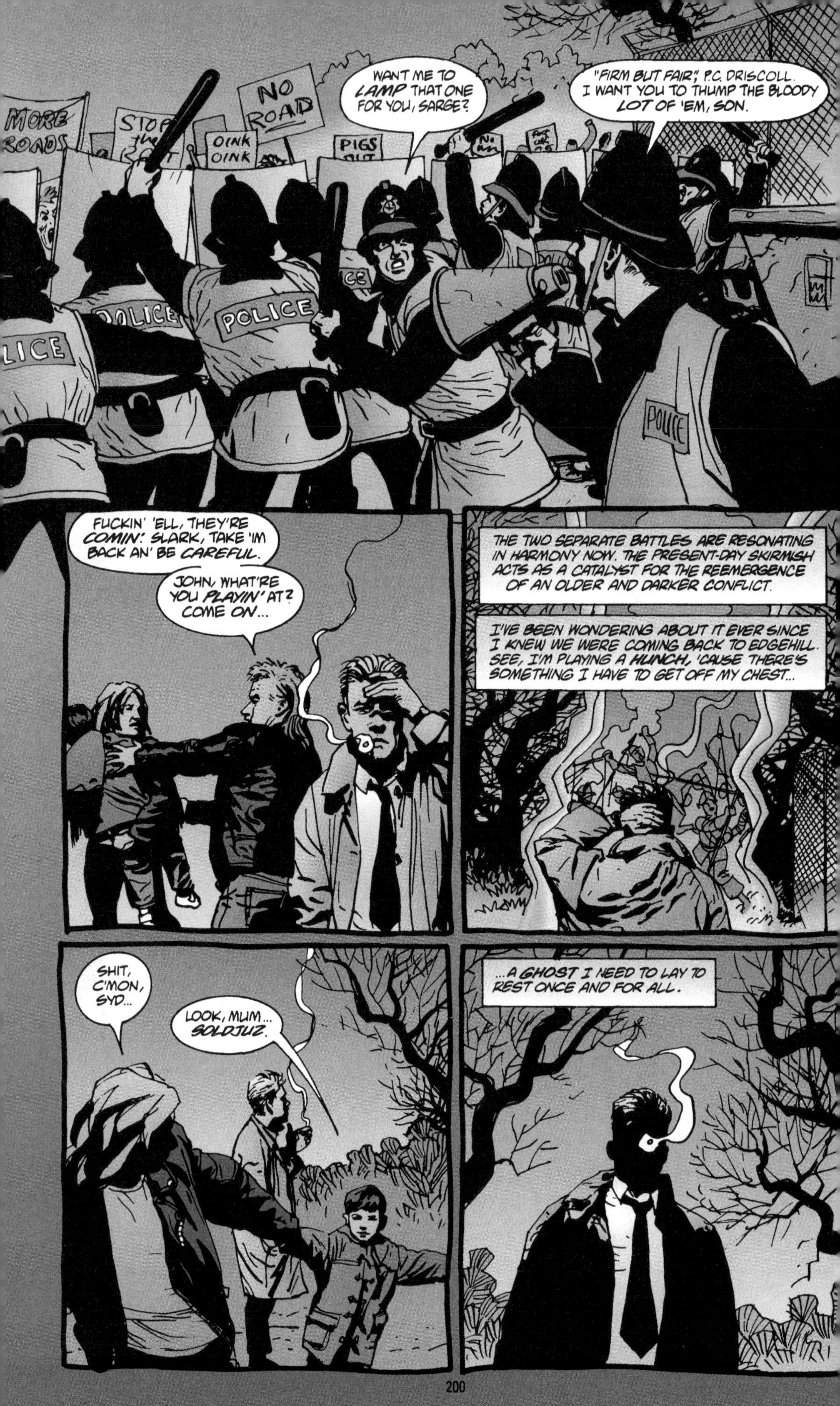
MORE ROADS
STOP the
NO ROAD
OINK OINK
PIGS OUT
WANT ME TO LAMP THAT ONE FOR YOU, SARGE?
"FIRM BUT FAIR," P.C. DRISCOLL. I WANT YOU TO THUMP THE BLOODY LOT OF 'EM, SON.
POLICE
POLICE
LICE
POLICE
POLICE
FUCKIN' 'ELL, THEY'RE COMIN'. SLARK, TAKE 'IM BACK AN' BE CAREFUL.
JOHN, WHAT'RE YOU PLAYIN' AT? COME ON...
THE TWO SEPARATE BATTLES ARE RESONATING IN HARMONY NOW. THE PRESENT-DAY SKIRMISH ACTS AS A CATALYST FOR THE REEMERGENCE OF AN OLDER AND DARKER CONFLICT.
I'VE BEEN WONDERING ABOUT IT EVER SINCE I KNEW WE WERE COMING BACK TO EDGEHILL. SEE, I'M PLAYING A HUNCH, 'CAUSE THERE'S SOMETHING I HAVE TO GET OFF MY CHEST...
SHIT, C'MON, SYD...
LOOK, MUM... SOLDJUZ.
...A GHOST I NEED TO LAY TO REST ONCE AND FOR ALL.

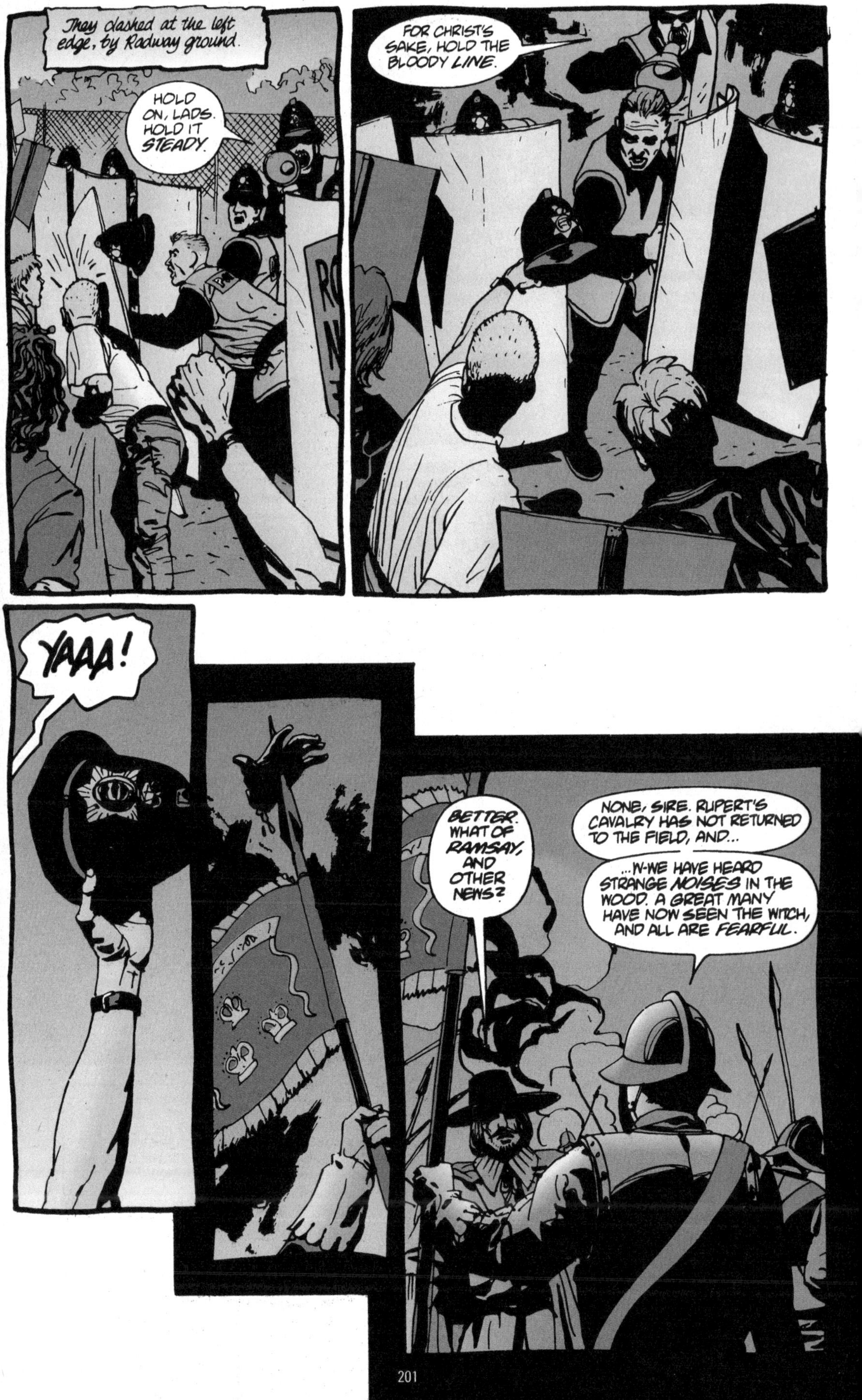
They clashed at the left edge, by Radway ground.
HOLD ON, LADS. HOLD IT STEADY.
FOR CHRIST'S SAKE, HOLD THE BLOODY LINE.
YAAA!
BETTER. WHAT OF RAMSAY, AND OTHER NEWS?
NONE, SIRE. RUPERT'S CAVALRY HAS NOT RETURNED TO THE FIELD, AND...
...W-WE HAVE HEARD STRANGE NOISES IN THE WOOD. A GREAT MANY HAVE NOW SEEN THE WITCH, AND ALL ARE FEARFUL.

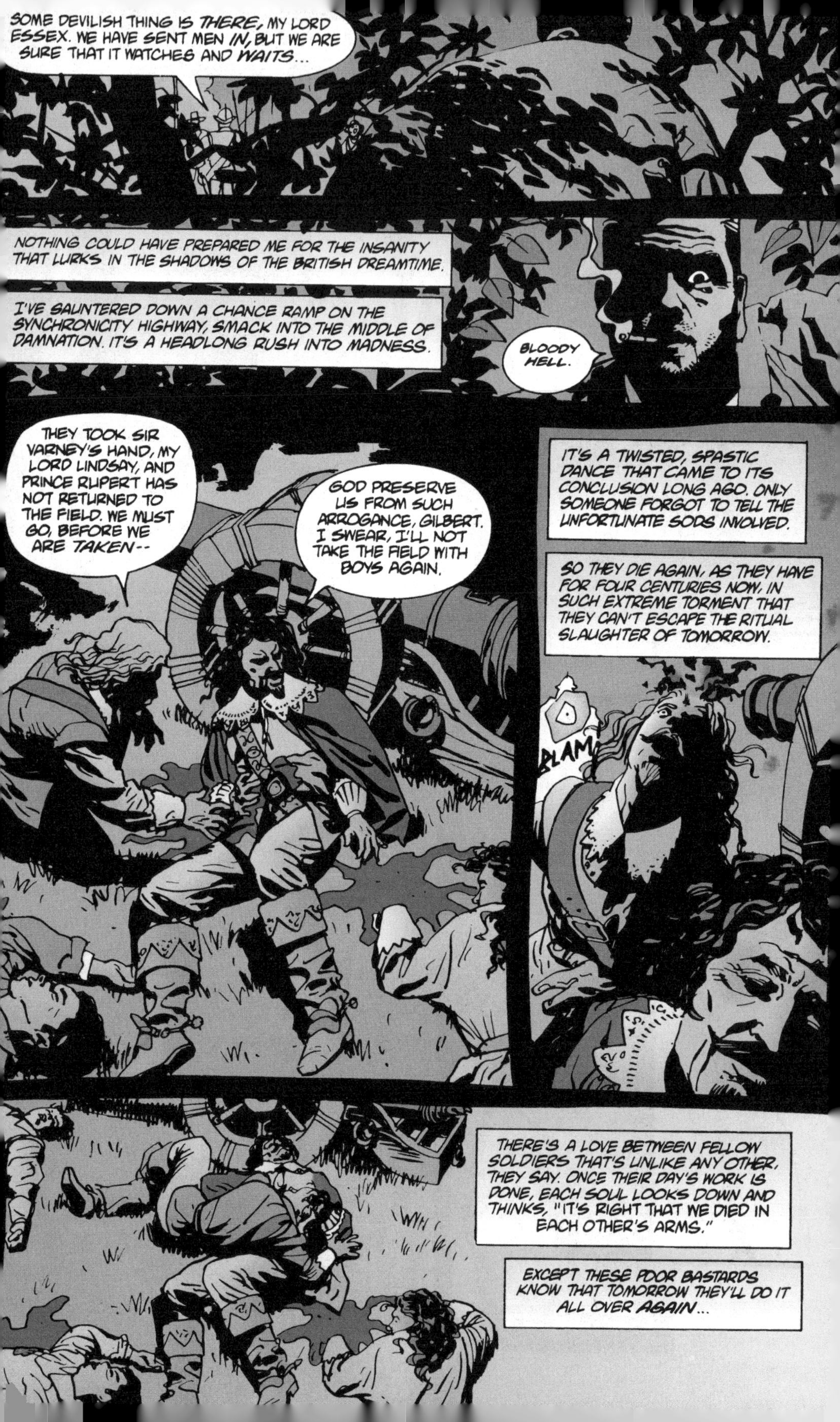
SOME DEVILISH THING IS THERE, MY LORD ESSEX. WE HAVE SENT MEN IN, BUT WE ARE SURE THAT IT WATCHES AND WAITS...
NOTHING COULD HAVE PREPARED ME FOR THE INSANITY THAT LURKS IN THE SHADOWS OF THE BRITISH DREAMTIME.
I'VE SAUNTERED DOWN A CHANCE RAMP ON THE SYNCHRONICITY HIGHWAY, SMACK INTO THE MIDDLE OF DAMNATION. IT'S A HEADLONG RUSH INTO MADNESS.
BLOODY HELL.
THEY TOOK SIR VARNEY'S HAND, MY LORD LINDSAY, AND PRINCE RUPERT HAS NOT RETURNED TO THE FIELD. WE MUST GO, BEFORE WE ARE TAKEN--
GOD PRESERVE US FROM SUCH ARROGANCE, GILBERT. I SWEAR, I'LL NOT TAKE THE FIELD WITH BOYS AGAIN.
IT'S A TWISTED, SPASTIC DANCE THAT CAME TO ITS CONCLUSION LONG AGO. ONLY SOMEONE FORGOT TO TELL THE UNFORTUNATE SODS INVOLVED.
SO THEY DIE AGAIN, AS THEY HAVE FOR FOUR CENTURIES NOW, IN SUCH EXTREME TORMENT THAT THEY CAN'T ESCAPE THE RITUAL SLAUGHTER OF TOMORROW.
BLAM
THERE'S A LOVE BETWEEN FELLOW SOLDIERS THAT'S UNLIKE ANY OTHER, THEY SAY. ONCE THEIR DAY'S WORK IS DONE, EACH SOUL LOOKS DOWN AND THINKS, "IT'S RIGHT THAT WE DIED IN EACH OTHER'S ARMS."
EXCEPT THESE POOR BASTARDS KNOW THAT TOMORROW THEY'LL DO IT ALL OVER AGAIN...

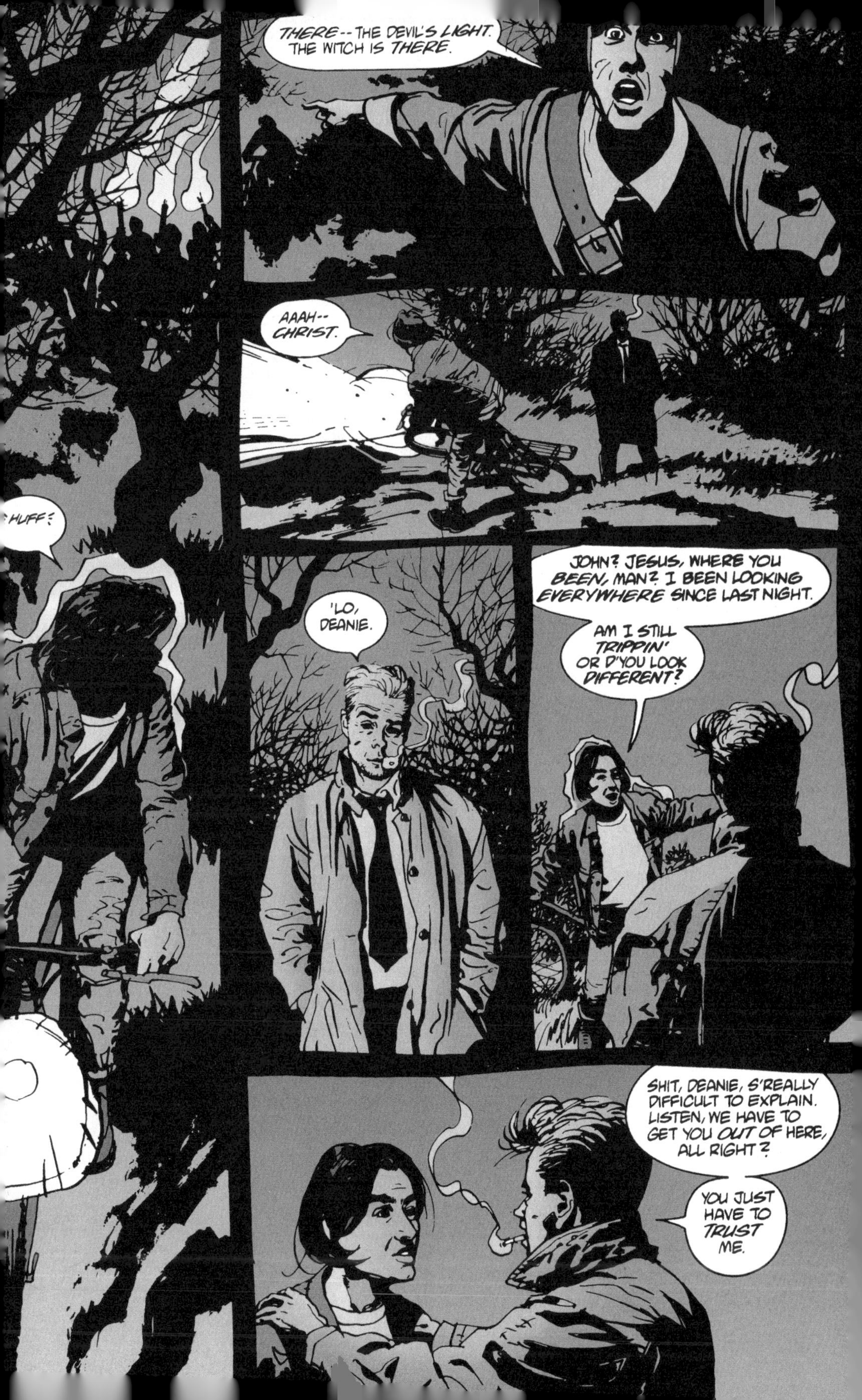
THERE -- THE DEVIL'S LIGHT. THE WITCH IS THERE.
AAAH-- CHRIST.
HUFF
'LO, DEANIE.
JOHN? JESUS, WHERE YOU BEEN, MAN? I BEEN LOOKING EVERYWHERE SINCE LAST NIGHT.
AM I STILL TRIPPIN' OR D'YOU LOOK DIFFERENT?
SHIT, DEANIE, S'REALLY DIFFICULT TO EXPLAIN. LISTEN, WE HAVE TO GET YOU OUT OF HERE, ALL RIGHT?
YOU JUST HAVE TO TRUST ME.

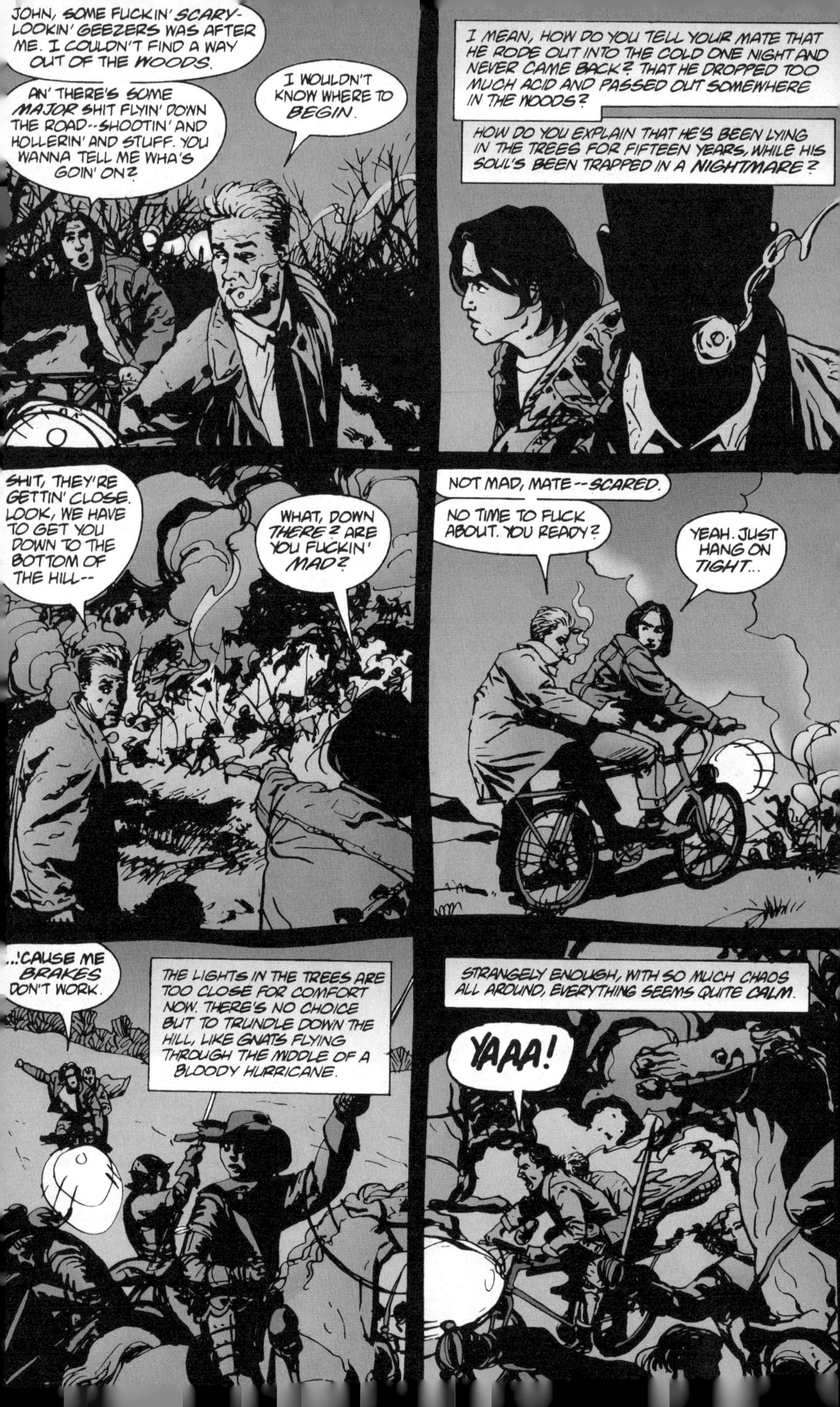

JOHN, SOME FUCKIN' SCARY-LOOKIN' GEEZERS WAS AFTER ME. I COULDN'T FIND A WAY OUT OF THE WOODS.
AN' THERE'S SOME MAJOR SHIT FLYIN' DOWN THE ROAD--SHOOTIN' AND HOLLERIN' AND STUFF. YOU WANNA TELL ME WHA'S GOIN' ON?
I WOULDN'T KNOW WHERE TO BEGIN.
I MEAN, HOW DO YOU TELL YOUR MATE THAT HE RODE OUT INTO THE COLD ONE NIGHT AND NEVER CAME BACK? THAT HE DROPPED TOO MUCH ACID AND PASSED OUT SOMEWHERE IN THE WOODS?
HOW DO YOU EXPLAIN THAT HE'S BEEN LYING IN THE TREES FOR FIFTEEN YEARS, WHILE HIS SOUL'S BEEN TRAPPED IN A NIGHTMARE?
SHIT, THEY'RE GETTIN' CLOSE. LOOK, WE HAVE TO GET YOU DOWN TO THE BOTTOM OF THE HILL--
WHAT, DOWN THERE? ARE YOU FUCKIN' MAD?
NOT MAD, MATE--SCARED.
NO TIME TO FUCK ABOUT. YOU READY?
YEAH. JUST HANG ON TIGHT...
...'CAUSE ME BRAKES DON'T WORK.
THE LIGHTS IN THE TREES ARE TOO CLOSE FOR COMFORT NOW. THERE'S NO CHOICE BUT TO TRUNDLE DOWN THE HILL, LIKE GNATS FLYING THROUGH THE MIDDLE OF A BLOODY HURRICANE.
STRANGELY ENOUGH, WITH SO MUCH CHAOS ALL AROUND, EVERYTHING SEEMS QUITE CALM.
YAAA!

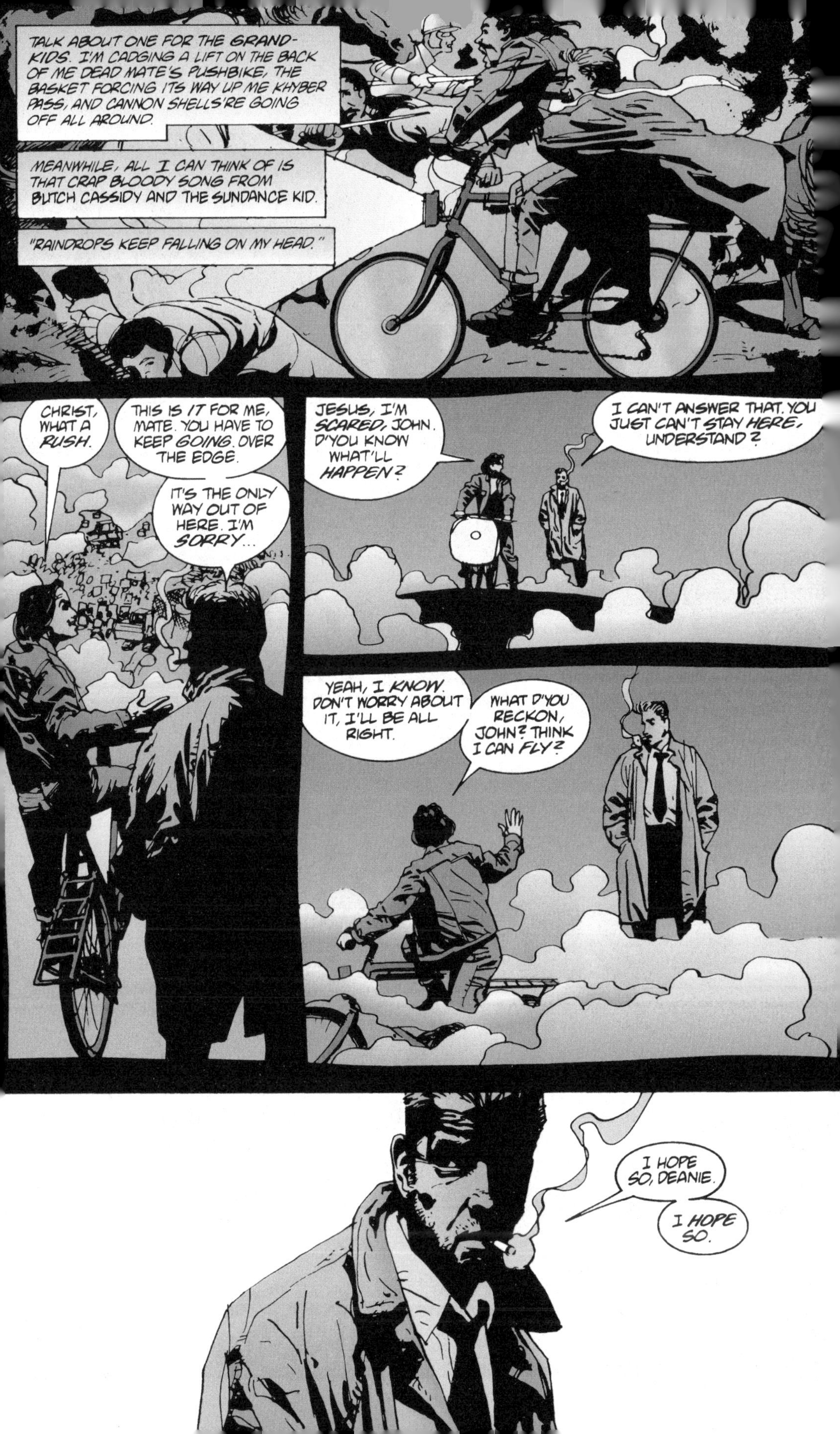

TALK ABOUT ONE FOR THE GRAND-KIDS. I'M CADGING A LIFT ON THE BACK OF ME DEAD MATE'S PUSHBIKE, THE BASKET FORCING ITS WAY UP ME KHYBER PASS, AND CANNON SHELLS'RE GOING OFF ALL AROUND.
MEANWHILE, ALL I CAN THINK OF IS THAT CRAP BLOODY SONG FROM BUTCH CASSIDY AND THE SUNDANCE KID.
"RAINDROPS KEEP FALLING ON MY HEAD."
CHRIST, WHAT A RUSH.
THIS IS IT FOR ME, MATE. YOU HAVE TO KEEP GOING. OVER THE EDGE.
IT'S THE ONLY WAY OUT OF HERE. I'M SORRY...
JESUS, I'M SCARED, JOHN. D'YOU KNOW WHAT'LL HAPPEN?
I CAN'T ANSWER THAT. YOU JUST CAN'T STAY HERE, UNDERSTAND?
YEAH, I KNOW. DON'T WORRY ABOUT IT, I'LL BE ALL RIGHT.
WHAT D'YOU RECKON, JOHN? THINK I CAN FLY?
I HOPE SO, DEANIE.
I HOPE SO.

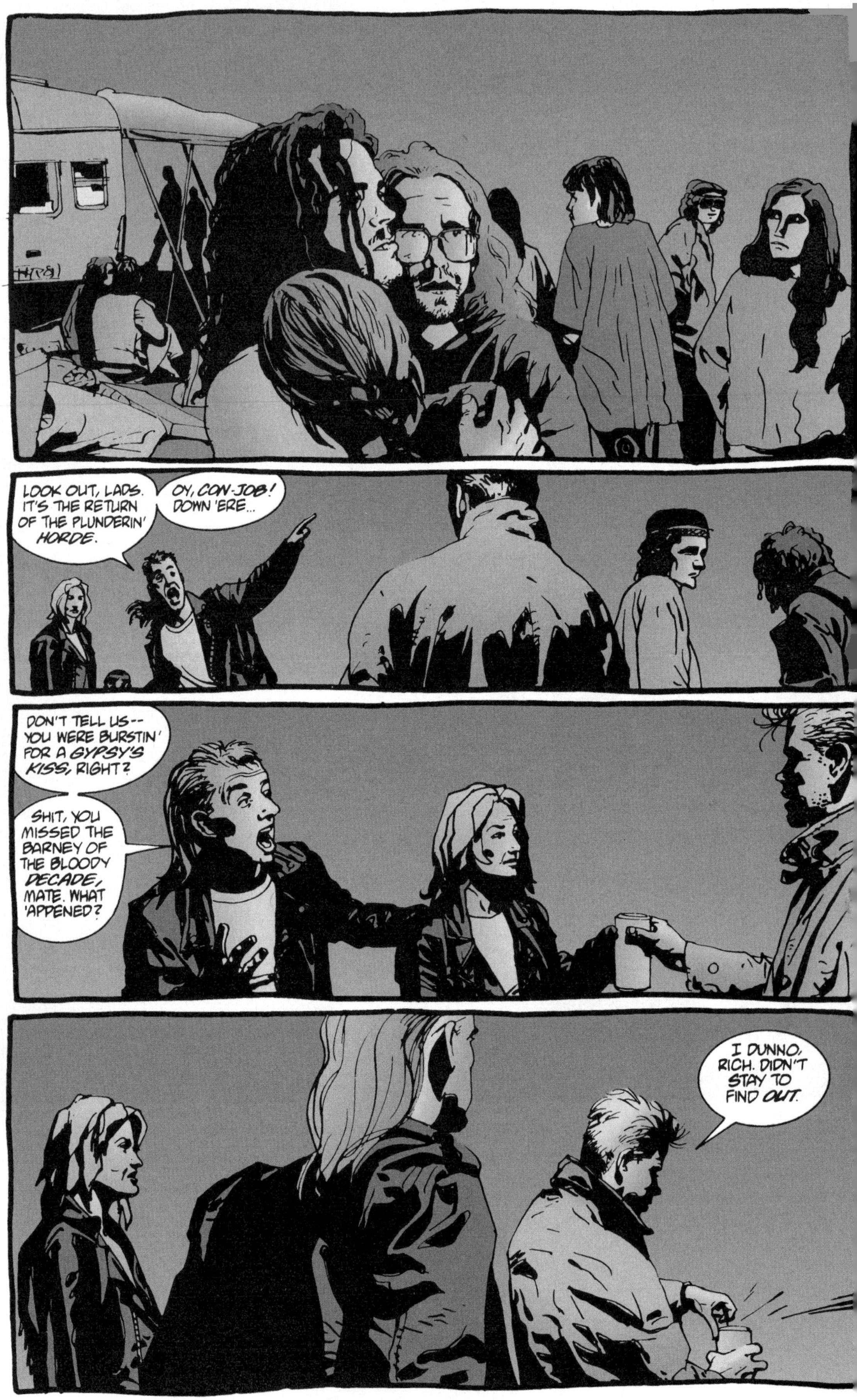
LOOK OUT, LADS. IT'S THE RETURN OF THE PLUNDERIN' HORDE.
OY, CON-JOB! DOWN 'ERE...
DON'T TELL US-- YOU WERE BURSTIN' FOR A GYPSY'S KISS, RIGHT?
SHIT, YOU MISSED THE BARNEY OF THE BLOODY DECADE, MATE. WHAT 'APPENED?
I DUNNO, RICH. DIDN'T STAY TO FIND OUT.

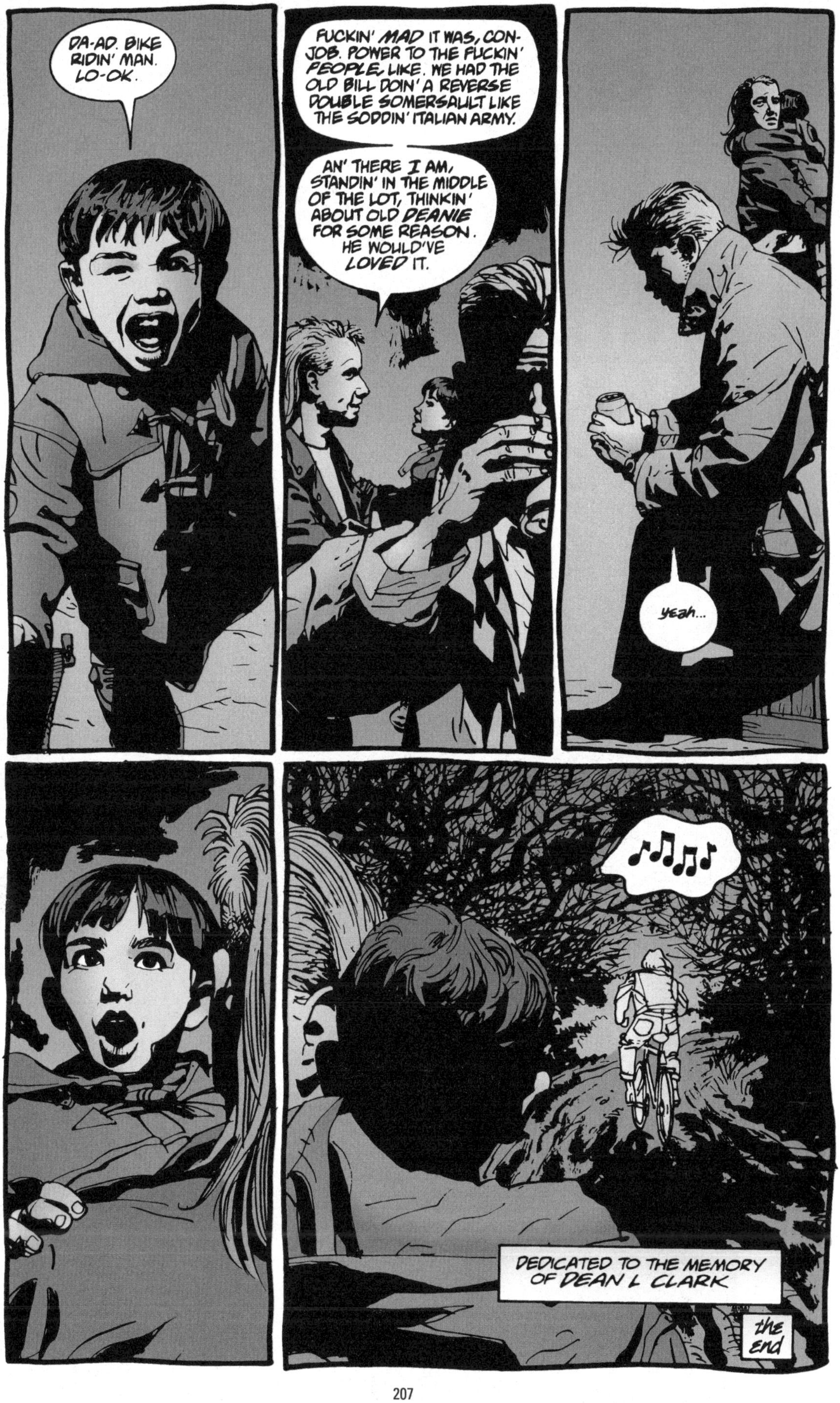
DA-AD. BIKE RIDIN' MAN. LO-OK.
FUCKIN' MAD IT WAS, CON-JOB. POWER TO THE FUCKIN' PEOPLE, LIKE. WE HAD THE OLD BILL DOIN' A REVERSE DOUBLE SOMERSAULT LIKE THE SODDIN' ITALIAN ARMY.
AN' THERE I AM, STANDIN' IN THE MIDDLE OF THE LOT, THINKIN' ABOUT OLD DEANIE FOR SOME REASON. HE WOULD'VE LOVED IT.
yeah...
DEDICATED TO THE MEMORY OF DEAN L CLARK
the end

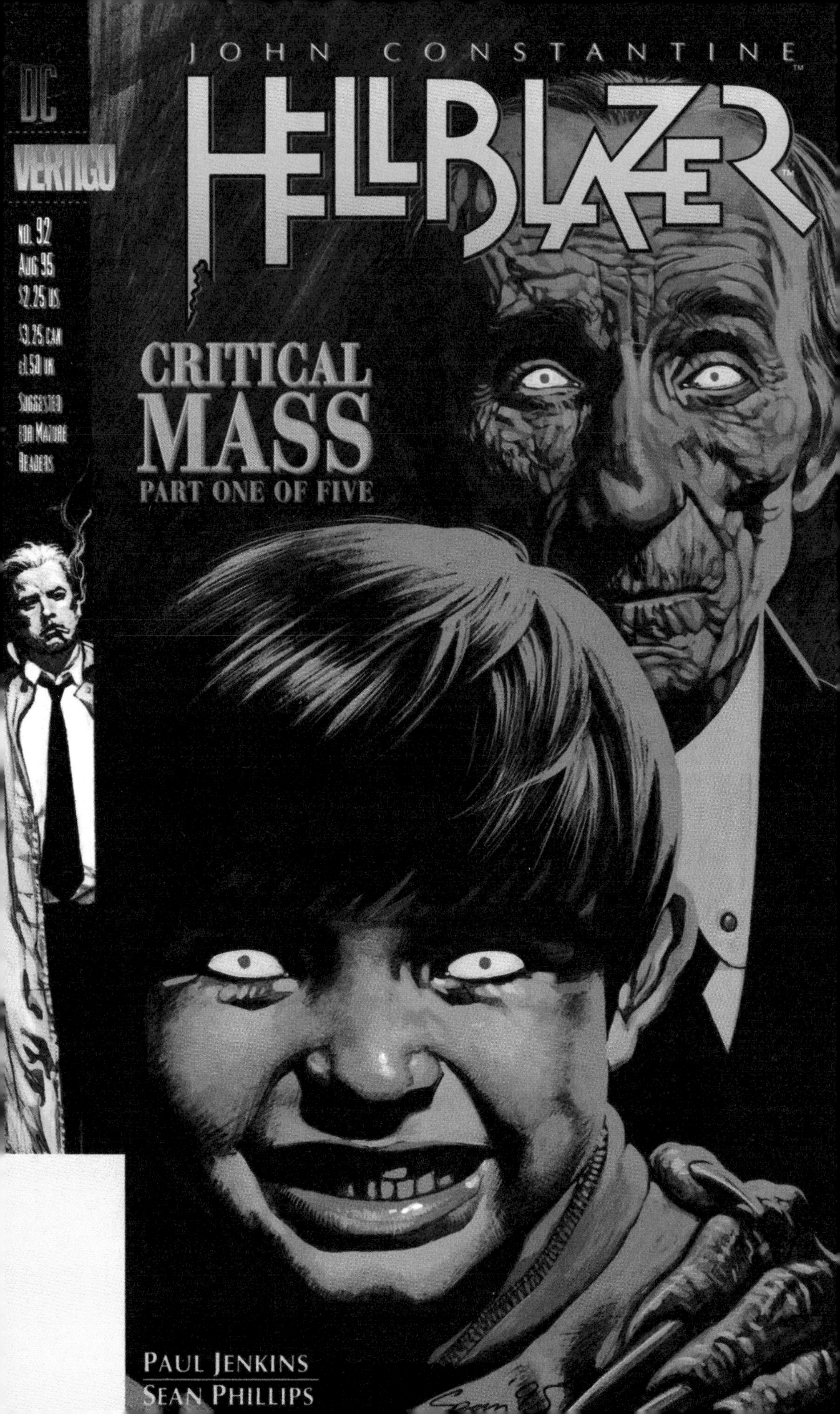
JOHN CONSTANTINE
HELLBLAZER
DC
VERTIGO
NO. 92
AUG 95
$2.25 US
$3.25 CAN
£1.50 UK
SUGGESTED FOR MATURE READERS
CRITICAL MASS
PART ONE OF FIVE
PAUL JENKINS
SEAN PHILLIPS

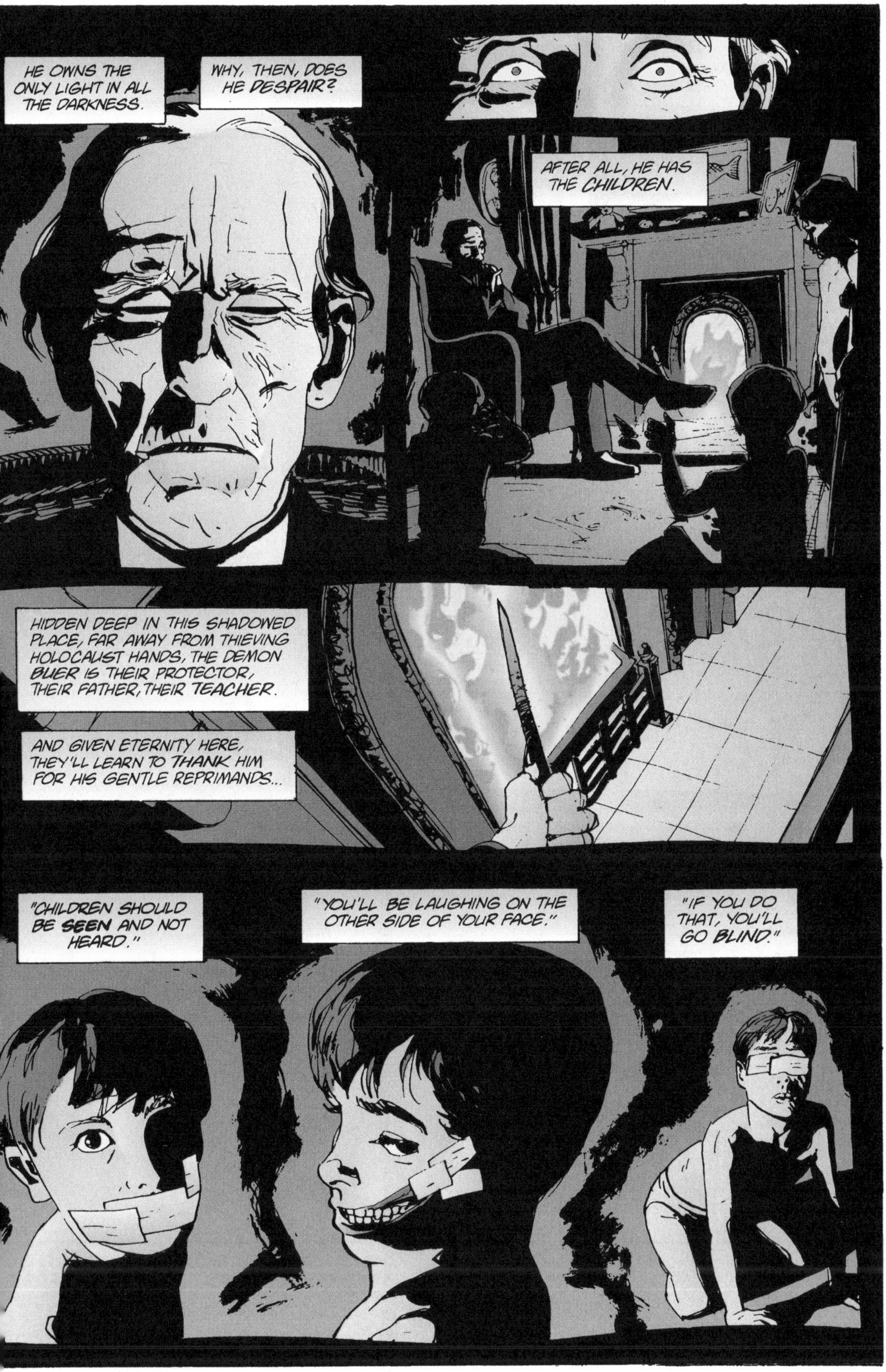

HE OWNS THE ONLY LIGHT IN ALL THE DARKNESS.
WHY, THEN, DOES HE DESPAIR?
AFTER ALL, HE HAS THE CHILDREN.
HIDDEN DEEP IN THIS SHADOWED PLACE, FAR AWAY FROM THIEVING HOLOCAUST HANDS, THE DEMON BUER IS THEIR PROTECTOR, THEIR FATHER, THEIR TEACHER.
AND GIVEN ETERNITY HERE, THEY'LL LEARN TO THANK HIM FOR HIS GENTLE REPRIMANDS...
"CHILDREN SHOULD BE SEEN AND NOT HEARD."
"YOU'LL BE LAUGHING ON THE OTHER SIDE OF YOUR FACE."
"IF YOU DO THAT, YOU'LL GO BLIND."

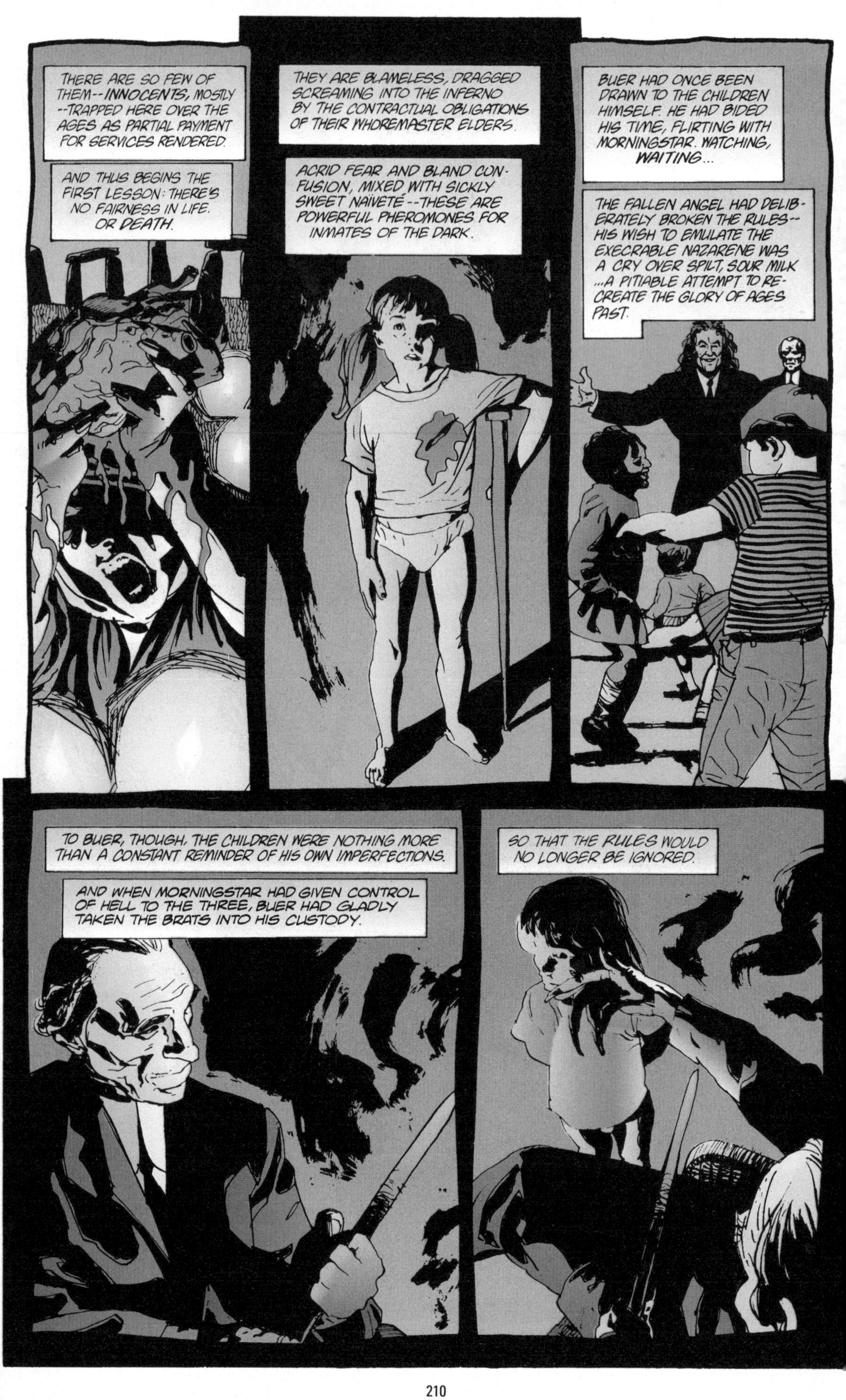
THERE ARE SO FEW OF THEM--INNOCENTS, MOSTLY --TRAPPED HERE OVER THE AGES AS PARTIAL PAYMENT FOR SERVICES RENDERED.
AND THUS BEGINS THE FIRST LESSON: THERE'S NO FAIRNESS IN LIFE. OR DEATH.
THEY ARE BLAMELESS, DRAGGED SCREAMING INTO THE INFERNO BY THE CONTRACTUAL OBLIGATIONS OF THEIR WHOREMASTER ELDERS.
ACRID FEAR AND BLAND CON-FUSION, MIXED WITH SICKLY SWEET NAÏVETÉ--THESE ARE POWERFUL PHEROMONES FOR INMATES OF THE DARK.
BUER HAD ONCE BEEN DRAWN TO THE CHILDREN HIMSELF. HE HAD BIDED HIS TIME, FLIRTING WITH MORNINGSTAR. WATCHING, WAITING...
THE FALLEN ANGEL HAD DELIB-ERATELY BROKEN THE RULES--HIS WISH TO EMULATE THE EXECRABLE NAZARENE WAS A CRY OVER SPILT, SOUR MILK ...A PITIABLE ATTEMPT TO RE-CREATE THE GLORY OF AGES PAST.
TO BUER, THOUGH, THE CHILDREN WERE NOTHING MORE THAN A CONSTANT REMINDER OF HIS OWN IMPERFECTIONS.
AND WHEN MORNINGSTAR HAD GIVEN CONTROL OF HELL TO THE THREE, BUER HAD GLADLY TAKEN THE BRATS INTO HIS CUSTODY.
SO THAT THE RULES WOULD NO LONGER BE IGNORED.

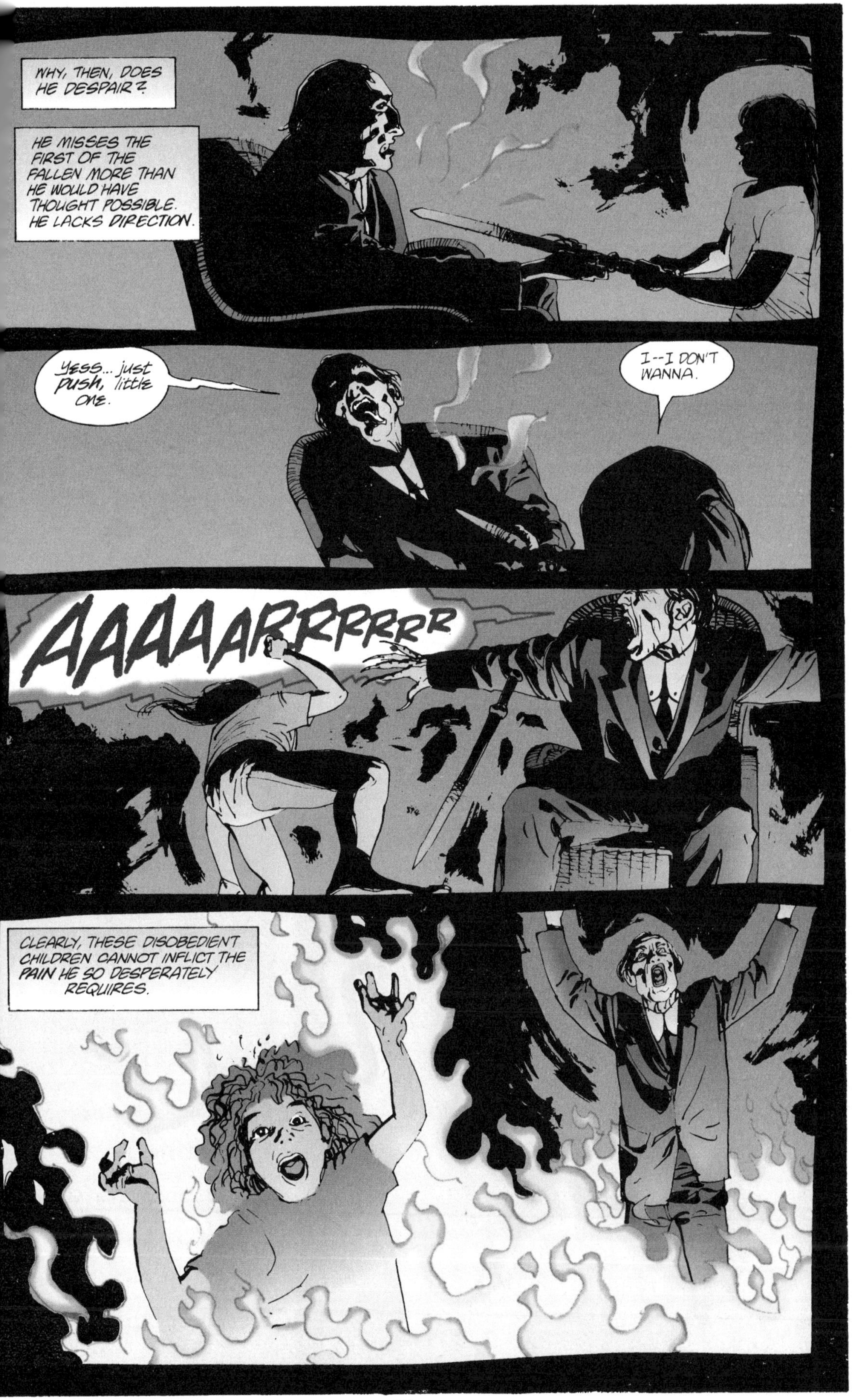
WHY, THEN, DOES HE DESPAIR?
HE MISSES THE FIRST OF THE FALLEN MORE THAN HE WOULD HAVE THOUGHT POSSIBLE. HE LACKS DIRECTION.
YESS... JUST PUSH, LITTLE ONE.
I--I DON'T WANNA.
AAAAARRRRRR
CLEARLY, THESE DISOBEDIENT CHILDREN CANNOT INFLICT THE PAIN HE SO DESPERATELY REQUIRES.

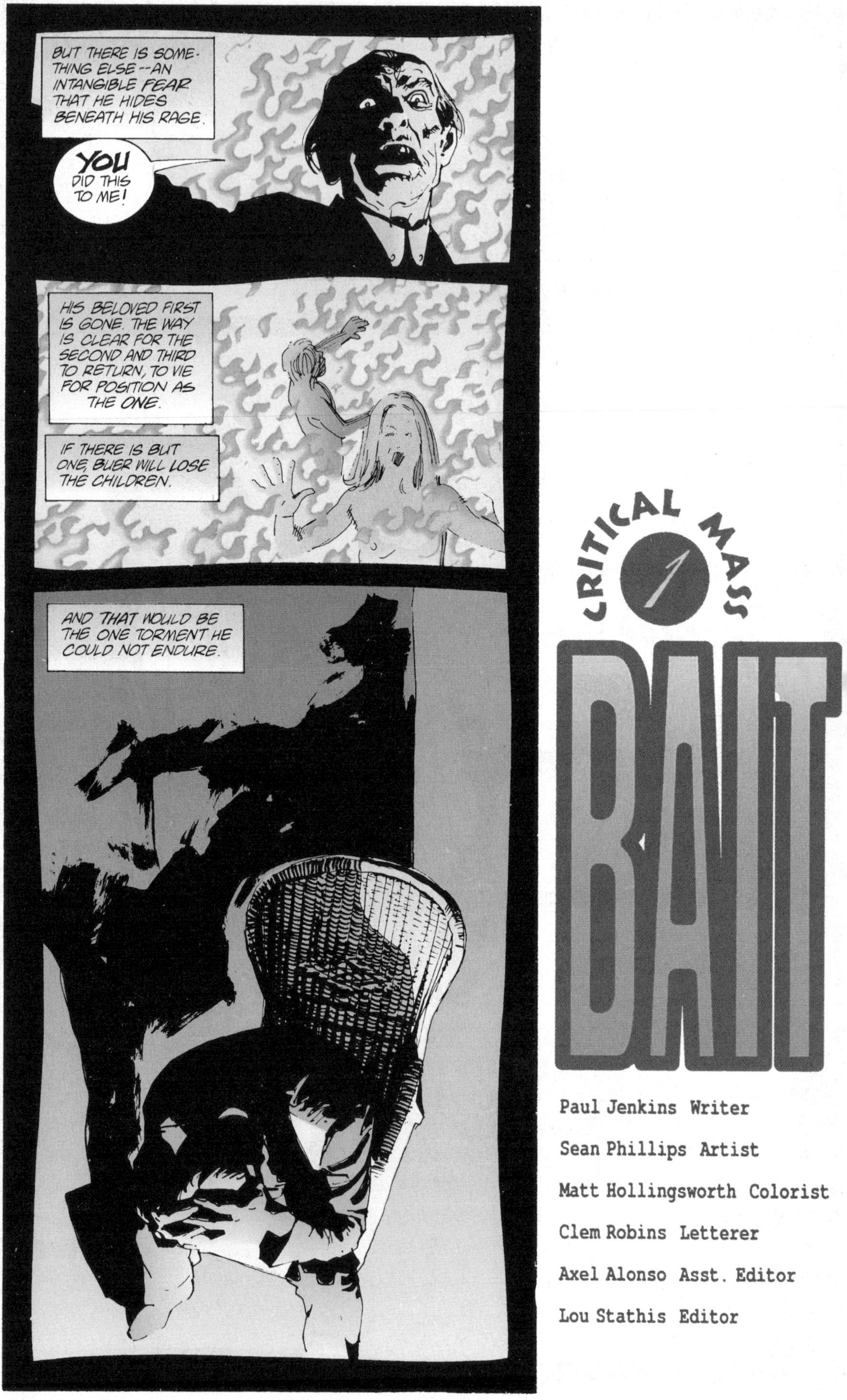

BUT THERE IS SOMETHING ELSE--AN INTANGIBLE FEAR THAT HE HIDES BENEATH HIS RAGE.
YOU DID THIS TO ME!
HIS BELOVED FIRST IS GONE. THE WAY IS CLEAR FOR THE SECOND AND THIRD TO RETURN, TO VIE FOR POSITION AS THE ONE.
IF THERE IS BUT ONE, BUER WILL LOSE THE CHILDREN.
AND THAT WOULD BE THE ONE TORMENT HE COULD NOT ENDURE.

CRITICAL MASS 1

BAIT

Paul Jenkins Writer

Sean Phillips Artist

Matt Hollingsworth Colorist

Clem Robins Letterer

Axel Alonso Asst. Editor

Lou Stathis Editor

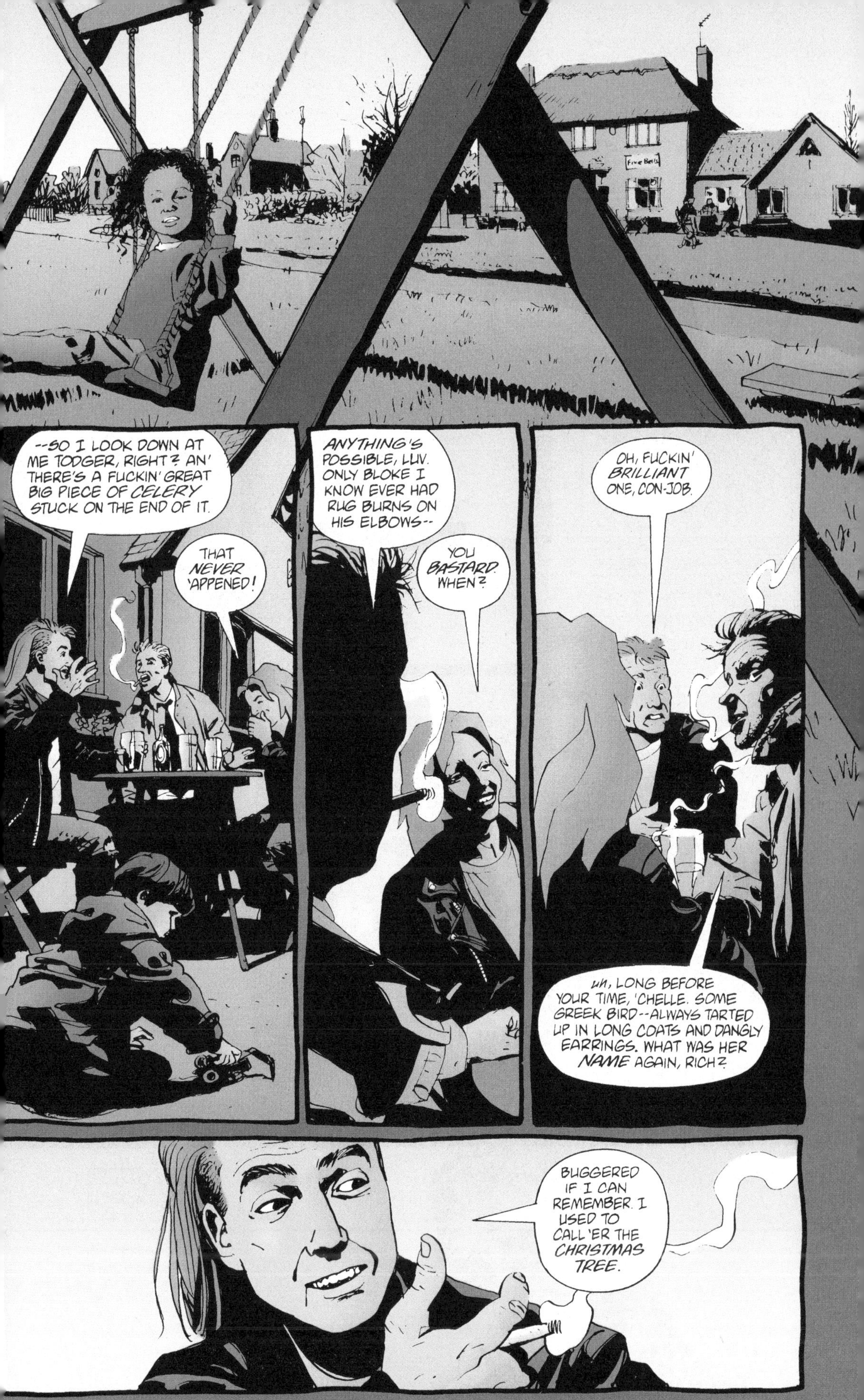
--SO I LOOK DOWN AT ME TODGER, RIGHT? AN' THERE'S A FUCKIN' GREAT BIG PIECE OF CELERY STUCK ON THE END OF IT.
THAT NEVER 'APPENED!
ANYTHING'S POSSIBLE, LUV. ONLY BLOKE I KNOW EVER HAD RUG BURNS ON HIS ELBOWS--
YOU BASTARD. WHEN?
OH, FUCKIN' BRILLIANT ONE, CON-JOB.
uh, LONG BEFORE YOUR TIME, 'CHELLE. SOME GREEK BIRD--ALWAYS TARTED UP IN LONG COATS AND DANGLY EARRINGS. WHAT WAS HER NAME AGAIN, RICH?
BUGGERED IF I CAN REMEMBER. I USED TO CALL 'ER THE CHRISTMAS TREE.

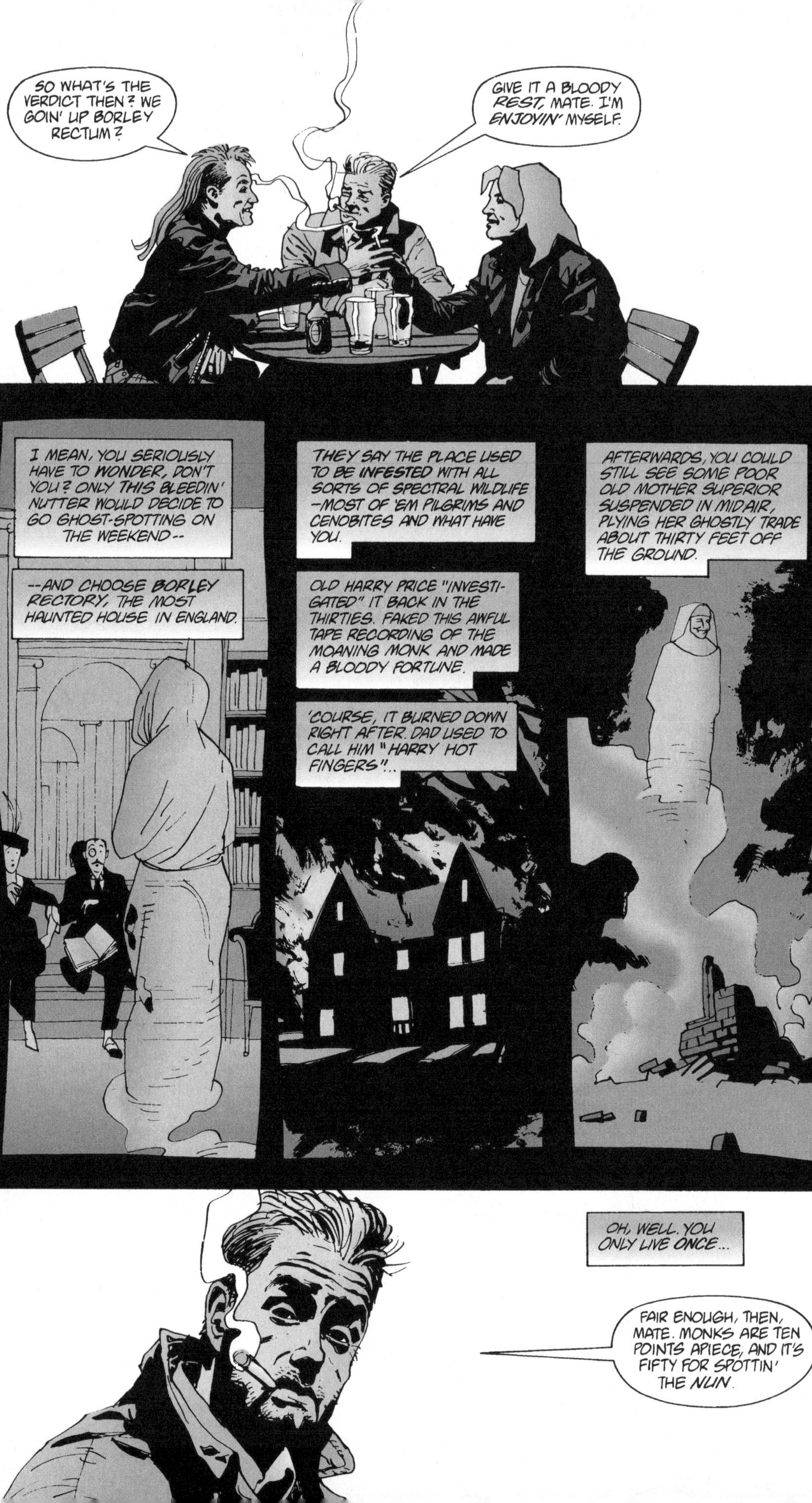

SO WHAT'S THE VERDICT THEN? WE GOIN' UP BORLEY RECTUM?
GIVE IT A BLOODY REST, MATE. I'M ENJOYIN' MYSELF.
I MEAN, YOU SERIOUSLY HAVE TO WONDER, DON'T YOU? ONLY THIS BLEEDIN' NUTTER WOULD DECIDE TO GO GHOST-SPOTTING ON THE WEEKEND--
--AND CHOOSE BORLEY RECTORY, THE MOST HAUNTED HOUSE IN ENGLAND.
THEY SAY THE PLACE USED TO BE INFESTED WITH ALL SORTS OF SPECTRAL WILDLIFE --MOST OF 'EM PILGRIMS AND CENOBITES AND WHAT HAVE YOU.
OLD HARRY PRICE "INVESTIGATED" IT BACK IN THE THIRTIES. FAKED THIS AWFUL TAPE RECORDING OF THE MOANING MONK AND MADE A BLOODY FORTUNE.
'COURSE, IT BURNED DOWN RIGHT AFTER. DAD USED TO CALL HIM "HARRY HOT FINGERS"...
AFTERWARDS, YOU COULD STILL SEE SOME POOR OLD MOTHER SUPERIOR SUSPENDED IN MIDAIR, PLYING HER GHOSTLY TRADE ABOUT THIRTY FEET OFF THE GROUND.
OH, WELL. YOU ONLY LIVE ONCE...
FAIR ENOUGH, THEN, MATE. MONKS ARE TEN POINTS APIECE, AND IT'S FIFTY FOR SPOTTIN' THE NUN.

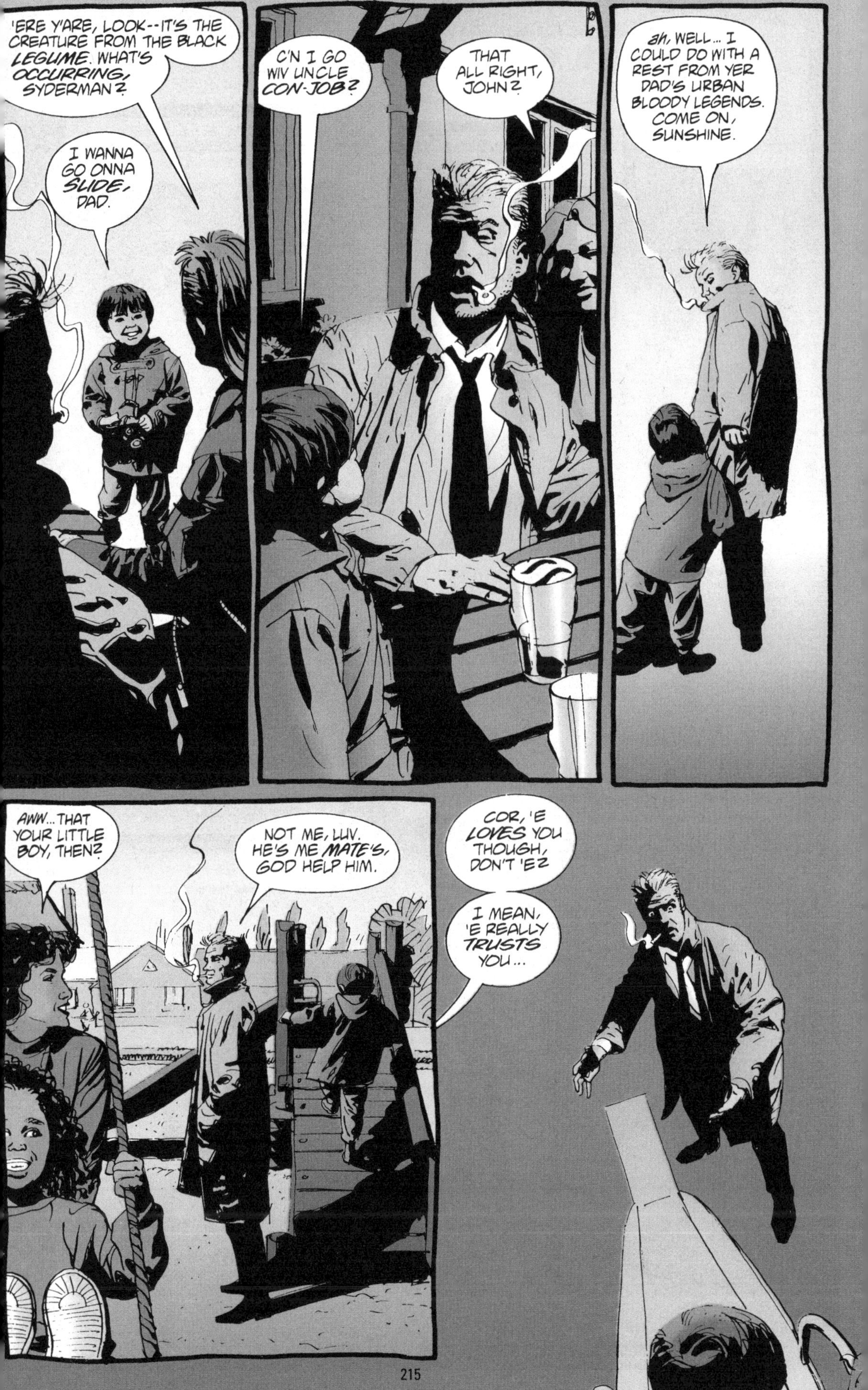
'ERE Y'ARE, LOOK--IT'S THE CREATURE FROM THE BLACK LEGUME. WHAT'S OCCURRING, SYDERMAN?
I WANNA GO ONNA SLIDE, DAD.
C'N I GO WIV UNCLE CON-JOB?
THAT ALL RIGHT, JOHN?
AH, WELL... I COULD DO WITH A REST FROM YER DAD'S URBAN BLOODY LEGENDS. COME ON, SUNSHINE.
AWW...THAT YOUR LITTLE BOY, THEN?
NOT ME, LUV. HE'S ME MATE'S, GOD HELP HIM.
COR, 'E LOVES YOU THOUGH, DON'T 'E?
I MEAN, 'E REALLY TRUSTS YOU...

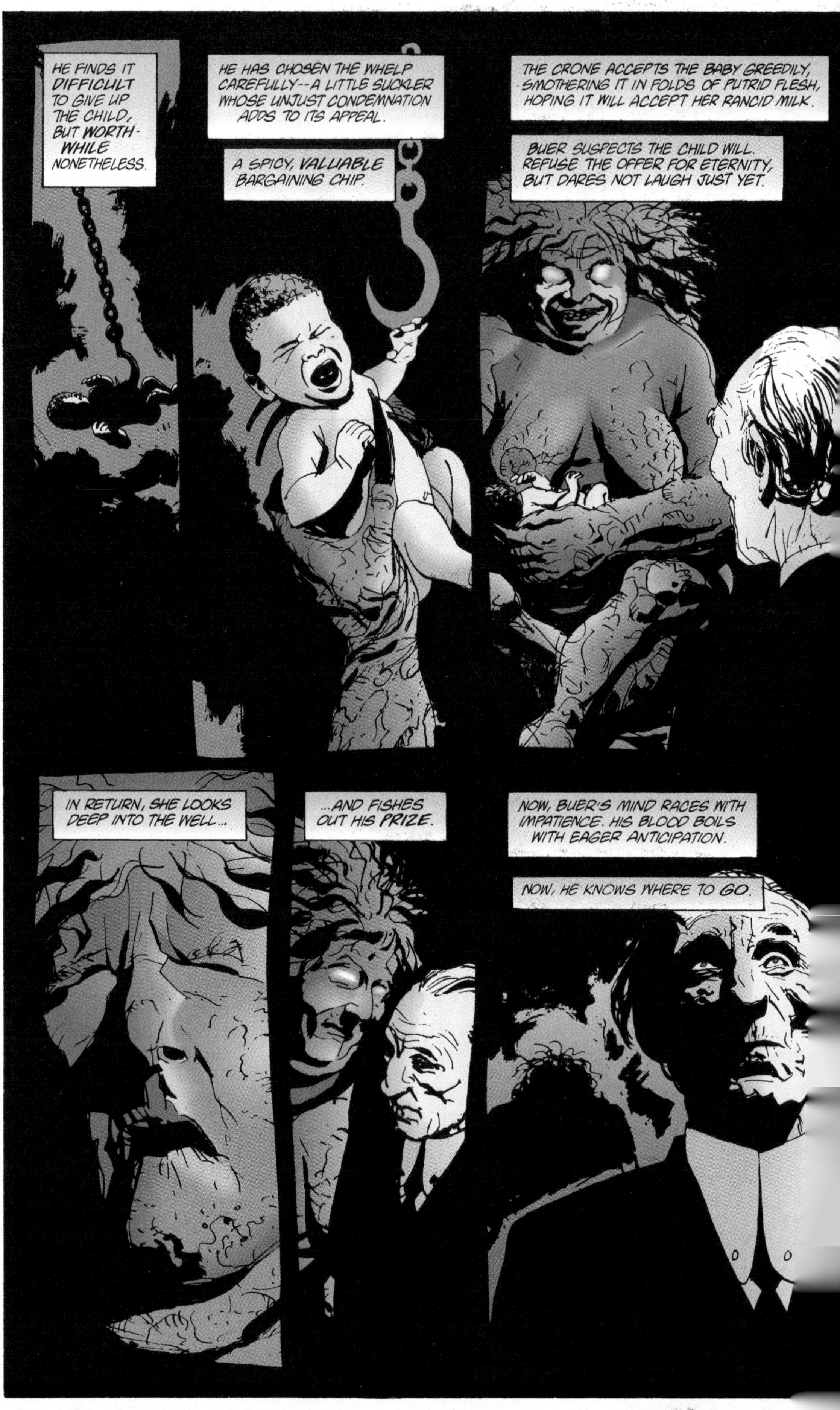
HE FINDS IT DIFFICULT TO GIVE UP THE CHILD, BUT WORTH-WHILE NONETHELESS.
HE HAS CHOSEN THE WHELP CAREFULLY--A LITTLE SUCKLER WHOSE UNJUST CONDEMNATION ADDS TO ITS APPEAL.
A SPICY, VALUABLE BARGAINING CHIP.
THE CRONE ACCEPTS THE BABY GREEDILY, SMOTHERING IT IN FOLDS OF PUTRID FLESH, HOPING IT WILL ACCEPT HER RANCID MILK.
BUER SUSPECTS THE CHILD WILL REFUSE THE OFFER FOR ETERNITY, BUT DARES NOT LAUGH JUST YET.
IN RETURN, SHE LOOKS DEEP INTO THE WELL...
...AND FISHES OUT HIS PRIZE.
NOW, BUER'S MIND RACES WITH IMPATIENCE. HIS BLOOD BOILS WITH EAGER ANTICIPATION.
NOW, HE KNOWS WHERE TO GO.

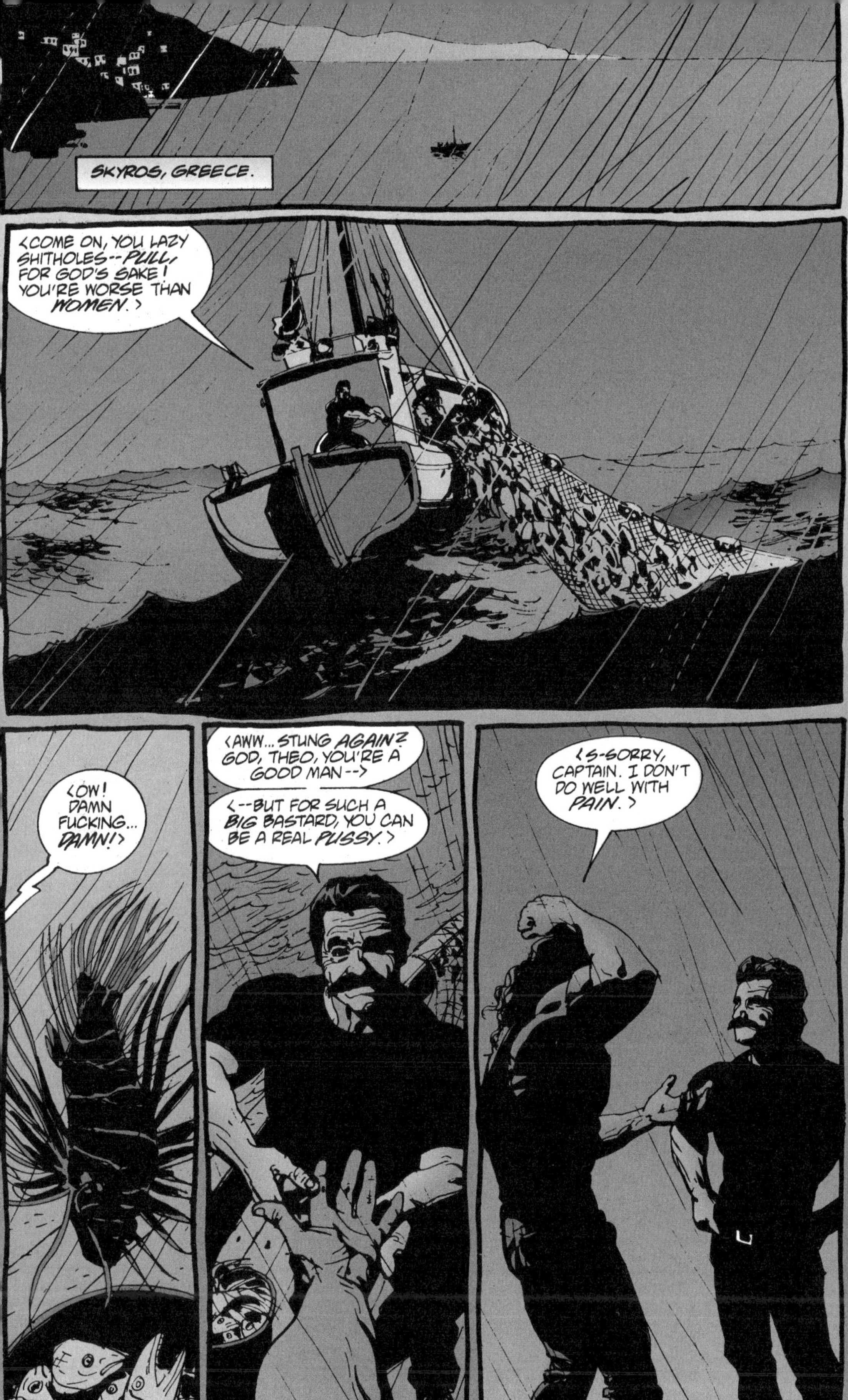
SKYROS, GREECE.
<COME ON, YOU LAZY SHITHOLES--PULL, FOR GOD'S SAKE! YOU'RE WORSE THAN WOMEN.>
<OW! DAMN FUCKING... DAMN!>
<AWW... STUNG AGAIN? GOD, THEO, YOU'RE A GOOD MAN-->
<--BUT FOR SUCH A BIG BASTARD, YOU CAN BE A REAL PUSSY.>
<S-SORRY, CAPTAIN. I DON'T DO WELL WITH PAIN.>

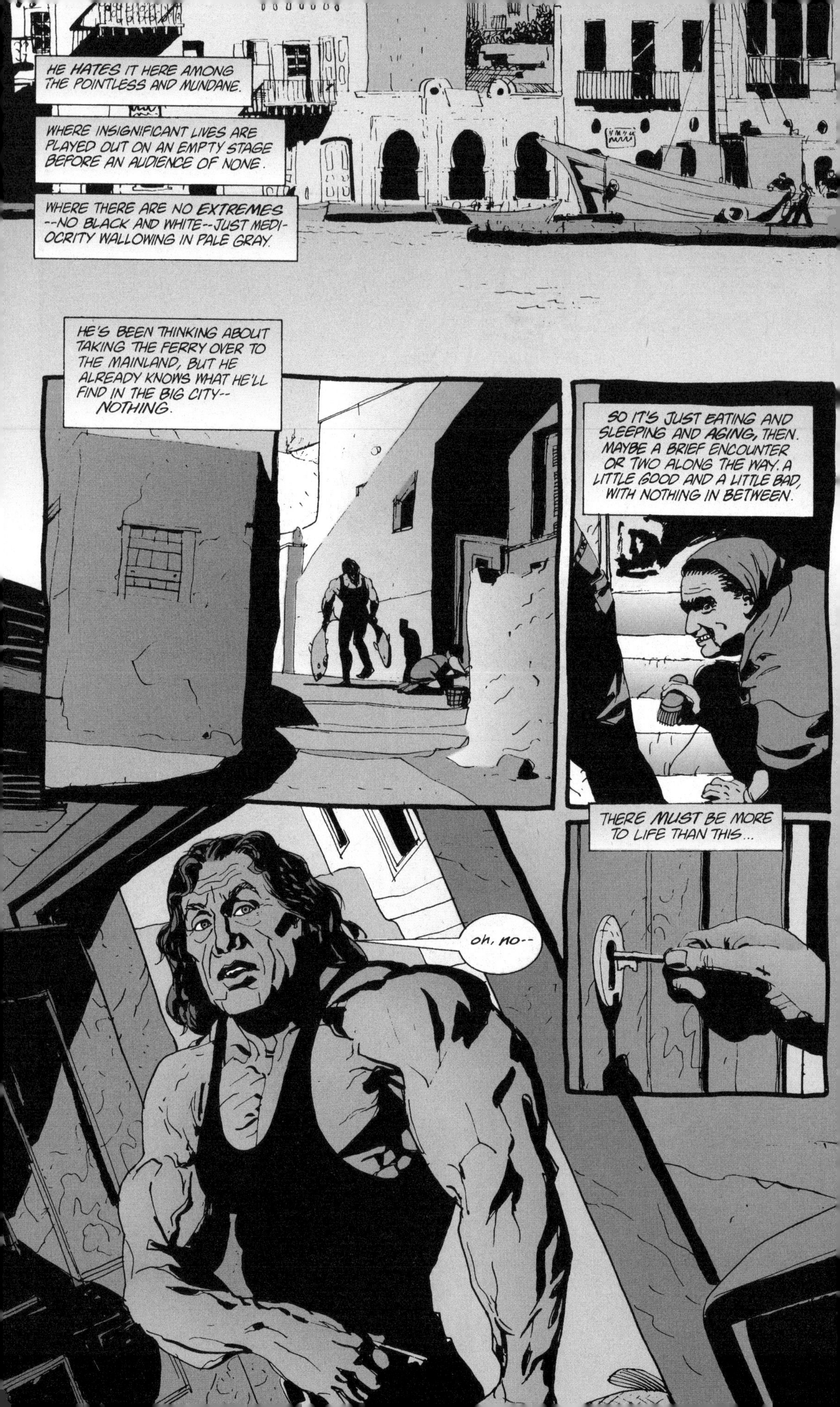
HE HATES IT HERE AMONG THE POINTLESS AND MUNDANE.
WHERE INSIGNIFICANT LIVES ARE PLAYED OUT ON AN EMPTY STAGE BEFORE AN AUDIENCE OF NONE.
WHERE THERE ARE NO EXTREMES --NO BLACK AND WHITE--JUST MEDIOCRITY WALLOWING IN PALE GRAY.
HE'S BEEN THINKING ABOUT TAKING THE FERRY OVER TO THE MAINLAND, BUT HE ALREADY KNOWS WHAT HE'LL FIND IN THE BIG CITY-- NOTHING.
SO IT'S JUST EATING AND SLEEPING AND AGING, THEN. MAYBE A BRIEF ENCOUNTER OR TWO ALONG THE WAY. A LITTLE GOOD AND A LITTLE BAD, WITH NOTHING IN BETWEEN.
THERE MUST BE MORE TO LIFE THAN THIS...
oh, no--

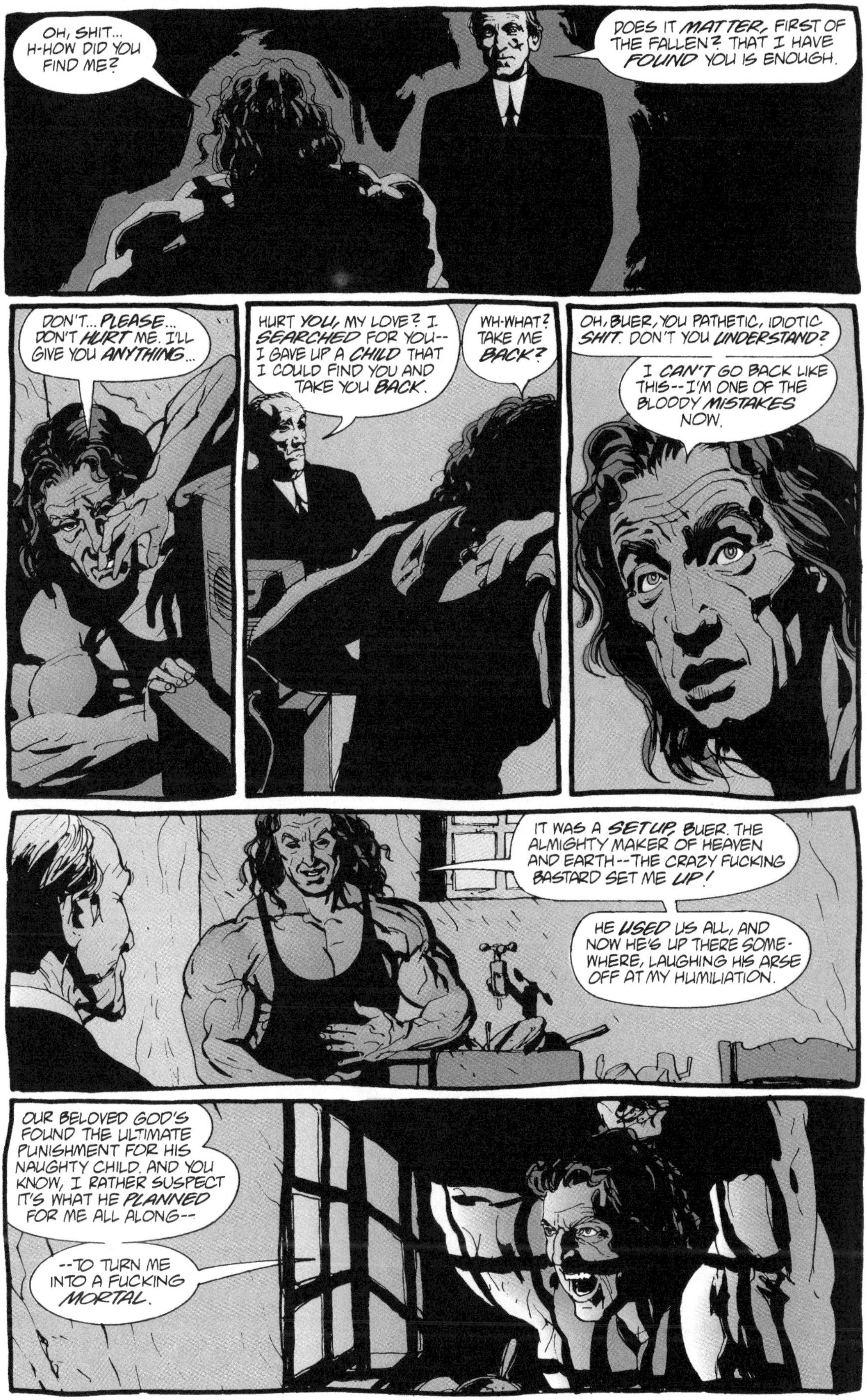
OH, SHIT... H-HOW DID YOU FIND ME?
DOES IT MATTER, FIRST OF THE FALLEN? THAT I HAVE FOUND YOU IS ENOUGH.
DON'T... PLEASE... DON'T HURT ME. I'LL GIVE YOU ANYTHING...
HURT YOU, MY LOVE? I. SEARCHED FOR YOU-- I GAVE UP A CHILD THAT I COULD FIND YOU AND TAKE YOU BACK.
WH-WHAT? TAKE ME BACK?
OH, BUER, YOU PATHETIC, IDIOTIC SHIT. DON'T YOU UNDERSTAND?
I CAN'T GO BACK LIKE THIS--I'M ONE OF THE BLOODY MISTAKES NOW.
IT WAS A SETUP, BUER. THE ALMIGHTY MAKER OF HEAVEN AND EARTH--THE CRAZY FUCKING BASTARD SET ME UP!
HE USED US ALL, AND NOW HE'S UP THERE SOME-WHERE, LAUGHING HIS ARSE OFF AT MY HUMILIATION.
OUR BELOVED GOD'S FOUND THE ULTIMATE PUNISHMENT FOR HIS NAUGHTY CHILD. AND YOU KNOW, I RATHER SUSPECT IT'S WHAT HE PLANNED FOR ME ALL ALONG--
--TO TURN ME INTO A FUCKING MORTAL.

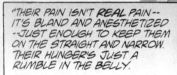

"YOU CAN'T BEGIN TO UNDERSTAND WHAT IT'S LIKE BEING AMONGST MORTALS, LITTLE DEMON. BUT I DO, AND NOW I HATE THEM EVEN *MORE*.

"THEIR PAIN ISN'T *REAL* PAIN-- IT'S BLAND AND ANESTHETIZED --JUST ENOUGH TO KEEP THEM ON THE STRAIGHT AND NARROW. THEIR HUNGER'S JUST A RUMBLE IN THE BELLY.

"*THAT'S* WHAT HE'S MADE THEM BY DESIGN--SAFE, SERVILE, AND *HARMLESS*..."

BUT YOU *CAN* RETURN, LORD. AS YOU KNOW, THERE ARE CERTAIN *RULES*--

AH, YES. *HIS* RULES.

THE "RULES" DON'T APPLY TO *HIM*, BUT THAT'S TO BE EXPECTED. AND, OF COURSE, HE'S OMNIPRESENT. OH YES... AND *OMNISCIENT*.

CALL IT PARANOIA IF YOU WILL--BUT YOU HAVE TO WONDER, DID HE MAKE *THIS* ONE UP ENTIRELY FOR ME?

AS I RECALL, I'M SUPPOSED TO WIN THE SOUL OF THE ONE-MOST-HATED, OR SOME SUCH NONSENSE. I HAD ALWAYS THOUGHT IT WOULD BE HIS BASTARD CHILD...

...BUT I WAS *WRONG*--IT'S BLOODY *CONSTANTINE*.

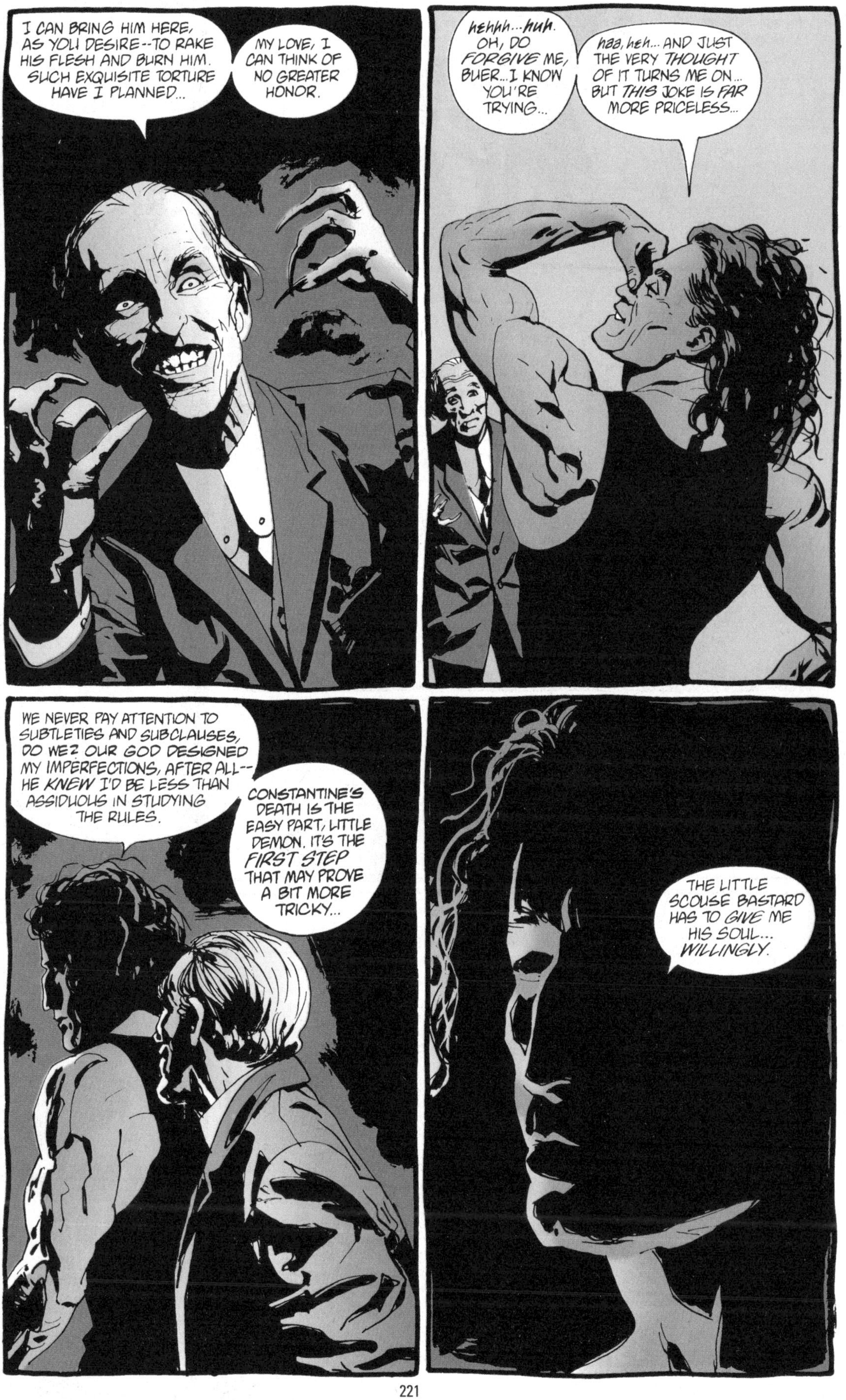
I CAN BRING HIM HERE, AS YOU DESIRE--TO RAKE HIS FLESH AND BURN HIM. SUCH EXQUISITE TORTURE HAVE I PLANNED...
MY LOVE, I CAN THINK OF NO GREATER HONOR.
hehhh...huh. OH, DO FORGIVE ME, BUER...I KNOW YOU'RE TRYING...
haa, heh... AND JUST THE VERY THOUGHT OF IT TURNS ME ON... BUT THIS JOKE IS FAR MORE PRICELESS...
WE NEVER PAY ATTENTION TO SUBTLETIES AND SUBCLAUSES, DO WE? OUR GOD DESIGNED MY IMPERFECTIONS, AFTER ALL-- HE KNEW I'D BE LESS THAN ASSIDUOUS IN STUDYING THE RULES.
CONSTANTINE'S DEATH IS THE EASY PART, LITTLE DEMON. IT'S THE FIRST STEP THAT MAY PROVE A BIT MORE TRICKY...
THE LITTLE SCOUSE BASTARD HAS TO GIVE ME HIS SOUL... WILLINGLY.

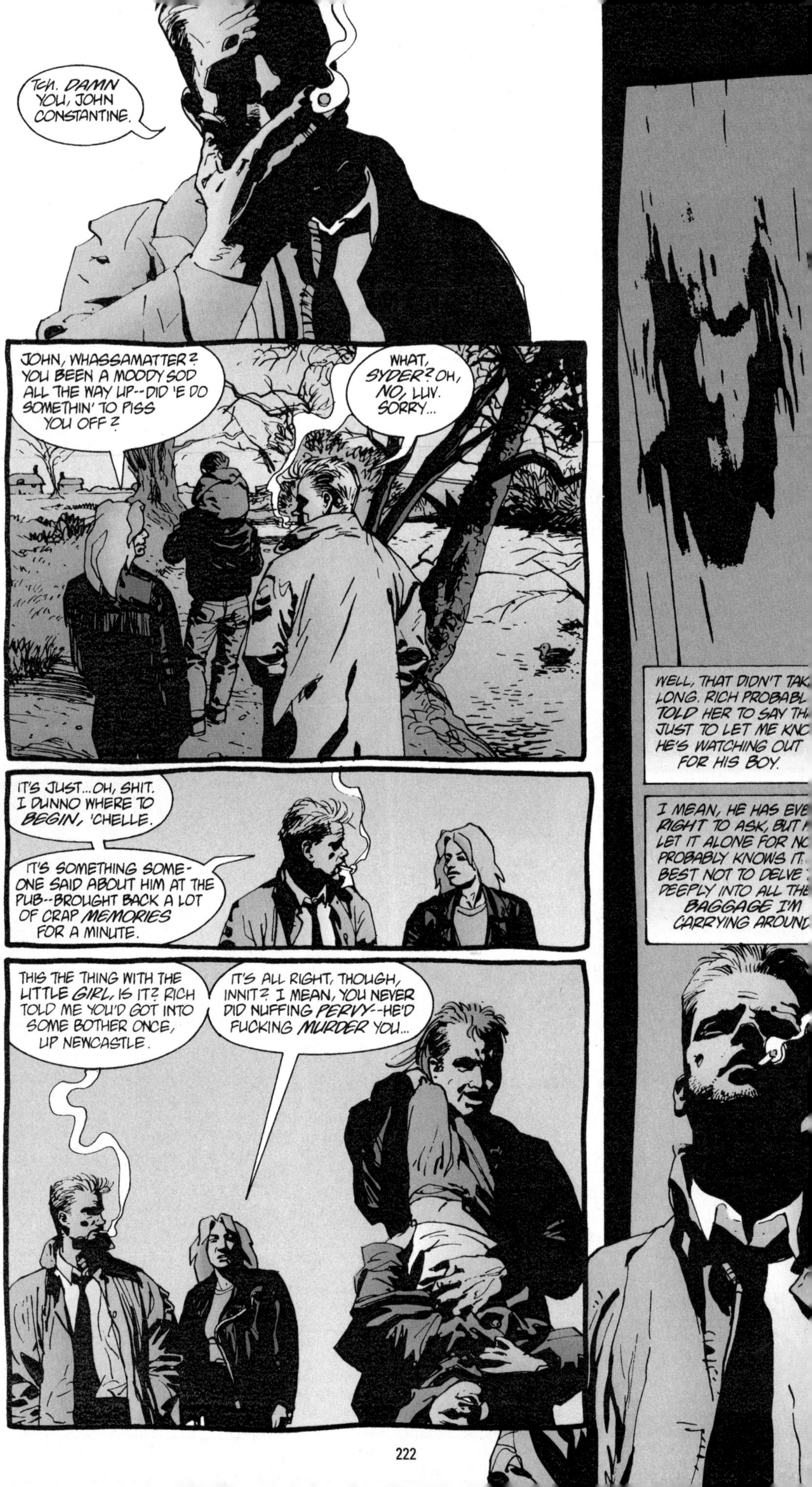
TCH. DAMN YOU, JOHN CONSTANTINE.
JOHN, WHASSAMATTER? YOU BEEN A MOODY SOD ALL THE WAY UP--DID 'E DO SOMETHIN' TO PISS YOU OFF?
WHAT, SYDER? OH, NO, LUV. SORRY...
WELL, THAT DIDN'T TAK LONG. RICH PROBABL TOLD HER TO SAY TH JUST TO LET ME KN HE'S WATCHING OUT FOR HIS BOY.
IT'S JUST...OH, SHIT. I DUNNO WHERE TO BEGIN, 'CHELLE.
IT'S SOMETHING SOME-ONE SAID ABOUT HIM AT THE PUB--BROUGHT BACK A LOT OF CRAP MEMORIES FOR A MINUTE.
I MEAN, HE HAS EVE RIGHT TO ASK, BUT LET IT ALONE FOR N PROBABLY KNOWS IT BEST NOT TO DELVE DEEPLY INTO ALL TH BAGGAGE I'M CARRYING AROUN
THIS THE THING WITH THE LITTLE GIRL, IS IT? RICH TOLD ME YOU'D GOT INTO SOME BOTHER ONCE, UP NEWCASTLE.
IT'S ALL RIGHT, THOUGH, INNIT? I MEAN, YOU NEVER DID NUFFING PERVY--HE'D FUCKING MURDER YOU...

"NEVER DID ANYTHING," EH? WELL, NOT THAT I COULD BE CONVICTED OF--BUT I WAS GUILTY ALL THE SAME.

GUILTY OF BEING JACK THE BLOODY LAD. GUILTY OF THINKING I COULD HANDLE IT ALL ON MY OWN.

AND WHEN PUSH CAME TO SHOVE-- WHEN THE NIGHTMARE JOSTLED ITS WAY INTO THE REAL WORLD-- I STEPPED UP TO KNOCK IT FOR SIX WITHOUT A SECOND THOUGHT.

I WANTED TO STARE DOWN THE DEMON IN HIS OWN BACKYARD --TO MAKE HIS EYES WATER AND DANCE OFF LIKE A JESTER INTO THE SUN. JUST TO PROVE I COULD.

THE CHILD, SHE WAS SIMPLY A PAWN IN THE GAME. SO I TOLD HER TO TRUST ME AS I TOOK HER HAND...

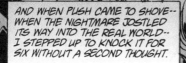

...AND LEFT THE REST OF HER IN HELL.

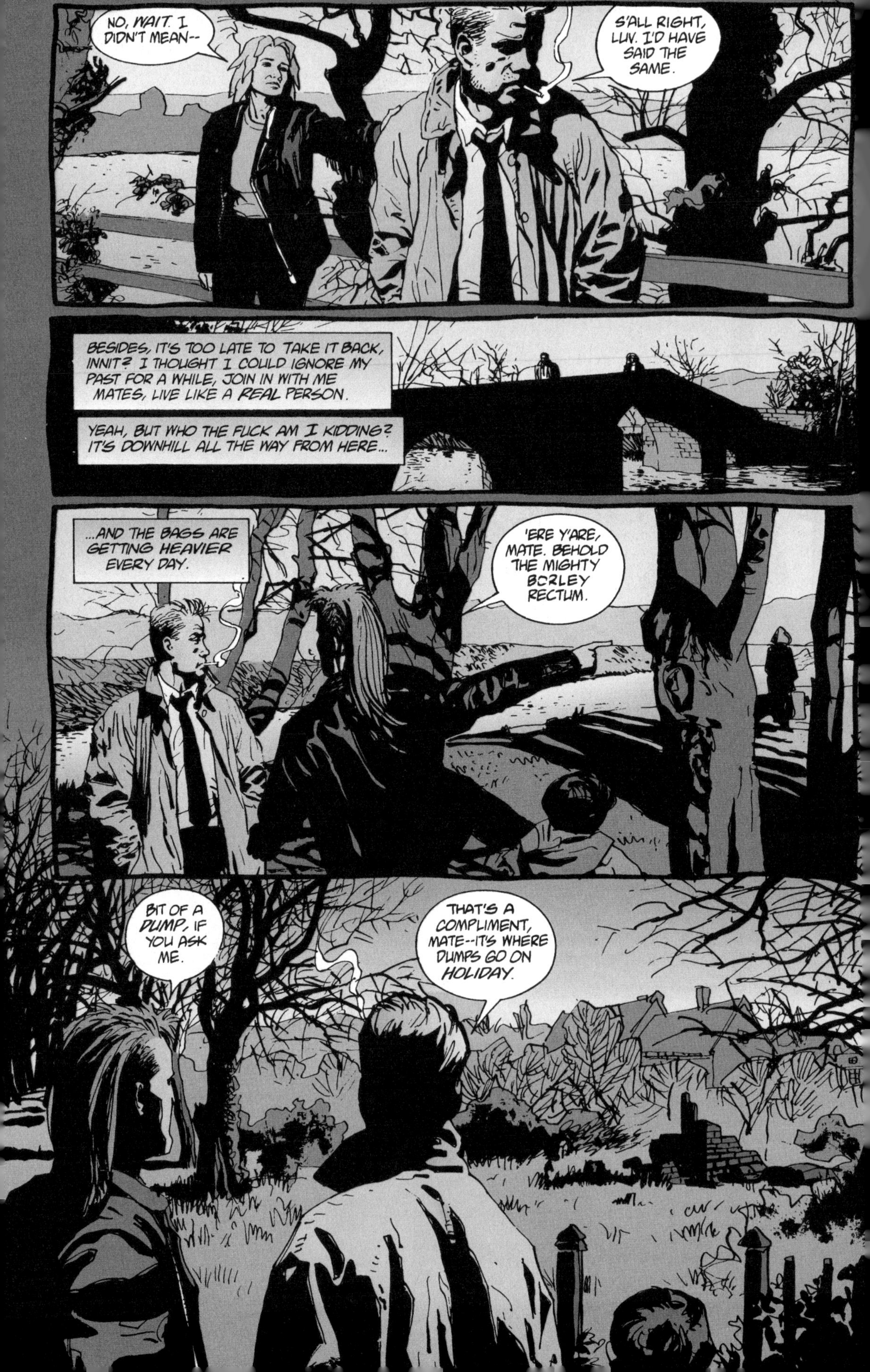
NO, WAIT. I DIDN'T MEAN--
S'ALL RIGHT, LUV. I'D HAVE SAID THE SAME.
BESIDES, IT'S TOO LATE TO TAKE IT BACK, INNIT? I THOUGHT I COULD IGNORE MY PAST FOR A WHILE, JOIN IN WITH ME MATES, LIVE LIKE A REAL PERSON.
YEAH, BUT WHO THE FUCK AM I KIDDING? IT'S DOWNHILL ALL THE WAY FROM HERE...
...AND THE BAGS ARE GETTING HEAVIER EVERY DAY.
'ERE Y'ARE, MATE. BEHOLD THE MIGHTY BORLEY RECTUM.
BIT OF A DUMP, IF YOU ASK ME.
THAT'S A COMPLIMENT, MATE--IT'S WHERE DUMPS GO ON HOLIDAY.

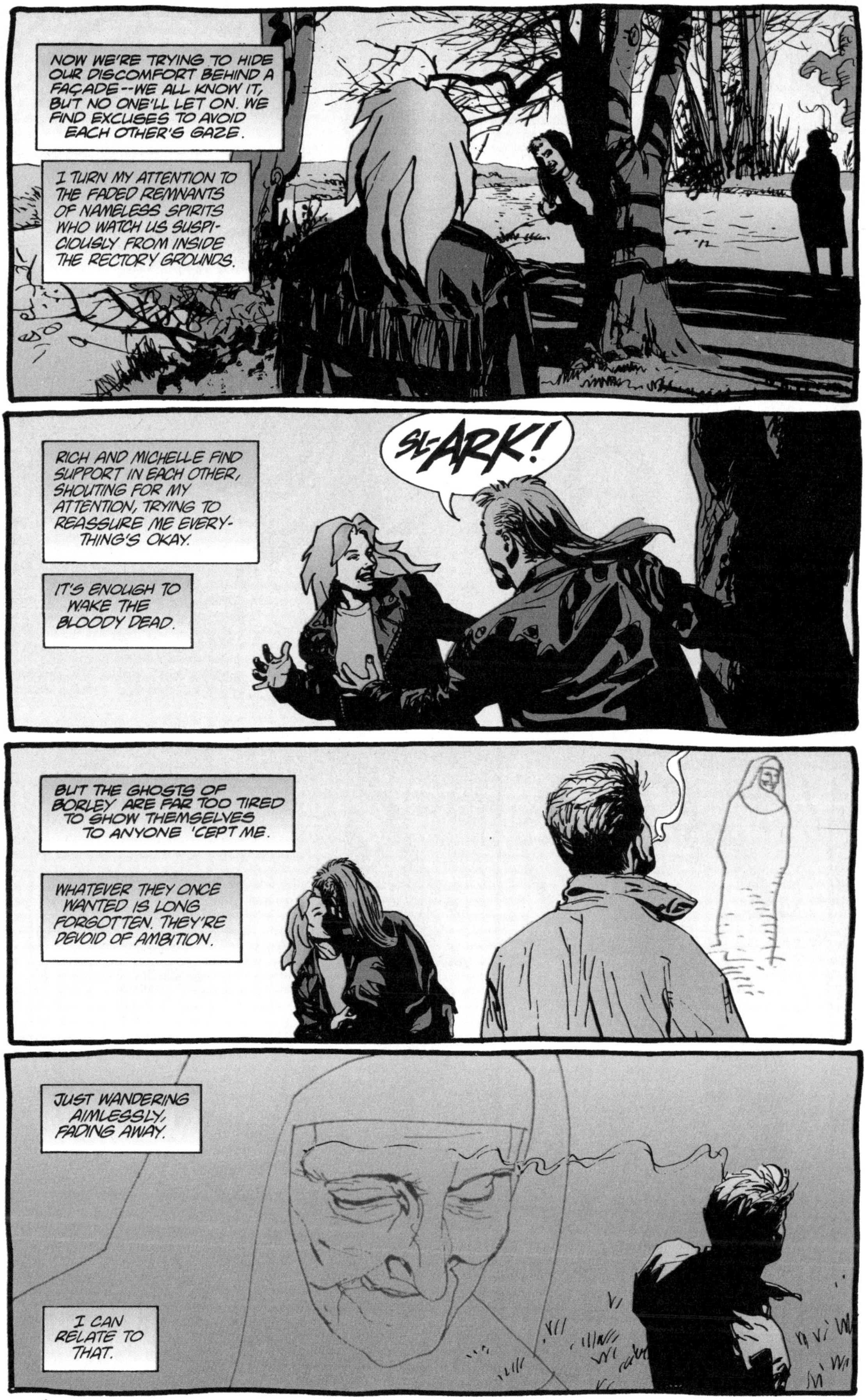
NOW WE'RE TRYING TO HIDE OUR DISCOMFORT BEHIND A FAÇADE--WE ALL KNOW IT, BUT NO ONE'LL LET ON. WE FIND EXCUSES TO AVOID EACH OTHER'S GAZE.
I TURN MY ATTENTION TO THE FADED REMNANTS OF NAMELESS SPIRITS WHO WATCH US SUSPICIOUSLY FROM INSIDE THE RECTORY GROUNDS.
RICH AND MICHELLE FIND SUPPORT IN EACH OTHER, SHOUTING FOR MY ATTENTION, TRYING TO REASSURE ME EVERYTHING'S OKAY.
SL-ARK!
IT'S ENOUGH TO WAKE THE BLOODY DEAD.
BUT THE GHOSTS OF BORLEY ARE FAR TOO TIRED TO SHOW THEMSELVES TO ANYONE 'CEPT ME.
WHATEVER THEY ONCE WANTED IS LONG FORGOTTEN. THEY'RE DEVOID OF AMBITION.
JUST WANDERING AIMLESSLY, FADING AWAY.
I CAN RELATE TO THAT.

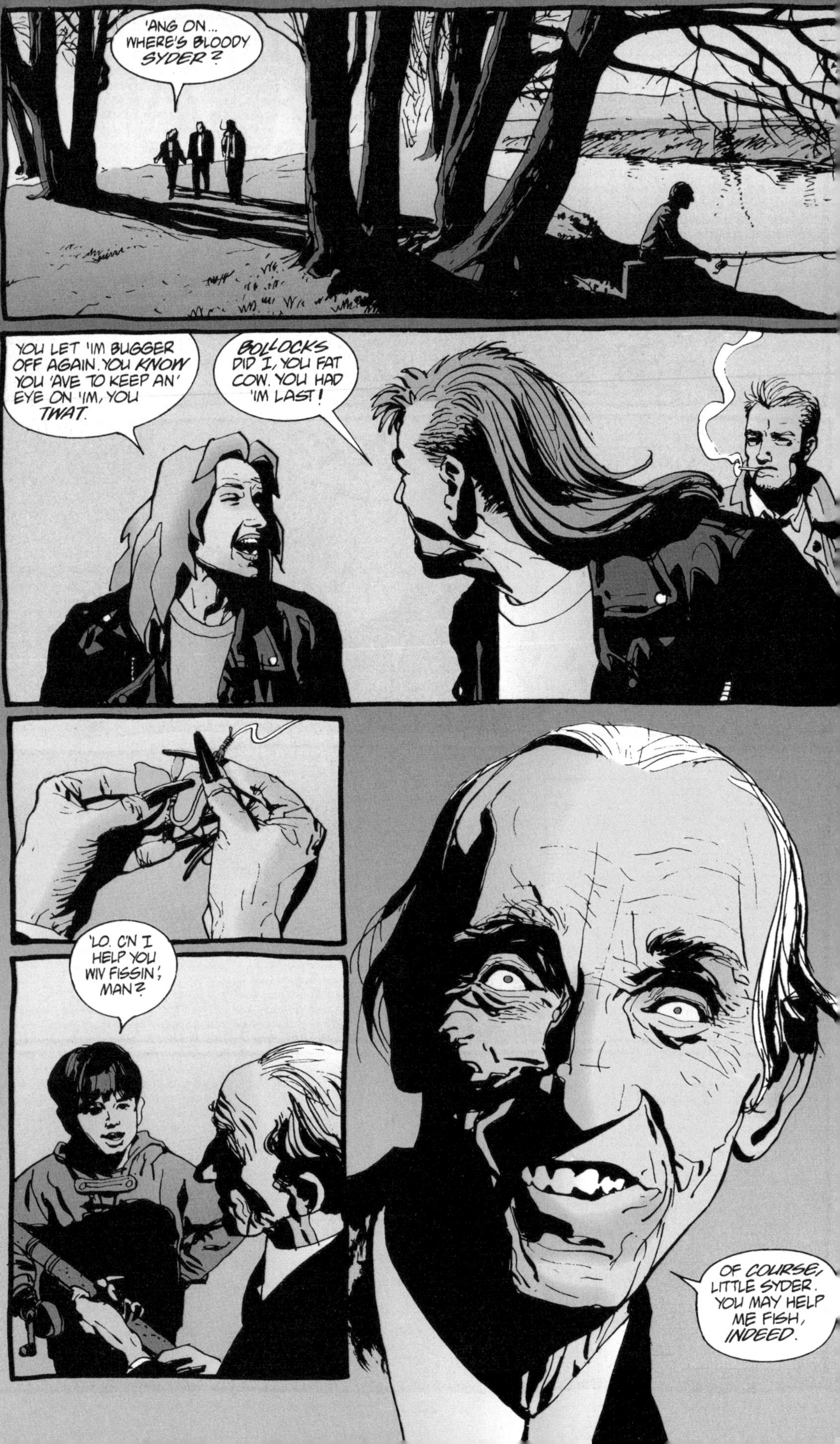
'ANG ON... WHERE'S BLOODY SYDER?
YOU LET 'IM BUGGER OFF AGAIN. YOU KNOW YOU 'AVE TO KEEP AN' EYE ON 'IM, YOU TWAT.
BOLLOCKS DID I, YOU FAT COW. YOU HAD 'IM LAST!
'LO. C'N I HELP YOU WIV FISSIN', MAN?
OF COURSE, LITTLE SYDER. YOU MAY HELP ME FISH, INDEED.

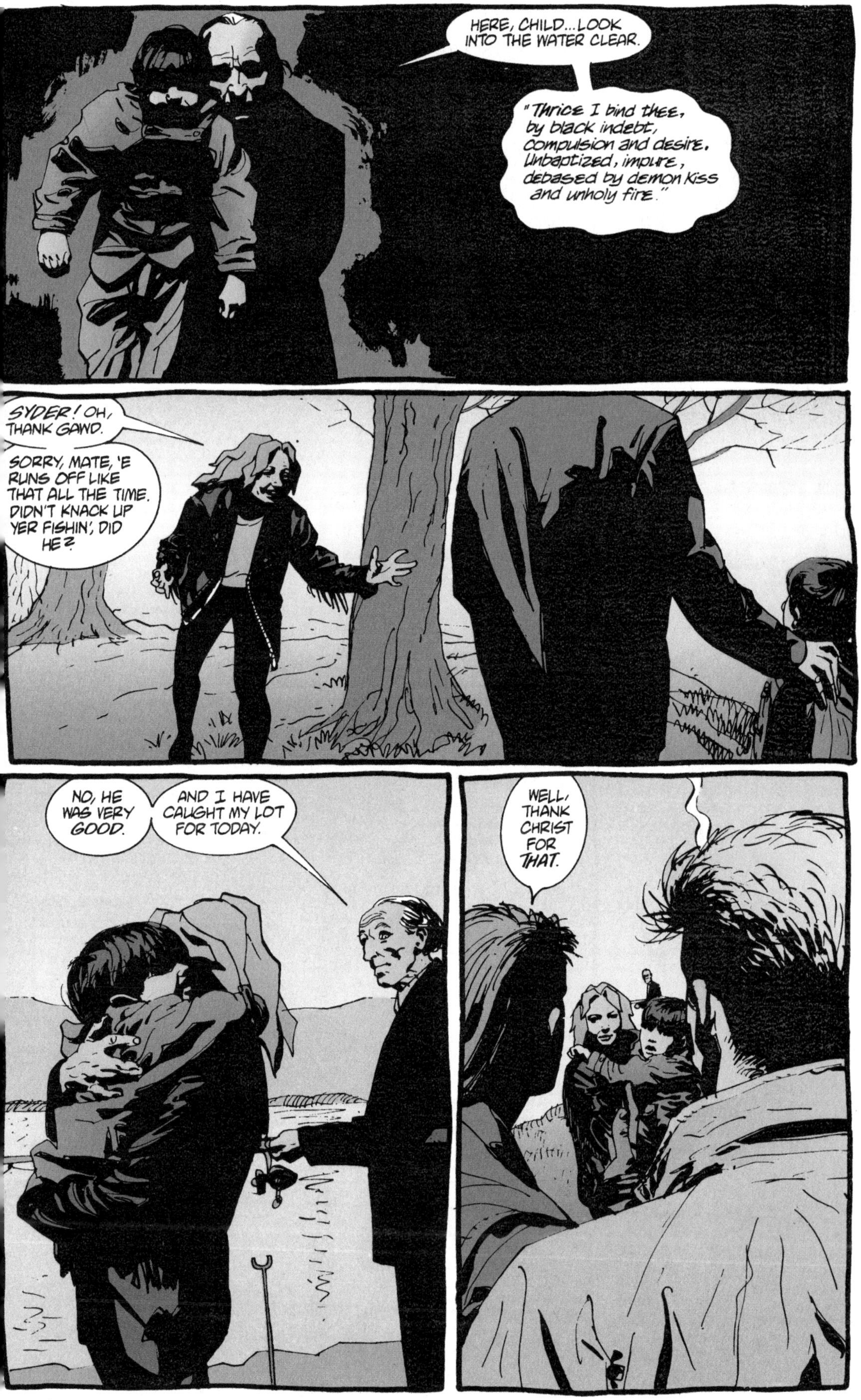
HERE, CHILD... LOOK INTO THE WATER CLEAR.
"Thrice I bind thee, by black indebt, compulsion and desire. Unbaptized, impure, debased by demon kiss and unholy fire."
SYDER! OH, THANK GAWD.
SORRY, MATE, 'E RUNS OFF LIKE THAT ALL THE TIME. DIDN'T KNACK UP YER FISHIN', DID HE?
NO, HE WAS VERY GOOD.
AND I HAVE CAUGHT MY LOT FOR TODAY.
WELL, THANK CHRIST FOR THAT.

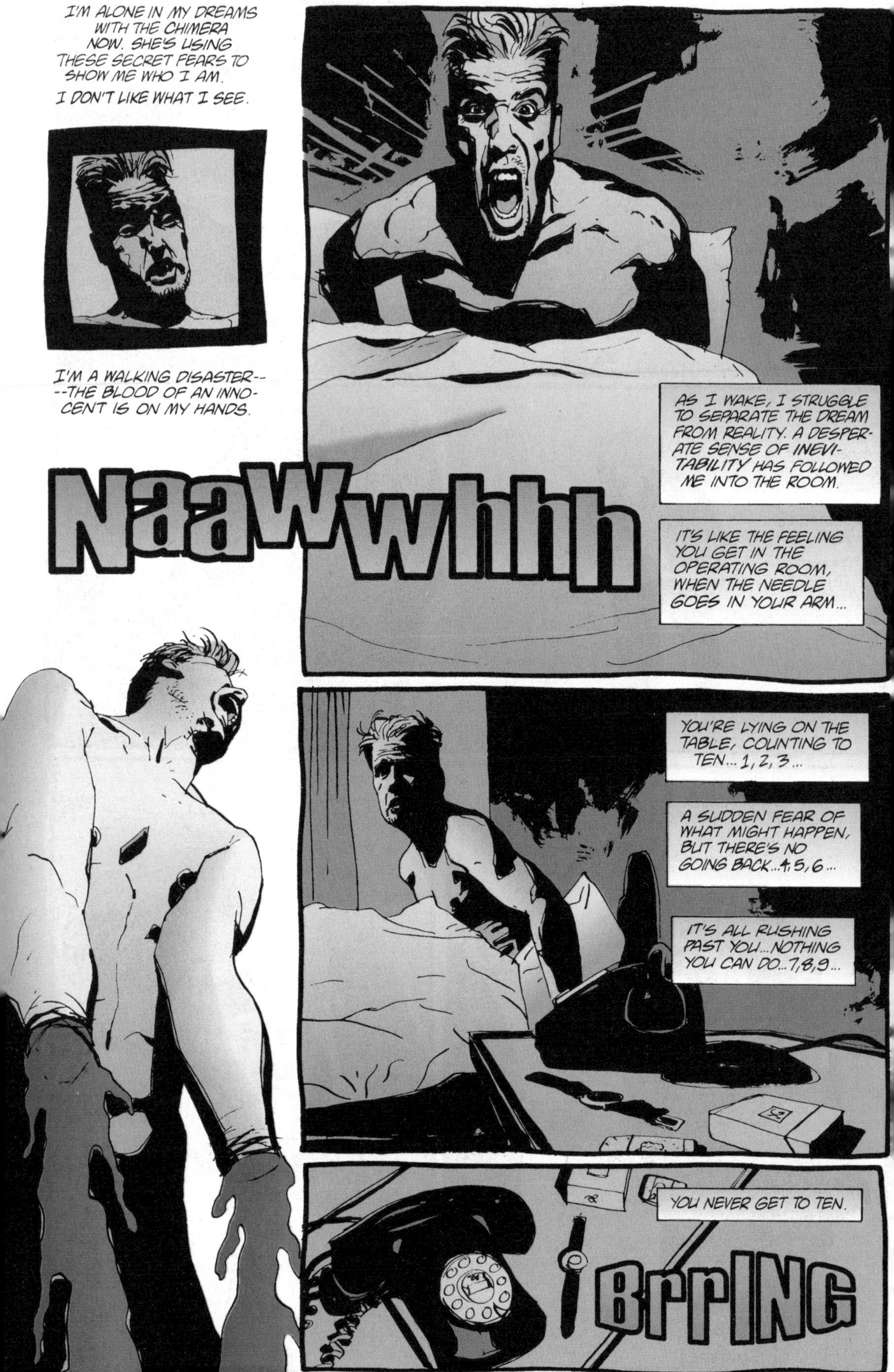
I'M ALONE IN MY DREAMS WITH THE CHIMERA NOW. SHE'S USING THESE SECRET FEARS TO SHOW ME WHO I AM.
I DON'T LIKE WHAT I SEE.
I'M A WALKING DISASTER-- --THE BLOOD OF AN INNOCENT IS ON MY HANDS.
NaaWwhhh
AS I WAKE, I STRUGGLE TO SEPARATE THE DREAM FROM REALITY. A DESPERATE SENSE OF INEVITABILITY HAS FOLLOWED ME INTO THE ROOM.
IT'S LIKE THE FEELING YOU GET IN THE OPERATING ROOM, WHEN THE NEEDLE GOES IN YOUR ARM...
YOU'RE LYING ON THE TABLE, COUNTING TO TEN... 1, 2, 3...
A SUDDEN FEAR OF WHAT MIGHT HAPPEN, BUT THERE'S NO GOING BACK...4, 5, 6...
IT'S ALL RUSHING PAST YOU...NOTHING YOU CAN DO...7, 8, 9...
YOU NEVER GET TO TEN.
BrrING

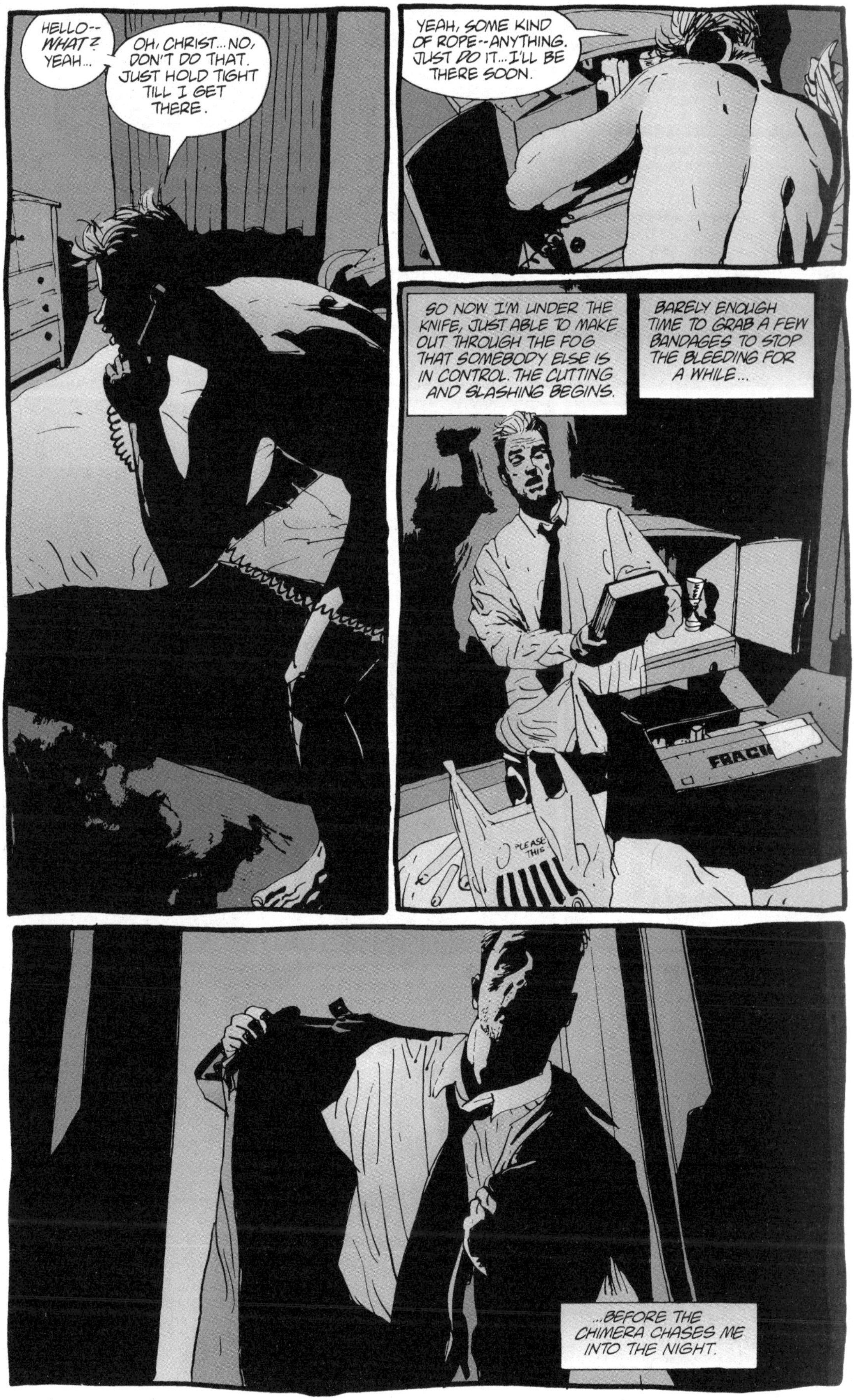
HELLO--
WHAT?
YEAH...
OH, CHRIST...NO, DON'T DO THAT. JUST HOLD TIGHT TILL I GET THERE.
YEAH, SOME KIND OF ROPE--ANYTHING. JUST DO IT...I'LL BE THERE SOON.
SO NOW I'M UNDER THE KNIFE, JUST ABLE TO MAKE OUT THROUGH THE FOG THAT SOMEBODY ELSE IS IN CONTROL. THE CUTTING AND SLASHING BEGINS.
BARELY ENOUGH TIME TO GRAB A FEW BANDAGES TO STOP THE BLEEDING FOR A WHILE...
...BEFORE THE CHIMERA CHASES ME INTO THE NIGHT.

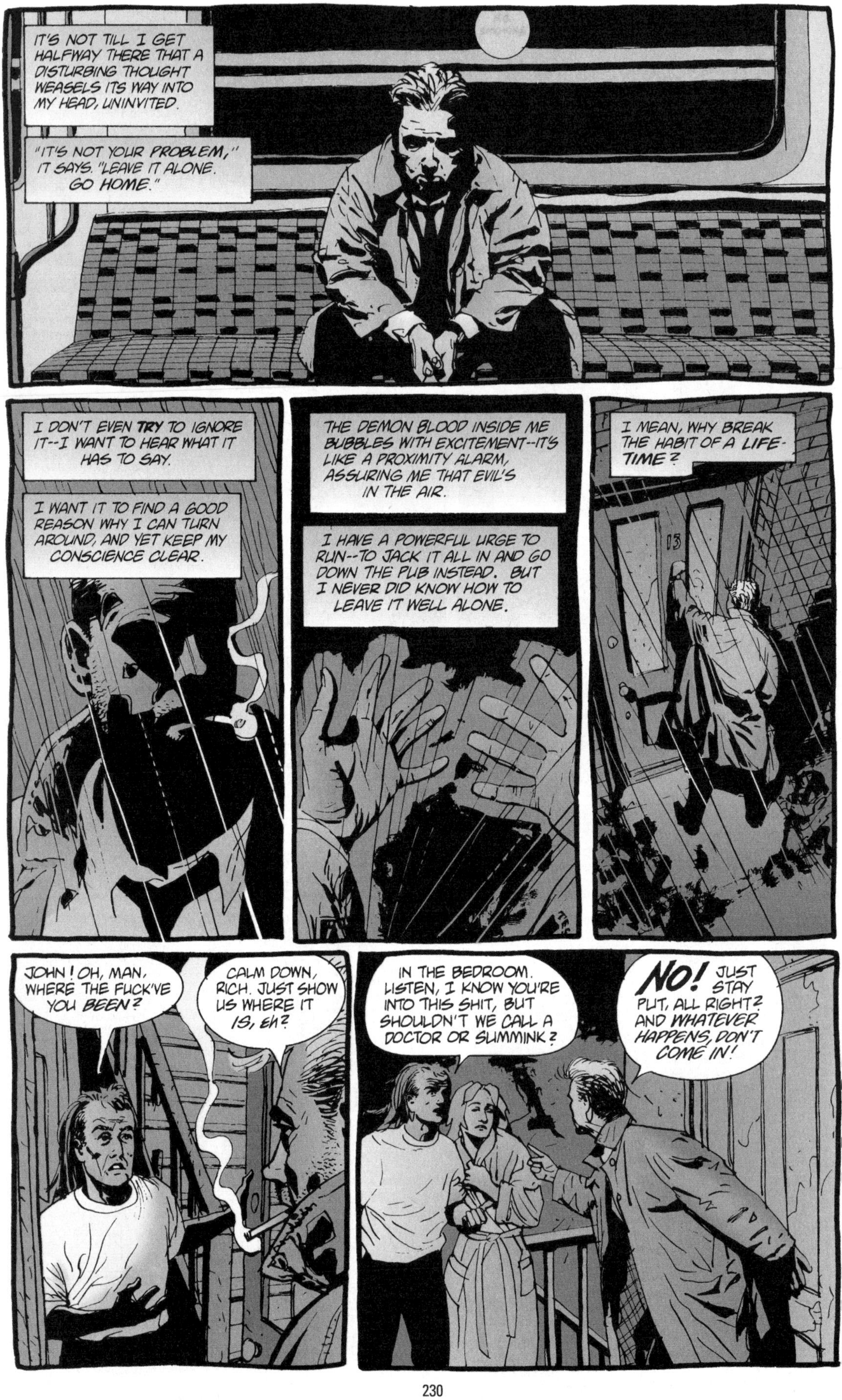
IT'S NOT TILL I GET HALFWAY THERE THAT A DISTURBING THOUGHT WEASELS ITS WAY INTO MY HEAD, UNINVITED.
"IT'S NOT YOUR PROBLEM," IT SAYS. "LEAVE IT ALONE. GO HOME."
I DON'T EVEN TRY TO IGNORE IT--I WANT TO HEAR WHAT IT HAS TO SAY.
I WANT IT TO FIND A GOOD REASON WHY I CAN TURN AROUND, AND YET KEEP MY CONSCIENCE CLEAR.
THE DEMON BLOOD INSIDE ME BUBBLES WITH EXCITEMENT--IT'S LIKE A PROXIMITY ALARM, ASSURING ME THAT EVIL'S IN THE AIR.
I HAVE A POWERFUL URGE TO RUN--TO JACK IT ALL IN AND GO DOWN THE PUB INSTEAD. BUT I NEVER DID KNOW HOW TO LEAVE IT WELL ALONE.
I MEAN, WHY BREAK THE HABIT OF A LIFE-TIME?
13
JOHN! OH, MAN, WHERE THE FUCK'VE YOU BEEN?
CALM DOWN, RICH. JUST SHOW US WHERE IT IS, EH?
IN THE BEDROOM. LISTEN, I KNOW YOU'RE INTO THIS SHIT, BUT SHOULDN'T WE CALL A DOCTOR OR SUMMINK?
NO! JUST STAY PUT, ALL RIGHT? AND WHATEVER HAPPENS, DON'T COME IN!

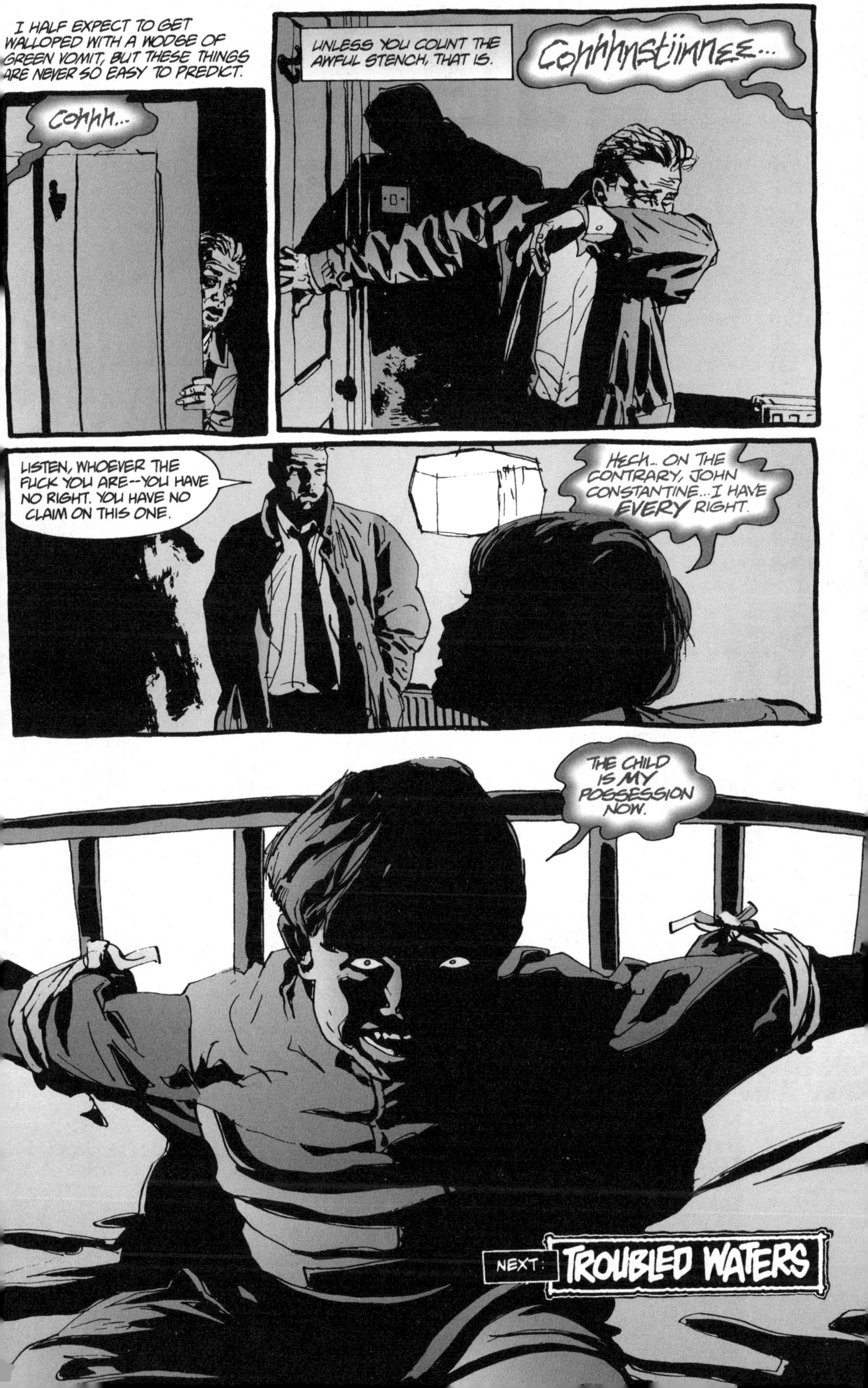
I HALF EXPECT TO GET WALLOPED WITH A WODGE OF GREEN VOMIT, BUT THESE THINGS ARE NEVER SO EASY TO PREDICT.
Cohhh...
UNLESS YOU COUNT THE AWFUL STENCH, THAT IS.
Cohhhnstiinnee...
LISTEN, WHOEVER THE FUCK YOU ARE--YOU HAVE NO RIGHT. YOU HAVE NO CLAIM ON THIS ONE.
HECH.. ON THE CONTRARY, JOHN CONSTANTINE...I HAVE EVERY RIGHT.
THE CHILD IS MY POSSESSION NOW.
NEXT: TROUBLED WATERS

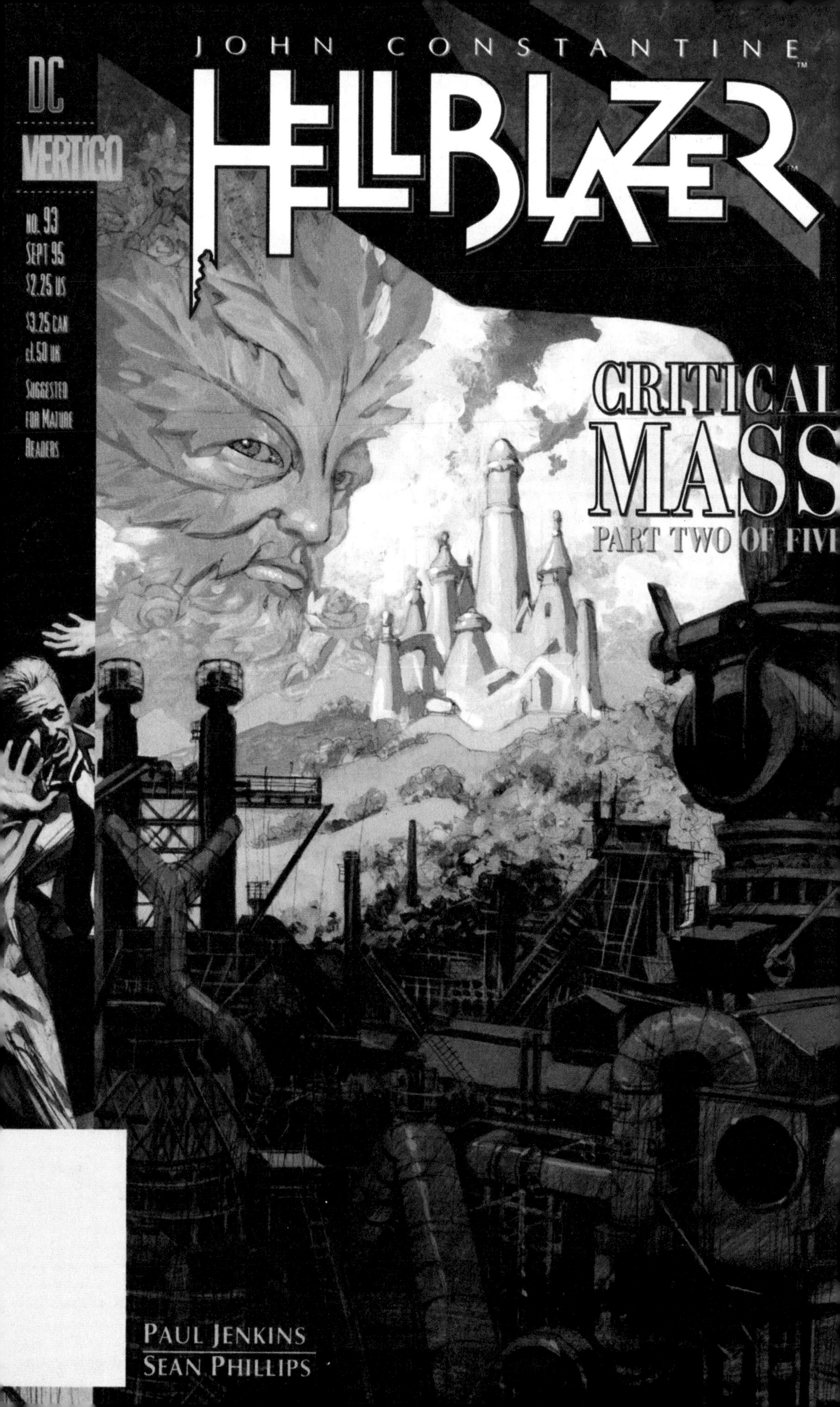
JOHN CONSTANTINE
HELLBLAZER
DC
VERTIGO
NO. 93
SEPT 95
$2.25 US
$3.25 CAN
£1.50 UK
SUGGESTED FOR MATURE READERS
CRITICAL MASS
PART TWO OF FIVE
PAUL JENKINS
SEAN PHILLIPS

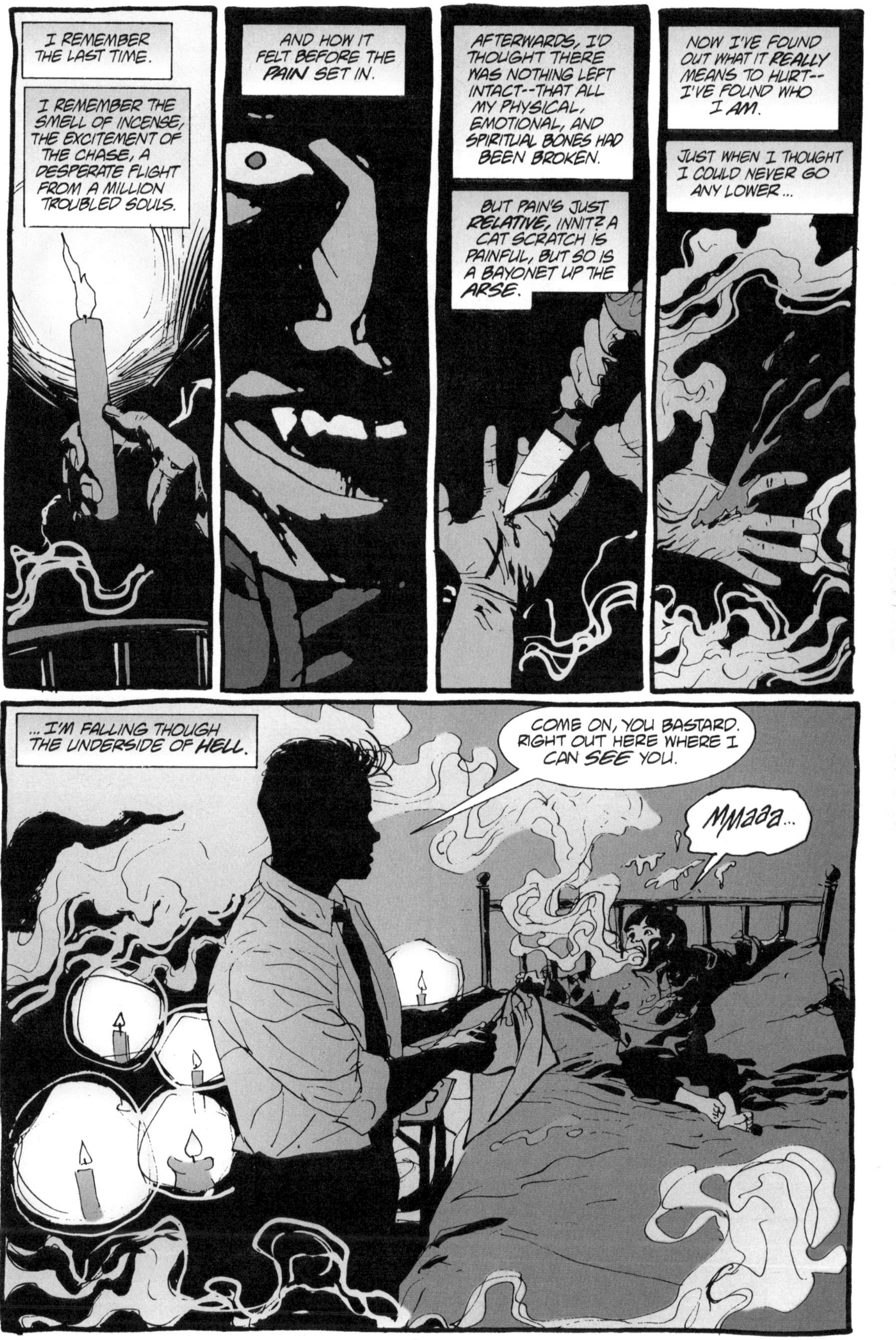
I REMEMBER THE LAST TIME.
I REMEMBER THE SMELL OF INCENSE, THE EXCITEMENT OF THE CHASE, A DESPERATE FLIGHT FROM A MILLION TROUBLED SOULS.
AND HOW IT FELT BEFORE THE PAIN SET IN.
AFTERWARDS, I'D THOUGHT THERE WAS NOTHING LEFT INTACT--THAT ALL MY PHYSICAL, EMOTIONAL, AND SPIRITUAL BONES HAD BEEN BROKEN.
BUT PAIN'S JUST RELATIVE, INNIT? A CAT SCRATCH IS PAINFUL, BUT SO IS A BAYONET UP THE ARSE.
NOW I'VE FOUND OUT WHAT IT REALLY MEANS TO HURT-- I'VE FOUND WHO I AM.
JUST WHEN I THOUGHT I COULD NEVER GO ANY LOWER ...
... I'M FALLING THOUGH THE UNDERSIDE OF HELL.
COME ON, YOU BASTARD. RIGHT OUT HERE WHERE I CAN SEE YOU.
MMaaa...

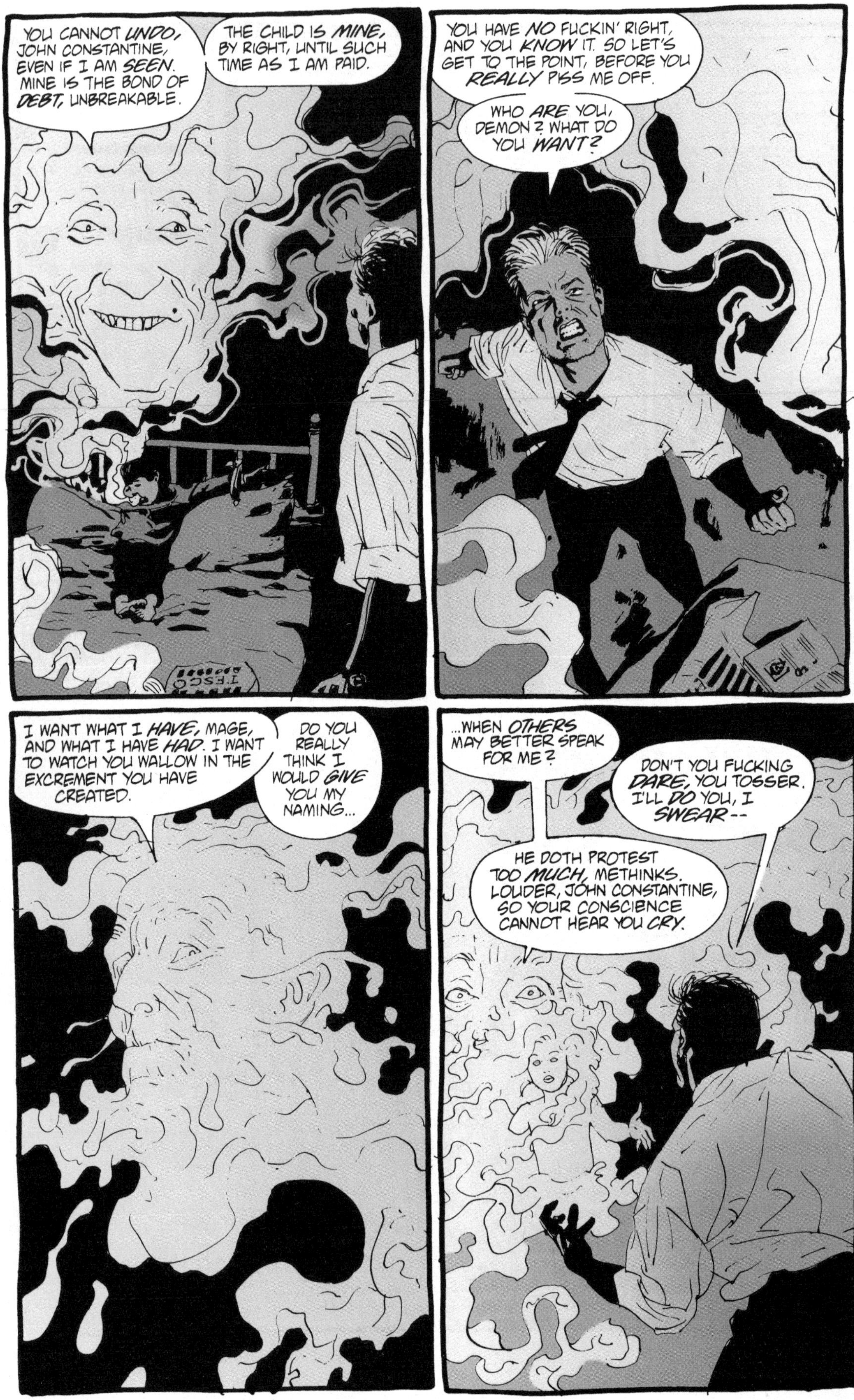
YOU CANNOT UNDO, JOHN CONSTANTINE, EVEN IF I AM SEEN. MINE IS THE BOND OF DEBT, UNBREAKABLE.
THE CHILD IS MINE, BY RIGHT, UNTIL SUCH TIME AS I AM PAID.
TESCO
YOU HAVE NO FUCKIN' RIGHT, AND YOU KNOW IT. SO LET'S GET TO THE POINT, BEFORE YOU REALLY PISS ME OFF.
WHO ARE YOU, DEMON? WHAT DO YOU WANT?
I WANT WHAT I HAVE, MAGE, AND WHAT I HAVE HAD. I WANT TO WATCH YOU WALLOW IN THE EXCREMENT YOU HAVE CREATED.
DO YOU REALLY THINK I WOULD GIVE YOU MY NAMING...
...WHEN OTHERS MAY BETTER SPEAK FOR ME?
DON'T YOU FUCKING DARE, YOU TOSSER. I'LL DO YOU, I SWEAR--
HE DOTH PROTEST TOO MUCH, METHINKS. LOUDER, JOHN CONSTANTINE, SO YOUR CONSCIENCE CANNOT HEAR YOU CRY.

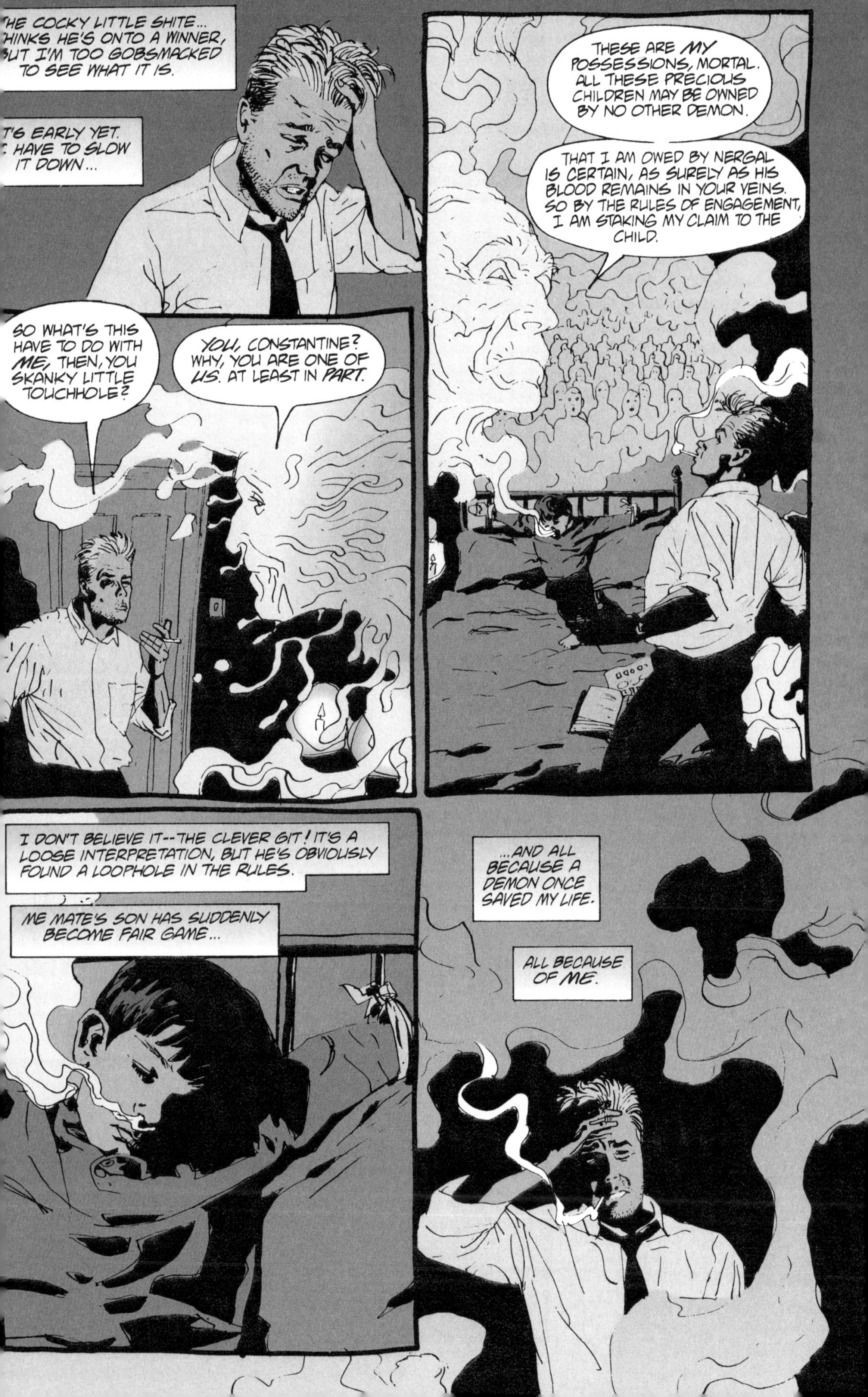
THE COCKY LITTLE SHITE... THINKS HE'S ONTO A WINNER, BUT I'M TOO GOBSMACKED TO SEE WHAT IT IS.
IT'S EARLY YET. I HAVE TO SLOW IT DOWN...
SO WHAT'S THIS HAVE TO DO WITH ME, THEN, YOU SKANKY LITTLE TOUCHHOLE?
YOU, CONSTANTINE? WHY, YOU ARE ONE OF US. AT LEAST IN PART.
THESE ARE MY POSSESSIONS, MORTAL. ALL THESE PRECIOUS CHILDREN MAY BE OWNED BY NO OTHER DEMON.
THAT I AM OWED BY NERGAL IS CERTAIN, AS SURELY AS HIS BLOOD REMAINS IN YOUR VEINS. SO BY THE RULES OF ENGAGEMENT, I AM STAKING MY CLAIM TO THE CHILD.
I DON'T BELIEVE IT--THE CLEVER GIT! IT'S A LOOSE INTERPRETATION, BUT HE'S OBVIOUSLY FOUND A LOOPHOLE IN THE RULES.
ME MATE'S SON HAS SUDDENLY BECOME FAIR GAME...
...AND ALL BECAUSE A DEMON ONCE SAVED MY LIFE.
ALL BECAUSE OF ME.

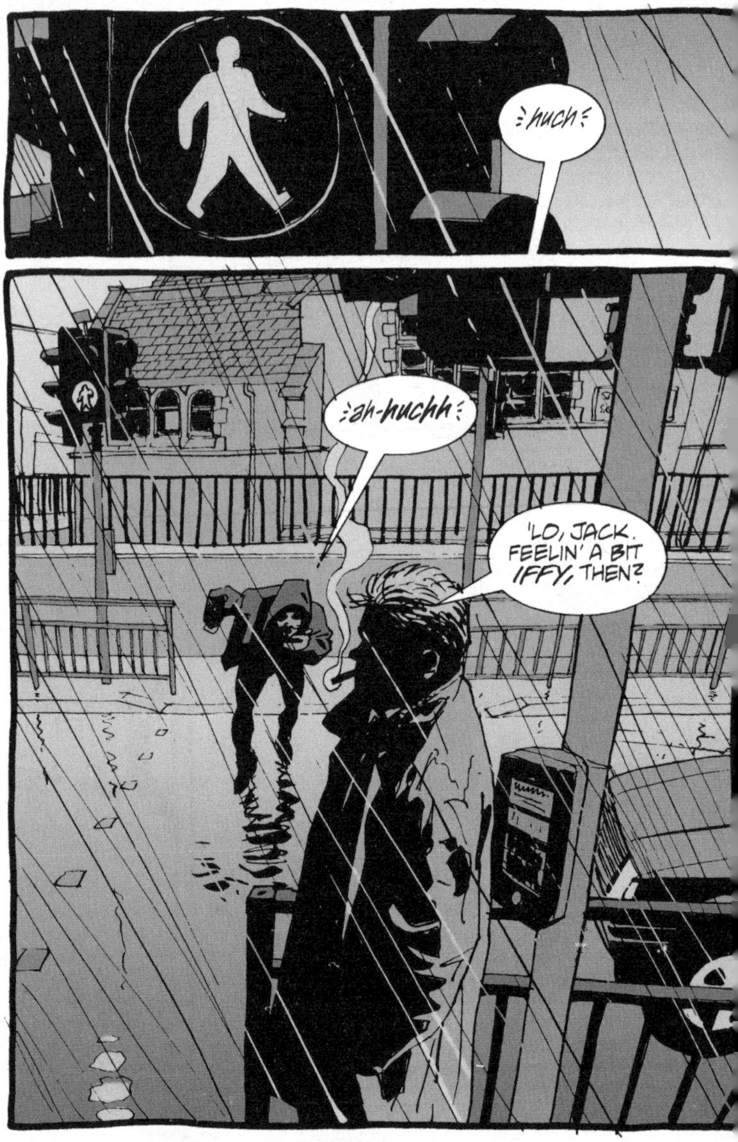
huch
ah-huchh
'LO, JACK. FEELIN' A BIT IFFY, THEN?

CRITICAL MASS 2

Troubled Waters

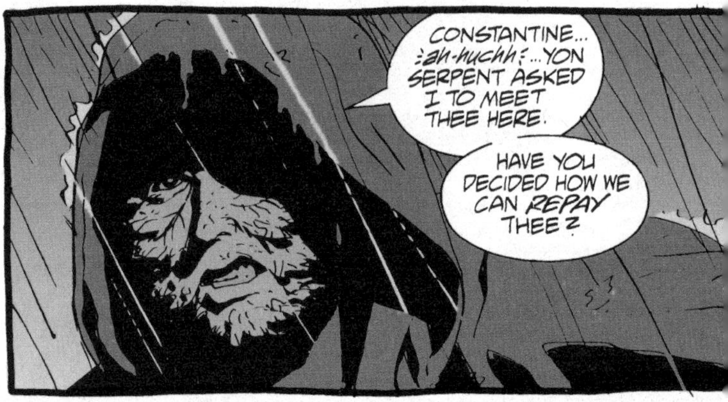
CONSTANTINE... ah-huchh ...YON SERPENT ASKED I TO MEET THEE HERE.
HAVE YOU DECIDED HOW WE CAN REPAY THEE?

Paul Jenkins Writer

Sean Phillips Artist

Matt Hollingsworth Colorist

Clem Robins Letterer

Axel Alonso Asst. Editor

Lou Stathis Editor

HOLD YER HORSES, MATE. ONE COFFIN NAIL AT A TIME, *eh?*

POOR SOD--IT'S NOT HIS FAULT, BUT I HAVE TO LET HIM *THINK* I'M IN CHARGE. TOO MUCH RIDING ON THIS...

:ah-*huchh*: CONS--:ah-*hecchh*:

I THOUGHT HE'D BE ALL WINDSWEPT AND INTERESTING. STANDS TO REASON HE'D LOOK LIKE *SHIT.*

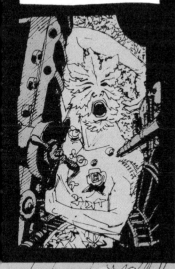

THESE DAYS, THE BRITISH COUNTRYSIDE'S REELING FROM THE EFFECTS OF CIVILIZA-TION. ALL THE MYSTICAL SITES ARE BEING REPLACED WITH COUNCIL HOUSES.

OUR DREAM'S GETTING SMALLER AND SMALLER, AND THE POOR OLD GREEN MAN--THE EMBODIMENT OF THE LAND ESSENCE --HE'S AS SICK AS A PARROT.

:ah-*huchh*:... YON SWAMP CREATURE--THE *ELEMENTAL* ... :ah-hucch: TOLD US YOU'D BE *DIFFICULT...*

YEAH, WELL WHAT DO YOU EXPECT FROM A CABBAGE?

:ah-*huchh*:...JOHN, *KNOW* THEE I CAN'T TARRY IN THIS PLACE...:ah-*huchh*: ...WHAT DO YOU *WANT?*

SIMPLE, MATE.

I WANT TO GO TO *ABATON.*

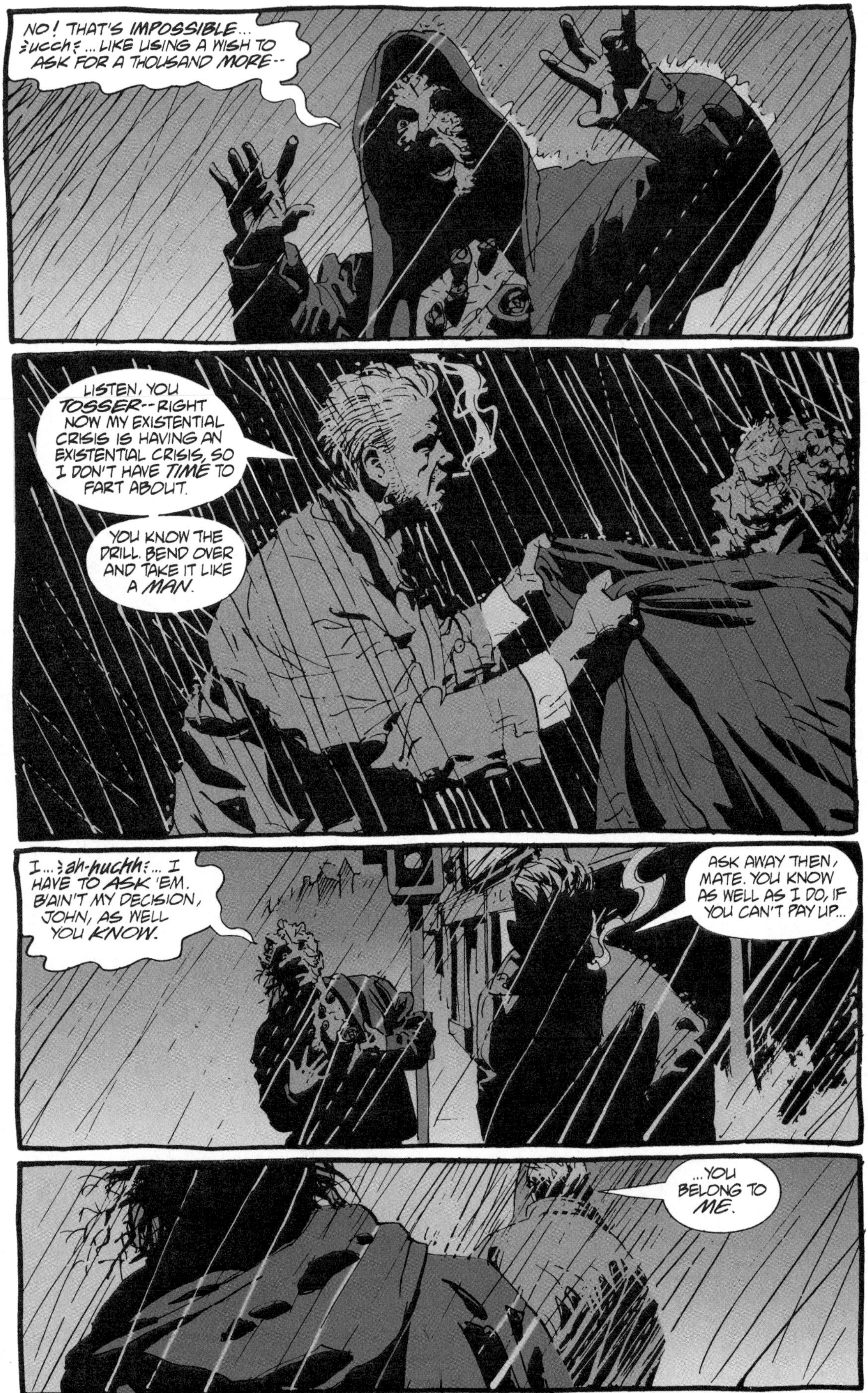
NO! THAT'S IMPOSSIBLE... ucch ... LIKE USING A WISH TO ASK FOR A THOUSAND MORE--
LISTEN, YOU TOSSER--RIGHT NOW MY EXISTENTIAL CRISIS IS HAVING AN EXISTENTIAL CRISIS, SO I DON'T HAVE TIME TO FART ABOUT.
YOU KNOW THE DRILL. BEND OVER AND TAKE IT LIKE A MAN.
I... ah-huchh ... I HAVE TO ASK 'EM. B'AIN'T MY DECISION, JOHN, AS WELL YOU KNOW.
ASK AWAY THEN, MATE. YOU KNOW AS WELL AS I DO, IF YOU CAN'T PAY UP...
...YOU BELONG TO ME.

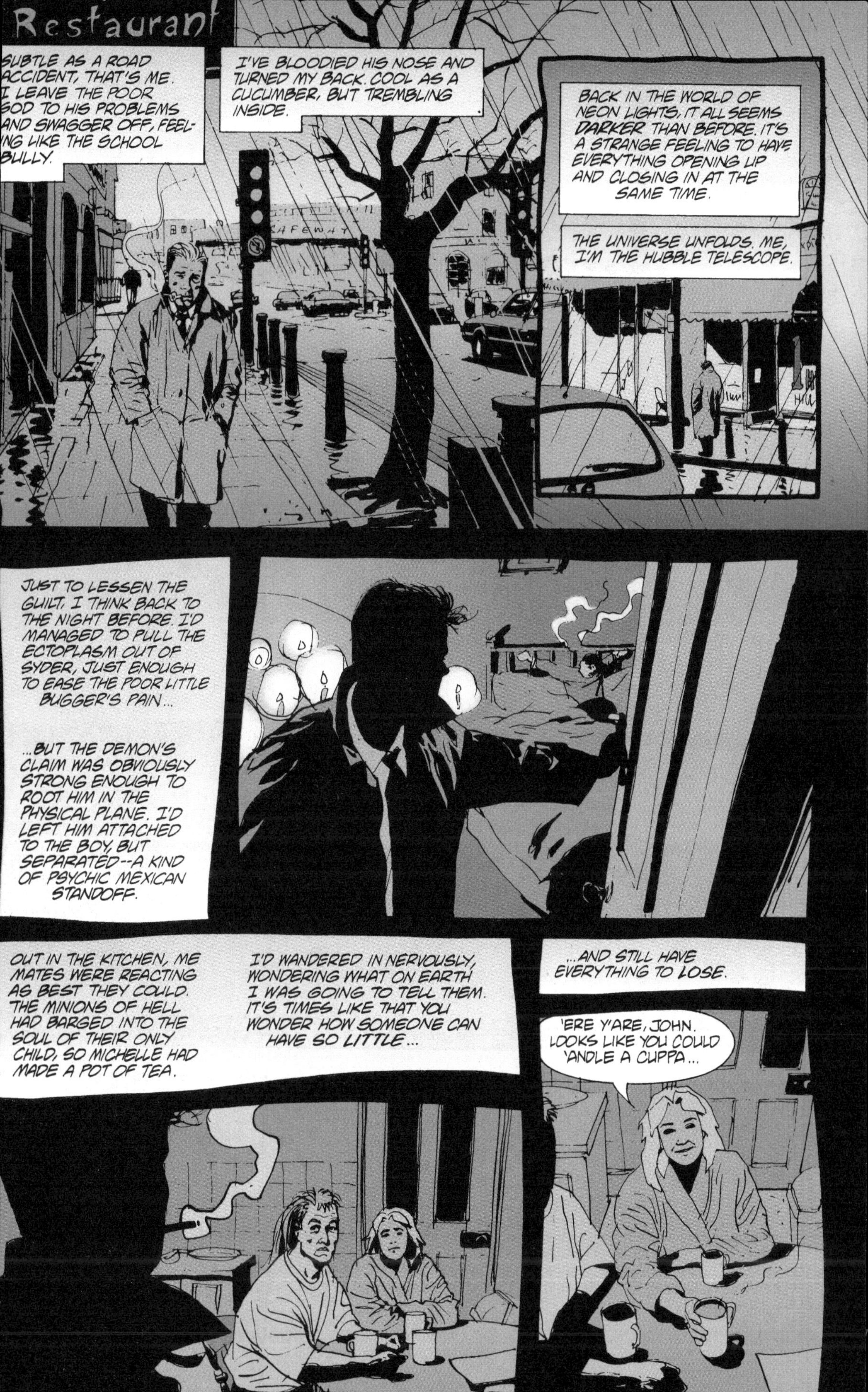

Restaurant
SUBTLE AS A ROAD ACCIDENT, THAT'S ME. I LEAVE THE POOR GOD TO HIS PROBLEMS AND SWAGGER OFF, FEELING LIKE THE SCHOOL BULLY.
I'VE BLOODIED HIS NOSE AND TURNED MY BACK. COOL AS A CUCUMBER, BUT TREMBLING INSIDE.
SAFEWAY
BACK IN THE WORLD OF NEON LIGHTS, IT ALL SEEMS DARKER THAN BEFORE. IT'S A STRANGE FEELING TO HAVE EVERYTHING OPENING UP AND CLOSING IN AT THE SAME TIME.
THE UNIVERSE UNFOLDS. ME, I'M THE HUBBLE TELESCOPE.
JUST TO LESSEN THE GUILT, I THINK BACK TO THE NIGHT BEFORE. I'D MANAGED TO PULL THE ECTOPLASM OUT OF SYDER, JUST ENOUGH TO EASE THE POOR LITTLE BUGGER'S PAIN...
...BUT THE DEMON'S CLAIM WAS OBVIOUSLY STRONG ENOUGH TO ROOT HIM IN THE PHYSICAL PLANE. I'D LEFT HIM ATTACHED TO THE BOY, BUT SEPARATED--A KIND OF PSYCHIC MEXICAN STANDOFF.
OUT IN THE KITCHEN, ME MATES WERE REACTING AS BEST THEY COULD. THE MINIONS OF HELL HAD BARGED INTO THE SOUL OF THEIR ONLY CHILD, SO MICHELLE HAD MADE A POT OF TEA.
I'D WANDERED IN NERVOUSLY, WONDERING WHAT ON EARTH I WAS GOING TO TELL THEM. IT'S TIMES LIKE THAT YOU WONDER HOW SOMEONE CAN HAVE SO LITTLE...
...AND STILL HAVE EVERYTHING TO LOSE.
'ERE Y'ARE, JOHN. LOOKS LIKE YOU COULD 'ANDLE A CUPPA...

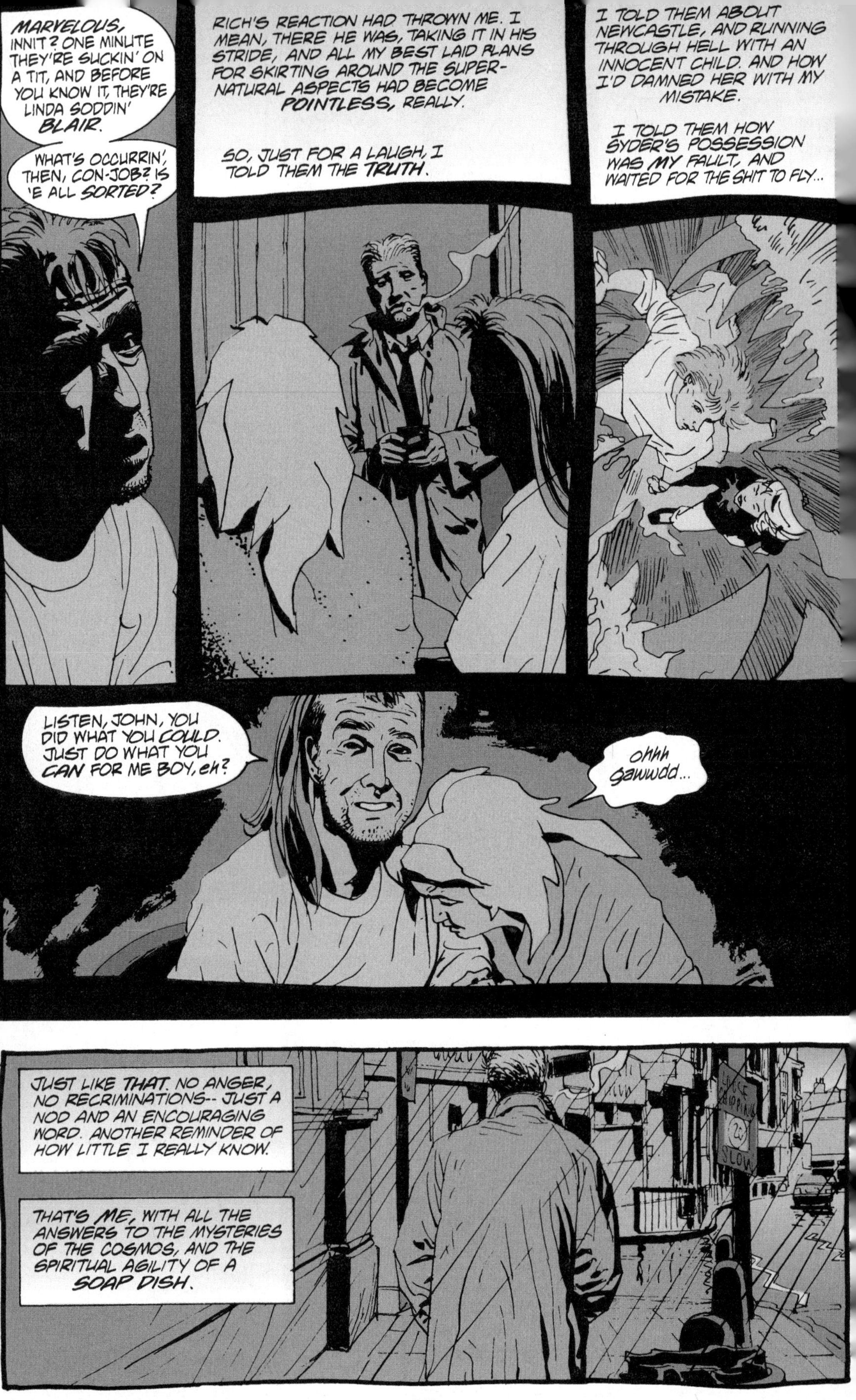
MARVELOUS, INNIT? ONE MINUTE THEY'RE SUCKIN' ON A TIT, AND BEFORE YOU KNOW IT, THEY'RE LINDA SODDIN' BLAIR.
WHAT'S OCCURRIN', THEN, CON-JOB? IS 'E ALL SORTED?
RICH'S REACTION HAD THROWN ME. I MEAN, THERE HE WAS, TAKING IT IN HIS STRIDE, AND ALL MY BEST LAID PLANS FOR SKIRTING AROUND THE SUPER-NATURAL ASPECTS HAD BECOME POINTLESS, REALLY.
SO, JUST FOR A LAUGH, I TOLD THEM THE TRUTH.
I TOLD THEM ABOUT NEWCASTLE, AND RUNNING THROUGH HELL WITH AN INNOCENT CHILD. AND HOW I'D DAMNED HER WITH MY MISTAKE.
I TOLD THEM HOW SYDER'S POSSESSION WAS MY FAULT, AND WAITED FOR THE SHIT TO FLY...
LISTEN, JOHN, YOU DID WHAT YOU COULD. JUST DO WHAT YOU CAN FOR ME BOY, eh?
ohhh gawwdd...
JUST LIKE THAT. NO ANGER, NO RECRIMINATIONS-- JUST A NOD AND AN ENCOURAGING WORD. ANOTHER REMINDER OF HOW LITTLE I REALLY KNOW.
THAT'S ME, WITH ALL THE ANSWERS TO THE MYSTERIES OF THE COSMOS, AND THE SPIRITUAL AGILITY OF A SOAP DISH.
SLOW

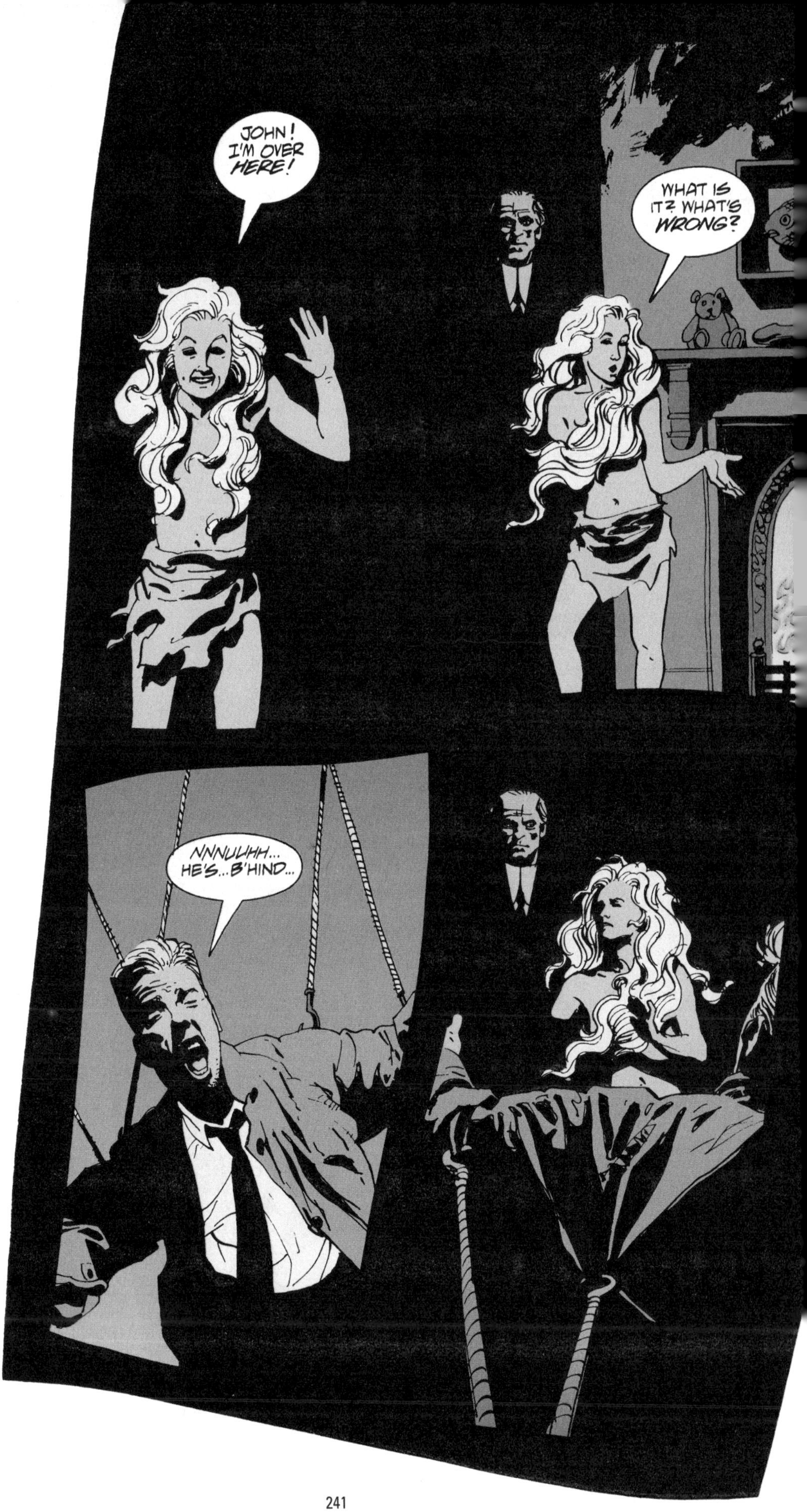
JOHN! I'M OVER HERE!
WHAT IS IT? WHAT'S WRONG?
NNNUUHH... HE'S...B'HIND...

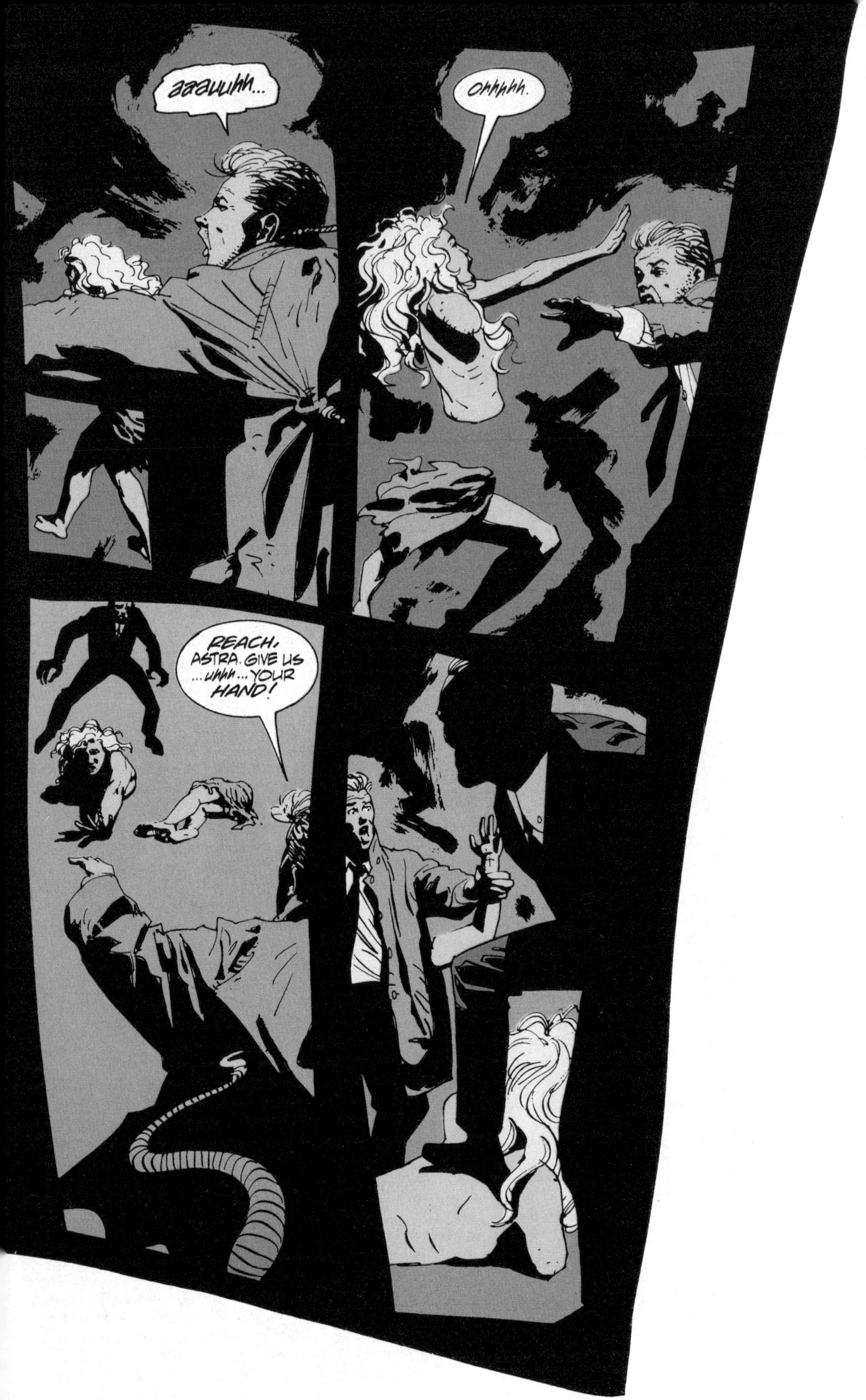
aaauuhh...
Ohhhhh.
REACH, ASTRA. GIVE US ...uhhh... YOUR HAND!

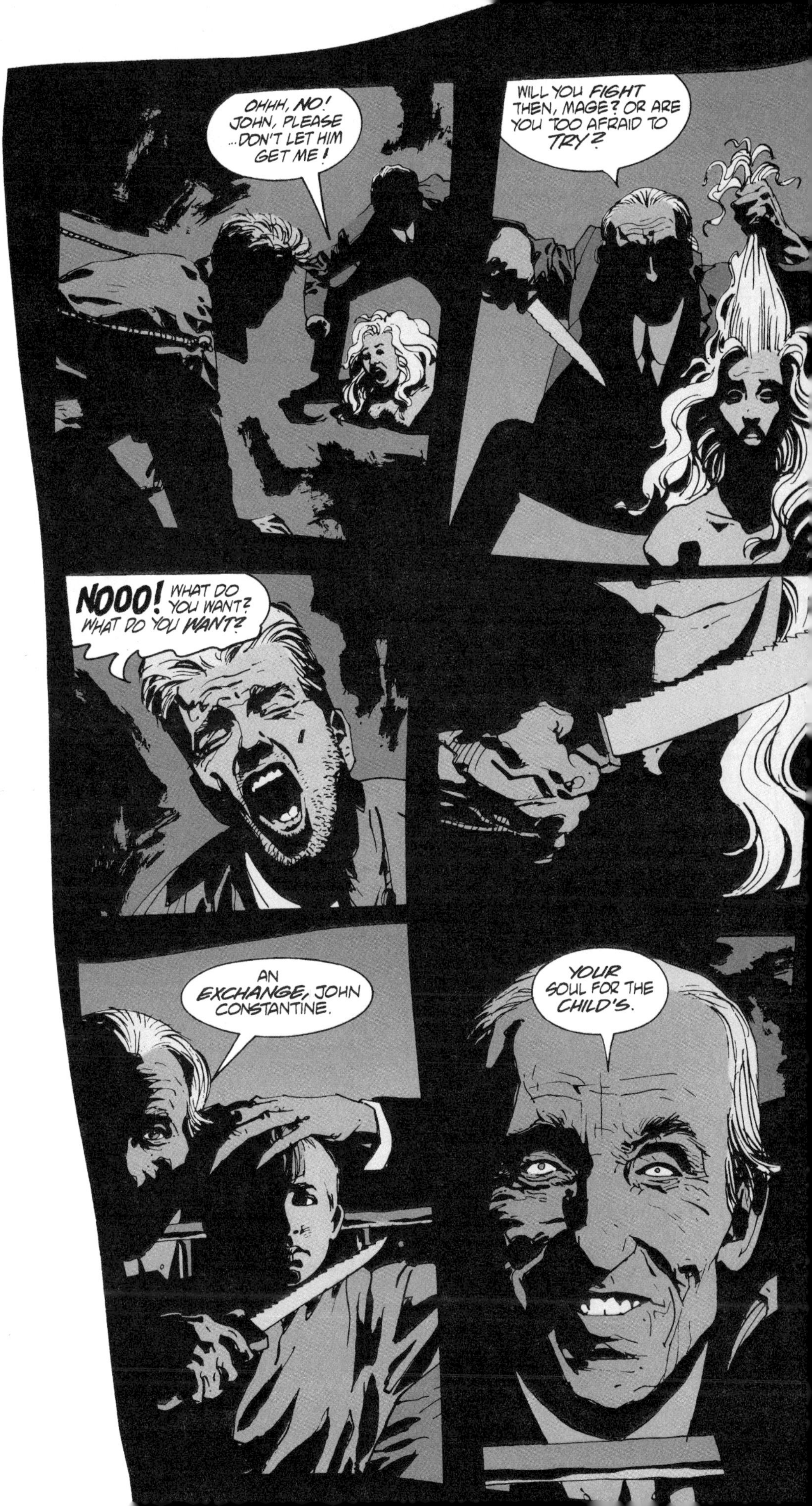
OHHH, NO! JOHN, PLEASE ...DON'T LET HIM GET ME!
WILL YOU FIGHT THEN, MAGE? OR ARE YOU TOO AFRAID TO TRY?
NOOO! WHAT DO YOU WANT? WHAT DO YOU WANT?
AN EXCHANGE, JOHN CONSTANTINE.
YOUR SOUL FOR THE CHILD'S.

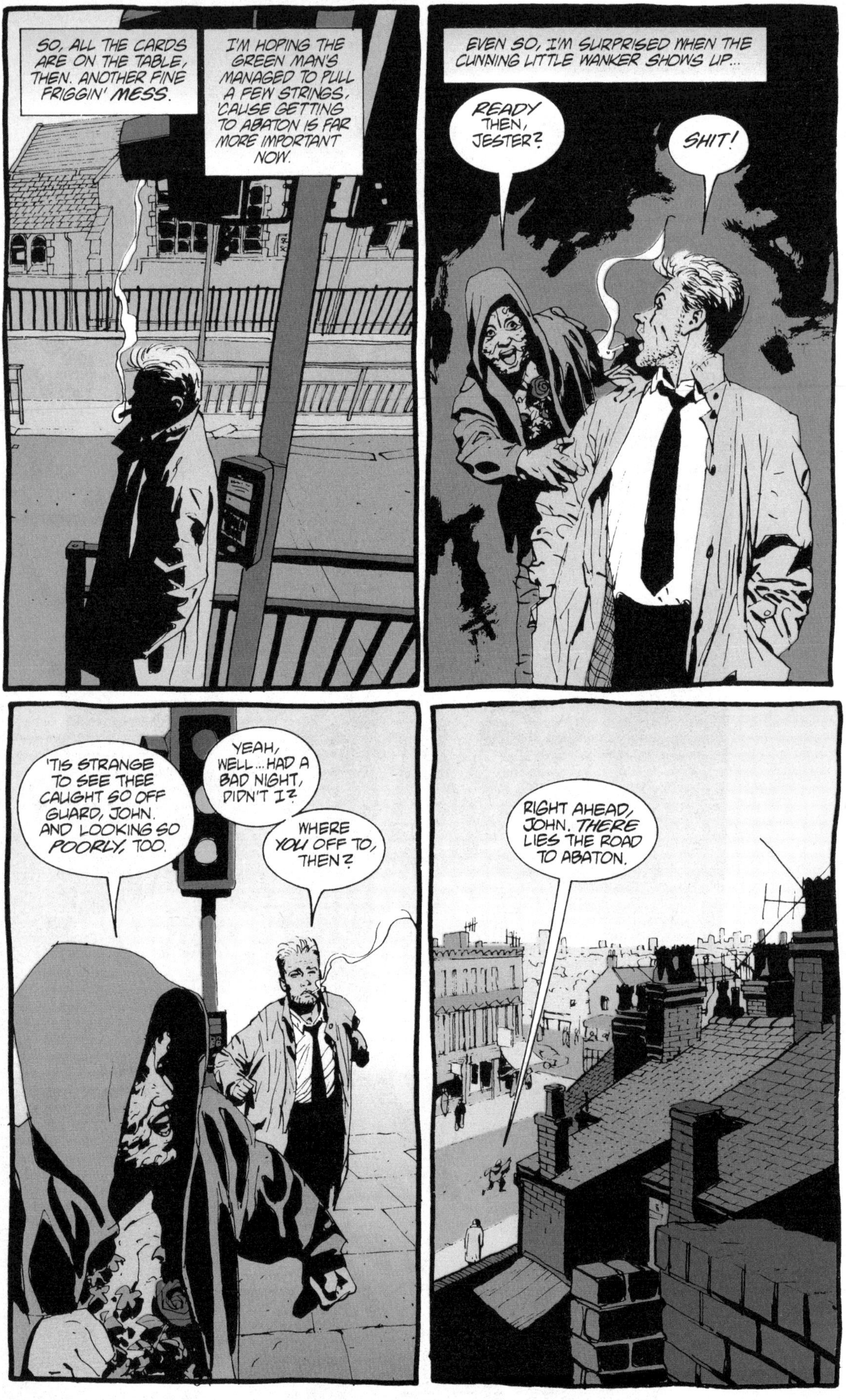
SO, ALL THE CARDS ARE ON THE TABLE, THEN. ANOTHER FINE FRIGGIN' MESS.
I'M HOPING THE GREEN MAN'S MANAGED TO PULL A FEW STRINGS, 'CAUSE GETTING TO ABATON IS FAR MORE IMPORTANT NOW.
EVEN SO, I'M SURPRISED WHEN THE CUNNING LITTLE WANKER SHOWS UP...
READY THEN, JESTER?
SHIT!
'TIS STRANGE TO SEE THEE CAUGHT SO OFF GUARD, JOHN. AND LOOKING SO POORLY, TOO.
YEAH, WELL... HAD A BAD NIGHT, DIDN'T I?
WHERE YOU OFF TO, THEN?
RIGHT AHEAD, JOHN. THERE LIES THE ROAD TO ABATON.

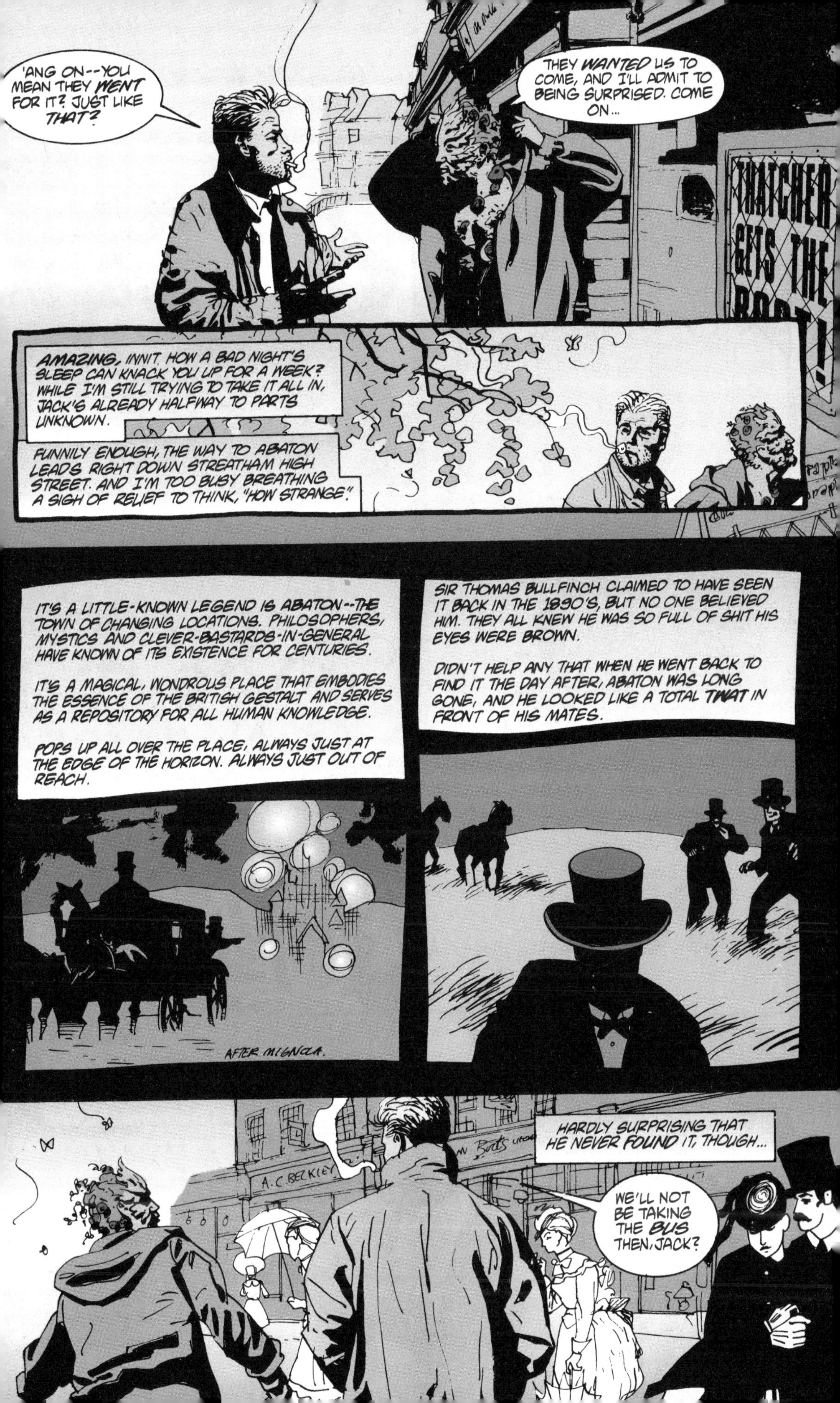
'ANG ON--YOU MEAN THEY WENT FOR IT? JUST LIKE THAT?
THEY WANTED US TO COME, AND I'LL ADMIT TO BEING SURPRISED. COME ON...
THATCHER GETS THE
AMAZING, INNIT, HOW A BAD NIGHT'S SLEEP CAN KNACK YOU UP FOR A WEEK? WHILE I'M STILL TRYING TO TAKE IT ALL IN, JACK'S ALREADY HALFWAY TO PARTS UNKNOWN.
FUNNILY ENOUGH, THE WAY TO ABATON LEADS RIGHT DOWN STREATHAM HIGH STREET. AND I'M TOO BUSY BREATHING A SIGH OF RELIEF TO THINK, "HOW STRANGE".
IT'S A LITTLE-KNOWN LEGEND IS ABATON--THE TOWN OF CHANGING LOCATIONS. PHILOSOPHERS, MYSTICS AND CLEVER-BASTARDS-IN-GENERAL HAVE KNOWN OF ITS EXISTENCE FOR CENTURIES.
IT'S A MAGICAL, WONDROUS PLACE THAT EMBODIES THE ESSENCE OF THE BRITISH GESTALT AND SERVES AS A REPOSITORY FOR ALL HUMAN KNOWLEDGE.
POPS UP ALL OVER THE PLACE, ALWAYS JUST AT THE EDGE OF THE HORIZON. ALWAYS JUST OUT OF REACH.
SIR THOMAS BULLFINCH CLAIMED TO HAVE SEEN IT BACK IN THE 1890'S, BUT NO ONE BELIEVED HIM. THEY ALL KNEW HE WAS SO FULL OF SHIT HIS EYES WERE BROWN.
DIDN'T HELP ANY THAT WHEN HE WENT BACK TO FIND IT THE DAY AFTER, ABATON WAS LONG GONE, AND HE LOOKED LIKE A TOTAL TWAT IN FRONT OF HIS MATES.
AFTER MIGNOLA.
HARDLY SURPRISING THAT HE NEVER FOUND IT, THOUGH...
A. C. BECKLEY
WE'LL NOT BE TAKING THE BUS THEN, JACK?

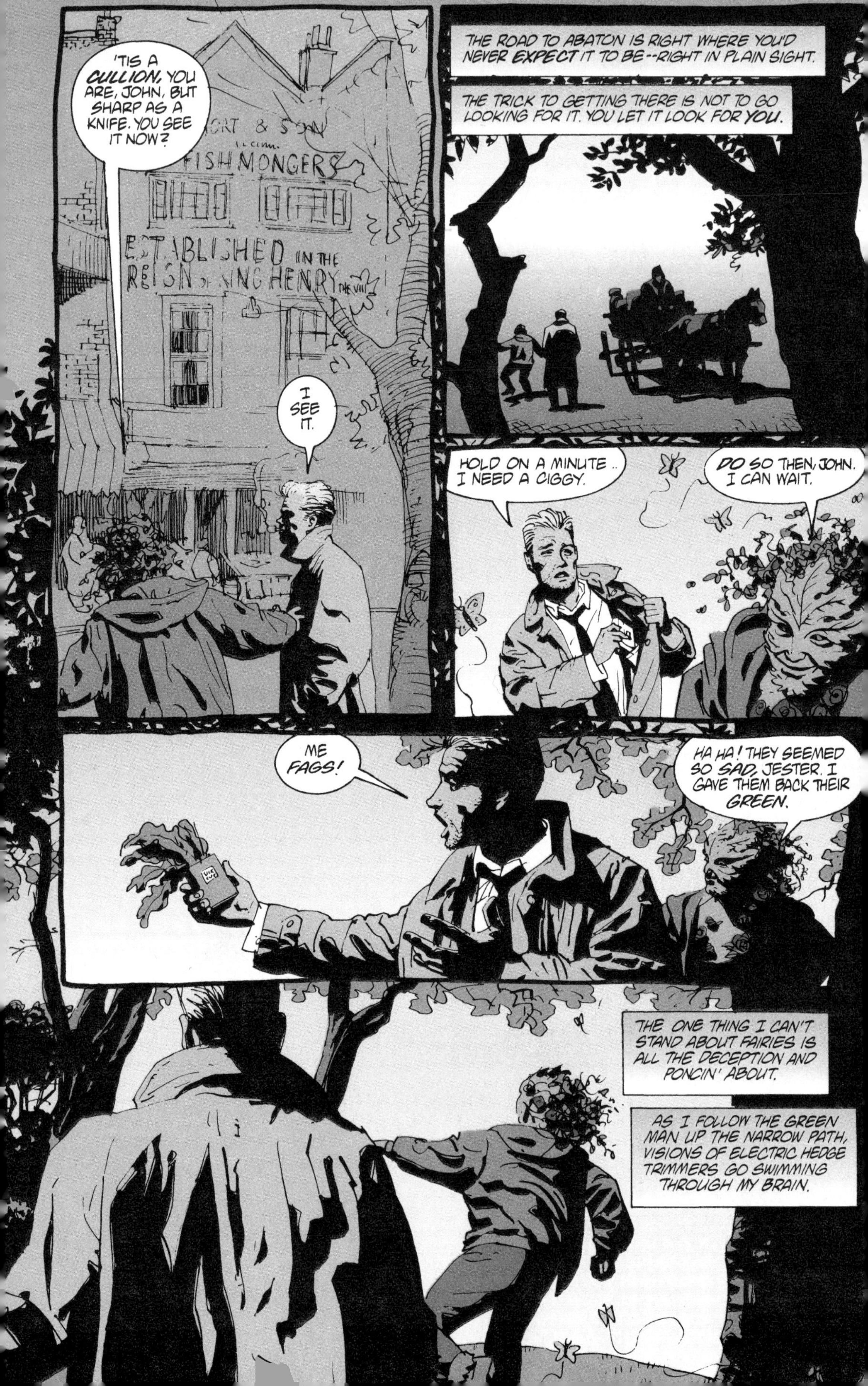
'TIS A CULLION, YOU ARE, JOHN, BUT SHARP AS A KNIFE. YOU SEE IT NOW?
FISHMONGERS
ESTABLISHED IN THE REIGN OF KING HENRY THE VIII
I SEE IT.
THE ROAD TO ABATON IS RIGHT WHERE YOU'D NEVER EXPECT IT TO BE--RIGHT IN PLAIN SIGHT.
THE TRICK TO GETTING THERE IS NOT TO GO LOOKING FOR IT. YOU LET IT LOOK FOR YOU.
HOLD ON A MINUTE .. I NEED A CIGGY.
DO SO THEN, JOHN. I CAN WAIT.
ME FAGS!
HA HA! THEY SEEMED SO SAD, JESTER. I GAVE THEM BACK THEIR GREEN.
THE ONE THING I CAN'T STAND ABOUT FAIRIES IS ALL THE DECEPTION AND PONCIN' ABOUT.
AS I FOLLOW THE GREEN MAN UP THE NARROW PATH, VISIONS OF ELECTRIC HEDGE TRIMMERS GO SWIMMING THROUGH MY BRAIN.

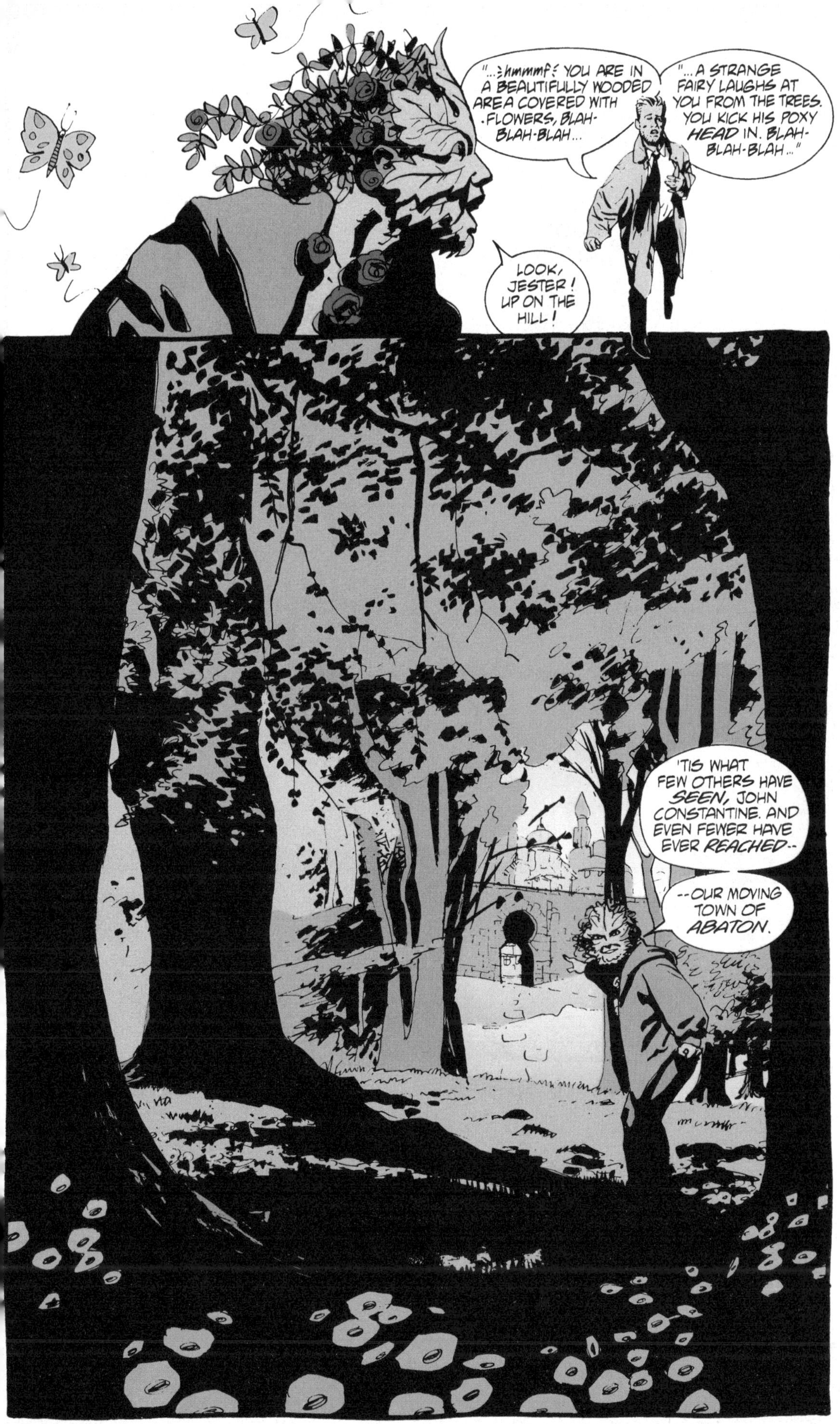
"...hmmmf: YOU ARE IN A BEAUTIFULLY WOODED AREA COVERED WITH FLOWERS, BLAH-BLAH-BLAH...
"...A STRANGE FAIRY LAUGHS AT YOU FROM THE TREES. YOU KICK HIS POXY HEAD IN. BLAH-BLAH-BLAH..."
LOOK, JESTER! UP ON THE HILL!
'TIS WHAT FEW OTHERS HAVE SEEN, JOHN CONSTANTINE. AND EVEN FEWER HAVE EVER REACHED--
--OUR MOVING TOWN OF ABATON.

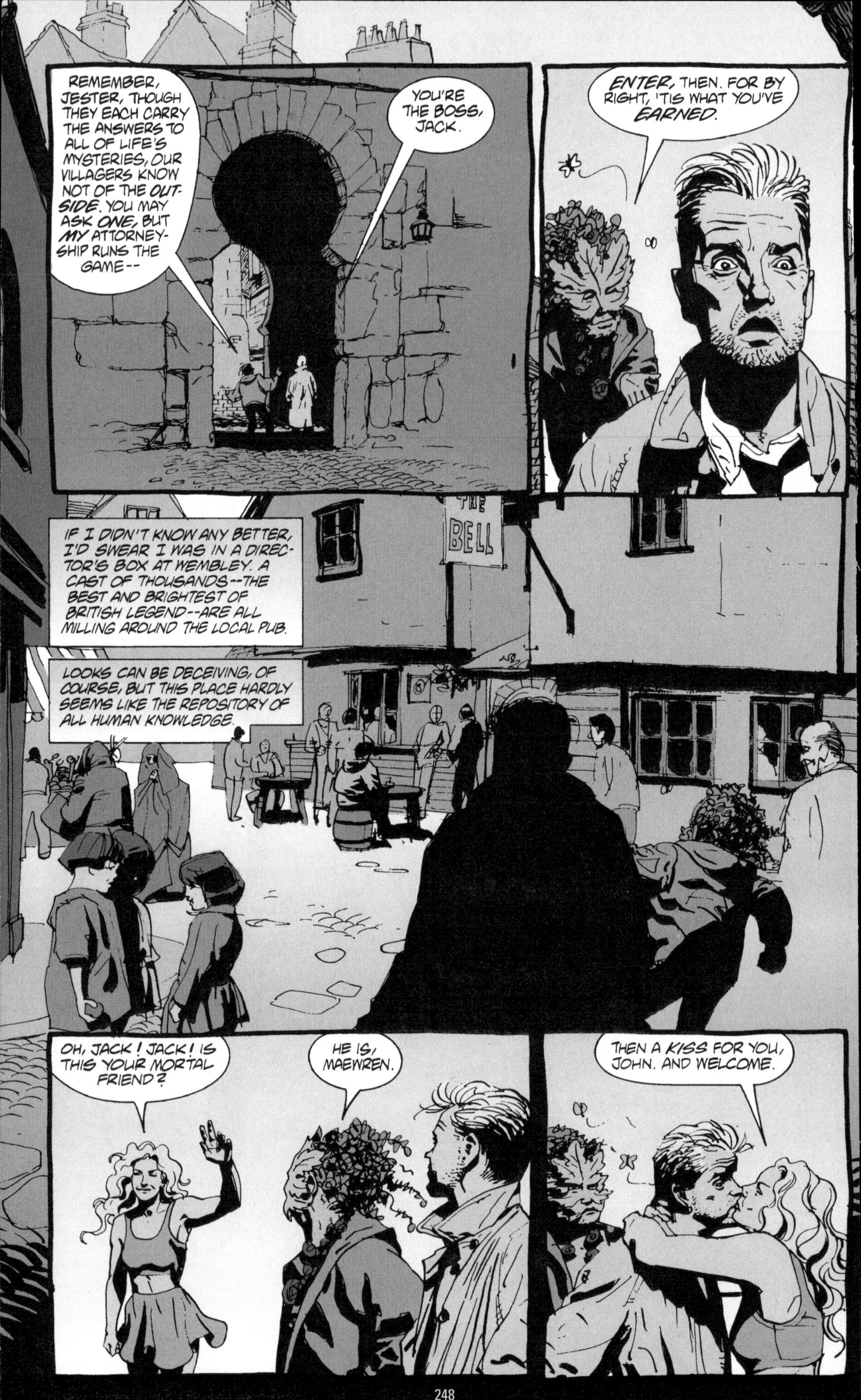
REMEMBER, JESTER, THOUGH THEY EACH CARRY THE ANSWERS TO ALL OF LIFE'S MYSTERIES, OUR VILLAGERS KNOW NOT OF THE OUTSIDE. YOU MAY ASK ONE, BUT MY ATTORNEYSHIP RUNS THE GAME--
YOU'RE THE BOSS, JACK.
ENTER, THEN. FOR BY RIGHT, 'TIS WHAT YOU'VE EARNED.
THE BELL
IF I DIDN'T KNOW ANY BETTER, I'D SWEAR I WAS IN A DIRECTOR'S BOX AT WEMBLEY. A CAST OF THOUSANDS--THE BEST AND BRIGHTEST OF BRITISH LEGEND--ARE ALL MILLING AROUND THE LOCAL PUB.
LOOKS CAN BE DECEIVING, OF COURSE, BUT THIS PLACE HARDLY SEEMS LIKE THE REPOSITORY OF ALL HUMAN KNOWLEDGE.
OH, JACK! JACK! IS THIS YOUR MORTAL FRIEND?
HE IS, MAEWREN.
THEN A KISS FOR YOU, JOHN. AND WELCOME.

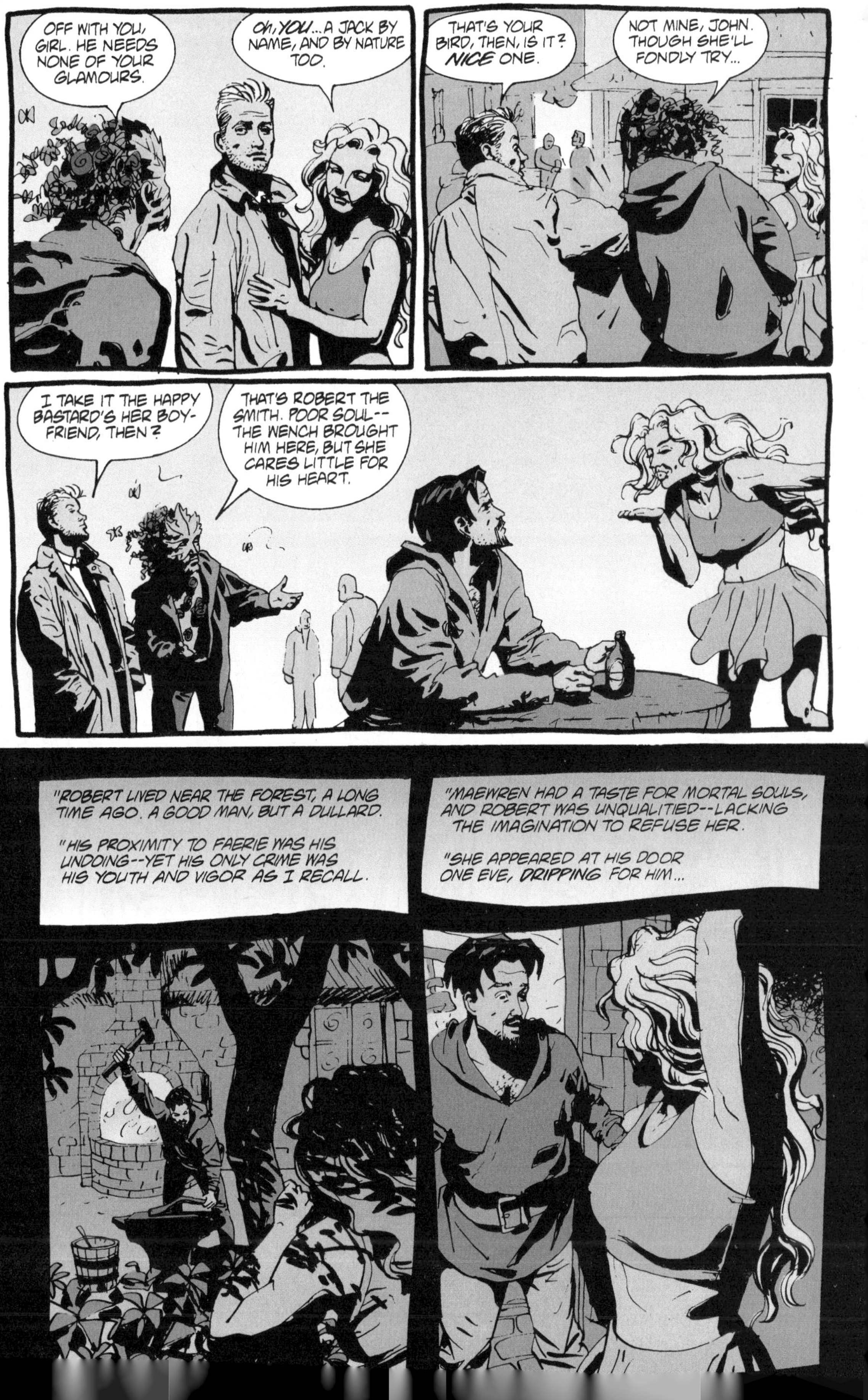
OFF WITH YOU, GIRL. HE NEEDS NONE OF YOUR GLAMOURS.
Oh, YOU... A JACK BY NAME, AND BY NATURE TOO.
THAT'S YOUR BIRD, THEN, IS IT? NICE ONE.
NOT MINE, JOHN. THOUGH SHE'LL FONDLY TRY...
I TAKE IT THE HAPPY BASTARD'S HER BOY-FRIEND, THEN?
THAT'S ROBERT THE SMITH. POOR SOUL-- THE WENCH BROUGHT HIM HERE, BUT SHE CARES LITTLE FOR HIS HEART.
"ROBERT LIVED NEAR THE FOREST, A LONG TIME AGO. A GOOD MAN, BUT A DULLARD.
"HIS PROXIMITY TO FAERIE WAS HIS UNDOING--YET HIS ONLY CRIME WAS HIS YOUTH AND VIGOR AS I RECALL.
"MAEWREN HAD A TASTE FOR MORTAL SOULS, AND ROBERT WAS UNQUALIFIED--LACKING THE IMAGINATION TO REFUSE HER.
"SHE APPEARED AT HIS DOOR ONE EVE, DRIPPING FOR HIM...

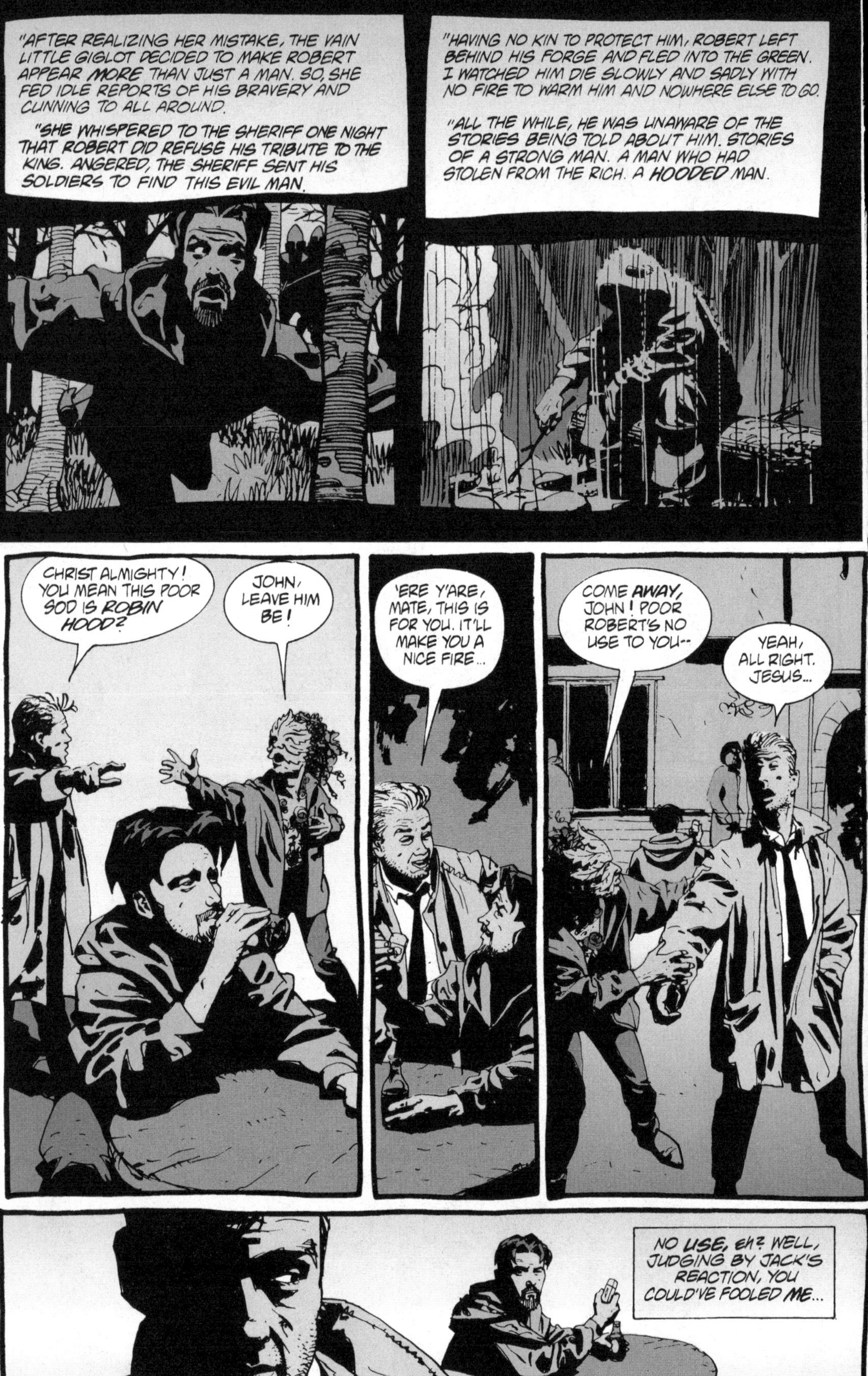
"AFTER REALIZING HER MISTAKE, THE VAIN LITTLE GIGLOT DECIDED TO MAKE ROBERT APPEAR MORE THAN JUST A MAN. SO, SHE FED IDLE REPORTS OF HIS BRAVERY AND CUNNING TO ALL AROUND.
"SHE WHISPERED TO THE SHERIFF ONE NIGHT THAT ROBERT DID REFUSE HIS TRIBUTE TO THE KING. ANGERED, THE SHERIFF SENT HIS SOLDIERS TO FIND THIS EVIL MAN.
"HAVING NO KIN TO PROTECT HIM, ROBERT LEFT BEHIND HIS FORGE AND FLED INTO THE GREEN. I WATCHED HIM DIE SLOWLY AND SADLY WITH NO FIRE TO WARM HIM AND NOWHERE ELSE TO GO.
"ALL THE WHILE, HE WAS UNAWARE OF THE STORIES BEING TOLD ABOUT HIM. STORIES OF A STRONG MAN. A MAN WHO HAD STOLEN FROM THE RICH. A HOODED MAN.
CHRIST ALMIGHTY! YOU MEAN THIS POOR SOD IS ROBIN HOOD?
JOHN, LEAVE HIM BE!
'ERE Y'ARE, MATE, THIS IS FOR YOU. IT'LL MAKE YOU A NICE FIRE...
COME AWAY, JOHN! POOR ROBERT'S NO USE TO YOU--
YEAH, ALL RIGHT. JESUS...
NO USE, EH? WELL, JUDGING BY JACK'S REACTION, YOU COULD'VE FOOLED ME...

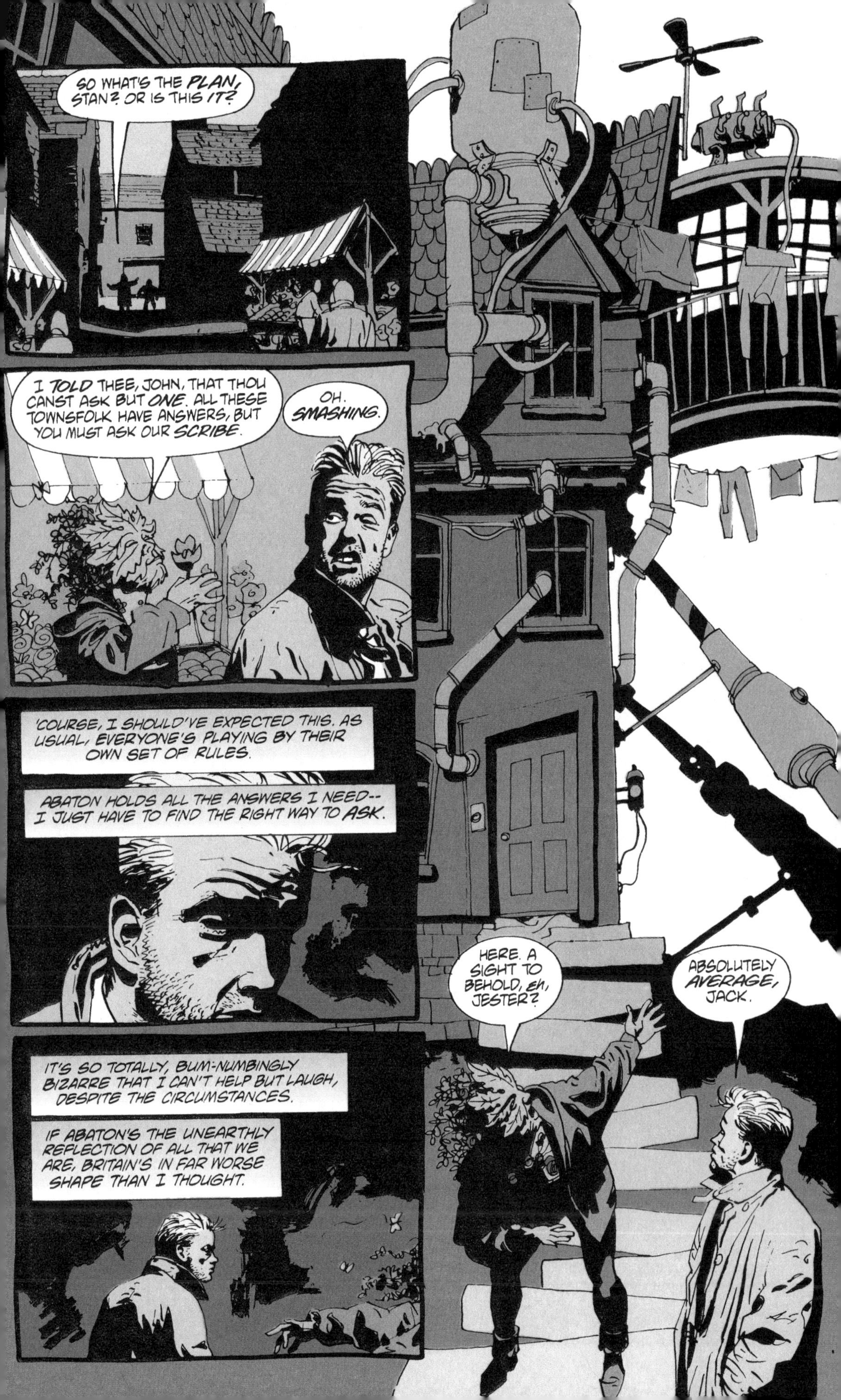
SO WHAT'S THE PLAN, STAN? OR IS THIS IT?
I TOLD THEE, JOHN, THAT THOU CANST ASK BUT ONE. ALL THESE TOWNSFOLK HAVE ANSWERS, BUT YOU MUST ASK OUR SCRIBE.
OH. SMASHING.
'COURSE, I SHOULD'VE EXPECTED THIS. AS USUAL, EVERYONE'S PLAYING BY THEIR OWN SET OF RULES.
ABATON HOLDS ALL THE ANSWERS I NEED-- I JUST HAVE TO FIND THE RIGHT WAY TO ASK.
IT'S SO TOTALLY, BUM-NUMBINGLY BIZARRE THAT I CAN'T HELP BUT LAUGH, DESPITE THE CIRCUMSTANCES.
IF ABATON'S THE UNEARTHLY REFLECTION OF ALL THAT WE ARE, BRITAIN'S IN FAR WORSE SHAPE THAN I THOUGHT.
HERE. A SIGHT TO BEHOLD, EH, JESTER?
ABSOLUTELY AVERAGE, JACK.

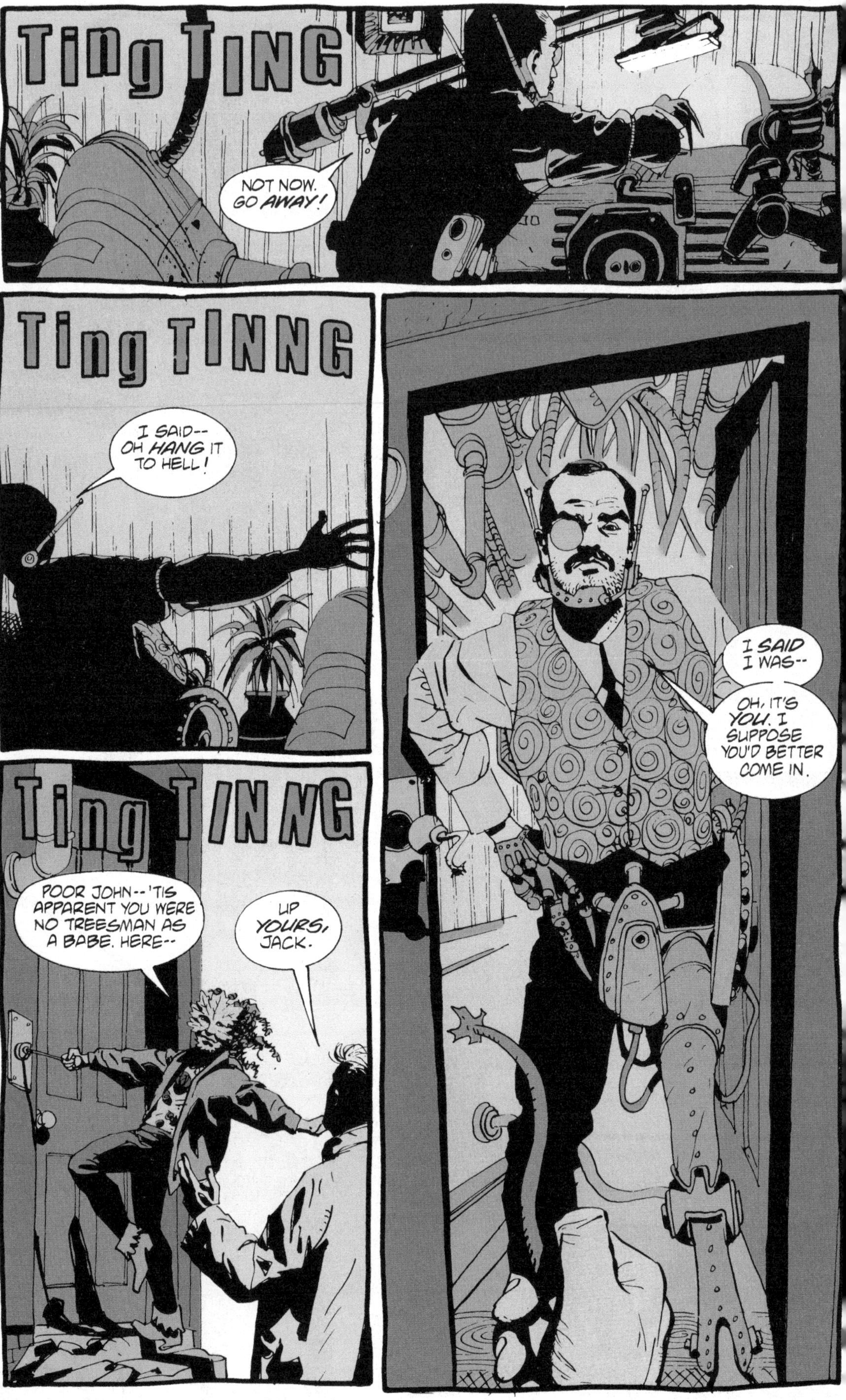
Ting TING
NOT NOW. GO AWAY!
Ting TINNG
I SAID-- OH HANG IT TO HELL!
Ting TINNG
POOR JOHN--'TIS APPARENT YOU WERE NO TREESMAN AS A BABE. HERE--
UP YOURS, JACK.
I SAID I WAS--
OH, IT'S YOU. I SUPPOSE YOU'D BETTER COME IN.

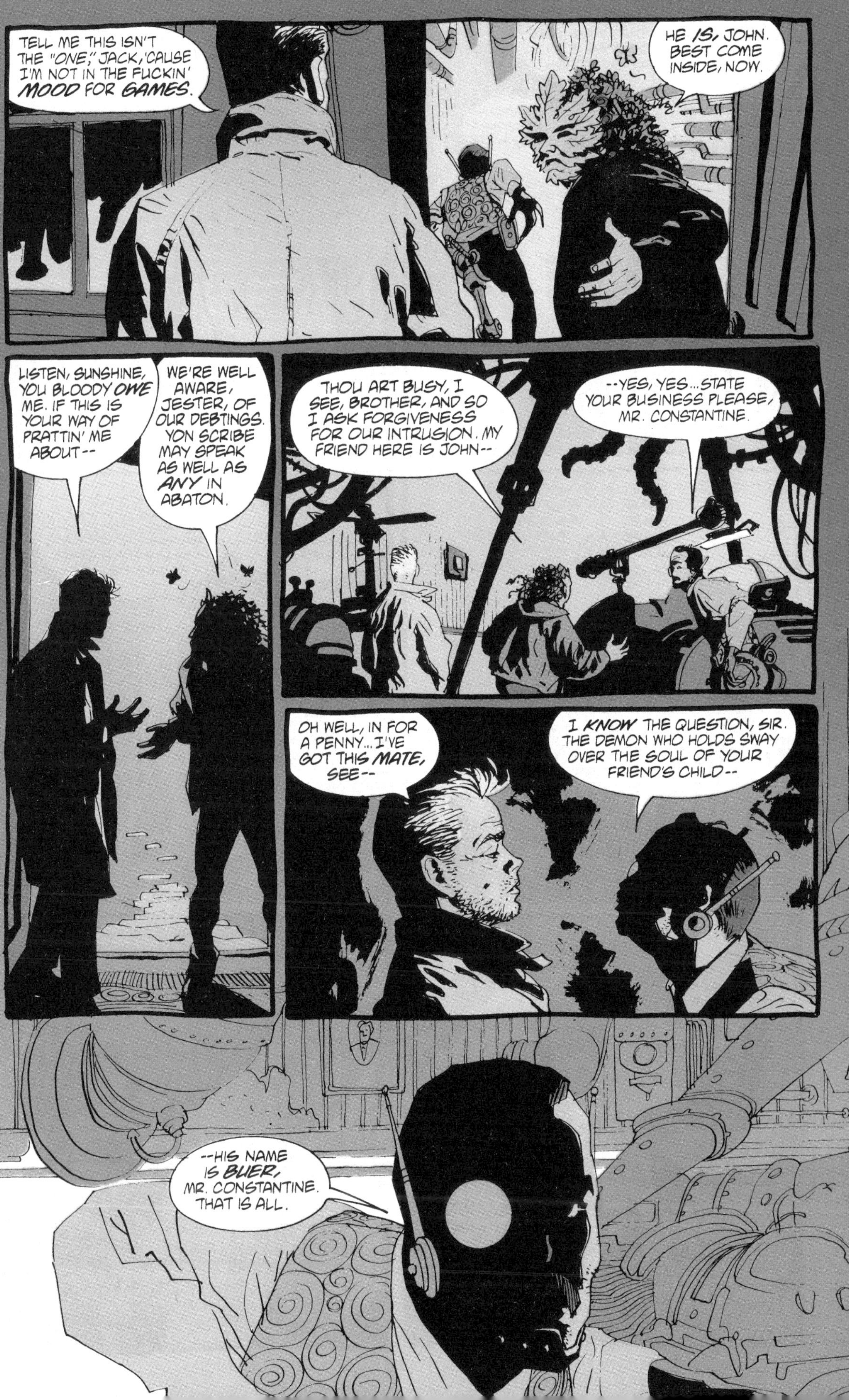
TELL ME THIS ISN'T THE "ONE," JACK, 'CAUSE I'M NOT IN THE FUCKIN' MOOD FOR GAMES.
HE IS, JOHN. BEST COME INSIDE, NOW.
LISTEN, SUNSHINE, YOU BLOODY OWE ME. IF THIS IS YOUR WAY OF PRATTIN' ME ABOUT--
WE'RE WELL AWARE, JESTER, OF OUR DEBTINGS. YON SCRIBE MAY SPEAK AS WELL AS ANY IN ABATON.
THOU ART BUSY, I SEE, BROTHER, AND SO I ASK FORGIVENESS FOR OUR INTRUSION. MY FRIEND HERE IS JOHN--
--YES, YES...STATE YOUR BUSINESS PLEASE, MR. CONSTANTINE.
OH WELL, IN FOR A PENNY...I'VE GOT THIS MATE, SEE--
I KNOW THE QUESTION, SIR. THE DEMON WHO HOLDS SWAY OVER THE SOUL OF YOUR FRIEND'S CHILD--
--HIS NAME IS BUER, MR. CONSTANTINE. THAT IS ALL.

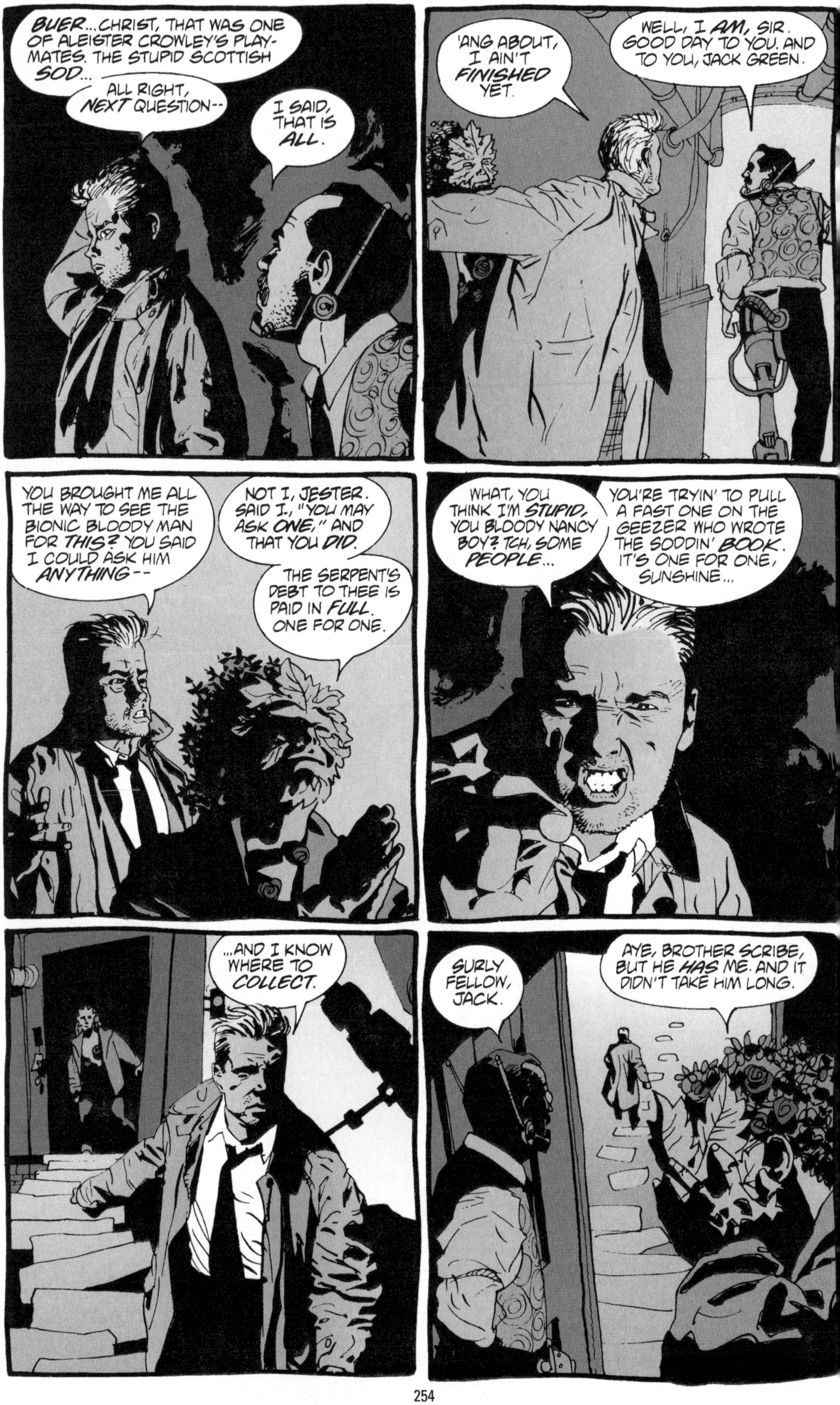
BUER... CHRIST, THAT WAS ONE OF ALEISTER CROWLEY'S PLAYMATES. THE STUPID SCOTTISH SOD...
ALL RIGHT, NEXT QUESTION--
I SAID, THAT IS ALL.
'ANG ABOUT, I AIN'T FINISHED YET.
WELL, I AM, SIR. GOOD DAY TO YOU. AND TO YOU, JACK GREEN.
YOU BROUGHT ME ALL THE WAY TO SEE THE BIONIC BLOODY MAN FOR THIS? YOU SAID I COULD ASK HIM ANYTHING--
NOT I, JESTER. SAID I, "YOU MAY ASK ONE," AND THAT YOU DID.
THE SERPENT'S DEBT TO THEE IS PAID IN FULL. ONE FOR ONE.
WHAT, YOU THINK I'M STUPID, YOU BLOODY NANCY BOY? TCH, SOME PEOPLE...
YOU'RE TRYIN' TO PULL A FAST ONE ON THE GEEZER WHO WROTE THE SODDIN' BOOK. IT'S ONE FOR ONE, SUNSHINE...
...AND I KNOW WHERE TO COLLECT.
SURLY FELLOW, JACK.
AYE, BROTHER SCRIBE, BUT HE HAS ME. AND IT DIDN'T TAKE HIM LONG.

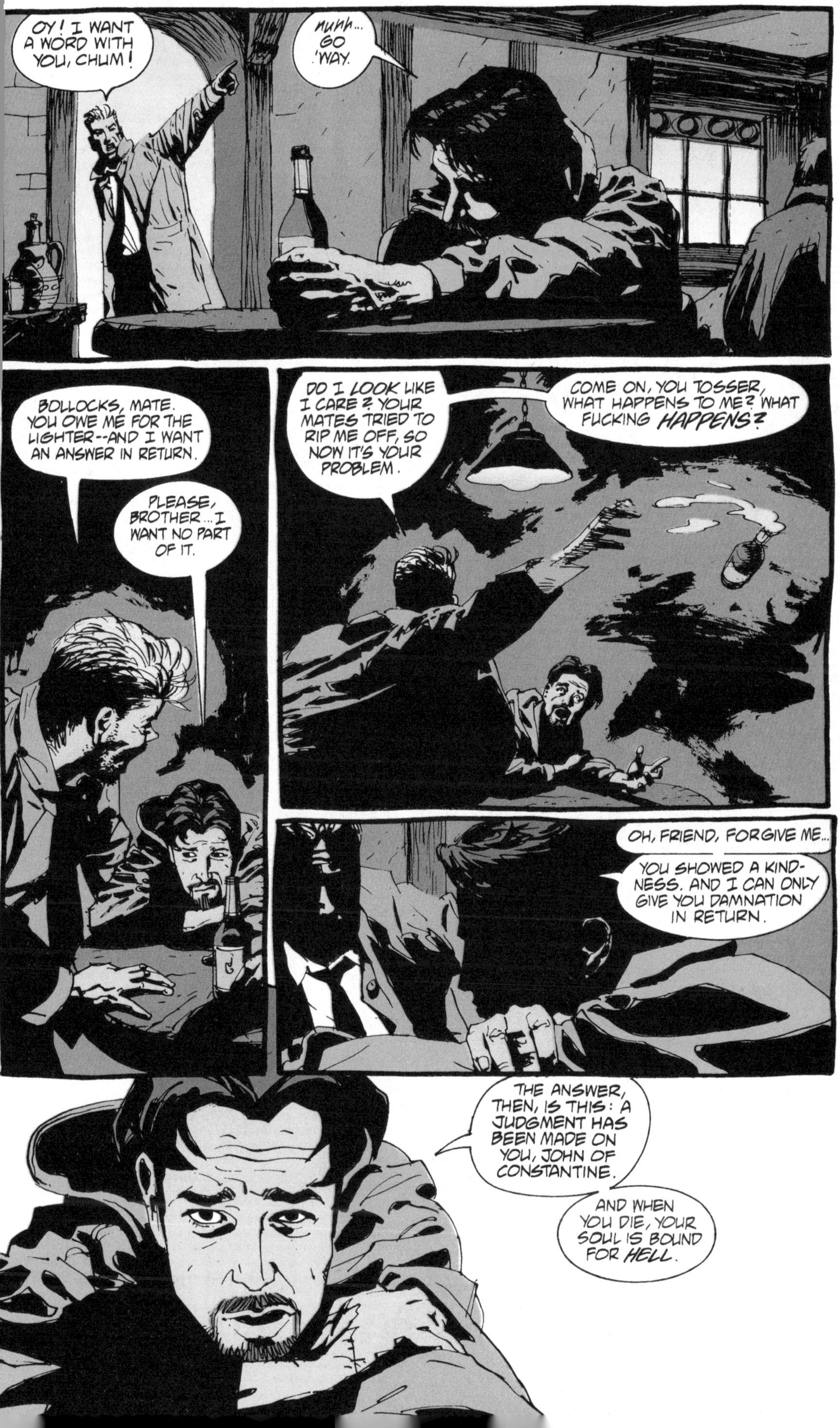

OY! I WANT A WORD WITH YOU, CHUM!
nuhh... GO 'WAY.
BOLLOCKS, MATE. YOU OWE ME FOR THE LIGHTER--AND I WANT AN ANSWER IN RETURN.
PLEASE, BROTHER... I WANT NO PART OF IT.
DO I LOOK LIKE I CARE? YOUR MATES TRIED TO RIP ME OFF, SO NOW IT'S YOUR PROBLEM.
COME ON, YOU TOSSER, WHAT HAPPENS TO ME? WHAT FUCKING HAPPENS?
OH, FRIEND, FORGIVE ME...
YOU SHOWED A KINDNESS. AND I CAN ONLY GIVE YOU DAMNATION IN RETURN.
THE ANSWER, THEN, IS THIS: A JUDGMENT HAS BEEN MADE ON YOU, JOHN OF CONSTANTINE.
AND WHEN YOU DIE, YOUR SOUL IS BOUND FOR HELL.

JOHN CONSTANTINE™
HELLBLAZER™
DC
VERTIGO
NO. 94
OCT 95
$2.25 US
$3.25 CAN
£1.50 UK
SUGGESTED FOR MATURE READERS
PAUL JENKINS
SEAN PHILLIPS
PAT McEOWN
CRITICAL MASS
PART THREE OF FIVE

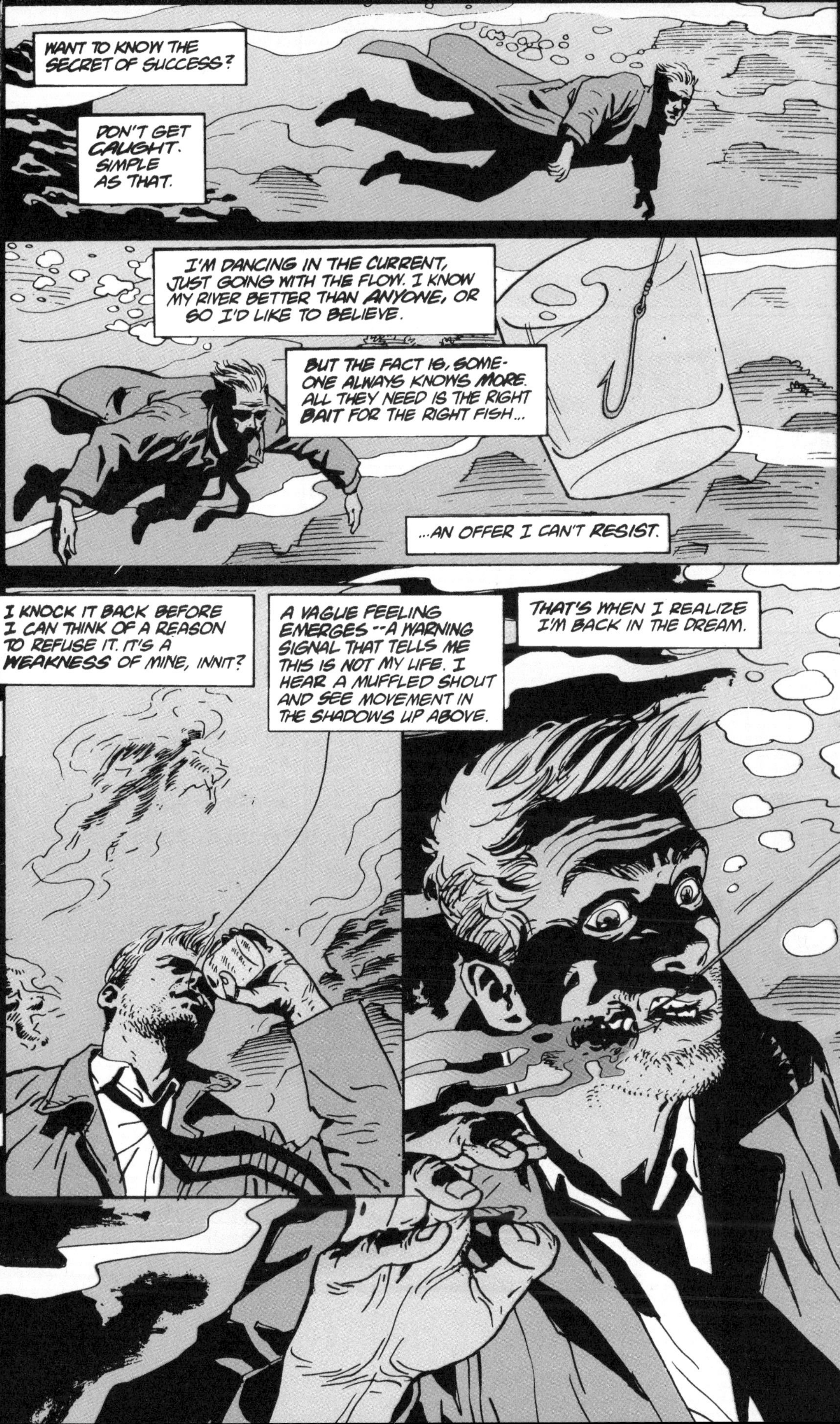
WANT TO KNOW THE SECRET OF SUCCESS?
DON'T GET CAUGHT. SIMPLE AS THAT.
I'M DANCING IN THE CURRENT, JUST GOING WITH THE FLOW. I KNOW MY RIVER BETTER THAN ANYONE, OR SO I'D LIKE TO BELIEVE.
BUT THE FACT IS, SOME-ONE ALWAYS KNOWS MORE. ALL THEY NEED IS THE RIGHT BAIT FOR THE RIGHT FISH...
...AN OFFER I CAN'T RESIST.
I KNOCK IT BACK BEFORE I CAN THINK OF A REASON TO REFUSE IT. IT'S A WEAKNESS OF MINE, INNIT?
A VAGUE FEELING EMERGES--A WARNING SIGNAL THAT TELLS ME THIS IS NOT MY LIFE. I HEAR A MUFFLED SHOUT AND SEE MOVEMENT IN THE SHADOWS UP ABOVE.
THAT'S WHEN I REALIZE I'M BACK IN THE DREAM.

THERE'S A CRY FROM SOMEWHERE OFF IN THE DISTANCE: "FISH ON THE LINE!"
AT FIRST, I'M UNABLE TO COMPREHEND A LIFE OUTSIDE THE WATER--BUT THE MEMORIES COME RUSHING BACK WHEN I BREAK THE SURFACE.

SUDDENLY, I KNOW WHERE I AM, AND I CAN'T BREATHE.

CRITICAL MASS 3

The Devil and the Deep Blue Sea

HHHKK. BLOODY HELLFIRE...

Paul Jenkins Writer

Pat McEown Pencils

Sean Phillips Inks

Matt Hollingsworth Colorist

Clem Robins Letterer

Axel Alonso Asst. Editor

Lou Stathis Editor

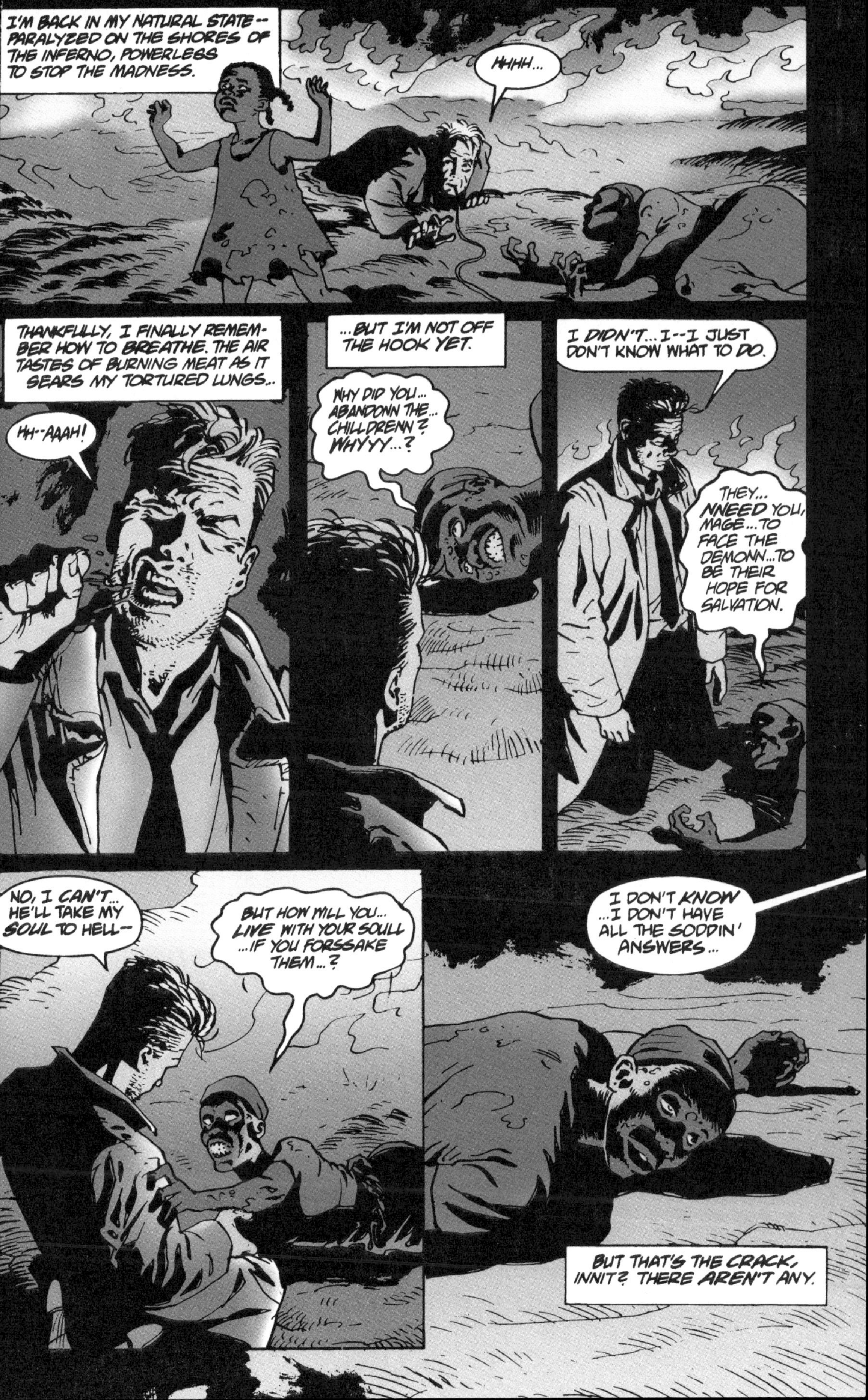
I'M BACK IN MY NATURAL STATE--PARALYZED ON THE SHORES OF THE INFERNO, POWERLESS TO STOP THE MADNESS.
HHHH...
THANKFULLY, I FINALLY REMEMBER HOW TO BREATHE. THE AIR TASTES OF BURNING MEAT AS IT SEARS MY TORTURED LUNGS...
HH--AAAH!
...BUT I'M NOT OFF THE HOOK YET.
WHY DID YOU... ABANDONN THE... CHILLDRENN? WHYYY...?
I DIDN'T... I--I JUST DON'T KNOW WHAT TO DO.
THEY... NNEED YOU, MAGE... TO FACE THE DEMONN... TO BE THEIR HOPE FOR SALVATION.
NO, I CAN'T... HE'LL TAKE MY SOUL TO HELL--
BUT HOW WILL YOU... LIVE WITH YOUR SOULL ...IF YOU FORSSAKE THEM...?
I DON'T KNOW ...I DON'T HAVE ALL THE SODDIN' ANSWERS...
BUT THAT'S THE CRACK, INNIT? THERE AREN'T ANY.

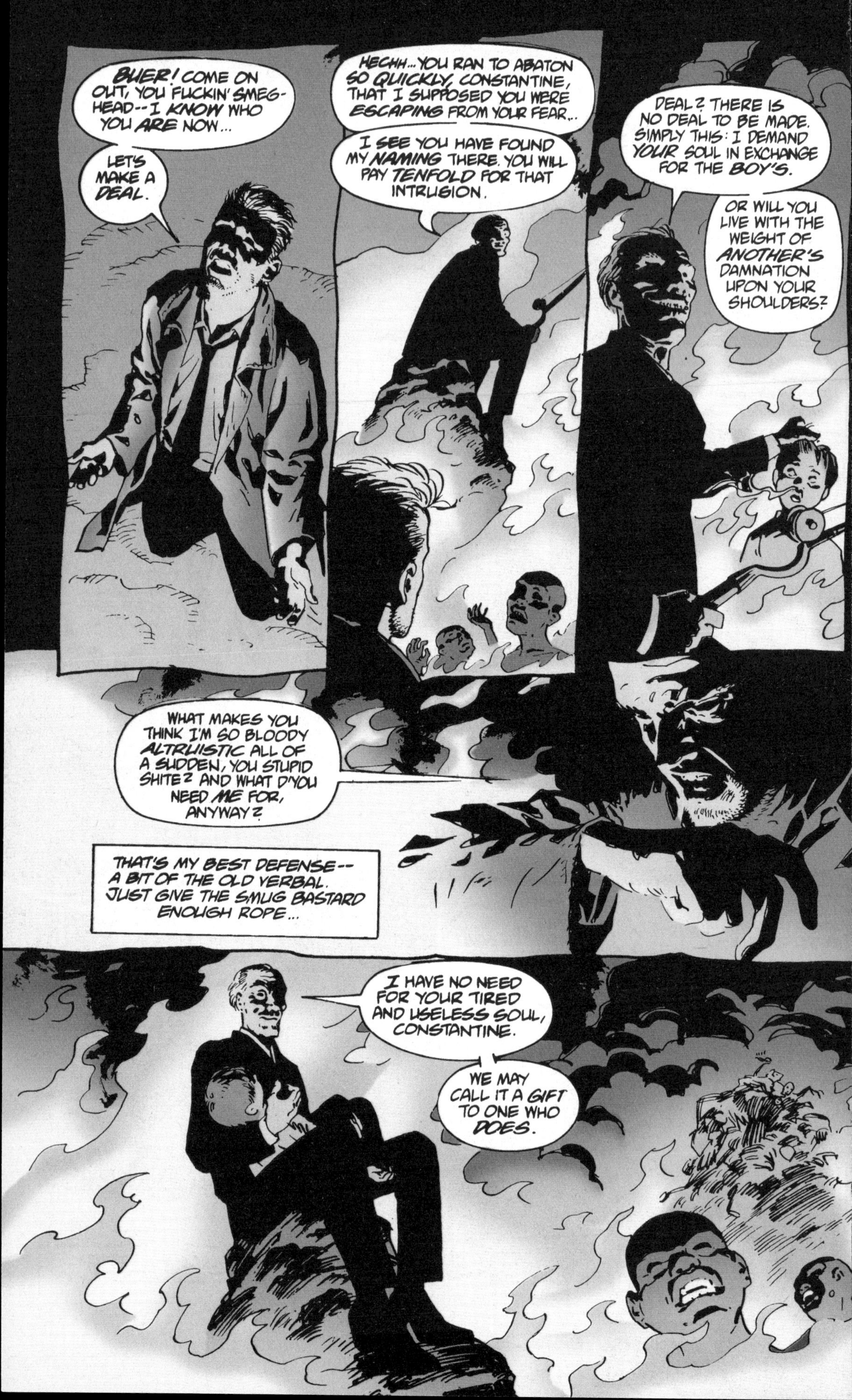
BUER! COME ON OUT, YOU FUCKIN' SMEG-HEAD--I KNOW WHO YOU ARE NOW...
LET'S MAKE A DEAL.
HECHH... YOU RAN TO ABATON SO QUICKLY, CONSTANTINE, THAT I SUPPOSED YOU WERE ESCAPING FROM YOUR FEAR...
I SEE YOU HAVE FOUND MY NAMING THERE. YOU WILL PAY TENFOLD FOR THAT INTRUSION.
DEAL? THERE IS NO DEAL TO BE MADE. SIMPLY THIS: I DEMAND YOUR SOUL IN EXCHANGE FOR THE BOY'S.
OR WILL YOU LIVE WITH THE WEIGHT OF ANOTHER'S DAMNATION UPON YOUR SHOULDERS?
WHAT MAKES YOU THINK I'M SO BLOODY ALTRUISTIC ALL OF A SUDDEN, YOU STUPID SHITE? AND WHAT D'YOU NEED ME FOR, ANYWAY?
THAT'S MY BEST DEFENSE-- A BIT OF THE OLD VERBAL. JUST GIVE THE SMUG BASTARD ENOUGH ROPE...
I HAVE NO NEED FOR YOUR TIRED AND USELESS SOUL, CONSTANTINE.
WE MAY CALL IT A GIFT TO ONE WHO DOES.

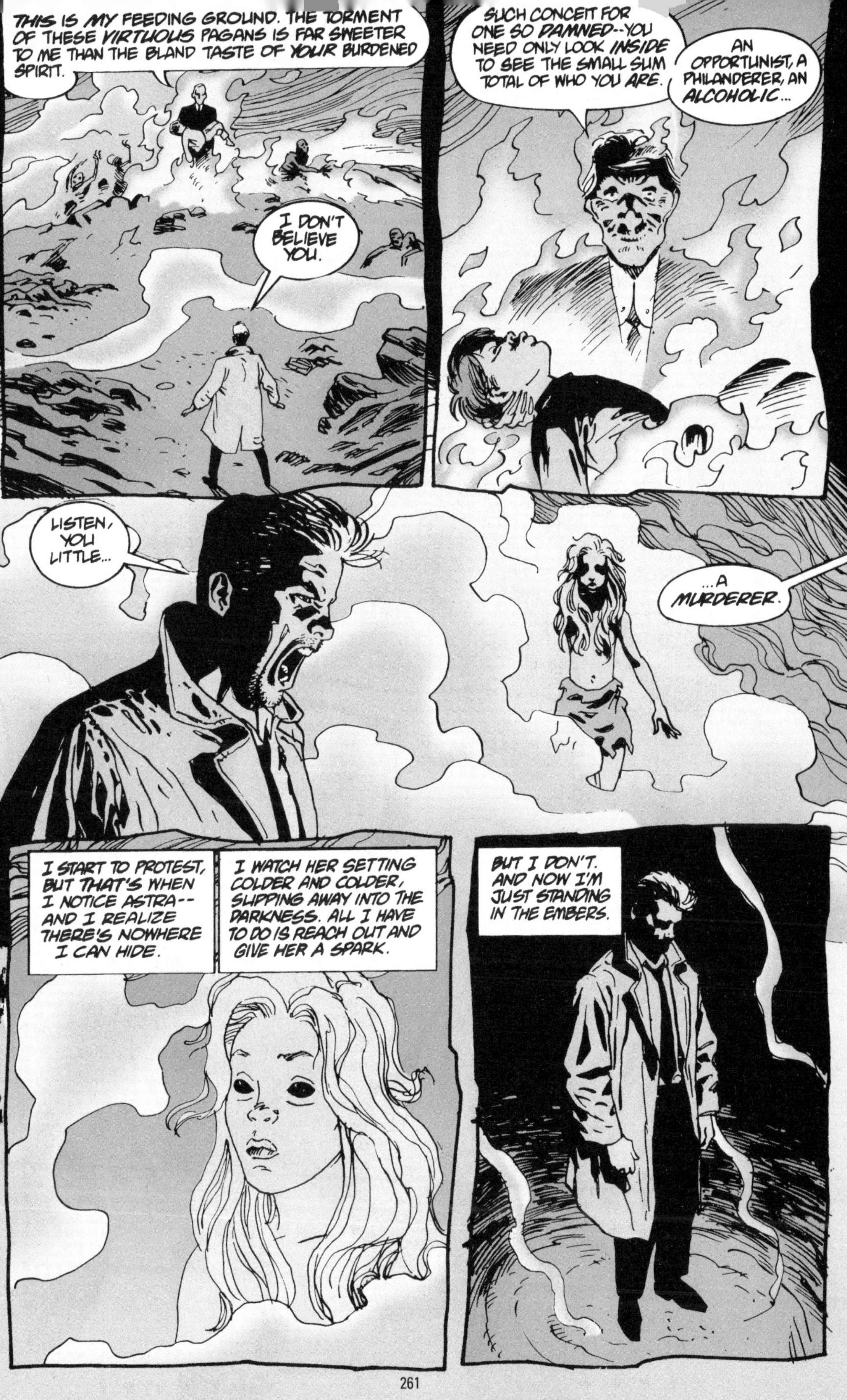

THIS IS MY FEEDING GROUND. THE TORMENT OF THESE VIRTUOUS PAGANS IS FAR SWEETER TO ME THAN THE BLAND TASTE OF YOUR BURDENED SPIRIT.
I DON'T BELIEVE YOU.
SUCH CONCEIT FOR ONE SO DAMNED--YOU NEED ONLY LOOK INSIDE TO SEE THE SMALL SUM TOTAL OF WHO YOU ARE.
AN OPPORTUNIST, A PHILANDERER, AN ALCOHOLIC...
LISTEN, YOU LITTLE...
...A MURDERER.
I START TO PROTEST, BUT THAT'S WHEN I NOTICE ASTRA-- AND I REALIZE THERE'S NOWHERE I CAN HIDE.
I WATCH HER SETTING COLDER AND COLDER, SLIPPING AWAY INTO THE DARKNESS. ALL I HAVE TO DO IS REACH OUT AND GIVE HER A SPARK.
BUT I DON'T. AND NOW I'M JUST STANDING IN THE EMBERS.

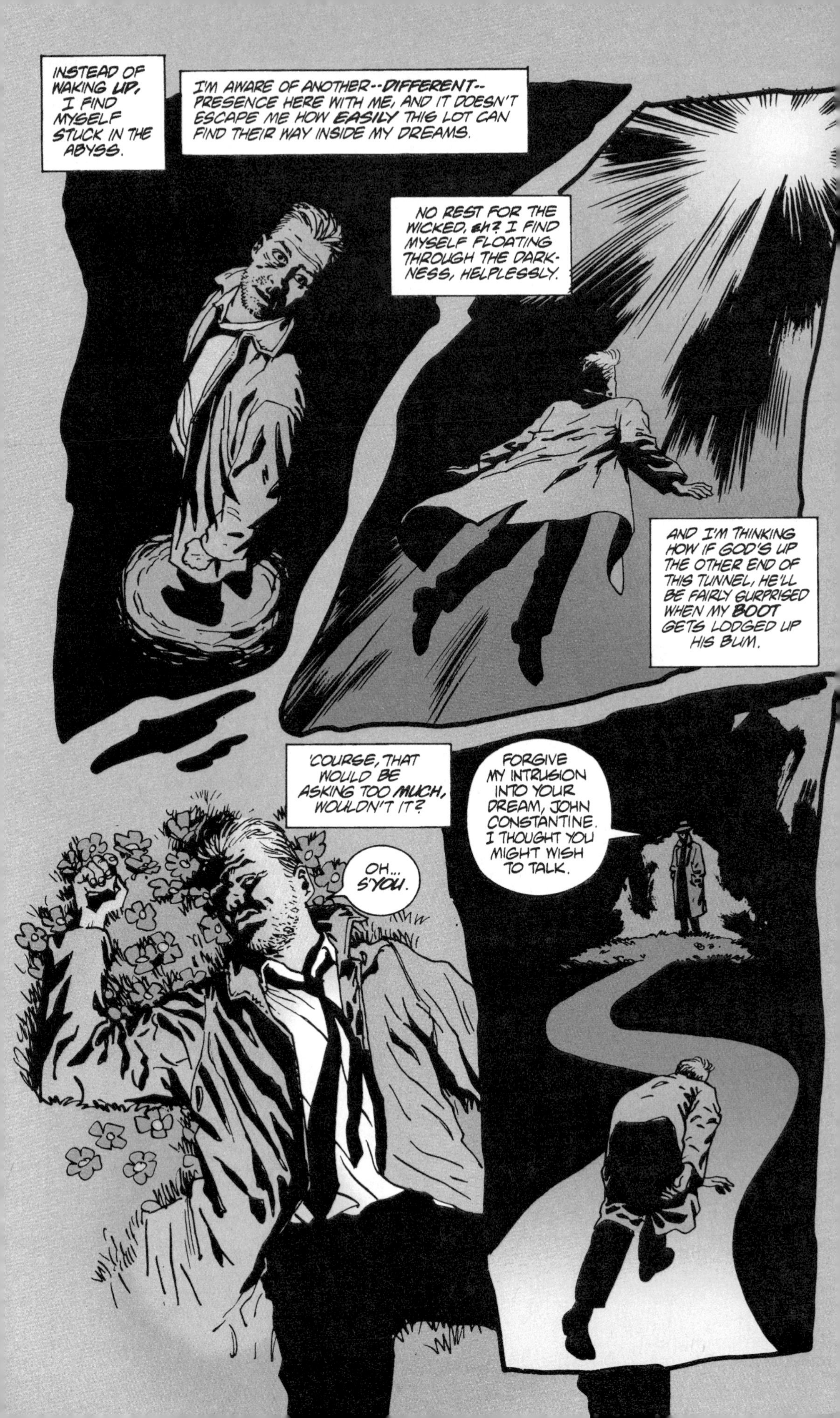
INSTEAD OF WAKING UP, I FIND MYSELF STUCK IN THE ABYSS.
I'M AWARE OF ANOTHER--DIFFERENT--PRESENCE HERE WITH ME, AND IT DOESN'T ESCAPE ME HOW EASILY THIS LOT CAN FIND THEIR WAY INSIDE MY DREAMS.
NO REST FOR THE WICKED, eh? I FIND MYSELF FLOATING THROUGH THE DARKNESS, HELPLESSLY.
AND I'M THINKING HOW IF GOD'S UP THE OTHER END OF THIS TUNNEL, HE'LL BE FAIRLY SURPRISED WHEN MY BOOT GETS LODGED UP HIS BUM.
'COURSE, THAT WOULD BE ASKING TOO MUCH, WOULDN'T IT?
OH... S'YOU.
FORGIVE MY INTRUSION INTO YOUR DREAM, JOHN CONSTANTINE. I THOUGHT YOU MIGHT WISH TO TALK.

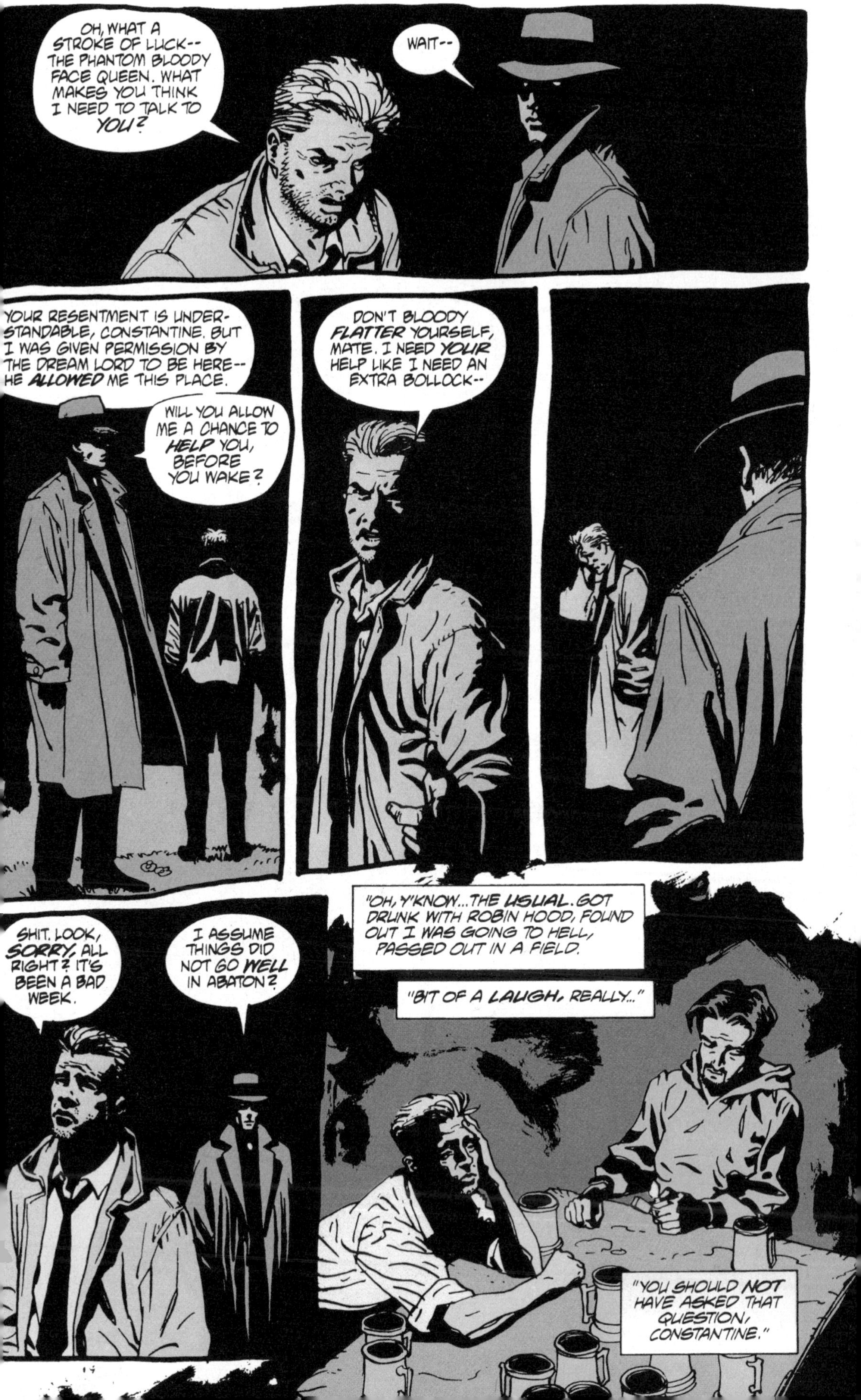
OH, WHAT A STROKE OF LUCK-- THE PHANTOM BLOODY FACE QUEEN. WHAT MAKES YOU THINK I NEED TO TALK TO YOU?
WAIT--
YOUR RESENTMENT IS UNDERSTANDABLE, CONSTANTINE. BUT I WAS GIVEN PERMISSION BY THE DREAM LORD TO BE HERE-- HE ALLOWED ME THIS PLACE.
WILL YOU ALLOW ME A CHANCE TO HELP YOU, BEFORE YOU WAKE?
DON'T BLOODY FLATTER YOURSELF, MATE. I NEED YOUR HELP LIKE I NEED AN EXTRA BOLLOCK--
SHIT. LOOK, SORRY, ALL RIGHT? IT'S BEEN A BAD WEEK.
I ASSUME THINGS DID NOT GO WELL IN ABATON?
"OH, Y'KNOW... THE USUAL. GOT DRUNK WITH ROBIN HOOD, FOUND OUT I WAS GOING TO HELL, PASSED OUT IN A FIELD.
"BIT OF A LAUGH, REALLY..."
"YOU SHOULD NOT HAVE ASKED THAT QUESTION, CONSTANTINE."

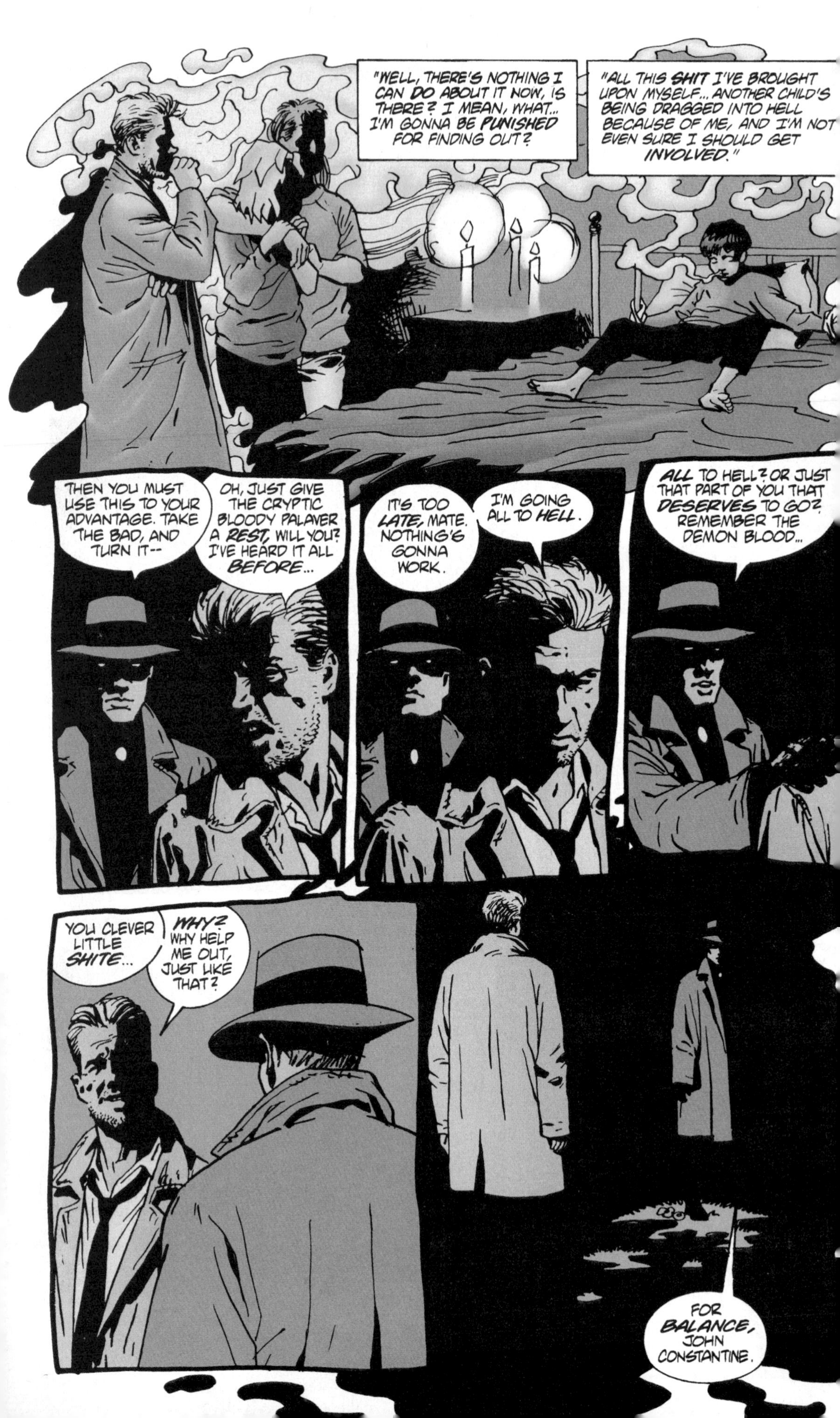
"WELL, THERE'S NOTHING I CAN DO ABOUT IT NOW, IS THERE? I MEAN, WHAT... I'M GONNA BE PUNISHED FOR FINDING OUT?
"ALL THIS SHIT I'VE BROUGHT UPON MYSELF... ANOTHER CHILD'S BEING DRAGGED INTO HELL BECAUSE OF ME, AND I'M NOT EVEN SURE I SHOULD GET INVOLVED."
THEN YOU MUST USE THIS TO YOUR ADVANTAGE. TAKE THE BAD, AND TURN IT--
OH, JUST GIVE THE CRYPTIC BLOODY PALAVER A REST, WILL YOU? I'VE HEARD IT ALL BEFORE...
IT'S TOO LATE, MATE. NOTHING'S GONNA WORK.
I'M GOING ALL TO HELL.
ALL TO HELL? OR JUST THAT PART OF YOU THAT DESERVES TO GO? REMEMBER THE DEMON BLOOD...
YOU CLEVER LITTLE SHITE...
WHY? WHY HELP ME OUT, JUST LIKE THAT?
FOR BALANCE, JOHN CONSTANTINE.

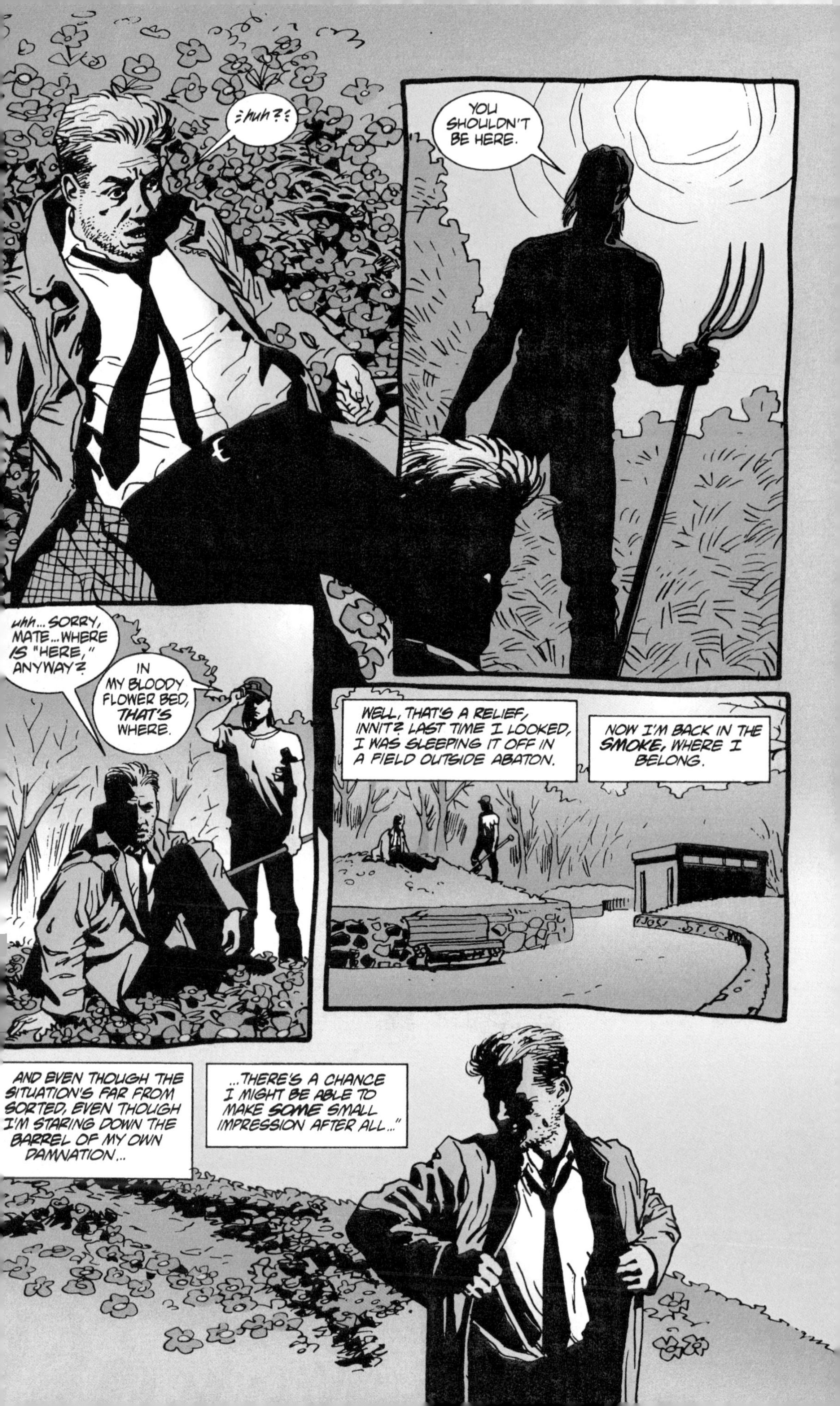

huh?
YOU SHOULDN'T BE HERE.
uhh... SORRY, MATE... WHERE IS "HERE," ANYWAY?
IN MY BLOODY FLOWER BED, THAT'S WHERE.
WELL, THAT'S A RELIEF, INNIT? LAST TIME I LOOKED, I WAS SLEEPING IT OFF IN A FIELD OUTSIDE ABATON.
NOW I'M BACK IN THE SMOKE, WHERE I BELONG.
AND EVEN THOUGH THE SITUATION'S FAR FROM SORTED, EVEN THOUGH I'M STARING DOWN THE BARREL OF MY OWN DAMNATION...
...THERE'S A CHANCE I MIGHT BE ABLE TO MAKE SOME SMALL IMPRESSION AFTER ALL..."

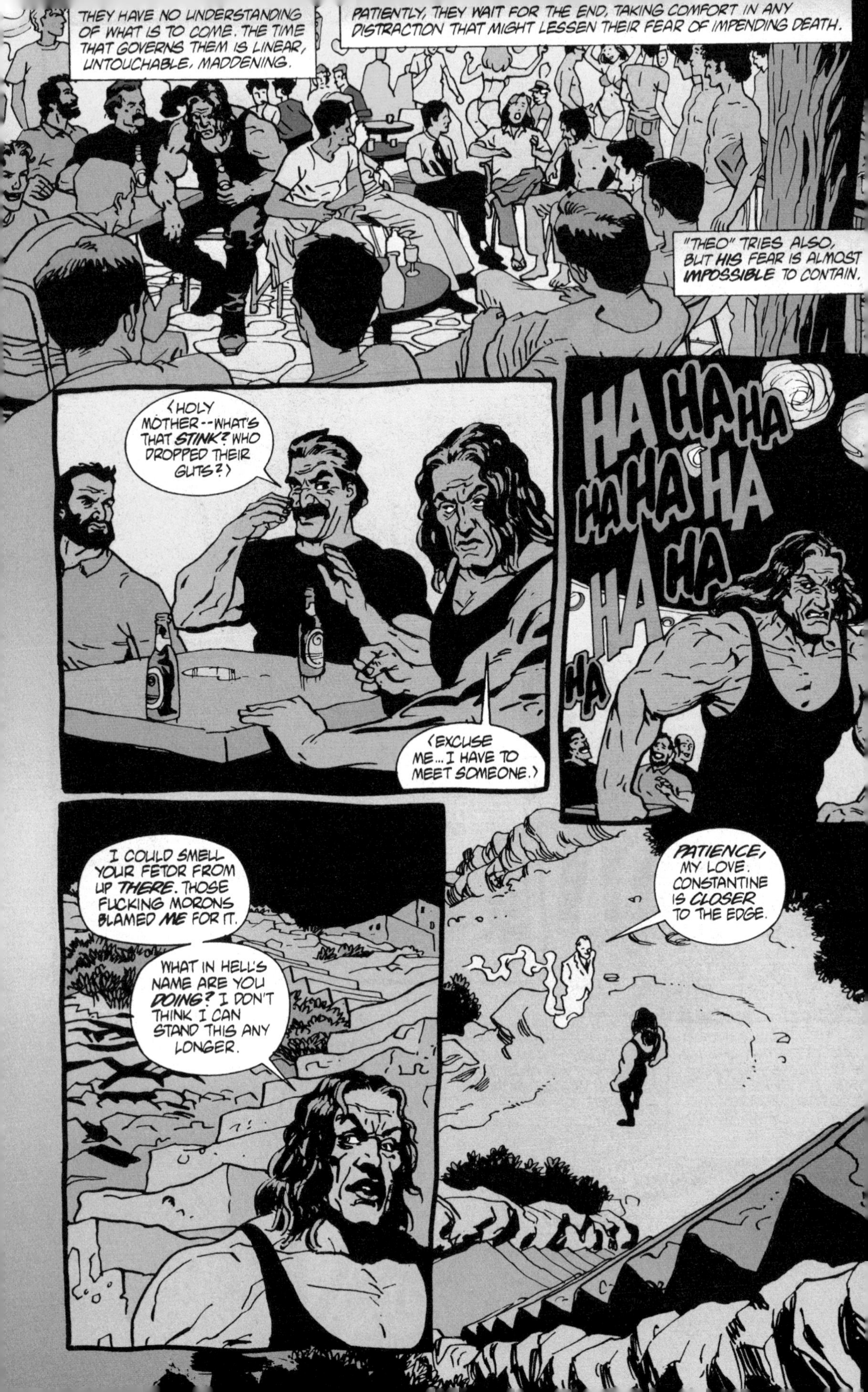
THEY HAVE NO UNDERSTANDING OF WHAT IS TO COME. THE TIME THAT GOVERNS THEM IS LINEAR, UNTOUCHABLE, MADDENING.
PATIENTLY, THEY WAIT FOR THE END, TAKING COMFORT IN ANY DISTRACTION THAT MIGHT LESSEN THEIR FEAR OF IMPENDING DEATH.
"THEO" TRIES ALSO, BUT HIS FEAR IS ALMOST IMPOSSIBLE TO CONTAIN.
‹HOLY MOTHER--WHAT'S THAT STINK? WHO DROPPED THEIR GUTS?›
‹EXCUSE ME... I HAVE TO MEET SOMEONE.›
HA HA HA HA HA HA HA HA HA HA
I COULD SMELL YOUR FETOR FROM UP THERE. THOSE FUCKING MORONS BLAMED ME FOR IT.
WHAT IN HELL'S NAME ARE YOU DOING? I DON'T THINK I CAN STAND THIS ANY LONGER.
PATIENCE, MY LOVE. CONSTANTINE IS CLOSER TO THE EDGE.

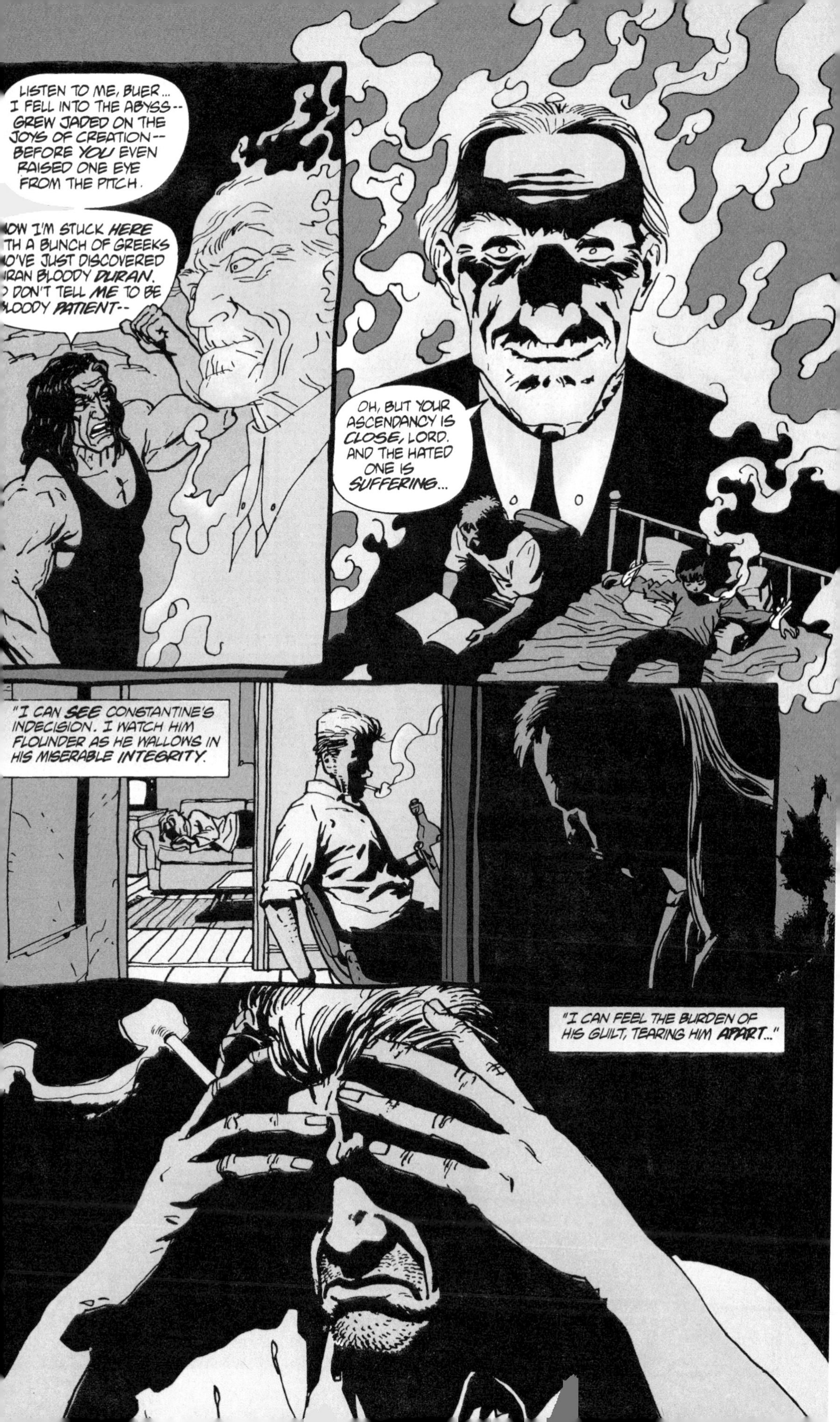
LISTEN TO ME, BUER... I FELL INTO THE ABYSS-- GREW JADED ON THE JOYS OF CREATION-- BEFORE YOU EVEN RAISED ONE EYE FROM THE PITCH.
OW I'M STUCK HERE TH A BUNCH OF GREEKS O'VE JUST DISCOVERED IRAN BLOODY DURAN. DON'T TELL ME TO BE LOODY PATIENT--
OH, BUT YOUR ASCENDANCY IS CLOSE, LORD. AND THE HATED ONE IS SUFFERING...
"I CAN SEE CONSTANTINE'S INDECISION. I WATCH HIM FLOUNDER AS HE WALLOWS IN HIS MISERABLE INTEGRITY.
"I CAN FEEL THE BURDEN OF HIS GUILT, TEARING HIM APART..."

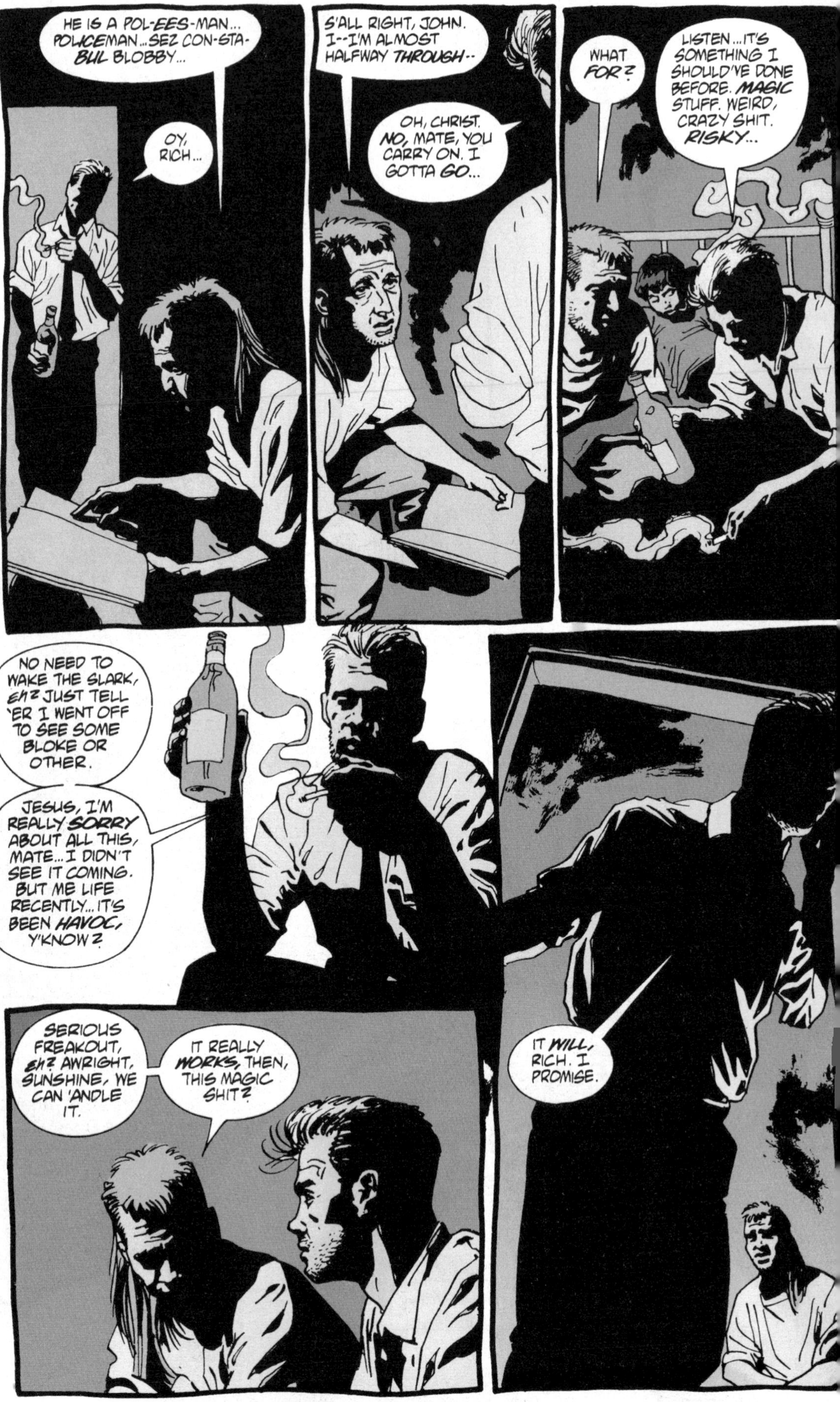
HE IS A POL-EES-MAN... POLICEMAN...SEZ CON-STA-BUL BLOBBY...
OY, RICH...
S'ALL RIGHT, JOHN. I--I'M ALMOST HALFWAY THROUGH..
OH, CHRIST. NO, MATE, YOU CARRY ON. I GOTTA GO...
WHAT FOR?
LISTEN...IT'S SOMETHING I SHOULD'VE DONE BEFORE. MAGIC STUFF. WEIRD, CRAZY SHIT. RISKY...
NO NEED TO WAKE THE SLARK, EH? JUST TELL 'ER I WENT OFF TO SEE SOME BLOKE OR OTHER.
JESUS, I'M REALLY SORRY ABOUT ALL THIS, MATE... I DIDN'T SEE IT COMING. BUT ME LIFE RECENTLY... IT'S BEEN HAVOC, Y'KNOW?
SERIOUS FREAKOUT, EH? AWRIGHT, SUNSHINE, WE CAN 'ANDLE IT.
IT REALLY WORKS, THEN, THIS MAGIC SHIT?
IT WILL, RICH. I PROMISE.

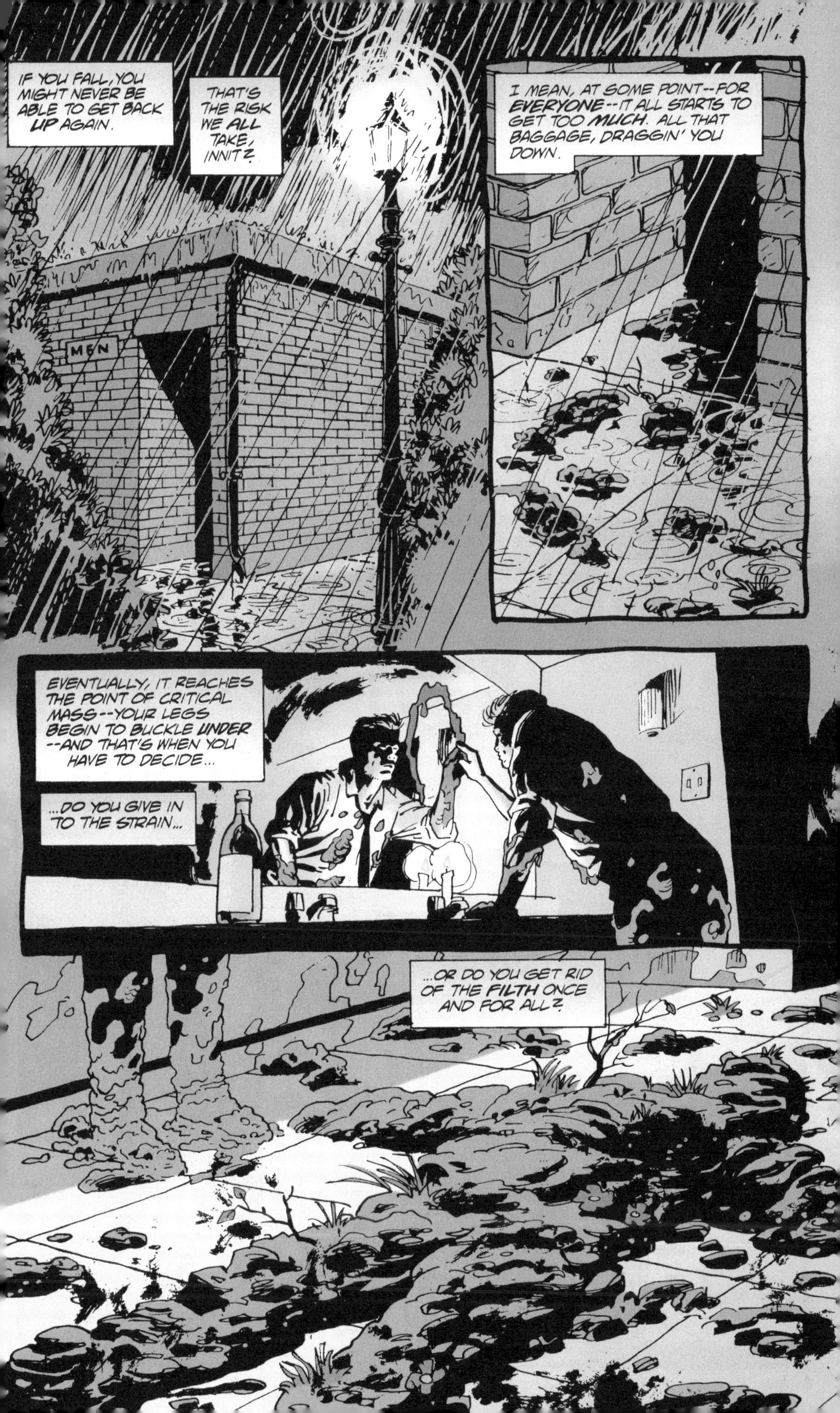
IF YOU FALL, YOU MIGHT NEVER BE ABLE TO GET BACK UP AGAIN.
THAT'S THE RISK WE ALL TAKE, INNIT?
MEN
I MEAN, AT SOME POINT--FOR EVERYONE--IT ALL STARTS TO GET TOO MUCH. ALL THAT BAGGAGE, DRAGGIN' YOU DOWN.
EVENTUALLY, IT REACHES THE POINT OF CRITICAL MASS--YOUR LEGS BEGIN TO BUCKLE UNDER--AND THAT'S WHEN YOU HAVE TO DECIDE...
...DO YOU GIVE IN TO THE STRAIN...
...OR DO YOU GET RID OF THE FILTH ONCE AND FOR ALL?

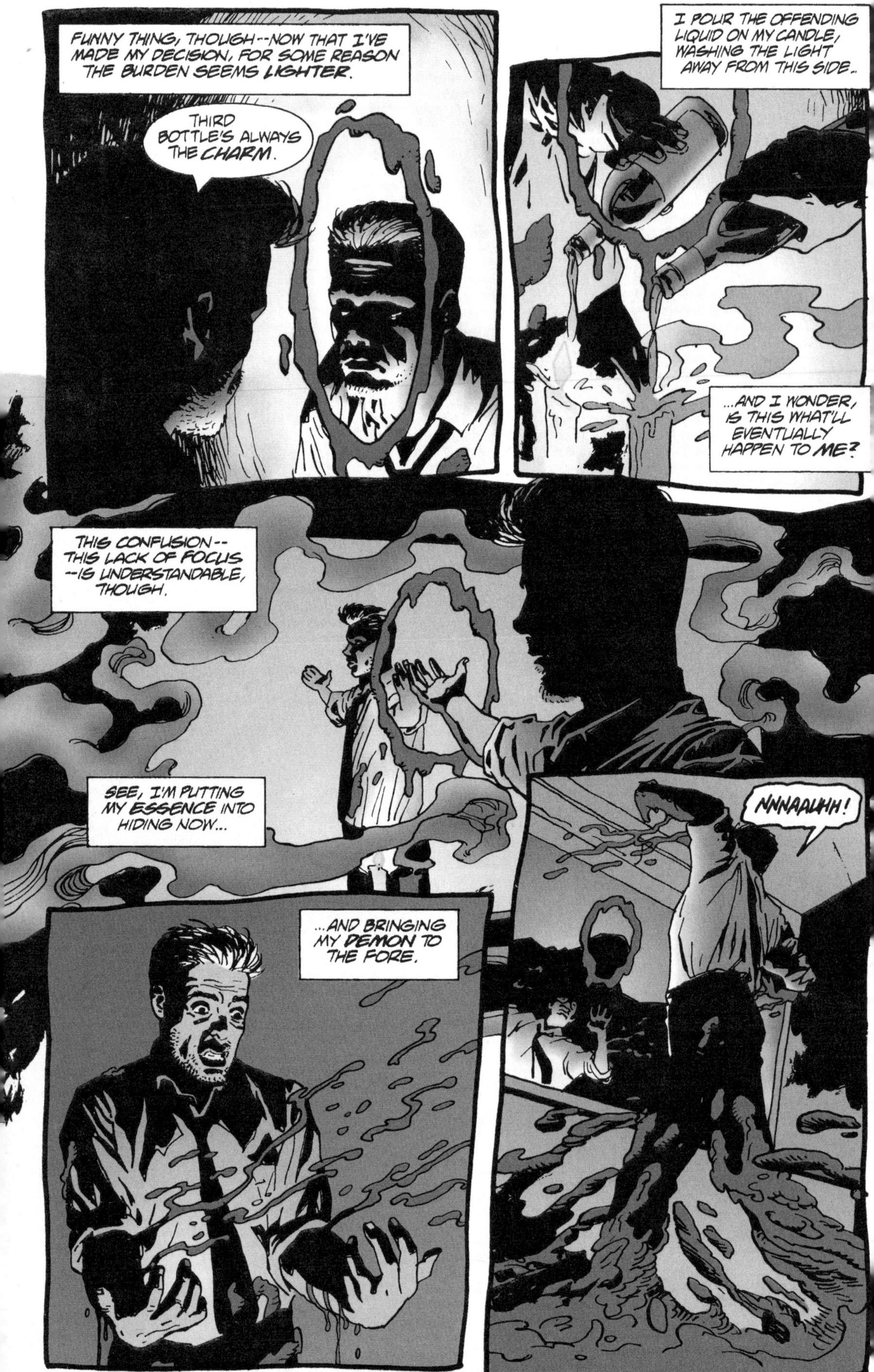

FUNNY THING, THOUGH--NOW THAT I'VE MADE MY DECISION, FOR SOME REASON THE BURDEN SEEMS LIGHTER.
THIRD BOTTLE'S ALWAYS THE CHARM.
I POUR THE OFFENDING LIQUID ON MY CANDLE, WASHING THE LIGHT AWAY FROM THIS SIDE..
...AND I WONDER, IS THIS WHAT'LL EVENTUALLY HAPPEN TO ME?
THIS CONFUSION-- THIS LACK OF FOCUS --IS UNDERSTANDABLE, THOUGH.
SEE, I'M PUTTING MY ESSENCE INTO HIDING NOW...
...AND BRINGING MY DEMON TO THE FORE.
NNNAAUHH!

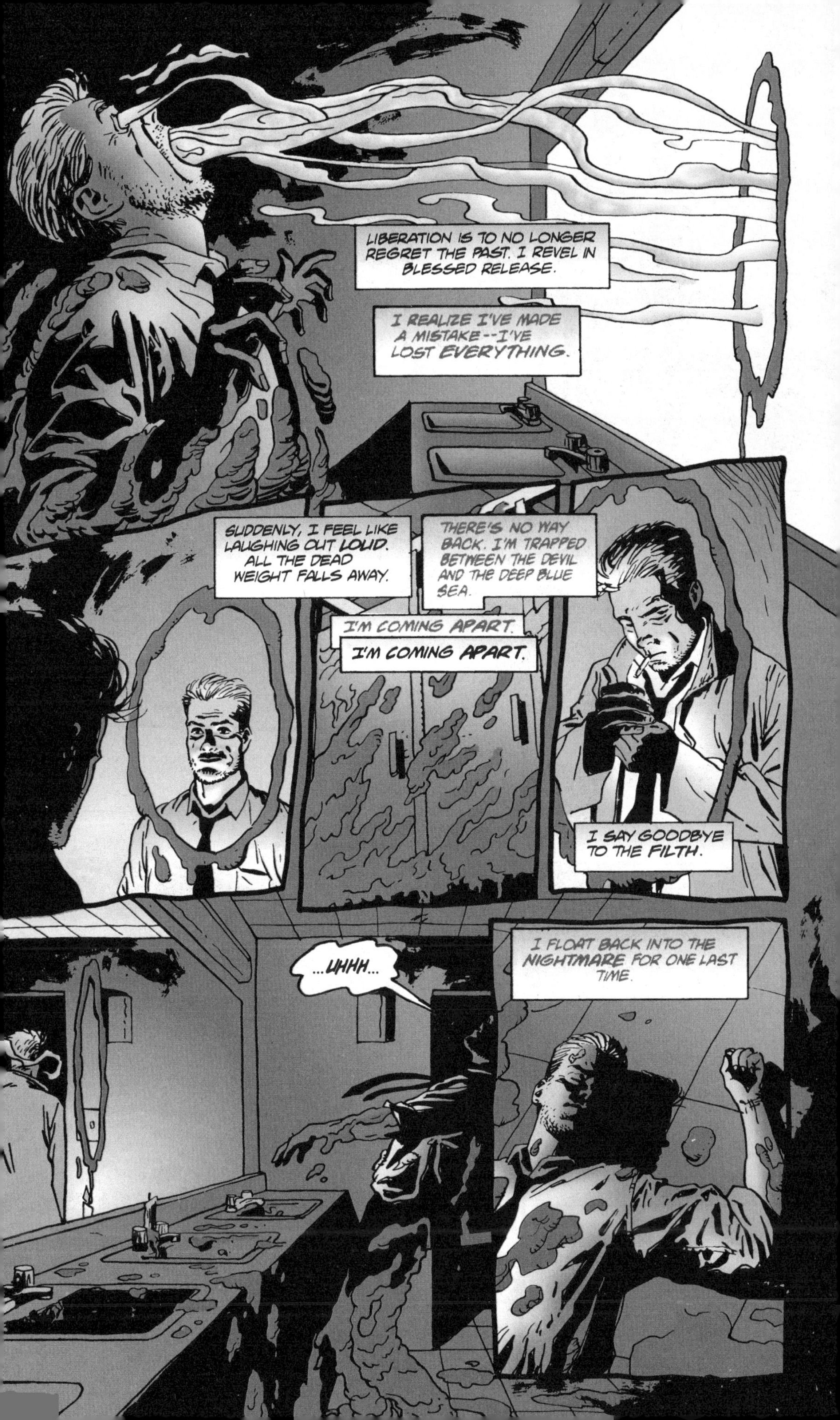
LIBERATION IS TO NO LONGER REGRET THE PAST. I REVEL IN BLESSED RELEASE.
I REALIZE I'VE MADE A MISTAKE--I'VE LOST EVERYTHING.
SUDDENLY, I FEEL LIKE LAUGHING OUT LOUD. ALL THE DEAD WEIGHT FALLS AWAY.
THERE'S NO WAY BACK. I'M TRAPPED BETWEEN THE DEVIL AND THE DEEP BLUE SEA.
I'M COMING APART.
I'M COMING APART.
I SAY GOODBYE TO THE FILTH.
...UHHH...
I FLOAT BACK INTO THE NIGHTMARE FOR ONE LAST TIME.

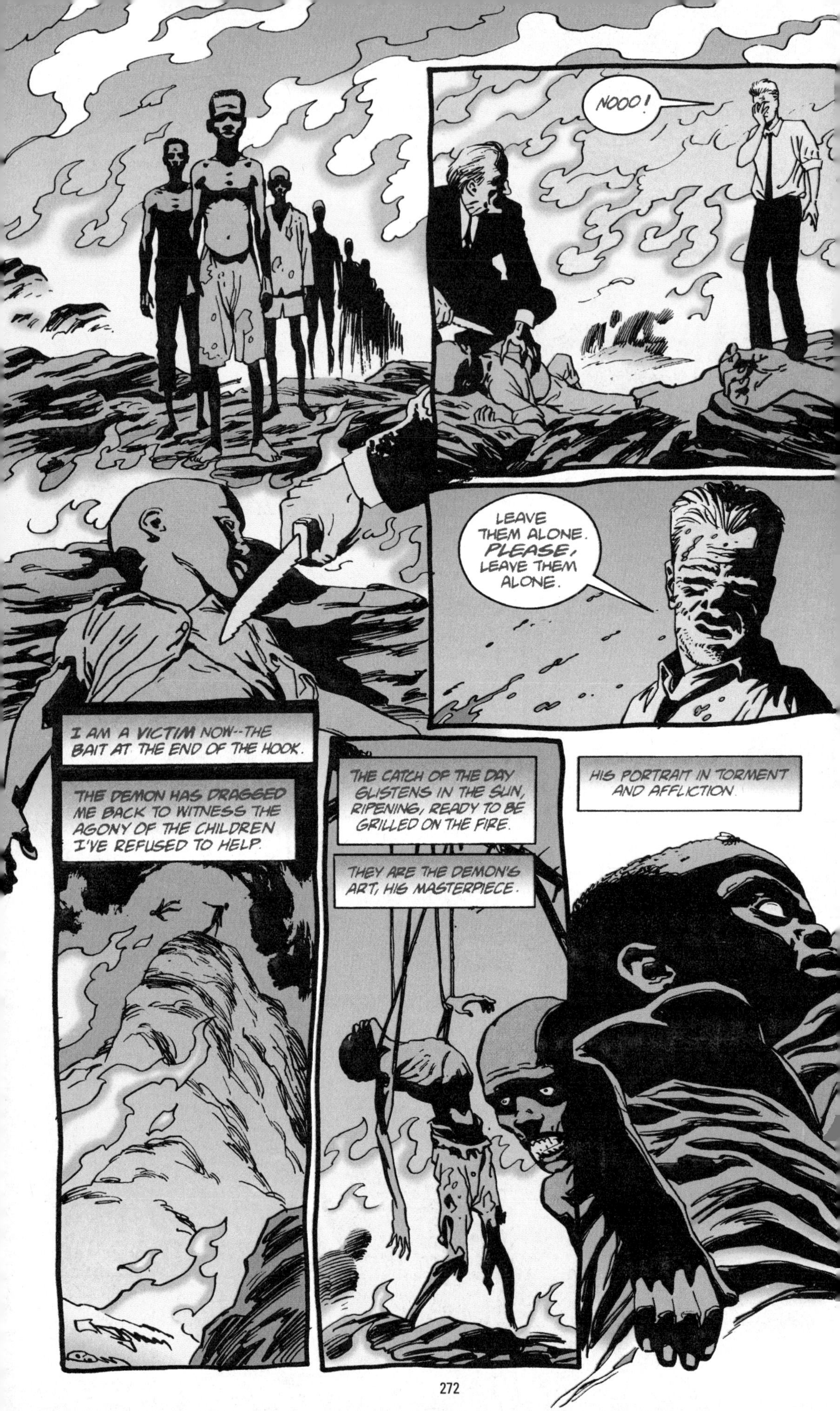
NOOO!
LEAVE THEM ALONE. PLEASE, LEAVE THEM ALONE.
I AM A VICTIM NOW--THE BAIT AT THE END OF THE HOOK.
THE DEMON HAS DRAGGED ME BACK TO WITNESS THE AGONY OF THE CHILDREN I'VE REFUSED TO HELP.
THE CATCH OF THE DAY GLISTENS IN THE SUN, RIPENING, READY TO BE GRILLED ON THE FIRE.
THEY ARE THE DEMON'S ART, HIS MASTERPIECE.
HIS PORTRAIT IN TORMENT AND AFFLICTION.

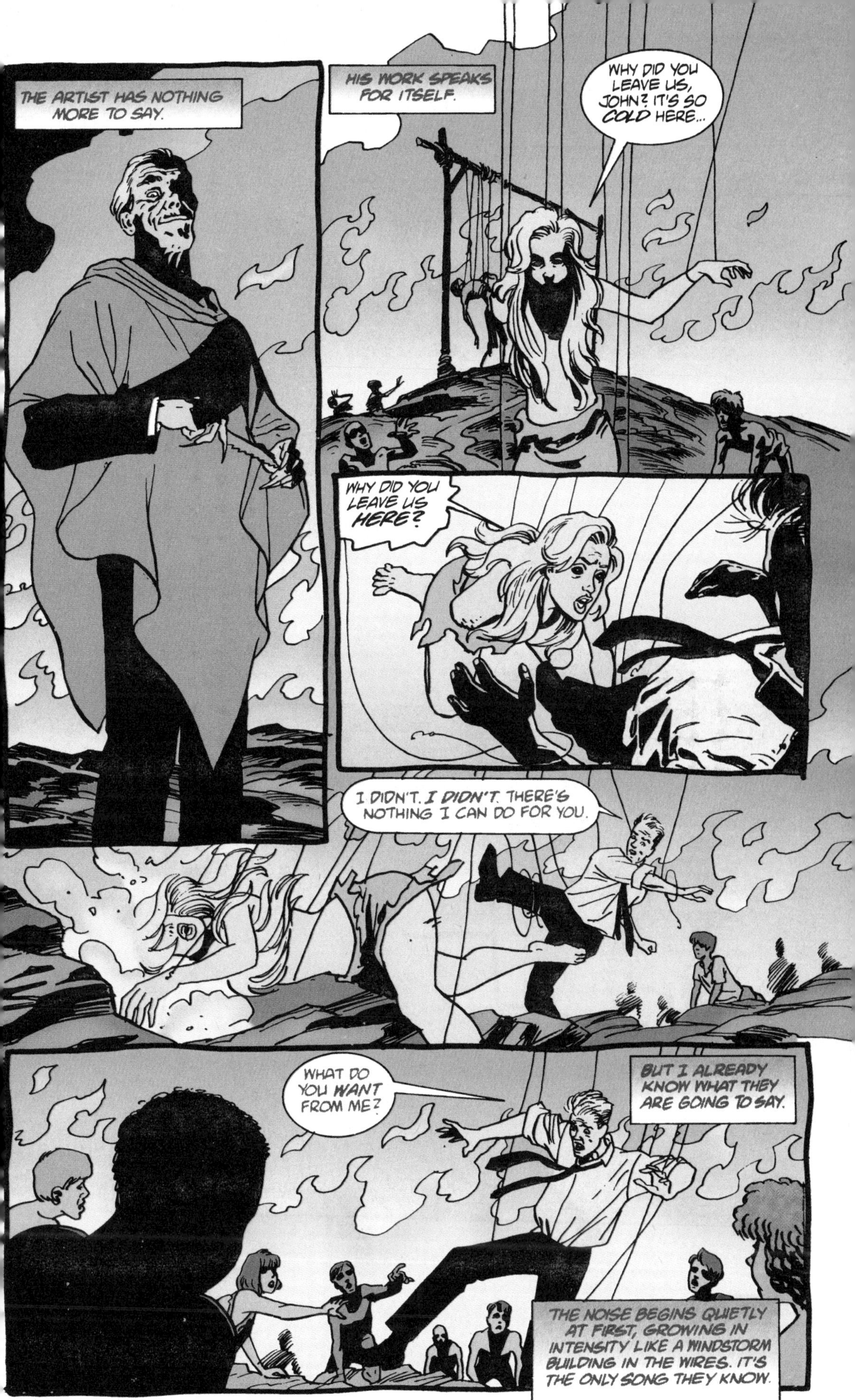
THE ARTIST HAS NOTHING MORE TO SAY.
HIS WORK SPEAKS FOR ITSELF.
WHY DID YOU LEAVE US, JOHN? IT'S SO COLD HERE...
WHY DID YOU LEAVE US HERE?
I DIDN'T. I DIDN'T. THERE'S NOTHING I CAN DO FOR YOU.
WHAT DO YOU WANT FROM ME?
BUT I ALREADY KNOW WHAT THEY ARE GOING TO SAY.
THE NOISE BEGINS QUIETLY AT FIRST, GROWING IN INTENSITY LIKE A WINDSTORM BUILDING IN THE WIRES. IT'S THE ONLY SONG THEY KNOW.

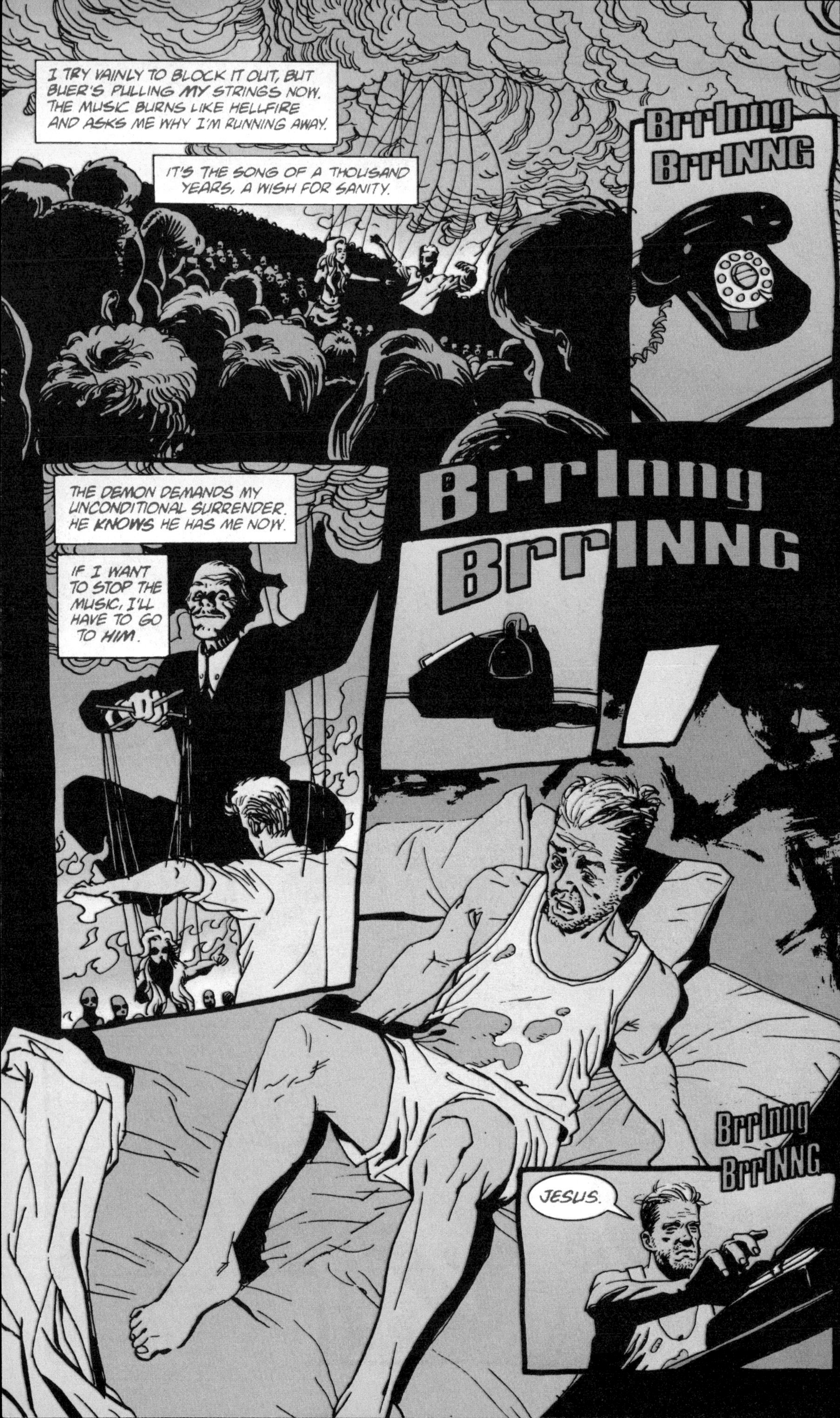
I TRY VAINLY TO BLOCK IT OUT, BUT BUER'S PULLING MY STRINGS NOW. THE MUSIC BURNS LIKE HELLFIRE AND ASKS ME WHY I'M RUNNING AWAY.
IT'S THE SONG OF A THOUSAND YEARS, A WISH FOR SANITY.
BrrInng BrrINNG
THE DEMON DEMANDS MY UNCONDITIONAL SURRENDER. HE KNOWS HE HAS ME NOW.
IF I WANT TO STOP THE MUSIC, I'LL HAVE TO GO TO HIM.
BrrInng BrrINNG
BrrInng BrrINNG
JESUS.

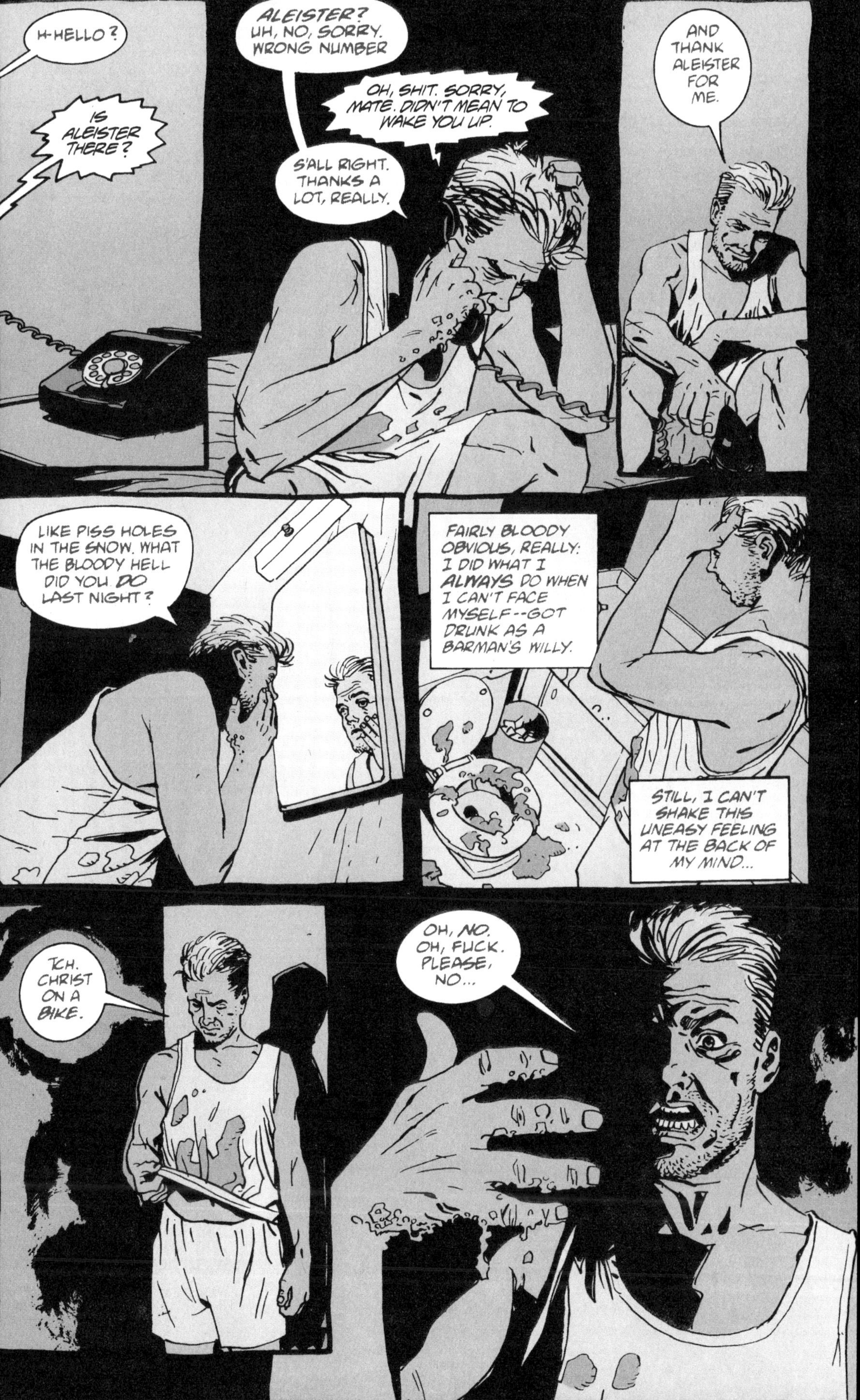
H-HELLO?
IS ALEISTER THERE?
ALEISTER? UH, NO, SORRY. WRONG NUMBER
OH, SHIT. SORRY, MATE. DIDN'T MEAN TO WAKE YOU UP.
S'ALL RIGHT. THANKS A LOT, REALLY.
AND THANK ALEISTER FOR ME.
LIKE PISS HOLES IN THE SNOW. WHAT THE BLOODY HELL DID YOU DO LAST NIGHT?
FAIRLY BLOODY OBVIOUS, REALLY: I DID WHAT I ALWAYS DO WHEN I CAN'T FACE MYSELF--GOT DRUNK AS A BARMAN'S WILLY.
STILL, I CAN'T SHAKE THIS UNEASY FEELING AT THE BACK OF MY MIND...
TCH. CHRIST ON A BIKE.
OH, NO. OH, FUCK. PLEASE, NO...

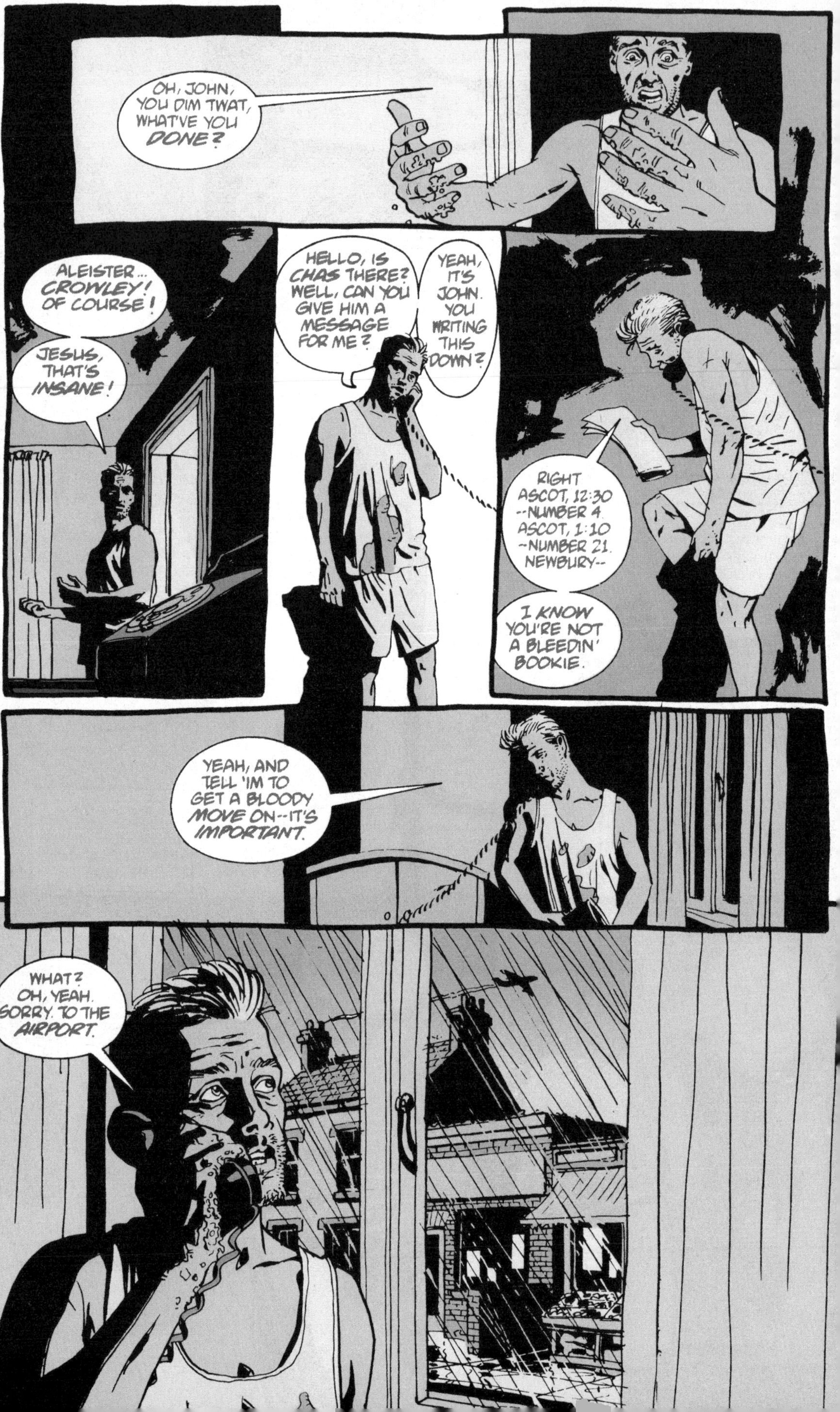
OH, JOHN, YOU DIM TWAT, WHAT'VE YOU DONE?
ALEISTER... CROWLEY! OF COURSE!
JESUS, THAT'S INSANE!
HELLO, IS CHAS THERE? WELL, CAN YOU GIVE HIM A MESSAGE FOR ME?
YEAH, IT'S JOHN. YOU WRITING THIS DOWN?
RIGHT ASCOT, 12:30 --NUMBER 4. ASCOT, 1:10 --NUMBER 21. NEWBURY--
I KNOW YOU'RE NOT A BLEEDIN' BOOKIE.
YEAH, AND TELL 'IM TO GET A BLOODY MOVE ON--IT'S IMPORTANT.
WHAT? OH, YEAH. SORRY. TO THE AIRPORT.

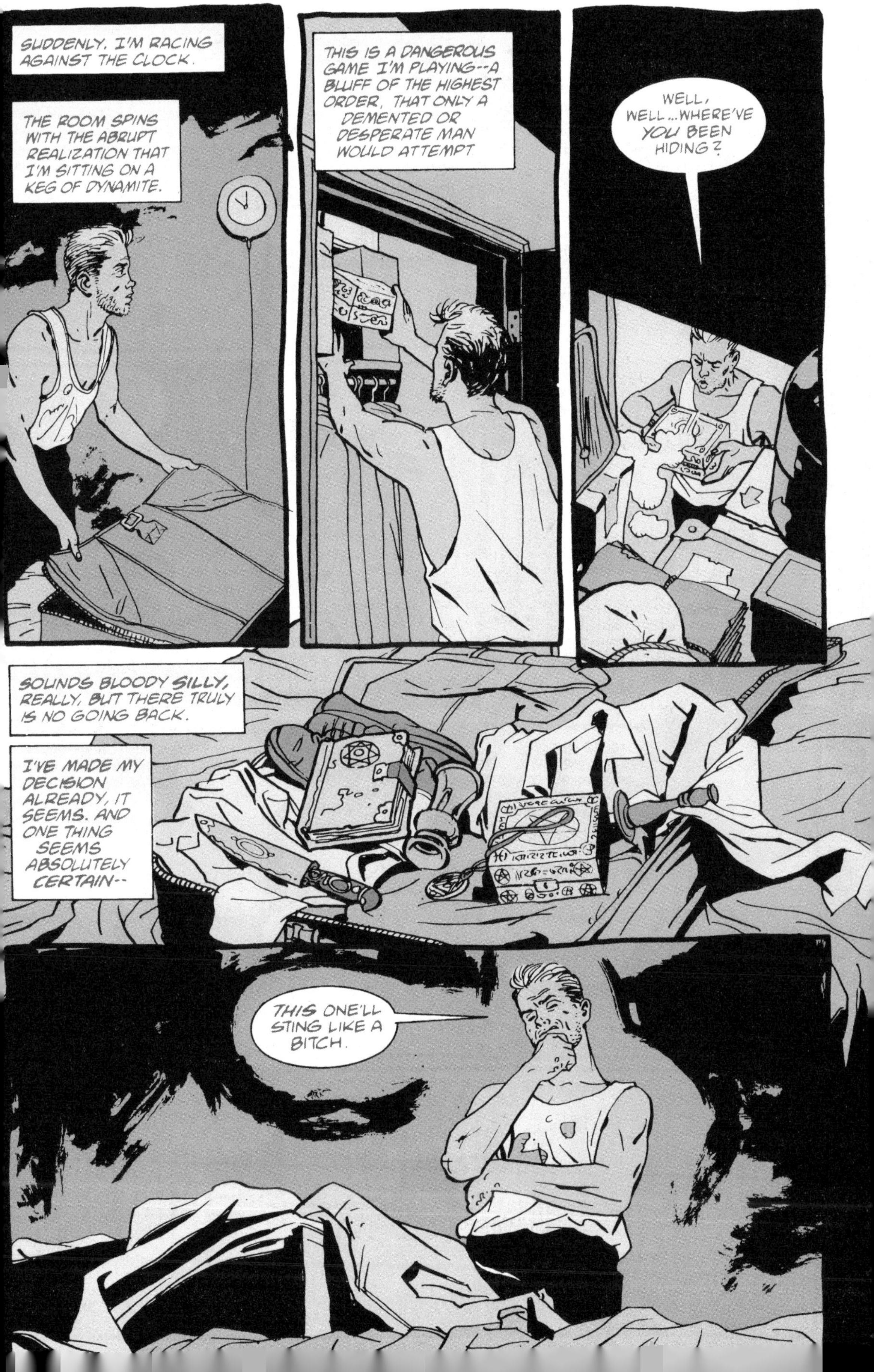
SUDDENLY, I'M RACING AGAINST THE CLOCK.
THE ROOM SPINS WITH THE ABRUPT REALIZATION THAT I'M SITTING ON A KEG OF DYNAMITE.
THIS IS A DANGEROUS GAME I'M PLAYING--A BLUFF OF THE HIGHEST ORDER, THAT ONLY A DEMENTED OR DESPERATE MAN WOULD ATTEMPT
WELL, WELL...WHERE'VE YOU BEEN HIDING?
SOUNDS BLOODY SILLY, REALLY, BUT THERE TRULY IS NO GOING BACK.
I'VE MADE MY DECISION ALREADY, IT SEEMS. AND ONE THING SEEMS ABSOLUTELY CERTAIN--
THIS ONE'LL STING LIKE A BITCH.

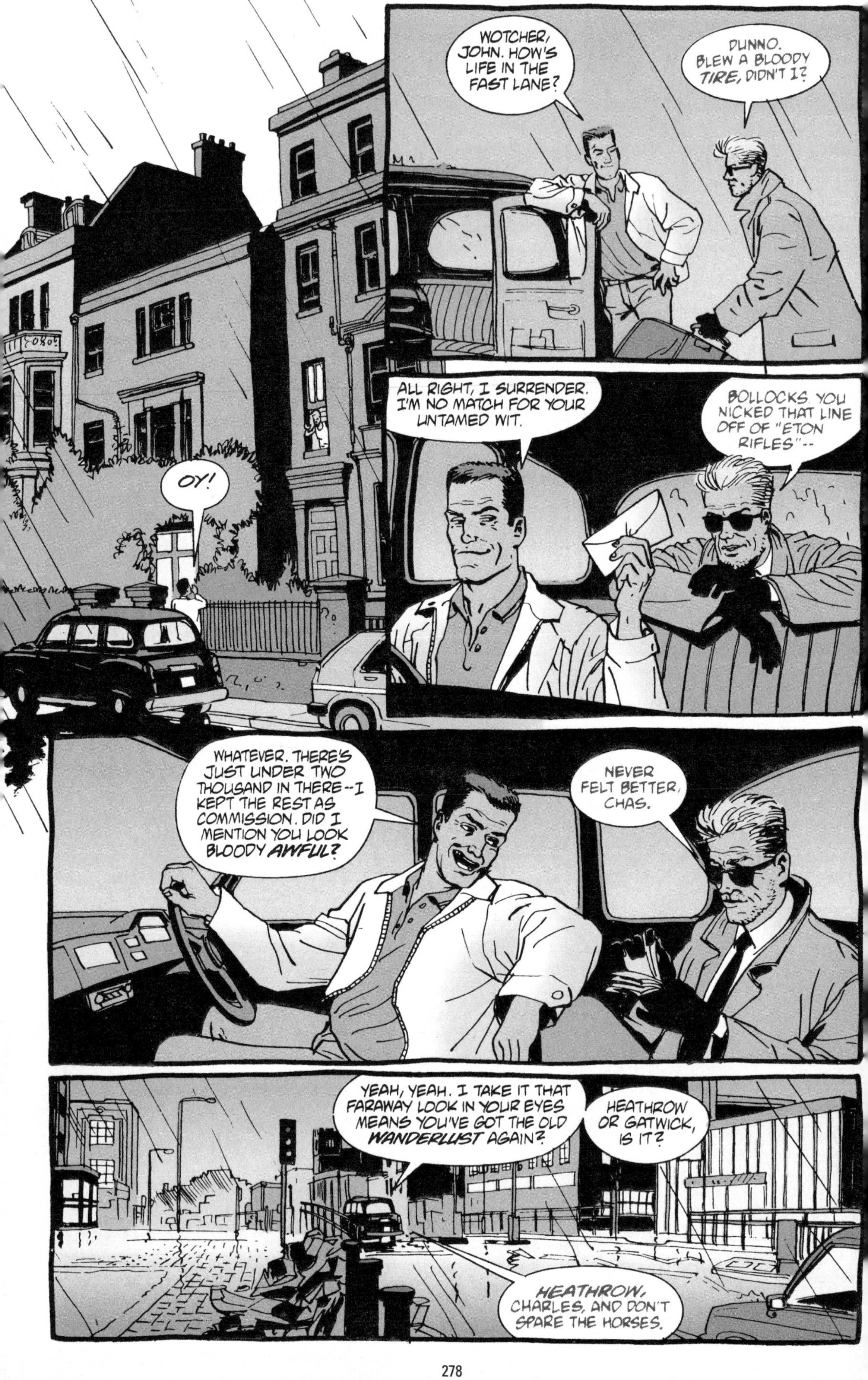
OY!
WOTCHER, JOHN. HOW'S LIFE IN THE FAST LANE?
DUNNO. BLEW A BLOODY *TIRE*, DIDN'T I?
ALL RIGHT, I SURRENDER. I'M NO MATCH FOR YOUR UNTAMED WIT.
BOLLOCKS. YOU NICKED THAT LINE OFF OF "ETON RIFLES"--
WHATEVER. THERE'S JUST UNDER TWO THOUSAND IN THERE--I KEPT THE REST AS COMMISSION. DID I MENTION YOU LOOK BLOODY *AWFUL*?
NEVER FELT BETTER, CHAS.
YEAH, YEAH. I TAKE IT THAT FARAWAY LOOK IN YOUR EYES MEANS YOU'VE GOT THE OLD *WANDERLUST* AGAIN?
HEATHROW OR GATWICK, IS IT?
HEATHROW, CHARLES, AND DON'T SPARE THE HORSES.

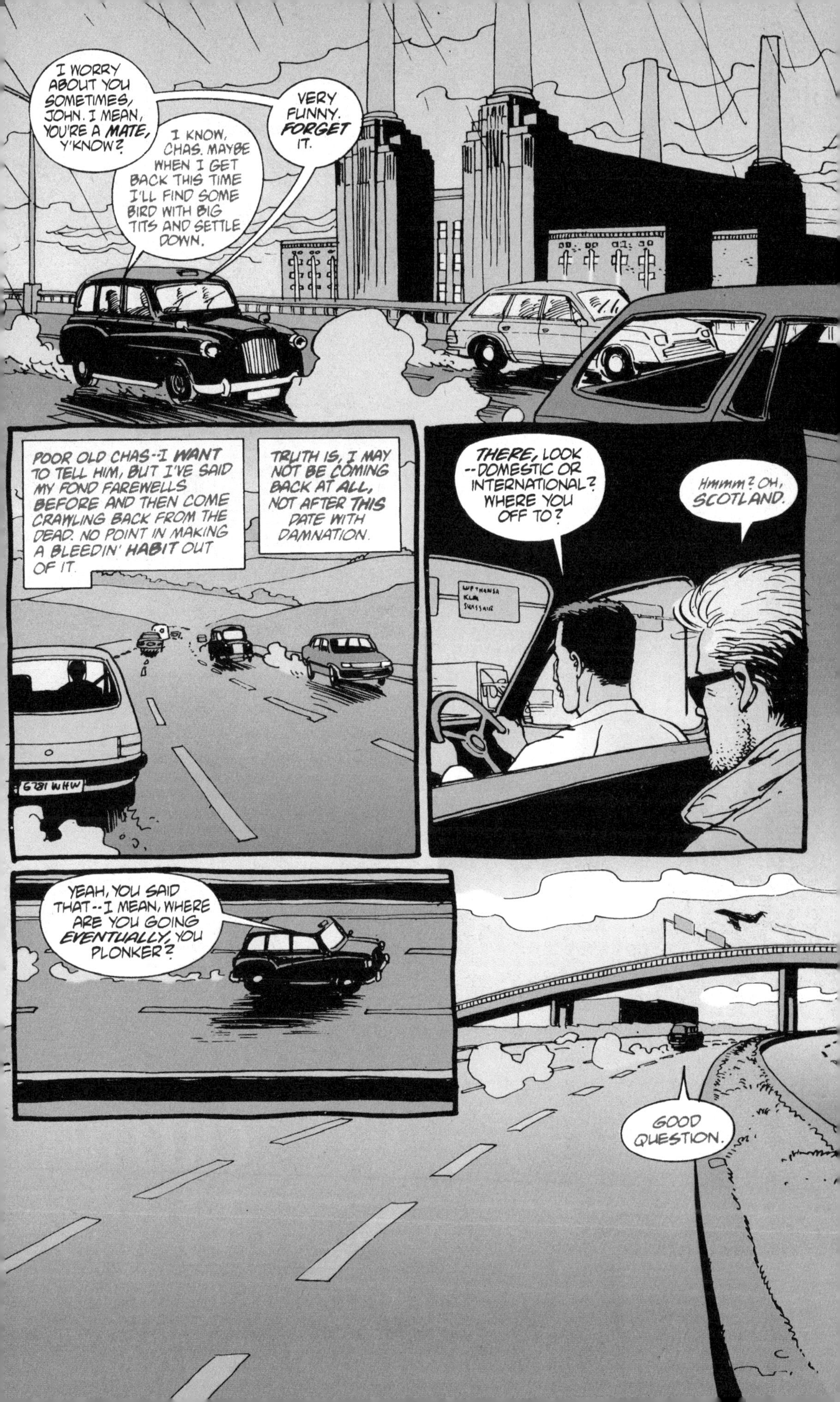
I WORRY ABOUT YOU SOMETIMES, JOHN. I MEAN, YOU'RE A MATE, Y'KNOW?
I KNOW, CHAS. MAYBE WHEN I GET BACK THIS TIME I'LL FIND SOME BIRD WITH BIG TITS AND SETTLE DOWN.
VERY FUNNY. FORGET IT.
POOR OLD CHAS--I WANT TO TELL HIM, BUT I'VE SAID MY FOND FAREWELLS BEFORE AND THEN COME CRAWLING BACK FROM THE DEAD. NO POINT IN MAKING A BLEEDIN' HABIT OUT OF IT.
TRUTH IS, I MAY NOT BE COMING BACK AT ALL, NOT AFTER THIS DATE WITH DAMNATION.
6781 WHW
THERE, LOOK --DOMESTIC OR INTERNATIONAL? WHERE YOU OFF TO?
Hmmm? OH, SCOTLAND.
YEAH, YOU SAID THAT--I MEAN, WHERE ARE YOU GOING EVENTUALLY, YOU PLONKER?
GOOD QUESTION.

JOHN CONSTANTINE
HELLBLAZER
CRITICAL
MASS
PART FOUR OF FIVE
PAUL JENKINS
SEAN PHILLIPS

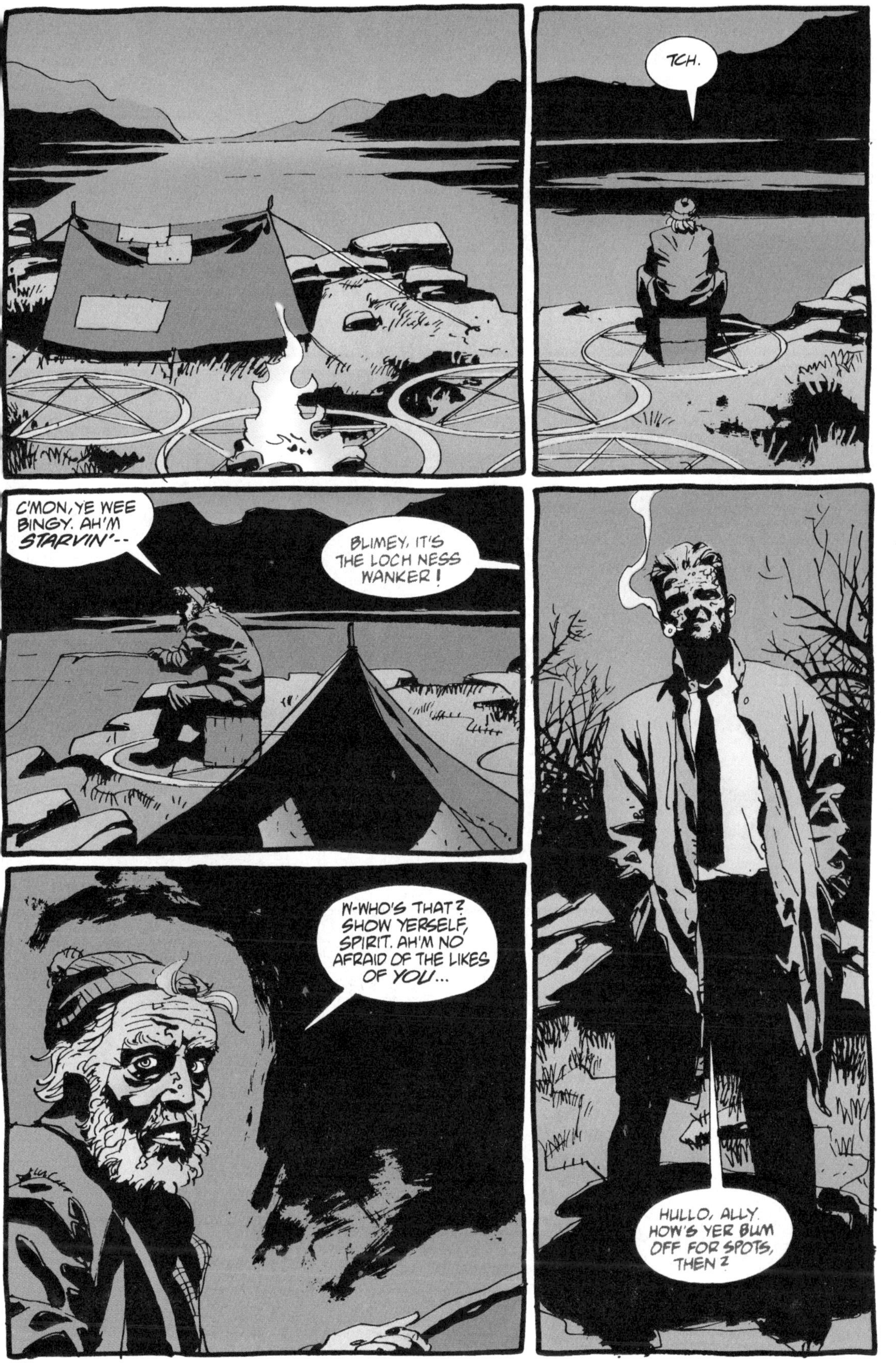
TCH.
C'MON, YE WEE BINGY. AH'M STARVIN'--
BLIMEY, IT'S THE LOCH NESS WANKER!
W-WHO'S THAT? SHOW YERSELF, SPIRIT. AH'M NO AFRAID OF THE LIKES OF YOU...
HULLO, ALLY. HOW'S YER BUM OFF FOR SPOTS, THEN?

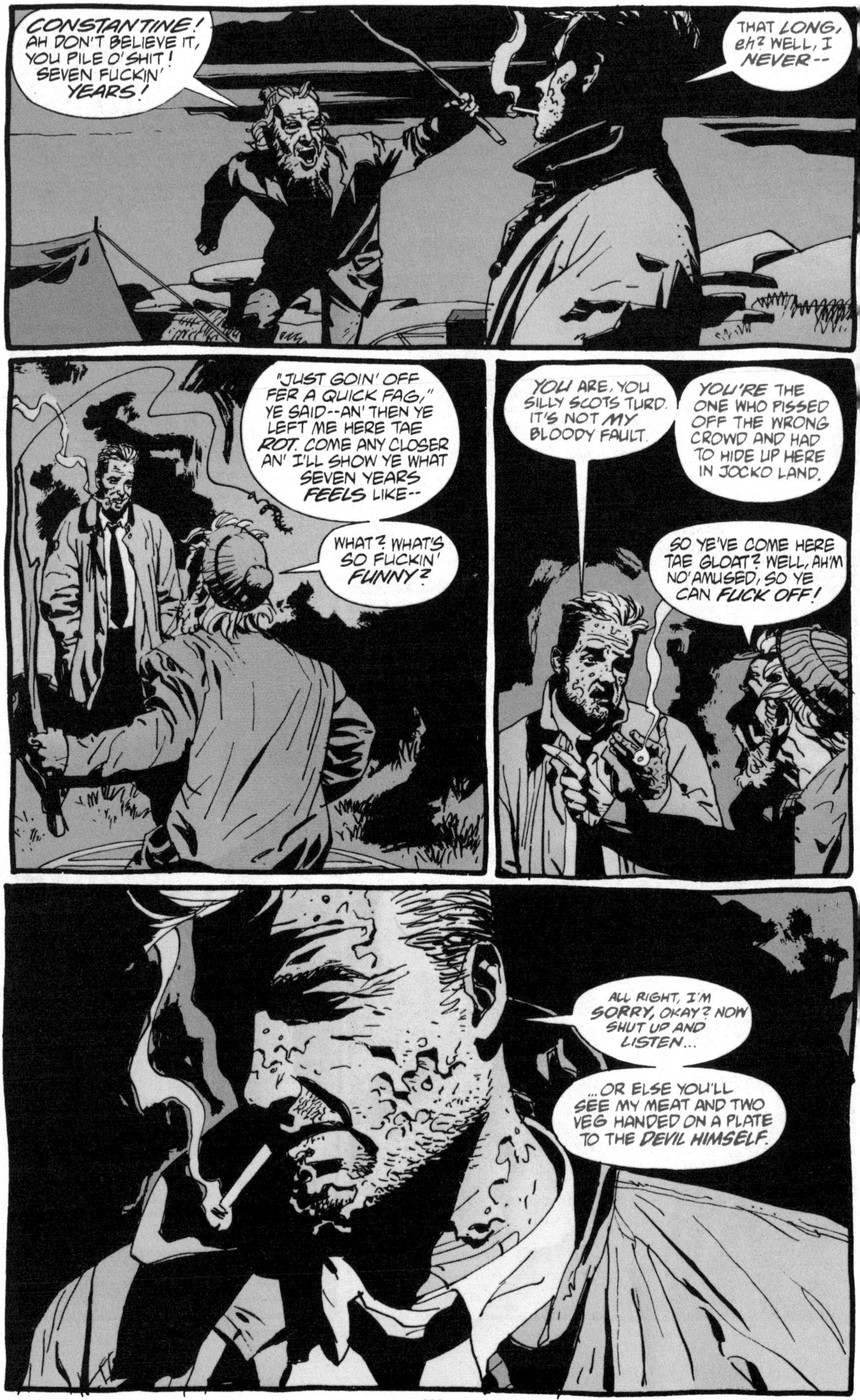
CONSTANTINE! AH DON'T BELIEVE IT, YOU PILE O'SHIT! SEVEN FUCKIN' YEARS!
THAT LONG, eh? WELL, I NEVER--
"JUST GOIN' OFF FER A QUICK FAG," YE SAID--AN' THEN YE LEFT ME HERE TAE ROT. COME ANY CLOSER AN' I'LL SHOW YE WHAT SEVEN YEARS FEELS LIKE--
WHAT? WHAT'S SO FUCKIN' FUNNY?
YOU ARE, YOU SILLY SCOTS TURD. IT'S NOT MY BLOODY FAULT.
YOU'RE THE ONE WHO PISSED OFF THE WRONG CROWD AND HAD TO HIDE UP HERE IN JOCKO LAND.
SO YE'VE COME HERE TAE GLOAT? WELL, AH'M NO'AMUSED, SO YE CAN FUCK OFF!
ALL RIGHT, I'M SORRY, OKAY? NOW SHUT UP AND LISTEN...
...OR ELSE YOU'LL SEE MY MEAT AND TWO VEG HANDED ON A PLATE TO THE DEVIL HIMSELF.

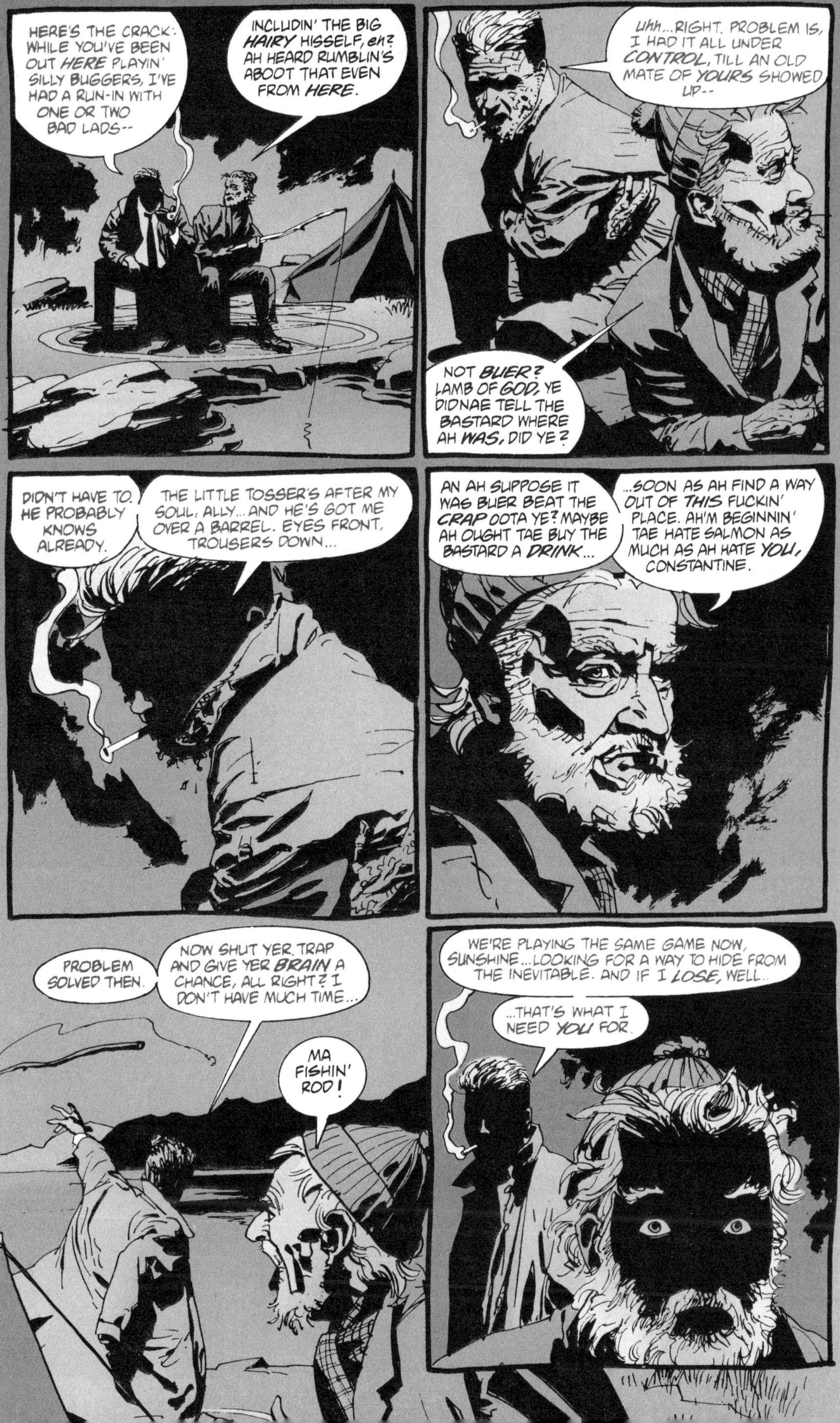
HERE'S THE CRACK: WHILE YOU'VE BEEN OUT HERE PLAYIN' SILLY BUGGERS, I'VE HAD A RUN-IN WITH ONE OR TWO BAD LADS--
INCLUDIN' THE BIG HAIRY HISSELF, eh? AH HEARD RUMBLIN'S ABOOT THAT EVEN FROM HERE.
Uhh...RIGHT. PROBLEM IS, I HAD IT ALL UNDER CONTROL, TILL AN OLD MATE OF YOURS SHOWED UP--
NOT BUER? LAMB OF GOD, YE DIDNAE TELL THE BASTARD WHERE AH WAS, DID YE?
DIDN'T HAVE TO. HE PROBABLY KNOWS ALREADY.
THE LITTLE TOSSER'S AFTER MY SOUL, ALLY... AND HE'S GOT ME OVER A BARREL. EYES FRONT, TROUSERS DOWN...
AN AH SUPPOSE IT WAS BUER BEAT THE CRAP OOTA YE? MAYBE AH OUGHT TAE BUY THE BASTARD A DRINK...
...SOON AS AH FIND A WAY OUT OF THIS FUCKIN' PLACE. AH'M BEGINNIN' TAE HATE SALMON AS MUCH AS AH HATE YOU, CONSTANTINE.
PROBLEM SOLVED THEN.
NOW SHUT YER TRAP AND GIVE YER BRAIN A CHANCE, ALL RIGHT? I DON'T HAVE MUCH TIME...
MA FISHIN' ROD!
WE'RE PLAYING THE SAME GAME NOW, SUNSHINE...LOOKING FOR A WAY TO HIDE FROM THE INEVITABLE. AND IF I LOSE, WELL...
...THAT'S WHAT I NEED YOU FOR.

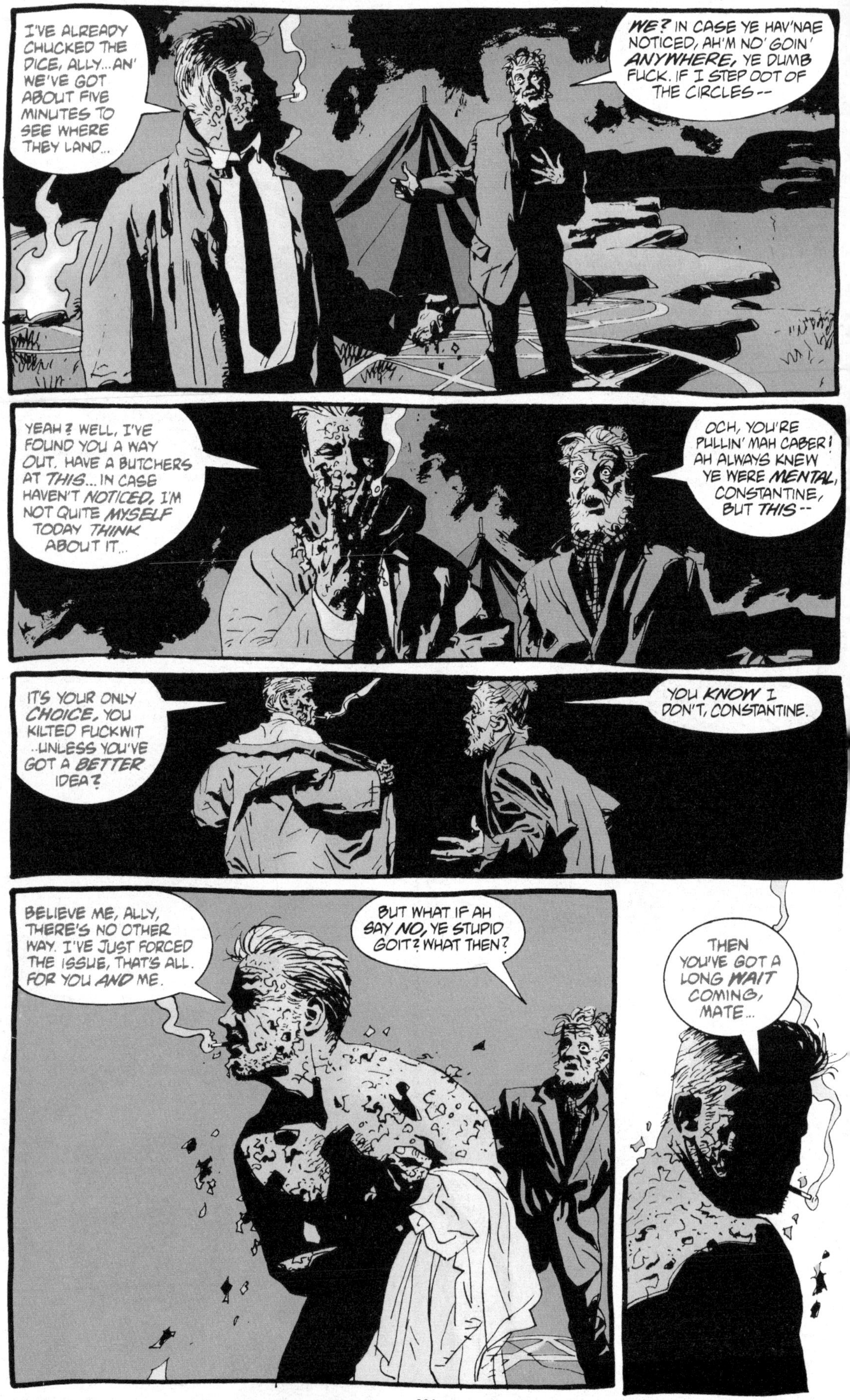

I'VE ALREADY CHUCKED THE DICE, ALLY...AN' WE'VE GOT ABOUT FIVE MINUTES TO SEE WHERE THEY LAND...
WE? IN CASE YE HAV'NAE NOTICED, AH'M NO' GOIN' ANYWHERE, YE DUMB FUCK. IF I STEP OOT OF THE CIRCLES --
YEAH? WELL, I'VE FOUND YOU A WAY OUT. HAVE A BUTCHERS AT THIS... IN CASE HAVEN'T NOTICED, I'M NOT QUITE MYSELF TODAY THINK ABOUT IT...
OCH, YOU'RE PULLIN' MAH CABER! AH ALWAYS KNEW YE WERE MENTAL, CONSTANTINE, BUT THIS --
IT'S YOUR ONLY CHOICE, YOU KILTED FUCKWIT ..UNLESS YOU'VE GOT A BETTER IDEA?
YOU KNOW I DON'T, CONSTANTINE.
BELIEVE ME, ALLY, THERE'S NO OTHER WAY. I'VE JUST FORCED THE ISSUE, THAT'S ALL. FOR YOU AND ME.
BUT WHAT IF AH SAY NO, YE STUPID GOIT? WHAT THEN?
THEN YOU'VE GOT A LONG WAIT COMING, MATE...

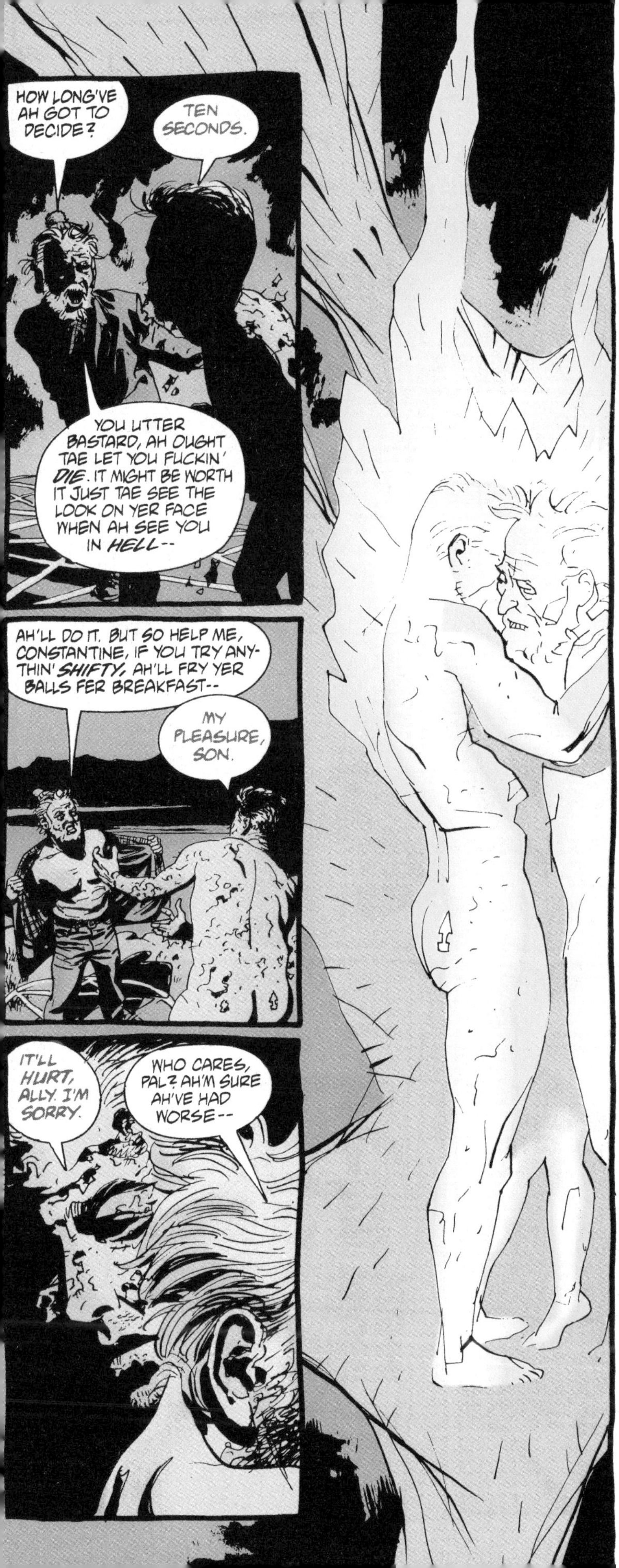
HOW LONG'VE AH GOT TO DECIDE?
TEN SECONDS.
YOU UTTER BASTARD, AH OUGHT TAE LET YOU FUCKIN' DIE. IT MIGHT BE WORTH IT JUST TAE SEE THE LOOK ON YER FACE WHEN AH SEE YOU IN HELL--
AH'LL DO IT. BUT SO HELP ME, CONSTANTINE, IF YOU TRY ANY-THIN' SHIFTY, AH'LL FRY YER BALLS FER BREAKFAST--
MY PLEASURE, SON.
IT'LL HURT, ALLY. I'M SORRY.
WHO CARES, PAL? AH'M SURE AH'VE HAD WORSE--

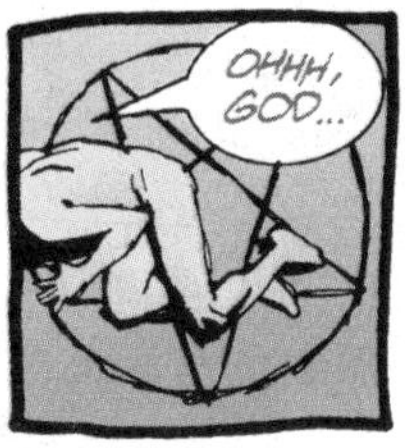
OHHH, GOD...

CRITICAL MASS 4

COMING UP FOR AIR

Paul Jenkins Writer

Sean Phillips Artist

Matt Hollingsworth Colorist

Clem Robins Letterer

Axel Alonso Asst. Editor

Lou Stathis Editor

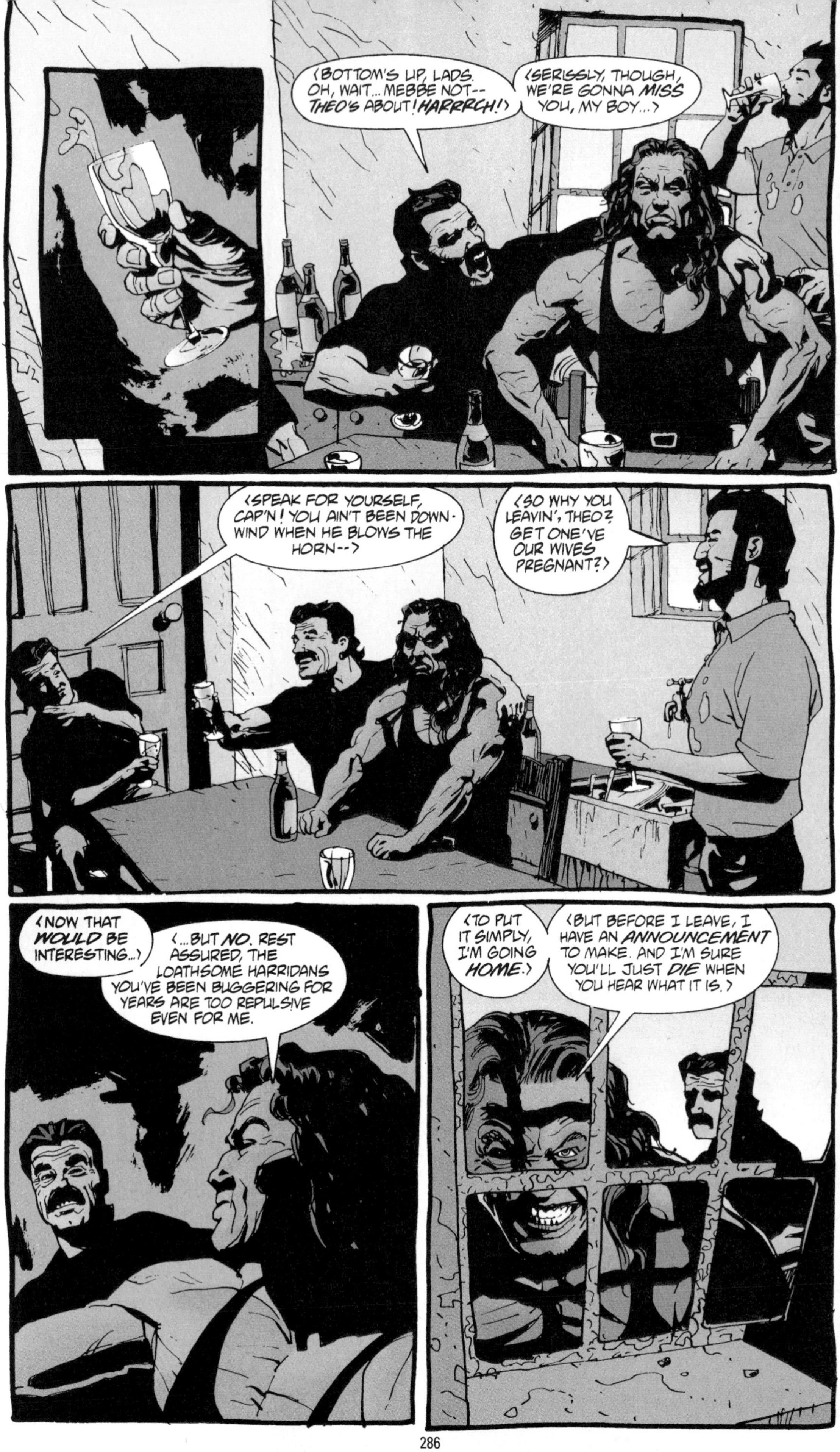

‹BOTTOM'S UP, LADS. OH, WAIT... MEBBE NOT-- THEO'S ABOUT! HARRRCH!›
‹SERISSLY, THOUGH, WE'RE GONNA MISS YOU, MY BOY...›
‹SPEAK FOR YOURSELF, CAP'N! YOU AIN'T BEEN DOWN-WIND WHEN HE BLOWS THE HORN--›
‹SO WHY YOU LEAVIN', THEO? GET ONE'VE OUR WIVES PREGNANT?›
‹NOW THAT WOULD BE INTERESTING...›
‹...BUT NO. REST ASSURED, THE LOATHSOME HARRIDANS YOU'VE BEEN BUGGERING FOR YEARS ARE TOO REPULSIVE EVEN FOR ME.
‹TO PUT IT SIMPLY, I'M GOING HOME.›
‹BUT BEFORE I LEAVE, I HAVE AN ANNOUNCEMENT TO MAKE. AND I'M SURE YOU'LL JUST DIE WHEN YOU HEAR WHAT IT IS.›

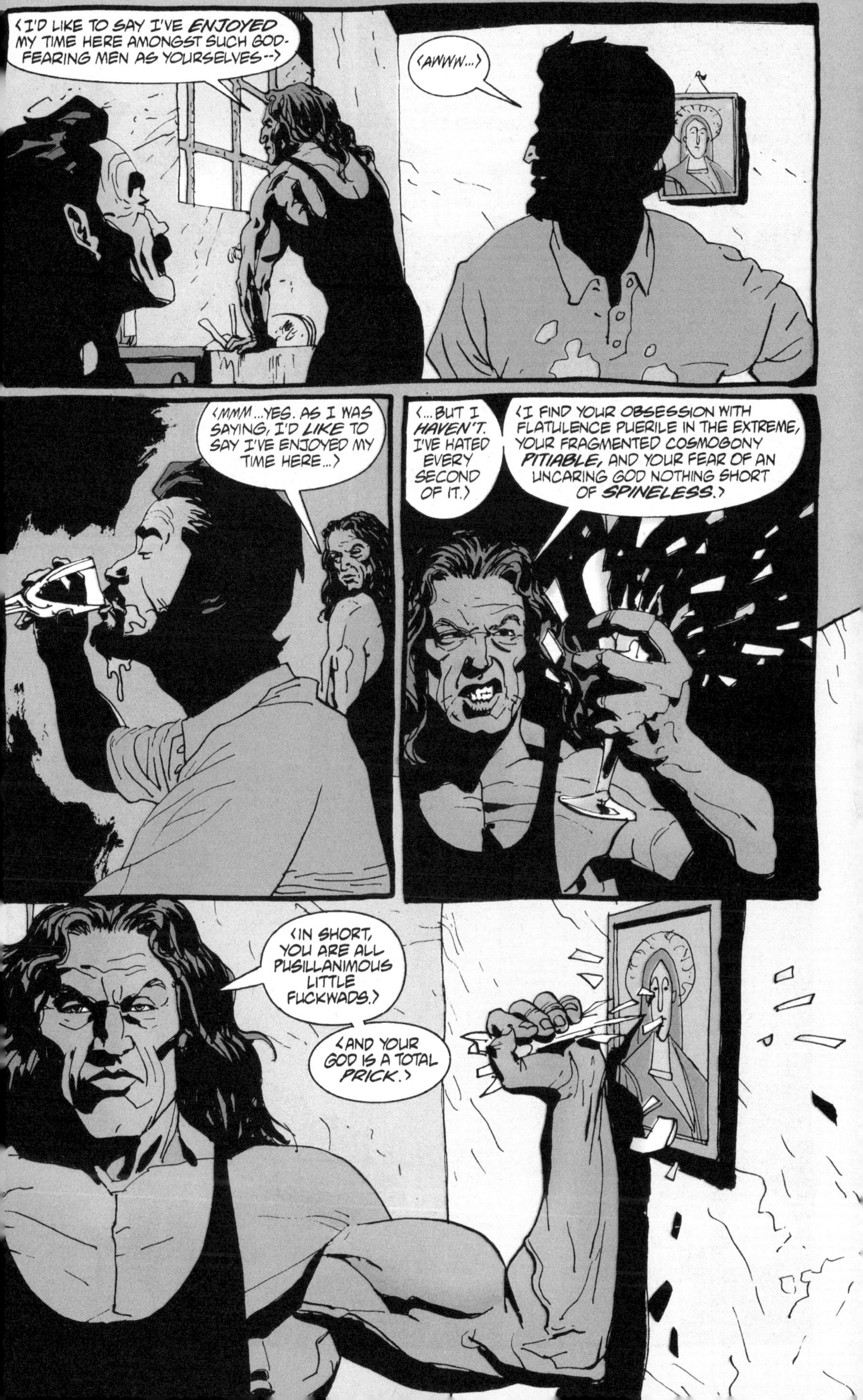

<I'D LIKE TO SAY I'VE ENJOYED MY TIME HERE AMONGST SUCH GOD-FEARING MEN AS YOURSELVES-->
<AWWW...>
<MMM...YES. AS I WAS SAYING, I'D LIKE TO SAY I'VE ENJOYED MY TIME HERE...>
<...BUT I HAVEN'T. I'VE HATED EVERY SECOND OF IT.>
<I FIND YOUR OBSESSION WITH FLATULENCE PUERILE IN THE EXTREME, YOUR FRAGMENTED COSMOGONY PITIABLE, AND YOUR FEAR OF AN UNCARING GOD NOTHING SHORT OF SPINELESS.>
<IN SHORT, YOU ARE ALL PUSILLANIMOUS LITTLE FUCKWADS.>
<AND YOUR GOD IS A TOTAL PRICK.>

⟨IF IGNORANCE IS BLISS, YOU WILL DIE HAPPY MEN INDEED-- AND THAT WILL *NEVER* DO. SO, WITHOUT FURTHER PREAMBLE, THE BIG ANNOUNCEMENT IS THIS--⟩

⟨DON'T DRINK THE RETSINA.⟩

⟨I POISONED IT.⟩

⟨BE SEEING YOU.⟩

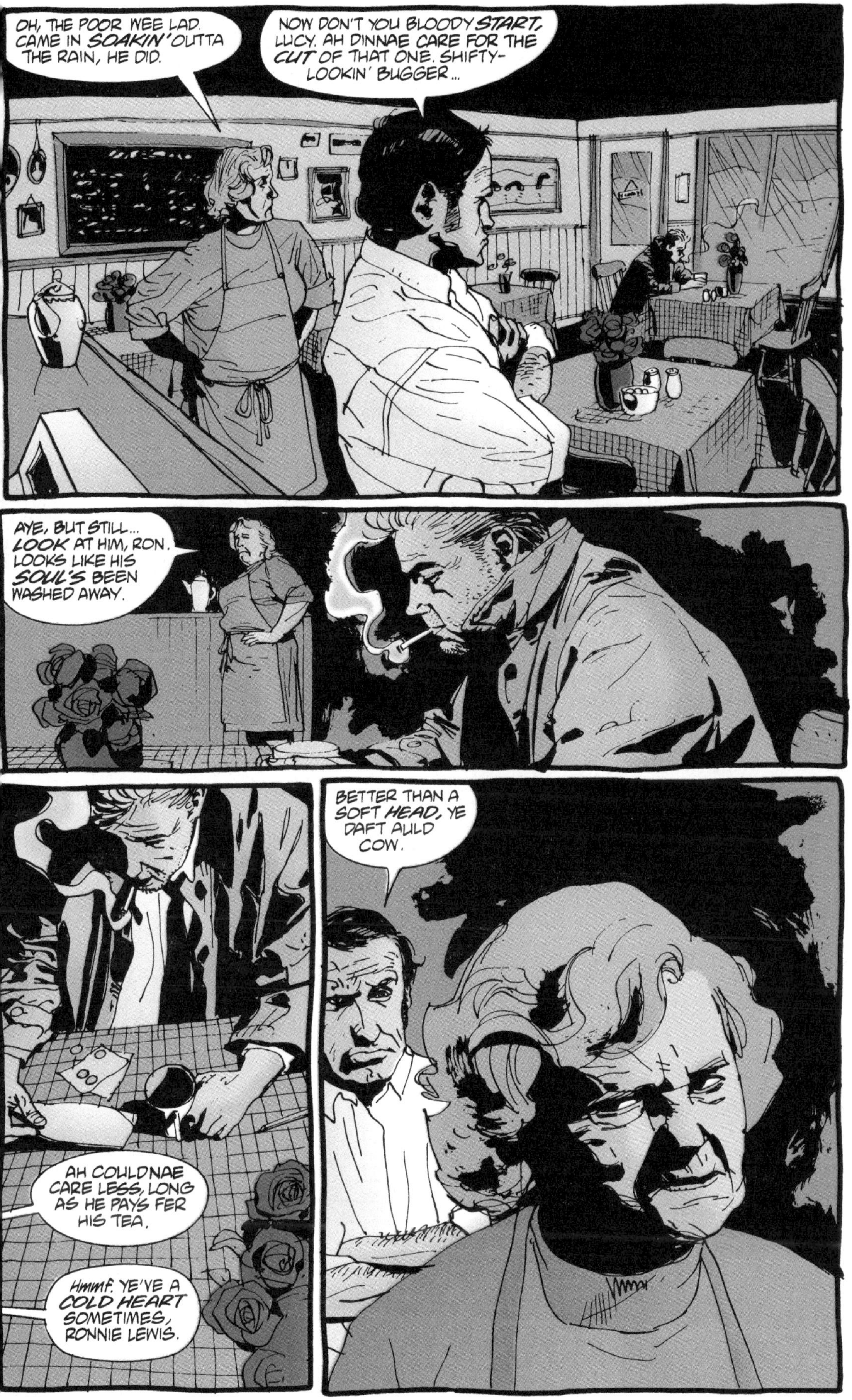
OH, THE POOR WEE LAD. CAME IN SOAKIN' OUTTA THE RAIN, HE DID.
NOW DON'T YOU BLOODY START, LUCY. AH DINNAE CARE FOR THE CUT OF THAT ONE. SHIFTY-LOOKIN' BUGGER...
AYE, BUT STILL... LOOK AT HIM, RON. LOOKS LIKE HIS SOUL'S BEEN WASHED AWAY.
AH COULDNAE CARE LESS, LONG AS HE PAYS FER HIS TEA.
HMMF. YE'VE A COLD HEART SOMETIMES, RONNIE LEWIS.
BETTER THAN A SOFT HEAD, YE DAFT AULD COW.

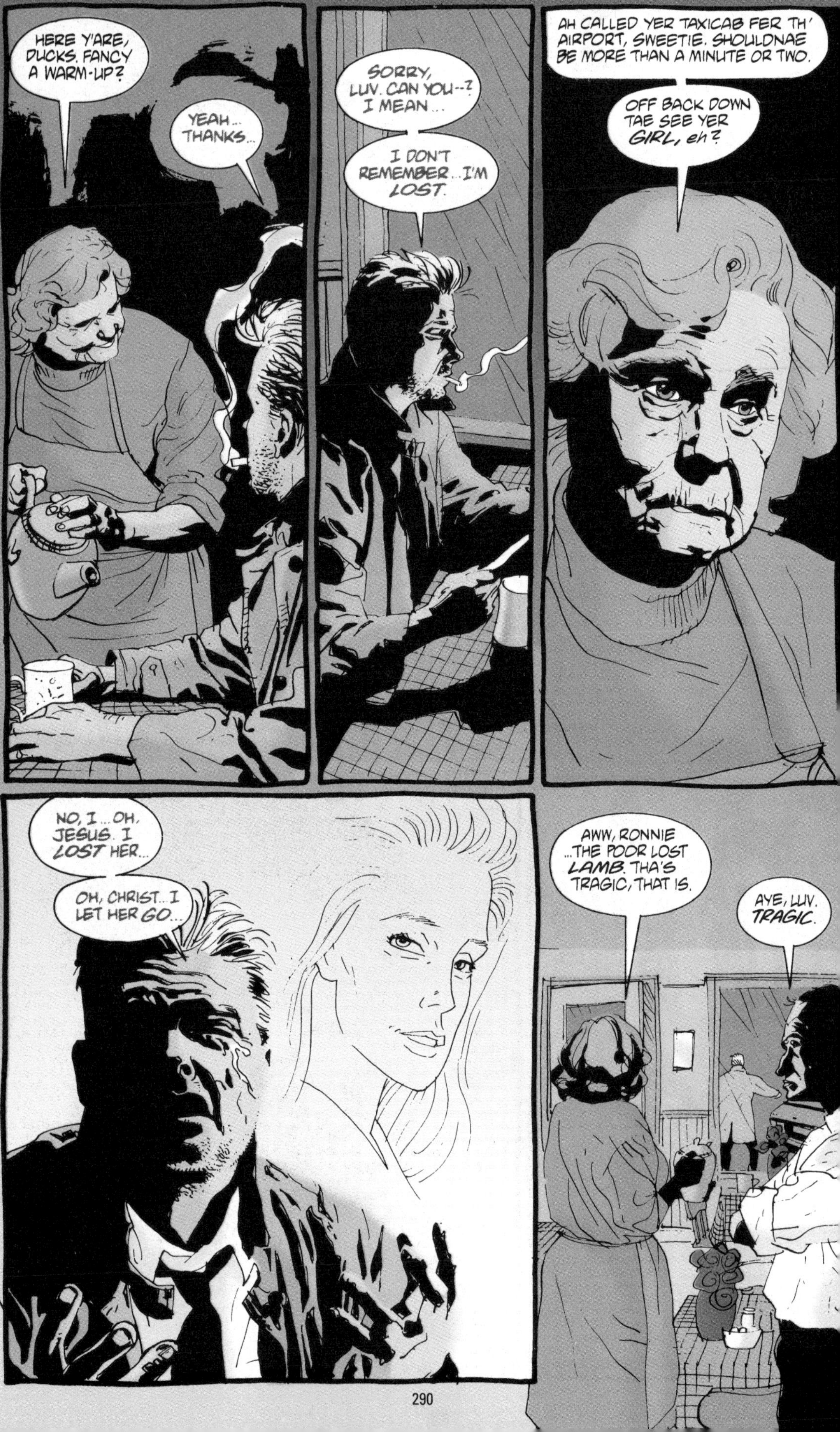
HERE Y'ARE, DUCKS. FANCY A WARM-UP?
YEAH... THANKS...
SORRY, LUV. CAN YOU--? I MEAN...
I DON'T REMEMBER... I'M LOST.
AH CALLED YER TAXICAB FER TH' AIRPORT, SWEETIE. SHOULDNAE BE MORE THAN A MINUTE OR TWO.
OFF BACK DOWN TAE SEE YER GIRL, eh?
NO, I... OH, JESUS. I LOST HER...
OH, CHRIST... I LET HER GO...
AWW, RONNIE ...THE POOR LOST LAMB. THA'S TRAGIC, THAT IS.
AYE, LUV. TRAGIC.

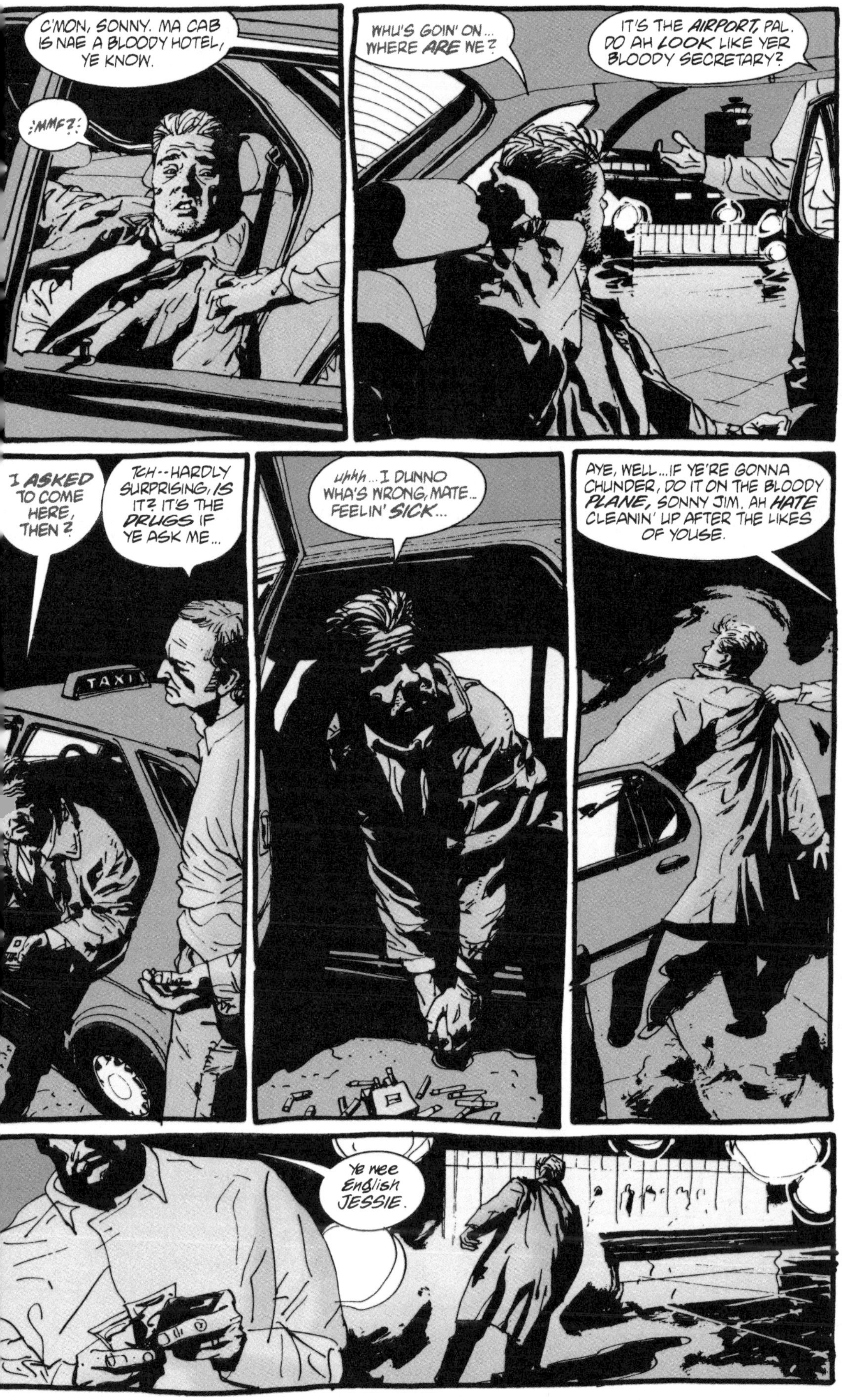
C'MON, SONNY. MA CAB IS NAE A BLOODY HOTEL, YE KNOW.
MMF?
WHU'S GOIN' ON... WHERE ARE WE?
IT'S THE AIRPORT, PAL. DO AH LOOK LIKE YER BLOODY SECRETARY?
I ASKED TO COME HERE, THEN?
TCH--HARDLY SURPRISING, IS IT? IT'S THE DRUGS IF YE ASK ME...
TAXI
uhhh... I DUNNO WHA'S WRONG, MATE... FEELIN' SICK...
AYE, WELL... IF YE'RE GONNA CHUNDER, DO IT ON THE BLOODY PLANE, SONNY JIM. AH HATE CLEANIN' UP AFTER THE LIKES OF YOUSE.
Ye wee English JESSIE.

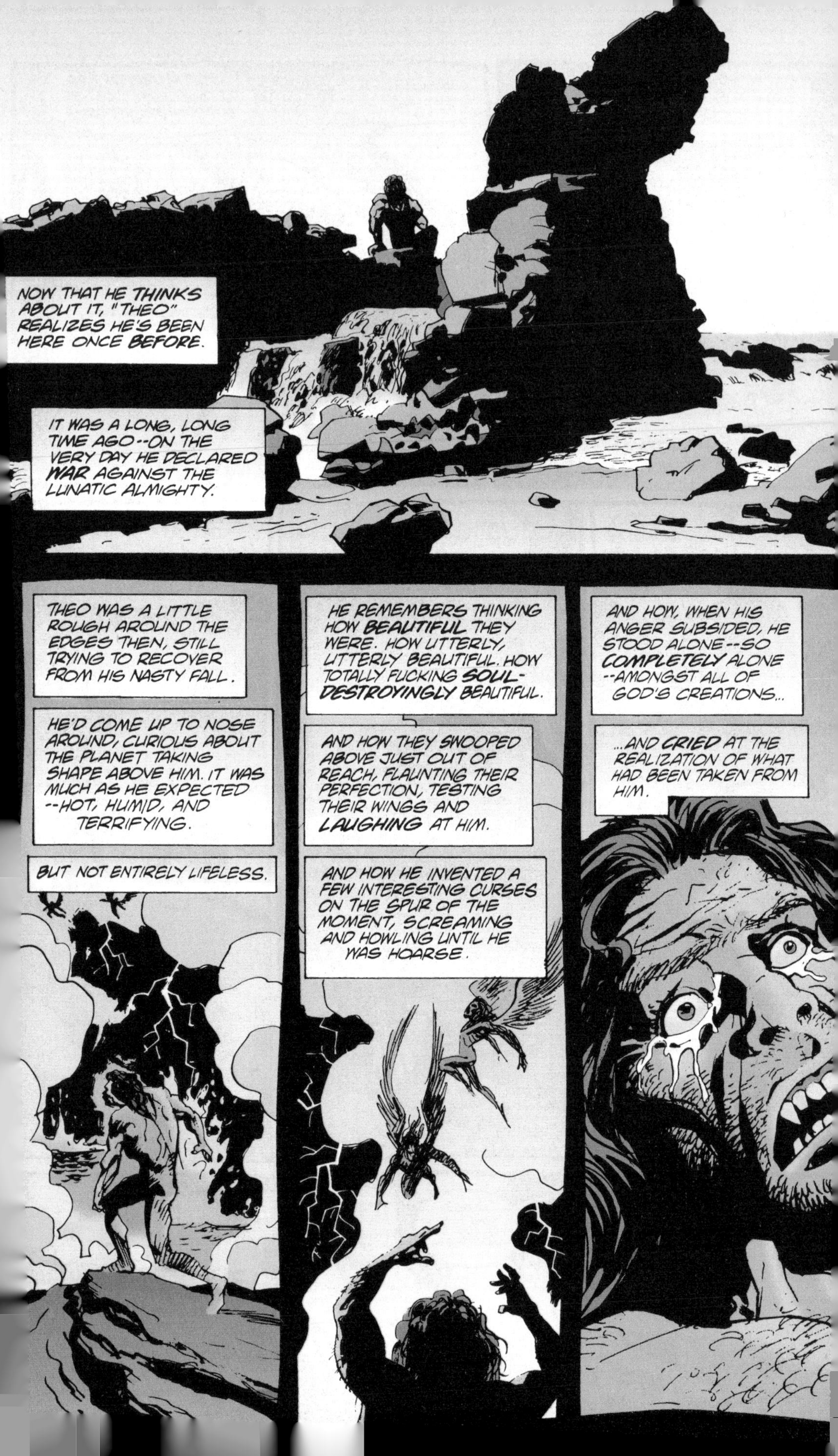
NOW THAT HE THINKS ABOUT IT, "THEO" REALIZES HE'S BEEN HERE ONCE BEFORE.
IT WAS A LONG, LONG TIME AGO--ON THE VERY DAY HE DECLARED WAR AGAINST THE LUNATIC ALMIGHTY.
THEO WAS A LITTLE ROUGH AROUND THE EDGES THEN, STILL TRYING TO RECOVER FROM HIS NASTY FALL.
HE'D COME UP TO NOSE AROUND, CURIOUS ABOUT THE PLANET TAKING SHAPE ABOVE HIM. IT WAS MUCH AS HE EXPECTED --HOT, HUMID, AND TERRIFYING.
BUT NOT ENTIRELY LIFELESS.
HE REMEMBERS THINKING HOW BEAUTIFUL THEY WERE. HOW UTTERLY, UTTERLY BEAUTIFUL. HOW TOTALLY FUCKING SOUL-DESTROYINGLY BEAUTIFUL.
AND HOW THEY SWOOPED ABOVE JUST OUT OF REACH, FLAUNTING THEIR PERFECTION, TESTING THEIR WINGS AND LAUGHING AT HIM.
AND HOW HE INVENTED A FEW INTERESTING CURSES ON THE SPUR OF THE MOMENT, SCREAMING AND HOWLING UNTIL HE WAS HOARSE.
AND HOW, WHEN HIS ANGER SUBSIDED, HE STOOD ALONE--SO COMPLETELY ALONE --AMONGST ALL OF GOD'S CREATIONS...
...AND CRIED AT THE REALIZATION OF WHAT HAD BEEN TAKEN FROM HIM.

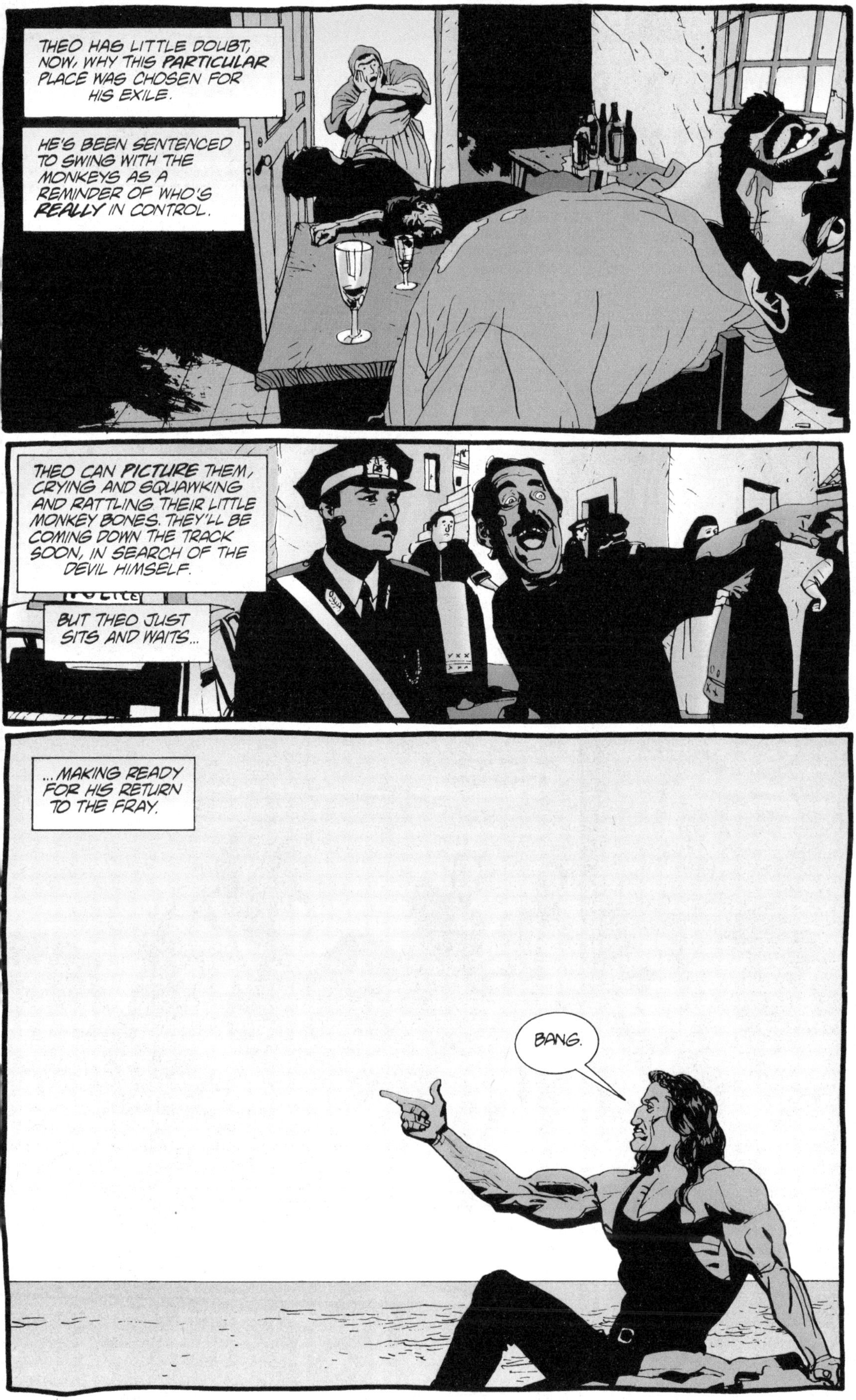
THEO HAS LITTLE DOUBT, NOW, WHY THIS PARTICULAR PLACE WAS CHOSEN FOR HIS EXILE.
HE'S BEEN SENTENCED TO SWING WITH THE MONKEYS AS A REMINDER OF WHO'S REALLY IN CONTROL.
THEO CAN PICTURE THEM, CRYING AND SQUAWKING AND RATTLING THEIR LITTLE MONKEY BONES. THEY'LL BE COMING DOWN THE TRACK SOON, IN SEARCH OF THE DEVIL HIMSELF.
BUT THEO JUST SITS AND WAITS...
...MAKING READY FOR HIS RETURN TO THE FRAY.
BANG.

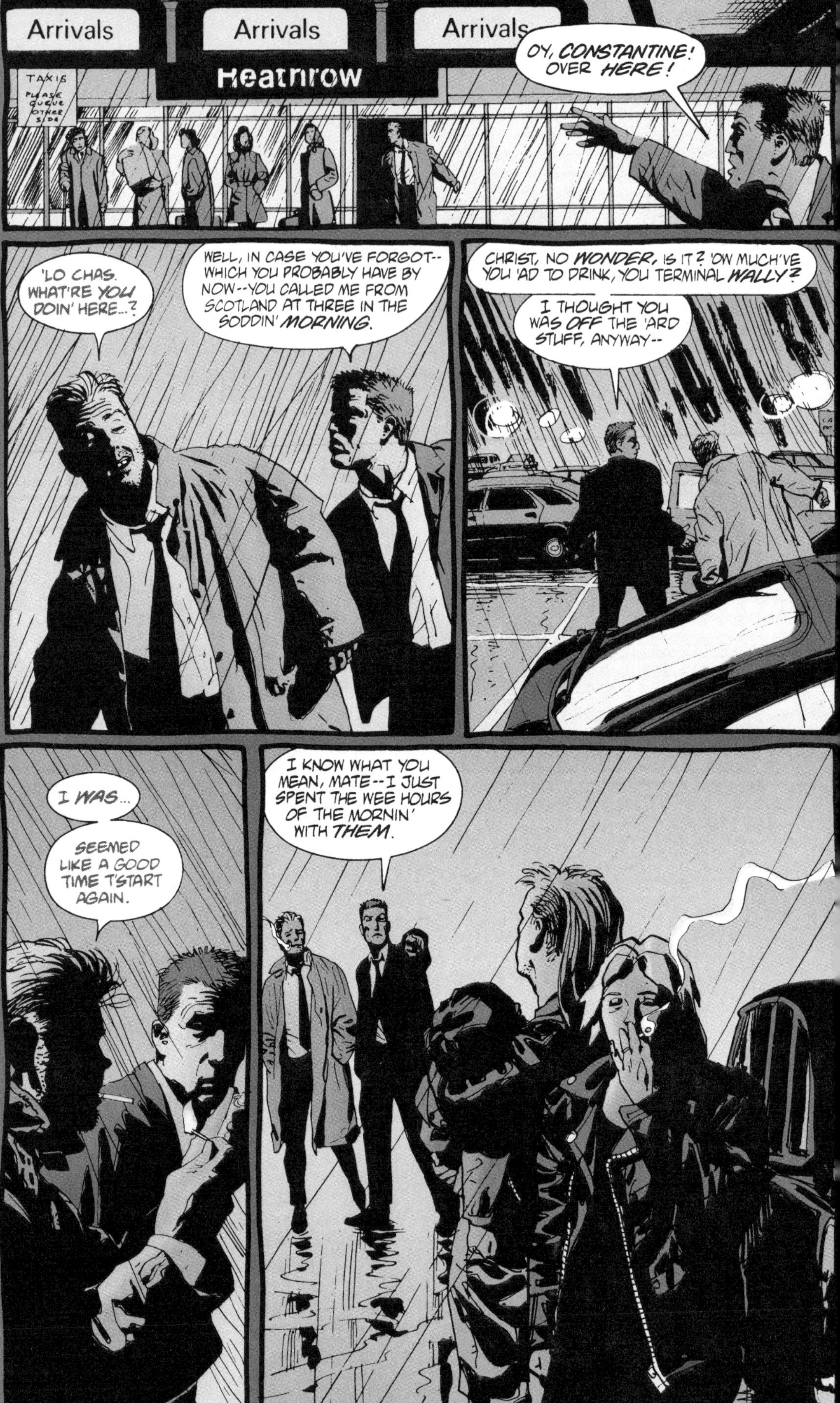

Arrivals
Arrivals
Arrivals
Heathrow
TAXIS PLEASE QUEUE OTHER SIDE
OY, CONSTANTINE! OVER HERE!
'LO CHAS. WHAT'RE YOU DOIN' HERE...?
WELL, IN CASE YOU'VE FORGOT-- WHICH YOU PROBABLY HAVE BY NOW--YOU CALLED ME FROM SCOTLAND AT THREE IN THE SODDIN' MORNING.
CHRIST, NO WONDER, IS IT? 'OW MUCH'VE YOU 'AD TO DRINK, YOU TERMINAL WALLY?
I THOUGHT YOU WAS OFF THE 'ARD STUFF, ANYWAY--
I WAS...
SEEMED LIKE A GOOD TIME T'START AGAIN.
I KNOW WHAT YOU MEAN, MATE--I JUST SPENT THE WEE HOURS OF THE MORNIN' WITH THEM.

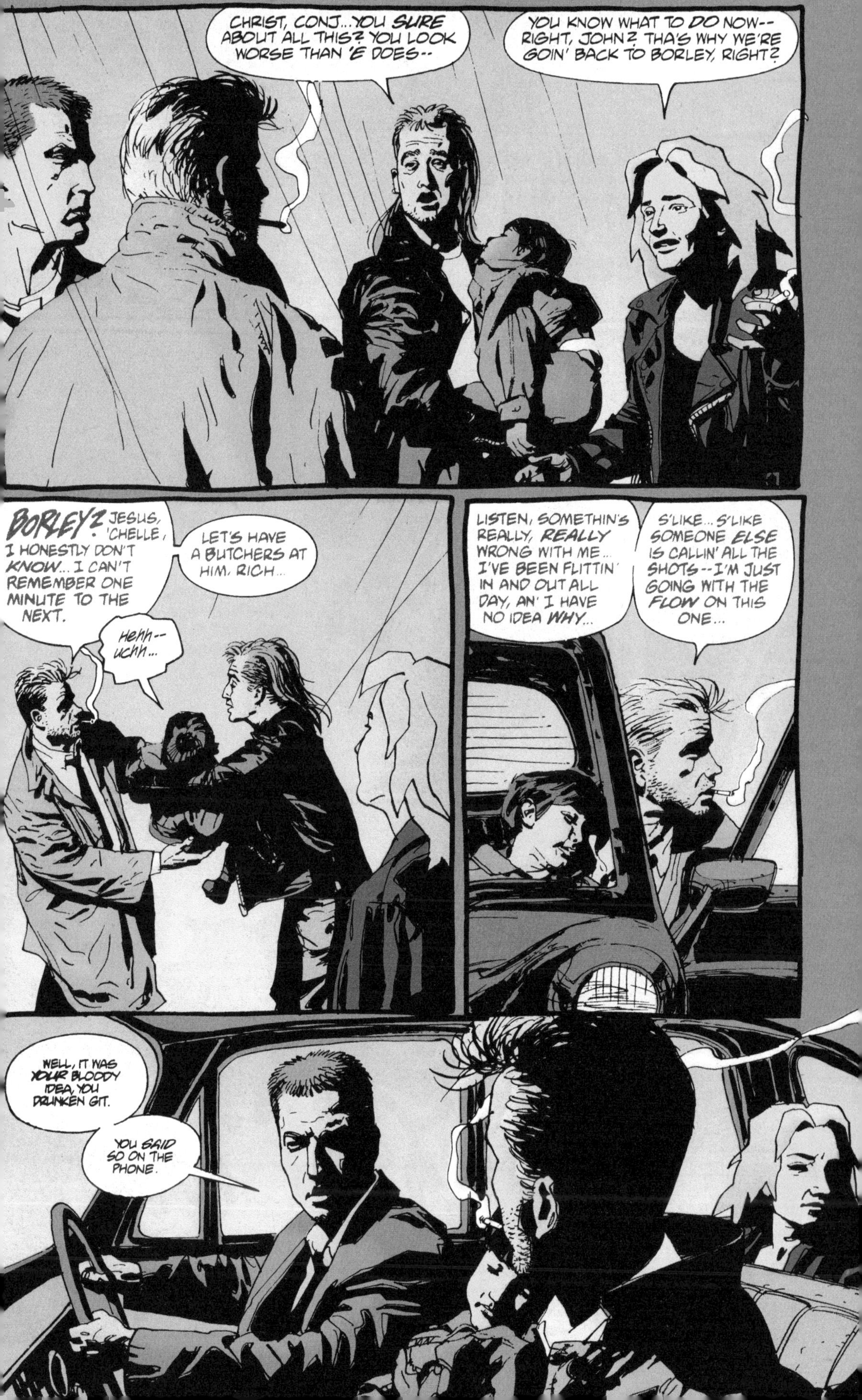
CHRIST, CONJ... YOU SURE ABOUT ALL THIS? YOU LOOK WORSE THAN 'E DOES--
YOU KNOW WHAT TO DO NOW-- RIGHT, JOHN? THA'S WHY WE'RE GOIN' BACK TO BORLEY, RIGHT?
BORLEY? JESUS, 'CHELLE, I HONESTLY DON'T KNOW... I CAN'T REMEMBER ONE MINUTE TO THE NEXT.
LET'S HAVE A BUTCHERS AT HIM, RICH...
Hehh-- uchh...
LISTEN, SOMETHIN'S REALLY, REALLY WRONG WITH ME... I'VE BEEN FLITTIN' IN AND OUT ALL DAY, AN' I HAVE NO IDEA WHY...
S'LIKE... S'LIKE SOMEONE ELSE IS CALLIN' ALL THE SHOTS--I'M JUST GOING WITH THE FLOW ON THIS ONE...
WELL, IT WAS YOUR BLOODY IDEA, YOU DRUNKEN GIT.
YOU SAID SO ON THE PHONE.

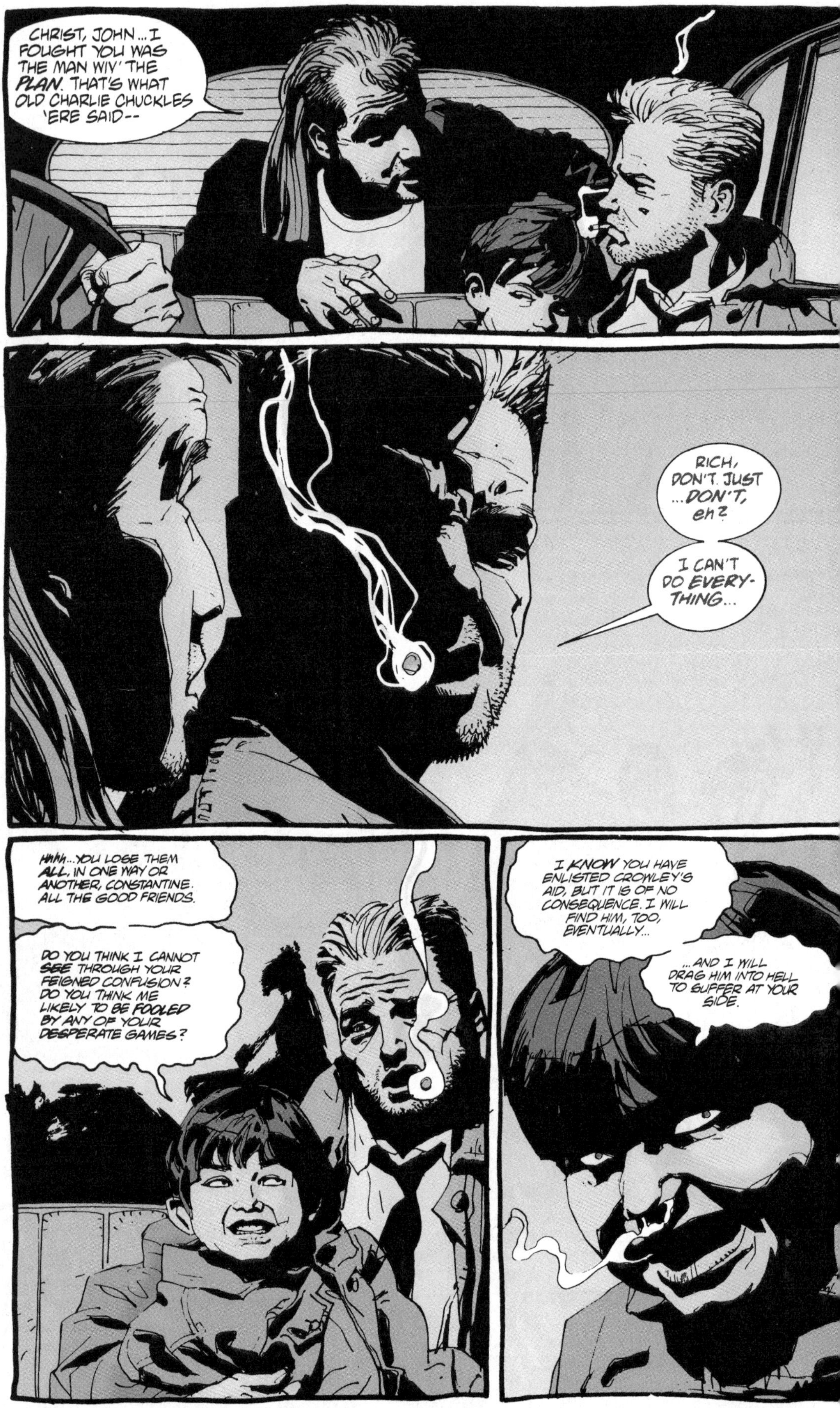
CHRIST, JOHN ... I FOUGHT YOU WAS THE MAN WIY' THE PLAN. THAT'S WHAT OLD CHARLIE CHUCKLES 'ERE SAID--
RICH, DON'T. JUST ...DON'T, eh?
I CAN'T DO EVERY-THING...
HHHH... YOU LOSE THEM ALL, IN ONE WAY OR ANOTHER, CONSTANTINE. ALL THE GOOD FRIENDS.
DO YOU THINK I CANNOT SEE THROUGH YOUR FEIGNED CONFUSION? DO YOU THINK ME LIKELY TO BE FOOLED BY ANY OF YOUR DESPERATE GAMES?
I KNOW YOU HAVE ENLISTED CROWLEY'S AID, BUT IT IS OF NO CONSEQUENCE. I WILL FIND HIM, TOO, EVENTUALLY...
...AND I WILL DRAG HIM INTO HELL TO SUFFER AT YOUR SIDE.

I'LL JUST CARRY ON, THEN, SHALL I? I MEAN, IT'S "CHAS DON'T NEED TO *KNOW*" ALL OVER AGAIN, *eh?*

KID'S POSSESSED BY A DEMON, CHAS. I'D LEAVE IT *ALONE* IF I WERE YOU.

'COURSE HE IS. DON'T WORRY ABOUT YOUR UNCLE JOHN, MATEY--HE'S A BIT'VE A SILLY SAUSAGE.

AWW, POOR LITTLE BLEEDER--HE DON'T HAVE A CLUE WHAT'S HAPPENIN', JOHN.

OH, BUT I *DO*, CHAS CHANDLER. HECCH...I KNOW ABOUT YOUR STASH OF FILTH ON THE TOP CUPBOARD IN THE LIVING ROOM, FOR EXAMPLE.

I KNOW THAT YOU MASTURBATE NIGHTLY TO "GASH STATION" WHILE YOUR OBESE WIFE WAITS PATIENTLY UPSTAIRS...

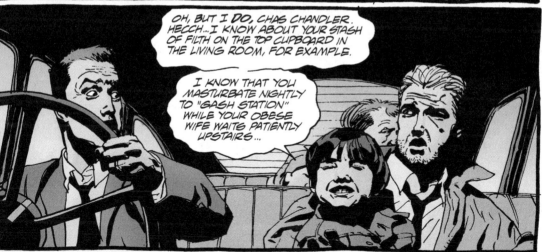

TOLD YA.

297

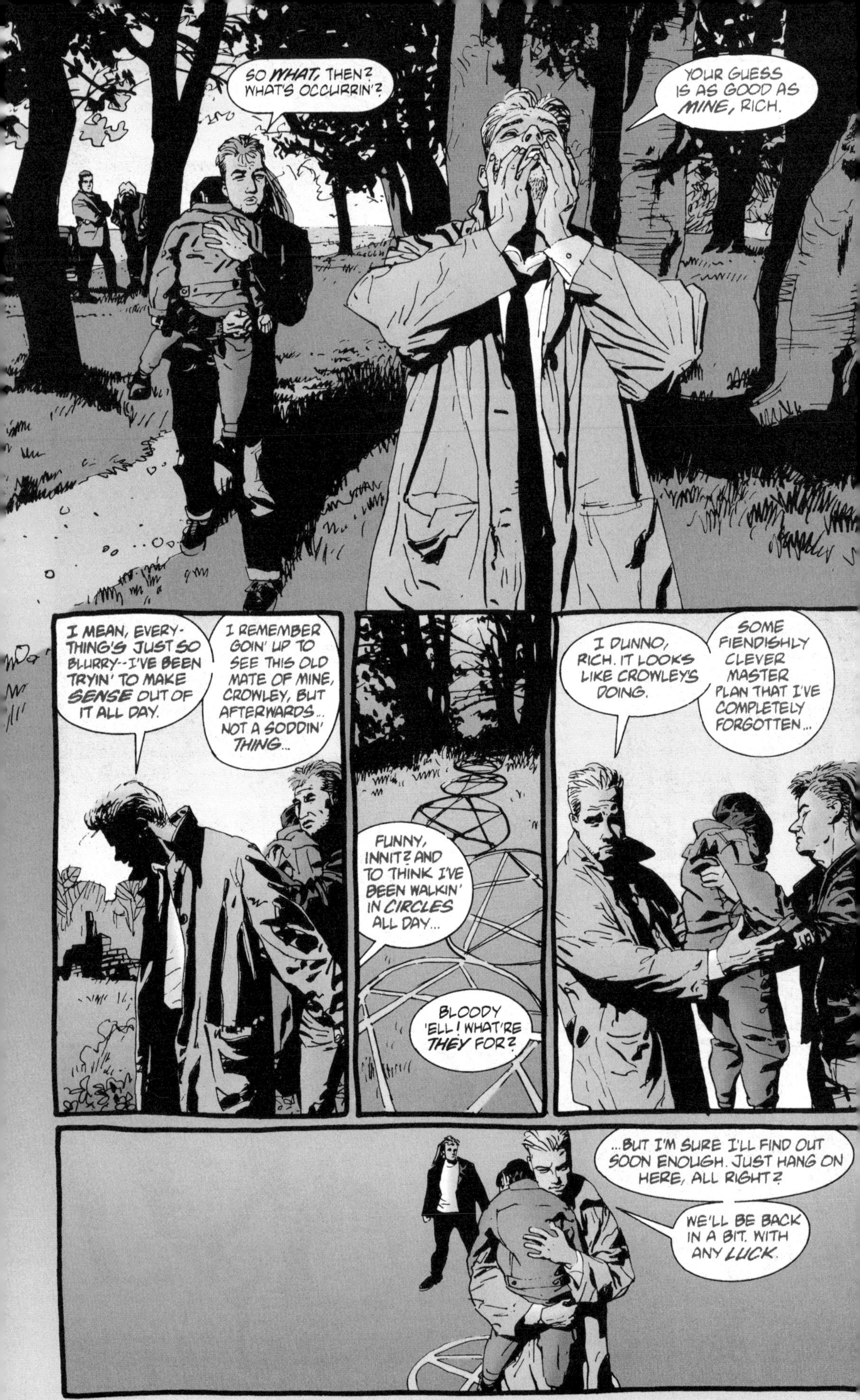
SO WHAT, THEN? WHAT'S OCCURRIN'?
YOUR GUESS IS AS GOOD AS MINE, RICH.
I MEAN, EVERY-THING'S JUST SO BLURRY--I'VE BEEN TRYIN' TO MAKE SENSE OUT OF IT ALL DAY.
I REMEMBER GOIN' UP TO SEE THIS OLD MATE OF MINE, CROWLEY, BUT AFTERWARDS... NOT A SODDIN' THING...
FUNNY, INNIT? AND TO THINK I'VE BEEN WALKIN' IN CIRCLES ALL DAY...
BLOODY 'ELL! WHAT'RE THEY FOR?
I DUNNO, RICH. IT LOOKS LIKE CROWLEY'S DOING.
SOME FIENDISHLY CLEVER MASTER PLAN THAT I'VE COMPLETELY FORGOTTEN...
...BUT I'M SURE I'LL FIND OUT SOON ENOUGH. JUST HANG ON HERE, ALL RIGHT?
WE'LL BE BACK IN A BIT. WITH ANY LUCK.

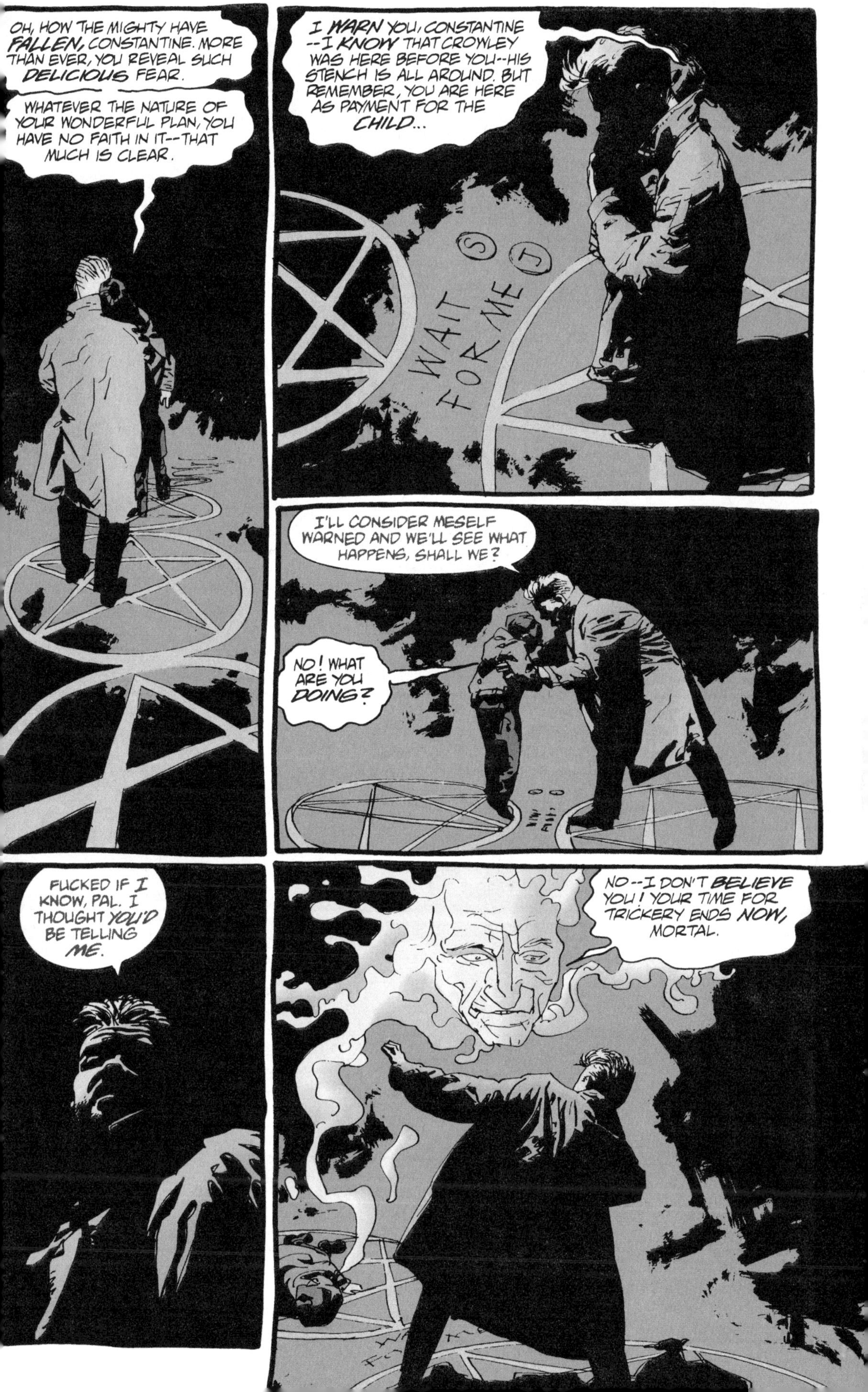
OH, HOW THE MIGHTY HAVE FALLEN, CONSTANTINE. MORE THAN EVER, YOU REVEAL SUCH DELICIOUS FEAR.
WHATEVER THE NATURE OF YOUR WONDERFUL PLAN, YOU HAVE NO FAITH IN IT--THAT MUCH IS CLEAR.
I WARN YOU, CONSTANTINE --I KNOW THAT CROWLEY WAS HERE BEFORE YOU--HIS STENCH IS ALL AROUND. BUT REMEMBER, YOU ARE HERE AS PAYMENT FOR THE CHILD...
S J
WAIT FOR ME
I'LL CONSIDER MESELF WARNED AND WE'LL SEE WHAT HAPPENS, SHALL WE?
NO! WHAT ARE YOU DOING?
FUCKED IF I KNOW, PAL. I THOUGHT YOU'D BE TELLING ME.
NO--I DON'T BELIEVE YOU! YOUR TIME FOR TRICKERY ENDS NOW, MORTAL.

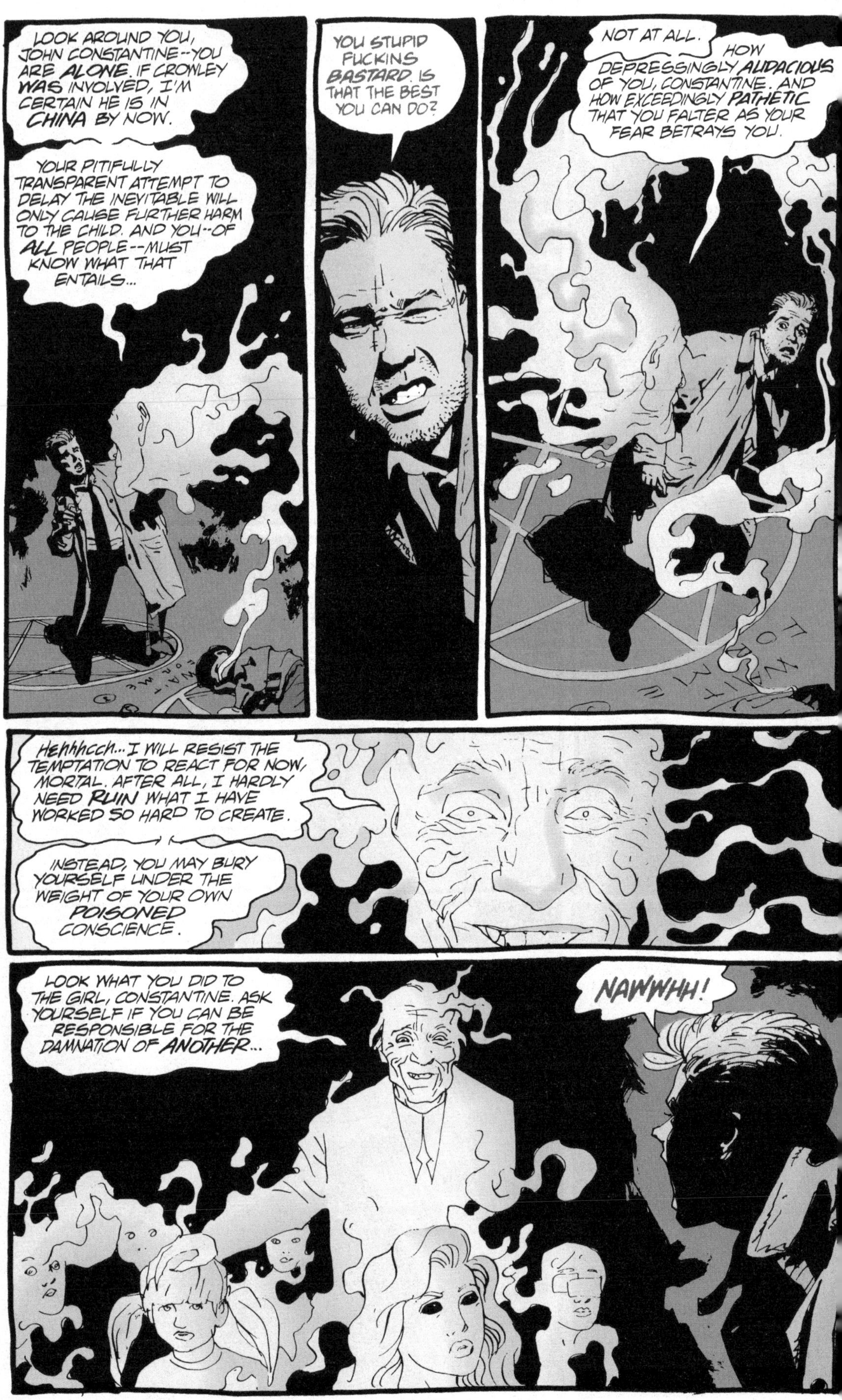
LOOK AROUND YOU, JOHN CONSTANTINE--YOU ARE ALONE. IF CROWLEY WAS INVOLVED, I'M CERTAIN HE IS IN CHINA BY NOW.
YOUR PITIFULLY TRANSPARENT ATTEMPT TO DELAY THE INEVITABLE WILL ONLY CAUSE FURTHER HARM TO THE CHILD. AND YOU--OF ALL PEOPLE--MUST KNOW WHAT THAT ENTAILS...
YOU STUPID FUCKING BASTARD. IS THAT THE BEST YOU CAN DO?
NOT AT ALL.
HOW DEPRESSINGLY AUDACIOUS OF YOU, CONSTANTINE. AND HOW EXCEEDINGLY PATHETIC THAT YOU FALTER AS YOUR FEAR BETRAYS YOU.
Hehhhcch... I WILL RESIST THE TEMPTATION TO REACT FOR NOW, MORTAL. AFTER ALL, I HARDLY NEED RUIN WHAT I HAVE WORKED SO HARD TO CREATE.
INSTEAD, YOU MAY BURY YOURSELF UNDER THE WEIGHT OF YOUR OWN POISONED CONSCIENCE.
LOOK WHAT YOU DID TO THE GIRL, CONSTANTINE. ASK YOURSELF IF YOU CAN BE RESPONSIBLE FOR THE DAMNATION OF ANOTHER...
NAWWHH!

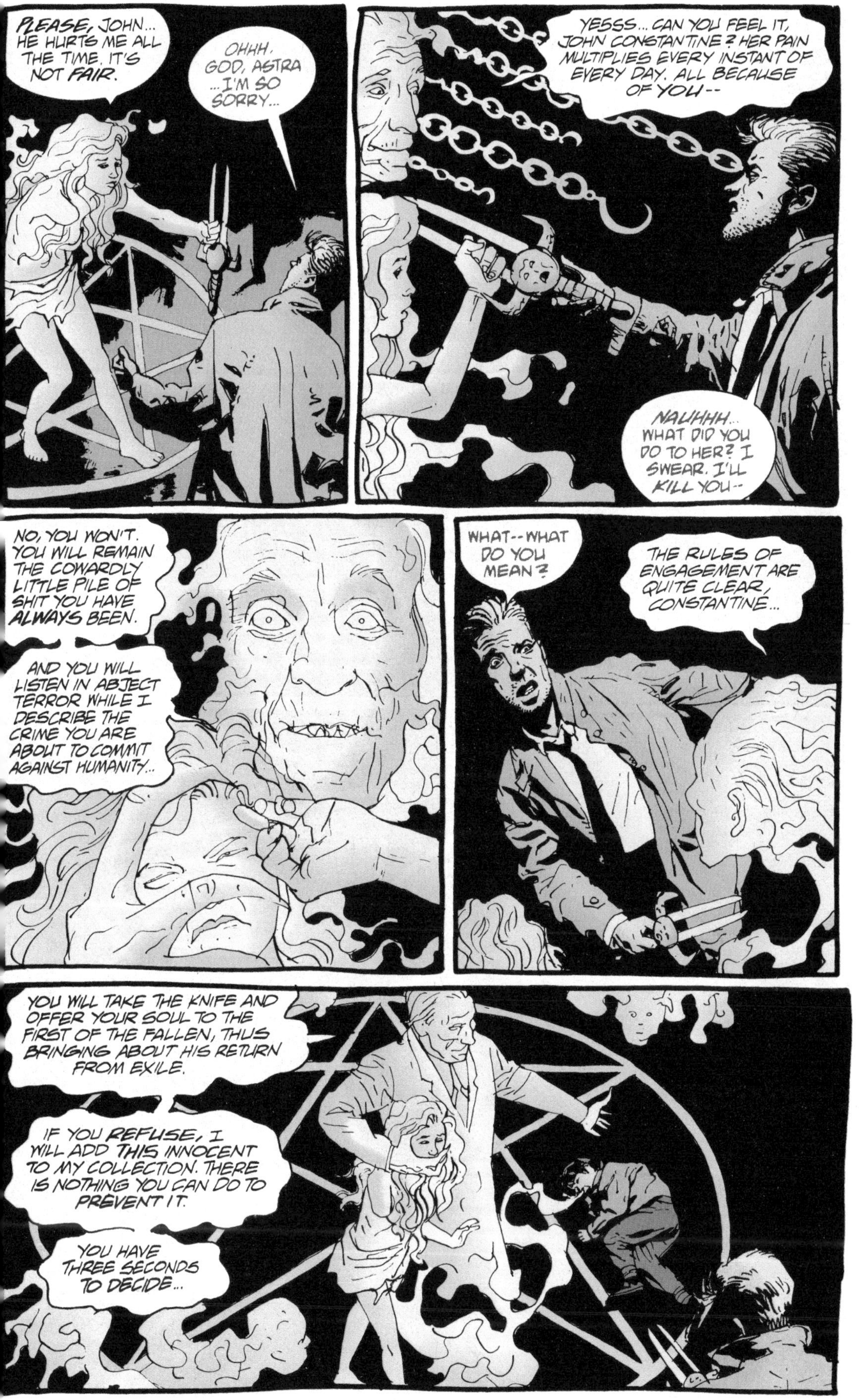
PLEASE, JOHN... HE HURTS ME ALL THE TIME. IT'S NOT FAIR.
OHHH, GOD, ASTRA ...I'M SO SORRY...
YESSS... CAN YOU FEEL IT, JOHN CONSTANTINE? HER PAIN MULTIPLIES EVERY INSTANT OF EVERY DAY. ALL BECAUSE OF YOU--
NAUHHH... WHAT DID YOU DO TO HER? I SWEAR, I'LL KILL YOU--
NO, YOU WON'T. YOU WILL REMAIN THE COWARDLY LITTLE PILE OF SHIT YOU HAVE ALWAYS BEEN.
AND YOU WILL LISTEN IN ABJECT TERROR WHILE I DESCRIBE THE CRIME YOU ARE ABOUT TO COMMIT AGAINST HUMANITY...
WHAT--WHAT DO YOU MEAN?
THE RULES OF ENGAGEMENT ARE QUITE CLEAR, CONSTANTINE...
YOU WILL TAKE THE KNIFE AND OFFER YOUR SOUL TO THE FIRST OF THE FALLEN, THUS BRINGING ABOUT HIS RETURN FROM EXILE.
IF YOU REFUSE, I WILL ADD THIS INNOCENT TO MY COLLECTION. THERE IS NOTHING YOU CAN DO TO PREVENT IT.
YOU HAVE THREE SECONDS TO DECIDE...

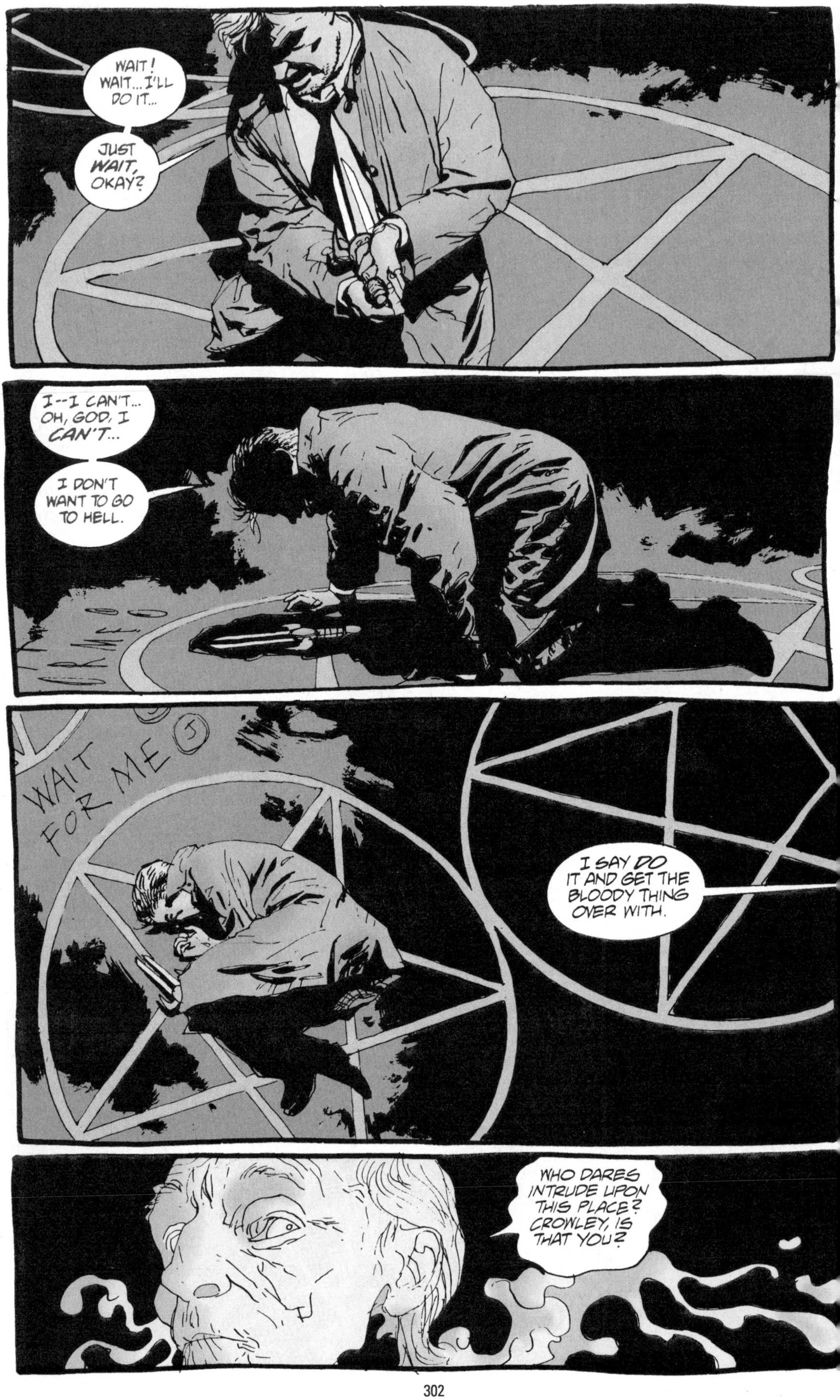
WAIT! WAIT... I'LL DO IT...
JUST WAIT, OKAY?
I--I CAN'T... OH, GOD, I CAN'T...
I DON'T WANT TO GO TO HELL.
WAIT FOR ME
I SAY DO IT AND GET THE BLOODY THING OVER WITH.
WHO DARES INTRUDE UPON THIS PLACE? CROWLEY, IS THAT YOU?

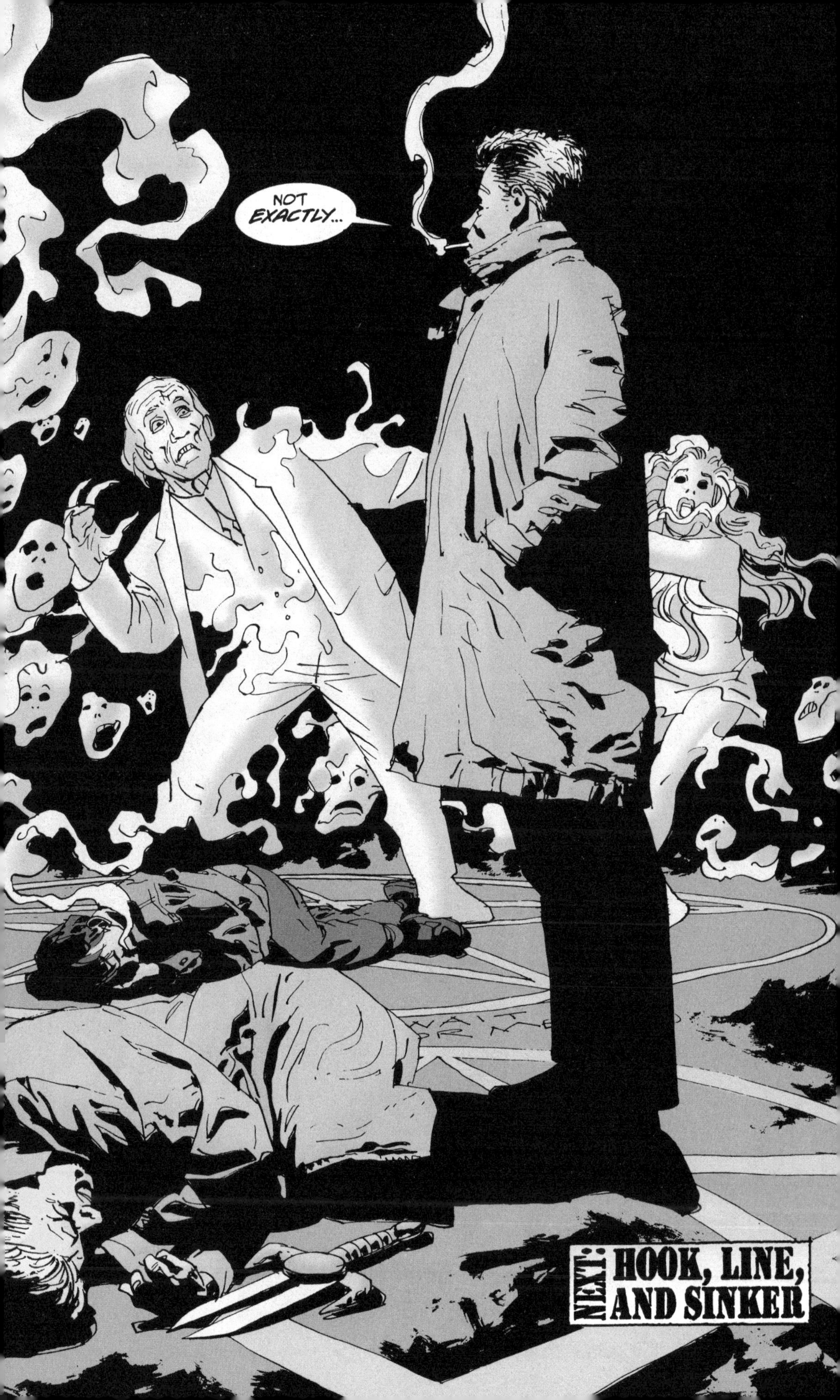
NOT EXACTLY...
NEXT: HOOK, LINE, AND SINKER

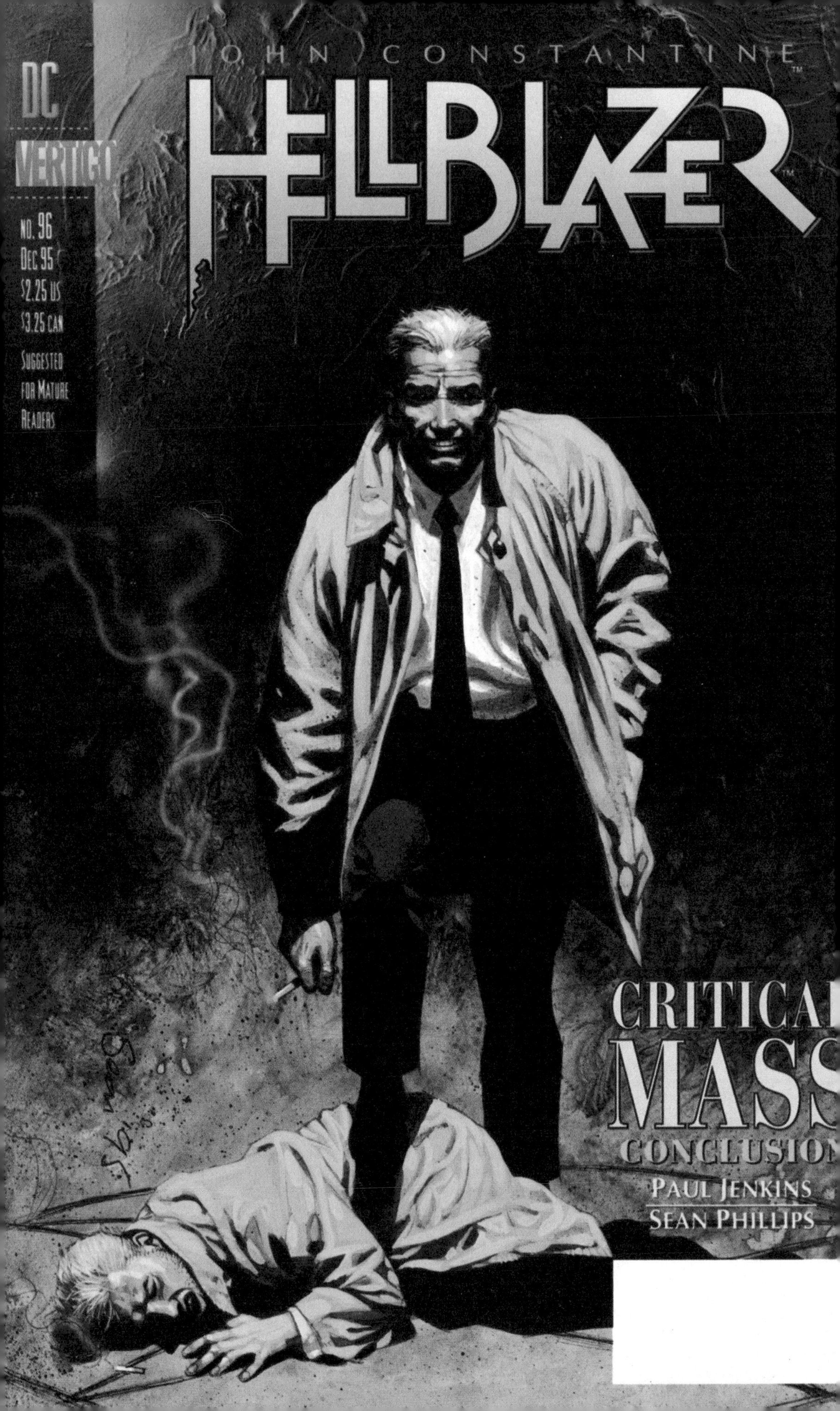
DC
VERTIGO
JOHN CONSTANTINE
HELLBLAZER
NO. 96
DEC 95
$2.25 US
$3.25 CAN
SUGGESTED FOR MATURE READERS
CRITICAL MASS
CONCLUSION
PAUL JENKINS
SEAN PHILLIPS

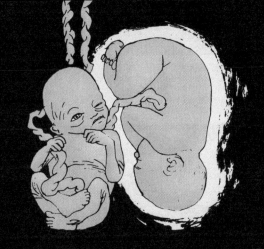

IT'S NOT THE **LENGTH** OF THE FALL THAT KILLS YOU--JUST THE HARD, DIRTY BIT AT THE **END**.

IF ONLY SOMEONE WOULD **EXPLAIN** THAT, MAYBE YOU'D CHUCK IT ALL IN BEFORE TAKING THE PLUNGE.

BUT YOU DON'T HAVE THAT CHOICE. YOUR FIRST LITTLE BABY THOUGHT IS A SUS-PICION THAT YOU'RE ALREADY DOOMED.

POWERLESS, YOU SCREAM TO THE HEAVENS IN DEFIANCE. NOBODY LISTENS TO YOUR CRIES...

YOU FALL FASTER. THERE'S NO SAFETY NET NOW--YOU'RE FLYING SOLO.

LIVE FOR **TODAY,** YOU THINK. TOMORROW NEVER COMES.

BUT TOMORROW **ALWAYS** COMES--JUST LIKE YOU KNEW IT WOULD.

NOW, YOU CAN ONLY FIND COMFORT IN OBLIVION. YOU TUMBLE THROUGH A CLOUD OF SELF-PITY AND DESPAIR, REGRETTING EVERY DECISION YOU EVER MADE.

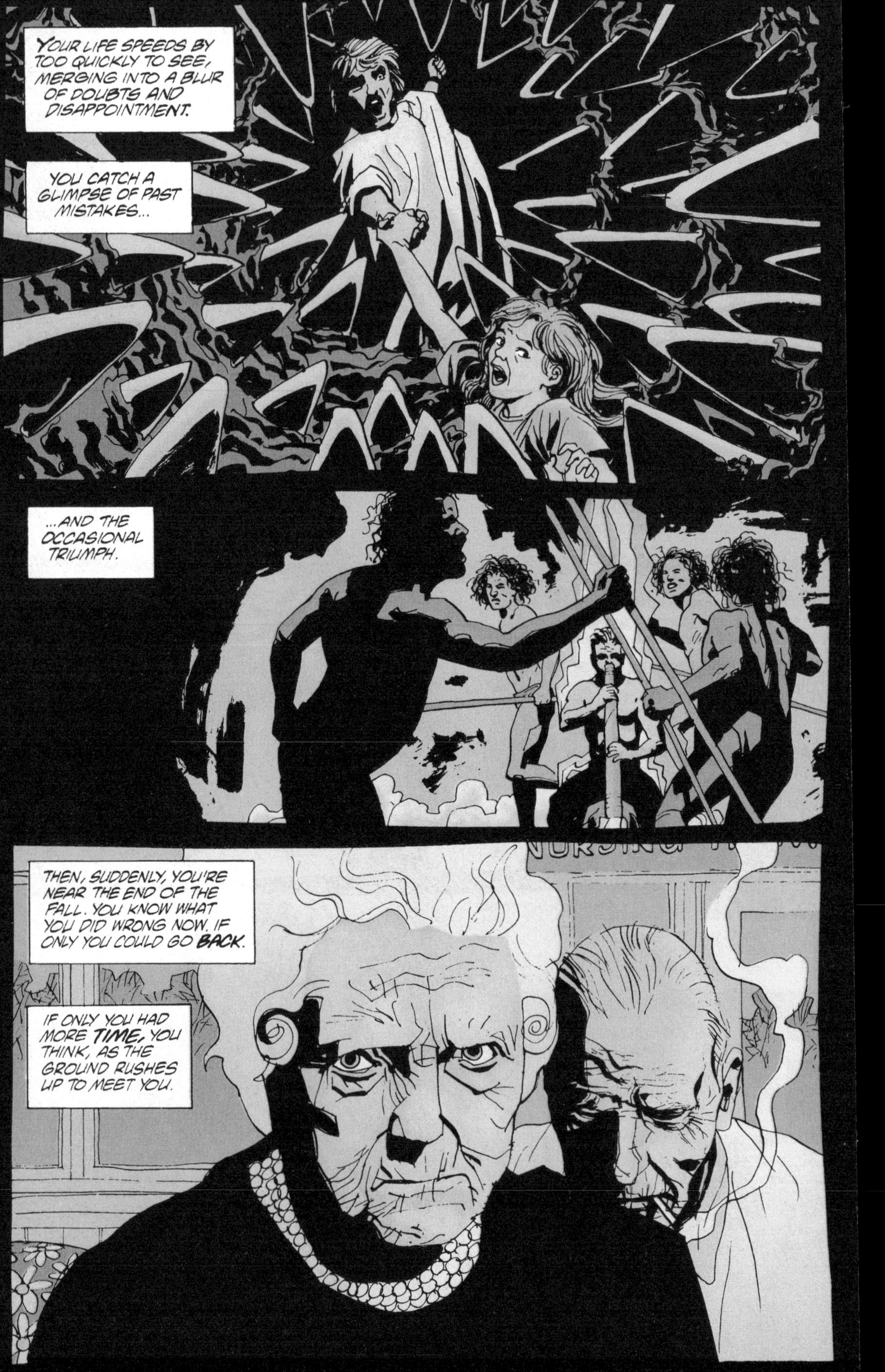
YOUR LIFE SPEEDS BY TOO QUICKLY TO SEE, MERGING INTO A BLUR OF DOUBTS AND DISAPPOINTMENT.
YOU CATCH A GLIMPSE OF PAST MISTAKES...
...AND THE OCCASIONAL TRIUMPH.
THEN, SUDDENLY, YOU'RE NEAR THE END OF THE FALL. YOU KNOW WHAT YOU DID WRONG NOW. IF ONLY YOU COULD GO BACK.
IF ONLY YOU HAD MORE TIME, YOU THINK, AS THE GROUND RUSHES UP TO MEET YOU.

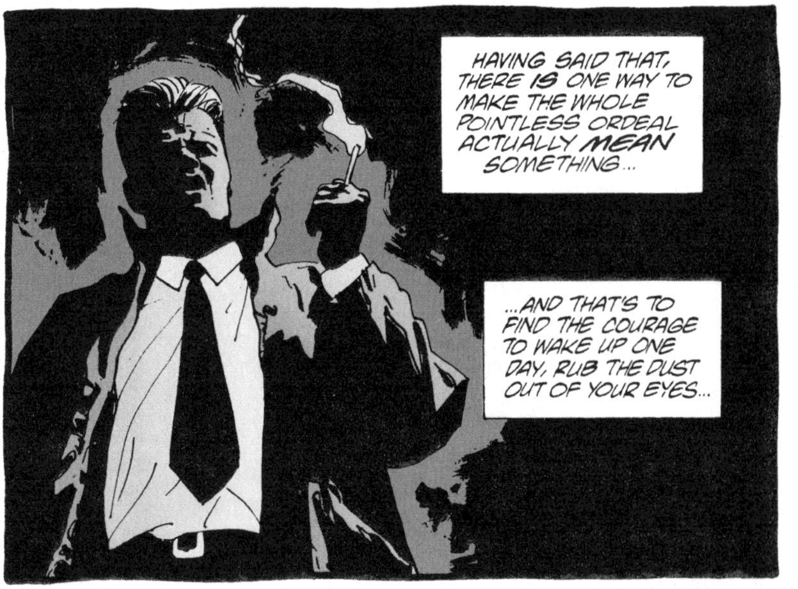
HAVING SAID THAT, THERE IS ONE WAY TO MAKE THE WHOLE POINTLESS ORDEAL ACTUALLY MEAN SOMETHING...
...AND THAT'S TO FIND THE COURAGE TO WAKE UP ONE DAY, RUB THE DUST OUT OF YOUR EYES...

CRITICAL MASS 5

Hook Line & Sinker

Paul Jenkins Writer

Sean Phillips Artist

Matt Hollingsworth Colorist

Clem Robins Letterer

Axel Alonso Asst. Editor

Lou Stathis Editor

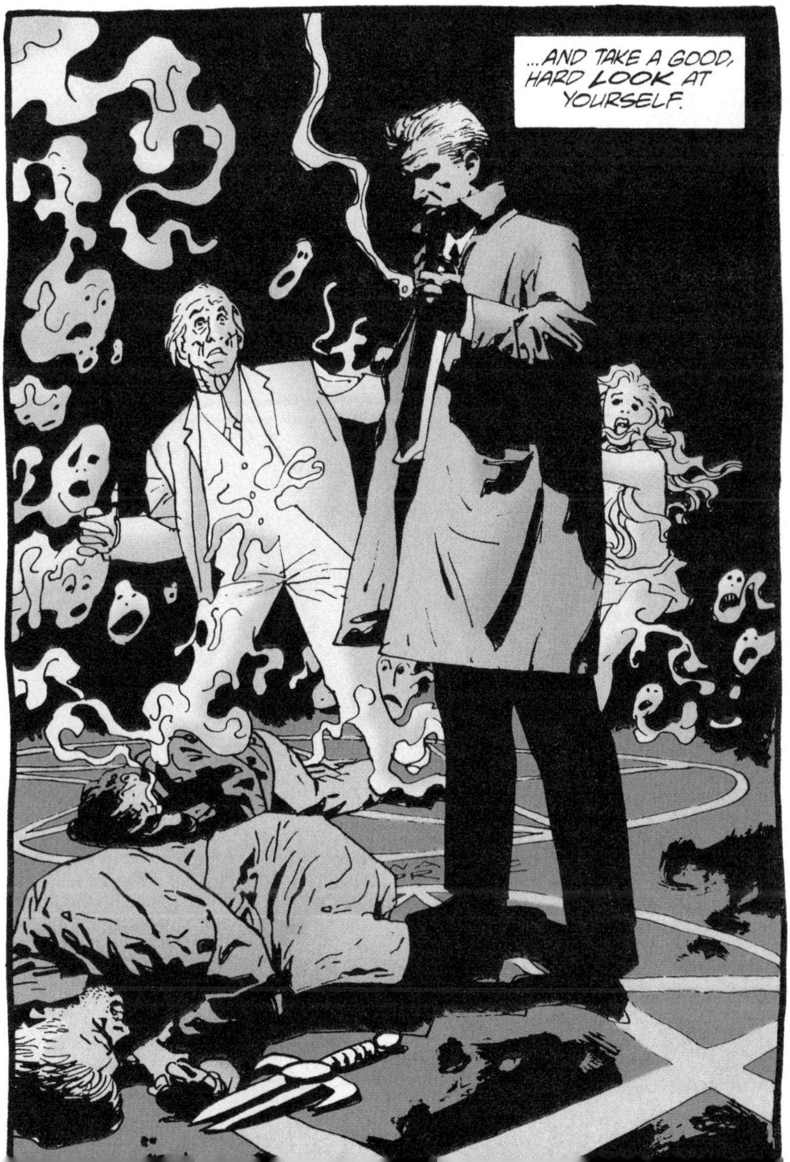
...AND TAKE A GOOD, HARD LOOK AT YOURSELF.

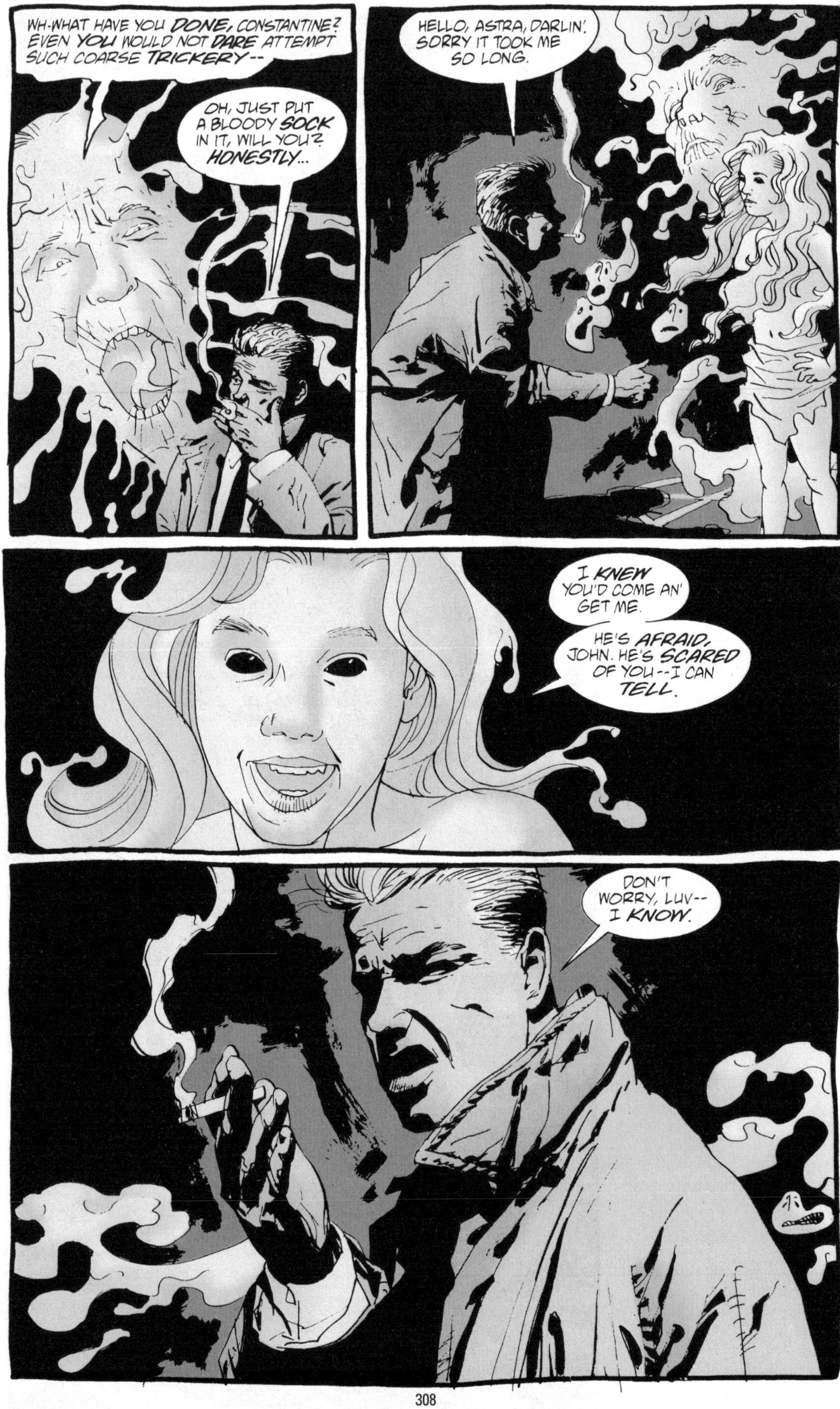
WH-WHAT HAVE YOU DONE, CONSTANTINE? EVEN YOU WOULD NOT DARE ATTEMPT SUCH COARSE TRICKERY--
OH, JUST PUT A BLOODY SOCK IN IT, WILL YOU? HONESTLY...
HELLO, ASTRA, DARLIN'. SORRY IT TOOK ME SO LONG.
I KNEW YOU'D COME AN' GET ME.
HE'S AFRAID, JOHN. HE'S SCARED OF YOU--I CAN TELL.
DON'T WORRY, LUV-- I KNOW.

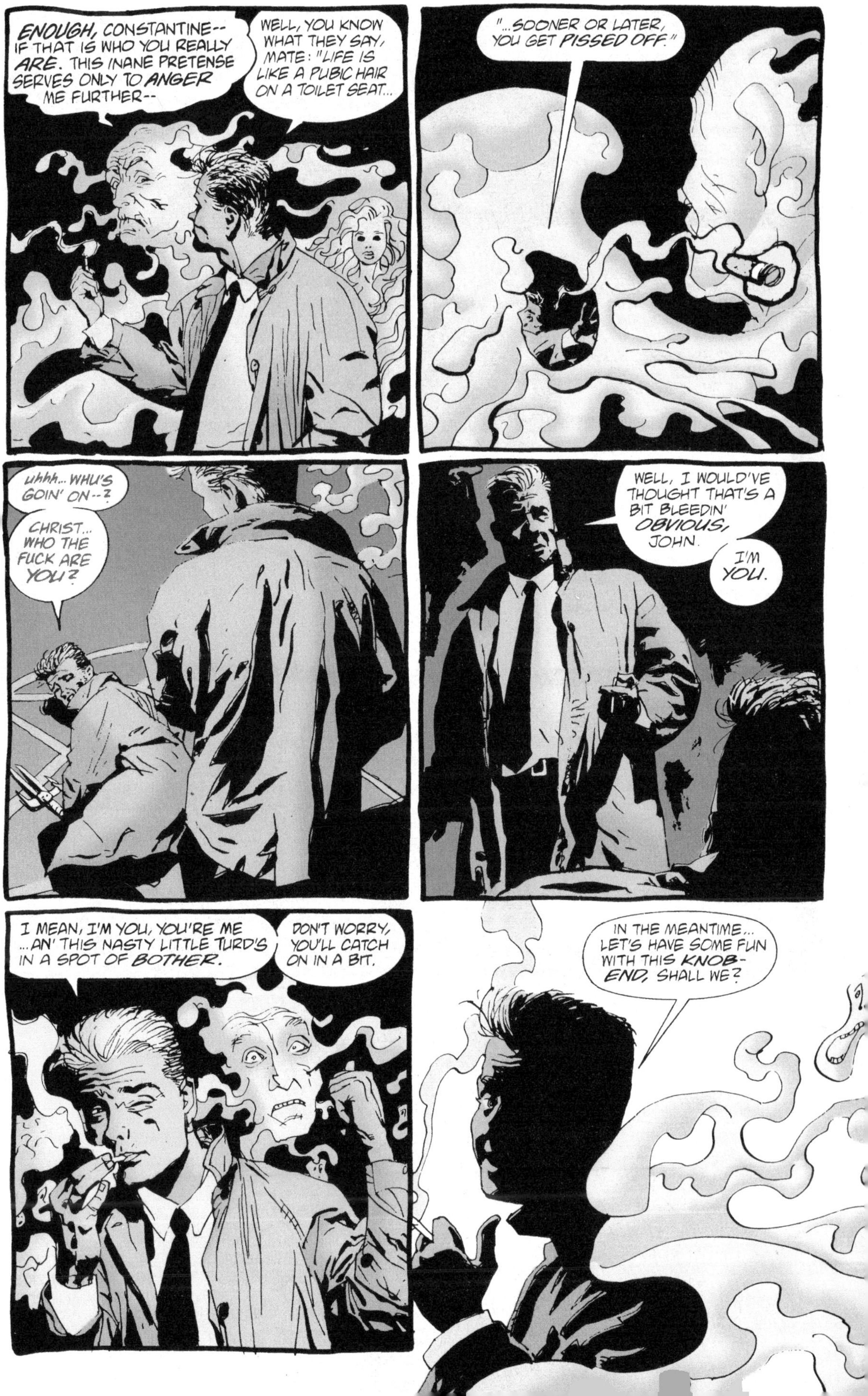
ENOUGH, CONSTANTINE-- IF THAT IS WHO YOU REALLY ARE. THIS INANE PRETENSE SERVES ONLY TO ANGER ME FURTHER--
WELL, YOU KNOW WHAT THEY SAY, MATE: "LIFE IS LIKE A PUBIC HAIR ON A TOILET SEAT...
"...SOONER OR LATER, YOU GET PISSED OFF."
uhhh... WHU'S GOIN' ON--?
CHRIST... WHO THE FUCK ARE YOU?
WELL, I WOULD'VE THOUGHT THAT'S A BIT BLEEDIN' OBVIOUS, JOHN.
I'M YOU.
I MEAN, I'M YOU, YOU'RE ME ...AN' THIS NASTY LITTLE TURD'S IN A SPOT OF BOTHER.
DON'T WORRY, YOU'LL CATCH ON IN A BIT.
IN THE MEANTIME... LET'S HAVE SOME FUN WITH THIS KNOB-END, SHALL WE?

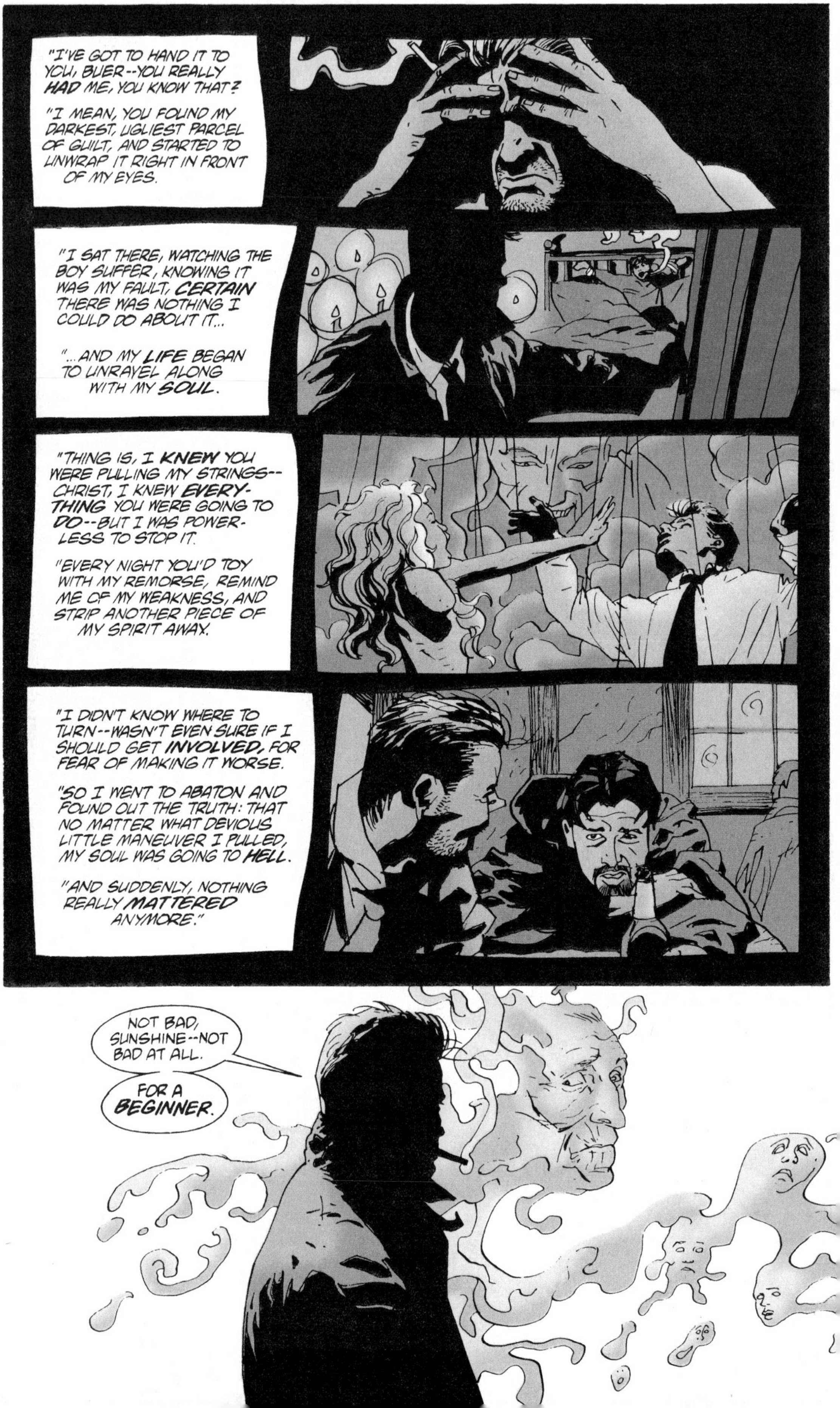
"I'VE GOT TO HAND IT TO YOU, BUER--YOU REALLY HAD ME, YOU KNOW THAT?
"I MEAN, YOU FOUND MY DARKEST, UGLIEST PARCEL OF GUILT, AND STARTED TO UNWRAP IT RIGHT IN FRONT OF MY EYES.
"I SAT THERE, WATCHING THE BOY SUFFER, KNOWING IT WAS MY FAULT, CERTAIN THERE WAS NOTHING I COULD DO ABOUT IT...
"...AND MY LIFE BEGAN TO UNRAVEL ALONG WITH MY SOUL.
"THING IS, I KNEW YOU WERE PULLING MY STRINGS--CHRIST, I KNEW EVERYTHING YOU WERE GOING TO DO--BUT I WAS POWERLESS TO STOP IT.
"EVERY NIGHT YOU'D TOY WITH MY REMORSE, REMIND ME OF MY WEAKNESS, AND STRIP ANOTHER PIECE OF MY SPIRIT AWAY.
"I DIDN'T KNOW WHERE TO TURN--WASN'T EVEN SURE IF I SHOULD GET INVOLVED, FOR FEAR OF MAKING IT WORSE.
"SO I WENT TO ABATON AND FOUND OUT THE TRUTH: THAT NO MATTER WHAT DEVIOUS LITTLE MANEUVER I PULLED, MY SOUL WAS GOING TO HELL.
"AND SUDDENLY, NOTHING REALLY MATTERED ANYMORE."
NOT BAD, SUNSHINE--NOT BAD AT ALL.
FOR A BEGINNER.

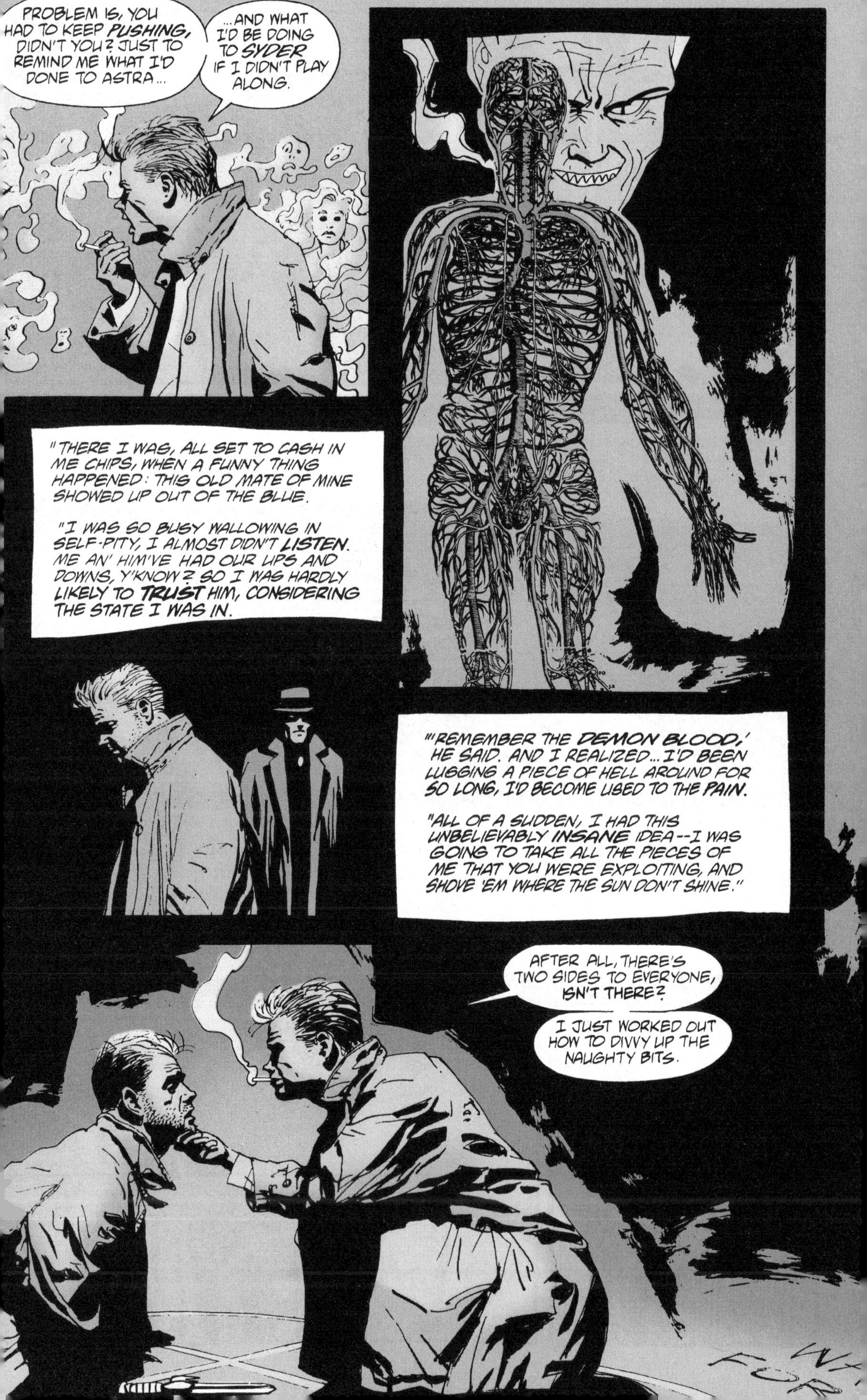
PROBLEM IS, YOU HAD TO KEEP PUSHING, DIDN'T YOU? JUST TO REMIND ME WHAT I'D DONE TO ASTRA...
...AND WHAT I'D BE DOING TO SYDER IF I DIDN'T PLAY ALONG.
"THERE I WAS, ALL SET TO CASH IN ME CHIPS, WHEN A FUNNY THING HAPPENED: THIS OLD MATE OF MINE SHOWED UP OUT OF THE BLUE.
"I WAS SO BUSY WALLOWING IN SELF-PITY, I ALMOST DIDN'T LISTEN. ME AN' HIM'VE HAD OUR UPS AND DOWNS, Y'KNOW? SO I WAS HARDLY LIKELY TO TRUST HIM, CONSIDERING THE STATE I WAS IN.
"'REMEMBER THE DEMON BLOOD,' HE SAID. AND I REALIZED... I'D BEEN LUGGING A PIECE OF HELL AROUND FOR SO LONG, I'D BECOME USED TO THE PAIN.
"ALL OF A SUDDEN, I HAD THIS UNBELIEVABLY INSANE IDEA--I WAS GOING TO TAKE ALL THE PIECES OF ME THAT YOU WERE EXPLOITING, AND SHOVE 'EM WHERE THE SUN DON'T SHINE."
AFTER ALL, THERE'S TWO SIDES TO EVERYONE, ISN'T THERE?
I JUST WORKED OUT HOW TO DIVVY UP THE NAUGHTY BITS.

A--A **WALK-IN!** YOU **PURGED** YOURSELF OF YOUR SOUL?

I--I REFUSE TO **BELIEVE** IT.

I **KNOW** YOU, CONSTANTINE ...YOU ARE NOT **THAT** PROFICIENT IN THE ARTS--

MAYBE SO, MATE, BUT I'VE GOT **YOU** BY THE SHORT AN' CURLIES, HAVEN'T I?

"NORMALLY, I'D KEEP MY DISTANCE FROM ALL THAT MASTER-OF-THE-MYSTIC-ARTS CRAP. BUT DESPERATE TIMES CALL FOR DESPERATE MEASURES...

"...AND I KNEW IT'D BE THE **LAST** THING YOU'D EXPECT. SO I WENT AHEAD AN' DID IT.

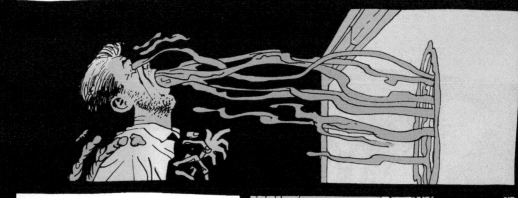

"IT'S THE ULTIMATE IN CATHARSIS, INNIT? I WASHED OUT ALL THE SMEGGY BITS OF MY SOUL, AND CHUCKED 'EM INTO A TEMPORARY VERSION OF MYSELF.

"NOW, I WAS FINALLY DOING SOME MANIPULATION OF MY OWN.

OH, YEAH, I ALMOST FORGOT... THE HOW'S AND WHY'S...

On The Transfer & Application of Souls

Aleister Crowley.

WELL, I DON'T JUST READ THE BEANO, NOW DO I?

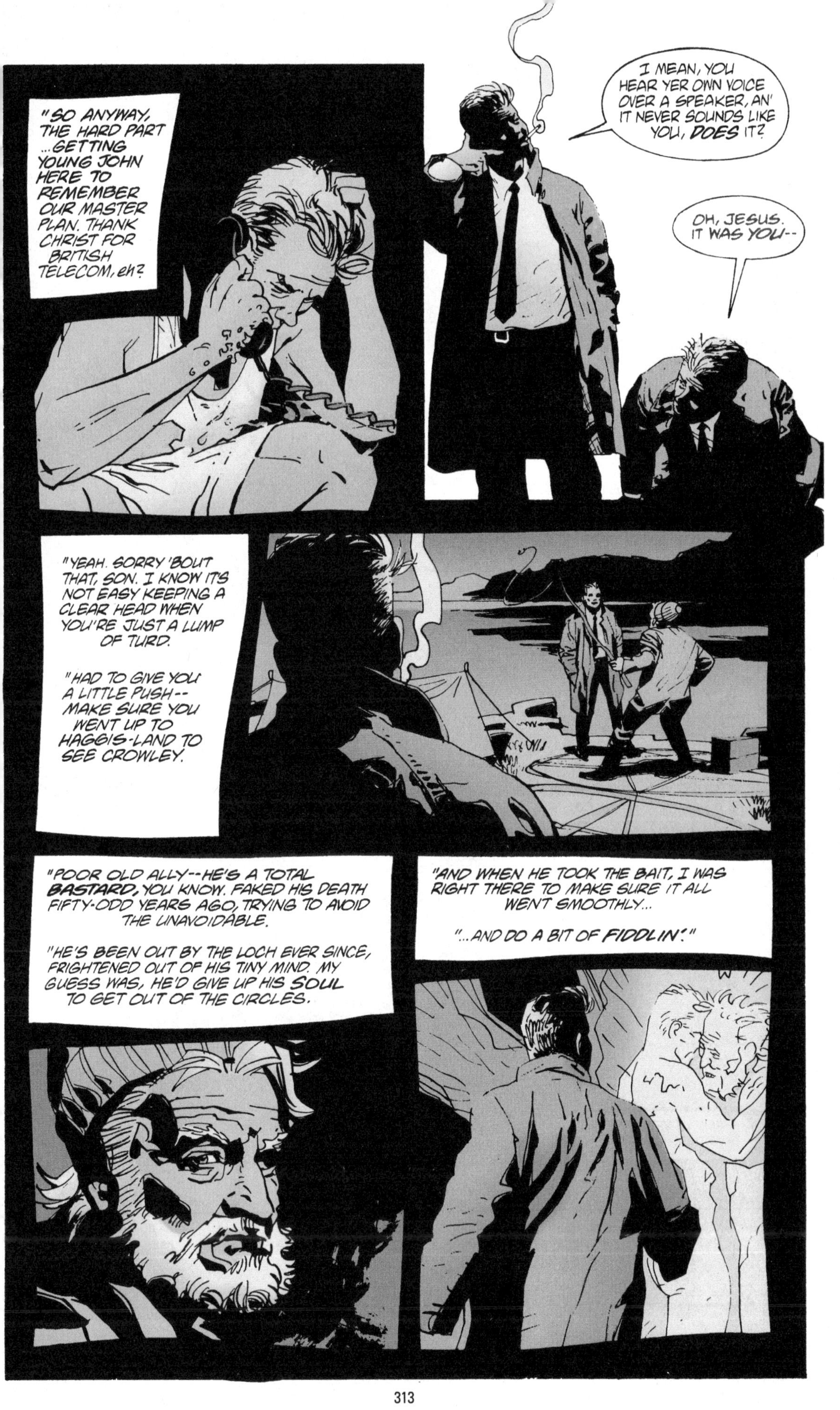
"SO ANYWAY, THE HARD PART ...GETTING YOUNG JOHN HERE TO REMEMBER OUR MASTER PLAN. THANK CHRIST FOR BRITISH TELECOM, eh?
I MEAN, YOU HEAR YER OWN VOICE OVER A SPEAKER, AN' IT NEVER SOUNDS LIKE YOU, DOES IT?
OH, JESUS. IT WAS YOU--
"YEAH. SORRY 'BOUT THAT, SON. I KNOW IT'S NOT EASY KEEPING A CLEAR HEAD WHEN YOU'RE JUST A LUMP OF TURD.
"HAD TO GIVE YOU A LITTLE PUSH-- MAKE SURE YOU WENT UP TO HAGGIS-LAND TO SEE CROWLEY.
"POOR OLD ALLY--HE'S A TOTAL BASTARD, YOU KNOW. FAKED HIS DEATH FIFTY-ODD YEARS AGO, TRYING TO AVOID THE UNAVOIDABLE.
"HE'S BEEN OUT BY THE LOCH EVER SINCE, FRIGHTENED OUT OF HIS TINY MIND. MY GUESS WAS, HE'D GIVE UP HIS SOUL TO GET OUT OF THE CIRCLES.
"AND WHEN HE TOOK THE BAIT, I WAS RIGHT THERE TO MAKE SURE IT ALL WENT SMOOTHLY...
"...AND DO A BIT OF FIDDLIN'."

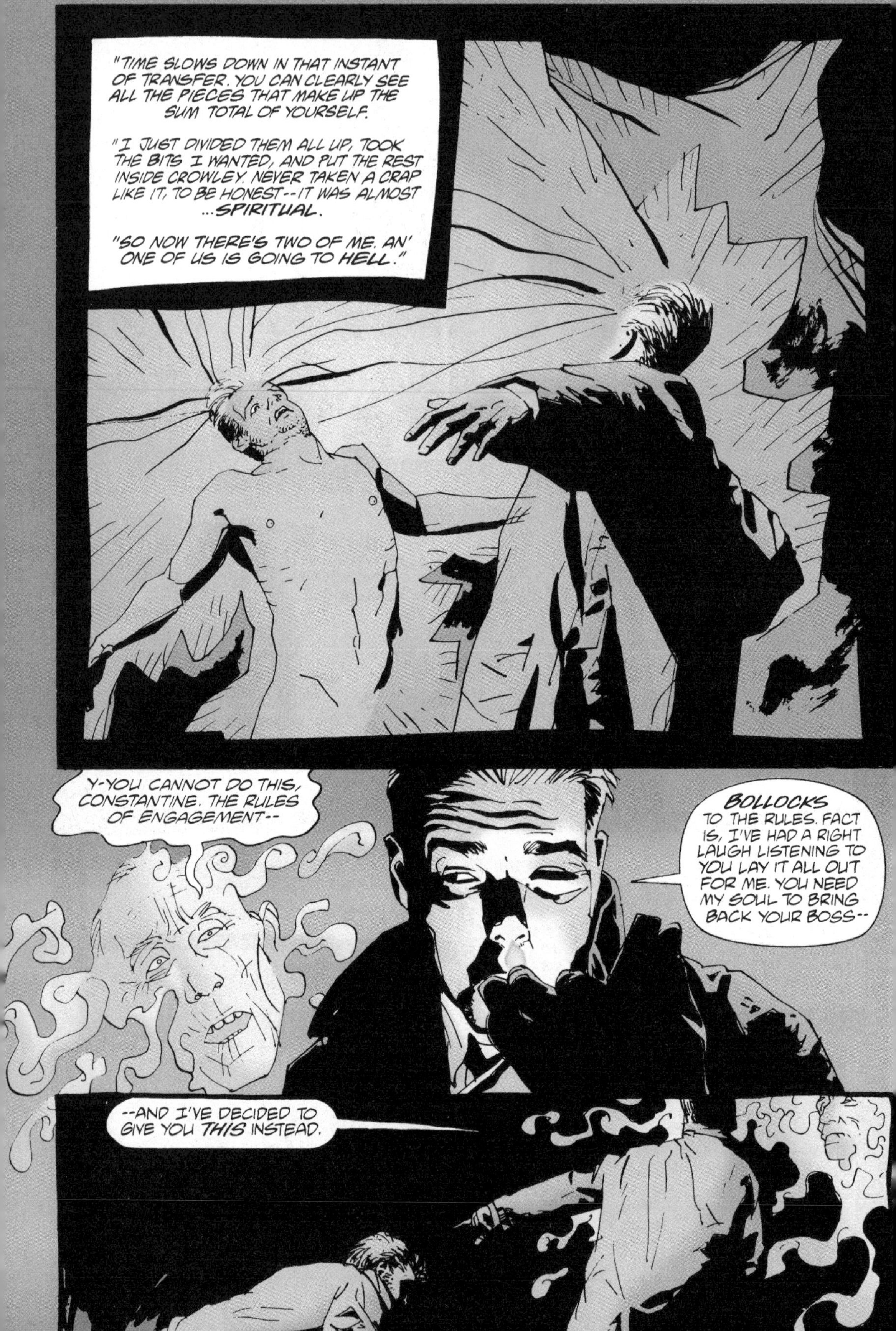
"TIME SLOWS DOWN IN THAT INSTANT OF TRANSFER. YOU CAN CLEARLY SEE ALL THE PIECES THAT MAKE UP THE SUM TOTAL OF YOURSELF.
"I JUST DIVIDED THEM ALL UP, TOOK THE BITS I WANTED, AND PUT THE REST INSIDE CROWLEY. NEVER TAKEN A CRAP LIKE IT, TO BE HONEST--IT WAS ALMOST ...SPIRITUAL.
"SO NOW THERE'S TWO OF ME. AN' ONE OF US IS GOING TO HELL."
Y-YOU CANNOT DO THIS, CONSTANTINE. THE RULES OF ENGAGEMENT--
BOLLOCKS TO THE RULES. FACT IS, I'VE HAD A RIGHT LAUGH LISTENING TO YOU LAY IT ALL OUT FOR ME. YOU NEED MY SOUL TO BRING BACK YOUR BOSS--
--AND I'VE DECIDED TO GIVE YOU THIS INSTEAD.

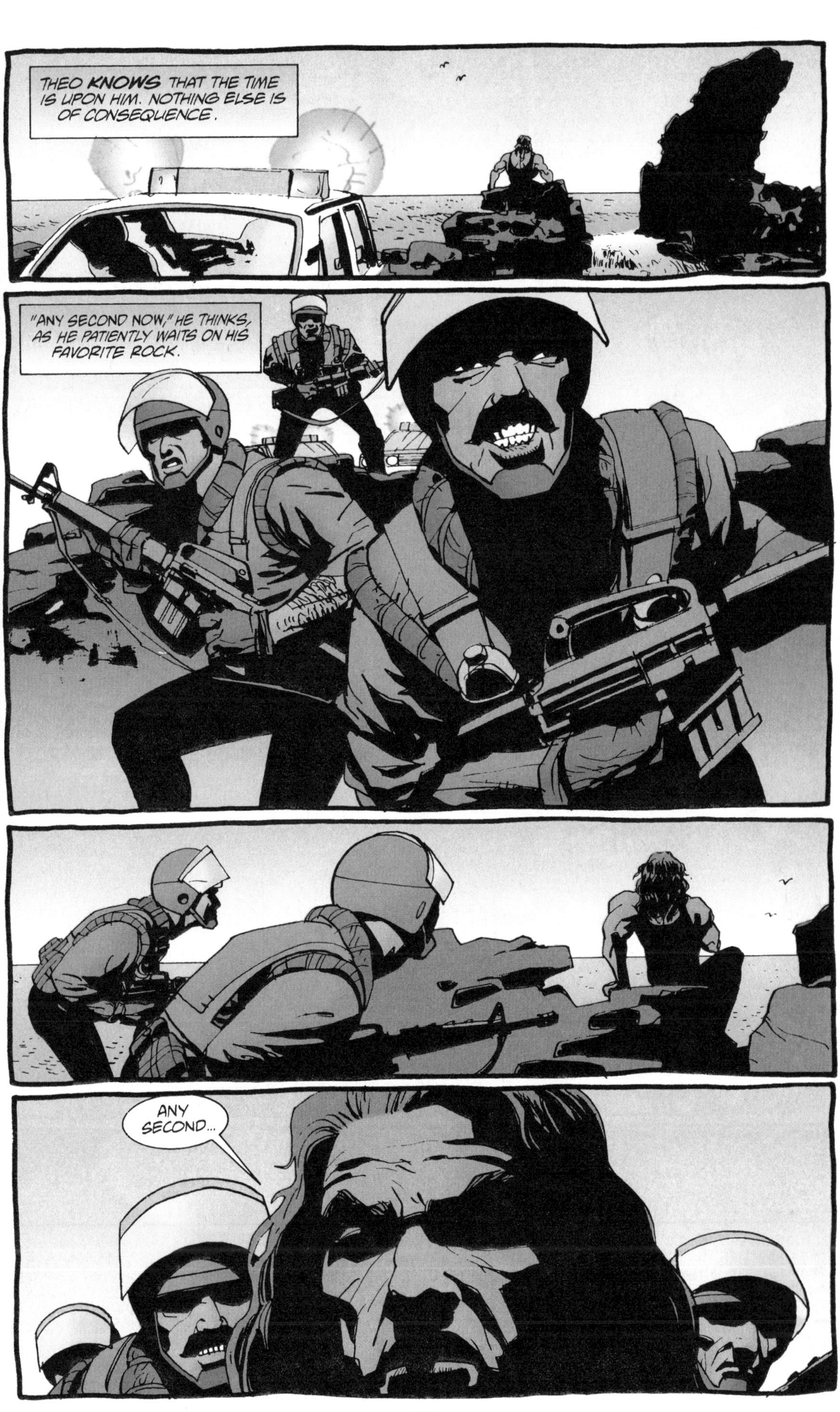
THEO **KNOWS** THAT THE TIME IS UPON HIM. NOTHING ELSE IS OF CONSEQUENCE.
"ANY SECOND NOW," HE THINKS, AS HE PATIENTLY WAITS ON HIS FAVORITE ROCK.
ANY SECOND...

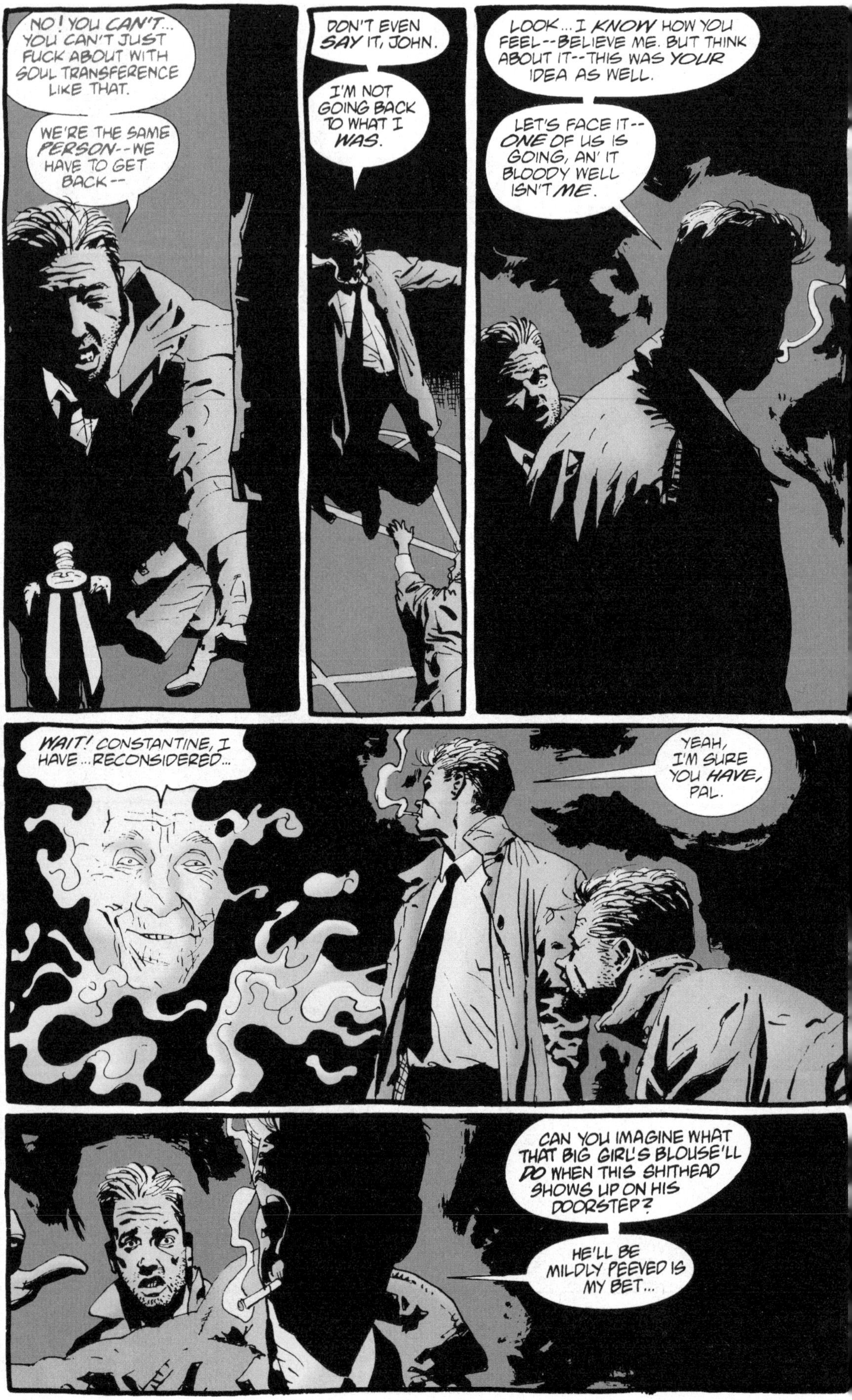
NO! YOU CAN'T... YOU CAN'T JUST FUCK ABOUT WITH SOUL TRANSFERENCE LIKE THAT.
WE'RE THE SAME PERSON--WE HAVE TO GET BACK--
DON'T EVEN SAY IT, JOHN.
I'M NOT GOING BACK TO WHAT I WAS.
LOOK... I KNOW HOW YOU FEEL--BELIEVE ME. BUT THINK ABOUT IT--THIS WAS YOUR IDEA AS WELL.
LET'S FACE IT--ONE OF US IS GOING, AN' IT BLOODY WELL ISN'T ME.
WAIT! CONSTANTINE, I HAVE...RECONSIDERED...
YEAH, I'M SURE YOU HAVE, PAL.
CAN YOU IMAGINE WHAT THAT BIG GIRL'S BLOUSE'LL DO WHEN THIS SHITHEAD SHOWS UP ON HIS DOORSTEP?
HE'LL BE MILDLY PEEVED IS MY BET...

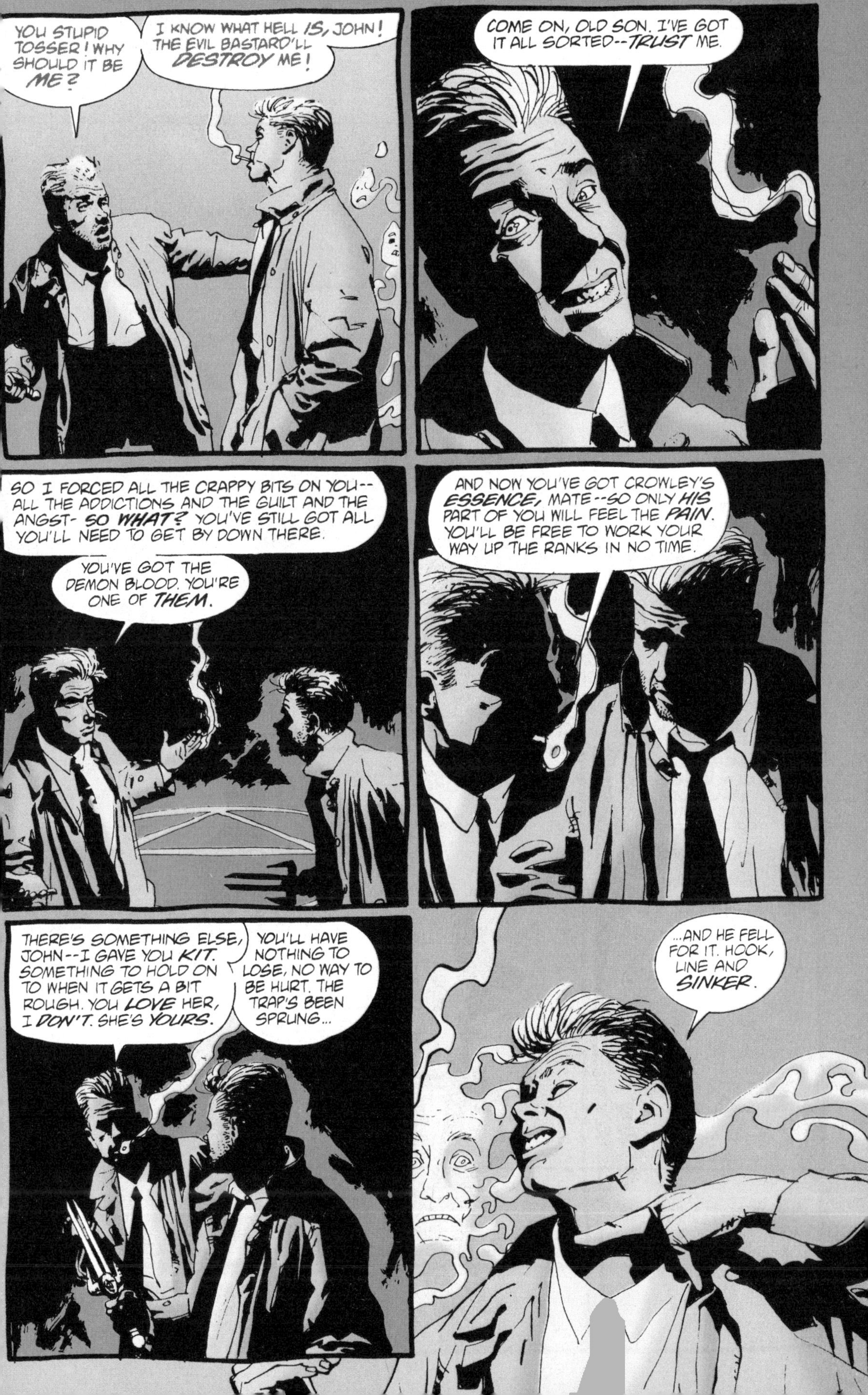

YOU STUPID TOSSER! WHY SHOULD IT BE ME?
I KNOW WHAT HELL IS, JOHN! THE EVIL BASTARD'LL DESTROY ME!
COME ON, OLD SON. I'VE GOT IT ALL SORTED--TRUST ME.
SO I FORCED ALL THE CRAPPY BITS ON YOU--ALL THE ADDICTIONS AND THE GUILT AND THE ANGST- SO WHAT? YOU'VE STILL GOT ALL YOU'LL NEED TO GET BY DOWN THERE.
YOU'VE GOT THE DEMON BLOOD. YOU'RE ONE OF THEM.
AND NOW YOU'VE GOT CROWLEY'S ESSENCE, MATE--SO ONLY HIS PART OF YOU WILL FEEL THE PAIN. YOU'LL BE FREE TO WORK YOUR WAY UP THE RANKS IN NO TIME.
THERE'S SOMETHING ELSE, JOHN--I GAVE YOU KIT. SOMETHING TO HOLD ON TO WHEN IT GETS A BIT ROUGH. YOU LOVE HER, I DON'T. SHE'S YOURS.
YOU'LL HAVE NOTHING TO LOSE, NO WAY TO BE HURT. THE TRAP'S BEEN SPRUNG...
...AND HE FELL FOR IT. HOOK, LINE AND SINKER.

I--I WANT NO PART OF THIS, CONSTANTINE.

PLEASE... FORGIVE ME ...THE CHILD IS YOURS.

AALLWGGH--

NNAHHH...WHERE'S MY DAAAAD?

S'OKAY, MATEY. YER UNCLE CON-JOB'S HERE.

FUCK YOU YOU BASTARD! THAT'S NOT ENOUGH!

LET THEM GO. ALL OF THEM--

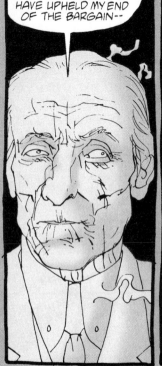

YOU DARE THREATEN ME, YOU WORTHLESS LITTLE VANDAL? I HAVE UPHELD MY END OF THE BARGAIN--

I NEVER BARGAINED WITH YOU, TOSSER. LET 'EM GO...

I'LL FUCKING DO IT, I SWEAR!

WAIT! I BEG OF YOU, PLEASE... STAY YOUR HAND.

I WILL DO AS YOU SAY... PLEASE...

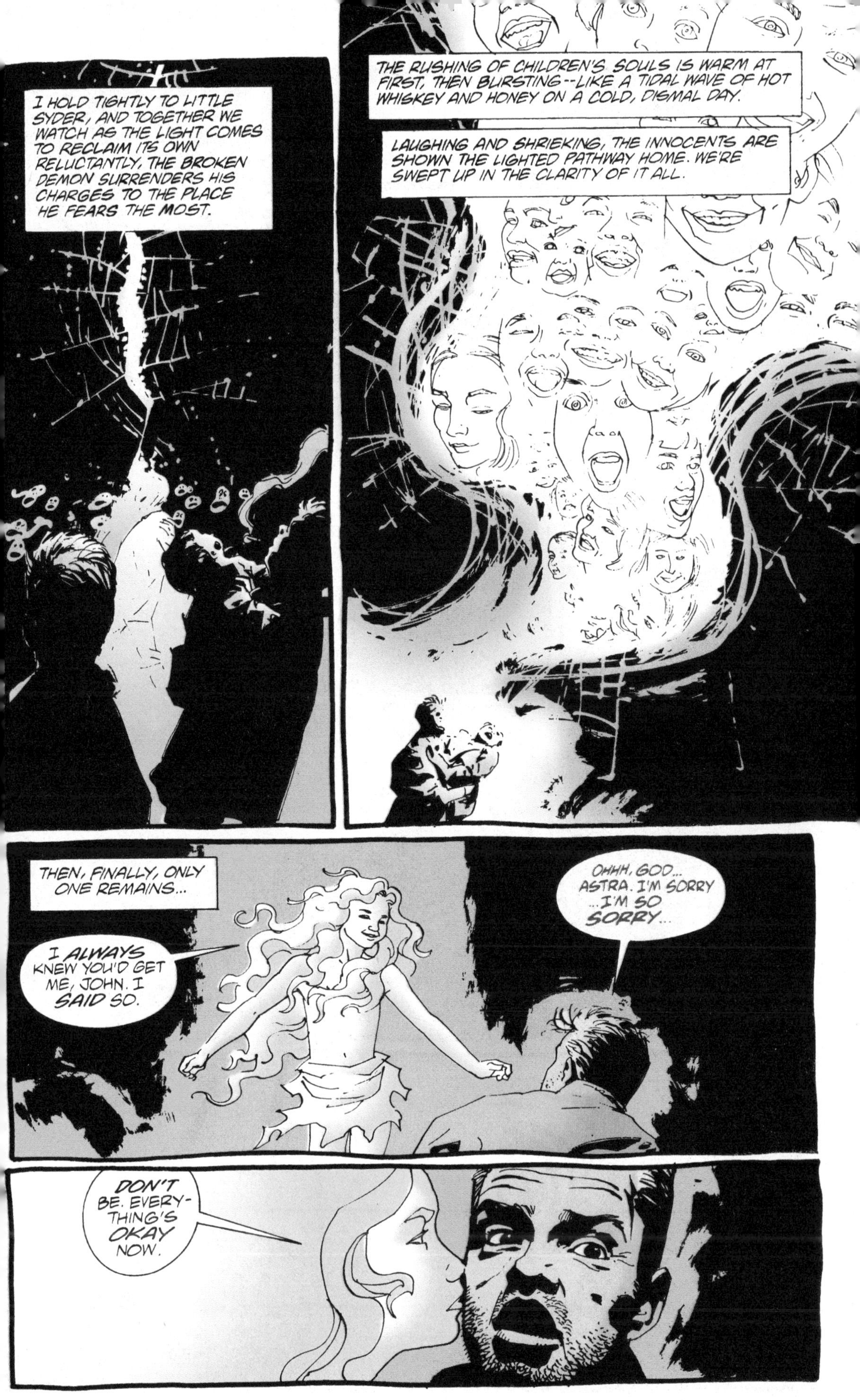
I HOLD TIGHTLY TO LITTLE SYDER, AND TOGETHER WE WATCH AS THE LIGHT COMES TO RECLAIM ITS OWN RELUCTANTLY, THE BROKEN DEMON SURRENDERS HIS CHARGES TO THE PLACE HE FEARS THE MOST.
THE RUSHING OF CHILDREN'S SOULS IS WARM AT FIRST, THEN BURSTING--LIKE A TIDAL WAVE OF HOT WHISKEY AND HONEY ON A COLD, DISMAL DAY.
LAUGHING AND SHRIEKING, THE INNOCENTS ARE SHOWN THE LIGHTED PATHWAY HOME. WE'RE SWEPT UP IN THE CLARITY OF IT ALL.
THEN, FINALLY, ONLY ONE REMAINS...
I ALWAYS KNEW YOU'D GET ME, JOHN. I SAID SO.
OHHH, GOD... ASTRA. I'M SORRY ...I'M SO SORRY...
DON'T BE. EVERYTHING'S OKAY NOW.

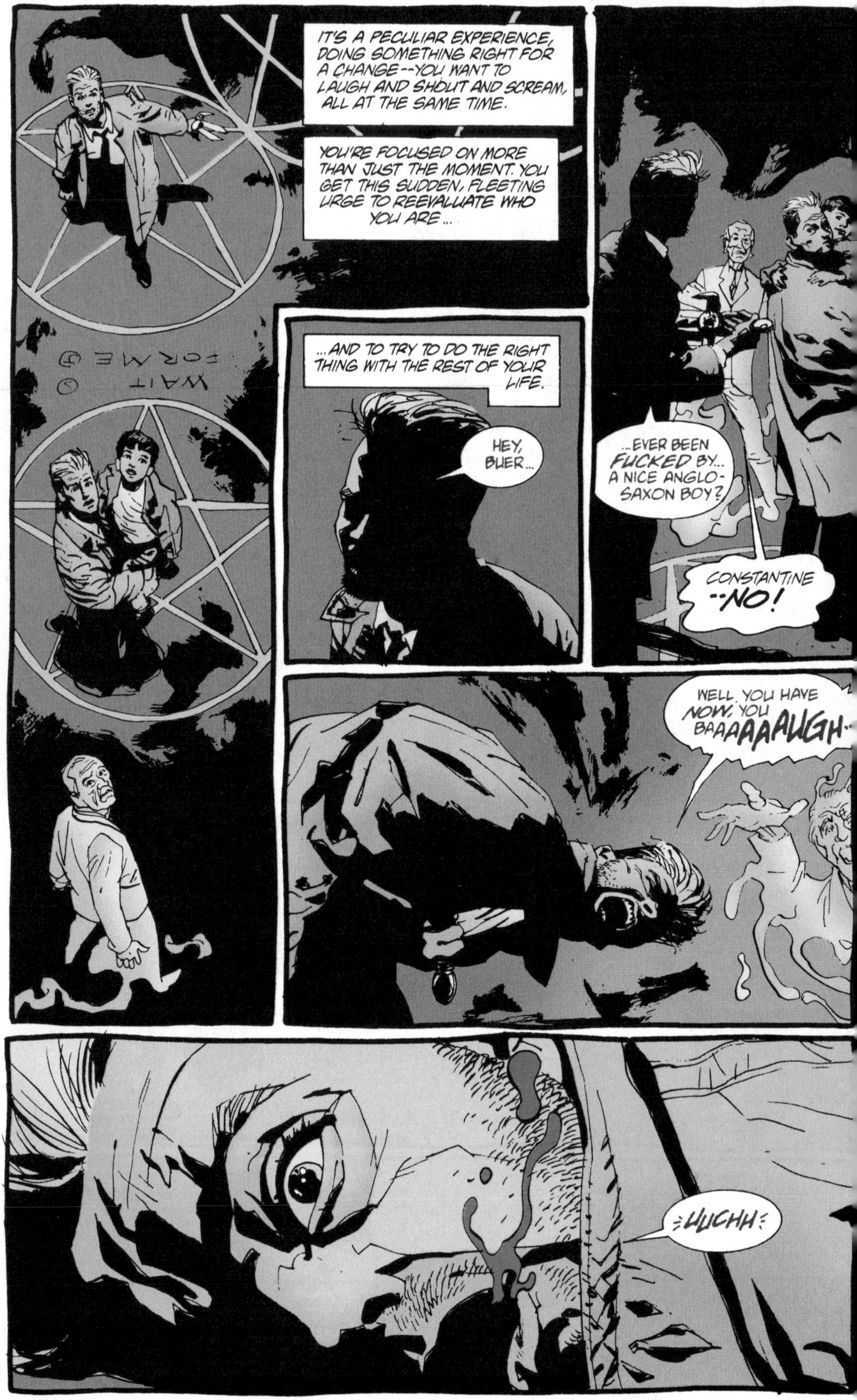
IT'S A PECULIAR EXPERIENCE, DOING SOMETHING RIGHT FOR A CHANGE--YOU WANT TO LAUGH AND SHOUT AND SCREAM, ALL AT THE SAME TIME.
YOU'RE FOCUSED ON MORE THAN JUST THE MOMENT. YOU GET THIS SUDDEN, FLEETING URGE TO REEVALUATE WHO YOU ARE...
WAIT FOR ME
...AND TO TRY TO DO THE RIGHT THING WITH THE REST OF YOUR LIFE.
HEY, BUER...
...EVER BEEN FUCKED BY... A NICE ANGLO-SAXON BOY?
CONSTANTINE --NO!
WELL, YOU HAVE NOW, YOU BAAAAAAUGH--
UUGHH

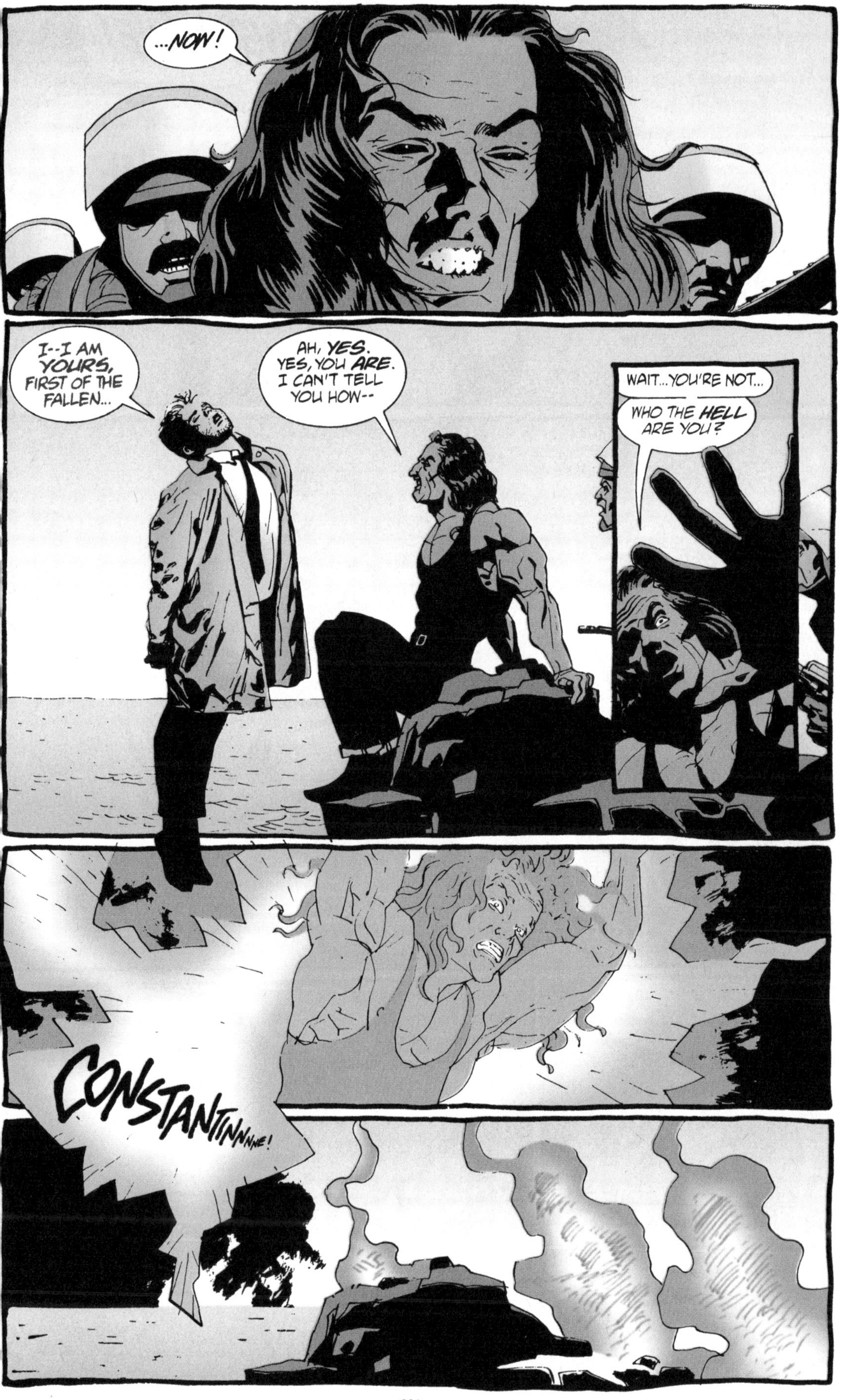
...NOW!
I--I AM YOURS, FIRST OF THE FALLEN...
AH, YES. YES, YOU ARE. I CAN'T TELL YOU HOW--
WAIT...YOU'RE NOT...
WHO THE HELL ARE YOU?
CONSTANTINNNNNE!

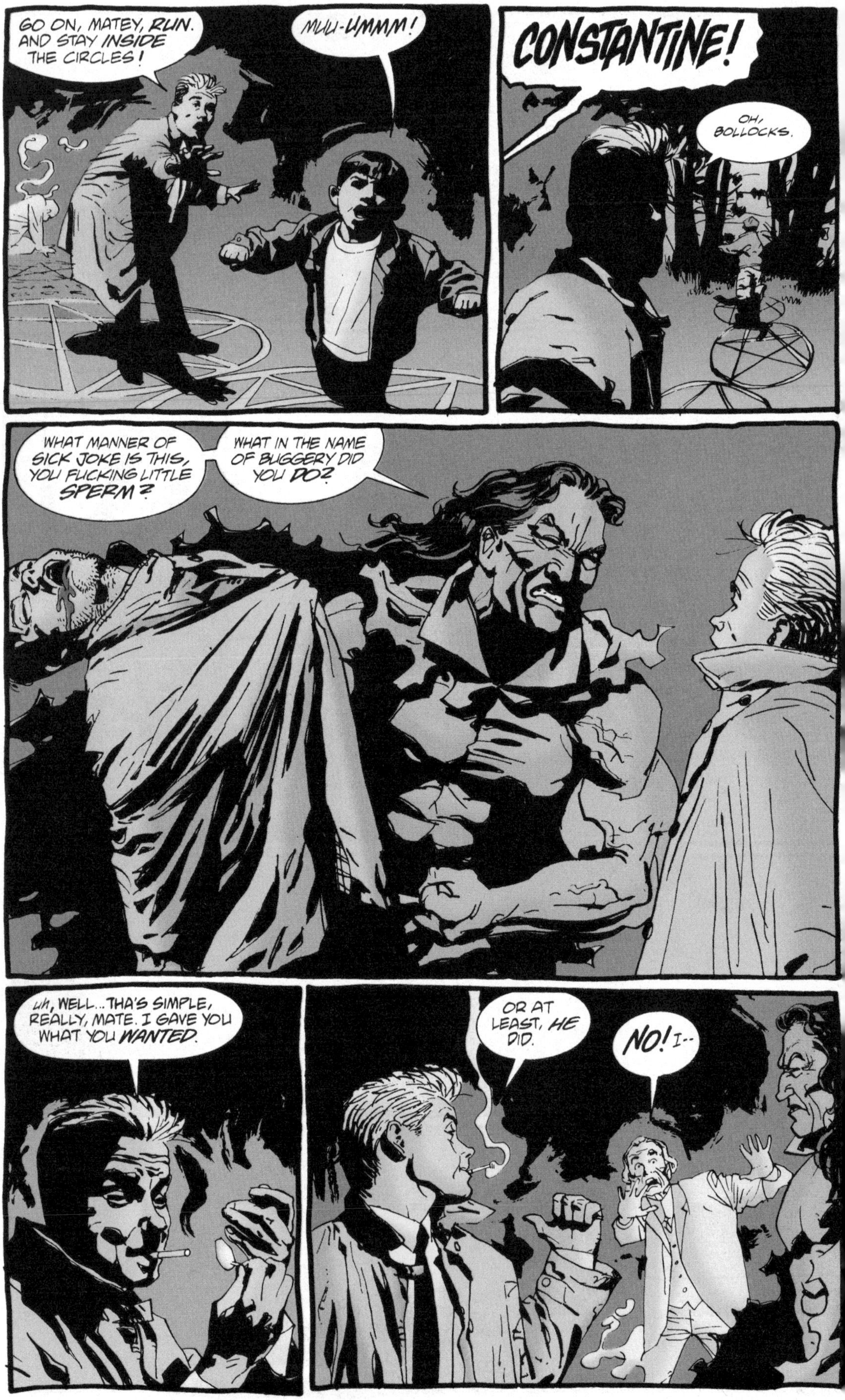
GO ON, MATEY, RUN. AND STAY INSIDE THE CIRCLES!
MUU-UMMM!
CONSTANTINE!
OH, BOLLOCKS.
WHAT MANNER OF SICK JOKE IS THIS, YOU FUCKING LITTLE SPERM?
WHAT IN THE NAME OF BUGGERY DID YOU DO?
UH, WELL... THA'S SIMPLE, REALLY, MATE. I GAVE YOU WHAT YOU WANTED.
OR AT LEAST, HE DID.
NO! I--

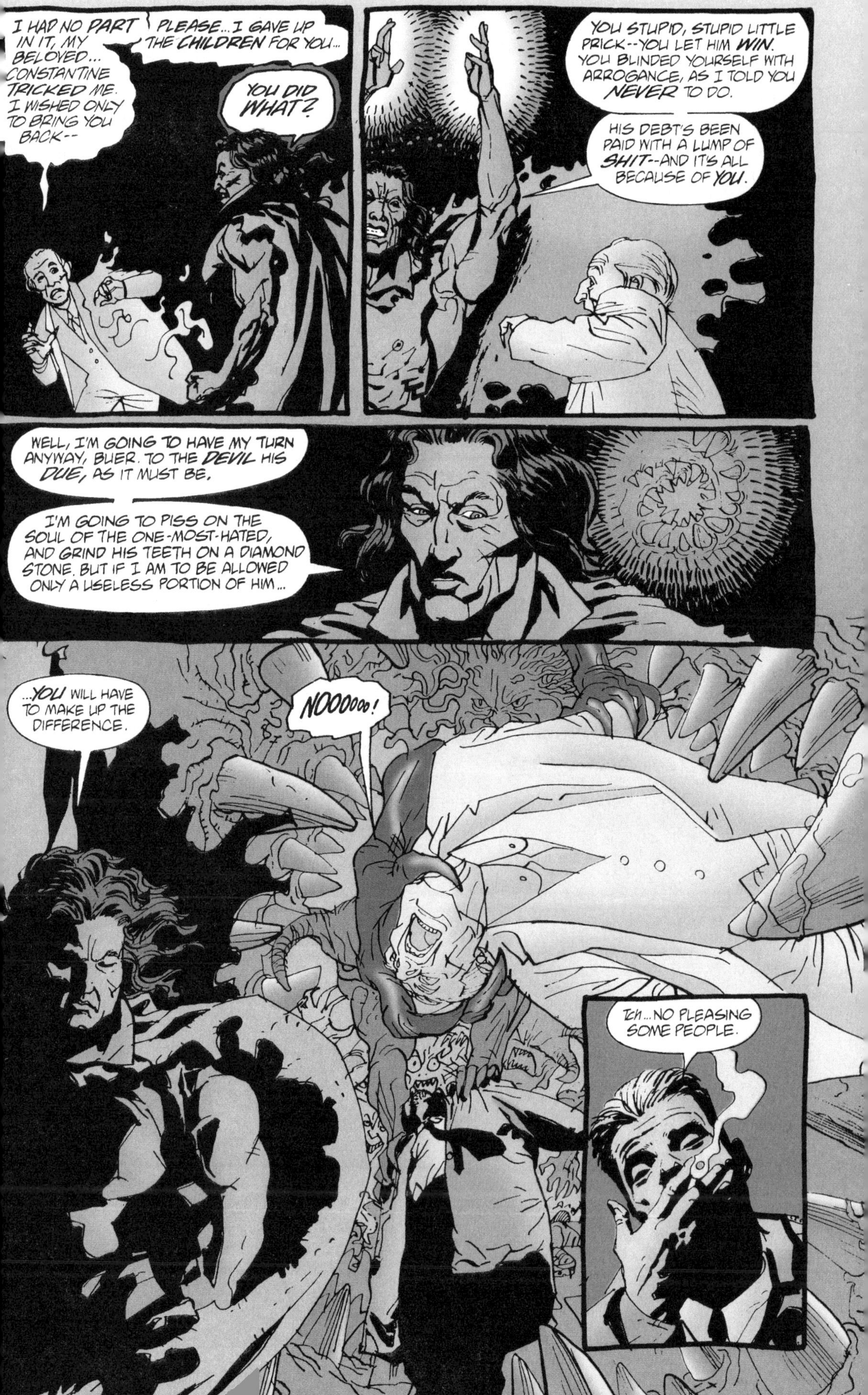
I HAD NO PART IN IT, MY BELOVED... CONSTANTINE TRICKED ME. I WISHED ONLY TO BRING YOU BACK--
PLEASE...I GAVE UP THE CHILDREN FOR YOU...
YOU DID WHAT?
YOU STUPID, STUPID LITTLE PRICK--YOU LET HIM WIN. YOU BLINDED YOURSELF WITH ARROGANCE, AS I TOLD YOU NEVER TO DO.
HIS DEBT'S BEEN PAID WITH A LUMP OF SHIT--AND IT'S ALL BECAUSE OF YOU.
WELL, I'M GOING TO HAVE MY TURN ANYWAY, BUER. TO THE DEVIL HIS DUE, AS IT MUST BE.
I'M GOING TO PISS ON THE SOUL OF THE ONE-MOST-HATED, AND GRIND HIS TEETH ON A DIAMOND STONE. BUT IF I AM TO BE ALLOWED ONLY A USELESS PORTION OF HIM...
...YOU WILL HAVE TO MAKE UP THE DIFFERENCE.
NOOOooo!
Tch...NO PLEASING SOME PEOPLE.

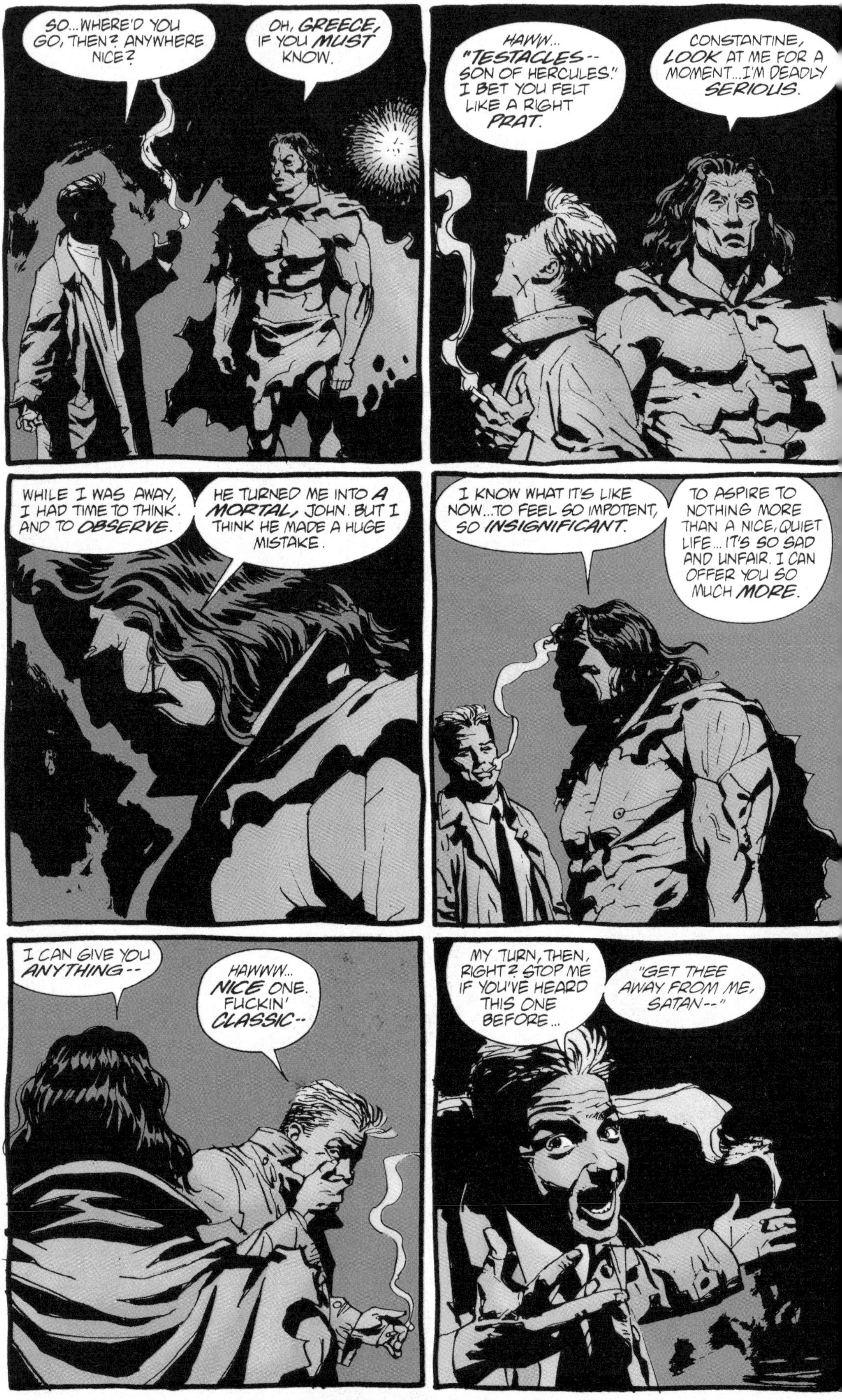

SO...WHERE'D YOU GO, THEN? ANYWHERE NICE?
OH, GREECE, IF YOU MUST KNOW.
HAWW... "TESTACLES-- SON OF HERCULES." I BET YOU FELT LIKE A RIGHT PRAT.
CONSTANTINE, LOOK AT ME FOR A MOMENT...I'M DEADLY SERIOUS.
WHILE I WAS AWAY, I HAD TIME TO THINK. AND TO OBSERVE.
HE TURNED ME INTO A MORTAL, JOHN. BUT I THINK HE MADE A HUGE MISTAKE.
I KNOW WHAT IT'S LIKE NOW...TO FEEL SO IMPOTENT, SO INSIGNIFICANT.
TO ASPIRE TO NOTHING MORE THAN A NICE, QUIET LIFE... IT'S SO SAD AND UNFAIR. I CAN OFFER YOU SO MUCH MORE.
I CAN GIVE YOU ANYTHING--
HAWWW... NICE ONE. FUCKIN' CLASSIC--
MY TURN, THEN, RIGHT? STOP ME IF YOU'VE HEARD THIS ONE BEFORE...
"GET THEE AWAY FROM ME, SATAN--"

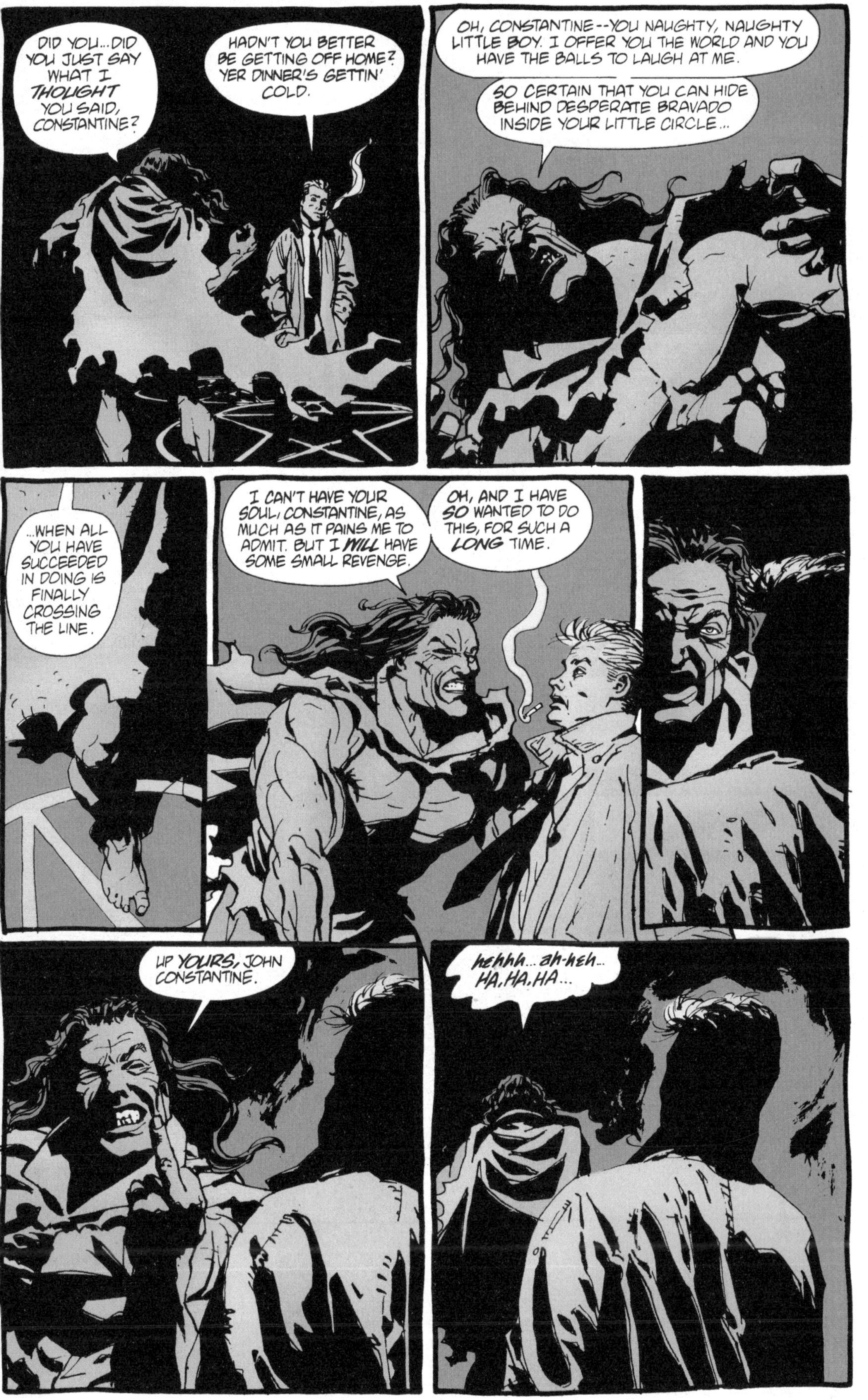
DID YOU...DID YOU JUST SAY WHAT I THOUGHT YOU SAID, CONSTANTINE?
HADN'T YOU BETTER BE GETTING OFF HOME? YER DINNER'S GETTIN' COLD.
OH, CONSTANTINE--YOU NAUGHTY, NAUGHTY LITTLE BOY. I OFFER YOU THE WORLD AND YOU HAVE THE BALLS TO LAUGH AT ME.
SO CERTAIN THAT YOU CAN HIDE BEHIND DESPERATE BRAVADO INSIDE YOUR LITTLE CIRCLE...
...WHEN ALL YOU HAVE SUCCEEDED IN DOING IS FINALLY CROSSING THE LINE.
I CAN'T HAVE YOUR SOUL, CONSTANTINE, AS MUCH AS IT PAINS ME TO ADMIT. BUT I WILL HAVE SOME SMALL REVENGE.
OH, AND I HAVE SO WANTED TO DO THIS, FOR SUCH A LONG TIME.
UP YOURS, JOHN CONSTANTINE.
hehhh... ah-heh... HA.HA.HA...

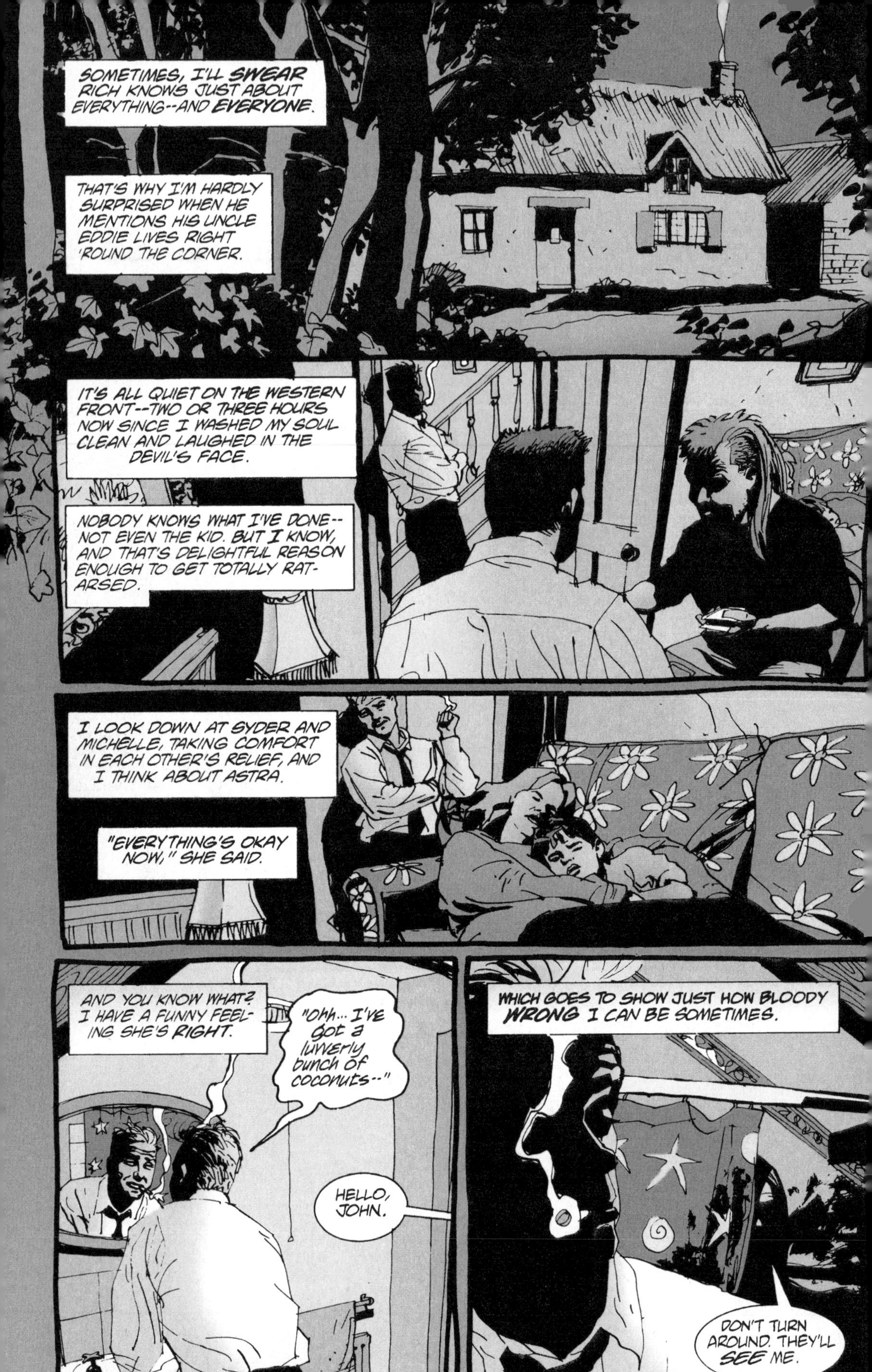
SOMETIMES, I'LL SWEAR RICH KNOWS JUST ABOUT EVERYTHING--AND EVERYONE.
THAT'S WHY I'M HARDLY SURPRISED WHEN HE MENTIONS HIS UNCLE EDDIE LIVES RIGHT 'ROUND THE CORNER.
IT'S ALL QUIET ON THE WESTERN FRONT--TWO OR THREE HOURS NOW SINCE I WASHED MY SOUL CLEAN AND LAUGHED IN THE DEVIL'S FACE.
NOBODY KNOWS WHAT I'VE DONE--NOT EVEN THE KID. BUT I KNOW, AND THAT'S DELIGHTFUL REASON ENOUGH TO GET TOTALLY RAT-ARSED.
I LOOK DOWN AT SYDER AND MICHELLE, TAKING COMFORT IN EACH OTHER'S RELIEF, AND I THINK ABOUT ASTRA.
"EVERYTHING'S OKAY NOW," SHE SAID.
AND YOU KNOW WHAT? I HAVE A FUNNY FEELING SHE'S RIGHT.
"Ohh... I've got a luvverly bunch of coconuts--"
HELLO, JOHN.
WHICH GOES TO SHOW JUST HOW BLOODY WRONG I CAN BE SOMETIMES.
DON'T TURN AROUND. THEY'LL SEE ME.

ELLIE! CHRIST, WHAT ARE *YOU* DOING HERE, LUV?

WHY, JOHN? WHY DID YOU *DO* IT?

ME? WHAT'D I DO?

YOU *BETRAYED* ME, YOU SON-OF-A-BITCH. I STUCK A KNIFE IN THE DEVIL'S BACK FOR YOU, AND YOU STUCK A KNIFE IN *MINE*.

HE'S GOING STARK, RAVING MAD DOWN THERE, JOHN--TURNING THE WHOLE DAMNED PLACE UPSIDE DOWN, TRYING TO FIND OUT WHO SENT HIM AWAY.

SO TELL ME--IF YOU CAN *LIE* QUICKLY ENOUGH--*WHY*?

'CAUSE YOU MADE YOURSELF A *CHOICE*, ELLIE. THE CHILDREN *DIDN'T*.

I'M SORRY.

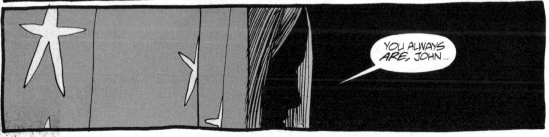

YOU ALWAYS *ARE*, JOHN...

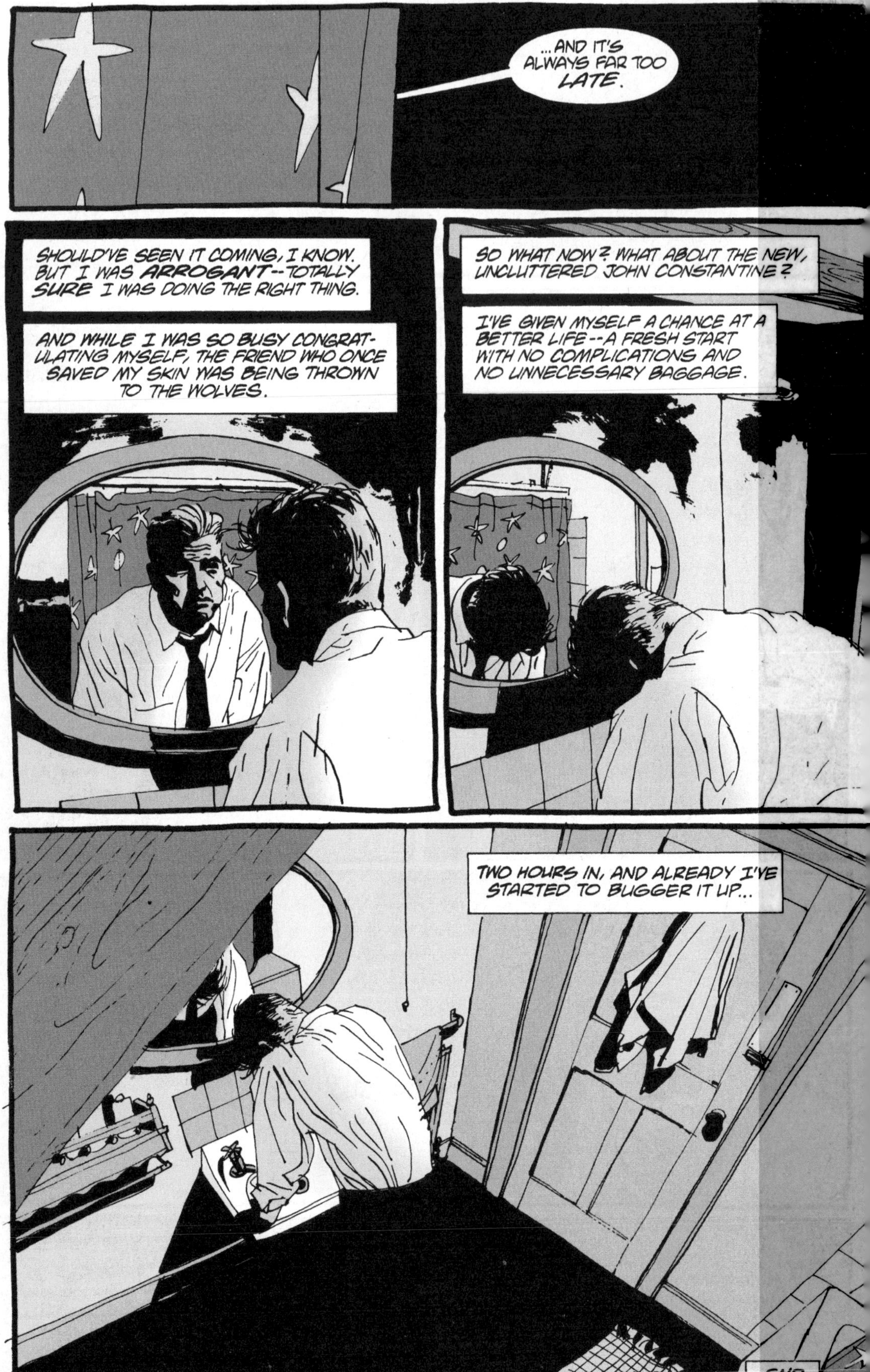
...AND IT'S ALWAYS FAR TOO LATE.
SHOULD'VE SEEN IT COMING, I KNOW. BUT I WAS ARROGANT--TOTALLY SURE I WAS DOING THE RIGHT THING.
AND WHILE I WAS SO BUSY CONGRATULATING MYSELF, THE FRIEND WHO ONCE SAVED MY SKIN WAS BEING THROWN TO THE WOLVES.
SO WHAT NOW? WHAT ABOUT THE NEW, UNCLUTTERED JOHN CONSTANTINE?
I'VE GIVEN MYSELF A CHANCE AT A BETTER LIFE--A FRESH START WITH NO COMPLICATIONS AND NO UNNECESSARY BAGGAGE.
TWO HOURS IN, AND ALREADY I'VE STARTED TO BUGGER IT UP...
END